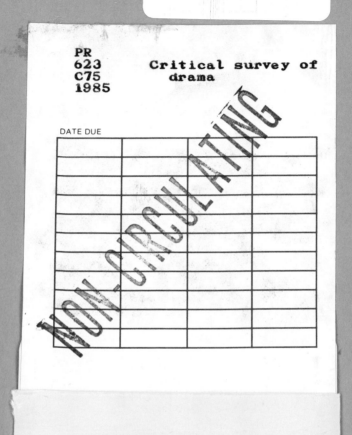

CRITICAL SURVEY
OF
DRAMA

CRITICAL SURVEY
OF
DRAMA

English Language Series

Authors

A-Con

1

Edited by
FRANK N. MAGILL

SALEM PRESS
Englewood Cliffs, N. J.

LIBRARY OF CONGRESS CATALOG CARD NUMBER: 85-50962

Complete Set: ISBN 0-89356-375-7
Volume 1: ISBN 0-89356-376-5

PRINTED IN THE UNITED STATES OF AMERICA

PREFACE

CRITICAL SURVEY OF DRAMA: *English Language Series* is the penultimate set in the Salem Press "Genre Series," a forty-five-volume project (when completed) devoted to a worldwide study of the major creative figures in the fields of short fiction, poetry, long fiction, and the drama. The final element—six volumes devoted to non-English-language drama—is scheduled for release in 1986.

The format of the individual articles in this set is consistent with that of the earlier volumes. Pertinent top matter is followed by a listing of the dramatist's plays, with dates of first release, a survey of publications in literary forms other than drama, a critical survey of the subject's professional achievements, a biographical sketch centered on the writer's dramatic development, and a rather extensive critical analysis of the subject's canon. Following these critical overviews appears a listing of major publications other than drama and a bibliography of significant criticism on the works of the subject dramatist.

In addition to individual articles on 198 dramatists, this set includes twenty-four extensive Essays on various aspects of English-language drama. Whereas the articles on individual dramatists explore the personal achievements in a most enlightening way—especially for students—the Essays cover aspects of the development and presentation of drama as a whole, including costumes, masks, lighting, directing, acting, and various other related elements necessary for the successful presentation of dramatic entertainment for an audience.

It is probably reasonable to hold that English-language drama sprang from the medieval mystery and miracle plays and the various cycles, such as York, Towneley, Coventry, and others, out of which eventually grew such secular plays as Nicholas Udall's *Ralph Roister Doister* (c. 1553), the farce *Gammer Gurton's Needle* (c. 1560), and other pure entertainments, which led into the magnificent era of Elizabethan and Jacobean drama, nourished by the shade of Christopher Marlowe and the presence of William Shakespeare and Ben Jonson. The richness of theatrical fare at this time could hardly have been surpassed, though its brilliance had begun to decline by the time the Puritans closed the theaters in 1642. During the closings, however, some playwrights and actors continued to offer plays—illegally—presenting many translated dramas, mostly from France.

After eighteen years the theaters were allowed to reopen, but a new, less classical, approach took over as the Restoration period began to modernize the language and revise the stage matter of the theater, not the least innovation being the introduction of women for female parts, formerly performed by boys. Restoration drama dispensed with any prudery that might have prevailed in earlier stage presentations, and audiences reveled in risqué lines and off-color innuendos. It was a spicy time for young blades and rakes, whose imagination encompassed every movement of Mrs. Bracegirdle and Nell Gwynn.

The eighteenth century was a period of great growth and development in the English theater. Improvements in stage techniques resulting from modernizations (lighting, enlargement and changes in stage shape, and a general break with tradition) accounted for a sharp increase in the number of theaters, playwrights, actors, and eager members of audiences. There was much back-and-forth relationship with the Continent (particularly France, Italy, and Germany), and the bawdiness of Restoration drama was toned down. Humanism became more important, and tragedy on the stage began to give way to a less gloomy mental approach toward life and a growing preference for comedy. Unfortunately, government licensing of English theaters closed down most of them, a "political" move that had a chilling effect on what was about to become an unprecedented burst of theatrical energy.

In the 1800's, however, more great strides were made in the modernization of production and staging. For stage lighting, gas replaced candles and oil lamps and changed forever what could be done onstage. Realism was beginning to make acting more "authentic," with engrossed audiences being made to feel that what they were seeing onstage might really be happening.

Part of this growing up of the theater resulted from a change in stage management. No longer were careless or incompetent actor-managers responsible for production. They were superseded by nonacting stage managers who became completely responsible for every aspect of the production: actors, script changes, stage sets, rehearsals—indeed, every part of the stage presentation, from start to finish. Thus, the theater had at least become professionalized.

The twentieth century has seen the flowering of English-language drama, but much is owed to the primitive beginnings in religious-based "plots" of medieval times that whetted the creative appetites of succeeding playwrights. The 198 articles in this set that deal with individual playwrights are unquestionably the core of the work. Not to be slighted, however, are the twenty-four background Essays, whose interpretations of the history of English-language drama are admirable, readable, and highly recommended.

As an example, consider the following excerpt from the Essay "Twentieth Century British Drama," which explores, among other topics, the many vital contributions to the genre by members of the Irish Renaissance:

> The Abbey Theatre . . . became known worldwide as the heart of the Celtic revival with productions such as Lady [Augusta] Gregory's *The Travelling Man* (pb. 1909), which invokes the mystical figure of the unconventional tramp; Rutherford Mayne's *The Turn of the Road* (pr. 1910), Padraic Colum's *Thomas Muskerry* (pr. 1910), and St. John Ervine's *Mixed Marriage* (pr. 1911) deal with the despair of the young under the domination of the old. Other plays critical of the Celtic mythos, such as those by [John

Millington] Synge or [Sean] O'Casey, evoked patriotic riots or indifference. Distinctively Celtic elements have defined the modern sense of drama, including plays by [William Butler] Yeats, remembered for his lyricism and symbolism; by Synge, for his Celtic linguistic patterns and ethos; and by O'Casey, for his prodigious experimentation. The Abbey also enriched the one-act play form, which in Ireland became the vehicle for expressing elemental human aspirations in such plays as Synge's *Riders to the Sea* (pb. 1903). Also to the Abbey's credit, or, rather, primarily to Yeats's, is the successful production of the verse play.

Such passages may ignite a spark of interest that can lead to a rewarding in-depth examination of a vital element in the study of British literary history.

Another striking example of the Essays' import—the opening words of "American Drama"—reveals the disappointment in America's early backward position in world drama yet implies the promise latent in the American conscience:

Until the post-World War I era, American drama, confronted with religious hostility and then by economic necessity and academic indifference, struggled to come into its own as a respected literary genre at home and as a force that made itself felt on foreign stages. A commonplace of American literary history is that the plays of Eugene O'Neill, in Walter J. Meserve's words, marked "America's full-scale arrival into the modern drama of western civilization."

In an article in a 1907 issue of *Atlantic Monthly,* John Corbin quoted Edmund Stedman, who proclaimed a literary declaration of independence for American drama: "Quote boldly, then, I prophesy the dawn of the American drama; and quite confidently, too, for the drama has already dawned. . . ."

The confidence implied by Mr. Stedman in 1907 was well founded. By the 1930's, Broadway was alive with good, and serious, dramas, and by the middle of the century, Broadway, Off-Broadway, and even Off-Off-Broadway had more opportunities for good scripts than their stages could handle.

Perhaps the advent of radio sparked the profusion of "playwrights," writers who rose to the demand for radio scripts. This need increased with the advent of television and its greed for more and more program material. The royalty level of this hierarchy was an original screenplay which saw production. There were never enough original screenplays to satisfy Hollywood's prodigious appetite, however, and this condition forced the industry to film stage plays and successful novels.

The new forms of public entertainment currently available are a far cry from medieval drama and, indeed, from the typical "Broadway" play, devoid as it is of electronic magic and retakes. Nevertheless, this study of English-language drama does include Essays on Radio Drama, Television Drama, and Cinema and Drama. It is true that at times one may hear complaints that the motion-picture medium, for example, cannot properly be equated with the dramatic experience drawn from the live stage—in short, that "movies aren't really drama." Using a conventional definition for the term "drama" (a story meant to represent life or one involving universally identifiable conflicts and passions), the two cinematic examples given in the Essay "Cinema and Drama" on pages 2513-2521, should provide ample substance for the argument that cinema is indeed "drama"—fully representative of the highest order of emotional transfer when seriously conceived and performed.

I wish to thank all those who have had a hand in the development of this extensive work—which is a "joint project" in the fullest sense.

FRANK N. MAGILL

CONTRIBUTORS

Writing Staff for Essays

Thomas Banks

Theodore Baroody

Robert Bensen

Elliott A. Denniston

William Frankfather

Irma M. Kashuba

John R. Lucas

Alan L. McLeod

Roger Manvell

Patricia Marks

Leslie B. Mittleman

Laurie P. Morrow

Cóilín D. Owens

Joseph Rosenblum

Valerie C. Rudolph

Susan Rusinko

David Sadkin

Laurence Senelick

Dale Silviria

Joseph H. Stodder

Craig Werner

Eugene P. Wright

Writing Staff for Author Articles

Howard C. Adams

Jacob H. Adler

Thomas P. Adler

Kwaku Amoabeng

Andrew J. Angyal

Stanley Archer

Edwin T. Arnold

William M. Baillie

Margaret Ann Baker

William Baker

Thomas Banks

Kirk H. Beetz

Anthony Bernardo

Harold Branam

Ward W. Briggs

Hallman B. Bryant

Elizabeth Buckmaster

Donald Burness

Douglas R. Butler

Ralph S. Carlson

Susan Carlson

John Carpenter

Lorna Clarke

Richard N. Coe

John W. Crawford

Carol Croxton

J. D. Daubs

J. Madison Davis

William A. Davis

Joan F. Dean

Elliott A. Denniston

Henry J. Donaghy

CRITICAL SURVEY OF DRAMA

Susan Duffy

Ted R. Ellis III

Jane Falco

Patricia A. Farrant

Edward Fiorelli

Benjamin Fisher

Howard Ford

Robert J. Forman

Lawrence S. Friedman

Steven H. Gale

Edward V. Geist

Donna Gerstenberger

Scott Giantvalley

Richard B. Gidez

E. Bryan Gillespie

Eleanor R. Goldhar

Peter Goslett

Peter W. Graham

Ira Grushow

Angela Hague

Jay Halio

Gertrude K. Hamilton

Robert D. Hamner

Maryhelen C. Harmon

Zia Hasan

William J. Heim

Gordon Henderson

Michael Hennessy

Janet S. Hertzbach

Holly Hill

Eril Barnett Hughes

Philip K. Jason

Vera Jiji

Millard T. Jones

Albert E. Kalson

Nancy Kearns

Arthur Kincaid

B. G. Knepper

Carrol Lasker

Kathleen Latimer

Norman Lavers

Perry Luckett

Michael McCully

John F. McDiarmid

James C. MacDonald

Christina Hunt Mahony

James E. Maloney

Stella Maloney

Patricia Marks

Walter J. Meserve

Raymond Miller, Jr.

Leslie B. Mittleman

Christian H. Moe

Michael D. Moore

Michael G. Moran

Laurie P. Morrow

Robert E. Morsberger

Gerald W. Morton

Mary C. Murphy

Evelyn S. Newlyn

George O'Brien

Robert H. O'Connor

Leslie O'Dell

Elizabeth Spalding Otten

Robert M. Otten

Cóilín D. Owens

Philip Oxley

Anthony F. R. Palmieri

Sidney F. Parham

Lisë Pedersen

Richard N. Ramsey

Steven Reese

Carl E. Rollyson, Jr.

Joseph Rosenblum

CONTRIBUTORS

Robert Ross

Valerie C. Rudolph

Victor Anthony Rudowski

Loren Ruff

Susan Rusinko

David Sadkin

Arthur M. Saltzman

Walter Shear

John C. Shields

Hugh Short

R. Baird Shuman

Charles L. P. Silet

Philip E. Smith II

Anthony Stephenson

Gerald H. Strauss

Edmund M. Taft

Daniel Taylor

Thomas J. Taylor

Christopher J. Thaiss

E. F. J. Tucker

A. Gordon Van Ness III

Doris Walters

Judith A. Weise

Craig Werner

David Allen White

Edwin W. Williams

Robert F. Willson, Jr.

Eugene P. Wright

Michael Zeitlin

LIST OF AUTHORS IN VOLUME 1

CRITICAL SURVEY
OF
DRAMA

JOSEPH ADDISON

Born: Milston, England; May 1, 1672
Died: London, England; June 17, 1719

Principal drama

Rosamond, pr., pb. 1707 (libretto; music by Thomas Clayton); *Cato*, pr., pb. 1713; *The Drummer: Or, The Haunted House*, pr., pb. 1716.

Other literary forms

Joseph Addison wrote in almost every genre flourishing in British literature during the reigns of William III and Queen Anne. In addition to his three plays, Addison wrote verse in Latin and in English, a travel book, a scholarly account of ancient Roman coins, political pamphlets, and hundreds of essays for *The Tatler*, *The Spectator*, and other periodicals. This variety reflects the active literary culture of the time, Addison's own wide learning, and his search for his proper niche.

Because of Addison's varied canon, there has yet to be a satisfactory complete edition. The first attempt, by Thomas Tickell in 1721, omitted some embarrassing early works and many of the periodical essays. Another collected edition a century later restored some early works and offered a fuller selection of essays. Two good modern critical editions cover most of Addison's corpus: A. C. Guthkelch's *The Miscellaneous Works* (1914) includes the plays as well as the poetry and nonperiodical prose works, and Donald Bond's *The Spectator* (1965) covers Addison's essays for the most famous periodical to which he contributed. Essays written for other journals await modern editions. Addison's *Letters*, an unrevealing collection, was published in 1941.

Achievements

Addison's literary reputation has risen and fallen cyclically for reasons that have little to do with his artistic achievement. His contemporaries and the next generation praised Addison highly for expressing not only Whig political principles but also classical qualities which gave English literature a dignity that it previously lacked. Readers and writers in the Romantic age, however, found Addison unoriginal and conventional. The Victorians restored Addison to the pedestal because he spoke well of virtue and painted the portrait of the Christian gentleman. Twentieth century critics often treat his work as a reflection of the values of the ascendant bourgeoisie; many personally dislike the man for accommodating himself to the class structure of eighteenth century England.

While such judgments affect how often Addison is reprinted and how much he is read, his place in literary history rests firmly on two achievements: his role in the development of the periodical essay and his prose style. Through his collaboration with Richard Steele on *The Tatler* (1709-1711), *The Spectator* (1711-1712, 1714), and *The Guardian* (1713), Addison helped to establish the periodical essay as a literary form. Seemingly informal and natural yet shaped by conscious art, Addison's prose style became for the next two centuries a model for novice writers: Stylists as diverse as Benjamin Franklin and Thomas Hardy began by imitating Addison. Samuel Johnson defined Addison's style in an immortal assessment: "Whoever wishes to attain an English style, familiar but not coarse, and elegant but not ostentatious, must give his days and nights to the volumes of Addison."

If Addison's primary achievement was in periodical prose, his plays rank second, his scholarly prose third, and his poetry last. His plays do not have all the virtues of successful drama but do show that two qualities of his prose—a light comic touch and a skill at putting the best words in the best order—were partially transferable to another genre. There is a consistency to Addison's drama: All three plays are quite competent and worth reading. Historically, the plays received varied reactions: *Rosamond* was a disaster, *Cato* was a huge success, and *The Drummer* was hardly noticed. The reactions to *Rosamond* and *Cato* had little to do with their literary merit, a fate common to other imaginative works in Augustan London, where politics, authorial popularity, and prejudice were often decisive.

Biography

Joseph Addison might easily have followed in his father's footsteps: attending Oxford University, becoming a minister of the Anglican Church, pursuing a series of increasingly important ecclesiastical posts, and supporting the divine right of Stuart kings. Addison, however, took a different path.

Two revolutionary currents swept up Addison while he was at Oxford. The first was an enthusiasm for the "New Philosophy," the scientific method that was challenging the supremacy of classical philosophy; the second was the Glorious Revolution of 1688, which brought William III to the throne in place of James II and established the principle that Parliament's choice for a king weighed equally with God's anointing of His earthly representative. Addison followed the traditional classical curriculum at Oxford (where he achieved his first literary reputation for Latin poetry), but with the idea of supporting a new English culture and political order. Based on the Roman concept of an educated citizenry, this new order, Addison and like-minded revolutionaries hoped, would be the greatest civilization England had yet known: a literate and cultured populace would sensibly cooperate in their own government in order to develop a thriving commercial economy at home and to achieve leadership among European nations.

While at Oxford, Addison expressed his enthusiasm for this new concept of England in poems that brought him to the attention of leading Whig politicians. In 1699, Lord Somers and Lord Halifax secured for Addison a grant from William III, allowing Addison to travel throughout the Continent in preparation for government service. Addison remained abroad until late 1703, when William's death ended the pension. He did little for the next year until, at the request of two of Queen Anne's ministers, he wrote *The Campaign* to celebrate the military victories of the Duke of Marlborough against the French. This successful poem, which was published in 1705, won for Addison a position as commissioner of appeals.

This post placed Addison in a circle of Whig politicians and writers called the Kit-Kat Club. The powerful politicians supported the writers by patronage; the writers helped the politicians gain or keep power by penning public-relations puffs and persuasive pamphlets. Addison's new acquaintances spurred his literary efforts. A Kit-Kat publisher brought out Addison's travels in 1705 to capitalize on the reputation of the author of *The Campaign*. Richard Steele, a Kit-Kat writer, urged Addison to dabble in the drama and to try his hand at an English opera to counteract London's then current passion for Italian opera. Addison's opera, *Rosamond*, was a failure, however, primarily because of Thomas Clayton's poor musical score.

Nevertheless, *Rosamond* was the only setback for Addison between 1705 and 1711. Political contacts at the Kit-Kat Club provided him with increasingly responsible appointments. He served as secretary to a number of important ministers and was elected to Parliament in 1708. His literary output in these years was limited to several political tracts and to a few contributions to the early numbers of Steele's *The Tatler*.

After the Whig ministry lost power in 1710, Addison became a regular partner with Steele in the later issues of *The Tatler* and shared responsibility for founding its successor, *The Spectator*. The new paper was spectacularly successful and was the talk of London's polite society; Addison provided most of the variety in the paper, writing sketches, fables, short stories, and poems in addition to the expository essays which were its staple.

Political events and Addison's high literary reputation conspired to return him to the theater in 1713. The country was torn by the question of the aging Queen Anne's successor: would the Protestant Prince George of Hanover succeed to the throne according to Parliament's wish, or would a Catholic Stuart attempt to assert his hereditary right by military force? Addison had begun sometime earlier a play about the Roman patriot Cato, who had resisted the dictatorial ambitions of Julius Caesar; his Whig friends encouraged Addison to finish the play and produce it as a clarion call to resist the return of Stuart absolutism. Addison reluctantly agreed and saw the play received with a passionate response from the party faithful. The Whigs' opponents, the Tories, ironically clapped up the play just as loudly, hailing it as a patriotic summons to resist a foreign prince. The play was produced at both London and Oxford with great success, although few paid attention to its literary qualities.

In 1714, the Protestant prince did ascend the English throne as George I, and Addison served as secretary to the council that oversaw the transition. Addison supported the new government with several poems and a political journal, *The Freeholder*. He tried his hand at the theater once more with *The Drummer* in 1716, but it ran for only three nights. Although not roundly scorned, as *Rosamond* had been, this "delicate" comedy (as Steele called it) did not impress audiences. In 1717, Addison reached the height of his political career by becoming secretary of state.

Political and literary success brought substantial rewards. Addison purchased a pleasant estate, Bilton Hall; married the widowed Countess of Warwick; and fathered a daughter, Charlotte. In 1718, however, illness forced him to resign from the government, and the last months of his life were marred by a pamphlet war with his former partner Steele over the Peerage Bill. On his deathbed, legend holds, Addison summoned his dissolute stepson to witness "how a Christian can die." Addison never lacked confidence in his religious, political, or literary convictions.

Analysis

Joseph Addison's three plays indicate important trends in eighteenth century British theater. *Rosamond* attempts to combine music and drama as a domestic alternative to Italian opera, an ambition not realized until two decades later, with the success of John Gay's *The Beggar's Opera* (1728). *Cato* represents a strain of classical tragedy that produced much declamation and little worth, "immortal in the closet" (as the saying went) but stale on the stage. *The Drummer* is an early sentimental comedy whose primary virtue was in being less maudlin than its successors.

None of Addison's plays is a landmark of drama—except *Cato*, by political accident—but none is bad. In fact, each play has its interesting aspects. All of them suffer from a common flaw, the lack of a central character whose plight engages the audience's sympathy, and each play suffers individual minor difficulties. Yet each play has distinctive virtues. *Rosamond* and *The Drummer* have enough comic characters and dialogue to justify, in conjunction with Addison's humorous papers in *The Spectator*, Samuel Johnson's observation: "If Addison had cultivated the lighter parts of poetry, he would probably have excelled." *Cato*'s blank verse, while no rival to Christopher Marlowe's or William Shakespeare's, is a solid achievement and is the best poetry that Addison ever wrote.

Rosamond's three acts tell of the love affair between Henry II and Rosamond Clifford. The main plot concerns Henry's conflict, his love for

Rosamond against his duty to Queen Elinor; the subplot concerns the man whom Henry has set to watch over Rosamond, Sir Trusty, himself in love with his charge and plagued with a shrewish wife, Grideline. Act 1 displays the characters in their frustrations: the queen jealous, the mistress guilty and lonely, the guardian melancholy. Only Henry, returning from France and eager to see Rosamond, seems pleased with the situation. In act 2, Grideline sends a page to spy on Sir Trusty, but the young man discovers instead Queen Elinor plotting to kill her husband's mistress. Hesitating for a moment because Rosamond's death may lead to Henry's, Elinor finally issues an ultimatum to her rival: be stabbed or drink poison. Rosamond chooses poison, and when Sir Trusty finds the corpse, he likewise drinks the fatal concoction. Act 3 begins with Henry asleep and dreaming of martial conquest. Spirits grant him a vision of England's future glory if he gives up his illicit love. Henry awakens and resolves to put Rosamond aside, but hearing of her death, he vows to die in battle. Elinor counters his rashness by revealing that the poison was only a sleeping potion and that Rosamond lives. She retires to a convent to expiate her sin, and Henry returns to Elinor and reestablishes domestic accord. Sir Trusty, awakening to find king and queen happily reunited, now devotes himself wholeheartedly to Grideline.

Addison's opera had several elements that ought to have made it congenial to audiences of the day. The plot came from English history, a strong appeal to the patriotic instincts of a generation locked in a long war with France. The characters were familiar dramatic types: The royal leads experienced the conflicts of love and honor so common to the protagonists of Restoration heroic tragedy, while Sir Trusty and Grideline knew the jealousies and philanderings fundamental to the Restoration comedy of manners. Finally, the play's third act offered a spectacular effect: In Henry's vision, there was a backdrop featuring Blenheim Castle, which was at that moment under construction. The play's theme—that married love conquers all—likewise accorded well with the sentiments for reform which had been growing increasingly fashionable since the accession of William III.

Contemporaries agreed that an atrocious musical score doomed the play, but it must also be admitted that Addison's arrangement of the parts must have seemed odd to his audience no matter how mellifluous the music. A plot recitation indicates those elements which were supposed to predominate: several romantic conflicts, a patriotic theme, an uplifting moral. A close reading of *Rosamond*, however, reveals that the author's best effects are in the comic elements. If the London stage of 1707 had been familiar with the musical comedy, as Bonamy Dobrée points out, Addison's opera would have been comprehensible. It is a play in which the major ingredients are wholesome and bland while the subplot and supporting characters are what the audience enjoys and remembers. The witty but foolish Sir

Trusty steals the show. His superficial passion and foolish suicide, meant to contrast with Henry's love and Elinor's jealousy, instead made the royal lovers look like caricatures. Surely the effect was unintentional; not until Gilbert and Sullivan's operettas would ridiculing the aristocracy become public dramatic entertainment.

The Drummer does not suffer from the same tension between main plot and subplot; in fact, the two are nicely harmonized, although the best character in the play is still the male protagonist of the subplot. What *The Drummer* lacks, in fact, is any strong tension at all. Although its situations and language produce numerous smiles, the play lacks the sharpness that memorable comedy demands.

Addison, drawing on his classical learning, borrowed the plot of *The Drummer* from the last several books of Homer's *Odyssey* (c. 800 B.C.). Like Homer's epic, Addison's play is about a soldier, supposedly dead in a war, who comes home in disguise to find his wife besieged by suitors and his only ally in a faithful servant.

Act 1 depicts the estate of Lady Trueman, supposedly haunted by the drumbeating ghost of her husband, Sir George, killed fourteen months before in battle. The ghost is actually a disguised suitor for the widow's hand in marriage, the London beau Fantome, who has secured the help of a servant, Abigail, in his plot to drive away another suitor, the foppish Tinsel. Though Lady Trueman acts kindly toward Tinsel, she in fact despises both men. When the real Sir George turns up alive in act 2, he enters the household disguised as a conjurer in order to observe his wife's behavior. Throughout act 3, Vellum, Sir George's faithful steward, attempts to help his master expose Tinsel and subvert Fantome by wooing Abigail. In act 4, Fantome disposes of his rival but unknowingly loses Abigail's assistance. In act 5, Sir George tests his wife to determine if she still loves her husband; convinced by her reaction, the real Sir George routs the pseudo-Sir George by appearing as the drumbeating ghost of himself. Sir George and Lady Trueman are reunited, and Vellum earns Abigail's love as well as her rich bribe from Fantome.

Sir George and Lady Trueman are more convincing lovers than Henry and Elinor. Since they do not begin so very far apart, reconciliation is natural. Though fearful that his widow may have been too quick to forget him, Sir George really knows all along that his spouse has more heart than the typically coquettish wife. Though Lady Trueman is quick to have suitors, she keeps them at a distance.

Vellum, not in love with the same woman as his lord, does not undercut Sir George's character as Trusty undercut Henry's. Vellum, in fact, is a reluctant lover, becoming a wooer of Abigail only to help his master and only after he discovers that she responds to his stewardly approach to love. A steward is a careful man who always itemizes and lists what is valuable and keeps an eye on it. Addison skillfully uses the steward mentality both to depict Vellum as a delightful eccentric and to use him as a weapon against the unstewardly figures Tinsel and Fantome, who know how to value nothing.

In addition to Vellum, who is the highlight of the play, Addison creates some humor with three bumbling servants—a butler, a coachman, and a gardener—of whose credulity Sir George takes advantage in order to pass himself off as a conjurer. These four, however, do not have enough stage lines to offset the blandness of the major characters. Sir George and Lady Trueman are loving but not very witty with each other; the fops Tinsel and Fantome are without any distinguishing or distinctive foolishness; Abigail, who has some tendency to be vixenish, slides without ado from corrupted betrayer to protective intriguer. *The Drummer* on the whole does not disappoint the reader, but it cannot lure one back for a second encounter.

If *Rosamond* and *The Drummer* show Addison's comic touch, *Cato* contains his best poetry. For several decades after its first performance, *Cato* maintained a firm stage reputation as well as a solid critical repute, but largely on the strength of its political appeal, the high esteem in which Addison was generally held, and a weakness for declamation among audiences that should have known better. In more recent times, the glaring discrepancy between the main plot and the subplot has become impossible to ignore and the absence of human feeling in the tragic protagonist too obvious to be obscured by the play's virtues. Only the language, which develops subtle and rich image patterns, saves the play from being a mere museum piece.

The main plot and subplot are so different that the play is better summarized in two parts than act by act. The hero is Cato, often praised as the ideal Roman magistrate, who as consul and senator opposed the dictatorial ambitions of Julius Caesar. Cato has led a senatorial army in defense of the Republic, but it is now reduced to a small force trapped at Utica. Like many other cornered generals, Cato confronts, in addition to the enemy, mutiny among his own troops and desertion by allied contingents. Cato personally faces a severe dilemma. Should he fight a glorious but futile battle, dying in defense of his principles? Should he slink out of Utica alone in hopes of raising new allies and a new army elsewhere so that he can carry on the struggle? Should he surrender his troops in order to avoid senseless bloodshed but commit suicide to prevent falling into his enemy's hands? After successfully combating mutiny in the ranks, Cato chooses suicide in order to remain the master of his own destiny.

The subplot, patterned after the romantic dilemmas of Restoration heroic tragedy, seems today to be made out of soap-opera materials. With Cato at Utica are his two sons Marcus and Portius, both of whom are in love with Lucia, the daughter of a Roman general. Portius knows he is his brother's rival and feels badly; Marcus does not know and spills his heart's love to Portius; Lucia knows that both men love her and refuses to choose one lest she make the other despair. With Cato, too, is his daughter Marcia, herself pursued by two suitors: the Roman senator Sempronius and the Numidian prince Juba. Marcia refuses to consider either until the army's fate is decided. Sempronius, however, refuses to wait and plans to revolt against Cato and carry off Marcia. The mutiny helps bring out all the lovers' true feelings. Marcia resists Sempronius and confesses to loving Juba, whom she mistakenly believes has been killed in the rebellion. Lucia refuses Marcus' proposal—painfully delivered by the torn Portius—and the rejected suitor throws himself bravely but recklessly into battle against Sempronius' rebels. Marcus' heroic death leaves Portius and Lucia free to wed, as are Juba and Marcia.

That Cato should have to see to his children happily married as the Republic collapses about him indicates one of the imbalances in the play. Addison, in apparent deference to the theatrical taste of the time, tried to combine a complicated love plot with a tragedy in the Senecan mold which discusses important political issues through declamation. The two plots never mix onstage: The oil of romance remains atop and befouls the waters of political philosophy.

Cato himself is a paragon of virtue. Addison follows most classical authors in depicting the Roman senator as the epitome of Stoic virtue. Seneca, Cicero, and Plutarch all described Cato as a human rock steadfast amid the storms of Fortune. Cato was an attractive model of secular, civic virtue to eighteenth century Englishmen who had seen the results of religious, sectarian virtue in the religious civil wars of the seventeenth century. Reviewing the text of *Cato* before its production, Lady Mary Wortley Montagu praised Cato's plain and great sentiments.

Yet for all the ideals that Cato represented to a contemporary audience, the dramatic fact is that he does not engage one's sympathy. As Samuel Johnson put it, the play's "hopes and fears communicate no vibrancy to the heart." Although Addison has created in the first three acts enough dilemmas to bring out a character's humanity, Cato shows none of it in the last two acts. His reaction to Marcus' death in act 4, glorying in the corpse's wounds as a sign of virtue, seems exaggerated and monstrous. In act 5, he contemplates the immortality of the soul before he commits suicide, but so superficially that he seems to be carrying out a ritual rather than reflecting on eternity. He advises Portius to retire to his estate—prudential wisdom indeed, but not consistent with his own fate or that of Marcus. Worst of all, as a contemporary reviewer observed, *Cato* lacks the reversal of fortune, the moment of realization by a despairing protagonist such as Oedipus which strikes an audience with terror and pity. Cato suffers throughout the play, but he never contributes to his downfall. He stands against superior armed forces and malevolent fate until he chooses no longer to be overwhelmed.

Although Cato's story is not tragic, it is not unmoving. It is a brave tale, a portrait of human greatness, and a paean to devotion to principle. The audience senses these qualities, however, more through the language of the play than through its action. Addison builds around a central metaphor a pattern of imagery that makes sense of otherwise discordant love complications and cardboard characters.

The central metaphor is that of the man who stands so calmly and resolutely amid the storms of civil war that his virtue shines like a beacon through the darkness, the wind, and the rain. Throughout the play, Addison images the forces of rebellion—Caesar, Sempronius, the mutinous troops—as storms that batter Cato. In contrast stands Cato's soul, whose virtuous flame never flickers amid the external mayhem. Shielded by virtue, Cato's soul is all placidity. In each act, this opposition of internal harmony and external chaos becomes an index by which the other characters in the play can be judged.

In language rich with contrasting images of harmony and discord, calm and storm, peace and battle, Addison measures each character against the standard, and with each character the loftiness of the standard becomes more apparent. Sempronius, though like Cato a senator, proves un-Roman because the outer storm of Caesar's rebellion sets off in him corresponding inner storms of rebellion against Cato and of lustful passion for Marcia. Marcus is inwardly as blown about by passion and resentment as is Sempronius, but at least Marcus directs his untamable energies into his country's cause. Juba, prince of a desert kingdom, accustomed to riding the whirlwind of his own desires, gradually acquires a Cato-like serenity by learning the Stoic philosophy.

The remaining characters—Portius, Marcia, and Lucia—are already Cato-like as the play opens. Despite their personal dilemmas about love, each focuses more on Cato's plight and resolves not to let personal fears or jealousies conquer as long as the great man's fate hangs in the balance. In the course of the play, none is lost to frustrated passion; having withstood the storms of civil war as well, each emerges at the play's end pure and rejuvenated:

> So the pure limpid stream when foul with stains,
> Of rushing torrents, and descending rains,
> Works itself clear, and as it runs, refines;
> 'Till by degrees, the floating mirrour shines,
> Reflects each flow'r that on the border grows,
> And a new Heaven in its fair bosom shows.

In keeping with the increasingly intellectual preoccupations of the middle class, Addison tried his hand at both the comic and the serious, the delicate and the moral, and the domestic and the philosophical. Even when light in tone, his works reflect the polite society of the day, while revealing an underlying common sense that informs his essays and drama alike. Drawing on his scholarly background, Addison synthesized popular and learned aspects of Augustan society. As a stylist, he gained the respect of his era, and he has continued to exert a formidable influence on later writers.

Other major works

SHORT FICTION: *The Tatler*, 1709-1711 (with Richard Steele; periodical essays); *The Spectator*, 1711-1712, 1714 (with Richard Steele; periodical essays); *The Guardian*, 1713 (with Richard Steele; periodical essays); *The Freeholder: Or, Political Essays*, 1715-1716 (periodical essays).

POETRY: *To Mr. Dryden*, 1693; *A Poem to His Majesty*, 1695; *Praelum Inter Pygmaeos et Grues Commisum*, 1699; *A Letter from Italy*, 1703; *The Campaign*, 1705; *To Her Royal Highness*, 1716; *To Sir Godfrey Kneller on His Portrait of the King*, 1716.

NONFICTION: *Remarks upon Italy*, 1705; *Dialogues upon the Usefulness of Ancient Medals*, 1721; *Letters*, 1941 (Walter Graham, editor).

TRANSLATION: *Fourth Georgic*, 1694 (of Vergil's *Georgics*).

MISCELLANEOUS: *The Miscellaneous Works*, 1914 (A. C. Guthkelch, editor); *The Spectator*, 1965 (Donald Bond, editor).

Bibliography

Bloom, Edward A., and Lillian D. Bloom. *Joseph Addison's Sociable Animal: In the Market Place, on the Hustings, in the Pulpit*, 1971.
Cohen, Michael C. "The Imagery of Addison's *Cato* and the Whig Sublime," in *CEA Critic*. XXXVIII (1976), pp. 23-25.
Dobrée, Bonamy. "The First Victorian," in *Essays in Biography: 1680-1762*, 1925.
Elioseff, Lee Andrew. *The Cultural Milieu of Addison's Literary Criticism*, 1963.
Johnson, Samuel. "Life of Addison," in *The Lives of the English Poets*, 1925.
Kelsall, M. M. "The Meaning of Addison's *Cato*," in *Review of English Studies*. XVII (1966), pp. 149-161.
Otten, Robert. *Joseph Addison*, 1982.
Rogers, Donald O. "Addison's *Cato*: Teaching Through Imagery," in *CEA Critic*. XXXVI (1974), pp. 17-18.

Robert M. Otten

EDWARD ALBEE

Born: Washington, D.C.; March 12, 1928

Principal drama

The Zoo Story, pr. 1959, pb. 1960; *The Death of Bessie Smith*, pr., pb. 1960; *The Sandbox*, pr., pb. 1960; *Fam and Yam*, pr. 1960, pb. 1963; *The American Dream*, pr., pb. 1961; *Bartleby*, pr. 1961 (libretto, with James Hinton, Jr.; music by William Flanagan; adaptation of Herman Melville's "Bartleby the Scrivener"); *Who's Afraid of Virginia Woolf?*, pr., pb. 1962; *The Ballad of the Sad Café*, pr., pb. 1963 (adaptation of Carson McCullers' novel *The Ballad of the Sad Café*); *Tiny Alice*, pr. 1964, pb. 1965; *A Delicate Balance*, pr. 1966, pb. 1967; *Malcolm*, pr., pb. 1966 (adaptation of James Purdy's novel *Malcolm*); *Everything in the Garden*, pr. 1967, pb. 1968 (adaptation of Giles Cooper's play *Everything in the Garden*); *Box and Quotations from Chairman Mao Tse-Tung*, pr. 1968, pb. 1969 (2 one-acts); *All Over*, pr., pb. 1971; *Seascape*, pr., pb. 1975; *Counting the Ways*, pr., pb. 1977; *Listening*, pr., pb. 1977; *The Lady from Dubuque*, pr., pb. 1980; *Lolita*, pr. 1981 (adaptation of Vladimir Nabokov's novel *Lolita*); *The Man Who Had Three Arms*, pr., pb. 1982; *Finding the Sun*, pr. 1983.

Other literary forms

Although Edward Albee has written the libretto for an unsuccessful operatic version of Herman Melville's story "Bartleby the Scrivener," as well as some occasional essays and a few adaptations, he is known primarily for his plays.

Achievements

Edward Albee is the only American playwright to emerge since the 1950's with any claim to being considered a major dramatist ranked among the pantheon of Eugene O'Neill, Thornton Wilder, Arthur Miller, and Tennessee Williams. In the quarter century since *The Zoo Story* first appeared, Albee has produced a sustained and varied body of work, often of considerably higher quality than his critical and popular reputation would suggest. In the introduction to his most experimental works, the two one-acts published together in *Box and Quotations from Chairman Mao Tse-Tung*, Albee sets forth the two "obligations" of a playwright: to illuminate the human condition and to make some statement about the art form itself by altering "the forms within which his precursors have had to work." Like O'Neill before him, Albee has always been an experimentalist, refusing to go back and repeat the earlier formulas simply because they have proved commercially and critically successful. Unlike O'Neill's last works in the mode of symbolic realism, which now are generally regarded as his best, Albee's later dramas have failed to garner the critical acclaim that his earliest ones received—though they are superior dramatically to the efforts of almost all of his American contemporaries. Although acutely disturbed by the downward spiral and paralysis of will that seem to have overtaken modern civilization, and committed to charting these in his work, Albee is not primarily a social playwright, and there is hardly a one of his plays which is totally naturalistic or realistic. In form and style, they range, indeed, from surrealism (*The Sandbox*) to allegory (*Tiny Alice*), from the quasi-religious drawing-room play (*A Delicate Balance*) to the fable (*Seascape*), from the picaresque journey (*Malcolm*) to the ritual deathwatch (both *All Over* and *The Lady from Dubuque*), and from scenes linked by cinematic techniques (*The Death of Bessie Smith*) to monodrama for a disembodied voice (*Box*).

Though he is touted sometimes as the chief American practitioner of the Absurd in drama, Albee only rarely combines in a single work both the techniques and the philosophy associated with that movement and is seldom as unremittingly bleak and despairing an author as Samuel Beckett. Yet the influence of Eugène Ionesco's humor and of Jean Genet's rituals can be discerned in isolated works, as can the battle of the sexes and the voracious, emasculating female from August Strindberg, the illusion/reality motif from Luigi Pirandello and O'Neill, and the poetic language of T. S. Eliot, Beckett (particularly of *Endgame*), and Harold Pinter, as well as the recessive action and lack of definite resolution and closure often found in Beckett and Pinter. As the only avant-garde American dramatist of his generation to attain a wide measure of popular success, Albee sometimes demonstrates, especially in the plays from the first decade of his career, the rather strident and accusatory voice of the angry young man. The outlook in his later works, however, is more that of the compassionate moralist, linking him—perhaps unexpectedly—with Anton Chekhov; one of the characters in *All Over*, recognizing the disparity between what man could become and what he has settled for, even echoes the Russian master's Madame Ranevsky when she says, "How dull our lives are." Even in his most technically and stylistically avant-garde dramas, however, Albee remains essentially very traditional in the values he espouses, as he underlines the necessity for human contact and communion, for family ties and friendships, which provide man with the courage to grow and face the unknown. Always prodding man to become more, yet, at the same time, sympathetically accepting his fear and anxiety over change, Albee has increasingly become a gentle apologist for human beings, who need one crutch after another, who need one illusion after another, so that—in a paraphrase of O'Neill's words—they can make it through life and comfort their fears of death.

Biography

Born on March 12, 1928, in Washington, D.C., Edward Franklin Albee was adopted at the age of two weeks by the socially prominent and wealthy New Yorkers Reed and Frances Albee. His adoptive father was the scion of the family who owned the Keith-Albee chain of vaudeville houses; his adoptive mother was a former Bergdorf high-fashion mannequin. Albee's deep-seated resentment of the natural parents who abandoned him finds reflection in the child motifs that pervade both his original plays and his adaptations: the orphan in *The Zoo Story* and *The Ballad of the Sad Café*, the mutilated twin in *The American Dream*, the intensely hoped-for child who is never conceived and the conceived child who is unwanted in *Who's Afraid of Virginia Woolf?*, the dead son in *A Delicate Balance*, the child in search of his father in *Malcolm*. Living with the Albees was Edward's maternal grandmother, Grandma Cotta, whom he revered and would later memorialize in *The Sandbox* and *The American Dream*. After his primary education at the Rye Country Day School, Albee attended a succession of prep schools (Lawrenceville School for Boys, Valley Forge Military Academy), finally graduating from Choate in 1946 before enrolling at Trinity College in Hartford, Connecticut, where he studied for a year and a half. While in high school, he wrote both poetry and plays.

In 1953, Albee was living in Greenwich Village and working at a variety of odd jobs when, with the encouragement of Thornton Wilder, he committed himself to the theater. *The Zoo Story*, written in only two weeks, premiered in Berlin on September 28, 1959; when it opened Off-Broadway at the Provincetown Playhouse on a double bill with Beckett's *Krapp's Last Tape* in January, 1960, it brought Albee immediate acclaim as the most promising of the new playwrights and won for him an Obie Award as Best Play of the Year. *Who's Afraid of Virginia Woolf?*, his first full-length work—and still his most famous—opened on Broadway in October, 1962, winning for him both the Drama Critics Circle Award and the Tony Award for the Best American Play of that season; the Drama Jury voted it the Pulitzer Prize, but the Advisory Board of Columbia University overturned the nomination because of the play's strong language, and, as a result, John Gassner and John Mason Brown resigned from the jury in protest. Albee went on, however, to win two Pulitzers, for *A Delicate Balance* and *Seascape*. Along with the New York productions of seven original one-act plays and eight original full-length works, Albee has done four adaptations for the stage: of Carson McCullers' 1951 novella *The Ballad of the Sad Café*; of James Purdy's 1959 novel *Malcolm*; of Giles Cooper's 1962 play *Everything in the Garden*; and of Vladimir Nabokov's 1981 novel *Lolita*.

From the time of his own early successes, Albee has actively encouraged the development of other young dramatists and, as part of a production team, has also brought the work of major avant-garde foreign dramatists to New York. Under the auspices of the State Department, he toured behind the Iron Curtain and in South America, and he has become a frequent and popular lecturer on the college circuit, as well as a director of revivals of his own plays.

Analysis

The major recurrent pattern in Edward Albee's plays finds his characters facing a test or a challenge to become more fully human. In *The Zoo Story*, Jerry arrives at a bench in Central Park to jar Peter out of his passivity and Madison Avenue complacence; in *The Death of Bessie Smith*, the black blues singer arrives dying at a Southern hospital only to be turned away because of racial prejudice; in *Tiny Alice*, Brother Julian arrives at Miss Alice's mansion to undergo his dark night of the soul; in *A Delicate Balance*, Harry and Edna arrive at the home of their dearest friends to test the limits of friendship and measure the quality of Agnes and Tobias' life; in *Seascape*, the lizards Leslie and Sarah come up from the sea to challenge Charlie to renewed activity and to try their own readiness for the human adventure; and in *The Lady from Dubuque*, the Lady and her black traveling companion arrive to ease Jo to her death and help her husband learn to let go.

In order to effect the desired change in Peter, Jerry in *The Zoo Story* must first break down the barriers that hinder communication. Accomplishing this might even require deliberate cruelty, since kindness by itself may no longer be enough; oftentimes in Albee, one character needs to hurt another before he can help, the hurt then becoming a creative rather than a destructive force. Along with the focus on lack of communication and on a love and concern that dare to be critical, Albee consistently pursues several additional thematic emphases throughout his works. *The American Dream*, which comments on the decline and fall from grace of Western civilization and on the spiritual aridity of a society that lives solely by a materialistic ethic, also decries the emasculation of Daddy at the hands of Mommy; to a greater or lesser degree, *The Death of Bessie Smith*, *Who's Afraid of Virginia Woolf?*, and *A Delicate Balance* all speak as well to what Albee sees as a disturbing reversal of gender roles (a motif he inherits from Strindberg), though Albee does become increasingly understanding of the female characters in his later works. Several plays, among them *Who's Afraid of Virginia Woolf?* and *A Delicate Balance*, consider the delimiting effect of time on human choice and the way in which man's potential for constructive change decreases as time goes on. Characters in both *A Delicate Balance* and *Tiny Alice* face the existential void, suffering the anxiety that arises over the possibility of there being a meaninglessness at the very core of existence, while characters in several others, including *Box and*

Quotations from Chairman Mao Tse-Tung, All Over, and *The Lady from Dubuque,* confront mortality as they ponder the distinction between dying (which ends) and death (which goes on) and the suffering of the survivor. Elsewhere, particularly in *Counting the Ways,* Albee insists on the difficulty of ever arriving at certainty in matters of the heart, which cannot be known or proved quantitatively. Finally, in such works as *Malcolm* and *Seascape,* he explores the notion that innocence must be lost—or at least risked—before there can be any hope of achieving a paradise regained.

If the mood of many Albee works is autumnal, even wintry, it is because the dramatist continually prods his audiences into questioning whether the answers which the characters put forward in response to the human dilemma—such panaceas as religion (*Tiny Alice*) or formulaic social rituals (*All Over*)—might not in themselves all be simply illusions in which man hides from a confrontation with the ultimate nothingness of existence. In this, he comes closer to the Absurdists, though he is more positive in his holding out of salvific acts: the sacrifice to save the other that ends *The Zoo Story,* the gesture of communion that concludes *Who's Afraid of Virginia Woolf?,* the affirmation of shared humanness that ends *Seascape,* the merciful comforting of the survivor that concludes *The Lady from Dubuque.* If Albee's characters often live a death-in-life existence, it is equally evident that man, God's only metaphor-making animal, can sometimes achieve a breakthrough by coming to full consciousness of his condition and by recognizing the symbolic, allegorical, and anagogical planes of existence.

Who's Afraid of Virginia Woolf?, which brought Albee immediate fame as the most important American dramatist since Williams and Miller, is probably also the single most important American play of the 1960's, the only one from that decade with any likelihood of becoming a classic work of dramatic literature. In this, his first full-length drama, Albee continues several strands from his one-act plays—including the need to hurt in order to help from *The Zoo Story,* the criticism of Western civilization from *The American Dream,* and the Strindbergian battle of the sexes from that play and *The Death of Bessie Smith*—while weaving in several others that become increasingly prominent in his work: excoriating wit, a concern with illusion/reality, the structuring of action through games and game-playing (here, "Humiliate the Host," "Hump the Hostess," "Get the Guests," and "Bringing Up Baby"), and a mature emphasis on the need to accept change and the potentially creative possibilities it offers.

Tightly unified in time, place, and action, *Who's Afraid of Virginia Woolf?* occurs in the early hours of Sunday morning in the home of George, a professor of history, and his wife, Martha, in the mythical eastern town of New Carthage. After a party given by her father, the college president, Martha invites Nick, a young biology teacher, and his wife,

Honey, back home for a nightcap. Through the ensuing confrontations and games that occasionally turn bitter and vicious, both the older and the younger couples experience a radical, regenerative transformation. George, who sees himself as a humanist who lives for the multiplicity and infinite variety that have always characterized history, immediately sets himself up against Nick, the man of science, or, better yet, of scientism, whose narrow, amoral view of inevitability—wherein every creature would be determined down to color of hair and eyes—would sound the death knell for civilization. Like the attractive, muscular young men from *The American Dream* and *The Sandbox*, Nick is appealing on the outside but spiritually vapid within. If his ethical sense is undeveloped, even nonexistent, and his intellect sterile, he is also physically impotent when he and Martha go off to bed, though his temporary impotence should probably be regarded mainly as symbolic of the general sterility of his entire life. George apparently intends, much as Jerry had in *The Zoo Story*, to jar Nick out of his present condition, which involves being overly solicitous of his mousey, infantile wife. Though experiencing a false pregnancy when Nick married her, Honey, slim-hipped and unable to hold her liquor—her repeated exits to the bathroom are adroitly managed to move characters on and off the stage—is frightened of childbirth. As George detects, she has been preventing conception or aborting without Nick's knowledge, and in this way unmanning her husband, preventing him from transmitting his genes. By the play's end, Nick and Honey have seen the intense emptiness that can infect a marriage without children, and Honey three times cries out that she wants a child. George and Martha were unable to have children—neither will cast blame on the other for this—and so, twenty-one years earlier, they created an imaginary son, an illusion so powerful that it has become, for all intents and purposes, a reality for them.

If not intellectually weak, George, who is in fact Albee's spokesman in the play, does share with Nick the condition of being under the emotional and physical control of his wife. Ever since the time when Martha's Daddy insisted that his faculty participate in an exhibition sparring match to demonstrate their readiness to fight in the war and Martha knocked George down in the huckleberry bush, she has taunted George with being a blank and a cipher. It is unlikely that he will ever succeed her father as college president—he will not even become head of the history department. Martha claims that George married her to be humiliated and that she has worn the pants in the family not by choice but because someone must be stronger in any relationship. George realizes that if he does not act decisively to change his life by taking control, the time for any possible action will have passed.

In a formulation of the evolutionary metaphor that Albee recurrently employs, George, who, like civilization, is facing a watershed, remarks that a person can descend only so many rungs on the ladder before there can be no turning back; he must stop contemplating the past and decide to "alter the future." Martha, too, seems to want George to take hold and become more forceful; she, indeed, is openly happy when he exerts himself, as when he frightens them all with a rifle that shoots a parasol proclaiming "Bang," in one of the absurd jokes of which Albee is fond. Martha, despite being loud and brash and vulgar, is also sensual and extremely vulnerable. She does indeed love George, who is the only man she has ever loved, and fears that someday she will go so far in belittling him that she will lose him forever.

The imaginary son has served not only as a uniting force in their marriage but also as a beanbag they can toss against each other. When George decides to kill the son whom they mutually created through an act of imagination, Martha desperately insists that he does not have the right to do this on his own, but to no avail. Even if the child, who was to have reached his twenty-first birthday and legal maturity on the day of the play, had been real, the parents would have had to let go and continue on alone, facing the future with only each other. As George says, "It was time." He kills the illusion, intoning the mass for the dead. It is Sunday morning, and Martha is still frightened of "Virginia Woolf," of living without illusion, but also of facing the unknown. "*Maybe* it will be better," George tells her, for man can never be totally certain of what is to come. Just as there can be no assurance—though all signs point in that direction—that Nick and Honey's marriage will be firmer with a child, there can be no certainty that George and Martha's will be better without their imaginary son, though George is now prepared to offer Martha the strength and support needed to see her through her fear. Finally, Albee seems to be saying, man must not only accept change but also actively embrace it for the possibilities it presents for growth. The future is always terrifying, an uncharted territory, yet if man does not walk into it, he has no other choice but death.

Tiny Alice is Albee's richest work from a philosophical point of view; it also represents his most explicit excursion into the realm of the Absurd. In it, Albee addresses the problem of how man comes to know the reality outside himself, even questioning whether there is, finally, any reality to know. To do this, Albee builds his play around a series of dichotomies: between faith and reason, between present memory and past occurrence, between symbol and substance. The play opens with a scene that could almost stand on its own as a little one-act play, demonstrating Albee's wit at its virulent best. A Lawyer and a Cardinal, old school chums and, apparently, homosexual lovers in their adolescence, attack each other verbally, revealing the venery of both civil and religious authority. The Lawyer has come as the emissary of Miss Alice, ready to bequeath to the Church one hundred million dollars a year for the next twenty years; the Cardinal's secretary, the lay Brother Julian, will be sent to her castle to complete the transaction. For Julian, this becomes an allegorical dark night of the soul, a period when his religious faith will be tempted and tested. On the literal level, the play seems preposterous at times and even muddled; the suspicion that all this has been planned by some extortion ring, though it is unclear what they hope to gain by involving Julian, or even, perhaps, that all this is a charade devised by Julian to provide himself with an opportunity for sacrifice, is never quite dispelled. On the metaphoric and symbolic levels, however, as a religious drama about contemporary man's need to make the abstract concrete in order to have some object to worship, *Tiny Alice* is clear and consistent and succeeds admirably.

Julian, who earlier suffered a temporary loss of sanity over the disparity between his own conception of God and the false gods that men create in their own image, is now undergoing a further crisis. His temptation now is to search out a personification of the Godhead in order to make the Unknowable knowable, by making it concrete through a symbol; he hopes to prove that God exists by making contact with an experiential representation of Him. To represent the Deity in this manner is, however, as the Lawyer insists, to distort and diminish It so that It can be understood in human terms. Up to this point, Julian has always fought against precisely such a reduction of the divine. The symbol that Julian now literally embraces—through a sexual consummation and marriage that is both religious and erotic—is Miss Alice, the surrogate for Tiny Alice. That God in Albee's play is named *"Tiny* Alice" points, in itself, to the strange modern phenomenon of a reduced and delimited rather than an expansive deity. Instead of the real (Miss Alice) being a pale shadowing forth of the ideal form (Tiny Alice), here the symbol (Alice) is *larger* than what it represents, just as the mansion in which the action after scene 1 occurs is larger than its replica, exact down to the last detail, that is onstage in the library. The Lawyer insists that man can never worship an abstraction, for to do so always results in worshiping only the symbol and never the substance or the thing symbolized. Furthermore, he causes Julian to question whether that substance has any tangible existence: Is it only the symbol, and not the thing symbolized, that exists? If so, then Julian faces the possibility of nothingness, of there being *nothing there*, of there being only the finite, sense-accessible dimension in which people live and no higher order that provides meaning.

In the face of this dilemma, Brother Julian can either despair of ever knowing his God, or he can make a leap of faith. When the financial arrangements have been completed, the Lawyer, who—like the Butler—has had Miss Alice as his mistress, shoots Julian, who has always dreamed of sacrificing himself for his faith. Martyrdom, the ultimate form of service to one's God, always involves questions of suicidal intent, of doing, as

Eliot's hero in *Murder in the Cathedral* knows, "the right deed for the wrong reason." Is one dying for self, or as a totally submissive instrument of God? As Julian dies in the posture of one crucified, he demands, in a paroxysm blending sexual hysteria and religious ecstasy, that the transcendent personify itself; indeed, a shadow moves through the mansion, accompanied by ever-increasing heartbeat and ever-louder breathing, until it totally envelops the room. As Albee himself commented, two possibilities present themselves: Either the transcendent is real, and the God Tiny Alice actually manifests itself to Brother Julian at the moment of his death, or Julian's desire for transcendence is so great that he deceives himself. Thus, the play's ending, while allowing for the person of faith to be confirmed in his or her belief about the spiritual reality behind the physical symbol, is at the same time disquieting in that it insists on the equally possible option that the revelation of transcendence is merely a figment of one's imagination. What Albee may well be suggesting, then, and what brings him to the doorstep of the Absurdists in this provocative work, is that there is, finally, nothing there except what man, through his illusions, is able to call up as a shield against the void.

A Delicate Balance, for which Albee deservedly won the Pulitzer Prize denied him by the Advisory Board four seasons earlier for *Who's Afraid of Virginia Woolf?*, is an autumnal play about death-in-life. A metaphysical drawing-room drama in the manner of Eliot and Graham Greene, it focuses on a well-to-do middle-aged couple, Agnes and Tobias, who are forced one October weekend to assess their lives by the unexpected visit of their closest friends, Harry and Edna (characters in Albee traditionally lack surnames). The latter couple arrives on Friday night, frightened by a sudden perception of emptiness. Having faced the existential void, they flee, terrified, to the warmth and succor of Agnes and Tobias' home, trusting that they will discover there some shelter from meaninglessness, some proof that at least the personal values of friendship and love remain. As the stage directions imply, an audience should not measure these visitors-in-the-night against the requirements of realistic character portrayal; they function, instead, as mirror images for their hosts, who, by looking at them, are forced to confront the emotional and spiritual malaise of their own lives. Agnes' live-in sister, the self-proclaimed alcoholic Claire—whose name suggests the clear-sightedness of this woman who stands on the sidelines and sees things as they are—understands the threat that Harry and Edna bring with them. Agnes fears that their guests come bearing the "plague," and Claire understands that this weekend will be spent waiting for the biopsy, for confirmation of whether some dread, terminal disease afflicts this family.

Agnes not only has no desire for self-knowledge but also deliberately guards against any diagnosis of the family's ills. As the fulcrum, she is able to maintain the family's status quo only by keeping herself and Tobias in a condition of stasis, insulated from the currents that threaten to upset the "delicate balance" that allows them to go on without ever questioning their assumptions. A somewhat haughty though gracious woman, whose highly artificial and carefully measured language reflects the controlled pattern of her existence and her inability to tolerate or handle the unexpected, Agnes muses frequently on sex roles. A dramatic descendant of Strindberg's male characters rather than of his female characters, she decries all of those things that have made the sexes too similar and have thus threatened the stability of the traditional family unit.

From her perspective, it is the wife's function to maintain the family *after* the husband has made the decisions: She only holds the reins; Tobias decides the route. It is Tobias' house which is not in order, and only he, she says, can decide what should be done. Tobias himself would claim that Agnes rules, but Agnes would counter that this is only his illusion. Clearly, Tobias seems to have relinquished his position of authority after the death of their son, Teddy; at that point, according to their oft-divorced daughter, Julia, now inopportunely home again after a fourth failed marriage, Tobias became a pleasant, ineffectual, gray *non*eminence. Undoubtedly, his insufficiencies as a father have had an adverse effect upon his daughter's relationships with men, and although Tobias rationalizes that he did not want another son because of the potential suffering it might have caused for Agnes, he might equally have feared his own inadequacy as a role model.

That Tobias lacks essential self-criticism and decisiveness is suggested by the motto he has cheerfully adopted: "We do what we can." In other words, he takes the path of least resistance, no longer exerting himself to do more than the minimum in his personal relationships. At one point in the play, Tobias tells a story about his cat and him—a parable similar to Jerry's tale of the dog in *The Zoo Story*—which illustrates Tobias' attitude toward having demands placed upon him and being judged. Believing that the cat was accusing him of being neglectful, and resenting this assessment, he turned to hating the cat, which he finally had put to sleep in an act Claire terms the "least ugly" choice. Now, with Harry and Edna's visit, Tobias is again having his motives and the depth of his concern measured. He realizes that if he does not respond positively to their needs, he will be tacitly admitting that his whole life, even his marriage to Agnes, has been empty. In one of the verbal arias for which Albee is justly famous, Tobias begs, even demands, that they remain, though he does not want this burden and disruption. When, despite his desperate entreaties, they insist on leaving, Agnes can calmly remark, "Come now; we can begin the day," satisfied that the dark night of terror is safely passed. Her closing line must, however, be understood as ironic. Although it is Sunday morning, there has been no resurrection or renewal; the opportunity for salvation has been missed, and Tobias must now live on with the knowledge that he has failed, that much of his life has been a sham.

As is true of the characters at the end of O'Neill's *Long Day's Journey into Night,* Tobias' tragedy is that he has come to self-knowledge too late to act upon the new recognition. This is perhaps Albee's central perception in *A Delicate Balance*: that time diminishes the possibilities for human choice and change. Try as he might, it is now too late for Tobias to break out of the pattern, and so he is condemned to living out his days with an awareness of how little he has become, since he lacks the comforting illusions of propriety and magnanimity that Agnes can call upon for solace. He has seen his soul, and he has found it wanting, and things can never be the same again. For Tobias, in what is Albee's most beautiful play, the "delicate balance" that everyone erects as a shelter has tipped, but not in his favor. As Agnes muses, "Time happens," and all that remains is rust, bones, and wind. These are Albee's hollow people for whom the dark never ends.

If *Tiny Alice* and *A Delicate Balance* are dark plays, *Seascape* is a play of light, Albee's most luminous work to date. An optimistic tone poem which won for Albee his second Pulitzer, *Seascape* might, indeed, profitably be seen as a reverse image of *A Delicate Balance*, which won for him his first. In the later play, Albee again focuses on a couple in their middle age who ask: Where do we go from here? Are change and growth still possible, or is all that remains a gradual process of physical and spiritual atrophy until death? Nearly the entire first act of *Seascape*—which is primarily a play of scintillating discussion rather than action—is a two-character drama, with the diametrically opposed viewpoints of Nancy and Charlie temporarily poised in a tenuous equilibrium. Nancy's inclination is to follow the urge to ever fuller life, while Charlie is seduced by the prospect of a painless withdrawal from all purposive activity. The "seascape" of the play's title is the literal setting, but it is also an "escape," for the sea lying beyond the dunes is the archetype of both life and death; if it once symbolized Charlie's will-to-life, it now communicates his willed desire for the inertia of death or, at least, for a kind of premoral existence in which life simply passes. The shadow of Albee's dark plays still falls over *Seascape* in Charlie's initial stance as a man experiencing existential angst, terrified by the premonition of loneliness if Nancy should no longer be with him, fearful that even life itself may be only an illusion. In the face of these terrors—symbolized by the recurrent sound of the jet planes passing overhead—death beckons as a welcome release for Charlie, since he has lived well. As his watchword, he chooses "we'll see," just another way of saying that things will be put off until they are blessedly forgotten. Nancy, on the other hand, refuses to vegetate by retreating from life and living out her remaining days in a condition equivalent to "purgatory *before* purgatory," insisting instead that they "*do something*." She understands that if nothing is ever ventured, nothing can be gained. If Charlie, like Agnes in *A Delicate Balance*, desires stasis, a condition comfortable precisely because it is known and therefore can be controlled, Nancy will make the leap of faith into the unknown, accepting change and flux as a necessary precondition for progress and growth. Nancy accuses Charlie of a lack of "interest in imagery"; if, as Albee has frequently said, it is man's metaphor-making ability that renders him truly human, then Charlie's deficiency in this regard signals his diminished condition.

No sooner has Nancy finished her admonition to Charlie that they "*try something new*" than the opportunity presents itself in the appearance of Leslie and Sarah, two great green talking lizards come up from the sea. Their arrival, a startling yet delightful *coup de théâtre*, raises the work to the level of parable and allegory: Leslie and Sarah, existing at some prehuman stage on the evolutionary scale, serve as recollections of what the older couple's heritage was eons ago—as well as of what Charlie desires to become once again. Leslie and Sarah, like Harry and Edna in *A Delicate Balance*, are afraid not of the prospect of dying and finding nothingness or the void but of the challenge of becoming more highly developed, which is to say more human and morally responsible creatures. Life in the sea, unterrifying because a known quantity, was also more restricted and limiting. What inspires them to seek something more are the inklings of a sense of wonder, of awe, and of a childlike enthusiasm—qualities Nancy possesses in abundance. Their choice, then, exactly parallels Charlie's: They can make do by settling for less than a full life, or they can expand their lives qualitatively by becoming conscious of themselves as thinking and feeling beings, though that, of course, requires a willingness to experience consciously suffering as well as joy.

Significantly, it is Charlie, himself afraid, who convinces Leslie and Sarah to remain up on earth rather than descend back into the deep. In the moment of convincing them, he himself undergoes a regenerative epiphany that saves him, too. At the climactic point in *Seascape*, Charlie, like Jerry in *The Zoo Story* and George in *Who's Afraid of Virginia Woolf?* before him, gives Leslie and Sarah a "survival kit." To accomplish this requires that he hurt them, especially Sarah. Since what separates man from the lower animals is precisely his consciousness of being alive, of being vulnerable, and of finally being mortal, Charlie realizes that he can help Leslie and Sarah complete their transformation from beast to man only by making them feel truly human emotions. Playing on Sarah's fear that Leslie might someday leave her and never return, he deliberately, in an action that recalls the necessary violence of Jerry toward Peter, makes Sarah cry; that, in turn, makes Leslie so defensive and angry that he hits and chokes

Charlie. Having tasted these human emotions of sorrow and wrath, Sarah and Leslie at first desire more than ever to return to the ooze, to the prehuman security of the sea. What quenches their fears is Nancy and Charlie pleading with them not to retreat, extending their hands to the younger couple in a gesture of compassion and human solidarity. In aiding Leslie and Sarah on the mythic journey from the womb into the world that, no matter how traumatic, must in time be taken, Charlie simultaneously leaves behind his desire to escape from life and asserts once more his will to live. If Charlie is a representative Everyman, fallen prey to ennui and despair, then Leslie's "Begin," on which the curtain falls, is a declaration of faith, trust, and determination, uttered not only for himself and Sarah but also for all humankind, who must periodically be roused and inspired to continue their journey.

The "Begin" that closes *Seascape* might also be seen as Albee's own motto and challenge to himself as a playwright. Despite a quarter-century-long career that has, especially in its second half, been marked by more critical downs than ups, he has not been satisfied to rest on his successes, such as *Who's Afraid of Virginia Woolf?*, nor has he been content simply to repeat the formulas that have worked for him in the past. Instead, he has continued to experiment with dramatic form, to venture into new structures and styles. In so doing, he has grown into a major voice in dramatic literature, the progress of whose career in itself reflects his overriding theme: No emotional or artistic or spiritual growth is possible without embracing the terror—and perhaps the glory—of tomorrow's unknown, for the unknown is contemporary man's only certainty.

Bibliography
Bigsby, C. W. E. *Albee*, 1969.
Debusscher, Gilbert. *Edward Albee: Tradition and Renewal*, 1967.
Hirsch, Foster. *Who's Afraid of Edward Albee?*, 1978.
Rutenberg, Michael E. *Edward Albee: Playwright in Protest*, 1969.
Stenz, Anita Maria. *Edward Albee: The Poet of Loss*, 1978.

Thomas P. Adler

MAXWELL ANDERSON

Born: Atlantic, Pennsylvania; December 15, 1888
Died: Stamford, Connecticut; February 28, 1959

Principal drama

White Desert, pr. 1923; *What Price Glory?*, pr. 1924, pb. 1926 (with Laurence Stallings); *Outside Looking In*, pr. 1925, pb. 1929; *First Flight*, pr. 1925, pb. 1926 (with Stallings); *Three American Plays*, pb. 1926; *Saturday's Children*, pr., pb. 1927; *Gypsy*, pr. 1929; *Elizabeth the Queen*, pr., pb. 1930 (adaptation of Lytton Strachey's history *Elizabeth and Essex*); *Night over Taos*, pr., pb. 1932; *Both Your Houses*, pr., pb. 1933; *Mary of Scotland*, pr., pb. 1933; *Valley Forge*, pr., pb. 1934; *Winterset*, pr., pb. 1935; *The Masque of Kings*, pb. 1936, pr. 1937; *High Tor*, pr., pb. 1937; *Knickerbocker Holiday*, pr., pb. 1938 (lyrics; music by Kurt Weill); *Key Largo*, pr., pb. 1939; *Eleven Verse Plays, 1929-1939*, pb. 1940; *Joan of Lorraine*, pr., pb. 1946; *Anne of the Thousand Days*, pr., pb. 1948; *Lost in the Stars*, pr., pb. 1949 (lyrics; music by Weill; adaptation of Alan Paton's novel *Cry, the Beloved Country*); *Barefoot in Athens*, pr., pb. 1951; *Bad Seed*, pr. 1954, pb. 1955 (adaptation of William March's novel); *The Day the Money Stopped*, pr., pb. 1958 (adaptation of Brendan Gill's novel); *The Golden Six*, pr. 1958, pb. 1961; *Four Verse Plays*, pb. 1959.

Other literary forms

Maxwell Anderson's reputation rests exclusively on his dramatic works. In addition to his works in various forms of drama, he wrote a number of essays on the theater, some of which are collected in *The Essence of Tragedy and Other Footnotes* (1939) and *Off Broadway: Essays About the Theatre* (1947). Anderson also published a collection of poetry, *You Who Have Dreams* (1925). Finally, he wrote a number of screenplays, including the screenplay for the film adaptation of *Joan of Lorraine*, entitled *Joan of Arc* (1948).

Achievements

Anderson was a prolific and versatile playwright, the author of poetic drama and historical drama, realistic plays and thesis plays, radio drama, screenplays, and musical drama (including two collaborations with composer Kurt Weill). At the peak of his success, during one season in the 1930's, he had three plays running on Broadway at the same time. During that same decade, he twice received the New York Drama Critics Circle Award and was also awarded a Pulitzer Prize.

Of the twelve Anderson plays produced on Broadway in his lifetime, nine are verse dramas—a remarkable feat in itself in the twentieth century, with verse drama long an endangered species. Indeed, it is as a rare modern practitioner of that form that Anderson is likely to be remembered.

Even Anderson's lesser achievements attest the enormous vitality of the American theater in his time: The sheer range of his work, including both failed experiments and commercial successes, the stretch of his ambition (even when one concedes that his theory of tragedy, for example, is an intellectual embarrassment)—all of this makes him one of the representative figures of a key period in the history of American drama.

Biography

James Maxwell Anderson was born the son of a Baptist minister in Atlantic, Pennsylvania, on December 15, 1888. The family moved frequently, but in time Maxwell enrolled at the University of North Dakota, where he wrote poetry and drama. Following graduation, in 1911, he married Margaret Haskett. After two years of teaching high school, he enrolled in a master's program at Stanford University and earned his M.A. degree in 1914. After having taught for five years, Anderson went into journalism, working for the *Chronicle* and the *Bulletin* in San Francisco. In 1918, he moved to New York, where he worked on the editorial staffs of *The New Republic*, *New York Evening Globe*, and *New York World*.

Anderson's playwriting did not begin until 1923, when, at the age of thirty-five, he wrote the verse tragedy *White Desert*. The play was a theatrical failure, but it interested another playwright, Laurence Stallings, at that time a successful book reviewer for *New York World*. In 1924, the two collaborated on an antiwar play, *What Price Glory?*, a realistic piece that was extremely well received.

Following this success, Anderson began to broaden his techniques, writing in both verse and prose. When subsequent collaborations with Stallings did not prove successful, Anderson parted company with him. He was to write six more plays before he achieved another success, with *Elizabeth the Queen* in 1930. In this play, Anderson's unusual combination of poetic, dramatic, and philosophical gifts finds brilliant expression in a dramatization of the love affair of Queen Elizabeth I of England and the ambitious Lord Essex.

Anderson's technique of illuminating contemporary issues with historical settings was so successful in *Elizabeth the Queen* that he wrote eight more plays using history for this purpose. *Night over Taos*, *Mary of Scotland*, *Valley Forge*, and *The Masque of Kings* are, like *Elizabeth the Queen*, verse plays, though none of these was as successful as the latter. One of Anderson's musicals, *Knickerbocker Holiday*, which takes as its point of departure Washington Irving's *A History of New York* (1809), also has a historical setting, used to shed a comic and satiric light on the political scene of the 1930's. *Barefoot in Athens* and the perennially popular *Anne of the Thousand Days* combine the historical drama with the drama of ideas, following the pattern of George Bernard Shaw but without Shaw's ability to dramatize intellectual issues. Finally, *Joan of Lorraine* is an examination of Joan's character through a rehearsal for a play during which the actress portraying the saint and the director disagree on the interpretation of her role.

In the 1940's and 1950's, Anderson devoted more of his time to matters outside the theater and produced fewer plays than he had during the 1930's. In 1940, he participated in Wendell Willkie's unsuccessful campaign for the presidency against Franklin Delano Roosevelt. In 1942, Anderson helped to raise money to buy High Tor, and in 1943, it was given to the state of New York for a park, thus saving the real mountain from the fate it suffered in the play of the same title. He spent part of 1943 touring army bases in North Carolina and Virginia, then in England and North Africa. In 1944, he devoted the summer and fall to campaigning against the United States congressman from his home district in New York State and was successful in that venture. In 1947, he toured Greece and wrote a series of essays about the political situation there.

Anderson's first wife had died in 1931, and in 1933 he had married the actress Gertrude Maynard. They had been estranged for some time when, in March, 1953, she committed suicide. In 1954, Anderson married Gilda Oakleaf. They established a new home in Stamford, Connecticut, where Anderson was to live until his death.

Burdened with tax problems, Anderson in the late 1950's wrote three plays primarily to bring in more money: *Bad Seed* in 1954, *The Day the Money Stopped* in 1958, and *The Golden Six* in the same year. Only *Bad Seed*, however, proved to be a commercial success.

Anderson died on February 28, 1959, following a stroke at his home in Stamford, Connecticut. On March 3, a memorial service was held for him at St. Paul's Chapel, Columbia University.

Analysis

Maxwell Anderson was one among several playwrights, including Eugene O'Neill, Elmer Rice, Sidney Howard, Robert E. Sherwood, George S. Kaufman, and Paul Green, who changed the world's perception of American drama. Before World War I, American drama was purely of local interest, and no great playwrights had appeared in the United States. By the end of the 1920's, however, New York City had become one of the most vital theater centers in the world, and American dramatists were enjoying a period of extraordinary creative flowering.

Although the American playwrights of this period were diverse in their points of view, many of them reflected the disillusionment that followed World War I. Anderson was among these; the basic philosophy of life that informs his drama is typical of the 1920's. In this view, modern man is deprived of religious faith or the opportunity for meaningful social action. Love, although fleeting, is the only thing that gives life meaning. Anderson's first successful play, *What Price Glory?*, on which he collaborated with Laurence Stallings, has affinities with many works of the 1920's; its critical look at the myths surrounding war brings to mind Ernest Hemingway's novel *A Farewell to Arms* (1929). The play centers on a squad of marines in the midst of some of the heaviest fighting in World War I.

The play's disillusioned attitude and profane dialogue may seem mild to today's readers, who are accustomed to stronger stuff, but to the audience of the 1920's, the play was shocking. Stallings and Anderson's soldiers talk like soldiers, and their profanity (toned down after objections from various groups, including the Marine Corps) epitomizes a thoroughgoing irreverence among the characters toward matters that traditionally had been treated with greater respect.

The play uses the war as a symbol for a world that is purposeless and chaotic. Act 1 shows the American marine unit awaiting a battle with the Germans in a French town; act 2 centers on the battle, emphasizing the suffering of Americans and Germans alike; and act 3 reveals the futility of the conflict. In act 1, Sergeant Quirk arrives to take over the duties of a longtime enemy, Captain Flagg, while Flagg goes on a brief leave. Quirk later becomes involved with a prostitute named Charmaine, unaware that Flagg also likes her. The inevitable happens: The girl's father eventually demands that his daughter's honor be saved by marriage. Quirk is threatened by Flagg with court-martial if he does not marry the girl, but the company is ordered to the front before the matter can be resolved. The girl is abandoned so that the men can continue to kill others, rather than themselves.

When *Elizabeth the Queen* was produced on November 3, 1930, Anderson launched the most productive decade of his career and for the first time showed the public the nature of his concern with poetic tragedy. The play was both a popular and a critical success—surprising, perhaps, considering that it was written in verse. The controlled expression of emotion through rhythm and image is well handled in the play, perhaps contributing to the acceptance of the poetic form by the audience. The idea of the play came from Lytton Strachey's history *Elizabeth and Essex*, published in 1928. Anderson, however, shifted the focus from historic transition to individual character. Evident here is a recurring theme in Anderson's Tudor plays: the lust for power in conflict with sexual passion.

The aging Queen Elizabeth suspects that her youthful lover Essex is as enamored of her throne as he is of her person. Two rival courtiers, Sir Robert Cecil and Sir Walter Raleigh, intrigue against Essex by intercepting Essex's and the queen's letters while he is in Ireland on a military expedi-

tion, thus sowing further distrust between the lovers. Their plot is successful: Essex is provoked into storming the palace, but once within the throne
room, he is outwitted by Elizabeth, who then orders his arrest and execution for treason. In the last act, Elizabeth anxiously waits for Essex to
return to her a ring as a sign of his repentence. Finally, she sends for him.
Her attempt to save him is futile, however, for Essex is too proud to beg
for his life and acknowledges that, were he freed, he would continue his
pursuit of the throne. Essex leaves, having accepted his fate, and Elizabeth
must wait, in anguish, for his now inevitable execution.

Anderson distrusted the system of government and of power politics in
the United States and elsewhere. He believed that men of goodwill are
usually destroyed by evil ones—a sentiment expressed here in the line,
"The rats inherit the earth." He saw, however, in the struggle of mankind
against powerful forces a magnificence in which he found inspiration. *Elizabeth the Queen* revolves around very strong characters motivated by great
passion, flawed characters who are nevertheless dignified through suffering.
Their sense of loneliness and alienation reflects the fragmentation and isolation of modern society; Elizabeth says "The years are long living among
strangers." Such recognition of the lonely state of man in a society in which
evil is a dominant force recurs throughout Anderson's work.

Soon after the success of *Elizabeth the Queen*, Anderson returned to
prose drama with the political satire *Both Your Houses*, which won for him
a Pulitzer Prize in 1933. Although the setting of the latter is modern Washington, D.C., rather than historical England, *Both Your Houses*, like its
predecessor, centers on the isolation of the honest individual in a predominantly evil society. Alan McClean is a freshman congressman who is
appalled by the graft and corruption he finds to be commonplace in Washington. As he explores this rampant corruption, he discovers not only that
his own election campaign is tainted but also that, if he votes according to
his conscience, he risks financially ruining his fiancé's father, a man whom
he admires. McClean is unsuccessful in an attempt to beat his colleagues at
their own game and is left, in his own eyes, with no choice but to resign.

Among Anderson's many plays of the 1930's, his most productive decade, one of the most interesting is *High Tor*. Perhaps it is so interesting
because the theme is an enduring one in American literature: conservation,
or, as it is now termed, ecology. High Tor is a real mountain peak over-
looking the Hudson River, near which Anderson lived at the time he wrote
the play.

Van Van Dorn, the individualistic owner of High Tor, is determined not
to sell his mountain despite the threats of two men who represent a mining
company that wants to buy High Tor. Van Dorn is aided in his efforts to
preserve the mountain by the ghosts of Henry Hudson's crew, who have
been wandering the slopes of High Tor for three hundred years, waiting for

their ship to return for them. When the company men are stranded on the mountain after dark, they take shelter in a steam shovel, which the ghosts then hoist high into the air. Morning finds the conflicts resolved. The spectral ship has returned for its crew, and Van Dorn finally agrees to sell High Tor, believing that, like the ghosts, the mountain has vanished overnight.

The play blends realism, fantasy, farce, and satire in a delightfully theatrical mix; it won for Anderson the New York Drama Critics Circle Award. Despite the play's entertaining qualities, however, it reminds the audience that the materialistic modern world will not allow the free and natural to survive.

Throughout his dramatic works, Anderson adhered to the Aristotelian principles of unity and the tragic hero as he explored the myths of his times. Producing the most important body of his work during the Depression era, he addressed social issues and injustices, though his primary purpose seems to have been to place them in their historical, literary, and mythological contexts rather than to raise the audience's awareness of such problems. Clearly, Anderson was interested in dramatic theory and history, and his plays exemplify his concerns with form as well as with theme.

Other major works

NOVEL: *Morning Winter and Night*, 1952 (as John Nairne Michaelson).

POETRY: *You Who Have Dreams*, 1925.

NONFICTION: *The Essence of Tragedy and Other Footnotes*, 1939; *Off Broadway: Essays About the Theatre*, 1947.

SCREENPLAYS: *All Quiet on the Western Front*, 1930 (with others; adaptation of Erich Maria Remarque's novel); *Joan of Arc*, 1948 (with Andrew Solt); *The Wrong Man*, 1957.

Bibliography

Avery, Laurence G., ed. *Dramatist in America: Letters of Maxwell Anderson, 1912-1958*, 1977.

Bailey, Mabel Driscoll. *Maxwell Anderson: The Playwright as Prophet*, 1957.

Gould, Jean. *Modern American Playwrights*, 1967.

Mersand, Joseph. *The American Drama Since 1930*, 1968.

Shivers, Alfred S. *The Life of Maxwell Anderson*, 1983.

_____ . *Maxwell Anderson*, 1976.

Taylor, William E., ed. *Modern American Drama*, 1968.

John W. Crawford

ROBERT ANDERSON

Born: New York, New York; April 28, 1917

Principal drama

Come Marching Home, pr. 1945; *All Summer Long*, pr. 1953, pb. 1955; *Tea and Sympathy*, pr., pb. 1953; *Silent Night, Lonely Night*, pr. 1955, pb. 1960; *The Days Between*, pr., pb. 1965; *You Know I Can't Hear You When the Water's Running*, pr., pb. 1967 (comprises four one-act plays: *The Footsteps of Doves*, *I'm Herbert*, *The Shock of Recognition*, and *I'll Be Home for Christmas*); *I Never Sang for My Father*, pr., pb. 1968; *Solitaire/Double Solitaire*, pr. 1971, pb. 1972.

Other literary forms

Robert Anderson has written numerous radio, television, and film scripts, including screen adaptations of Kathryn Hulme's 1956 novel *The Nun's Story* (1959), of Richard McKenna's 1962 novel *The Sand Pebbles* (1966), and of his own *I Never Sang for My Father* (1970). The only one of these that has been published, however, is the screenplay of *I Never Sang for My Father*. Many interviews with Anderson and essays by him on the practice of playwriting and the state of the theater have been published in various newspapers and journals, but these interviews and essays have not been collected. He has also published two novels: *After* (1973) and *Getting Up and Going Home* (1978).

Achievements

Considering Robert Anderson's lifelong devotion to the theater, the number of his plays receiving wide notice has been relatively small. Although he wrote *The Days Between* with Broadway in mind, Anderson offered it to the newly formed American Playwrights Theater when that organization was having difficulty getting good new plays to offer its member theaters. As a result, *The Days Between* was produced during 1965-1966 in fifty regional theaters but was never produced on Broadway. *Come Marching Home*, which did have a short New York run, was never published.

Although Anderson's plays are to some extent marred by imitativeness and by a lack of variation in theme and motif, they nevertheless represent a solid, if modest, achievement. Anderson has created several memorable characters—for example, the rigid, domineering, irascible, charming, and pathetic Tom Garrison of *I Never Sang for My Father*, a self-made man who in his old age is unable to admit to himself, much less communicate to his family, his need for them and his loneliness; the comic, anxiously adaptable actor Richard Pawling of *The Shock of Recognition*, also pathetic in his eagerness to be or to do anything at all in order to get a part in a play; and the middle-class, middle-aged, anguished Chuck of *I'll Be Home for Christmas*, suddenly, by a letter from his son, brought face to face with his own fears about the meaninglessness of his existence.

In addition, Anderson has been willing to take chances in his plays, and in so doing has helped enrich both in subject and in technique the possibilities open to the theater. In subject, for example, *Tea and Sympathy* was the first American play to deal explicitly with homosexuality, and *Double Solitaire* carries frankness in the discussion of sexual experiences to what is probably the limit of public acceptability on the stage; in stage technique, *The Shock of Recognition* introduced for the first time the possibility of presenting male frontal nudity in the theater (though not itself actually presenting such nudity); and in format, his *You Know I Can't Hear You When the Water's Running* successfully defied the well-entrenched belief that a group of one-act plays could not achieve commercial success on Broadway. These accomplishments have established Anderson's reputation as a dramatist seriously interested in making stage depictions of life correspond more closely to real life.

Biography

Robert Woodruff Anderson was born in New York City in April, 1917, to James Hewston and Myra Grigg Anderson. His father was a self-made man who twice made his way from poverty to financial success. Perhaps as a consequence, James Anderson had great respect for the so-called "manly" virtues of self-reliance, determination, and physical courage, but shared none of the aesthetic values which his wife instilled in young Robert. The resultant unhappy relationship between a husband and wife unable to appreciate each other's values has been mirrored in several of Anderson's plays, notably *All Summer Long*, *Tea and Sympathy*, and *I Never Sang for My Father*. The strained relationship between a father with a purely materialistic bent and a son whose artistic and literary bent embarrasses and bewilders his father forms a secondary motif in several of Anderson's plays and provides the central conflict in *I Never Sang for My Father*.

Anderson was educated in private elementary schools; at Phillips Exeter Academy, in Exeter, New Hampshire, where he wrote his first plays; and at Harvard, where he wrote plays, theater reviews, and a senior honors thesis entitled "The Necessity for Poetic Drama." He completed his undergraduate work at Harvard in 1939 and his work for the master's degree in 1940, and continued work toward a Ph.D. there until he entered the navy in 1942. While a graduate student at Harvard, he served as a teaching assistant and also taught drama courses in several small local colleges. During his navy service in World War II, Anderson wrote several plays, including *Come Marching Home*, which won the National Theater Conference Prize in 1945 for the best play written by a serviceman overseas and which subsequently had a very brief run Off Broadway in New York. This prize helped him to obtain a scholarship to study playwriting under John Gassner, who later became one of Anderson's staunchest supporters among drama critics.

In 1940, Anderson married Phyllis Stohl, a woman ten years older than he, who was beloved in theatrical circles and who all of their married life was working for the theater in one capacity or another—as teacher, director, radio scriptwriter, producer, and finally as a literary agent for playwrights. They had no children, and the last five years of their sixteen-year marriage were dominated for both by the emotional turmoil of her long, and eventually unsuccessful, struggle against cancer. The trauma of this experience and his subsequent feelings of grief and guilt haunted Anderson for many years, leaving its impact on several of his plays, until he finally exorcised it in the pages of a very autobiographical novel, *After*. In 1959, Anderson married another theater personality, the stage and screen actress Teresa Wright, who later originated the role of Alice in the stage version of *I Never Sang for My Father*. This marriage produced no children, although Wright had two children from a previous marriage.

To date, only three of Anderson's plays have had any great degree of commercial and critical success: *Tea and Sympathy*, *You Know I Can't Hear You When the Water's Running*, and *I Never Sang for My Father*. The others have had short runs and mixed reviews. In addition to writing for the theater, however, he has produced numerous scripts for radio, television, and motion pictures, many of them highly successful in production, and has been a teacher of drama and playwriting in colleges and universities. In the 1970's, he turned to the writing of novels.

Analysis

Robert Anderson is a heavily autobiographical playwright. His focal character is usually male, is usually a writer, often also a teacher, is misunderstood or not properly appreciated by someone close to him—most often his father or his wife—and is sometimes suffering from a tragedy associated with his wife. This character is young in the plays written when Anderson was young—in *All Summer Long*, he is only twelve, and in *Tea and Sympathy*, he is almost eighteen—but in the plays written as Anderson grew older, the focal character also is older: in *Silent Night, Lonely Night*, he is in his early forties; in *The Days Between*, he is split into two characters, both of whom are around forty; in three of the four one-act plays which make up *You Know I Can't Hear You When the Water's Running*, he is middle-aged, though in one of these he is not a writer; in *I Never Sang for My Father*, he is forty; in *Solitaire*, he is around fifty and, though not a writer since writing is obsolete in his society, a recorder of tapes in a library; and in *Double Solitaire*, he is forty-three.

Anderson's themes derive from the circumstances of this character in various incarnations. One of his most common themes is the incompatibility of a husband and wife, particularly a middle-aged couple who were once madly in love with each other. Their incompatibility may or may not be in values or goals, but its major symptom is always an unhappy sex life. In some cases, it even results in a complete cessation of any sex life within the marriage. Closely related to this theme is the theme of the importance of good sexual experiences in and of themselves, even outside marriage. Sex is seen as therapeutic, and it becomes a charitable obligation for kind and selfless people to fulfill the sex needs which they discern in lonely people with whom they have a mental or spiritual rapport. Another common theme of the plays is an unhappy father-son relationship, usually stemming from the inability of a materialistic, forceful, athletically inclined father to understand or appreciate properly the nature or accomplishments of a more sensitive, thoughtful, artistic son. Two other themes are inherent in these unhappy relationships, whether marital or father-son: the theme of guilt and hostility within the failing or failed relationship, and the theme of loneliness—the loneliness of an individual who is unable to achieve with another a sharing of values, goals and aspirations, tenderness and love.

Surprisingly for a writer so personal in theme and character, Anderson has seldom been innovative in plot, style, or technique. Perhaps because of his many years of formal education in drama, his works are much influenced by earlier writers, particularly Anton Chekhov, John Van Druten, and Tennessee Williams. *All Summer Long*, for example, follows Chekhov's *The Cherry Orchard* (pr. 1904) not only in its slow pace and in the lassitude of its ineffectual characters, but also in the loss of the family home, which literally slides into a river because the adults in the family have been unable to put aside their petty personal desires and take some positive action to prevent the erosion of the soil under the house. *Tea and Sympathy* has an equally heavy debt to Van Druten's *Young Woodley* (pr. 1925), and *I Never Sang for My Father* owes several of its important elements to Williams' *The Glass Menagerie* (pr. 1944). Anderson has, however, not been wedded to any particular format or technique, but has been willing to experiment with various techniques introduced by others, using for his settings in some plays the highly realistic, conventional scene behind the proscenium arch and in others settings which are to varying degrees illusionistic and nonrepresentational; using an almost bare stage in some of the one-act plays; and using a narrator-chorus figure in *I Never Sang for My Father*. His attempts to make the theater more frank and open in its treatment of sex stem from his desire to see it become more adult and honest in its treatment of human relationships, particularly the marital and extramarital sexual relationships on which his plays so often center.

The autobiographical influences on *Tea and Sympathy* are readily apparent. The setting is a New England preparatory school similar to the one
Anderson attended. Young Tom Lee has an artistic and sensitive nature
and aesthetic interests which make him seem an "off-horse" to some of the
other boys, to his housemaster, and to his father, who has sent Tom to this
school in the hope that the housemaster will develop in Tom what the
father considers a more manly character. Tom is not a writer, although in
his elementary school days when his class needed a poet he was apparently
the automatic choice. His real interest is in music, however, and he hopes
for a career as a folksinger. Anderson's own first interest had also been
music, and only after a sinus condition ruined his voice did he turn to the
writing of plays. Tom falls in love with Laura Reynolds, a woman almost
ten years older than he. Like Anderson's first wife, Phyllis, Laura is sympathetic to young people and eager to encourage talent in the young. Anderson's dedication of the play to Phyllis, "whose spirit is everywhere in
this play," suggests that Laura resembles Phyllis in many other respects.

In addition to this strong autobiographical influence, however, there are
also several strong literary influences on the play. One such influence,
although a minor one, is Williams' *A Streetcar Named Desire*. In Williams'
play, the young, sensitive first husband of Blanche kills himself when she
discovers he is homosexual. His suicide scars Blanche for life, leaving her
with feelings of guilt and remorse which she attempts to expiate by having
sex with teenage boys even later in life when she is much older than they.
In *Tea and Sympathy*, the young, sensitive first husband of Laura, because
of some incident unknown to Laura which called his courage and manliness
into question, in effect kills himself by risking his life unnecessarily in battle to prove to others that he is not a coward. His death scars Laura and
may lead to her desire to experience sexual love with the teenage Tom Lee.

Two more important literary influences are Van Druten's *Young Woodley*
and George Bernard Shaw's *Candida*. *Tea and Sympathy* is, in fact, so
similar to *Young Woodley* that it might almost be considered an adaptation.
In both plays, the young protagonist, a student at a boarding school, is
disliked by his housemaster and teased by some of the students because he
does not conform to their concept of manliness. Both housemasters hope
eventually to become housemasters of their schools; both housemasters are
apparently projecting their own weaknesses and self-doubts on the protagonists. In both, the protagonist has been deprived of his mother early in life,
in *Young Woodley* by her death and in *Tea and Sympathy* by the divorce of
the parents. In both, the student is in love with the housemaster's young
wife (in both plays named Laura), whose nature and values are far different from those of her husband. In both, Laura encourages the young
man in his artistic pursuits. In both, the young man visits the town prosti-

tute, with resultant feelings of self-disgust, though for different reasons. In both, the young man, in a rage of frustration and despair, makes an attack with a butcher knife, Woodley an attack on another student and Tom an attempt at suicide. One important difference between the two plays is that in the last analysis, Woodley's father is far more helpful and sympathetic to his son than is Tom's father, a difference which reflects the lack of sympathetic understanding between Anderson and his own father. Another major difference is in the ending; Anderson gave his play a conclusion which, for that period in American theatrical history, was quite sensational.

This ending stems from the inspiration which Shaw's play *Candida* gave to Anderson's play. When Candida, the older married woman in Shaw's play, speculates on the effect which her rejection of the young, poetic Marchbanks will ultimately have on him, she wonders whether Marchbanks will forgive her for selfishly maintaining her own purity and chastity instead of initiating him into the mysteries of sexual love. She concludes that Marchbanks will forgive her if some other good woman teaches him about such love, but will not forgive her if he has the disillusioning experience of learning about sexual love from a "bad woman." In *Tea and Sympathy*, Tom asks Laura if she thinks Candida was right to send Marchbanks away, and Laura replies that Shaw "made it seem right." Later, when Tom, overcome by emotion, impulsively embraces and kisses Laura, she momentarily rejects his kisses, and he flees to the arms of the local prostitute, where his repulsion for the prostitute makes him unable to perform sexually and fills him with self-disgust. Laura, hearing about Tom's wretched experience, feels responsible for it, saying that she wishes she had let Tom prove his sexual prowess with her rather than sending him off to such a sordid experience. She has, thus, decided that Candida was wrong after all, and the play concludes as she is offering herself to Tom so that he will be able to prove to himself that he can indeed perform sexually as a man.

Here, Anderson is developing one of his favorite themes—the immorality and selfishness of allowing conventional mores to prevent one from offering a loving sexual experience to a kindred spirit who is lonely and in need of such love. The offering of a spirit of love and understanding is not enough in such circumstances; the truly loving person will feel the obligation to offer the full consummation of a sexual experience and will feel guilty for withholding such an offer. This theme provides the major conflict of Anderson's next play, *Silent Night, Lonely Night*, in which two lonely, unhappy people meet by chance on Christmas Eve, and, though both remain committed to their own unhappy marriages, help and strengthen each other by experiencing together a full sexual communion for that night only. Each has regrets for times in the past when he or she should have offered such an experience but withheld it through mindless obedience to an inappropriate system of morality, and both are seen at the conclusion of the play as better persons because they have learned to overcome such rigid principles. In this play, the Christmas Eve setting seems intended to give a religious sanction to Anderson's thesis.

Not only the morality but also the validity of this thesis can be, and indeed have been, questioned. Gerald Weales has branded it as belonging to the "fashionable sex-as-therapy" school of drama, which he finds unrealistic, and even John Gassner pointed out the strong possibility that in reality, the awe in which Tom Lee held Laura would prevent him from performing sexually with her and would thus compound, instead of alleviating, his trauma. Others have noted the lengths to which Anderson went to make the sensational ending seem right: that he divided his characters for the most part along melodramatic lines into the good and the bad, with both Laura and Tom clearly in the category of the good and with the vicious housemaster clearly in the category of the bad; that the housemaster is revealed as a latent homosexual himself; that Laura unequivocally breaks off her marriage to him before she offers herself to Tom; and even that her seduction of Tom takes place on his eighteenth birthday, so that she cannot be accused of contributing to the delinquency of a minor.

Tea and Sympathy thus takes up all the major themes of Anderson's later plays: the unhappy marital relationship, the unhappy father-son relationship, the feelings of guilt and loneliness deriving from the failure of such relationships, and the moral imperative of offering sexual experiences generously under certain circumstances. While derivative in plot and technique, it does break new ground in treating homosexuality explicitly rather than by innuendo and in the sexual frankness of the scene on which the curtain drops.

Though produced the year after *You Know I Can't Hear You When the Water's Running*, *I Never Sang for My Father* was written earlier and represents an earlier stage in Anderson's development. It is his most thorough and most successful attempt at exploring a difficult father-son relationship. Again, the autobiographical elements of the play are obvious. Tom Garrison, the father in the play, is like Anderson's father in many respects. He is a self-made man; he loves athletics and athletic values; he was once a mayor (Anderson's father once ran for the office of mayor of New Rochelle); and he has never understood or appreciated the artistic and literary interests of either his wife or his son. The son, Gene Garrison, is like Anderson in being both a writer and a college professor, in having had a wife who died slowly of a lingering illness, in being much closer to his mother than to his father, and in trying unsuccessfully to establish a satisfying relationship with his father.

The most important literary influence on the play is Williams' *The Glass Menagerie*. Anderson's play was first written as a movie script, and when Anderson sought a way of giving the play version a fluidity of movement from short scene to short scene, he borrowed the narrator-chorus figure which Williams had used so successfully in *The Glass Menagerie*. In addition, the two plays are similar in that both protagonists are trying to free their lives from the claims which parents are trying to impose on them, that both do eventually reject those claims and escape their parents' domination, and that neither succeeds in throwing off the consequent feelings of guilt and remorse.

In addition to the unsatisfactory father-son relationship, *I Never Sang for My Father* develops at some length the incompatibility of the interests and values of Margaret and Tom Garrison, thus providing yet another example of Anderson's interest in the theme of the unhappy marital relationship. As in his earlier treatments of this theme, the incompatibility of values is reflected in an unsatisfactory sex life, though this aspect of their lives is barely hinted at by Margaret Garrison.

In its exploration of both the father-son and the marital relationship, *I Never Sang for My Father* is probably Anderson's best play. The characters are real, and the anguish that they experience as they try unsuccessfully to reach one another is deep and moving. Gene's reactions ring true as those of a middle-aged son who loves his mother and tries to love his father but is appalled by the inevitable dependence of both on him. Gene and his mother understand each other well, and their shared understanding of Tom intensifies their closeness. Gene and his father, on the other hand, are diametrically opposed in temperament and values, so that all Gene's efforts at reaching some rapport with his father fail miserably. Nevertheless, Gene continues to try, partly because he feels it his duty to do so, partly because his nature craves a father he can love, and partly—as his sister Alice suggests—because he has never gotten over the fact that he does not measure up to his father's idea of manliness. Tom views with contempt all Gene's accomplishments as a writer and teacher, and only once in his life, when Gene was in the Marines, has Tom felt proud of his son.

Tom is the most rigid character in the play, yet Anderson treats him fairly, showing that his character and attitudes stem from a bad relationship with his own father and from the resultant hardship of his life as a child and as a young man. His unreasonableness is believable, and his son's simultaneous desire and inability to break through it are convincing. Alice is also convincingly complex as the daughter who has succeeded in escaping Tom's domination, partly because his opposition to her marriage gave her an excuse to do so with a clear conscience, but who in one vulnerable moment unexpectedly reveals how deeply she has been affected by the lack of love from her father.

Although there is nothing new in this play—the characters, their circumstances, and their helpless and mostly ineffectual attempts to deal with those circumstances are very familiar—*I Never Sang for My Father* will probably be remembered for its complex and credible characters and for the sincerity of the emotion the play generates.

In *You Know I Can't Hear You When the Water's Running*, Anderson returned to a form which he evidently found very congenial, the one-act play. Of approximately twenty-four plays which he wrote in his Harvard years, some twenty were one-act plays, and the one nonmusical play he wrote at Exeter was a one-act play. Of the four plays which make up *You Know I Can't Hear You When the Water's Running*, two—*The Footsteps of Doves* and *I'm Herbert*—are mere entertainments, little more than skits. The other two—*The Shock of Recognition* and *I'll Be Home for Christmas*— have much greater significance in acuteness of observation and validity and interest of characterization.

The Footsteps of Doves derives its title from a saying of Friedrich Nietzsche to the effect that major changes in one's life are not announced dramatically, with thunderous crescendos, but slip up on one almost imperceptibly, like the footsteps of doves—a saying which Anderson had used earlier, in *Silent Night, Lonely Night*, and would use again in his novel *After*. In this play, the footsteps are heard only by the husband when a middle-aged couple, George and Harriet, are buying a new bed and Harriet insists on twin beds despite all of George's arguments for the double bed. George and Harriet's sex life has deteriorated badly since the time of their youthful happiness together, and George sees the purchase of the twin beds as symbolic of an utter lack of hope that it will improve. When the younger, more vital Jill appears and makes a thinly veiled offer to share a double bed with George, it becomes apparent that he will accept this offer and thus will thenceforth accept her, rather than his wife, as his permanent sex partner.

This play expresses Anderson's oft-reiterated belief in the importance of a happy sex life to a good marriage, but it is new in its isolation of that element from all the other elements which go into making a good marriage. In his earlier plays, an unhappy sex life is seen as the result of other kinds of incompatibility in the marriage—personality clashes, value clashes, clashes in beliefs and goals—but in this play, one knows nothing about the couple except their sex life.

I'm Herbert also focuses on the sex life of a couple as the sole index of the happiness of their marriage. Some critics have found in the play that theme so common among absurdist playwrights, the lack of communication in modern society; this interpretation, however, is negated by the fact that the lack of communication in *I'm Herbert* stems neither from the specific conditions of modern society nor from the perennial human condition but solely from senility, a specific medical problem found only in some elderly people. Thomas P. Adler sees the play as almost a paean to a happy marriage which has "passed beyond physical sexuality"; this interpretation, however, is negated by the fact that the old couple in the play remember nothing at all about their former or present mates but the sexual experiences they shared, and that the sexual experiences they remember are not attached to any particular person in their minds but are remembered simply for themselves. Love is nowhere to be found in this play, which focuses entirely on the theme of the importance of sexual excitement and gratification. In the absence of any greater depth of meaning, then, it seems to be no more than an extended and tasteless joke based on a highly unfair and inaccurate stereotype of the elderly. *I'm Herbert* is, thus, the least satisfying of the plays in the quartet.

The Shock of Recognition is the first of Anderson's plays to center on the discussion of a particular theatrical issue. Jack Barnstable is an autobiographical character in that he is a writer of plays arguing for a position which Anderson supported, the acceptance in the theater of greater honesty and realism in dealing with sex. Herb Miller is a stereotype of the kind of opponent such a position often meets: a man who prides himself on his virility and who thinks of sex as the appropriate subject for dirty jokes told among men and for broad innuendoes used to embarrass naïve young women, but not as something which can be discussed openly and objectively among adult men and women or can be presented in such a fashion onstage. The really interesting character in this play, however, is Richard Pawling, the actor who will sacrifice anything to get a part in a play. Both ludicrous and pathetic in his eagerness and determination to please, he is Anderson's most richly comic character, and the play is memorable more for this character than for any other element, even the then shocking but now passé idea of presenting male frontal nudity onstage.

I'll Be Home for Christmas, though beginning as comedy and presumably intended to maintain the comic tone to complement the tone of the other plays in this group, is at times too moving and real in its pain to be funny. Chuck's hurt and anguish, his real fear that his life has no meaning, are too strong. Like the other plays in this group, *I'll Be Home for Christmas* deals with the importance of sex, but unlike the others, it demonstrates that a healthy marriage needs more than sexual gratification. Chuck, the middle-aged husband, is appalled at the mechanical, even clinical, view which his wife Edith has of sex, which she considers an extremely important part of a wholesome married life. He is revolted as she discusses the sex education which she has been giving and proposes to continue giving to their children. He has a much more romantic view of sex and demands much more meaning, not only in his marriage but in his entire life, than he discerns around him. Unfortunately, the one-act format works against the play on this point. There has not been room to develop any notion of the values which Chuck has stood for in the past. The values of Edith are, however, both apparent and repugnant, so that as Chuck sits brooding over a letter in which his son Donny has rejected Chuck's way of life as meaningless, the audience is likely to wonder why Donny did not address the letter to his mother, rather than to his father.

The success of this quartet of one-act plays led Anderson to try the one-act format once again in two short plays on the theme of family life, *Solitaire/Double Solitaire*. The lack of success of this duet on Broadway may have helped to push Anderson in the direction of writing novels. Another very important element in his turning to novels, however, was certainly the fact that in *Double Solitaire* he had carried frankness in the discussion and portrayal of sex to the limits which it could reach on the stage. As Anderson has acknowledged, the autobiographical, even confessional, nature of the content of *After* required "so much explicit sex" and "so many interior monologues" that he had to give up his attempts to present it in the form of a play and turn to the novel instead.

In discussing the writing of *After*, Anderson said, "I have always been obsessed with the themes of love and sex and death and marriage." The sources of this obsession in the experiences of his own life are readily apparent, and it well may be that the autobiographical nature of his work has made it difficult for him to achieve the aesthetic distance necessary for effective drama. At the same time, however, this autobiographical impulse is probably what has enabled him to create with sympathy and compassion the characters and scenes on which his reputation as a dramatist rests.

Other major works

NOVELS: *After*, 1973; *Getting Up and Going Home*, 1978.

SCREENPLAYS: *The Nun's Story*, 1959 (adaptation of Kathryn Hulme's novel); *The Sand Pebbles*, 1966 (adaptation of Richard McKenna's novel); *I Never Sang for My Father*, 1970 (adaptation of his play).

Bibliography

Adler, Thomas P. *Robert Anderson*, 1978.

Bentley, Eric Russell. *The Dramatic Event: An American Chronicle*, 1954.

Gassner, John. *Theatre at the Crossroads: Plays and Playwrights of the Mid-Century American Stage*, 1960.

Lewis, Allan. *American Plays and Playwrights of the Contemporary Theater*, 1965.

Sievers, W. David. *Freud on Broadway: A History of Psychoanalysis and the American Drama*, 1955.

Weales, Gerald. *American Drama Since World War II*, 1962.

Wharton, John F. *Life Among the Playwrights: Being Mostly the Story of the Playwrights Producing Company*, 1974.

Lisë Pedersen

JOHN ARDEN

Born: Barnsley, England; October 26, 1930

Principal drama

All Fall Down, pr. 1955; *The Waters of Babylon*, pr. 1957, pb. 1964; *Live Like Pigs*, pr. 1958, pb. 1964; *When Is a Door Not a Door?*, pr. 1958, pb. 1967; *Serjeant Musgrave's Dance: An Unhistorical Parable*, pr. 1959, pb. 1960; *The Business of Good Government*, pr. 1960, pb. 1963 (with Margaretta D'Arcy); *The Happy Haven*, pr. 1960, pb. 1964; *Ironhand*, pr. 1963, pb. 1965 (adaptation of Johann Wolfgang von Goethe's *Goetz von Berlichingen*); *The Workhouse Donkey*, pr. 1963, pb. 1964; *Armstrong's Last Goodnight: An Exercise in Diplomacy*, pr. 1964, pb. 1965; *Ars Longa, Vita Brevis*, pr. 1964, pb. 1965 (with D'Arcy); *Fidelio*, pr. 1965 (adaptation of libretto of Ludwig van Beethoven's opera); *Left-Handed Liberty*, pr., pb. 1965; *Friday's Hiding*, pr. 1966, pb. 1967 (with D'Arcy); *The Royal Pardon*, pr. 1966, pb. 1967 (with D'Arcy); *The Vietnam War-Game*, pr. 1967 (with D'Arcy); *Harold Muggins Is a Martyr*, pr. 1968 (with Cartoon Archetypal Slogan Theater and D'Arcy); *The Hero Rises Up*, pr. 1968, pb. 1969 (with D'Arcy); *The Soldier's Tale*, pr. 1968 (adaptation of libretto by Ramuz; music by Igor Stravinsky); *The True History of Squire Jonathan and His Unfortunate Treasure*, pr. 1968, pb. 1971; *The Ballygombeen Bequest*, pr., pb. 1972 (with D'Arcy); *The Island of the Mighty*, pr. 1972, pb. 1974 (trilogy; with D'Arcy); *Henry Dubb Show*, pr. 1973 (with D'Arcy), *Portrait of a Rebel*, pr. 1973 (with D'Arcy); *The Non-Stop Connolly Show* (6 parts), pr. 1975, pb. 1977-1978 (5 volumes; with D'Arcy); *The Little Gray Home in the West*, pr. 1978, pb. 1982 (with D'Arcy; revision of *The Ballygombeen Bequest*); *Vandaleur's Folly: An Anglo-Irish Melodrama*, pr. 1978, pb. 1981 (with D'Arcy).

Other literary forms

An important work for understanding the dramaturgy and politics of John Arden is *To Present the Pretence* (1977), a collection of his essays which originally appeared in various publications over a number of years. Many of Arden's plays are also accompanied by informative prefaces, especially concerning the genesis and composition of individual plays, their production, and the dramatist's own sometimes stormy relations with the professional theatrical world. Finally, Arden's first novel, *Silence Among the Weapons*, was published in Great Britain in 1982.

Achievements

Along with John Osborne, Arnold Wesker, and Harold Pinter, John Arden is one of the early leading playwrights of the so-called New Wave (or New Renaissance) of British drama. Encouraged primarily by the English Stage Company, directed by George Devine at London's Royal Court Theatre, the playwrights of the New Wave have given Britain some of the most lively drama in the contemporary world. Arden has been an important part of the movement, both through his own work and through his influence on later dramatists.

Throughout his career, Arden has been a controversial figure in his own country. None of his plays has enjoyed commercial success, and some have been violently attacked by critics. His best-known work, *Serjeant Musgrave's Dance*, lost ten thousand pounds at the Royal Court; the critic Harold Hobson called the play "another frightful ordeal" and *Punch* dubbed it a "lump of absurdity." Arden's early critics complained that he sermonized and that his sermons were not clear. Audiences had trouble identifying with his central characters, and his plays were even called amoral. These confused reactions say as much about the ingrown nature of British drama at the time as they do about the plays themselves, though it is true that in his early plays the young playwright was struggling with his own uncertainties. Arden generally wrote in a mode resembling the "epic theater" of Bertolt Brecht, filling his plays with ballads, narration, emblematic actions and sets, and other "alienating" (that is, deliberately theatrical) effects. Arden's mode also draws on an older tradition in Britain: Besides Brecht, Arden has acknowledged the influence of Ben Jonson, William Shakespeare, and medieval drama. Part of Arden's achievement is that he has helped break down audience expectations of naturalistic drama to reintroduce the British to their own traditions.

Despite the initial critical reception of his work, Arden's reputation grew. Harold Hobson changed his opinion about *Serjeant Musgrave's Dance* as the play became popular with university theater groups; eventually, it reached the status of a set text for secondary school examinations in English. Arden attained a peak of official acceptance in 1965 when the Corporation of the City of London commissioned him to write *Left-Handed Liberty* for the seven hundred fiftieth anniversary of the signing of the Magna Carta. Thereafter, whether by choice or otherwise, Arden gradually drifted further away from the London professional theater, writing mostly in collaboration with his wife, Margaretta D'Arcy, and becoming more involved in experimental, community, and political theater. His new activities also aroused controversy.

Meanwhile, Arden's reputation spread abroad (particularly to Germany), and he has become a subject of scholarly study, including several books. This attention is deserved, even though Arden's work is uneven in quality. For example, the ambitious three-part work *The Island of the Mighty* is a disappointment, and some of the less ambitious short pieces are of minor interest. So far, Arden's best plays seem to be several modern comedies, *The Waters of Babylon* and *The Workhouse Donkey*, and the historical parables *Serjeant Musgrave's Dance*, *Armstrong's Last Goodnight*, *The Hero Rises Up*, and *Vandaleur's Folly*. The key to Arden's best work is the same quality that appeals to university audiences: a combination of Dionysian energy with treatment of the big issues in today's world. Since those issues will not go away soon, it is likely that Arden's reputation will continue to grow.

Biography

John Arden's development as a playwright can be explained in part by his background, which differs significantly from the London working-class background typical of fellow New Wave dramatists. The product of a Yorkshire middle-class family, Arden was educated at Sedbergh, a private boarding school in Yorkshire's remote northwest dales (where he had been sent to escape World War II bombing raids), took a degree in architecture from Cambridge University (1953), and proceeded to further study of architecture at Edinburgh College of Art, receiving his diploma from that institution in 1955. Between Sedbergh and Cambridge, the future author of *Serjeant Musgrave's Dance* and writer for *Peace News* served in the military, mostly in Edinburgh, where he attained the rank of lance-corporal in the Army Intelligence Corps.

Arden's background in the North Country, home of medieval drama and balladry and the setting of most of his best work, is a major source of strength in his plays, as is evident from the salty language used in them. His background suggests that Arden was not born to his Socialist sentiments but arrived at them through a lengthy process of observation and deliberation. Such a process of development, involving constant challenge and considerable self-examination, would help account for the ambiguities in his earlier works and for Arden's characterizations of himself as having been a wishy-washy liberal, a sort of Hamlet of the New Wave. Possibly the young playwright also had mixed reactions to the new welfare state in Britain and to the prevailing doctrinaire atmosphere, especially in the universities, where left-wing evangelizing, with its assumptions and jargon, was sometimes reminiscent of Bible-belt fundamentalism: The New Jerusalem did not tolerate its sinners easily, and it found its American devils handy. Although polite and mild-mannered, Arden has always been strongly independent in his thinking. He chose, for example, to study architecture rather than English in order to avoid compromising his creativity as a writer.

Arden's architectural study did not go to waste: It has contributed to his sense of dramatic structure and sometimes to the content of his plays. His education also gave him perhaps the strongest intellectual background of any of the New Wave playwrights. He practiced architecture in London for only two years, however, until his playwriting career was launched by the Royal Court's 1957 presentation of *The Waters of Babylon*.

That same year, Arden married Margaretta D'Arcy, an actress of Irish background. Not only have they had four sons, but D'Arcy has also been closely associated with Arden's career, first as a friendly critic/consultant and later as a collaborator. (An important distinction among their collaborative works is marked by the designations "by Arden and D'Arcy" and "by D'Arcy and Arden.") D'Arcy has influenced Arden's involvement in experimental, community, and political drama and his use of Irish material. Their travels together have also been influential, particularly two trips to the United States (Arden held guest lectureships at New York University in 1967 and, with D'Arcy, at the University of California at Davis in 1973), where they led politically controversial drama projects, and a stay in India (for the centennial celebrations of Mahatma Gandhi's birth), where they were shocked by the depth of that country's poverty.

Since the 1960's, the Ardens' residence in the west of Ireland (County Galway) has seemed to symbolize their distance from the London political and theatrical Establishment—a 'distance which became manifest in their much-publicized dispute with the Royal Shakespeare Company over its 1972 production of *The Island of the Mighty*. The Ardens ended up picketing the production. How much this unfortunate dispute affected Arden's career is hard to say, but it was certainly controversial.

Analysis

The controversy accompanying John Arden's career has tended to obscure his rather old-fashioned views of the proper role of the playwright. He draws not only on an older dramatic tradition but also on an older concept of the dramatist: the playwright as burgher. Arden is an immensely civic-minded playwright, a citizen who chooses to dramatize his concern for the commonweal. This concept of the dramatist—almost antithetical to the commercial theater as it now exists—belongs to an older tradition which embraces Shakespeare, the medieval theater, and the Greek dramatists. In Arden and D'Arcy's three-part Arthurian *The Island of the Mighty*, the ancient poets are not merely entertainers but also political advisers. Arden's concept of the dramatist explains his interest in community theater; increasingly, in the global village, his concerns have become international in scope.

Arden's concept of the dramatist means that his drama has been almost exclusively political, but his politics have changed and his involvement developed over time. In his early plays, although he treated parochial issues, he tended not to take a stand; rather, like the architect he had trained to be, he was merely concerned with how people live, as indicated by such titles as *Live Like Pigs* and *The Happy Haven*. If any stand was implied, it was likely to be anti-Socialist—for example, to condemn heavy-handed administration of the welfare state. Soon, however, through his historical parables, Arden expanded his vision: He began to connect local issues to world issues and to historical processes, and he began to deal either directly or indirectly with pacifist and Socialist concerns: militarism, colonialism, economic and social injustice. Finally, the plays written with D'Arcy take a more militant, partisan approach toward these same issues and others (such as sexism), condemning the imperialist/militarist/capitalist/exploitative mentality and viewing the Irish situation as a prime result of this mentality.

For Arden, the development in his thinking is summed up in the crisis of the liberal: the conflict between revolution and reform, and the fear that reform is only refining and strengthening an exploitative system. His thinking is influenced not only by the world scene but also specifically by Britain's past experience of empire. Also, Arden's thinking is not unique in contemporary Britain but is only one aspect of a political mood evoked by the title of the first New Wave play, John Osborne's *Look Back in Anger* (pr. 1956).

In three early social comedies, *The Waters of Babylon*, *Live Like Pigs*, and *The Happy Haven*, one sees the young dramatist struggling to find his way. All three plays are generally comic in tone, but some terrible things happen in each one. Some of the humor is undergraduate, but when these were written, the playwright had, after all, only recently been a student (and his most appreciative audience was students). Despite flashes of energy, the action drags in both *Live Like Pigs* and *The Happy Haven*, and both plays mix modes awkwardly: *Live Like Pigs* combines naturalism with the Brechtian mode, while *The Happy Haven* mixes naturalism with a Theater-of-the-Absurd parable.

Live Like Pigs and *The Happy Haven* are notable, however, for their implied criticism of the welfare state, new to Britain after World War II and hence somewhat raw. A coercive bureaucracy and pressures to conform are revealed in *Live Like Pigs* when the Sawneys, a raffish family living in an old tramcar down by the tracks, are forced by officials to move into a public housing estate. The Sawneys turn their new house into a pigsty, offend their proper neighbors, and provoke a bloody riot. The insensitive treatment of people as objects is even more obvious in *The Happy Haven*: Here, the nursing-home setting can be seen as a satire on the welfare state, complete with a presiding doctor who performs experiments on the old people—for their own good, of course (he is perfecting an elixir of youth). Such is the bureaucratic best of all possible worlds.

A much better play is *The Waters of Babylon*, which sticks closer to the Brechtian mode and has a wider scope, showing postwar Britain's legacy of colonialism, militarism, and capitalism. While Britain was building a welfare state, it was being flooded by refugees and immigrants, represented in this play by the Poles, Irish, and West Indians. Their world, as the play's title suggests, is a world of dislocation and exile. Moreover, their world is the true postwar world, a world full of Sawneys, and it is impinging on the tidy British, whether they like it or not. Some do not, a group represented by the insular Englishman Henry Ginger. Others do, represented by Alexander Loap, a Member of Parliament who keeps an expensive redheaded Irish mistress, and by Charles Butterthwaite, a former Yorkshire politician who finds a corrupt mate in Krank, the Polish slum landlord.

Above all, it is Krank, one of Arden's most colorful characters, who represents the soul of postwar Great Britain. His full name, Sigismanfred Krankiewicz, sums up the European history with which Britain has tried not to be involved. Krank himself wants to be uninvolved, left alone, but meanwhile he profits from his own little British empire, a run-down apartment house where he takes in immigrants and operates a prostitution ring. The chickens come to roost for Krank as they do for the British Empire: It is discovered that he spent the war in Buchenwald, all right, but as a German soldier rather than a prisoner, and he is shot by the Polish patriot Paul. Before he dies, however, Krank admits his complicity in recent human history—a lesson, Arden suggests, that we could all learn.

If *The Waters of Babylon* shows some aftereffects of the British Empire, *Serjeant Musgrave's Dance* goes to the Empire's heart, showing its workings. The play is Brechtian in mode, but with an elemental, mythic quality. The time is the Victorian era, around 1880. The place is a wintry North Country coal town, snowbound and starving, in the middle of a strike, the coldness of the setting suggesting the coldness of the empire's discipline. This discipline is maintained in the town by a triumvirate of mayor (who, conveniently, also owns the coal mine), parson, and constable, assisted by the distractions of Mrs. Hitchcock's pub (where a man can purchase grog and the ministrations of Annie). Abroad in the colonies, discipline is even less subtle: It is maintained by the Queen's army, which collects troublemakers at home to turn them loose on troublemakers in the colonies. In an emergency, the troops can also be used against the home folks. Thus, in the name of prosperity, patriotism, and good order, blessed by religion, the ruthless forces of capitalism, colonialism, and militarism operate together in a vast but tightly enclosed system which benefits the few at the expense and suffering of the many. The ballad chorus captures the spirit of the system: "The Empire wars are far away/ For duty's sake we sail away/ Me arms and legs is shot away/ And all for the wink of a shilling and a drink."

A desperate challenge to this brutal system is mounted by four soldiers who appear in the coal town, ostensibly to recruit but in reality to bring home the truth. The truth about the system is symbolized by the skeleton of Billy Hicks, a young soldier from the town. Billy was murdered in a far-off British "protectorate," and the British army retaliated by indiscriminately wounding thirty-four natives and killing five in a bloody night raid. Now the soldiers, led by Serjeant Musgrave, hoist Billy's skeleton on a market cross in the town square, train rifles and a Gatling gun on the town's citizens (actually, on the play's audience), and proceed to lecture them about the evils of the system and their complicity in it. At first the citizens think Musgrave, who does a little dance under the skeleton, is merely balmy, but then the striking colliers heed his call for solidarity. Not unnaturally, however, they draw back when Musgrave announces plans to kill twenty-five townspeople in retaliation for the five dead protectorate natives. The final straw comes when the crowd learns that one of the four soldiers is missing, dead at the hands of his comrades. The townspeople are saved by disagreement among the remaining soldiers and by the arrival of the dragoons. The temporarily challenged system starts up again, symbolized by a dance in which all join hands and sing a mindless round, led by the grotesque Bargee, who has been Musgrave's shadow throughout the play.

The trouble is that Musgrave himself is twisted by the system. His intentions are good, but his methods are terrible. He thinks he is led by God, but he is instead moved by the military logic he opposes, as indicated by the discipline he maintains over the soldiers even after they are all deserters. His protest takes the form of a military exercise, complete with military mathematics. As the soldier Attercliffe notes, Musgrave tries to end war "by its own rules: no bloody good . . . you can't cure the pox by whoring." Yet it is a protest which will be remembered by the townspeople—and by the people who see the play.

Like *Serjeant Musgrave's Dance*, *Armstrong's Last Goodnight* is "an unhistorical parable"—that is, both plays were suggested by current events: *Serjeant Musgrave's Dance* by events in Cyprus in 1958, *Armstrong's Last Goodnight* by the situation in the Congo in 1961. Setting the plays in the past provides distance from current events but at the same time raises ironic parallels. For example, *Armstrong's Last Goodnight* is ironically subtitled *An Exercise in Diplomacy*, suggesting that much diplomacy has been and is still an exercise in treachery. In *Armstrong's Last Goodnight*, it resides in early sixteenth century Scotland, a vicious land of constant feuding, plotting, and shifting alliances (rather like the early sixteenth century English court described in the play's epigraph from the poet John Skelton), a land where the biggest freebooter prevails.

In *Armstrong's Last Goodnight*, the prescribed strategy is to invite your enemy to go hunting, offer him some of the local brew, shake hands with him, swear friendship forever, and then kill him at the first safe opportunity. Johnnie Armstrong of Gilknockie, a colorful border strongman, does this to James Johnstone of Wamphray, and then James V of Scotland does it to Armstrong. To entice Armstrong, King James needs the help of his scheming ambassador, Sir David Lindsay (another poet who was involved in politics), and of Lindsay's mistress, an earthy lady who even gets used to the smell in Armstrong's castle and who describes her sexuality in terms of a hot pot of red-herring broth (boiling over, of course). This play too has its elemental, mythic qualities, qualities enhanced by the Scots dialect in which it is written, but its overriding reminder is that international relations are still conducted on the primitive level of relations among early Scotch lairds.

Authored by D'Arcy and Arden, *Vandaleur's Folly* has a dialectic pattern familiar from *Serjeant Musgrave's Dance*: thesis, antithesis, fiasco. Here the exploitative system is the prototypical plantation colony of 1830's Ireland, a country of whiskey-drinking British gentry and thirsty Irish tenantry, where the absentee landlords gamble in Dublin's Hell Fire Club and visit their estates occasionally to conduct a "fox" hunt using a lively Irish lass. The play draws parallels between the treatment of the Irish, the American slave trade, and the treatment of women. For example, the slave-trader Wilberforce is the business partner of Major Baker-Fortescue, the vicious Orangeman landlord. The two are opposed by Roxana, an American abolitionist who is part black, and by Micheal, an Irishman who leads the Lady Clare Boys, a peasant guerrilla group.

The most important challenge to the plantation system, however, is Ralahine, a Socialist cooperative set up by Vandaleur, an enlightened landowner. Ralahine, where landowner and tenant share equally and have equal rights, is a financial success and brings peace to the countryside, yet it drives the other landowners wild. The Commune's opponents finally destroy it by taking advantage of a fatal flaw in its makeup: Like Musgrave, Vandaleur is still infected by the system; he retains private ownership of the experimental estate and, in a fit of gambling fever, loses it to Baker-Fortescue in a faro game at the Hell Fire Club.

Subtitled *An Anglo-Irish Melodrama*, *Vandaleur's Folly* fits the description. Its one-sided characterizations result in some loss of artistic power, and the language of the play is not spiced with dialect. Yet *Vandaleur's Folly* is entertaining melodrama, and there is no trouble understanding its partisan point: Private property is wrong, and so is any arrangement which treats people as property.

Like the forthright *Vandaleur's Folly*, Arden's work generally is meant to stir people to think about the issues of today's world and perhaps to take action. One of the current writers most attuned to those issues, Arden is very much a practical playwright: He does not merely look back in anger, but looks forward with hope. As this description implies, he is also a playwright for the young. Although his work embodies prophetic warnings, it does not reflect the despairing tone of earlier twentieth century literature, with its recurring visions of the wasteland; rather, Arden looks beyond the crisis of modern civilization toward solutions.

Other major works

NOVEL: *Silence Among the Weapons*, 1982 (also as *Vox Pop: Last Days of the Roman Republic*, 1983).

NONFICTION: *To Present the Pretence*, 1977.

TELEPLAYS: *Soldier, Soldier*, pr. 1960, pb. 1967; *Wet Fish*, pr. 1961, pb. 1967.

RADIO PLAYS: *The Life of Man*, pr. 1956; *The Dying Cowboy*, pr. 1961; *The Bagman*, pr. 1970, pb. 1971; *Keep Those People Moving*, pr. 1972 (with D'Arcy); *Pearl*, pr. 1978, pb. 1979; *To Put It Frankly...*, pr. 1979; *Don Quixote* (2 parts), pr. 1980; *Garland for a Hoar Head*, pr. 1982; *The Old Man Sleeps Alone*, pr. 1982.

Bibliography

Gray, Frances. *John Arden*, 1982.
Hunt, Albert. *Arden: A Study of His Plays*, 1974.
Itzin, Catherine. *Stages in the Revolution*, 1980.
Leeming, Glenda. *John Arden*, 1974.
Page, Malcolm. *John Arden*, 1984.
Taylor, John Russell. *Anger and After*, 1962, 1969.
Trussler, Simon. *John Arden*, 1973.

Harold Branam

W. H. AUDEN

Born: York, England; February 21, 1907
Died: Vienna, Austria; September 29, 1973

Principal drama

Paid on Both Sides: A Charade, pb. 1930, pr. 1931; *The Dance of Death*, pb. 1933, pr. 1934; *The Dog Beneath the Skin: Or, Where Is Francis?*, pb. 1935, pr. 1936 (with Christopher Isherwood); *The Ascent of F6*, pb. 1936, pr. 1937 (with Isherwood); *On the Frontier*, pr., pb. 1938 (with Isherwood); *Paul Bunyan*, pr. 1941, pb. 1976 (libretto; music by Benjamin Britten); *The Rake's Progress*, pr., pb. 1951 (libretto, with Chester Kallman; music by Igor Stravinsky); *Delia: Or, A Masque of Night*, pb. 1953 (libretto, with Kallman; not set to music); *For the Time Being*, pr. 1959 (oratorio; musical setting by Martin David Levy); *Elegy for Young Lovers*, pr., pb. 1961 (libretto, with Kallman; music by Hans Werner Henze); *The Bassarids*, pr., pb. 1966 (libretto, with Kallman; music by Henze); *Love's Labour's Lost*, pb. 1972, pr. 1973 (libretto, with Kallman; music by Nicolas Nabokov; adaptation of William Shakespeare's play *Love's Labour's Lost*); *The Entertainment of the Senses*, pr. 1974 (libretto, with Kallman; music by John Gardiner).

Other literary forms

Although well regarded as a playwright and librettist, W. H. Auden is known chiefly as a poet. During his lifetime, he published more than twenty collections of poetry, establishing himself as a major voice in twentieth century literature. His work includes a remarkable variety of lyric poems, notable for their range of thought and technique. Auden also wrote several longer poems, including *For the Time Being* and *The Sea and the Mirror*, both of which appeared in a 1944 collection, and *The Age of Anxiety* (1947). The shorter as well as the longer poems are in *Collected Poems* (1976) and *The English Auden* (1977), both edited by Edward Mendelson.

In addition to plays, librettos, and poetry, Auden produced a substantial amount of nonfiction prose. Many of his best essays, reviews, lectures, and introductions are collected in *The Dyer's Hand and Other Essays* (1962), *Secondary Worlds* (1969), and *Forewords and Afterwords* (1973). Auden also wrote several scripts for film and radio and worked extensively as an editor and translator. In addition to the two collections already issued by Mendelson, the Auden estate plans to publish definitive editions of Auden's complete poetry, prose, and dramatic writing.

Achievements

Though W. H. Auden is not regarded as a major playwright, he and his collaborators produced a body of work that is recognized today as a significant contribution to modern drama and opera. His plays with Christopher Isherwood have survived as period pieces and are well regarded as experiments in poetic, didactic drama, written at a time when the English theater offered little more than uninspired Naturalism. *The Dog Beneath the Skin*, probably the most lasting of the Auden-Isherwood collaborations, contains some of Auden's finest verse written for the stage and, though often raw and uneven, remains engaging in its mixture of popular, high-spirited comedy and political satire. Michael Sidnell, while suggesting that personal and artistic difficulties kept Auden and Isherwood from fully committing themselves to the theater, argues, nevertheless, that they "were in advance of their time in using poetry, song, dance, and fable for serious dramatic purposes in a way that did not become common on the English stage until the late 1950's, when the strong influence of Brecht was belatedly felt."

Auden's work for the operatic stage is more difficult to assess, partly because of the complex interdependence of the librettos and their musical settings. Auden saw the librettist's role as clearly secondary to the composer's, yet his librettos with Chester Kallman are regarded by some as significant dramatic and poetic texts in their own right. John Blair, for example, treating *The Rake's Progress* as an "operatic poem," suggests that the libretto can be "seen as an epitome of Auden's mature poetic mode." As opera, the Auden-Kallman collaborations have had mixed success; *The Rake's Progress* (with music by Igor Stravinsky) is generally conceded to be their best and, as Humphrey Carpenter points out, is apparently "one of the very few modern operas to become a permanent addition to the repertoire." In the two years following its premiere, it was staged more than two hundred times.

Biography

Wystan Hugh Auden was born into a middle-class English family in 1907, the son of George Auden, a medical doctor, and Constance Bicknell Auden, a nurse. Auden grew up in an atmosphere that fostered intellectual and cultural growth, and his parents, both the children of clergymen, gave him and his two older brothers a strong sense of traditional religious values. His father was the strongest influence on his early intellectual life, teaching Auden about classical and Norse mythology and encouraging his interest in science. Auden maintained this interest throughout his life, often using scientific concepts and images in his poetry.

In 1915, when he was eight, Auden went as a boarder to St. Edmund's School in Surrey, where he met Christopher Isherwood, later his close friend and collaborator. After St. Edmund's, Auden attended Gresham's School, an institution with a strong reputation in the sciences. During his time there, Auden began to question the religion of his childhood and to distance himself from the traditional values of his middle-class, public-school upbringing. At Gresham's, he acknowledged his homosexuality, and, by the time he left, he had abandoned his faith.

Auden's interest in writing, begun at Gresham's, flourished at Oxford, where he went to read science in 1925. He soon changed to English studies and, before finishing his undergraduate career, resolved to make poetry his vocation. While at Oxford and in the remaining years of the 1930's, Auden established a considerable reputation as a poet and experimental dramatist. In 1928, he wrote his first dramatic work, *Paid on Both Sides,* a brief "charade" that draws heavily on his English public-school experience, his fascination with the lead-mining country of his youth, and the Icelandic legends he learned from his father. Four years later, in 1932, he again turned to theater. In the summer of that year, the ballet dancer Rupert Doone and the painter Robert Medley (whom Auden had known at Gresham's) proposed to Auden the idea of forming an experimental theater company that Doone hoped could be "self-sufficient and independent of any purely commercial considerations." The founders of what came to be known as the Group Theatre wanted to bring to the stage a combination of dance, music, and speech; they also saw in the theater a potential for left-wing social commentary, an idea that appealed to Auden, whose political leanings had become increasingly leftist during the 1930's.

At the urging of Doone and Medley, Auden produced for the Group Theatre a ballet-drama on Marxist themes. In the next several years, he collaborated with Christopher Isherwood on three more plays for the Group, the first of them *The Dog Beneath the Skin*, a work that developed out of earlier dramatic experiments by the two writers—their joint effort, "Enemies of a Bishop" (written in 1929), and two works by Auden, "The Fronny" (written in 1930) and "The Chase" (written in 1934). These plays were not published or performed, and only a few scraps of "The Fronny" survive. By the end of the 1930's, Auden and Isherwood had collaborated on a second and third play for the Group Theatre, both of them more theatrically conventional than their first one.

In 1939, Auden's life took a major turn. He and Isherwood left England for the United States, and, within two years of his arrival, Auden rejoined the Anglican communion, a reaffirmation of his childhood faith toward which he had been moving for some time. From this point in his life, his writing was informed by a Christian perspective spelled out most explicitly in the long poems he wrote during the 1940's, particularly his Christmas oratorio, *For the Time Being.* Though clearly not intended for the stage, his long poems of this period make considerable use of dramatic techniques. Auden's only theatrical work of the time was a brief libretto that he wrote for the British composer Benjamin Britten; *Paul Bunyan* was performed once in 1941 but remained unpublished until after Auden's death.

Auden's dramatic career entered its second phase near the end of the 1940's, when he began the first of his several collaborations with his friend and lifelong companion Chester Kallman, whom he had met shortly after his arrival in America. Together, they wrote for Stravinsky a libretto for *The Rake's Progress* and, later, a briefer one called *Delia*, for which Stravinsky never provided a score. In the last twenty years of his life, Auden continued to write extensively both poetry and prose, living part of each year in New York City and part in Europe. He and Kallman continued their productive collaboration, translating a number of librettos and writing several of their own, two for the German composer Hans Werner Henze and one for the Russian-born composer Nicolas Nabokov. Their final work for the stage, written in the last month of Auden's life, was *The Entertainment of the Senses,* a brief "antimasque" commissioned for the composer John Gardiner. Shortly after completing this piece, Auden left his summer home in Kirchstetten, Austria, to return to Oxford, where he had taken up winter residence the year before. On the way to England, he and Kallman stopped in Vienna for a poetry reading that Auden was scheduled to give there. He died there, suddenly; he is buried, as he wished, in Kirchstetten.

Analysis

W. H. Auden's writing for the stage falls into two distinct categories: the plays of the 1930's, written mostly in collaboration with Christopher Isherwood, and the opera librettos, all but one written with Chester Kallman after Auden's move to America in 1939.

The plays of the 1930's are essentially political and didactic; Auden saw them as a means of reaching a wider audience than he could with his poetry, a way to reunite, as Mendelson puts it, "the private world of the poet with the public world of the theatre." Hence, the plays set forth various psychological and political positions he adopted during the 1930's, offering audiences lessons in the history of their time and awakening them to the possibility of personal and social renewal. Written in a mixture of poetry and prose, Auden's plays borrow theatrical devices from a variety of unlikely sources: ballet, conventional melodrama, music-hall comedy, the variety show, and the cabaret sketch. He combines these devices with serious poetry (often spoken by a chorus), using a blend of popular and literary writing as a vehicle for antiestablishment political commentary. At times, the didacticism outweighs theatrical effectiveness, as it does in *On the Frontier*, a topical and technically conventional play that lacks the energy of Auden's other collaborations with Isherwood. At their best, however, the plays manage to handle political and social themes with a considerable amount of dramatic vitality.

This vitality is best represented in *The Dog Beneath the Skin,* generally recognized as the most successful of the three Auden-Isherwood plays. An odd blend of fable and farce, the plot centers on the quest of Alan Norman to find Sir Francis Crewe, missing heir to the late squire of the English village of Pressan Ambo. Each year, the villagers gather to select by lot a young man to search for Sir Francis (whom they perceive as a sort of idealized lost leader); the ten youths who precede Alan fail in their quest, and two of them never return to the village (though both appear briefly during Alan's quest).

The first part of the play evokes the complacency of the staid and deceptively idyllic English village, whose leading citizens are the town vicar, the pompous General Hothan—a retired military man—and Iris Crewe, Sir Francis' sister, who lives at Honeypot Hall, the family estate. This trio is the object of the play's satire against the established social order. Representing religious, military, and class authority, they begin as conventional reactionaries, but, by the end of the play (and in Alan's absence), they turn to Fascism, establishing a militaristic youth brigade in the village. After a quest that takes up most of the play's action, Alan returns with Sir Francis to discover the altered state of affairs in Pressan Ambo. The lost heir, who had in fact been living in disguise among the villagers for the past ten years, denounces them as "obscene, cruel, hypocritical, mean, vulgar creatures." Taking Alan and a small band of villagers with him, Sir Francis leaves Pressan Ambo to "be a unit in the army of the other side," presumably a political and social order opposite the Fascism now established in the village. Though some argue that Sir Francis does not speak for a specific political doctrine, others such as John Fuller, see his joining of the "other side" as an explicit reference to the Communist Party. His and Alan's conversion represents, in any case, a move away from personal and political stagnation toward an active commitment to regeneration and change, an idea that Auden was working with in his poetry at the time.

Along with its explicit critique of Fascist politics, the play makes a broader political statement on the entire capitalist system. The extent to which Auden embraced Marxism is not entirely clear, but he did for a time sympathize with many of its key tenets. His first play for the Group Theatre, *The Dance of Death*, is an avowedly political one, illustrating the decline and eventual death of the bourgeoisie. In *The Dog Beneath the Skin*, his intent is somewhat less overt, but the bulk of the play (and most of its vitality) comes in the quest scenes, which burlesque the moral and economic decay of European capitalism.

At the beginning of his quest, Alan is joined by a large dog that gives the play its title, provides much of its farcical humor, and, in the end, carries much of the play's thematic weight. The dog, it turns out, is Sir Francis Crewe, the object of Alan's quest. The missing heir of Pressan Ambo has been living in disguise for ten years among the villagers and is now

Alan's companion. In the middle section of the play, the two of them travel together, observing the corruption of the established social order, a corruption that had previously seduced and destroyed two young men from the village; though Alan is temporarily lured toward decadence, he manages— with the help of his dog—to escape, having learned along the way the lessons that lead to his personal salvation.

The scenes that satirize capitalist decay borrow an array of theatrical devices from the popular stage. Using slapstick, farce, burlesque, cabaret songs, doggerel, and a host of other devices, Auden and Isherwood provide a kind of comic revue of modern political corruption and personal decadence. The loosely connected comic scenes are separated by a number of choral poems that develop in a more serious fashion the implications of the play's high-spirited satire. The bulk of the satiric pieces are set in Ostonia, a decadent monarchy in Eastern Europe, and Westland, a Fascist state with clear parallels to Nazi Germany. (Both of these nations reappear in the other Auden-Isherwood collaborations.) In Ostonia, Alan and the dog— accompanied by two journalists—witness a grotesquely comic execution of four workers accused of inciting revolution. The satiric point is unmistakable, as it is later in Westland, where the political system becomes an asylum that "the leader" rules by speaking to the inmates through a megaphone attached to his picture.

One of the most memorable sequences in the play occurs at the Ninevah Hotel, where Alan watches a cabaret act in the hotel restaurant, an act which, as John Fuller points out, "burlesques the sexual tyranny and . . . militant philistinism of the rich." At the end of the first sketch, which includes a crude song performed by the Ninevah Girls, one of the wealthy hotel patrons selects a willing chorus girl and orders her cooked and prepared for his dinner. This satire of wealth and sexual domination is followed by another sketch, in which Destructive Desmond uses a penknife to destroy an original Rembrandt while "a piece of third-rate Victorian landscape painting" stands unharmed beside it. The wealthy patrons applaud ecstatically at this grand entertainment, asserting their aggressive distaste for high culture.

With their "brutal, noisy vulgarity and tasteless extravagance" (as the stage directions put it), the Ninevah Hotel scenes have a comic vitality that prevents the play's didacticism from becoming ponderous. Finally, such scenes, with the chorus's commentary, allow Auden and Isherwood to illustrate pointedly the essential decadence and egotism of modern man, his inability to love and sympathize with his fellowman. This theme, which is implicit throughout the play, becomes overt in a scene at Paradise Park, where Alan meets a poet who insists that he is "the only real person in the world," a notion echoed later in the chorus's warning to the audience: "Beware of yourself:/ Have you not heard your own heart whisper: 'I am the nicest person in this room'?"

If the play finally has a significance beyond social satire, it lies in Auden's suggestion that political solutions are useless without personal regeneration. At the end of the play, back in Pressan Ambo and revealed as the missing heir, Sir Francis tells the gathered villagers that for ten years he had a "dog's eye view" of them, "seeing people from underneath," observing their essential hypocrisy, their lack of common human sympathy. After he, Alan, and a few converted villagers leave for the ill-defined "other side," the chorus offers the audience a choice, suggesting that personal change must precede political action: "Choose therefore that you may recover: both your charity and your place/ Determining/ ... Where grace may grow outward and be given praise." As in much of Auden's work of the 1930's, the exact nature of the proposed solution to personal and political ills is clouded; at the time, Auden was a diagnostician, not a healer. The ending of *The Dog Beneath the Skin* gestures toward an ill-defined "love" that is "loath to enter." Only in his later work, and after his return to Christianity, did Auden arrive at a less clouded notion of love as a means of personal and social redemption.

That notion of love is defined most clearly in the long poems that Auden wrote during the 1940's, a time when his interest in stage drama subsided. Aside from *Paul Bunyan*, the brief libretto written for Britten in 1939, Auden did no writing for the stage until Stravinsky approached him in 1947 about the possibility of doing an opera based on William Hogarth's series of engravings *A Rake's Progress*. Auden agreed to the project and wrote with Chester Kallman the first of their several librettos. Auden saw in opera a logical fulfillment of his earlier interest in poetic drama. In a 1966 interview for the British Broadcasting Corporation, he suggested that "opera is the proper place for lyric theatre, rather than the spoken drama." The "job of the librettist," he wrote in *Secondary Worlds*, "is to furnish the composer with a plot, characters and words." Clearly in a supporting role, the verbal text "is to be judged ... by its success or failure in exciting the musical imagination of the composer."

Though Auden tended to minimize the role of the librettist, his operatic works with Kallman have considerable merit apart from their musical settings. *The Rake's Progress* is particularly well regarded both as a stage opera and as an independent poetic text. The libretto illustrates many of the central themes of Auden's mature work and suggests that several of the techniques he and Isherwood used in the 1930's plays were naturally suited for the operatic stage: the reliance on fable and myth, the use of overstatement and grand gesture, and the emphasis on idea and spectacle rather than character.

The libretto is essentially a moral fable, illustrating in religious terms the Fall and Redemption of man. Auden suggests that through an act of free will, man can choose selfless love (*agape*) and, in doing so, find grace and redemption. This theme is worked out in the fate of the opera's hero, Tom Rakewell, described by Edward Callan as "an aesthetic personality who relies on fortune and believes in his own superior destiny." Auden illustrates the folly of Tom's egotism by giving him three wishes (after the pattern of the archetypal quest hero), each of which leads him further from Anne Truelove, the libretto's symbolic embodiment of selfless love. Rakewell's first wish (for money) is, like his other wishes, fulfilled by Nick Shadow, a satanic servant who secretly aims to damn Rakewell's soul. Removed by his first wish from the redemptive powers of Anne's love, Tom makes a second wish (for happiness), which leads him to an *acte gratuit*, an existential choice to marry Baba, a bearded lady from a fair; Shadow has convinced him that such an act could bring true happiness by freeing him from the demands of necessity. According to Fuller, Auden uses Rakewell's absurd act as a critique of the Existentialist view of free will; his marriage is "a grotesque parody of the true Christian choice" he will make later.

Tom's final wish (to have a magical bread-making machine he has dreamed of) brings about his final ruin. Left at the mercy of Shadow, he is offered—in a Faustian scene—a last, yet apparently hopeless, chance for salvation; recalling Anne's love, he makes an irrational choice when Shadow asks him to name three cards: "I wish for nothing else./ Love, first and last, assume eternal reign;/ Renew my life, O Queen of Hearts, again." The choice is, in effect, a leap of faith, a genuine acceptance of love. The memory of Anne thus saves Rakewell from damnation. Denied Rakewell's soul, Shadow condemns him to madness, but in the concluding scene, Tom (imagining himself as Adonis) is symbolically redeemed from his suffering by Anne (as Venus) and dies reconciled to her.

In a sense, *The Rake's Progress* is a thematic extension of the ideas raised by the Auden-Isherwood plays of the 1930's. Auden's Christianity, his embracing of *agape*, provides a new perspective on the personal and social ills diagnosed in *The Dog Beneath the Skin*. In the later work, Auden sees human failings in personal and religious terms; social and political malaise originates, he seems to suggest, by human imperfection, in man's fallen nature. Only by appealing to powers outside himself can man find redemption.

Auden's dramatic works—both the political plays and the librettos—are concerned at base with the exposition of ideas. In his plays, as in his poetry, he pursues a range of philosophical positions with relish and zest, and his writing for the stage is remarkable, finally, for its managing to bring dramatic vitality to political and theological concepts. His inventiveness, his willingness to experiment, and his masterful use of conventional forms (popular theater as well as opera) guarantee Auden and his collaborators a significant place in the history of modern drama.

Other major works

POETRY: *Poems*, 1930; *The Orators*, 1932; *Look, Stranger!*, 1936 (also as *On This Island*, 1937); *Letters from Iceland*, 1937 (poetry and prose, with Louis MacNeice); *Spain*, 1937; *Journey to a War*, 1939 (poetry and prose, with Christopher Isherwood); *Another Time*, 1940; *The Double Man*, 1941 (also as *New Year Letter*, 1941); *For the Time Being*, 1944 (collection); *The Collected Poetry*, 1945; *The Age of Anxiety*, 1947; *Collected Shorter Poems, 1930-1944*, 1950; *Nones*, 1951; *The Shield of Achilles*, 1955; *Homage to Clio*, 1960; *About the House*, 1965; *Collected Shorter Poems 1927-1957*, 1966; *Collected Longer Poems*, 1968; *City Without Walls and Other Poems*, 1969; *Epistle to a Godson and Other Poems*, 1972; *Thank You, Fog*, 1974; *Collected Poems*, 1976 (Edward Mendelson, editor); *Selected Poems*, 1979 (Edward Mendelson, editor).

NONFICTION: *Letters from Iceland*, 1937 (poetry and prose, with Louis MacNeice); *Journey to a War*, 1939 (poetry and prose, with Christopher Isherwood); *The Enchafèd Flood*, 1950; *The Dyer's Hand and Other Essays*, 1962; *Selected Essays*, 1964; *Secondary Worlds*, 1969; *A Certain World*, 1970; *Forewords and Afterwords*, 1973.

ANTHOLOGIES: *The Oxford Book of Light Verse*, 1938; *The Portable Greek Reader*, 1948; *Poets of the English Language*, 1950 (5 volumes, with Norman Holmes Pearson); *The Faber Book of Modern American Verse*, 1956; *Selected Poems of Louis MacNeice*, 1964; *Nineteenth Century British Minor Poets*, 1966; *A Choice of Dryden's Verse*, 1973.

MISCELLANEOUS: *The English Auden: Poems, Essays and Dramatic Writings, 1927-1939*, 1977 (Edward Mendelson, editor).

Bibliography

Blair, John. *The Poetic Art of W. H. Auden*, 1965.

Bloomfield, B. C., and Edward Mendelson. *W. H. Auden: A Bibliography*, 1973.

Callan, Edward. *Auden: A Carnival of Intellect*, 1983.

Carpenter, Humphrey. *W. H. Auden: A Biography*, 1981.

Fuller, John. *A Reader's Guide to W. H. Auden*, 1970.

Hynes, Samuel. *The Auden Generation*, 1977.

Kerman, Joseph. *Opera as Drama*, 1956.

Mendelson, Edward. *Early Auden*, 1981.

Osborne, Charles. *W. H. Auden: The Life of a Poet*, 1979.

Sidnell, Michael J. "W. H. Auden," in *Dictionary of Literary Biography: Modern British Dramatists, 1900-1945*, 1982.

Spears, Monroe K. *The Poetry of W. H. Auden: The Disenchanted Island*, 1963.

Spender, Stephen. *W. H. Auden: A Tribute*, 1975.

Stravinsky, Igor, and Robert Craft. *Memories and Commentaries*, 1960.

_____ . *Retrospectives and Conclusions*, 1969.
Symons, Julian. *The Thirties: A Dream Revolved*, 1960.

Michael Hennessy

ALAN AYCKBOURN

Born: Hampstead, England; April 12, 1939

Principal drama

The Square Cat, pr. 1959 (as Roland Allen); *Love After All*, pr. 1959 (as Roland Allen); *Relatively Speaking*, pr. 1967, pb. 1968 (originally as *Meet My Father*, pr. 1965); *How the Other Half Loves*, pr. 1969, pb. 1972; *Time and Time Again*, pr. 1971, pb. 1973; *Absurd Person Singular*, pr. 1972, pb. 1974; *The Norman Conquests*, pr. 1973, pb. 1975 (includes *Table Manners*, *Living Together*, and *Round and Round the Garden*); *Absent Friends*, pr. 1974, pb. 1975; *Bedroom Farce*, pr. 1975, pb. 1977; *Just Between Ourselves*, pr. 1976, pb. 1978; *Ten Times Table*, pr. 1977, pb. 1978; *Joking Apart*, pr. 1978, pb. 1979; *Men on Women on Men*, pr. 1978 (lyrics; music by Paul Todd); *Sisterly Feelings*, pr. 1979, pb. 1981; *Taking Steps*, pr. 1979, pb. 1981; *First Course*, pr. 1980 (lyrics; music by Paul Todd); *Season's Greetings*, pr. 1980; *Making Tracks*, pr. 1981 (lyrics; music by Paul Todd); *Way Upstream*, pr. 1981; *Intimate Exchanges*, pr. 1982.

Other literary forms

Alan Ayckbourn is chiefly known for his plays, including several musicals on which he has collaborated with English composer Paul Todd.

Achievements

Often compared to Noël Coward, Ayckbourn has emerged during the 1970's as the most popular and prolific comic dramatist writing for the English stage, particularly since the spectacular success of his two London productions in 1972-1973, *Absurd Person Singular* and *The Norman Conquests*, both of which brought immediate and widespread recognition in the form of numerous awards and televised productions. The comparison with Coward, however, is misleading. Both playwrights use typically English settings, characters, and humor, and both gained immense popularity; unlike Coward, however, Ayckbourn is not essentially a satirist of high society, nor is he much concerned with social and political issues. His deepest interests lie in the exploration of the most fundamental human relationships: husband-wife, parent-child, brother-sister, and employer-employee. Even those plays which are based upon social and political issues, such as *Ten Times Table*, which involves a Marxist attempt to use a local arts festival for subversive purposes, focus greater attention upon the humdrum and thwarted lives of those individuals victimized by society and politicians. If the Marxists prevail in *Ten Times Table*, it is owing to the lack of imagination and creative skill of the typical person who serves on such committees as the Pendon Arts Council.

Ayckbourn's drama has been translated into more than twenty-five foreign languages and has been performed in most European countries. Coming to the playwright's craft after several years of experience in acting, stage managing, and directing, Ayckbourn has specialized in writing for theater-in-the-round and has served as the chief playwright for the Stephen Joseph Theatre at Scarborough, Yorkshire, England. His plays reveal a genius for innovative uses of theatrical form and technique. *Absurd Person Singular* and *The Norman Conquests* brilliantly explore the possibilities of utilizing offstage characters and action. *Bedroom Farce* and *Taking Steps* employ split scenes and simultaneous action. *Sisterly Feelings* and *Intimate Exchanges* are both structured upon the basis of arbitrary choices which determine the form of a play on a given night. In *Sisterly Feelings*, for example, the action depends upon the flip of a coin to decide whether Abigail or Dorcas will go home with the athletic Simon, and a further variation occurs when one or the other of the sisters will make a choice concerning her relationship with Simon and with her husband or boyfriend. Thus, the play can be staged in four different ways on four different nights purely on the basis of chance or whim. *Intimate Exchanges*, an immensely complex play (or complex of plays) about marital infidelity involving the staff of a boys' boarding school, allows for nearly twenty such permutations in plot. In spite of the structural difficulties involved in the performance or reading of Ayckbourn's plays, their substance invariably presents a searching, often sardonic study of human character when placed in unusual or even improbable situations. It is this deep insight into human relationships, together with Ayckbourn's intriguing exploration of the boundaries between comedy and farce, which will ensure his continuing appeal to audiences all over the world.

Biography

Alan Ayckbourn's father was a talented musician and deputy leader of the London Symphony Orchestra, and his mother was a free-lance journalist who contributed hundreds of articles to popular women's journals. When Ayckbourn was only five, his parents divorced, and he was left in his mother's care. Even though she remarried, domestic relations did not improve, and Ayckbourn spent his formative years attending local boarding schools. At the age of twelve, he received a Barclays Bank scholarship to attend public school at Haileybury, where, under the tutelage of Edgar Matthews, he discovered drama. It was Matthews who introduced the young Ayckbourn to men such as Donald Wolfit and Robert Flemyng, who helped him land his first jobs in the theater.

Ayckbourn served his apprenticeship as an assistant stage manager at Worthing before he moved to Scarborough, where he joined the Theatre-in-the-Round company managed by Stephen Joseph, for whom he wrote, in 1959, his first plays, *The Square Cat* and *Love After All*. Although he had learned much by his association with the brilliantly innovative Joseph, he left Scarborough to found the Victoria Theatre Company at Stoke-on-Trent and later to work for the BBC as a producer of radio drama. He continued to write occasional comedies for the Scarborough company but did not return in a full-time capacity until 1970, when he assumed the post of Director of Productions. In the meantime, he had also experienced his first successes outside of Scarborough when *Meet My Father* (retitled *Relatively Speaking*), starring Celia Johnson, and *How the Other Half Loves*, starring Robert Morley, were produced in London. These comedies did not receive widespread critical acclaim, however, for like most of Ayckbourn's work, they did not readily adapt to the star system and the large stage format of West End theater. Now that he is able to exert a stronger influence over the direction of his plays, or direct them himself, his reputation has become well established. Most of his plays are now produced in London, and many have been televised. In spite of these triumphs, Ayckbourn must be viewed as a writer who is chiefly committed to writing for the small and balanced casts of the Theatre-in-the-Round at Scarborough and for the audiences attracted to that solidly middle-class seaside resort.

Analysis

One of the most distinctive features of Alan Ayckbourn's drama is his inclusion, by manipulating the structure, of action which the audience does not normally see. For example, in *Absurd Person Singular*, continuous action takes place in both the living room and the kitchen, although the audience only *sees* what transpires in the kitchen while a party is in progress in the next room. Snatches of dialogue are heard from the front room whenever a character enters or leaves the kitchen, and one of the couples, the Potters, is never seen, although they become the object of much discussion among those who make their way into the kitchen. While the play is outrageously funny and explores a number of important themes, it does not successfully fulfill Ayckbourn's structural purposes because it is quite clear that the major interests in the comedy do, in fact, develop in the kitchen scenes.

The Norman Conquests, however, comes much closer to achieving the dramatist's structural purposes in terms of offstage action because ultimately very little is left to speculation. *The Norman Conquests* is a trilogy of plays, each of which presents the offstage action that occurs during the other two. In other words, the first play (*Table Manners*) details action in the dining room, while the second (*Living Together*) presents simultaneous events in the living room, and the third (*Round and Round the Garden*) extends the action into the adjoining garden. Thus, when a character leaves the setting of one play, he usually enters the action of one of the other two, that is, unless he goes upstairs to one of the bedrooms or leaves the area entirely. In order to understand the action in its totality, it is necessary to see or read all three plays, although Ayckbourn has managed to make each play capable of standing as a dramatic entity. A reader, of course, has the advantage of following the action as it progresses during each time sequence from play to play. For example, the action begins with the first scene of *Round and Round the Garden*, then moves into the first scene of *Table Manners* before picking up in scene 1 of *Living Together.* It does not matter in what order one chooses (or happens) to read or see the plays; presumably, with a large enough stage, all three plays could be blocked simultaneously, or they could be shown on three separate television screens.

Underlying the entire plot is the unseen yet living presence of the "ailing" mother who keeps to her bed upstairs and whose needs must be tended to by one of her children: Annie, who lives with her, Ruth, or Reg. In *Table Manners*, the audience learns that Annie has made a date to run off with Norman, her sister Ruth's husband, for a weekend in Hastings (the scene of the historical Norman Conquest), but she is angry because Norman has booked them for East Grinstead instead. She confesses the whole plan to her sister-in-law Sarah, who, in order to facilitate Annie's holiday, has arrived to nurse her mother-in-law. Annie offers no explanation except that she is tired of looking after her cantankerous mother and that she is frustrated by her erstwhile boyfriend, Tom, who appears unlikely to break his long, awkward silence with any proposal of marriage. A veterinarian, "poor" Tom pays more attention to the family cat than he does to Annie. The officious Sarah, the self-appointed head of the family, determines that Annie will not go anywhere with the nefarious Norman but will spend the weekend resting at home, and she devotes much energy to prevent Norman from being alone with Annie. Sarah also informs her husband, Reg, of his sister's immoral intentions and telephones Ruth in a zealous effort to thwart Norman's plans. Nevertheless, it appears that Sarah is thoroughly frustrated by her own unromantic husband, and she accuses him of being unappreciative of her efforts to rear their two children and to keep him happy. While this action unfolds, Norman is heard in the next room, becoming increasingly inebriated. The whole first scene is a series of quarrels, between Sarah and Reg, and Annie and Tom, mostly over trifles. In one important sequence, Reg, who seems amused at Annie's lecherous desires, discusses their mother's continual infidelities and recalls how she had chased after everything in pants behind their father's back. They imply that Mother has decided to remain bedridden because she has lost her ability to attract men and therefore sees no further reason to live.

Norman makes his first appearance onstage in the second scene of *Table Manners*, although he has been the catalyst of everything that has transpired in the opening scene. After driving both Annie and Sarah from the breakfast table with a torrent of abuse, he is interrupted by the arrival of Ruth, who is indignant because she has been called away from her professional work. Norman attributes the whole situation to his marital disillusionment and accuses Ruth of treating their relationship as though it were a mere legal contract. She expresses impatience with Norman's sexual importunities and explodes into uncontrollable laughter when informed that he had planned a weekend with Annie in East Grinstead.

The second act begins with Annie rejecting further romantic advances by Norman, while Sarah appeals to both Norman and Reg not to fuel any more quarrels during the evening. Alone with Sarah, Norman implies that they share a common fate, as in-laws, in being deliberately misunderstood and in standing outside family concern. With Norman professing love to all, the family assembles for dinner, Sarah presiding. It is not long before warfare erupts, and Sarah goes berserk trying to maintain calm. The scene finishes with Tom launching a punch at Norman for insulting Annie, and Ruth giving Sarah a tongue-lashing for being an interfering bitch. Once again, Norman and Sarah console each other for being victims of a vicious family.

In the final scene, Norman and Sarah find themselves conveniently alone at breakfast. He heaps praise upon her for her loving devotion to her miraculous children, and he finally suggests that it would make her happy to spend a weekend with him at Bournemouth. Although she feigns hesitancy, she agrees to discuss the idea with him over the phone later. The play closes with all the visitors making hasty preparations for departure and Norman returning to find Annie alone in the kitchen. She flies into his arms and confesses that she does relish the idea of going to East Grinstead with him after all. Norman willingly acquiesces to the renewed assignation.

Living Together, which shows the action taking place in the living room during the same time period, quickly sketches in the same expository details; it provides the additional interest of an early confrontation between Norman and Sarah, who expresses disgust with Norman for seducing Annie on the living-room rug last Christmas while her sister had been ill in bed upstairs. Norman at first dismisses the whole affair as the natural outcome of the Yuletide spirit but then claims that he is in love with Annie. When he turns the tables on Sarah and asks if she is happy with the lackluster Reg, she claims that she is too busy to notice whether she is happy, having so many responsibilities. After Annie gives an unsatisfactory explanation of her decision to stay at home, Norman immediately launches into a drunken spree with Tom, heard as offstage sound in act 1 of *Table Manners*. Norman also persuades Tom that he could gain greater respect from Annie if he treated her with masculine disdain, by giving her the "metaphorical boot." While the rest of the family quarrel over coffee and a boring game which Reg has invented, Norman snores all the way to the end of the second scene before arising to make an inarticulate telephone call to Ruth (who had also been called by Sarah during the same time interval in *Table Manners*). When Annie picks on Tom, he takes Norman's advice and stalks out of the house, but not before telling her she's ill-dressed and needs a hefty belt across the ear.

The second scene begins with a tirade by Ruth, who is extremely irritated at being interrupted from her work. She appears little concerned about Norman's "gestures" and even suggests that he might have saved Annie from "a fate worse than marriage": eternal engagement to such a nonentity as Tom. After much debate, the family all decide to go up to bed. Later, Annie allows Norman to maneuver her onto the infamous rug, but they are interrupted by Sarah, who sneaks back into the room, probably motivated by similar feelings of frustration and desire for Norman. She explodes into a paroxysm of rage at what she discovers and orders Annie from the room. Annie, objecting to the title of "whore," engages Sarah in open conflict. While Norman enjoys the spectacle of two women fighting over him, Ruth returns to the room and orders both combatants to bed. She then launches into Norman for his "deceitful, odious, conceited, self-centered, selfish, inconsiderate, and shallow" behavior in humiliating her in front of the family. Norman pleads the excuse that he is driven to it because Ruth has rejected him in favor of her work. As her anger fades, Norman entices her onto the rug with the promise that in the future it will be *their* rug. In the final scene, Reg discovers them the next morning snuggled together on the rug, and they extract a vow of secrecy from him. Tom returns to make a sheepish apology to a most nonchalant Annie, and Norman persuades Ruth to take off time from work to spend a day at home with him. The other members of the family exchange farewells with the departing Ruth and Norman, and the play ends with Sarah, much to Reg's astonishment, wondering what it might be like in Bournemouth at this time of year.

Round and Round the Garden opens with Tom trying to coax the cat down from the tree and Annie anxiously awaiting the arrival of Reg and Sarah. She is surprised to find Norman hiding among the brambles, and she insists he meet her at the appointed time. Before he has a chance to comply, however, he is intercepted by Tom, then Reg, and finally by Sarah, who triumphantly announces that Annie has decided not to go away after all. Norman believes that Annie's defection is all Sarah's fault. In the second scene, Reg and Sarah carry Norman (who has become drunk onstage at the end of the first scene of *Living Together*) into the garden to sober up, but when Reg accuses her of interfering, Sarah imperiously orders him back into the house. She then begins to scold Norman, who gradually and insistently works upon her own frustrations to the point that she falls into his arms in a long passionate embrace. Amazed at herself, she beats a hasty retreat, leaving Norman alone with Annie, who apologizes to him for being such a coward. Although she is a coward about going to hotels, she invites him to spend the night with her. He promises to mess up his own bed before joining her, in order to allay any suspicions Sarah may entertain. He continues his pretense of being drunk, and Reg and Sarah carry him into the house. The second act opens with Sarah intercepting Ruth in the garden and Ruth wondering what all the fuss is about. After all, she has become accustomed to Norman's gesturing and compares him to a large, unmanageable, but lovable dog, always getting into mischief, who only jumps up and licks those like Annie and Sarah who encourage him. In the hope of improving Tom's chances with Annie, Ruth begins a counseling session, but Tom, whose brain receives messages like unfiled memos in a vast civil service department, takes her words of advice as expressions of her own feelings and believes that Ruth is carrying a torch for him. Thus, when Annie and Norman use a game of catch as an excuse for a roll in the grass, Tom furiously kisses Ruth, shouting "Two can play at that." The final scene reveals Norman overplaying his hand and losing the attention of all three conquests. Left alone, he shouts in bewildered indignation that he only wanted to make them happy.

The Norman Conquests presents an intriguing character study of three women who find themselves, actually or potentially, trapped by marriage. Ruth finds protection from Norman's infidelity in her professional work, and while she recognizes Norman's incorrigibility, she cloaks her feelings in an air of profound cynicism and apparent nonchalance. Fully aware of Norman's antics, she perseveres until she is confronted with her own humiliation. Annie is to some extent a reflection of "the evil woman upstairs," to whom she has to read erotic romances. Her desire for "a *really* dirty weekend" with Norman is simply a reaction to the frustration she feels in her impotent relationship with Tom. Thoroughly conventional, driven by a sense of duty, Sarah is secretly fascinated by Norman and needs the affection he offers. She does not respect Reg, or love him, because, like Tom, he is completely incapable of romantic passion, and yet she despises what she feels. This self-disgust is reflected in the string of epithets she directs at Annie in the rug scene. Norman, on the other hand, is the litmus paper which produces the predictable chemical reaction. His conquests are possible because he possesses a natural, animallike instinct for recognizing the sexual needs of the vanquished. He *is* a lovable dog, and he prevails because he is there.

In most of Ayckbourn's comedies, there are women driven to distraction by insensitive partners: the drunken Marion and the suicidal Eva in *Absurd Person Singular*, Diana in *Absent Friends*, Vera in *Just Between Ourselves*, Elizabeth in *Taking Steps*, and Belinda in *Season's Greetings*. If any of the

Ayckbourn wives escape this fate, it is usually because they are too ob-
tuse, conventional, passionless, or inured by routine to notice or to care.
The only characters who transcend such emotional entrapments are those
mavericks who disregard the conventions or prevail by challenging them.
Joking Apart, however, provides an interesting twist to these themes. In
the first scene, an apparently happily married couple, Richard and Anthea
Clarke, are visited by Hugh Emerson, the new vicar, and his wife, Louise.
Richard and Anthea, the visitors discover, are simply living together and,
ironically, occupy the old vicarage, whereas Hugh and Louise live in a new
house across the garden fence. These four are joined by Sven and Olive
Holmenson, who are involved in business with the Clarkes, and by Brian
and his girlfriend Melody, in order to celebrate Guy Fawkes Day. Richard
busies himself entertaining the children (who can be heard offstage), but
Louise, who is so highly strung that she cannot stand the firecrackers, has
to hurry off with their uncontrollable brat, Christopher. Melody acts surly
because she resents Brian, who is using her in an effort to make Anthea
jealous, since Anthea has remained impervious to Brian's infatuation. Sven
is an assertive individual whose self-importance impresses only his wife, Olive. Sven insists that he is an authority on virtually every subject; Richard
and Anthea indulge his fancies but otherwise ignore him.

The second scene takes place four years later and involves an offstage
game of croquet in addition to the ever-present tennis. Little has changed
except that Brian has a new girl, Mandy, who paints and pouts throughout
the scene, while Sven complains that Richard ignores his professional
advice and yet makes good profits for The Scandinavian Craftware Company Limited, in which he has become virtually the silent partner. Hugh's
ministry has not fared well, because of his dull sermons, and Louise feels
that her husband's reputation suffers because he relies upon the unorthodox Anthea for parish chores. Sven suggests that Richard and Anthea exercise an invidious power over the people they collect, but their chief vice
seems to be that they insist upon being themselves and responding to the
needs of others.

Act 2 repeats the garden scene four years later in a celebration of Box-
ing Day, which features a game of tennis (mostly offstage). Again nothing
has changed. Brian has brought a new girlfriend, Mo, who gets drunk after
Brian explains that he has been in love with Anthea for ten years. Sven is
even more depressed by Richard's business successes; his "excellent partner
runs the whole business in his sleep" and always makes the right decisions,
without any help from Sven. Bragging about his former status as junior
tennis champion of Finland, Sven challenges Richard to a set, over Olive's
pleading that he not overexert himself, and then wins the match, only to
find out that Richard has given him an edge by playing him left-handed.
As the match progresses, Hugh confesses that he has fallen in love with

Anthea, who only listens patiently to his protestations and tells him to go home and forget such silly notions, which are not appropriate for the Church Militant.

In the final scene, four years later at the eighteenth birthday party of Richard and Anthea's daughter Debbie, the audience learns that Sven's exertions have led to a coronary and that he is forced to take life easy. Brian has run out of girlfriends but still yearns for Anthea. Sven has re-lapsed into a settled bitterness and calls himself a "middle-aged medioc-rity," an unworthy opponent for a man such as Richard, fortune's favorite. Hugh and Louise's son has now become quite a scholar but despises his parents and never speaks to them. Louise lives on whatever miracle drugs her doctor is currently peddling and ranges from being soporific to suicidal, completely out of touch with Hugh, who keeps a respectful distance from Anthea. When the guests all depart, Debbie asks her parents if they have any normal friends and tells her mother that she finds Brian disgusting. Anthea explains that Brian is "a nothing, a neutral," and quite harmless, and that it is always as well to be charitable to those whose lives are less fortunate.

Like Norman, Richard and Anthea only want to make people happy, but their tragedy is that their good-natured success serves as a constant re-proach to the conventional couples who depend upon them. Hugh and Louise represent the failure of traditional Christian marriage, a failure con-firmed when their only son rejects them. Hugh sees the attractions on the other side of the fence but is fettered to the empty life he leads with Lou-ise by virtue of the office he holds. Sven's earlier assurance merely cloaked his mediocrity. His relationship with Richard, like Brian's with Anthea, is basically masochistic. The constant reminder of Richard and Anthea's un-orthodox happiness is a source of self-laceration, a measure of their own failures. Only Richard and Anthea escape the gradual erosion of marital ideals and the collapse of fantasies; they escape because they refuse to be bound by the constricting norms of conventional relationships. One senses that they will impart the secrets of freedom and charity to their own chil-dren, Debbie and Giles.

Ayckbourn's theater demonstrates an admirable sense of the dramatically functional; there is almost never any wasted material in his plays. They reveal their author's keenly developed practical sense not only of what will be effective onstage, but also of that often more elusive matter of provid-ing an audience with what it needs to imagine, what is *not* represented. Ayckbourn's talent for farce, his technical facility and inventiveness in terms of plot, structure, and character development, should not obscure the complexity, even sorrow, which lies beneath his comic vision. Man's foi-bles are indeed ridiculous and worthy of scorn, but they result from a pro-found and tragic blindness to the realities of the world in which he lives.

Bibliography
Elsom, John. *Post-War British Theatre*, 1976.
Hayman, Ronald. *British Theatre Since 1955*, 1979.
Kerensky, Oleg. *The New British Drama*, 1977.
Taylor, John Russell. *The Second Wave*, 1971.
Watson, Ian. *Conversations with Ayckbourn*, 1981.

E. F. J. Tucker

JAMES BALDWIN

Born: New York, New York; August 2, 1924

Principal drama

The Amen Corner, pr. 1954, pb. 1968; *Blues for Mister Charlie*, pr., pb. 1964.

Other literary forms

Best known for his novels and essays, James Baldwin has contributed to every contemporary genre except poetry. Baldwin established his literary reputation with *Go Tell It on the Mountain* (1953), a novel which anticipates the thematic concerns of *The Amen Corner*. Subsequent novels, including *Another Country* (1962), *If Beale Street Could Talk* (1974), and *Just Above My Head* (1979), along with the brilliant story "Sonny's Blues" (1957) confirmed Baldwin's stature as a leading figure in postwar American fiction. Several of Baldwin's early essays, collected in *Notes of a Native Son* (1955) and *Nobody Knows My Name: More Notes of a Native Son* (1961), are today recognized as classics; his essays on Richard Wright, "Everybody's Protest Novel" (1949) and "Many Thousands Gone" (1951), occupy a central position in the development, during the 1950's, of "universalist" Afro-American thought. *The Fire Next Time* (1963), perhaps Baldwin's most important work of nonfiction, is an extended meditation on the relationship of race, religion, and the individual experience. Emphasizing the failure of the United States to heed the warning of *The Fire Next Time*, *No Name in the Street* (1971) asserts the more militant political stance articulated in *Blues for Mister Charlie*. Less formal and intricate, though in some cases more explicit, statements of Baldwin's positions can be found in *A Rap on Race* (1971), an extended discussion with Margaret Mead, and *A Dialogue: James Baldwin and Nikki Giovanni* (1975). Of special interest in relation to Baldwin's drama are the unfilmed scenario *One Day, When I Was Lost: A Scenario Based on Alex Haley's "The Autobiography of Malcolm X"* (1972) and *The Devil Finds Work: An Essay* (1976), which focuses on Baldwin's personal and aesthetic frustrations with the American film industry.

Achievements

Baldwin's image as an Afro-American racial spokesman during the 1950's and 1960's guarantees his place in American cultural history. His fiction and essays, both aesthetically and as charts of the movement from universalism to militancy in Afro-American thought, have earned for him serious and lasting attention. Nevertheless, Baldwin's significance as a dramatist remains problematic. In large part because of Baldwin's high public visibility, *Blues for Mister Charlie* was greeted as a major cultural event when it opened on Broadway at the ANTA Theater on April 23, 1964. Baldwin's most direct expression of political anger to that time, the play echoed the warning to white America sounded in *The Fire Next Time*, the play that had catapulted Baldwin to prominence in the mass media. Despite its immediate impact, however, *Blues for Mister Charlie* failed to win lasting support. Numerous Afro-American critics, particularly those associated with the community theater movement of the late 1960's, dismissed the play as an attempt to attract a mainstream white audience. Mainstream critics, drawing attention to the contradiction between Baldwin's political theme and his attack on protest writing in "Everybody's Protest Novel," dismissed the play as strident propaganda. Critics of diverse perspectives united in dismissing the play as theatrically static. The play's closing, following a four-month run, underscored its failure to realize the early hopes for a new era in Afro-American theater on Broadway. Ironically, Baldwin's reputation as a dramatist now rests primarily on *The Amen Corner*, a relatively obscure play written in the early 1950's, produced under the direction of Owen Dodson at Howard University in 1954, and brought to Broadway for a twelve-week run only in April, 1965, as an attempt to capitalize on the interest generated by *Blues for Mister Charlie*. Examining the tension between religious and secular experience, *The Amen Corner* maintains some interest as an anticipation of the thematic and structural use of music in Afro-American plays during the Black Arts Movement. Although Baldwin's drama fails to live up to the standards set by his prose, the heated public discussion surrounding *Blues for Mister Charlie* attests its historical importance as one element in the political and aesthetic transition from the nonviolent universalism of Afro-American thought in the 1950's to the militant nationalism of the 1960's.

Biography

James Baldwin once dismissed his childhood as "the usual bleak fantasy." Nevertheless, the major concerns of his writing consistently reflect the social context of his family life in Harlem during the Depression. The dominant figure of Baldwin's childhood was his stepfather, David Baldwin, who worked as a manual laborer and preached in a storefront church. Clearly the model for Gabriel Grimes in *Go Tell It on the Mountain*, David Baldwin had moved from New Orleans to New York City, where he married James's mother, Emma Berdis. The oldest of what was to become a group of nine children in the household, James assumed a great deal of the responsibility for the care of his half brothers and sisters. Insulated somewhat from the brutality of Harlem street life by his domestic duties, Baldwin sought refuge in the Church. Following a conversion experience in

1938, Baldwin preached as a youth minister for several years. At the same time, he began to read, immersing himself in works such as Harriet Beecher Stowe's *Uncle Tom's Cabin* (1852) and the novels of Charles Dickens. Both at his Harlem junior high school, where the Afro-American poet Countée Cullen was one of his teachers, and at his predominantly white Bronx high school, Baldwin contributed to student literary publications. The combination of family tension, economic hardship, and religious vocation provides the focus of much of Baldwin's greatest writing, most notably *Go Tell It on the Mountain*, *The Fire Next Time*, and *Just Above My Head*.

If Baldwin's experience during the 1930's provided his material, his life from 1942 to 1948 shaped his characteristic approach to that material. After he was graduated from high school in 1942, Baldwin worked for a year as a manual laborer in New Jersey, an experience which increased both his understanding of his stepfather and his insight into America's economic and racial systems. Moving to Greenwich Village in 1944, Baldwin worked during the day and wrote at night for the next five years; his first national reviews and essays appeared in 1946. The major event of the Village years, however, was Baldwin's meeting with Richard Wright in the winter of 1944-1945. Wright's interest helped Baldwin acquire a Eugene F. Saxton Memorial Trust Fellowship and then a Rosenwald Fellowship, enabling him to move to Paris in 1948.

After his arrival in France, Baldwin experienced more of the poverty which had shaped his childhood. Simultaneously, he developed a larger perspective on the psychocultural context conditioning his experience, feeling at once a greater sense of freedom and a larger sense of the global structure of racism, particularly as reflected in the French treatment of North Africans. In addition, he formed many of the personal and literary friendships which contributed to his later public prominence. Baldwin's well-publicized literary feud with Wright, who viewed the younger writer's criticism of *Native Son* (1940) as a form of personal betrayal, helped establish Baldwin as a major presence in Afro-American letters. Although Baldwin's first novel, *Go Tell It on the Mountain*, was well received critically, it was not so financially successful that he could devote his full time to creative writing. Returning to the United States briefly in 1954-1955, he saw Dodson's production of *The Amen Corner* at Howard University. For several years, he continued to travel widely, frequently on journalistic assignments, while writing the novel *Giovanni's Room* (1956), which is set in France and involves no black characters.

Returning to the United States as a journalist covering the civil rights movement, Baldwin made his first trip to the American South in 1957. The essays and reports describing that physical and psychological journey propelled Baldwin to the position of public prominence that he maintained for more than a decade. During the height of the movement, Baldwin lectured widely and was present at major events such as the march on Washington and the voter registration drive in Selma, Alabama. In addition, he met with most of the major Afro-American activists of the period, including Martin Luther King, Jr., Elijah Muhammad, James Meredith, and Medgar Evers. Attorney General Robert Kennedy requested that Baldwin bring together the most influential voices in the black community; even though the resulting meeting accomplished little, the request testifies to Baldwin's image as a focal point of Afro-American opinion. In addition to this political activity, Baldwin formed personal and literary relationships—frequently tempestuous ones—with numerous white writers, including William Styron and Norman Mailer. A surge in literary popularity, reflected in the presence of *Another Country* and *The Fire Next Time* on the best-seller lists throughout most of 1962 and 1963, accompanied Baldwin's political success and freed him from financial insecurity for the first time. His experiences with the civil rights movement shaped both the narrative material and the political perspective of *Blues for Mister Charlie.*

Partly because of Baldwin's involvement with prominent whites and partly because of the sympathy for homosexuals evinced in his writing, several black militants, most notably Eldridge Cleaver, attacked Baldwin's position as "black spokesman" beginning in the late 1960's. As a result, nationalist spokesmen such as Amiri Baraka and Bobby Seale gradually eclipsed Baldwin in the literary and political spotlight. Nevertheless, Baldwin, himself sympathetic to many of the militant positions, has continued his involvement with public issues, such as the fate of the Wilmington, North Carolina prisoners—an issue which he addressed in an open letter to Jimmy Carter shortly after Carter's election to the presidency. In the early 1980's, Baldwin returned to the South to assess the changes of the last three decades and to examine the meaning of events such as the Atlanta child murders.

Analysis

James Baldwin's plays, like his best prose, examine the self-defeating attempts of characters to protect themselves against suffering by categorizing experience in terms of simplistic dichotomies. Like *Go Tell It on the Mountain, The Amen Corner* concentrates on the failure of the dichotomy between "Temple" and "Street" to articulate the experience of the congregation of a Harlem storefront church. Like *The Fire Next Time* and *Another Country, Blues for Mister Charlie* emphasizes the black-white dichotomy shaping the murderous racial conflict that devastates both blacks and whites psychologically. Where Baldwin's fiction ultimately suggests some means of transcending these tensions, however, his plays frequently remain enmeshed in dramatic structures which inadvertently perpetuate the dichotomies they ostensibly challenge. Paradoxically, Baldwin's problems as a playwright derive from his strengths as a novelist. His use of the tradition of Afro-American folk preaching as the base for a narrative voice capable of taking on a powerful presence of its own frequently results in static didacticism when linked to a character on stage. Similarly, the emphasis on the importance of silence in his novels highlights the tendency of his plays to make explicit aspects of awareness which his characters would be highly unlikely to articulate even to themselves. As a result, conceptually powerful passages in which characters confront the tension between their ideals and experiences tend to freeze the rhythm onstage. As Afro-American playwright Carlton Mollette observed in a comment that applies equally well to *Blues for Mister Charlie*, "*The Amen Corner* is at its worst as a play precisely when it is at its best as literature."

Nowhere are these difficulties seen more clearly than in Baldwin's treatment of the tension between institutionalized religion and moral integrity in *The Amen Corner*. Like *Go Tell It on the Mountain*, *The Amen Corner* challenges the dichotomy between the holy Temple and the sinful Street, a tension which shapes the play's entire dramatic structure. Accepted unquestioningly by most members of Sister Margaret Alexander's congregation, the dichotomy reflects a basic survival strategy of blacks making the transition from their rural Southern roots to the urban North during the Great Migration. By dividing the world into zones of safety and danger, church members attempt to distance themselves and, perhaps more important, their loved ones from the brutalities of the city. As Baldwin comments in his introduction to the play, Sister Margaret faces the dilemma of "how to treat her husband and her son as men and at the same time to protect them from the bloody consequences of trying to be a man in this society." In act 1, Margaret attempts to resolve the dilemma by forcing her son David, a musician in his late teens, into the role of servant of the Lord while consigning her estranged husband Luke, a jazz musician, to the role of worldly tempter. Having witnessed the brutal impact of Harlem on Luke, she strives to protect her son by creating a world entirely separate from his father's. Ultimately, however, the attempt fails as David's emerging sense of self drives him to confront a wider range of experience; meanwhile, Luke's physical collapse, which takes place in the "safe zone," forces Margaret to acknowledge her own evasions. The most important of these, which reveals Margaret's claim to moral purity as self-constructed illusion, involves her claim that Luke abandoned his family; in fact, she fled from him to avoid the pain caused by the death of a newborn daughter, a pain associated with sexuality and the Street.

As he did in *Go Tell It on the Mountain*, Baldwin treats the collapse of the dichotomies as a potential source of artistic and spiritual liberation. David recognizes that his development as a musician demands immersion in both the sacred and the secular traditions of Afro-American music; Margaret attempts to redefine herself in terms not of holiness but of an accepting love imaged in her clutching Luke's trombone mouthpiece after his death. Both resolutions intimate a synthesis of Temple and Street, suggesting the common impulse behind the gospel music and jazz which sound throughout the play. The emotional implications of the collapse of the dichotomies in *The Amen Corner* are directly articulated when, following her acknowledgment that the vision on which she bases her authority as preacher was her own creation, Margaret says: "It's a awful thing to think about, the way love never dies!" This second "vision" marks a victory much more profound than that of the church faction which casts Margaret out at the end of the play. Ironically, the new preacher, Sister Moore, seems destined to perpetuate Margaret's moral failings. Although Sister Moore's rise to power is grounded primarily in the congregation's dissatisfaction with Margaret's inability to connect her spiritual life with the realities of the Street (Margaret refuses to sympathize with a woman's marital difficulties or to allow a man to take a job driving a liquor truck), she fails to perceive the larger implications of the dissatisfaction. Sister Moore's inability to see the depth of Margaret's transformed sense of love suggests that the simplifying dichotomies will continue to shape the congregation's experience.

Thematically and psychologically, then, *The Amen Corner* possesses a great deal of potential power. Theatrically, however, it fails to exploit this potential. Despite Baldwin's awareness that "the ritual of the church, historically speaking, comes out of the theater, the *communion* which is the theater," the structure of *The Amen Corner* emphasizes individual alienation rather than ritual reconciliation. In part because the play's power in performance largely derives from the energy of the music played in the church, the street side of Baldwin's vision remains relatively abstract. Where the brilliant prose of *Go Tell It on the Mountain* suggests nuances of perception which remain only half-conscious to John Grimes during his transforming vision, David's conversations with Luke and Margaret focus almost exclusively on his rebellion against the Temple while leaving the terms of the dichotomy unchallenged. In act 3, similarly, Margaret's catharsis seems static. The fact that Margaret articulates her altered awareness in her preacher's voice suggests a lingering commitment to the Temple at odds with Baldwin's thematic design. Although the sacred music emanating from the church is theoretically balanced by the jazz trombone associated with Luke, most of the performance power adheres to the gospel songs that provide an embodied experience of call and response; taken out of its performance context, the jazz seems a relatively powerless expression. As a result, *The Amen Corner* never escapes from the sense of separation it conceptually attacks.

Blues for Mister Charlie reconsiders the impact of simplistic dichotomies in explicitly political terms. Dedicated to the murdered civil rights leader

Medgar Evers and the four black children killed in a 1963 Birmingham terrorist bombing, the play reflects both Baldwin's increasing anger and his continuing search for a unified moral being. Loosely basing his plot on the case of Emmett Till, a black youth murdered for allegedly insulting a white woman in Mississippi, Baldwin focuses his attention on the unpunished white murderer of Richard Henry, who is killed after returning to his minister father's Southern home to recover from a drug addiction. Baldwin establishes a black-white division onstage as an extension of the sacred-secular dichotomy; the two primary sets are a black church and a white courthouse, both of which are divided into two areas, Whitetown and Blacktown. Underscoring the actual interdependence of the constituting terms, Baldwin insists in his stage directions that the audience be aware of the courthouse flag throughout scenes set in the church and of the Cross during scenes set in the courthouse. Periodically, the dialogue brings the connections between seemingly disparate realities into the foreground. Richard's father, Meridian, responds to the liberal white newspaperman Parnell's surprise over the intensity of rage and hatred in the black community following Richard's death: "You've heard it before. You just never recognized it before. You've heard it in all those blues and spirituals and gospel songs you claim to love so much." The tentative rapprochement of Parnell, Meridian, and Richard's lover Juanita at the end of the play provides an image of a potential community capable of acknowledging the complexity of transforming both the rage and the past failures of perception into a political and moral action. When Parnell, employing a term with particularly charged meaning in the context of the Southern civil rights movement, asks if he can "join you on the march," Juanita's tempered acceptance—"we can walk in the same direction"—represents a profound attempt not to invert the black-white dichotomy following the acquittal of Richard's murderer, Lyle Britten, an acquittal in which Parnell is implicated by his inability to challenge the underlying structure of the white legal system.

As background for this resolution, Baldwin develops three central themes: the growing anger of young blacks; the impact of this anger on the older members of the black community; and the white psychology which enables apparently normal individuals to perpetrate atrocities without remorse. The theme of anger focuses on Richard, whose experiences both in New York and Mississippi generate an intense bitterness against all whites. Articulating a militant credo which Baldwin finds emotionally comprehensible but morally inadequate, Richard tells his grandmother, "I'm going to treat every one of them as though they were responsible for all the crimes that ever happened in the history of the world—oh, yes! They're responsible for all the misery I've ever seen ... the only way the black man's going to get any power is to drive all the white men into the sea."

Backed up by his vow to carry a gun with him at all times, Richard's militancy comes into direct conflict with his grandmother's and his father's traditional values of endurance, hope, and Christian compassion. Ironically, Richard's compassion for his grandmother leads him to give his gun to his father, an act which leaves him defenseless when attacked by Lyle. Baldwin suggests that some adjustment between unbridled violence and naïve faith will be necessary if blacks are to put an end to their victimization without emulating the moral failures of their white persecutors.

Baldwin's comments on *Blues for Mister Charlie* emphasize the importance of the portrait of the white persecutor to his overall design. Attributing his reluctance to write drama to a "deeper fear," Baldwin stresses his desire to overcome his own dichotomizing impulses and "to draw a valid portrait of the murderer." Unfortunately, the dramatic presentation of Lyle Britten in many ways fails to fulfill this desire. Obsessed with racial honor, especially as it involves white women, Lyle seems more sociological exemplar than rounded individual. Despite the fact that he has had at least one sexual relationship with a black woman, Lyle's obsession with interracial sex, grounded in a deep insecurity which leads him to respond violently to any perceived threat to his sense of masculine superiority, dominates every aspect of his character. While sociological works such as Joel Kovel's *White Racism: A Psychohistory* (1970) and Calvin Hernton's *Sex and Racism in America* (1965) support the general accuracy of the diagnosis, Baldwin nevertheless fails to demonstrate its relation to aspects of Lyle's experience not directly involved with the obsession. Lyle's monologues on his poor white heritage and his sexual experience sound stilted and contrived, especially when juxtaposed to a generally unconvincing presentation of whites in the play. Parnell's monologue on "the holy, the liberating orgasm," for example, seems more a didactic parody of Norman Mailer's *The White Negro* (1957) than an aspect of his character.

Although in his fiction Baldwin demonstrates a profound understanding of the psychological reality and aesthetic power of silence, *Blues for Mister Charlie* veers sharply toward an overelaboration which undercuts the validity of his portrait of the white persecutors. This in turn weighs the play more heavily than Baldwin intended toward the black perspective, reinforcing rather than challenging the underlying dichotomy. The conversations among Parnell, Lyle, and Lyle's wife, Jo, concerning their attitudes toward race and sex seem wooden and static largely because they articulate attitudes that if consciously acknowledged would dictate changes in behavior in any realistic, as opposed to demoniac, characters. Although it would be possible to interpret the monologues as Eugene O'Neill-style "stream-of-unconsciousness" passages, the dialogue subverts the effectiveness of the technique, suggesting that Baldwin has simply failed to come to terms with the silence of his characters' personalities. Although *Blues for Mister Char-*

78 *Critical Survey of Drama*

lie advances Baldwin's belief that imposing dichotomies on experience leads inexorably to emotional and physical violence, it nevertheless perpetuates a dichotomy between abstract statement and concrete experience. Baldwin's decision not to return to drama after *Blues for Mister Charlie* seems an acknowledgment that he is much more comfortable with forms in which his voice can assume a concrete reality of its own, transforming tensions that in his drama remain unresolved.

Other major works

NOVELS: *Go Tell It on the Mountain*, 1953; *Giovanni's Room*, 1956; *Another Country*, 1962; *Tell Me How Long the Train's Been Gone*, 1968; *If Beale Street Could Talk*, 1974; *Just Above My Head*, 1979.

SHORT FICTION: *Going to Meet the Man*, 1965.

NONFICTION: *Notes of a Native Son*, 1955; *Nobody Knows My Name: More Notes of a Native Son*, 1961; *The Fire Next Time*, 1963; *No Name in the Street*, 1971; *A Rap on Race*, 1971; *A Dialogue: James Baldwin and Nikki Giovanni*, 1975; *The Devil Finds Work: An Essay*, 1976.

SCREENPLAYS: *One Day, When I Was Lost: A Scenario Based on Alex Haley's "The Autobiography of Malcolm X,"* 1972 (unfilmed); *The Inheritance*, 1973.

Bibliography

Eckman, Fern. *The Furious Passage of James Baldwin*, 1966.
Kinnamon, Kenneth. *James Baldwin: A Collection of Critical Essays*, 1974.
Mitchell, Loften. *Black Drama*, 1970.
O'Daniel, Therman B., ed. *James Baldwin: A Critical Evaluation*, 1977.
Pratt, Louis H. *James Baldwin*, 1978.
Sylvander, Carolyn Wedin. *James Baldwin*, 1980.

Craig Werner

JOHN BALE

Born: Cove, England; November 21, 1495
Died: Canterbury, England; November, 1563

Principal drama

King Johan, wr. 1531(?), pb. 1538, pr. 1539(?); *Three Laws*, wr. 1531(?), pb. 1547; *God's Promises*, wr. 1538, pb. 1547; *John Baptist*, wr. 1538, pb. 1547; *The Temptation*, wr. 1538, pb. 1547; *The Dramatic Writings of John Bale*, pb. 1907 (John S. Farmer, editor).

Other literary forms

A Carmelite friar and scholar turned Protestant propagandist, John Bale wrote literary history, chronicle history, and religious polemics as well as verse drama. While a Carmelite, he edited some devotional works and compiled several Latin-language catalogs of the Order's practices and history in England. His *Illustrium Maioris Britanniae Scriptorum* (famous writers of Great Britain), first issued in 1548, subsequently revised and retitled in 1557, gave biographical information about the important writers of England, Scotland, and Wales and listed the titles and dates of their works.

Bale wrote chronicles of persons he deemed noteworthy Protestant martyrs: *A Brief Chronicle of Sir John Oldcastle, the Lord Cobham* (1544), *The First Examination of Anne Askew* (1546), and *The Latter Examination of Anne Askew* (1547).

A bitter opponent of the traditional Catholicism, from which he converted in mid-life, Bale wrote polemics combining dialogue with diatribe. He interpreted the pope as the Antichrist in *The Image of Both Churches* (part 1, 1541; part 2, 1545; part 3, 1547). In *The Acts of English Votaries* (1546), Bale attacked the behavior of those in religious orders. He disputed the positions of various Catholic apologists in the verse tract *An Answer to a Papistical Exhortation* (1548), and in prose in *An Expostulation Against the Blasphemies of a Frantic Papist* (1552) and *The Apology of John Bale Against a Rank Papist* (c. 1555). Bale attacked the papacy in *Acta Romanorum Pontificum* (1558; acts of the Roman pontiffs), and he criticized opponents nearer to home in his book *A Declaration Concerning the Clergy of London* (1561).

Bale edited a work on the sacrament of Holy Communion by John Lambert, *A Treatise to Henry VIII* (c. 1548). In 1538, he translated from the German Thomas Kirchmayer's Protestant play *Pammachius*, though his translation is not extant. Bale's *The True History of the Christian Departing of Martin Luther* (1546) is a translation of German accounts originally collected by Justus Jonas, Michael Cellius, and Joannes Aurifaber.

Achievements

A controversialist living in chaotic times, Bale is known less for originality in his own work than for setting precedents which other talents brought to flower.

Bale's own literary catalogs include a sprinkling of medieval trivia, such as attribution of certain literary works to the biblical Adam, yet his work provided a model for persistence in research, acknowledgment of sources, and comparative thoroughness in the entries on the writers of his own era. Modern literary biographers are still drawing on Bale's *Illustrium Maioris Britanniae Scriptorum* and its expanded editions for information on sixteenth century writers.

In his time, Bale was known for his Protestant propaganda, which attacked various doctrines and practices of Roman Catholic tradition as well as the views of other Protestants whom Bale believed to be extreme or misguided. Hence, in all genres, dogmatic Protestant zeal motivated his writing.

Bale's chronicle on Sir John Oldcastle was intended to rehabilitate the fourteenth century nobleman's reputation. As a follower of early reformer and Bible translator John Wycliffe, Oldcastle was depicted unfavorably in traditional records. Bale's wish that Protestant martyrs be viewed sympathetically was not unique, but according to his friend John Foxe, Bale's chronicle influenced in perspective and substance the histories written by Edward Hall and Raphael Holinshed, as well as Foxe's *The Book of Martyrs* (1559). All three writers reflected to some degree a break from traditional Catholic perspectives, and the chronicles of Hall and of Holinshed were to become sources for William Shakespeare's history plays.

Although Bale recorded titles of twenty-one plays that he wrote, only five are extant. The titles of the lost works, such as *Against Adulterators of God's Word, Christ's Passion*, and *Simon the Leper*, imply that the lost plays share the dogmatic purpose and medieval conventions of the plays that survive.

The extant play *King Johan*, however, includes a basic innovation which later writers worked to full advantage. Among the familiar walking, talking abstractions of the morality play's virtue and vice characters, Bale placed the thirteenth century monarch King Johan (King John) and a few of his historical enemies. King Johan's ill repute easily outlasted Bale's attempt to make him a Protestant saint and hero of English sovereignty and therefore a villain to Roman Catholic historians. Still, *King Johan* is a prototype drama including historical persons and events in English theater. The history plays of Shakespeare and Christopher Marlowe display far greater sophistication in plot, characterization, and theatricality, but Bale set the precedent for the history play as a type. He also, in perspective and substance, influenced the chronicle histories of Hall and Holinshed that Shakespeare used extensively in writing his history plays and stirred the debate over Sir John Oldcastle's true character that gave Shakespeare material for his rascal Falstaff.

Biography

John Bale included autobiographical notes in his literary catalogs. Beginning with those entries, then studying correspondence between Bale and his contemporaries and reviewing official records of the era, Jesse W. Harris has provided considerable background data in his book *John Bale: A Study in the Minor Literature of the Reformation* (1940), to which the following summary is indebted.

Bale was born to Henry and Margaret Bale at Cove, County Suffolk, near Dunwich, England. At age twelve, he began study with the Carmelite friars at Norwich, whose monastery had a good library. Bale learned Latin, the rites and customs of the Order, and the principles of careful study and research.

In 1514, Bale entered Jesus College in Cambridge University. College policy apparently required that he reside at Jesus College rather than with fellow Carmelites in lodgings that the order maintained at the university. When Bale arrived at Cambridge, interest in the New Learning was high and Continental Reformation influences were strong; Erasmus, the Dutch theologian and New Testament scholar, was in residence there. A number of Bale's fellow students, including Hugh Latimer, Thomas Cranmer, Stephen Gardiner, and Matthew Parker, were to become important figures in the religious and political struggles that erupted when Henry VIII assumed control of the English Church and that did not significantly subside until after the accession of Elizabeth I.

Bale took his bachelor of divinity in 1529 and his doctor of divinity not long afterward. He served briefly as prior of the Carmelite monastery in Maldon in 1530, then moved to the priory at Doncaster. In 1533, he became prior at Ipswich, not far from his hometown of Cove; by then, he had a reputation for unorthodox teaching. One William Broman, when questioned about his religious views in 1535, testified that Bale had taught him in Doncaster in 1531 that Christ was not physically present in the Eucharist.

At Ipswich, Bale grew close to Thomas Wentworth, an active Protestant who led the unorthodox friar to act more decisively on his reform convictions. Bale converted to Protestantism, left the priesthood, and married a young woman named Dorothy. On the strength of some fourteen Protestant plays already written for patron John de Vere, Wentworth recommended Bale to Thomas Cromwell, a major power in the Protestant movement. Cromwell encouraged Bale to continue writing plays and other materials to further the Protestant cause. On at least two occasions, Bale's outspoken views brought sanctions from authorities. He even spent time in Greenwich jail, but Cromwell was able to bring pressure to bear on the authorities involved, and Bale was released.

For several years, the nature of the Church in England was fiercely debated. Henry VIII's assumption of headship did not eradicate in one stroke all the centuries of Roman Catholic tradition in England, and among those who called for reform, there was no consensus on how much reform was enough. The relative influence of various factions waxed and waned. For a time, Cromwell's influence was substantial. Anne Boleyn's execution in 1536, however, set off a wave of pro-Catholic activity. By 1540, Henry VIII was less worried about the definition of the national Church than he was about the deep divisions within the body politic. He moved to solve his political problems as he had his personal problems—by execution. To be fair, he beheaded or burned three Catholic and three Protestant leaders, including Cromwell.

His patron gone, Bale fled with his wife and children to the Continent in 1540. He presumably spent time in Holland, Switzerland, and northern Germany. The publication notices in books he issued while in Europe cite places of publication such as Basle, Switzerland; Antwerp, Belgium; and Wesel, Germany. Collateral evidence indicates that he sometimes published in cities where he lived at the time. On occasion, too, whether because of a publishing opportunity or because of concern for personal safety, his works were published in cities where he did not reside. A few items were issued under pseudonyms.

In Europe, Bale developed further contacts with various reform leaders and continued his relationship with a number of exiled English Protestants as well. Meanwhile, his writings continued to stir controversy at home in England. In 1546, his books were banned along with the writings of several other authors, including the Bible translators John Wycliffe and Miles Coverdale. Bale's work on Anne Askew was particularly disturbing to the authorities.

In 1547, Henry VIII was succeeded by his nine-year-old son, Edward VI. The council of regents advising the boy-king was predominantly Protestant. Bishop Stephen Gardiner, who had strongly opposed Bale's writings, was imprisoned in the Tower of London. Bale then returned to England.

Through 1551, Bale continued research for his literary histories and continued writing in support of the Reformation. He was appointed rector of Bishopstoke, Hampshire, in June of 1551, and later of Swaffham, Norfolk. In August of 1552, Edward VI appointed Bale Bishop of Ossory in Ireland. Given the staunch Catholic convictions among most of the Irish clergy and laity in his bishopric, Bale provoked continually bitter conflict by attempting to limit or abolish various traditional customs and forms of worship.

Edward VI died in July of 1553 to be succeeded by Mary I, also known as Bloody Mary because of the number of executions carried out during her reign. The Catholic queen brought a return of Catholic influence to the court and to the English Church. Mary released Bishop Stephen Gardiner from the Tower to be her Lord Chancellor. Thereafter, an English translation of Gardiner's *De Vera Obedientia* (1553; of true obedience) began to circulate in England. Written in earlier days to support King Henry VIII's break with Rome, the book was a certain irritant to the older and more conservative Gardiner, in service to a Catholic queen. Bale is suspected of having done the English translation.

During 1554 and 1555, Bale lived in Frankfurt, Germany. When the English exile Church in Frankfurt split over issues of forms of worship, Bale and his friend John Foxe moved to Switzerland and stayed with a printer, Johannes Oporinus, who issued Bale's literary histories in 1557 and 1559.

Elizabeth I succeeded Mary in 1558. In 1559, Bale returned to England. Other Protestant churchmen were appointed to bishoprics. Bale was named to a prebendary, a modest position at Canterbury. He continued research and writing, though ill, and made many appeals to friends and officials for help in recovering books and manuscripts he had left in Ireland in 1553. Unfortunately, not even a letter from Queen Elizabeth could produce results. Bale died at Canterbury in November of 1563.

Analysis

Discussion of John Bale's drama requires some background on the theatrical conventions of the times. At festivals, common folk enjoyed song, dance, games, and ritual skits satirizing the nobility and the clergy. Some plays were enacted, drawing from English folklore. Also in medieval England there had developed a tradition of religious instruction through drama. Certain towns presented annual cycles of plays, productions lasting three days and made up of individual plays dramatizing selected Bible stories. Such series were designed to present a Christian worldview from the creation of Adam through the life of Christ and on to the Last Judgment. The religious purpose, however, did not preclude use of humorous, even bawdy, stage business and dialogue. Depictions of saints' lives and of moral fables were also common.

Medieval religious drama, which provided a rich heritage for English Renaissance drama, included three major categories: the mystery play, the miracle play, and the morality play. The mystery play drew on liturgy and on episodes of the life of Christ, dramatizing the "mysteries" of divine intervention in the temporal world. The miracle play presented events from lives of saints or martyrs for the purpose of asserting the virtue of faith in divine power and intervention. The morality play personified abstractions such as hope and charity in conflict with vices such as pride or greed in simple stories designed to teach moral, ethical, or theological premises.

Bale's verse drama *God's Promises* fits expectations of the mystery play. While it does not focus on the life of Christ directly, it presents a pattern of biblical characters—Old Testament personalities and John the Baptist from the New Testament—as the essential preface to Christ's coming. It is understood to be a play that Bale would use as the first in a trilogy. Second and third plays would cover Christ's life, death, and resurrection and possibly the Second Coming and Last Judgment.

God's Promises consistently embodies a Christian vision of pre-Christian scriptures as the record of preparation for and prophecy of Christ's appearance on earth. Ancient and medieval theology included searches for proofs of divine order both in the natural world and in Scripture. Numerological formulas were invoked to prove the divine source of Scripture. The number one, for example, was the number of God; three represented the trinity of Father, Son, and Holy Spirit. Six was the number of mortals, while seven, combining the mortal and the divine, was the perfect number.

Bale includes himself as a commentator in *God's Promises*, but the scriptural characters of this seven-act verse drama are seven in number—one divine, *Pater Coelestis* (Heavenly Father), and six mortal: *Adam Primus Homo* (Adam, the First Man), *Justus Noah* (Noah the Righteous), *Abraham Fidelis* (Abraham the Faithful), *Moseh Sanctus* (Moses the Holy), *David Rex Pius* (David the Pious King), *Esaias Prophetas* (Isaiah the Prophet), and *Joannes Baptista* (John the Baptist). Hence, the very structure of the play projects a conventional Christian view of pre-Christian history consisting of six eras leading to a seventh in which Christ appears.

Although one might expect a play featuring Old Testament figures to begin with material from Genesis, Heavenly Father's opening is a Trinitarian self-description that seems a creedal expansion of the first chapter of the Gospel of John. Following Heavenly Father's introduction, which includes references to Adam's fall and God's judgment on both man and woman, Adam enters to plead for mercy. The second act summarizes the era of Noah. Heavenly Father recites the evils which provoked his judgment on mortals, and Noah, like Adam, pleads for mercy. Heavenly Father, in the third act, expresses displeasure over the depravity of Noah's descendants, particularly their falling to idolatry and sodomy. Abraham, on behalf of his nephew Lot, who lives in the vicinity of Sodom and Gomorrah, appeals for mercy. He bargains with Heavenly Father until he secures a promise that God will spare the cities if ten righteous citizens can be found in them. Despite the flood of Noah's era, and despite the witness of faith in Abraham, mortals continue to sin. In the fourth act, Heavenly Father gives the Law to Moses for the people of Israel and for all nations. Dialogue in the fourth act reviews major events of Moses' life—the plagues of Egypt, the Exodus and provision of manna in the desert, Israel's apostasy with the golden calf, and so on. For Israel's idolatry, Heavenly Father again pronounces judgment but tempers his decree with the promise of a prophet to come.

The fifth act sets Heavenly Father in dialogue with David the Pious King. Their exchanges survey the leadership of priests and prophets between the time of Moses and the accession of Saul, David's predecessor. Heavenly Father condemns David for taking the wife of Uriah the Hittite and for taking a national census (a sign of faith in mortal strength rather than in divine protection). David must choose a punishment, but again the judgment is linked with a promise. In David's case, the promise is for the greatness of his son Solomon. Heavenly Father, in the sixth act, discourses with the prophet Isaiah, recounting the infidelity of Israel after Solomon, the split into the kingdoms of Israel and Judah, the Babylonian conquest, and the Babylonian captivity of Israel as punishment for recurrent idolatry. Isaiah, continuing the pattern that Bale has set for his mortal characters in dialogue with Heavenly Father, appeals for mercy. In response, Heavenly Father cites messianic verses from the Old Testament book of Isaiah which Christian tradition has long held to be predictions of Christ's birth.

With John the Baptist, in the seventh act, Heavenly Father surveys events from the time of the Babylonian Captivity through the age of latter prophets, giving special note to the restoration of the temple in Jerusalem and to the religious renewal under King Josiah. In closing, Heavenly Father names John the Baptist the messenger to announce the coming of Christ. In a very clear paraphrase of reactions to divine call in the biblical stories of Moses, Isaiah, and others, John objects, contending that he lacks the learning and eloquence necessary for such awesome duties, but Heavenly Father prevails.

The text of *God's Promises*, then, employs close paraphrase of Scripture and creedal statements throughout. For each era in the schema, Heavenly Father is a rigorous judge, punishing idolatry yet promising some form of relief to come. The emphases in dramatizing these particular characters in dialogue with, and in service to, Heavenly Father are not only traditionally messianic but also decidedly Protestant in their management.

As a friar who left holy orders to marry, Bale offers an interesting view of the Fall of Adam and Eve. Medieval tradition includes much misogynistic coloring of the Fall. Some interpreters made much of Eve's yielding to desire and then inducing Adam to yield to desire as well. Bale, however, poses Heavenly Father attributing Adam's Fall to a failure to use reason. Such a stance might be expected from a reformer quite given to scholarship and seeing in literacy and clear thinking a means to escape what he considered decadent superstition in religion. Furthermore, keeping the responsibility with Adam rather than with Eve, Bale sidesteps a conventional argument for clerical celibacy—namely, that a married cleric would be more concerned with a wife than with his religious duties.

Bale's focus on the Sodom and Gomorrah episode from Abraham's era is a means for him to stress divine judgment upon sodomy. Bale insisted that the rule of celibacy for those in holy orders simply led many to engage in homosexual or illicit heterosexual activity—observing the letter of the vow but not the spirit. Also, every act of *God's Promises* includes condemnation of idolatry. As a Protestant strongly opposed to veneration of saints and sacred relics, Bale keeps the anti-idolatry theme dominant.

In aspects of form other than the structural symbolism mentioned above, *God's Promises* is typical of Bale's style. The lines of verse are roughly pentametric, sometimes straggling into six- or seven-beat lines. End rhymes appear in various groupings, often approximating stanzas of five, seven, or nine lines by interlocking couplets, tercets, and quatrains of sometimes exact, sometimes slant rhyme. The verse functions mainly to keep the great patches of biblical and creedal paraphrase memorable for actors faced with long, set speeches and dialogues only occasionally relieved by some stage business. Religious songs between acts provide some variety, though the texts of certain songs do not seem wholly pertinent to the issues in the bracketing acts. The music itself may be a counter to the radical reform views which minimized or eliminated the role of music in worship.

For *Three Laws*, Bale used the morality play format. The opening is given by *Baleus Prolocutor* (Bale the Commentator). The first act stages the lead character *Deus Pater* (God the Father) calling out the three laws: *Lex Naturae* (the Natural Law), *Moseh Lex* (the Law of Moses, sometimes termed the Law of Bondage), and *Christi Lex* (the Law of Christ, sometimes termed the Law of Grace). At first, as in *God's Promises*, the divinity, God the Father, defines his Triune nature. He then defines each law. The Natural Law has sway in human hearts for three ages: from Adam to Noah, from Noah to Abraham, and from Abraham to Moses. The Law of Moses obtains in another three ages: from Moses to David, from David to the Babylonian Exile, and from the Exile to the appearance of Christ. The Law of Christ dominates the last age. Hence, though the characters staged are abstractions rather than biblical characters, *Three Laws* shares with *God's Promises* Bale's structural reinforcement of numerological symbols. The two sets of three eras equal the mortal number six, and the age of Christ brings the sum to the perfect seven, adding the divine number, one, to the mortal number.

The second act sets Natural Law in dialogue with *Infidelitas* (Infidelity). Natural Law declares, "A knowledge I am whom God in man does hide/ In his whole working to be to him a guide." Infidelity debates the very existence of Natural Law. If, indeed, God has created such an orderly world, why are there severe storms or wild animals that attack people or other extreme disruptions of order? Natural Law answers that such events are divine punishment for disregard of God. Having failed to best Natural Law in debate, Infidelity conjures the demons *Sodomismus* (Sodomy) and *Idolatrias* (Idolatry), who help him overcome Natural Law.

The third act brings the Law of Moses as a successor to Natural Law. To counter the force of the Law of Moses, Infidelity brings in *Avaritia* (Covetousness) and *Ambitio* (Ambition), who render the Law of Moses lame and blind. *Evangelium* (Christ's Gospel) enters in the fourth act to oppose Infidelity. The vice again produces assistants, *Pseudodoctrina* (False Doctrine) and *Hypocrisis* (Hypocrisy), and these three vice characters burn Christ's Gospel at the stake.

Vindicta Dei (God's Wrath) takes the lead in the fifth act. Infidelity offers God's Wrath a bribe to avoid conflict but is confronted and overcome. God the Father recalls the three laws for renewal and cleansing, after which the three sing praise. God the Father then announces restoration of "true faith and religion" and calls in *Fides Christiano* (Christian Faith) for closing doctrinal explanations.

Three Laws includes some passing references to historical figures, such as a comparison of King Henry VIII to the Hebrew reformer-king Josiah, but does not include those historical figures as active characters in the play.

While Bale's anti-Catholicism is occasionally stated outright in *God's Promises*, it runs rampant in *Three Laws*. Costuming notes at the play's end call for visual parodies. Sodomy is to be dressed as a monk, False Doctrine as a "popish doctor," and Hypocrisy as a Gray Friar. Infidelity frequently uses oaths such as "by the mass," and "by St. Stephen"; he also makes a number of coarse, offensive remarks to which the virtuous characters take exception.

Infidelity's introduction of Idolatry continues the anti-Catholic matter. Idolatry is credited with curing toothache, ague, and pox and with conjuring the Devil by saying the Hail Mary. The entrance and introduction of Sodomy carries similar attacks. Sodomy claims that clergy in Rome and elsewhere turn to him because they lack wives and do not fear divine retribution.

Bale builds a long list of Protestant propaganda charges into *Three Laws*: Veneration of saints equals idol worship; the doctrine of purgatory is a device to rob the poor; Latin rites, Scriptures, and prayers censor the true message of the Scriptures, while English is used for those customs and practices which bring cash to church coffers. Bale gives Covetousness a parodic creed that avers faith in the pope rather than faith in God, then continues listing various usages which Bale believed served a corrupt religious establishment while faithful parishioners were misled. Other writers and thinkers in the troubled times of the Reformation and the Counter-Reformation may have been opinionated, even bigoted. Among English writers of his day, Bale was so aggressive that he became known to succeeding generations as "Bilious Bale."

Bale's more noted play, *King Johan*, was probably written several years before 1538, its year of publication. The extant manuscript is likely two or three removes from the original, as its closing lines refer to Queen Elizabeth. The play consists of two long acts, the first with a shift of scene from England to Rome. The entrances and exits of characters, a bit of song, and various opportunities for stage business allow some relief from the steady onslaught of didactic dialogue. Formally, the play lacks the structural concern for symbolism found in *God's Promises* or for the classical convention of five acts as found in *Three Laws*. The political purpose of the drama seems its major shaping force.

The play opens with King Johan declaring that citizens should be loyal to their king, thus following the example of Christ's obedience to civil authorities. England, a widow, enters, complaining that the clergy has abused her rights and estranged her from God, her spouse, by refusing to honor God's word. Sedition derides England, then boasts to King Johan that he, Sedition, has papal authority to overcome secular rulers. King Johan confronts Nobility, Clergy, and Civil Order with the problem. Nobility says that his oath of knighthood requires that he defend the Church. Echoing Peter's denial of Christ, Nobility three times denies knowing Sedition. Civil Order declares loyalty to the king. In debate over the legitimacy of the many religious orders in a single church, Civil Order supports King Johan while Nobility sides with Clergy. The king contends that prayers and masses for the dead counter the premise that Christ's death was efficacious once for all. Nobility, Civil Order, and Clergy all submit to the king and vow to defend the realm. King Johan and Civil Order leave, and Clergy then persuades Nobility to reverse himself and believe what the Church teaches rather than reason for himself.

The scene shifts to Rome. Sedition meets Dissimulation, who, singing a litany, prays to be freed of King Johan. The two vices identify themselves as cousins, sons of Falsehood and Privy Treason, respectively, and as grandsons of Infidelity. Together they boast of various forms that the Church establishment can use for deceit. To help preserve the system, Dissimulation calls in Private Wealth. With Sedition's help, the latter two vices bring in Usurped Power, who reveals that he is Pope Innocent III in unofficial garb. Dissimulation asks the pope's blessing, then reports Clergy's complaints against King Johan of England. He has taxed the clergy, has held them accountable to civil justice rather than leaving offending clergy to ecclesiastical justice, and has forbidden bishops to appeal to Rome. Four English bishops have already pronounced the king excommunicated. He has seized church properties and has collected the revenues from salaries owed to exiled clergy. While the other characters move offstage for costume change, Dissimulation expounds on the measures which the pope will take to counter King Johan.

Returning to stage, the other vices have changed both appearances and identities. Usurped Power has become Pope Innocent III both in costume and in name. Sedition has become Steven Langton, Archbishop of Canterbury. The pope performs a ritual cursing King Johan with bell, book, and candle and declares him excommunicated. To close the first act, an Interpreter appears and summarizes the consequences in England of the king's excommunication and the interdiction of the realm (the banning of the Sacraments in the nation's churches).

In the second act, Nobility bemoans the conflict between king and clergy. Sedition, calling himself Good Perfection, offers Nobility pardon for sin in exchange for support of the Church. Nobility makes confession in rather general terms, but Sedition withholds absolution until Nobility again pledges to oppose King Johan. Met by Clergy and Civil Order, Sedition identifies himself as Archbishop Steven Langton. Clergy kneels for absolution and is presented with parodic relics including a louse and a "turd" from certain saints.

Absolution complete, Langton orders Clergy to provoke insurrection in England. Civil Order, formerly loyal to the king, now sides with the opposition. If the fortunes of the Church decline, so will the fortunes of lawyers.

Private Wealth, dressed as a cardinal, demands that King Johan restore all church property he has seized, accept Langton as Archbishop of Canterbury, and allow the return of all exiled clergy. The king insists that, in taxing the clergy, he is simply following biblical precedent. He offers to accept exiled clergy but balks at the appointment of Langton. At this, Private Wealth officially invokes the papal curse and excommunication of the king as well as the interdiction of the nation.

Nobility, Clergy, and Civil Order report the consequences of the excommunication. King Johan insists that the authority of Scripture is superior to the authority of the pope. He cites instances of Old Testament kings appointing priests. Still, he gains no support from his hearers, who reiterate their ties to the Church.

England again appeals to the king. She brings Commonality, who represents the populace and who is afflicted with poverty and blindness. As cardinal, Private Wealth orders Commonality to leave and advises King Johan to capitulate. Papal influence has raised threats of invasion from Scotland, France, and other lands. The danger is too great for King Johan. He regretfully surrenders his crown to the cardinal, submitting to papal authority and consenting to pay heavy fines.

Treason enters in chains. He recites a catalog of Catholic beliefs and practices in parody as his "crimes," then ends the list with civil felonies including "coin clipping" and counterfeiting. King Johan invokes civil justice and orders him hanged. Treason, however, is a priest. The cardinal releases him and demands that King Johan sign over a third of his realm to a sister-in-law. Widow England, in rebuttal, reports that the woman is dead. Johan confirms his submission to the pope. Sedition leaves to stir up trouble in France. Under the name Simon of Swinsett, Dissimulation concocts poison and drinks half the cup himself in order to ensure that King Johan drinks the rest. Each dies justifying himself. Dissimulation, too, relies on anticipatory pardon for his deed and on prayers and masses being said for his soul.

Verity appears to explain that in chronicles written by traditional churchmen, King Johan cannot but have a bad reputation. Nobility, Clergy, and Civil Order debate the quality of the dead king's life, then repent of their failure to support him. Next appears Imperial Majesty, who presses the trio to support their monarch, not to please the ruler personally, but on biblical authority. Sedition, threatened with hanging, also repents but, once pardoned, insists that papal supporters will continue to seek control of England. Imperial Majesty then reinstates the sentence, and Sedition is taken to be hanged. Nobility, Civil Order, and Clergy repent once more and accept the primacy of Imperial Majesty. They label the pope the Antichrist.

By parody in plot and characterization, Bale offers *King Johan* as another play to declare his usual Protestant arguments and to vilify his Roman Catholic opposition. Thematically, it varies somewhat from *Three Laws* and *God's Promises*, as it raises the issue of English sovereignty to the fore. Nevertheless, by structure and dialogue, it emphasizes the familiar anti-Catholic rant apparent in Bale's other plays. In versification and style, it is no more refined. The stiff convention of keeping two characters in extended dialogue, with only occasional exchanges among three or more, is employed in *King Johan* as in Bale's other works. His reliance on paraphrase of Scripture, creeds, and traditional ceremonies is equally evident.

While Bale seems not to have carried dramatic innovation any further in his extant plays, he did set a significant premise by setting the thirteenth century English king and his opponents onstage to enact historical events. His interpretation is warped by his propagandistic intent, and his flair for theatricality and creative characterization, evident in certain parodic scenes, is always subordinate to his doctrinal persuasion. It therefore remained for playwrights more concerned with drama as an art form, more willing to let their characters enact or show, rather than tell, their discoveries in life, and able to present life in its complexities onstage, rather than to reduce it to a set of foregone conclusions, to move further. Indeed, playwrights such as Shakespeare and Marlowe moved well beyond Bale's first mixture of a historical king and his enemies with the stock virtue and vice characters of the medieval morality play. They carried the history play to full development on the Renaissance stage.

Other major works

NONFICTION: *The Image of Both Churches*, 1541 (part 1), 1545 (part 2), 1547 (part 3); *A Brief Chronicle of Sir John Oldcastle, the Lord Cobham*, 1544; *The Acts of English Votaries*, 1546; *The First Examination of Anne Askew*, 1546; *The Latter Examination of Anne Askew*, 1547; *An Answer to a Papistical Exhortation*, 1548; *Illustrium Maioris Britanniae Scriptorum*, 1548; *An Expostulation Against the Blasphemies of a Frantic Papist*, 1552; *The Apology of John Bale Against a Rank Papist*, c. 1555; *Illustrium Maioris Britanniae Catalogus*, 1557, 1559 (revision of *Illustrium Maioris Britanniae Scriptorum*); *Acta Romanorum Pontificum*, 1558 (in Latin), 1561 (in French), 1571 (in German), 1574 (in English as *The Pageant of the Popes*); *A Declaration Concerning the Clergy of London*, 1561.

TRANSLATIONS: *Pammachius*, 1538 (of Thomas Kirchmayer's German play; no longer extant); *The True History of the Christian Departing of Martin Luther*, 1546 (from German accounts collected by Justus Jonas, Michael Cellius, and Joannes Aurifaber).

Bibliography

Bevington, David. *Tudor Drama and Politics*, 1968.
Blatt, Thora. *The Plays of Bale*, 1968.
Campbell, Lily B. *Divine Poetry and Drama in Sixteenth Century England*, 1959.
Craig, Hardin. *English Religious Drama of the Middle Ages*, 1955.
Fairfield, Leslie. *Bale, Mythmaker for the English Reformation*, 1976.
Harris, Jesse W. *John Bale: A Study in the Minor Literature of the Reformation*, 1940.
MacCusker, Honor. *Bale, Dramatist and Antiquary*, 1942.
Sanders, Norman, Richard Southern, T. W. Craik, and Lois Potter. *The Revels History of Drama in English, Volume II: 1500-1576*, 1980.

Ralph S. Carlson

AMIRI BARAKA
Everett LeRoi Jones

Born: Newark, New Jersey; October 7, 1934

Principal drama

The Baptism, pr. 1964, pb. 1966; *Dutchman*, pr., pb. 1964; *The Slave*, pr., pb. 1964; *The Toilet*, pr. 1964, pb. 1966; *Experimental Death Unit #1*, pr. 1965, pb. 1969; *Jello*, pr. 1965, pb. 1970; *A Black Mass*, pr. 1966, pb. 1969; *Arm Yourself or Harm Yourself*, pr., pb. 1967; *Great Goodness of Life (A Coon Show)*, pr. 1967, pb. 1969; *Madheart*, pr. 1967, pb. 1969; *Slave Ship: A Historical Pageant*, pr., pb. 1967; *The Death of Malcolm X*, pb. 1969; *Bloodrites*, pr. 1970, pb. 1971; *Junkies Are Full of (SHHH...)*, pr. 1970, pb. 1971; *A Recent Killing*, pr. 1973; *S-1*, pr. 1976, pb. 1978; *The Motion of History*, pr. 1977, pb. 1978; *The Sidney Poet Heroical*, pb. 1979 (originally as *Sidnee Poet Heroical*, pr. 1975); *What Was the Relationship of the Lone Ranger to the Means of Production?*, pr., pb. 1979.

Other literary forms

Amiri Baraka is a protean literary figure, equally well-known for his poetry, drama, and essays. In addition, he has written short stories, collected in *Tales* (1967), and an experimental novel, *The System of Dante's Hell* (1965), which includes numerous poetic and dramatic passages. Baraka's early volumes of poetry *Preface to a Twenty Volume Suicide Note* (1961) and *The Dead Lecturer* (1964) derive from his period of involvement with the New York City avant-garde. Later volumes such as *Black Magic* (1969) and *It's Nation Time* (1970) reflect his intense involvement with black nationalist politics. More recent volumes, such as *Hard Facts* (1975) and *Reggae or Not!* (1981), reflect his developing movement to a leftist political position and have generally failed to appeal to either his avant-garde or his black nationalist audience. Baraka's critical and political prose has been collected in *Home: Social Essays* (1966), *Raise Race Rays Raze: Essays Since 1965* (1971), *Selected Plays and Prose* (1979), and *Daggers and Javelins: Essays* (1984). *The Autobiography of LeRoi Jones/Amiri Baraka* was published in 1984.

Achievements

One of the most politically controversial playwrights of the 1960's, Amiri Baraka is best known for his brilliant early play *Dutchman* and for his contribution to the development of a community-based black nationalist theater. Throughout his career, he has sought dramatic forms for expressing the consciousness of those alienated from the psychological, economic, and racial mainstream of American society. Even though no consensus exists concerning the success of his experiments, particularly those with ritualistic forms for political drama, his challenge to the aesthetic preconceptions of the American mainstream and the inspiration he has provided younger black playwrights such as Ed Bullins and Ron Milner guarantee his place in the history of American drama.

Already well-known as an avant-garde poet, Baraka, then LeRoi Jones, first rose to prominence in the theatrical world with the 1964 productions of *The Baptism*, *Dutchman*, *The Slave*, and *The Toilet*, which established him as a major Off-Broadway presence. Shortly after winning the Obie Award for *Dutchman*, however, Baraka broke his ties with the white avant-garde to concentrate on the creation of a militant Afro-American theater. Turning away from the psychological complexity of his early plays, most of which treat race simply as one aspect of a disorienting reality, Baraka openly denounced the racism of American culture, endorsing a militant and, if necessary, violent black response. Although mainstream critics harshly denounced his new work, Baraka continued to experiment with radical theatrical forms. Political plays such as *Madheart* and *Slave Ship* are in some ways more technically innovative than his earlier works. As Baraka's mainstream reputation declined, he gained recognition as a leading voice of the Black Arts Movement, ultimately assuming a position of public political visibility matched by only a handful of American literary figures.

Biography

Everett LeRoi Jones, known as Amiri Baraka since 1967, was born into a black middle-class family in Newark, New Jersey. An excellent student whose parents encouraged his intellectual interests, Jones was graduated from Howard University of Washington, D.C., in 1954, at the age of nineteen. After spending two years in the United States Air Force, primarily in Puerto Rico, he moved to Greenwich Village, where he embarked on his literary career in 1957. During the early stage of his career, Jones associated closely with numerous white avant-garde poets, including Robert Creeley, Allen Ginsberg, Robert Duncan, and Dianne DiPrima, and, with DiPrima, he founded the American Theatre for Poets in 1961. Marrying Hettie Cohen, a white woman with whom he edited the magazine *Yugen* from 1958 to 1963, Jones established himself as an important young poet, critic, and editor. Among the many magazines to which he contributed was the jazz journal *Downbeat*, where he first developed the interest in Afro-American musical culture which helped shape his theatrical "rituals." The political interests that were to dominate Jones's later work were unmistakably present as early as 1960, when he toured Cuba with a group of black intellectuals. This experience sparked his perception of the United States as a corrupt bourgeois society and seems particularly significant in relation to his subsequent Socialist stance. Jones's growing political interest influenced his first produced plays, including the Obie Award-winning *Dutchman*, which anticipated the first major transformation of Jones's life.

Separating from Hettie Cohen and severing ties with his white associates, Jones moved from Greenwich Village to Harlem in 1965. Turning his attention to direct action within the black community, he founded the Black Arts Theatre and School in Harlem and, following his return to his native city in 1966, the Spirit House in Newark. After marrying a black woman, Sylvia Robinson (Amina Baraka), in 1966, Jones adopted a new name, Amiri (which means "prince") Baraka ("the blessed one"), to which he added the honorary title "Imamu." Over the next half-dozen years, Baraka helped found and develop organizations such as the Black Community Development and Defense Organization, the Congress of African Peoples (convened in Atlanta in 1970), and the National Black Political Convention (convened in Gary, Indiana, in 1972). As a leading spokesman of the Black Arts Movement, Baraka provided personal and artistic support for young black poets and playwrights, including Larry Neal, Ed Bullins, Marvin X, and Ron Milner. During the Newark riots of 1967, Baraka was arrested for unlawful possession of firearms. Although convicted and given the maximum sentence after the judge read the jury his poem "Black People!" as an example of incitement to riot, Baraka was later cleared on appeal.

Baraka supported Ken Gibson's campaign to become the first black mayor of Newark in 1970, but later broke with him over what he perceived as the Gibson Administration's bourgeois values. This disillusionment with black politics within the American system and Baraka's attendance at the Sixth Pan-African Conference at Dar es Salaam in 1974 precipitated the next stage of his political evolution. While not abandoning his commitment to confronting the special problems of Afro-Americans in the United States, Baraka began interpreting these problems within the framework of an overarching "Marxist-Leninist-Mao Tse-tung" philosophy. In conjunction with this second transformation, Baraka dropped the title Imamu and changed the name of his Newark publishing firm from Jihad to People's War. Since that time, he has taught at universities such as Yale and the State University of New York at Stony Brook while performing with an experimental jazz/poetry group. Although he has had some difficulty finding publishers for his Socialist writings, he has continued to speak publicly both inside and outside the Afro-American community.

Analysis

Working with forms ranging from the morality play to avant-garde Expressionism, Amiri Baraka throughout his career has sought to create dramatic rituals expressing the intensity of the physical and psychological violence which dominates his vision of American culture. From his early plays on "universal" alienation through his black nationalist celebrations to his multimedia proletarian pageants, Baraka has focused on a variety of sacrificial victims as his central dramatic presences. Some of these victims remain passive scapegoats who allow a corrupt and vicious system to dictate their fate. Others assume the role of heroic martyr in the cause of community consciousness. Yet a third type of victim is the doomed oppressor whose death marks the transformation of the martyr's consciousness into a ritual action designed to free the community from continuing passive victimization.

The dominant type in Baraka's early plays, the passive scapegoats unaware of their participation in ritual actions, condemn themselves and their communities to blind repetition of destructive patterns. Their apparent mastery of the forms of Euro-American cultural literacy simply obscures the fact of their ignorance of the underlying reality of oppression. Responding to this ironic situation, Baraka's black nationalist plays emphasize the new forms of consciousness, their roots in Africa rather than Europe, needed to free the Afro-American community from the historical and psychological forces which enforce such blind repetition. Inverting the traditional moral symbolism of Euro-American culture, Baraka creates rituals which substitute symbolically white scapegoats for the symbolically black victims of his earlier works. These rituals frequently reject the image of salvation through self-sacrifice (seen as a technique for the pacification of the black masses), insisting instead that only an active struggle can break the cycle of oppression.

Because the rituals of Baraka's black nationalist plays frequently culminate in violence directed against whites, or symbolically white members of the black bourgeois, or aspects of the individual black psyche, numerous critics have attacked him for perpetuating the violence and racism he ostensibly criticizes. These critics frequently condemn him for oversimplifying reality, citing his movement from psychologically complex ironic forms to much more explicit allegorical modes in his later drama; the most insistent simply dismiss his post-*Dutchman* plays as strident propaganda, lacking all aesthetic and moral merit. Basing their critiques firmly on Euro-American aesthetic assumptions, such critics in fact overlook the central importance of Baraka's changing sense of his audience. Repudiating the largely white avant-garde audience which applauded his early work, Baraka turned almost exclusively to an Afro-American audience more aware of the storefront preacher and popular music groups such as the Temptations than of August Strindberg and Edward Albee. In adopting a style of performance in accord with this cultural perception, Baraka assumed a didactic voice intended to focus attention on immediate issues of survival and community or class defense.

First produced in leading New York theaters such as St. Mark's Play-house (*The Slave* and *The Toilet*), the Cherry Lane Theatre (*Dutchman*), and the Writers' Stage Theatre (*The Baptism*), Baraka's early plays clearly reflect both his developing concern with issues of survival and his fascina-tion with Euro-American avant-garde traditions. *The Baptism*, in particular, draws on the conventions of Expressionist theater to comment on the absurdity of contemporary American ideas of salvation, which in fact sim-ply mask a larger scheme of victimization. Identified only as symbolic types, Baraka's characters speak a surreal mixture of street language and theological argot. While the slang references link them to the social reality familiar to the audience, their actions are dictated by the sudden shifts and thematic ambiguities characteristic of works such as Strindberg's *A Dream Play* and the "Circe" chapter of James Joyce's *Ulysses*.

The play's central character, named simply the Boy, resembles a tradi-tional Christ figure struggling to come to terms with his vocation. Baraka treats his protagonist with a mixture of irony and empathy, focusing on the ambiguous roles of the spirit and the flesh in relation to salvation. Pres-sured by the Minister to deny his body and by the cynical Homosexual to immerse himself in the profane as a path to the truly sacred, the Boy vacil-lates. At times he claims divine status; at times he insists, "I am only flesh." The chorus of women, at once holy virgins and temple prostitutes, reinforces his confusion. Shortly after identifying him as "the Son of God," they refer to him as the "Chief Religious jelly roll of the universe." Given these irreconcilable roles, which he is expected to fulfill, the Boy's destiny as scapegoat and martyr seems inevitable; the dramatic tension revolves around the question of who will victimize him and why. Baraka uses a sequence of conflicting views of the Boy's role, each of which momentarily dominates his self-image, to heighten this tension.

Responding to the Homosexual's insistence that "the devil is a part of creation like an ash tray or senator," the Boy first confesses his past sins and demands baptism. When the Women respond by elevating him to the status of "Son of God/ Son of Man," he explicitly rejects all claim to spiri-tual purity. The ambiguous masquerade culminates in an attack on the Boy, who is accused of using his spiritual status to seduce women who "wanted to be virgins of the Lord." Supported only by the Homosexual, the Boy defends himself against the Women and the Minister, who clamor for his sacrifice, ostensibly as punishment for his sins. Insisting that "there will be no second crucifixion," the Boy slays his antagonists with a phallic sword, which he interprets as the embodiment of spiritual glory. For a brief mo-ment, the figures of Christ as scapegoat and Christ as avenger seem recon-ciled in a baptism of fire.

Baraka undercuts this moment of equilibrium almost immediately. Hav-ing escaped martyrdom at the hands of the mob (ironically, itself victimized), the Boy confronts the Messenger, who wears a motorcycle jacket embellished with a gold crown and the words "The Man." In Baraka's dream allegory, the Man can represent the Roman/American legal system or be a symbol for God the Father, both powers that severely limit the Boy's control over events. The Boy's first reaction to the Messenger is to reclaim his superior spiritual status, insisting that he has "brought love to many people" and calling on his "Father" for compassion. Rejecting these pleas, the Messenger indicates that "the Man's destroying the whole works tonight." The Boy responds defiantly: "Neither God nor man shall force me to leave. I was sent here to save man and I'll not leave until I do." The allegory suggests several different levels of interpretation: social, psychological, and symbolic. The Boy rejects his responsibility to concrete individuals (the mob he kills, the Man) in order to save an abstract entity (the mob as an ideal, man). Ultimately, he claims his right to the martyr's death which he killed the mob in order to avoid, by repudiating the martyr's submission to a higher power. Losing patience with the Boy's rhetoric, the Messenger responds not by killing him but by knocking him out and dragging him offstage. His attitude of boredom effectively deflates the allegorical seriousness of the Boy's defiance, a deflation reinforced by the Homosexual's concluding comment that the scene resembles "some really uninteresting kind of orgy."

The Baptism's treatment of the interlocking themes of sacrifice, ritual, and victimization emphasizes their inherent ambiguity and suggests the impossibility of moral action in a culture that confuses God with the leader of a motorcycle gang. The encompassing irony of the Christ figure sacrificing his congregation to assure universal destruction recalls T. S. Eliot's treatment of myth in *The Waste Land* and his essay "Ulysses: Myth and Order." Eliot's use of classical allusions and mythic analogies to underscore the triviality of modern life clearly anticipates Baraka's ironic vision of Christian ritual. Baraka's baptism initiates the Boy into absurdity rather than responsibility. If any sins have been washed away, they are resurrected immediately in pointless ritual violence and immature rhetoric. Although he does not develop the theme explicitly in *The Baptism*, Baraka suggests that there is an underlying philosophical corruption in Euro-American culture, in this case derived from Christianity's tendency to divorce flesh from spirit. Increasingly, this philosophical corruption takes the center of Baraka's dramatic presentation of Western civilization.

Widely recognized as Baraka's greatest work in any genre, *Dutchman* combines the irony of his avant-garde period with the emotional power and social insight of his later work. Clay, a young black man with a highly developed sense of self, occupies a central position in the play analogous to that of the Boy in *The Baptism*. The central dramatic action of the play involves Clay's confrontation with a young white woman, Lula, who may in fact be seen as an aspect of Clay's own self-awareness. In both thematic emphasis and dramatic structure, *Dutchman* parallels Edward Albee's *The Zoo Story* (pr. 1959). Both plays focus on a clash between characters from divergent social and philosophical backgrounds; both comment on the internal divisions of individuals in American society; both culminate in acts of violence which are at once realistic and symbolic. What sets *Dutchman* apart, however, is its intricate exploration of the psychology that leads Clay to a symbolic rebellion which ironically guarantees his real victimization. Clay *thinks* he exists as an autonomous individual struggling for existential awareness. Baraka implies, however, that this Euro-American conception of self simply enforces Clay's preordained role as ritual scapegoat. As the Everyman figure his name suggests, Clay represents all individuals trapped by self-deception and social pressure. As a black man in a racist culture, he shares the more specific problem of those whose self-consciousness has been determined by white definitions.

The stage directions for *Dutchman* emphasize the link between Clay's situation and the decline of Euro-American culture, describing the subway car where the action transpires as "the flying underbelly of the city . . . heaped in modern myth." Lula enters eating an apple, evoking the myth of the Fall. Together, these allusions contribute a literary dimension to the foreboding atmosphere surrounding the extended conversation which leads to Clay's sacrifice at the hands of Lula and the subway riders, mostly white but some black. Throughout, Lula maintains clear awareness of her symbolic and political intentions, while Clay remains effectively blind. Lula's role demands simply that she maintain the interest of the black man until it is convenient to kill him. Meanwhile, Clay believes he can somehow occupy a position of detachment or spiritual superiority. Changing approach frequently, Lula plays the roles of temptress, intellectual, psychologist, racist. Clay responds variously to these gambits, sometimes with amusement, ultimately with anger and contempt. Consistently, however, he fails to recognize the genocidal reality underlying Lula's masquerade, unwittingly assuming his preordained role in the controlling ritual of black destruction. Much like the legendary ghost ship for which it was named, the "Dutchman," Baraka implies, will continue to sail so long as blacks allow the white world to control the premises of the racial debate.

This rigged debate reflects Baraka's reassessment of his universalist beliefs and his movement toward black nationalism. Clay resembles the early LeRoi Jones in many ways: Both are articulate natives of New Jersey with aspirations to avant-garde artistic success. *Dutchman* implies that both are subject to fantasies about the amount of meaningful success possible for them in the realm of Euro-American culture. Lula alternately reduces Clay to a "well-known type" and condemns him for rejecting his roots and embracing "a tradition you ought to feel oppressed by." During the first

act, Clay stays "cool" until Lula sarcastically declares him the "Black
Baudelaire" and follows with the repeated phrase "My Christ. My Christ."
Suddenly shifting emphasis, she immediately denies his Christ-like stature
and insists, "You're a murderer," compressing the two major attributes of
the Boy in *The Baptism*, this time with a specifically social resonance. The
sudden shift disrupts Clay's balance. Ironically restating and simplifying the
thesis of Ralph Ellison's universalist novel *Invisible Man*, Lula concludes
the opening act with an ironic resolution to "pretend the people cannot see
you . . . that you are free of your own history. And I am free of my history."
The rapid movement from Clay as Christ and murderer—standard black
roles in the fantasy life of white America—to the *pretense* of his freedom
underscores the inevitability of his victimization, an inevitability clearly dictated by the historical forces controlling Lula, forces which Clay steadfastly
refuses to recognize.

Clay's lack of awareness blinds him to the fact that the subway car, occupied only by himself and Lula during act 1, fills up with people during
act 2. Continuing to manipulate Clay through rapid shifts of focus, Lula
diverts his attention from the context, first by fantasizing a sexual affair
with him and then by ridiculing him as an "escaped nigger" with absurd
pretensions to cultural whiteness. Abandoning his cool perspective for the
first time, Clay angrily takes "control" of the conversation. His powerful
soliloquy establishes his superior understanding of his interaction with Lula,
but only in the theoretical terms of Euro-American academic discourse.
Admitting his hatred for whites, Clay claims a deep affinity with the explosive anger lying beneath the humorous surface of the work of the great
black musicians Bessie Smith and Charlie Parker. Ridiculing Lula's interpretation of his psychological makeup, Clay warns her that whites should
beware of preaching "rationalism" to blacks, since the best cure for the
black neurosis would be the random murder of whites. After this demonstration of his superior, and highly rational, awareness, Clay turns to go.
He dismisses Lula with contempt, saying, "we won't be acting out that little
pageant you outlined before." Immediately thereafter, Lula kills him. The
murder is in fact the final act of the real pageant, the ritual of black sacrifice. Seen from Lula's perspective, the entire conversation amounts to an
extended assault on Clay's awareness of the basic necessities of survival.
Seen from Baraka's viewpoint, the heightened racial awareness of Clay's final speech is simply an illusion, worthless if divorced from action. Clay's
unwilling participation in the pageant of white mythology reveals the futility of all attempts to respond to white culture on its own terms. Regarded
in this light, Baraka's subsequent movement away from the theoretical
avant-garde and from Euro-American modes of psychological analysis
seems inevitable.

Baraka's black nationalist plays, many of them written for community theater groups such as Spirit House Movers and the San Francisco State College Black Arts Alliance, occasionally employ specific avant-garde techniques. His earlier works take the techniques "seriously," but even his most experimental nationalist plays, such as *Experimental Death Unit #1*, clearly attempt to subvert the values implied by the Euro-American aesthetic. Determined to communicate with his community through its own idiom, Baraka sought new forms in the Afro-American aesthetic embodied in dance and music, African chants, experimental jazz, rhythm and blues, and reggae. Particularly when performed in predominantly black contexts, his work in this idiom creates an emotional intensity difficult to describe in standard academic terms, an atmosphere often extremely uncomfortable for white viewers. Even while embracing and exploiting the aesthetic potential of the idiom, however, Baraka attempts to purify and transform it. Repudiating his earlier vision of universal alienation and victimization, Baraka no longer sympathizes with, or even tolerates, passive scapegoats such as Clay and the Boy. He does not, however, remove the victim from the center of his drama. Rather, he emphasizes two new types of victims in his nationalist rituals: the clearly heroic Afro-American martyr in *Great Goodness of Life (A Coon Show)* and *The Death of Malcolm X*, and the whitewashed black and overthrown white oppressor in *Madheart* and *Slave Ship*, portrayed as deserving their death.

Madheart and *Great Goodness of Life (A Coon Show)* employ different constellations of these figures to criticize the failure of the black community to purge its consciousness of Euro-American values. Like *A Black Mass*, *Madheart* borrows the image of the "white devil" from the theology of the Nation of Islam (sometimes referred to inaccurately as the Black Muslims) to account for the fallen condition of black awareness. Beginning with a confrontation between allegorical characters identified as Black Man and Devil Lady, *Madheart* focuses on the Devil Lady's influence over the Black Man's Mother and Sister, whose red and blonde wigs indicate the extent of their corruption. Aided by the supportive Black Woman, Black Man rejects and sacrifices the Devil Lady, symbolically repudiating white culture. Mother and Sister, however, refuse to participate in the ritual of purification. Sister loses consciousness, believing that the death of the Devil Lady is also her own death. Lamenting over her daughter, Mother calls on white "saints" such as Tony Bennett, Beethoven, and Batman for deliverance. Clinging to their belief in whiteness, Mother and a revived Sister descend to the level of slobbering animals. Motivated by love rather than hatred, Black Man turns a firehose on them as the play ends. His concluding speech echoes Baraka's basic attitude toward his suffering community: "This stuff can't go on. They'll die or help us, be black or white and dead. I'll save them or kill them." To avoid being sacrificed like Clay, Baraka implies, the Afro-American community must repudiate its internal whiteness. The elimination of the white "devil," far from being an end in itself, is simply a preliminary step toward the purification of the black self-image.

Extending this critique of the internalization of white corruption, *Great Goodness of Life (A Coon Show)*, with its title ironic at several levels, focuses on the trial of Court Royal, a middle-aged black man accused of unspecified crimes. An offstage voice, supported by a sequence of increasingly respectable-looking Ku Klux Klan figures, echoes Lula in *Dutchman*, claiming that Court Royal has been harboring a murderer. Although Court Royal interprets the claim in concrete terms, the voice seeks primarily to bring about his repudiation of his black identify. Manipulating his fear of personal loss, the voice forces Court to preside over the ritual murder of a black martyr whose body is carried onstage to the accompaniment of projected slides showing Afro-American martyrs such as Malcolm X and Patrice Lumumba. Ordering the disposal of the corpse, the voice says: "Conceal the body in a stone. And sink the stone deep under the ocean. Call the newspapers and give the official history. Make sure his voice is in that stone too." In fact, the primary aim of the voice is to silence the Afro-American cultural tradition by encouraging individuals to see their own situations as divorced from that of their community. Despite Court Royal's dim awareness that the "body" is that of a collective figure, the voice forces him to deny his sense that "there are many faces." After Court Royal acquiesces to this Euro-American vision of individualism, the voice declares him "free," stipulating only that he "perform the rite." The rite is the execution of the "body."

Assuring Court Royal that the murderer is already dead, the voice nevertheless demands that he actively contribute to the destruction of the Afro-American tradition by sacrificing the "murderer" within. To distract Court Royal from the genocidal reality of his act, the voice delivers an intricate statement on the nature of ritual action. Court, caught in the trap of Euro-American rhetoric, ironically assumes the role of the white God and executes his symbolic son; the young black man cries out "Papa" as he dies. His soul "washed white as snow," Court merely returns to his night-out bowling. His voice sunk beneath the sea, he can only echo the white voice which commands his passive acceptance of Euro-American rituals. Where Clay was killed by white society directly, the martyr in *Great Goodness of Life (A Coon Show)* is killed by white society acting indirectly through the timorous and self-deluded black bourgeois. Ritual murder metamorphoses into ritual suicide. Baraka clearly intimates the need for new rituals that will be capable of presenting new alternatives not under the control of the white voice.

Slave Ship, Baraka's most convincing and theatrically effective black nationalist play, develops both the form and the content of these rituals.

Thematically, the play places the perceptions of *Madheart* and *Great Good-ness of Life (A Coon Show)* in a broader historical perspective. Beginning in West Africa and progressing through the American Civil War, Baraka traces the evolution of Afro-American culture, stressing the recurring scenes of betrayal in which traitors, frequently preachers, curry favor with their white masters by selling out their people. Such repeated betrayals, coupled with scenes of white violence against blacks, create a tension which is released only with the sudden ritual killing of the white voice and the black traitor. This sacrifice emphasizes Baraka's demand for an uncompro-mising response to the forces, inside and outside the community, responsi-ble for centuries of black misery.

The real power of *Slave Ship*, however, stems from its performance style, which combines lighting, music, at times even smell, to create an encom-passing atmosphere of oppression which gives way to an even more over-whelming celebration. The sound of white laughter and black singing and moaning surrounds the recurring visual images which link the historical vi-gnettes. A drumbeat reasserts itself at moments of tension and seeming despair, suggesting the saving presence of the African heritage. The drum, joined by a jazz saxophone as the black community rises to break its chains, initiates the celebratory chant: "When we gonna rise up, brother/ When we gonna rise above the sun/ When we gonna take our own place, brother/ Like the world had just begun?" Superimposed on the continuing background moaning, the chant inspires a communal dance which com-bines African and Afro-American styles. Invoking the choreography of the "Miracles/Temptations dancing line," Baraka calls the dance the Boogaloo-yoruba, compressing historical past and present in a ritual designed to cre-ate a brighter future. Following the climactic sacrifice, the severed heads of black traitor and white oppressor are cast down on the stage. Given ideal context and performance, the dancing of the Boogalooyoruba will then spread through the audience. *Slave Ship* thus exemplifies Afro-American ritual drama of the 1960's; merging aesthetic performance and political statement, it marks the culmination of Baraka's black nationalist work.

Baraka's more recent plays express the Marxist-Leninist-Mao Tse-tung philosophy he embraced in the mid-1970's. Gauging the success of monu-mental dramas such as *The Motion of History* and *The Sidney Poet Heroical* is difficult, in part because they are rarely performed, in larger part because of a generally hostile political climate. The texts of the plays reflect Baraka's continuing interest in multimedia performance styles, incorporating a great deal of musical and cinematic material. Both plays comprise numerous brief scenes revealing the action of historical forces, primarily economic in *The Motion of History* and primarily racial in *The Sidney Poet Heroical*. Both present images of martyr-heroes and oppressor-scapegoats. On the page, however, both appear programmatic and somewhat naïvely ideological. The climaxes, for example, feature mass meetings intended to inspire the audience to political commitment, a technique anticipated in proletarian dramas of the 1930's such as Clifford Odets' *Waiting for Lefty* (pr. 1935). The cries "Long live socialist revolution" and "Victory to Black People! Victory to all oppressed people!" which conclude *The Motion of History* and *The Sidney Poet Heroical* obviously require both a sensitive production and a politically sympathetic audience to work their desired effect. In the political climate of the late 1970's and 1980's, neither element has been common, and Baraka's plays of this period could be considered closet dramas.

Other major works

NOVEL: *The System of Dante's Hell*, 1965.

SHORT FICTION: *Tales*, 1967.

POETRY: *Spring and Soforth*, 1960; *Preface to a Twenty Volume Suicide Note*, 1961; *The Dead Lecturer*, 1964; *Black Art*, 1966; *A Poem for Black Hearts*, 1967; *Black Magic: Poetry 1961-1967*, 1969; *It's Nation Time*, 1970; *In Our Terribleness: Some Elements and Meaning in Black Style*, 1970 (with Fundi [Billy Abernathy]); *Spirit Reach*, 1972; *Afrikan Revolution*, 1973; *Hard Facts*, 1975; *Selected Poetry*, 1979; *Reggae or Not!*, 1981.

NONFICTION: *Blues People: Negro Music in White America*, 1963; *Home: Social Essays*, 1966; *Raise Race Rays Raze: Essays Since 1965*, 1971; *The New Nationalism*, 1972; *Selected Plays and Prose*, 1979; *The Autobiography of LeRoi Jones/Amiri Baraka*, 1984; *Daggers and Javelins: Essays*, 1984.

ANTHOLOGIES: *The Moderns: New Fiction in America*, 1963; *Black Fire: An Anthology of Afro-American Writing*, 1968 (with Larry Neal).

MISCELLANEOUS: *African Congress: A Documentary of the First Modern Pan-African Congress*, 1972 (editor).

Bibliography

Benston, Kimberly W. *Baraka: The Renegade and the Mask*, 1976.

_____ , ed. *Imamu Amiri Baraka (LeRoi Jones): A Collection of Critical Essays*, 1978.

Brown, Lloyd W. *Amiri Baraka*, 1980.

Hudson, Theodore. *From LeRoi Jones to Amiri Baraka: The Literary Works*, 1973.

Margolies, Edward. *Native Sons: A Critical Study of Twentieth-Century Negro American Authors*, 1968.

Sollors, Werner. *Amiri Baraka/LeRoi Jones: The Quest for a "Populist Modernism,"* 1978.

Craig Werner

JAMES NELSON BARKER

Born: Philadelphia, Pennsylvania; June 17, 1784
Died: Washington, D.C.; March 9, 1858

Principal drama

Tears and Smiles, pr. 1807, pb. 1808; *The Embargo: Or, What News*, pr. 1808 (no longer extant); *The Indian Princess: Or, La Belle Sauvage*, pr., pb. 1808 (libretto; music by John Bray); *Travellers: Or, Music's Fascination*, pr. 1808 (adaptation of Andrew Cherry's play; no longer extant); *Marmion: Or, The Battle of Flodden Field*, pr. 1812, pb. 1816 (based on Sir Walter Scott's poem); *The Armourer's Escape: Or, Three Years at Nootka Sound*, pr. 1817 (no longer extant); *How to Try a Lover*, pb. 1817, pr. 1836 (as *The Court of Love*; based on Pigault-Lebrun's novel *La Folie espagnole*); *Superstition: Or, The Fanatic Father*, pr. 1824, pb. 1826.

Other literary forms

Although known chiefly as a dramatist, James Nelson Barker wrote some occasional verse, political poems and orations, and several newspaper essays on contemporary drama. His six biographical essays on notable Americans, including DeWitt Clinton, Robert Fulton, and John Jay, appeared in *Delaplaine's Repository of the Lives and Portraits of Distinguished Americans* (1817).

Achievements

In the first half of the nineteenth century, when many American writers were struggling against a literary inferiority complex, Barker was among the earliest of American dramatists to break new ground. His *The Indian Princess*, which took the story of Pocahontas as its central theme, was the first American "Indian" play ever to be performed. It began a dramatic tradition, providing a motif for American playwrights for the next fifty years. Not until the eve of the Civil War, when drama turned more toward realism, had the Pocahontas material run its course. Barker's use of the Indian as a literary motif predates by more than ten years the depiction of the Indian in the novels of James Fenimore Cooper and in the works of his contemporaries.

Barker was thus among the first American writers to use native material as a corrective to what was perceived as the American writer's servile dependence on European, particularly British, literary influence. His most creative period, from 1808 to 1824, coincided with America's growing sense of literary nationalism, that sentiment by which American authors sought to produce a native literature that reflected the nation's character, customs, manners, and ideals. The forceful preface to his *Tears and Smiles*, for example, condemns the reverent attitude of American critics toward European standards. Denouncing these reviewers as "mental colonists," intellectually submissive to British opinion, Barker calls for a sort of declaration of literary independence, a repudiation of foreign models and an embracing of national cultural material.

Tears and Smiles, Barker's first play, contributed to the development of the stage Yankee, that bumbling yet shrewd New Englander whose individualism was distinctively American. Only twenty years after Royall Tyler introduced the stage Yankee in *The Contrast* (pr. 1787), Barker created the character of "Nathan Yank," a major link in the chain of Yankee plays that were to remain popular throughout the first half of the nineteenth century.

Barker's crowning achievement was the last of his five extant plays. First performed in 1824, *Superstition* is one of the earliest dramas to use colonial history as its source. Dealing primarily with the bigotry and fears of a New England village in the late seventeenth century, the play is a tragedy that anticipates some of the ideas and characters later to be found in the works of Nathaniel Hawthorne. It is the most controlled of Barker's dramas, and in its fusion of historical material with convincing character motivation, it remains the best American play of its time.

In his use of native material, then, together with his lifelong advocacy of a native American theater, Barker must be considered a significant influence in the history of American drama.

Biography

The fourth son of John Barker, one of Philadelphia's foremost citizens, James Nelson Barker was educated in public schools and became, in his early teens, a wide reader. Though he did not go to college, he was familiar enough with some of the world's great authors to begin, at the age of twenty, his first play, based on a story by Miguel de Cervantes. This play, "The Spanish Rover," was left unfinished and has not survived. By 1805, Barker had completed two acts of a proposed tragedy entitled "Attila," suggested by his reading of Edward Gibbon's five-volume work, *The History of the Decline and Fall of the Roman Empire* (1776, 1781, 1788); this play has also been lost. The only knowledge of these early efforts comes from Barker's autobiographical account of his dramatic career, written for William Dunlap's *History of the American Theatre* (1832).

Though these fledgling works attest Barker's early interest in the drama and indicate the scope of his reading, they also make a point about his creative imagination. The subject matter, the setting, even the characters of both works were foreign. Attila's Rome and Cervantes' seventeenth century Spain were far removed from the bumptious America of the early Republic; the results were therefore simple false starts. In contrast, when the occasion arose for the writing of a play with an American milieu as its setting, Barker's imagination took fire.

That occasion was a hunting trip in 1806. One of Barker's companions, a theater manager, knowing of the young man's dramatic interests, asked Barker to write an American play, and a prominent actor of the day, Joseph Jefferson, who specialized in Yankee characterizations, asked that Barker include a Yankee type. Barker set to work, and in forty-three days he completed his first play, *Tears and Smiles*, produced the following year. In his preface to the published work, Barker derides the popular opinion among critics that a successful drama had to be European in plot, setting, and character. As if poking fun at himself and his two earlier, abortive efforts, he quotes a fictitious friend who suggests that he, Barker, abandon his scheme of delineating American manners and instead "write a melodrama [*sic*] and lay [your] scene in the moon."

With one successful play behind him, Barker, now only in his early twenties, turned his youthful exuberance into more worldly pursuits. At this time, the city of Philadelphia had fallen under the spell of a sort of soldier of fortune, General Don Francisco de Miranda. Miranda wanted to liberate Venezuela and in time secure independence for all South America. In pursuit of this goal, he was seeking enlistments, promising wealth and glory to all who volunteered for the cause of freedom. Whether Barker was moved by the democratic fervor of the times or had merely surrendered to the swashbuckling Byronism of the scheme, he nevertheless left for the port of New York in August, 1806, with the idea of joining the expedition in Trinidad, West Indies. News of Miranda's defeat, however, and a series of letters from his father urging him to come home resulted in Barker's return to Philadelphia early in 1807.

This frustrated adventure can be seen as a catalyst in Barker's creative process, for his next play, first acted in March, 1808, was a political satire, *The Embargo*. Borrowing extensively from a British play by Arthur Murphy, *The Upholsterer* (1757), Barker's comedy was to be the most topical of his works. Never printed and since lost, the play was probably heavily allusive to President Thomas Jefferson's embargo of British shipping, in commercial retaliation for British seizures of American vessels during this period when Britain was engaged in a war with France, led by the Emperor Napoleon Bonaparte. Little else is known about what was probably Barker's least important work.

In April, 1808, Barker's third completed play was produced. *The Indian Princess* was a historically significant production, the first dramatization of the Pocahontas story. The play was enormously influential—so popular, in fact, that, by Barker's own account to Dunlap, it was eventually acted in every theater in the country. It was also the first original American play to be performed in England after its premiere in the United States.

Barker's next dramatic work was a trivial affair, an adaptation of *Travel-*

lers: Or, Music's Fascination (pr. 1806), by British author Andrew Cherry. A kind of musical panorama, the play was never printed, and though it was a modest success when performed during the Christmas season of 1808, it was, by Barker's admission, only "a little less absurd" than its original. It has been deservedly forgotten.

After this flurry of dramatic activity, Barker began to sow the seeds of his own political future, probably at the urging and with the help of his father, who was by 1809 the mayor of Philadelphia. Becoming active in the Democratic party of the city, Barker was sent to Washington with letters of introduction from his father to President James Madison. There he served as his father's lobbyist and listening post; his letters to the mayor, from his arrival in the capital in December, 1809, to his departure in March, 1810, are filled with political gossip, reports of evening balls and social entertainments, and frequent pleas for more money, always postscripted by appropriately filial apologies.

Returning to Philadelphia, Barker met and married Mary Rogers in 1811, took up portrait painting as a hobby, and wrote *Marmion*. The product of his reading of Sir Walter Scott, the play was not only a dramatization of Scott's poem of the same title but also a skillful conflation of other sources relating to the subject. In particular, Barker used material from the chronicles of Raphael Holinshed; the result was a play that was fast-paced and tightly structured. *Marmion* turned out to be Barker's longest-running stage work; it is interesting that it was his first successful drama on a nonnative subject, and this on the eve of the War of 1812, when national pride and patriotism were rising.

As it did for many, the war enabled Barker to develop his political career. Appointed a regimental captain of artillery, Barker soon saw active service at Fort Erie and at Buffalo, New York. Returning to Philadelphia, he became a principal recruiting officer in the region, mustering several hundred men; served as captain in the Artillery Corps; and was appointed brevet major by 1814.

At the war's end, Barker ran for the Pennsylvania Assembly on the Democratic ticket. Though defeated, he made many political friends, who helped him a short time later to be appointed a city alderman. It was a crucial political position, for only two years later, in 1819—and like his father—Barker himself became the mayor of Philadelphia. His one-year term, from October, 1819, to October, 1820, was marked by honesty, efficiency, and courage. He trimmed the city budget, cutting his own salary first; raised money for national relief programs; and reorganized the city's police and militia during a time of civil unrest.

Defeated for reelection, Barker also suffered a deep personal loss: Over the next two years, three of his children died. Barker's loyalty to the Democratic party was remembered, however, when Andrew Jackson became president and named Barker to the post of collector of the port of Philadelphia, a political plum, one of the choicest fruits of Jackson's spoils system. Barker held this post from 1829 to 1838.

Meanwhile, Barker's literary career continued to flourish. In the midst of his political activities leading to his post as alderman, Barker returned to a native subject for a play. *The Armourer's Escape* was a dramatization of John Jewitt's narrative of his captivity among the Nootkian Indians. Captivity narratives, real or fictional, were popular in England and in the United States during the late seventeenth and eighteenth centuries; Jewitt was counting on such literary precedent to promote the sales of his own adventures. His book was a failure, however, and he turned to the dramatist for help. The play was never printed and is now lost.

How to Try a Lover, though written shortly after the Jewitt dramatization, was not produced until almost twenty years later, though Barker remarked to Dunlap that it was the play with which he was most satisfied. Set in thirteenth century Spain, this comedy of love forsworn and finally consummated was based on Pigault-Lebrun's novel *La Folie espagnole* (1801). It is a charming, extremely actable play but not representative of that aspect of Barker's work which is most notable—namely, his use of native material.

Barker's use of such native sources resulted in his finest work, *Superstition*. In this work, the use of history meshes with sound dramatic instinct; the drama is regarded as one of the best American plays of the period. Serious, dark, and intense, the play shows a control of plot, character, and language that few dramatists had yet attained and which gains in effectiveness when one remembers that Barker wrote the play in the years immediately following the deaths of his children and his defeat for reelection to the mayoralty.

Although *Superstition* was Barker's last play, he continued, throughout the next decade, to supply newspapers and magazines with pedestrian occasional verse, patriotic centennial odes on such themes as the birthday of George Washington and on the founding of the state of Pennsylvania.

The last twenty years of Barker's life were spent in various positions in the United States Treasury Department in Washington, D.C. The demands of such service effectively curtailed his literary career. He remained a respected figure in Washington until his death on March 9, 1858.

Analysis

James Nelson Barker's earliest play, *Tears and Smiles*, succeeds on two counts. It is, first, a quickly moving, sprightly work, filled with the youthful exuberance of an author in his early twenties. Exuberance, indeed, is a crucial ingredient, for the recipe of plot and character is otherwise spoiled by convention and claptrap. Second, the piece has some genuine historical value as an early example of the portrayal of the stage Yankee, here named Nathan Yank.

Influenced by Tyler's *The Contrast*, *Tears and Smiles* relies on traditional elements of melodrama. Louisa Campdon, the heroine, has been promised by her father to the delicate dandy, Mr. Fluttermore, whose very name is suggestive of characters from Restoration drama. Louisa, however, is in love with Sydney, a young man of recognized valor but uncertain parentage who has returned from Tripoli and the wars against the Turkish pirates to reclaim her love. The Turkish allusions show how alert Barker was to literary and theatrical trends. Tyler had used the motif in his novel *The Algerine Captive* (1797), and the Turkish or Oriental motif had been popular in the early Gothic romances; in addition, operatic composers such as Christoph Gluck, Wolfgang Amadeus Mozart, and Gioacchino Rossini (Barker's contemporary) had staged Turkish operas.

By the end of the comedy, thanks to the intercession of characters such as General Campdon (Louisa's uncle) and the Widow Freegrace, the lovers are united and the fop appropriately chastened. Sydney is also reunited with his long-lost parents, who have been separated for years and suffered from pirates, slavery, and family disapproval. Such characters and situations were typical of the drama of the period, and *Tears and Smiles* is grievously weakened as art by its heavy reliance on them.

Still, the play is worthy of attention for its lively humor and satire as Barker pokes fun at Americans' seduction by European modes and manners. The opening scene quickly clears the ground for satire when Louisa's uncle protests her proposed marriage to Fluttermore, who, when he left America, was a clever, honest fellow but who has returned from his travels abroad "a puppy . . . with a pale face and a hearty contempt for everything this side of the water." Meanwhile, Barker skillfully delays Fluttermore's entrance until near the end of act 1, when Fluttermore saunters onstage with Monsieur Galliard, a combination companion and valet. The scene is deliciously funny, with bluff Jack Rangely, the second lead, shaking hands so cordially that he knocks the powder from Fluttermore's wig. By giving Fluttermore "Frenchified" rather than Anglicized affectations, Barker provides a variation on the standard portrayal of the British fop and makes a topical point about French influence on American fashion and theater at the time. "I can't conceive what you possibly do in this corner of the globe," says Fluttermore, disparaging American manners. "No opera; no masquerade, nor *fête*, nor *conversazione*." Later, writers from Hawthorne to Henry James would seriously lament America's lack of European refinement, that sense of history and rich cultural precedent, a lack which they saw as a limiting force on the American imagination. Yet here, at the dawn of American literary nationalism, foppish Fluttermore's denigration of American culture is distinctly comic.

Of special comic interest in *Tears and Smiles* is Nathan Yank, the first stage Yankee of the nineteenth century. Introduced in Tyler's *The Contrast*, this comic figure was to be one of the most popular and enduring types on the American stage. He was generally depicted as an honest, homespun bumpkin who very often was the butt as well as the perpetrator of jokes and whose comic antics were often dramatic set pieces, independent of the main action. Actors such as Joseph Jefferson, George Handel Hill, and Joshua Silsbee made their living playing Yankee characters. "Yankee" Hill was particularly notable for delivering Yankee monologues or yarns, a device that surely must have provided comic precedent for Mark Twain.

Barker's Nathan Yank added little to the characterization already drawn by Tyler some twenty years before. Nathan retains his predecessor's bumptiousness, for example, and holds the same status, that of servant, but whereas Tyler's Jonathan is boorish, he is also his own man. Jonathan shows a Puritan reliance on biblical precept as well as a practical sense of getting on in the world. His love scenes with Jenny, his social equal, prove him to be a man as well as a clown, a man of independent temperament, despite his status as servant.

In contrast, Nathan Yank never goes beyond the range of low comedian. He misdirects his master, Rangely, for example, by mistaking one house for another, and he indulges in a series of puns at the expense of Rangely's lover. To Rangely, who does not know her name, she is his "incognita," but Nathan henceforth refers to her as "Cognita." Inexplicably, Barker drops Nathan from the action by act 4, and Nathan is noticeably absent at the finale in act 5.

Although Nathan's shallow, one-dimensional buffoonery and his rather peripheral position in the action seem to represent a retrogression or at least a pause in the development of the stage Yankee, there is, on a closer reading of the play, an important advance in his use of dialect. While Tyler's Jonathan used dialect inconsistently, shifting arbitrarily from formal English to homely solecism, Nathan Yank is almost always dialectical, more consistently ungrammatical. From his first "I reckon" in act 1 to his "tarnal long" in his last appearance, Yank speaks strictly homespun American. This move toward a more consistent use of dialect was an important step in the transmission of the Yankee type.

If *Tears and Smiles* is notable for its exuberance, *The Indian Princess* is marked by a self-consciousness and a nationalistic sense of purpose. The very preface to the printed edition begins with a plea to both critics and theatergoers to take American drama seriously. Barker laments the poor reception American plays have received from critics and publishers, decrying the fact that acknowledged American productions simply die, like orphans, from "total neglect." As for *The Indian Princess* in particular, he urges the public not to denigrate the play simply because it "cannot lisp the language of Shakespeare." Like all living things, he says, American drama must first creep before it can walk. Finally, in a tone which adumbrates the pronouncements of Ralph Waldo Emerson and Walt Whitman, Barker predicts that America will bring forth "a dramatic genius" once the "stagnant atmosphere of entire apathy" is dispelled.

Though Barker's remarks may be seen as a self-serving acknowledgment of his pioneering role in the development of native drama, *The Indian Princess* is far from the work of genius predicted so confidently by its author. Despite its numerous failures, however, the play has genuine merit.

The first play in the literature to use the story of Pocahontas as its central idea, *The Indian Princess* was also the first of Barker's plays based on an authentic historical text. The advertisement to the 1808 edition credits Captain John Smith's *The Generall Historie of Virginia, New England, and the Summer Isles* (1624) as being the principal source, adding that the author has preserved "as close an adherence to historic truth" as the demands of the drama allowed.

An examination of Smith's account reveals just how cannily Barker used his source material. The Pocahontas episode in Smith (which in the opinion of some historians is of questionable truth) is narrated in the third person and is quickly told in a brief paragraph. The central scene in which Pocahontas puts her own head on the block to save Smith takes only a sentence. Barker casts this somewhat fleeting, almost offhand reference into the central episode of the play. It comes in the opening of act 2, not quite halfway through the three-act drama. Some critics, among them Arthur Hobson Quinn, have suggested that this crucial scene comes too early in the play, with the result that the third act tends to be rather anticlimactic.

If the statement in the advertisement about adhering to historical truth is taken as significant of Barker's intention, then the scene is rightly placed, for it serves as the central link in the chain of historical events that follow—namely, John Rolfe's love of the Indian Princess and their subsequent marriage, which cemented the bond between the English colonists and an important Indian tribe in the region, headed by Pocahontas' father, Chief Powhatan. Historically, Powhatan did seek English allies for his fight against the Susquehannocks, and in the closing scenes of Barker's play such an alliance takes place, both historically and symbolically, when all the lovers are united: Rolfe with Pocahontas; Robin (one of Smith's men) with Nima, Pocahontas' lady in waiting; and no less than three other pairs of lovers, Indian and white.

At the end of the play, Smith praises America as the new Eden, a new world "disjoined from old licentious Europe." This idea of America as a fresh start, an innocent, uncorrupted land untainted by history and therefore rich in human possibility, was a common thread in the skein of American literature during the nineteenth century. Barker's use of the idea so early in the century points out once again his pioneering sense of literary nationalism.

For all of its dramatic interest, however, the play is not without serious flaws. As in *Tears and Smiles*, Barker relies on conventional characters and situations, particularly in the scenes involving the minor pairs of lovers, such as Larry, the stage Irishman who loves Kate and who carries a potato in his pocket and commits execrable puns.

The play was originally intended as a straight drama, but Barker was persuaded to turn it into an opera—"an operatic melodrame," as the title page announces. As a result, some of the scenes are mere interludes, set pieces of vapid verse, set to music by a composer named Bray, which do little to advance the action or to discover character.

The most damaging weakness of *The Indian Princess* is Barker's inability to render effective, believable dialogue. The Indians speak, like their white counterparts, in blank verse or in orotund periods. Only on rare occasions does Barker even attempt to distinguish the speech of Indians from that of whites. These attempts often result in such rhetorical infelicities as Powhatan's exclamation at seeing Captain Smith for the first time: "Behold the white being." The love scene between Pocahontas and Rolfe is tender, evocative, and romantic, but echoes of William Shakespeare's *Romeo and Juliet* make Pocahontas' blank verse difficult to credit:

> Thou art my life!
> I lived not till I saw thee, love; and now
> I live not long in thine absence . . . .

Barker's failure to treat the Indian in other than romantic terms (even the evil medicine man, Grimosco, and the rival, Miami, are but red-skinned Gothic villains) typifies the problem faced by the early American writer who recognized the Indian as a legitimate literary property but who could not properly assimilate him into a creditable literary context because of subversive cultural differences.

For his finest work, *Superstition*, Barker once again turned to authentic colonial records. Drawing its main outlines from Thomas Hutchinson's *The History of Massachusetts* (1795), *Superstition* is set in a New England village in 1675. Ravensworth, the minister, is a zealous but cold man who is obsessed with what he sees as "the dark sorcery" practiced by Isabella, a late arrival to the village, who "scorns the church's discipline" and holds herself aloof from the neighbors. Isabella's son Charles is in love with Ravensworth's daughter Mary, an added motive feeding Ravensworth's obsession.

To this basic plot situation Barker successfully fuses a second motif, based also on a historical incident. A small group of Puritans who had presided over the execution of Charles I in January, 1649, were forced to flee

England at the restoration of Charles II in 1660. Though the majority were later granted amnesty, some were excepted and lived under assumed identities in the New World. Barker drew on this theme of the so-called regicides for the creation of the character of the Unknown, a mysterious figure living in exile in a cave deep in the wilderness. As the play unfolds, the Unknown saves the village from Indian attack by instilling courage and leading the colonists in a counter-offensive. In the end, he turns out to be a regicide and Isabella's long-lost father, in search of whom she has come to the New World.

The melodramatic elements inherent in this character and in his discovered relationship with Isabella seriously mar the aesthetic integrity of the play. Similarly, Ravensworth, whose obsession ultimately causes the deaths of Charles, Isabella, and his own daughter, has much of the melodramatic one-sidedness of a Gothic villain.

Yet the power of *Superstition* is undeniable. Its effectiveness lies in Barker's complete mastery in fusing historical event with psychological motivation. The characters' behavior and their various fates are dramatically represented as largely the results of the historical forces at work; there is an inevitability to the action. Action and character, in fact, are inseparable, as in all effective tragedy. Ravensworth's single-minded determination to root out "with an unsparing hand/ The weeds that choke the soil," his conviction that "the powers of darkness are at work among us," is made clear in the opening scene, and this obsession hangs over the characters and the action as a central, remarkably sustained idea.

Finally, there is strong temptation to speculate on the influence of *Superstition* on Hawthorne, who was an undergraduate at Bowdoin College when the play was first produced. Hawthorne, indeed, would later use the theme of the regicides in his short story "The Gray Champion," and Ravensworth's obsession is anticipatory of the diabolic singleness of purpose of Roger Chillingworth in Hawthorne's *The Scarlet Letter* (1850); even the similarity of surnames is notable. It could be argued, as well, that Isabella's independent piety and relative isolation are strongly suggestive of the character of Hester Prynne.

Regardless of whether *Superstition* was a direct early influence on Hawthorne, it stands on its own as a convincing treatment of a dark episode in American colonial history and as solid evidence of James Nelson Barker's legacy to the American theater.

Other major works

NONFICTION: "Peyton Randolph," "Thomas Jefferson," "John Jay," "Rufus King," "DeWitt Clinton," "Robert Fulton," in *Delaplaine's Repository of the Lives and Portraits of Distinguished Americans*, 1817.

Bibliography
Heffner, Hubert C., ed. *History of the American Theatre*, 1966.
Hughes, Glenn. *A History of the American Theatre 1700-1950*, 1951.
Moses, Montrose J., ed. *Representative Plays by American Dramatists*, 1921, 1964.
Musser, Paul. *James Nelson Barker*, 1929, 1969.
Quinn, Arthur Hobson. *A History of the American Drama from the Beginning to the Civil War*, 1923, 1943.

Edward Fiorelli

SIR JAMES BARRIE

Born: Kirriemuir, Scotland; May 9, 1860
Died: London, England; June 19, 1937

Principal drama

Ibsen's Ghost: Or, Toole Up to Date, pr. 1891, pb. 1939; *Richard Savage*, pr., pb. 1891 (with H. B. M. Watson); *Walker, London*, pr. 1892, pb. 1907; *The Professor's Love Story*, pr. 1892, pb. 1942; *The Little Minister*, pr. 1897, pb. 1942 (adaptation of Barrie's novel); *The Wedding Guest*, pr., pb. 1900; *Quality Street*, pr. 1902, pb. 1913; *The Admirable Crichton*, pr. 1902, pb. 1914; *Little Mary*, pr. 1903, pb. 1942; *Peter Pan: Or, The Boy Who Wouldn't Grow Up*, pr. 1904, pb. 1928; *Alice-Sit-by-the-Fire*, pr. 1905, pb. 1919; *Josephine*, pr. 1906; *Punch*, pr. 1906; *What Every Woman Knows*, pr. 1908, pb. 1918; *The Twelve-Pound Look*, pr. 1910, pb. 1914; *The Will*, pr. 1913, pb. 1914; *Der Tag: Or, The Tragic Man*, pr., pb. 1914; *The New Word*, pr. 1915, pb. 1918; *A Kiss for Cinderella*, pr. 1916, pb. 1920; *Dear Brutus*, pr. 1917, pb. 1923; *The Old Lady Shows Her Medals*, pr. 1917, pb. 1918; *Barbara's Wedding*, pb. 1918, pr. 1927; *A Well-Remembered Voice*, pr., pb. 1918; *Mary Rose*, pr. 1920, pb. 1924; *Shall We Join the Ladies?*, pr. 1921, pb. 1927; *The Boy David*, pr. 1936, pb. 1938; *Representative Plays*, 1954.

Other literary forms

The sheer volume of Sir James Barrie's literary output, together with the fact that his most successful and enduring works were written for the stage, tends to obscure recognition of his talent in other genres. His success as a playwright came when he was already launched as a writer. The vignettes and anecdotes of his literary apprenticeship had formed the basis for the successful *Auld Licht Idylls* (1888), and Barrie might have been content to continue drawing on his Scottish experiences in the form of articles and essays in the then popular "Kailyard" (cabbage-patch) style but for his determination to write a novel. Success in this genre came eventually with *The Little Minister* (1891), written in the same vein as the *Auld Licht Idylls*.

Barrie returned to the Scottish setting in *Margaret Ogilvy* (1896), a biography based on sentimental recollections of his mother. Questions were raised as to the genre of the work, and reviewers in Scotland were shocked by the detailed ruthlessness of his observation. No less revealing is the largely autobiographical novel *Sentimental Tommy* (1896), which, together with its sequel, *Tommy and Grizel* (1900), throws considerable light on Barrie's complex personality.

The novel *The Little White Bird* (1902) contained a blueprint for the development of the Peter Pan theme, but it was the successful dramatization of *The Little Minister* which finally channeled Barrie's literary efforts away from the novel toward the stage. The foundation of Barrie's career as a playwright was his determination to master the novel and to capitalize on his potentially limiting Scottish background and childhood experiences.

Achievements

Barrie was a prolific and versatile writer who enjoyed great popularity in his day, but he tends to be remembered only as the creator of *Peter Pan*. This enduringly popular work was the most successful play of Barrie's entire career, but it is uncharacteristic of his writing in that it was aimed at a children's audience. The secret of its undiminished popularity lies in Barrie's ability to appeal on different levels to both adults and children.

The bulk of Barrie's writing has now sunk into relative obscurity. It may be that his other works, and particularly his plays, are too closely tied to the spirit of the age in which they were conceived, or that their psychology is too naïve and their characters too transparent for modern taste. Nevertheless, Barrie's achievements as a playwright should not be assessed on the merits of *Peter Pan* alone.

Taken in the context of his dramatic works as a whole, *Peter Pan* can be seen to be a natural development of an escapist tendency which frequently motivates Barrie's plays. Often his plots center on a juxtaposition of a fantasy world with the "real" world as it is represented on the stage—real for the characters themselves and accepted as such by the audience. Barrie's preoccupation with psychological escapism can be attributed to his own tendency to fantasize in his closest personal relationships. Additionally, by involving his characters in the mechanics of a fantasy world as distinct from a theatrical representation of the real world, Barrie gives himself much greater scope for social criticism: Fantasy worlds are used to highlight the shortcomings of the real world.

Biography

James Matthew Barrie was of humble origins, the seventh of the eight surviving children of David Barrie, a Scottish weaver. Barrie's mother, Margaret Ogilvy, was a strict Puritan, reared in the fundamentalist beliefs of the Auld Lichts (Old Lights), a sect of the Presbyterian Church of Scotland. The unusual strength of the influence she exerted over Barrie throughout his life was detrimental to him in many ways. When he was six, his older brother David, aged nearly fourteen and his mother's favorite, died after a skating accident. Margaret Ogilvy was desolate in her loss, and the young James made a conscious effort to become a substitute for David, to help her overcome her grief. This was the beginning of the sharp division for Barrie between home, where he was acting out a fantasy in his most intimate relationship, and the outside, real world.

Barrie entered Dumfries Academy in 1873, and while there he began to be interested in all aspects of the theater. He was a founding member of a school dramatic society, and left school intent on becoming a writer. Family opposition was strong, however, and reluctantly he entered Edinburgh University, graduating in 1882. During his years as an undergraduate, he wrote as a free-lance drama critic for the Edinburgh *Courant*. After an unsuccessful year spent in Edinburgh researching a book on the early satirical poetry of Great Britain, he answered an advertisement for a job as leader-writer for the *Nottingham Journal*. Editorial supervision was virtually nonexistent, and Barrie wrote extensively for the paper under a variety of names. He began sending articles to London, undaunted by frequent rejections.

In 1884, Barrie returned to Scotland, where he wrote up his mother's childhood memories. "An Auld Licht Community" was published in the *St. James's Gazette*, and the editor requested more in the same vein, which Barrie found easy to provide. The following year, he decided that to make a career of writing he would have to be in London, so he moved south. He managed to sell articles steadily and before long was making a respectable living. His first successful book, a collection of Scottish articles, *Auld Licht Idylls*, appeared in 1888; together with *A Window in Thrums* (1889), it raised a storm of protest in Scotland, but Barrie was undeterred.

Barrie was now writing furiously, working simultaneously on a novel, *The Little Minister*, and a play. The part of the second leading lady in *Walker, London* went to Mary Ansell, whom Barrie ultimately married in 1894. The marriage, apparently unconsummated, ended in divorce in 1909, their companionship having been disrupted by the extraordinary way that Barrie was attracted to the Llewelyn Davies family, initially to the children, George (born 1893), Jack (born 1894), and Peter (born 1897), but later to Sylvia Jocelyn Llewelyn Davies, their mother. Barrie met her at a dinner party in 1897 and subsequently met the children in Kensington Gardens. They were enchanted by his stories, and he would frequently accompany them home. It was not long before he was behaving like a member of the family, despite the reluctance of their father, Arthur Llewelyn Davies, to accept this situation.

The year 1900 saw the birth of the Llewelyn Davies' fourth son, Michael, and Mary Barrie's purchase of Black Lake Cottage on the outskirts of Farnham, Surrey. Here Barrie and the three older Davies boys spent the summer of 1901 enacting adventures and fantasies in the overgrown gardens, setting the scene for *Peter Pan*; it was not until 1903, however, after the success of *Quality Street*, *The Admirable Crichton*, and *Little Mary*, that Barrie began the play which was to make him a household name.

In 1906, two years after the birth of his fifth son, Nicholas, Arthur Llewelyn Davies was diagnosed as having cancer. Unable to earn at the

Bar, he had no alternative but gratefully to accept Barrie's offer of financial support for his family. Barrie was by now spending almost all of his free time with the Davies family, leaving his own wife, Mary, very much alone. In the three-year period between Arthur's death and her own in 1910, Sylvia Davies received continuous support and attention from Barrie, and when she died Barrie took upon himself the guardianship of her sons— "My Boys," as he called them. Of the five, he seems to have been closest to George, killed in France in 1915, and Michael, drowned at Oxford in 1921. Michael's death prostrated Barrie, but he was helped over it by Lady Cynthia Asquith, who had been acting as his personal assistant since 1917. Barrie's relationship with her developed along similar lines to his relationship with Sylvia Llewelyn Davies. He frequently assisted the Asquiths out of financial difficulties with generous presents to Cynthia, and became imperceptibly an extension of their family, in the face of the opposition and dislike of Herbert (Beb) Asquith, an aspiring writer.

For a shy man, Barrie was by this time a very prominent figure. Having declined a knighthood in 1909, he had accepted a baronetcy in 1913 and was awarded the Order of Merit in 1922. He was unfailingly generous with his money, and during World War I he funded and organized the establishment of a home for refugee mothers and children in France. He continued a voluminous correspondence even after being forced by pain in his right hand to train himself to write with his left.

Barrie's last play, *The Boy David*, written for the Austrian actress Elisabeth Bergner, received highly critical notices. Cynthia Asquith arranged a command performance which should have been a triumph for Barrie but ended up as an unremarkable matinee, and the playwright died shortly afterward, a disappointed man.

Analysis

Walker, London was Sir James Barrie's third attempt at writing for the stage, but the first to meet with any real success. The idea for the setting came from a summer Barrie had spent on a houseboat on the Thames, and the play captures the lazy indolence of life moored to the riverbank. It is not by any means an outstanding work but is of interest as an early approach to the question of the relationship between fantasy and the real world, which was to become a constant preoccupation in Barrie's subsequent works.

The pleasant lethargy of the party on the houseboat is disturbed but not spoiled by an uninvited guest, an undistinguished London barber by the name of Jason Phipps. Phipps has run away from the reality of his everyday life, and for the duration of his holiday, which should have been his honeymoon, has decided to assume the identity of one of his customers, the celebrated African explorer Colonel Neil. Mrs. Golightly and the other members of the houseboat party are indebted to the newcomer for his ostensibly heroic action in saving Bell Golightly from drowning in a punting accident, and they are delighted to be able to offer hospitality to one so famous. The audience, however, is well aware that Neil is an impostor. He has bribed the only witness of the accident to support the heroic version of the episode, and he is being diligently searched for by his jilted fiancée. During the week that Phipps spends on board the houseboat, he regales the company with vivid descriptions of the adventures he has had on his explorations, drawing his listeners unwittingly into the fantasy he is building. As Neil, Phipps makes proposals to both Bell Golightly and her cousin Nanny O'Brien—proposals which they find difficult to reject, because they are caught up in the fantasy, too; as himself, however, Phipps realizes that the girl for him is the faithful Sarah, who catches up with him in the end. The last act is virtually pure farce and ends with Phipps making a quick exit into his everyday life before he can be unmasked.

Barrie had originally intended the play to be entitled "The Houseboat," but there was another work in existence by that title and thus a new one had to be found. As Phipps leaves the stage for the last time he is asked for his address. He gives it as Walker, London, the new title of the play: "Walker" was a slang word meaning a hoaxer.

The theme of assumed identity recurs in *Quality Street*, which was first produced in October, 1902, only one month before the equally successful *The Admirable Crichton*, enjoying a run of fourteen months. As with *Walker, London*, the definitive title of the play was a later alteration. The working title was "Phoebe's Garden," but Quality Street, the name of an actual town between Leith and North Berwick, appealed to Barrie; the final title subtly reinforces the notions of hidebound respectability with which the play deals.

The action takes place in Quality Street during the Napoleonic Wars. The heroine, Miss Phoebe Throssel, has fallen in love with a local doctor, Valentine Brown. Both Phoebe and her sister Susan, an old maid, expect that "V. B.," as they refer to him, is calling to make his declaration and ask for Phoebe's hand. Unfortunately, it becomes apparent that he has other news: He has enlisted in the army and will be leaving forthwith to join the campaign against the French. The Misses Throssel cover their disappointment admirably and, as convention demands, say nothing of love.

The second act takes place ten years later. The blue and white frilliness of the Throssel parlor has been subordinated to the requirements of a classroom. It transpires that Phoebe and Susan, having invested their money according to Brown's advice, have suffered a substantial loss and have been forced to earn their living by opening a school. Phoebe appears to have aged much more than ten years, assuming prematurely the garb and attitudes of the old maid she seems destined to become. The sisters' new way of life is highly distasteful to them, but for respectable women in their position, society offers no other choice. Their drab existence is suddenly brightened by the return of Valentine Brown and the rest of the troops. The doctor is visibly struck by the change in Phoebe when he calls on the Throssels unexpectedly, for she is at her most severe in her schoolmistress attire. Phoebe suddenly realizes that she no longer has to act older than her years. They have caught up with her, and she has come a long way from being the pretty girl that she was when the troops left for the war.

When Phoebe next appears on the stage, she has discarded her cap and drab clothes and has pulled out all her ringlets, so that she is virtually her former self, except for what she has experienced during the ten years. It is in this guise that Brown sees her next. She is inspired to pass herself off as her own niece, Miss Livvy, a ploy which her sister is pushed into supporting. The mechanics of the deception give rise to some comic scenes, particularly when the sisters find themselves having to deceive their gossipy and envious friends, the Misses Willoughby. By wearing the same fashionable veil as her friend, which can be opened or closed at will by the wearer, Phoebe is accepted as Miss Livvy, but the ladies sense a mystery and are desperate to find out what is happening.

Phoebe daringly sets out on a round of balls given to celebrate the victory, and act 3 shows her in full swing, acting in her assumed identity in an outrageously flirtatious way and turning the heads of all the men present. She is determined to take revenge on Valentine Brown for having forgotten that he kissed her once, ten years before. For all of those years she treasured both the memory of the kiss and her guilt at the impropriety of having allowed him to kiss her, only to find upon his return that he does not even remember the event. The climax comes when it looks as though Brown is going to propose to Livvy, and she is preparing to reject him out of hand. Much to her surprise, however, he confesses that it is her aunt Phoebe whom he really loves; in courting her, so much like her aunt in appearance but so different in behavior, he has come to realize where his affections really lie, and where they have always lain.

The sisters now have to find a way of getting rid of the unwanted Livvy. She takes to her bed and Phoebe reappears, but the Misses Willoughby are extremely solicitous. As it seems inevitable that the deception will be discovered, the tension rises until Valentine Brown, in his capacity as a doctor, goes into Livvy's bedroom and reappears to report on the progress of the patient who does not exist. He then joins forces with the sisters to dispose of Livvy. He wraps the phantom up and takes her out to his carriage, which is sent off with the maidservant in attendance to convey the sick Livvy home. The suspicions of the watching neighbors are lulled and the way is clear for Valentine Brown to make his proposal and for it to be accepted by his beloved Phoebe.

In *Quality Street*, the assumption of a new identity is not a *fait accompli* as in *Walker, London*. It is a deliberate ploy, but it is seen to happen on-stage in direct response to a development in external circumstances affecting the character. Whereas the character assumed by Jason Phipps was based on an idealization of the attributes of a person unknown to the audience, Phoebe finds her model in her own past, so her escape from her own personality is more pragmatic and less fanciful; the essence of her assumed nature has lain dormant within her. It is only in her uncharacteristic coquetry that Livvy is different from Phoebe, and in this there is a large measure of making up for lost opportunity, a foreshadowing of the development of this theme in *Dear Brutus*.

The approach to fantasy in *The Admirable Crichton* is quite different. In this play, Barrie draws a definite line between the "real" world, where the characters originate, and the fantasy one, where they end up after the shipwreck. The desert island, however, is only fantasy to the audience; for the characters, it becomes reality, and they journey from the reality of the "real" world to the reality of the fantasy and back again in the course of the play.

The Admirable Crichton, one of Barrie's most successful plays, is a comedy with a social message. The dominant theme is the equality of man. As a philosophical ideal, the concept that all men are naturally equal is espoused by the Earl of Loam and is fashionably exploited in the peer's unprecedented declaration that one day a month all of his servants will meet the other members of his household on equal terms. Thus, the first act of the play opens on one such day, when the house is in a turmoil. It is immediately apparent to the audience that both masters and servants alike find the imposition of equality frustrating and unnatural. For the daughters of the house, it is a tiresome bore to receive their servants in the drawing room and address them as social equals using a respectful form of address. When "Miss" Fisher, Lady Mary's maid, is piqued by not taking precedence over the lower-ranking Tweeny, the audience may laugh at such trivial preoccupation with position in circumstances of albeit temporary, but nevertheless total, equality, but Barrie is reminding them how deeply ingrained in society are the distinctions of rank and privilege.

The second act takes place a short time after the first, but the setting is a remote desert island. The main characters have been shipwrecked, and they appear on the stage immediately after the catastrophe; a particular feature of the set is that unidentified objects drop at intervals from the trees to the ground, adding to the strangeness and hostility of the environment in which the castaways now find themselves. It is not long before both the audience and the characters become aware that the man best equipped to lead the castaways in their survival effort is not the earl, the socially superior and conventionally obvious candidate, but Crichton the butler. Crichton is a man who knows his place both with respect to his employers, to whom he knows he is inferior, but also with respect to his fellow servants, to whom he is undoubtedly superior. His progressive assumption of authority on the island is a natural extension of his regular duties, and he is accustomed to having other people under his authority. What is unforeseen, but very funny, is the total inability of the upper-class members of the shipwrecked party to make any practical contribution to attending to their immediate survival needs. Even with three minutes' warning of the impending disaster, they were unable to dress themselves suitably and have only one pair of boots between them. The most useful contribution the Honorable Ernest can make is to compose exasperating epigrams, and the three young ladies seem unaware of the seriousness of their predicament as they bemoan the loss of their hairpins. Such concern for trivia in the face of a desperate situation does not inspire confidence in their ability to survive.

That the relationship between master and servant is already becoming strained is apparent from the way Crichton follows the example of the peer's daughters and criticizes him for having left behind the hairpin he found on the beach. While the girls cannot see beyond the normal function of the hairpin, Crichton can visualize its use in a number of ways. The Earl of Loam is quick to realize that Crichton may be stepping out of line, and a discussion of leadership develops, with the peer and the butler arguing from exactly opposite viewpoints from the ones they took in the first act. Indignantly, the upper-class members of the party decide to go it on their own, despite having saved nothing at all from the wreck. That anything was salvaged was only because of the foresight and industry of Crichton, and in due course the smell of his stew wafting along the beach brings the others crawling back to the campfire.

The events of the third act take place after a lapse of three years or so. The physical conditions of the party have taken a turn for the better, and they are comfortably housed and well fed. A number of ingenious contraptions have been devised to improve the quality of their lives, and it transpires that this is all because of the drive and ability of "the Guv." The audience may suspect that Crichton is "the Guv" but does not know for certain until he appears on the stage, a distinctly regal figure. There has been much discussion among the women prior to his appearance about who will have the honor of serving him, and the honor falls to Lady Mary, now known as Polly, who begs Tweeny to let her wear "It" for the occasion. "It" is the skirt Tweeny was prudent enough to put on the night they escaped from the wreck, the only such garment on the island.

While the audience may have admired Crichton's quiet efficiency and obvious leadership potential in act 2, the figure he cuts in act 3 is disquieting.

Despite the order and efficiency he has imposed on life on the island, despite the benefits he has brought to the others who clearly would not have survived long without him, he is, nevertheless, a dictator, and it is galling to see the women courting his attentions. At a time when the Labour movement was gathering strength and the Fabians were active, Barrie may well have intended a warning to the upper echelons of society of impending social change. After all, he, himself, was nearing the top of the social ladder, having started off on its lowest rungs. It is reassuring to see the old order restored in the last act, with a return to the status quo.

Having seen a more worthy side of the upper-class characters in their newly found identities on the island, the audience might expect to see them retain some of their improved qualities, but this is not to be. When they regain their former position of social superiority, they also become subject once again to the shallow conventions and superficial moral preoccupations of society, as exemplified by the attitudes of the dowager. The distorted account that emerges of their life on the island is not a willful fabrication by the characters. It is a fantasizing of the reality of the fantasy. It is what would be expected of them by society, and in this deception it is society that should be condemned. Through the medium of humor, Barrie thus succeeds in criticizing both the philosophy that all men are equal and the idea that any kind of social revolution would be an improvement on the existing social order. That the existing social order is not without its defects is freely admitted, but any social critique is subordinate to the primary purpose of the play, which is to entertain and amuse.

Reality and fantasy coexist in *Peter Pan,* also, but in contrast to *The Admirable Crichton,* the boundaries between the two states are fluid and indistinct. Barrie is concerned above all with the progression from the one to the other, and in most cases this is the progression from the imaginative existence of the child into the prosaic life of the adult. At first, adult reality and childhood fantasy seem diametrically opposed and mutually exclusive, but it soon becomes apparent that the degree to which the characters in *Peter Pan* are able to enter into and become part of the fantasy is directly dependent on their distance from childhood. Wendy, like her mother, will always retain a childlike streak in her nature which will ensure that her memory of Never Land will never fade completely, no matter how old she becomes, but Peter Pan will never leave Never Land because of his refusal to progress to adulthood.

The archetypal boy who never grew up, Peter Pan evolved in the stories of Kensington Gardens with which Barrie enchanted the Davies boys. The earliest literary version of these stories was a novel, *The Little White Bird,* which, contrary to Barrie's original plan, came to be dominated by Peter Pan. Barrie was increasingly attracted by this new character as his ties with the Davies family became even closer, and in 1903 he grew absorbed in writing a new play which would have Peter Pan as the central character. The scene for the play had already been set two years earlier in the gardens of Black Lake Cottage. At that time, Barrie had made a photographic record of the boys' adventures, with a preface ostensibly written by Peter Llewelyn Davies, whose name the hero of the new play assumed. Using the working title of "Peter and Wendy," Barrie offered his play to Herbert Beerbohm Tree, knowing it would entail an elaborate and expensive production, but he was not interested. It was Barrie's American associate, the impresario Charles Frohman, who grasped the play's potential and spared no effort to make it a success. He engaged the talented Dion Boucicault as producer, a recent innovation in the theatrical world, where production had traditionally been the concern of the actor-managers, and the play opened at the Duke of York's Theatre on December 27, 1904.

The plot of *Peter Pan* is calculated to appeal to the imaginations of the young. The Darling children, Wendy, John, and Michael, are induced by the intriguing, magical boy Peter Pan and his fairy acolyte Tinker Bell to abandon their comfortable nursery and savor the delights and perils of Never Land. The climax of the first act comes as they fly out the nursery window.

In the second act, the children become acquainted with the other inhabitants of Never Land. The Lost Boys, children without mothers who as babies fell out of their baby carriages, recognize Peter as their natural leader. They are permanently in danger from the Pirates, a motley crew led by the dastardly Captain Hook. The Redskins are enemies of both the Lost Boys and the Pirates until Peter and the Lost Boys rescue the belle of the tribe from death by marooning at Hook's hands. The appeal of the island is enhanced by the antics of the mermaids, the threat of the wolves and the Never Bird, not to mention the ticking crocodile which follows Hook inexorably around and around the island, waiting for the moment when it can finish making a meal of him.

In the fourth act, a great battle between the Redskins and the Pirates ends in victory for Hook, and it is then very easy for him to abduct Wendy and the Lost Boys as they prepare to leave Never Land. Only Peter can rescue them from the pirate ship before they are made to walk the plank, and this he does with great enthusiasm. Hook meets his nemesis, the crocodile, and the Darling children return to the security of their nursery.

Peter is unique among the characters in his insistence that he does not want to grow up. The Lost Boys have no fixed opinion on the subject and are easily talked into going back with Wendy and her brothers to be adopted, and Wendy herself realizes that growing up is inevitable. It is easy to see the parallel between Peter's refusal to countenance even the thought of growing up with the singular circumstances of Barrie's own childhood. Physically, he remained a child longer than most of his contemporaries and was marked throughout his adulthood by his short stature (he was just over five feet tall); on the other hand, carefree childhood ended abruptly for him at the age of six when he embarked on the fantasy relationship with his mother, trying to live up to her expectations for his older brother.

Barrie's emphasis on the reluctance of Peter Pan to grow up is often interpreted as a disenchantment with adult life and an idealization of childhood, but Never Land offers only a temporary refuge from, and not a permanent solution to, the problems of growing up; childhood as epitomized by Peter, and to a lesser extent, the Lost Boys, is not ideal. Peter is callous and self-centered. He is illogical, inconsiderate, irresponsible, and irrepressible, but nevertheless endearing. His insouciance sets him apart from Wendy, who is already burdened with responsibilities and is happy to assume more.

If Peter Pan is a combination of Barrie himself and the characteristics that most appealed to him in the children of whom he was so fond, then Wendy must surely be a distillation of elements from the women in Barrie's life. The strongest parallel is with his mother, particularly as she emerged for him in her stories of her early childhood. Domestic responsibility came early to her, and she was already mothering her younger brother at the age of eight. The theme of motherhood is very strong in Peter Pan, and the maternal qualities of Sylvia Llewelyn Davies with her five sons must have served as a model for the scenes of Wendy and the Lost Boys. At the same time, Wendy's commonsense organization of the unpredictabilities of life in Never Land does not exclude her from participating in the great adventure. She is still a child and eligible to enjoy the delights of this children's preserve. She is already marked by feminine intuition, however, and if she is mother to the Lost Boys, then she expects Peter to be the father, a role of which he is particularly wary. The whole of the scene in the house underground in act 4 is built around Wendy's enactment of an adult role into which she will inevitably grow and Peter's avoidance of the parallel one which he will never accept.

Dreams are the substance of *Peter Pan*, and Barrie leaves the skeptical with the option of interpreting the fantasy on this level. On the other hand, even Mrs. Darling knows that Peter's shadow has substance: She has rolled it up and put it away in a drawer, and Tinker Bell's remarkable recovery after drinking the poison intended for Peter convinces every child in the audience, at least for the duration of the play, that fairies do exist.

If Peter Pan epitomizes childhood, then Lob in *Dear Brutus* is the essence of worldly experience. He is likened, by the other characters in the play at the beginning of the first act, to Puck, or what Puck would have looked like if he had forgotten to die. He is thus at the opposite end of the age spectrum to Peter but like Peter is instrumental in strangely altering the lives of the other characters. The first act opens in a darkened room in his house, looking out onto a moonlit garden, a pertinent reversal of the usual situation. When the main characters enter the dark room the lights go up and the ladies of the house party attempt to discover why they, particularly, have been invited. The butler, Matey, is blackmailed into giving them as much information as he knows, which is little. All he can say is to beware of the wood, and not to venture out beyond the garden. His advice sounds ridiculous, because as the characters all know there is no wood for miles around, but it is Midsummer's Eve, and strange tales are told about a magic wood and its properties. When the men of the party join the ladies, they are full of enthusiasm for a project clearly suggested by Lob—namely, to go out to find the fabled wood.

During the remainder of this act, it becomes apparent that the lives of all the guests are marred in some way. Purdie, for example, cannot help being attracted to women other than his wife, and the current object of his attentions is Joanna Trout; Will Dearth is a failure and an alcoholic who is despised by his wife; Coade has achieved nothing at all in his life and even confuses his second wife with the memory of his first. Will Dearth observes that there are three things generally viewed as never returning to men: the spoken word, past life, and neglected opportunity. They would all welcome a second chance at life, and this the wood could provide. The climax to the first act is the discovery that the mysterious wood now entirely surrounds Lob's house, and one by one the characters venture out into it.

Act 2 shows how the characters react to the boon of a second chance to live their lives. It is entirely predictable that they will repeat the mistakes of their lives in the real world, and this they proceed to do. Purdie, married to Joanna, chases after Mabel, in reality Mrs. Purdie; Alice Dearth has married her other suitor, and although she is the Honorable Mrs. Finch-Fallowe in name she is now only a vagrant. Of all of them, only Will Dearth has benefited, possibly because the value of his life only declined once his wife saw him as a failure. He now delights in the daughter he wanted, but never had in reality.

The third act takes place back in Lob's house. The characters drift in from the wood, leaving their fantasy existence, and in Dearth's case, his darling Margaret, behind. Their return to reality is gradual, however, and they are able to compare their two states, to arrive at some profound but depressing conclusions about the flaws in their characters which have made their lives what they are. It is Purdie, the now self-confessed philanderer, who quotes the lines from Julius Caesar that furnish the elliptical title of the play: "The fault, dear Brutus, is not in our stars, but in ourselves. . . ."

Only once (in *Der Tag*) did Barrie abandon comedy as his medium of expression. His plays are known for their lighthearted whimsicality, and are enjoyed for the elements of farce that even the more serious ones, such as *Dear Brutus*, contain. The majority of his characters are little more than caricatures, but Barrie nevertheless succeeds in capturing the essence of each, not least because of the careful notes about them which usually form part of the text of a given play. Comedy of character is augmented by verbal humor and a deft handling of the comic situation to put the theme of the play across to the audience with a minimum of effort. The result is that a Barrie play seems light, almost flippant, with the underlying social message only fleetingly apparent. Although the tenor and atmosphere of his plays faithfully reflect the society that filled the theaters when they were first produced, Barrie's themes and preoccupations are no less relevant today.

Other major works

NOVELS: *Better Dead,* 1887; *When a Man's Single,* 1888; *The Little Minister,* 1891; *Sentimental Tommy,* 1896; *Tommy and Grizel,* 1900; *The Little White Bird,* 1902.

SHORT FICTION: *Auld Licht Idylls,* 1888; *A Window in Thrums,* 1889.

NONFICTION: *Margaret Ogilvy,* 1896.

Bibliography

Asquith, Cynthia. *Portrait of Barrie,* 1954.

Birkin, A. *J. M. Barrie and the Lost Boys: The Love Story That Gave Birth to Peter Pan,* 1979.

Blake, G. *Barrie and the Kailyard School,* 1951.

Dunbar, Janet. *J. M. Barrie: The Man Behind the Image,* 1970.

Green, Roger L. *Fifty Years of Peter Pan,* 1954.

Mackail, Denis. *Barrie: The Story of J. M. B.,* 1941.

Zia Hasan

PHILIP BARRY

Born: Rochester, New York; June 18, 1896
Died: New York, New York; December 3, 1949

Principal drama

Autonomy, pr. 1919 (one act); *A Punch for Judy*, pr. 1921, pb. 1925; *You and I*, pr. 1923 (originally as *The Jilts*, pr. 1922); *The Youngest*, pr. 1924, pb. 1925; *In a Garden*, pr. 1925, pb. 1926; *White Wings*, pr. 1926, pb. 1927; *John*, pr. 1927, pb. 1929; *Paris Bound*, pr. 1927 (as *The Wedding*), pb. 1929; *Cock Robin*, pr. 1928, pb. 1929 (with Elmer Rice); *Holiday*, pr. 1928, pb. 1929; *Hotel Universe*, pr., pb. 1930; *Tomorrow and Tomorrow*, pr., pb. 1931; *The Animal Kingdom*, pr., pb. 1932; *The Joyous Season*, pr., pb. 1934; *Bright Star*, pr. 1935; *Spring Dance*, pr., pb. 1936 (adaptation of Eleanor Golden and Eloise Barrington's play); *Here Come the Clowns*, pr. 1938, pb. 1939 (adaptation of his novel, *War in Heaven*); *The Philadelphia Story*, pr., pb. 1939; *Liberty Jones*, pr., pb. 1941; *Without Love*, pr. 1942, pb. 1943; *Foolish Notion*, pr. 1945; *My Name Is Aquilon*, pr. 1949 (adaptation of Jean Pierre Aumont's play *L'Empereur de Chine*); *Second Threshold*, pr., pb. 1951 (completed by Robert E. Sherwood).

Other literary forms

Philip Barry published one novel, *War in Heaven* (1938), which was dramatized as *Here Come the Clowns*, and a short story in *Scribner's Magazine* in 1922 that, along with his juvenilia and some nonfiction works, constitute his only literary output other than his plays.

Achievements

Barry will always be regarded primarily as a writer of superb drawing-room comedies, full of wit and sophistication and charm; indeed, Barry did write such skillful comedies of manners. Even during his own lifetime, however, critics perceived a duality in his dramatic output and were somewhat perplexed by the variety of Barry's experimentation on the stage. As easy as it would have been for him to stick to a comedic formula, grinding out comedies year after year, Barry proved an adventuresome dramatist and thereby cast confusion among the critical community. In spite of repeated failure at the box office, Barry continued with engaging persistence to write and produce serious drama in a variety of forms—serious drama, tragedy in some cases, which in retrospect is of considerable interest even if it is far less pleasurable to study than are the mannered comedies.

Barry was neither as funny as George S. Kaufman nor as deeply brooding (or tedious) as Eugene O'Neill. His comedies, especially *You and I*, *Paris Bound*, *Holiday*, and *The Philadelphia Story*, attracted widespread attention when they were first produced and are still regularly revived by amateur theatrical groups. His serious dramas for the most part met with scant critical recognition and usually even less financial success, but such plays as *In a Garden, Hotel Universe, Tomorrow and Tomorrow, Here Come the Clowns*, and *Foolish Notion* are well within the traditions more fully exploited by such contemporaries as O'Neill, Robert E. Sherwood, Lillian Hellman, and Elmer Rice. What is often overlooked when discussing Barry's career is that he, too, was in on the beginnings of the new American drama, interested in many of the same innovations that were more highly publicized in the works of others. Partly because of his reticence, partly because his working methods eschewed the obvious, the self-consciously "serious" elements that were highlighted in the work of his contemporaries, Barry's message was often concealed by the charm of his characters and the smoothness of his dialogue.

Barry was among the earliest of American playwrights to incorporate the new Freudian psychology into his drama. Barry also did much to adapt Maeterlinckian fantasy for the Broadway stage, as in *In a Garden*. Symbolism, tragedy, realism, and poetic drama were used by Barry in his various dramatic experiments. Even social criticism forms a central part of his plays, and although he was criticized for not joining in the political movements of the 1930's, his work presents one of the most sustained and devastating critiques of the narrowness and aridity of American capitalism in the history of modern theater. All of this Barry accomplished without the intellectual posing or the critical backstabbing so often associated with the theater. In spite of these credentials, however, Barry's drama has all but disappeared from American literature—a fate that raises some awkward questions for anyone interested in assessing his work. In part it can be attributed to the lack of homogeneity among his plays. He skipped from one form to another and, except for high comedy, never seemed completely successful at any. He lacked the consistent vision of O'Neill, the virtuosity of Kaufman, the social commitment of Hellman and Clifford Odets. Finally, the diffidence which allowed him social mobility denied him the passionate engagement that might have made him a great rather than merely a fascinating playwright.

Biography

Outwardly, Philip Barry led a charmed life: He married the right woman, made lots of money, and ran with the rich and famous. Inwardly, however, his life was not as fortunate. By the time Barry died in 1949, at the comparatively young age of fifty-three, he had experienced more failures on Broadway than successes, and he was plagued by depression and religious doubts severe enough to disrupt his otherwise disciplined and orderly work habits. In addition, all of his life Barry remained on the periphery of the upper-class world he depicted in so many of his plays and emulated in his life. As Brendan Gill has perceptively noted, Barry, like such other Irish-Catholic writers of his generation as Eugene O'Neill, F. Scott Fitzgerald, and John O'Hara, spent his creative career striving for the perquisites and assurance of his Protestant betters.

Philip James Quinn Barry was born on June 18, 1896, in Rochester, New York, to James Corbett Barry and Mary Agnes Quinn. He was the youngest of four children. His father, who emigrated from Ireland as a boy, became wealthy in a marble and granite business, and when he married Mary Agnes, they brought together two well-to-do Irish families who were obviously going to make their mark in the prospering Upstate city. Unfortunately, James Barry died the year after Philip's birth, leaving his youngest son to be brought up by his sister and mother and under increasingly reduced circumstances, for despite the best efforts of the two older Barry sons, the granite business gradually declined. Barry attended Nazareth Hall Academy, a Roman Catholic secondary school, and East High School in Rochester. He attempted his first three-act play, "No Thoroughfare," in 1909, but other than a story, "Tab the Cat," which he wrote for publication in the *Rochester Post Express*, the young Philip did not show any precocious literary talent. In the autumn of 1913 he entered Yale.

The combination of East High and Yale did much to broaden Barry's world beyond the rather narrow Catholicism of his family. Especially at Yale, where he was thrown in among the Protestant elite, Barry decided to work his way into the larger, more sophisticated world of money. Because of defective eyesight, he had not been an athlete in school, so Barry turned to writing, and over the next three years he contributed poetry, short stories, and editorials to the *Yale Literary Magazine*. World War I disrupted Barry's education, and he went to work for the American Embassy in London as a code clerk after he was rejected for military service. He used the time to advantage, however, completing a three-act play, which he unsuccessfully tried to get produced. In March of 1919, he was back at Yale, his work done in London, and in June the Dramatic Club produced his only known one-act play, *Autonomy*. That September, after receiving his degree, Barry enrolled in George Pierce Baker's Workshop 47 at Harvard, and during the next year he wrote another three-act play, *A Punch for Judy*. Temporarily out of funds, Barry wrote copy for a year at W. A. Erickson, an advertising agency. During this time, he became engaged to Ellen Semple, daughter of a wealthy international lawyer, Lorenzo Semple, who with his wife lived in New York City and Mt. Kisco, New York. In the summer, Barry received word that *A Punch for Judy* would be produced by Workshop 47, would open in New York, and would go on tour. In the fall, Barry left advertising and returned to Baker's Workshop 47, where during the next few months he wrote the drafts of two plays, *The Jilts*, later retitled *You and I*, and "Poor Richard," which underwent several title changes before being published as *The Youngest*. On July 15, 1922, he married Ellen Semple, and they spent the rest of the summer honeymooning in Europe. On the return voyage, Barry, who had few prospects for employment, learned that *The Jilts* had won the Herndon Prize for the best full-length play written in Workshop 47 and that it would be produced on Broadway early in the new year. Retitled *You and I*, Barry's play became a rousing success and established him as one of the rising stars of the new American theater. Later that same year, his first son was born.

In spite of his impressive beginning, over the next few years Barry's plays were increasingly unsuccessful. *The Youngest* ran for 104 performances, *In a Garden* survived for seventy-four performances, *White Wings* ran for twenty-seven, and *John* lasted only eleven performances. During the summer of 1927, however, while Barry was living at Cannes in Southern France, his luck changed.

On the trip over, Barry and Rice had begun collaboration on a mystery play, *Cock Robin*, which Barry completed along with *Paris Bound* during his stay in France. *Paris Bound* opened in December and *Cock Robin* in January, 1928, both to good audiences. Barry followed these successes in the fall with *Holiday*, his eighth Broadway production, and it ran 230 performances at the Plymouth Theater. Thereafter, although his plays would often have a disappointing box office or receive mediocre reviews, Barry was at least financially secure. He earned increasing sums from the sale of his properties to Hollywood, and amateur performances continued to boost the revenues on each play he wrote. His second son was born in 1926. Although Barry's mother had died in 1927, his marriage, the most fortunate part of his exceptionally fortunate life, continued to provide him with sustenance. As one critic has described it, his marriage was itself "Barryesque," full of charm, intelligence, wit, and concern.

The 1930's treated Barry, professionally at least, much in the same way the 1920's had. He began strong with the successful run of *Tomorrow and Tomorrow*, slumped downward during the middle of the decade, his career reaching what was perhaps its nadir when *Bright Star* closed after seven performances, only to rise spectacularly in 1939 with the overwhelming success of *The Philadelphia Story*. The latter, starring Katharine Hepburn, ran for more than four hundred performances and is credited with restoring to solvency the Theatre Guild, which Barry had joined a decade earlier. Barry also published his only novel, *War in Heaven*, in 1938, and earlier in the decade he spent a brief stint in Hollywood as a screenwriter for Metro-Goldwyn-Mayer.

Barry came under increasing criticism during this period of social and political unrest. He was roundly condemned for writing frivolous plays at a time when many critics felt that all artists should be engaged in the struggle for economic and social justice. In particular, his refusal to write overtly about political causes lost him support among the younger drama critics of the period. In addition, Barry suffered two personal losses in these years: Both his brother, Edmund, and an infant daughter died.

World War II suspended the Barrys' routine of living most of the year in Southern France, but it hardly diminished Barry's output: He produced plays in 1941 (*Liberty Jones*), in 1942 (*Without Love*), and in 1945 (*Foolish Notion*). When the war was over, the Barrys returned to France. For the next three years, Barry had nothing running on Broadway, but in 1949 his adaptation of Jean Pierre Aumont's *L'Empereur de Chine, My Name Is Aquilon*, opened as his twentieth Broadway production and, as it would turn out, his last. After submitting the draft of his next play, *Second Threshold*, to the Theatre Guild, Barry died suddenly of a heart attack at his apartment in New York City. On December 5, a requiem mass was said at the Church of St. Vincent Ferrer, and he was buried at East Hampton, Long Island. *Second Threshold* was completed by Robert E. Sherwood in 1951 and, in the same year, it opened at the Morosco Theatre and ran for 126 performances.

Although Barry shared certain accidents of birth and background with other Irish-Catholic writers of his generation, he succeeded, unlike many of the others, in gaining acceptance into the moneyed world of the Protestant upper class. Even so, he always remained apart; the role of an observer was congenial to him. In the end, perhaps, Barry saw the upper classes clearly not only because of his proximity but also because of his restraint; by avoiding the excesses of O'Hara, Fitzgerald, and O'Neill, he was able to cross the social and financial barriers into the world which receded before the others like Gatsby's rolling prairie out into the night.

Analysis

Philip Barry made his mark in American theater as a writer of high comedy and as an experimentalist, and during three decades of playwriting he explored to the full both of these artistic tendencies in his work. In the process, he came to occupy a kind of middle ground between dramatic extremes; in the words of John Gassner, Barry tried to arrive at a point of reasonableness in an unreasonable world. As a theatrical moderate, he faced a much more difficult task than did the more extreme dramatists of the period between the two world wars. Neither a social satirist nor a vacuous entertainer, a partisan politico nor a know-nothing fool, an unthinking realist nor a muddled metaphysician, Barry's art was a healing art and his mission to reduce the dissonance of the modern American theater. Barry's diffidence, however, made him difficult to classify, and literary history has not treated him well. Often misunderstood when he was alive, he now resides in a critical limbo in American theatrical history. As a Catholic, it is a position he would have understood and perhaps relished.

Barry established his reputation with his play *You and I*, which under the working title *The Jilts* had won an award as the best play of Baker's Workshop 47. Under the terms of the award, the play chosen was to be produced on Broadway and then taken on tour. *You and I* was a resounding success, both in New York and on tour, and set the pattern for Barry's other drawing-room comedies, most notably *Paris Bound*, *Holiday*, and *The Philadelphia Story*. With witty dialogue and a modish plot, the play revealed the essentially corrupt spirit of capitalism and concluded with a realistic vision of life's limitations. The action centers on Maitland White, a fortyish businessman who decides to give up his comfortable advertising job in a soap company and return to the ambition of his youth, to become a painter. His wife rather generously agrees to give up her affluent life-style in order to help him realize his dream. His son, who is just embarking on his own life, has fallen in love with a girl and is about to give up his ambition to become an architect and go to work for the firm his father has just quit. The play concludes as the father returns to work, thereby freeing the son both to marry and to realize his dream of studying architecture in Paris. Matey realizes by the play's end that time has robbed him of any chance to become anything but a mediocre artist and that his family obligations must take precedence over his individual desires. Dreams, ambition, and talent can all die with age and obligation; such is the rather sobering resolution to Barry's witty plot.

This pattern of hope, loss, and reconciliation (or resignation) marked all of Barry's most famous and successful comedies. *Paris Bound*, which was produced in 1927 following a series of increasingly unsuccessful dramas, also contains a cautionary ending. Jim and Mary Hutton have been married for six years when Mary learns that her husband has committed casual adultery. Deeply hurt at such a betrayal, she leaves for Paris to sue for divorce. In spite of her "modern" attitude about such things, announced on her wedding day, Mary is now prepared to forsake her liberality in favor of a more conventional morality—until she, too, is faced with temptation by Richard, a bright, attractive, young composer. Although she does not have an affair with Richard, she learns the ease of such venial sins and accepts her husband back without revealing her own involvement. She has learned that the spiritual bond within marriage should be valued above mere physical fidelity. Again, Barry's dialogue was praised by the critics, while audiences were titillated by his unconventional attitude toward extramarital affairs. A smash hit on Broadway, the play was also included in the ten best list for 1927, and screen rights were purchased by Pathé. Once again, Barry's wit and charm obscured a more serious theme, one that would surface again and again in his later plays—namely, the question of marriage and resolutions to marriages in trouble. Like that of Tracy Lord in *The*

Philadelphia Story, Mary Hutton's resolution in *Paris Bound* strikes one as a little too pat for the anguish that has been expended. The problem of divorce and broken relationships was of considerable social interest during the 1920's, but Barry declined to confront it head-on.

Indeed, Barry was always able in his high comedies to skirt popular and often controversial issues by placing them in warm and sunny settings. One of the ways in which he used the upper-middle-class milieu for which he became famous was to couch radical themes in comfortable surroundings and thereby make them more palatable to his audiences. A case in point is his next broadly successful comedy, *Holiday*. Returning to the theme of a young man's dreams, *Holiday* deals with Johnny Case, who wants to risk his small fortune in order to go off and find himself, in spite of the fact that he has just met and fallen in love with the wealthy Julia Seaton. The play's plot hinges on whether Johnny, who has little prospect of earning a living and no money to fall back on, will withstand the financial and sexual pressures of Julia in order to be true to himself. As it turns out, Johnny does break off with Julia but is followed on his travels by the less frivolous and more understanding Linda, Julia's sister. Like *You and I*, the play centers on the various pulls made on the young hero by competing value systems and by competing girls. More upbeat than the earlier play, *Holiday* seems to suggest that it is possible to have it all but that such ventures are not without risks and finally entailments, albeit not necessarily strangling ones. Barry was saying that money should not be an end in itself and that all people should have the opportunity to make life choices for themselves and to assume responsibility for such choices. His point was well taken but came at a particularly inappropriate moment: The year after the play was produced, the stock market crashed, plunging the United States into unparalleled financial decline. The ensuing Depression denied to millions the opportunities afforded Johnny, and the optimism of *Holiday* rang hollow.

Barry was not to write another successful comedy of this type for four years. By 1932, the Depression was well established, with no end in sight. *The Animal Kingdom*, produced in that year, was originally written for a young Hepburn, then just beginning her stage career. For a variety of reasons, Hepburn was dropped from the cast of *The Animal Kingdom* at the last minute, but the play is now seen to be an earlier version of her hit *The Philadelphia Story*. *The Animal Kingdom* also bears a resemblance to *Paris Bound*. Tom Collier, a publisher, who has been living with Daisy Sage, a journalist, for three years, falls in love with and marries Cecelia Henry. Cecelia seduces Tom into publishing trash for a quick profit, to the damnation of his publisher's soul. Realizing the immorality of their marriage, Tom leaves Cecelia, who is more mistress than helpmate, to return to his mistress, Daisy, who is more wife than paramour. Daisy's love for Tom wins out over Cecelia's manipulation of his affection for profit. Again, Barry suggests that a marriage built only on the appetites of the animal kingdom is not a true marriage, and Daisy's pure love finally gives Tom the strength to free himself and discover who he really is. By rejecting the dictates of society, Tom is able, unlike Matey, to regain his individual integrity.

For the rest of the 1930's, Barry seemed unable to write anything that would capture the imagination of his public. In 1939, however, with a second chance to work with Hepburn, Barry wrote the play for which he is probably best remembered, *The Philadelphia Story*. For Hepburn, Barry, and the Theatre Guild, which produced it, the new play was crucial. None of the principals should have worried: *The Philadelphia Story* saved the Guild financially, helped establish Hepburn's career, and rescued Barry's reputation.

As the play begins, Tracy Lord is preparing to marry for the second time, but her plans are complicated by a series of family entanglements: Her boozy ex-husband shows up, a reporter from a national magazine arrives to do an in-depth piece on the family, her father has developed an attachment to a lady of questionable (or perhaps "unquestionable" would be better) morals, her sister's behavior is erratic, and her uncle goes around pinching young girls. Tracy's high moral principles match the priggishness of her husband-to-be until she gets roaring drunk one night and swims nude with the journalist who is covering the family. Like Mary in Barry's *Paris Bound*, Tracy learns tolerance. Rejecting her intolerant would-be second husband, she is reunited with her estranged father and former husband. Human warmth and understanding, Barry implies, are worth more than unthinking moral rectitude, and people with social position and wealth have no hold on individual morality, as the uprightness of the young reporter has proved. *The Philadelphia Story* was to be the last of Barry's high comedies and the last of his successful plays, for although two of Barry's later plays performed creditably at the box office, their success was nothing compared to that of *The Philadelphia Story*. The film version of the play, starring Hepburn as well, became one of the most successful screwball comedies of the late 1930's, while the 1956 musical film version, *High Society*, was a successful vehicle for a girl from Philadelphia, Grace Kelly.

Although Barry will probably always be known primarily for his high comedies, he was proudest, as John Mason Brown has written, of his failures, his experimental dramas. Underneath his surface gaiety and wit, Barry was a serious student of the theater, one who was in touch with the current trends in European as well as American avant-garde drama. His so-called failures represent that audacious, unconventional side of his theatrical nature. It must be understood that in all of his plays, Barry experimented. He played with dialogue, setting, character, and most of all subject matter, but those comedies which established his reputation in the American theater tended to be the least audacious stylistically. Then as now, audiences did not like to be jolted out of their complacency by too radical a form. Change the language, the plots, the themes, but do not change the form of the drama. When Barry wrote a play without an intermission, when he introduced allegory or fantasy, his audiences did not respond as fully as they did to his more conservative comedies.

Barry's first obviously experimental drama, *In a Garden*, not only employed a play within a play (in itself not a radical device) but also incorporated a deliberately poetic plot and dealt in a more overt way with self-consciously "serious" topics, two elements which Barry had kept discreetly in the background of his previous plays. There is an element of Luigi Pirandello in the fey qualities of the characters, especially the girl, Lissa, and several of the critics likened Barry's work to Henrik Ibsen's *A Doll's House* (pr. 1879). The play closed after seventy-four performances.

Barry followed *In a Garden* with another, even more fantastic play. *White Wings* is almost totally symbolic, dealing with a family of street cleaners whose livelihood is passing with the coming of the automobile and the disappearance of the horse. Although the play intrigued the critics, it baffled the public and ran for only twenty-seven performances. Clearly, *White Wings* is concerned with modernity's impact on traditional values, but the play's symbolic manner leaves Barry's precise intentions in doubt. One critic has suggested that Barry's faith had been called into question by his rereading of the Gospels and that the "faith of the fathers" which is portrayed and undercut in *White Wings* is the Catholicism of Barry's youth. Whatever the sources of *White Wings*, Barry continued in this vein in his next play, *John*, based on the life of John the Baptist.

John, the most serious work Barry had yet attempted, reflected the religious turmoil that he was experiencing at the time. Running for only eleven nights, the play was a disaster from the beginning; in particular, its language was too colloquial for its biblical subject matter. Still, in retrospect, the play looks better than its initial reception would indicate. The dialogue is less off-putting to the contemporary sensibility than it was to audiences in the late 1920's; indeed, *John* has affinities with Archibald MacLeish's highly successful *J. B.* (pr. 1958). Nevertheless, Barry was sufficiently discouraged by the failure of *John* to agree to collaborate with Rice on a mystery play, *Cock Robin*, which, along with *Paris Bound* and *Holiday*, managed to reestablish Barry's career at the end of the decade.

Hotel Universe was Barry's first play of the 1930's, a play which captured the critics' fancy but was only mediocre at the box office. A parable that mixes Freudianism and Christianity, *Hotel Universe* is set in a large house that once was a hotel. Ann Field has assembled a number of guests who have in various ways rebelled against society but who have achieved only purposeless personal freedom and who now face the emptiness of their lives with increasing despair. Running without intermissions, the play is an extended psychodrama in which the various characters reenact scenes from the past, experiencing catharsis in the process. Barry's parable, however skillfully presented, did not attract an audience. Its failure with the public followed the pattern set by his earlier experimental dramas, a pattern to which most of his later serious plays were also subject.

It is difficult to sum up Barry's career. He became one of the United States' most financially successful playwrights, earning enough money to allow him to live in the manner of one of his own characters. He was perhaps the most accomplished writer of high or sophisticated comedy between the wars, a period notable for its witty comedies of manners. He was among the most innovative American playwrights working on Broadway during the 1920's and the 1930's. In spite of all of these accomplishments, however, Barry remains largely excluded from serious discussions of American literature. The reasons for this are complex but center on Barry's need to be a maverick, an eccentric in a world dominated by corporate mentalities. Barry's plays, for all their commonality of themes, are just quirky enough to avoid easy synthesis. Both experimental and traditional, comic and serious, religious and skeptical, Barry's work provides enough ambiguity and variety to place him in his own category, which is to say, by himself, alone. It is a position Barry would have welcomed, for like so many of his characters he eschewed easy answers and sought salvation on his own terms.

Other major works

NOVEL: *War in Heaven*, 1938.

SHORT FICTION: "Meadow's End," 1922.

NONFICTION: *The Dramatist and the Amateur Public*, 1927; "Here Come the Clowns," 1938; "Liberty Jones," 1941.

CHILDREN'S LITERATURE: "Tab the Cat," 1905; "The Toy Balloon," 1917.

Bibliography

Brown, John Mason. "The American Barry," in *Saturday Review of Literature*. XXXII (December, 1949), pp. 24-27.

Cajetan, Brother. "The Pendulum Starts Back," in *Catholic World*. CXL (March, 1935), pp. 650-656.

Clark, Barrett H. "Philip Barry: The Development of a Distinguished Dramatic Talent," in *Theatre Guild Magazine*. VII (May, 1930), pp. 21-26.

Dickinson, Donald Hugh. "Mr. Eliot's *Hotel Universe*," in *Drama Critique*. I (February, 1958), pp. 33-44.

Flexner, Eleanor. *American Playwrights: 1918-1938*, 1938.

Gassner, John. "Philip Barry—Civilized Dramatist," in *Theatre Arts*. XXXV (December, 1951), pp. 48-49.

Gill, Brendan. "The Dark Advantage," in *States of Grace: Eight Plays by*

Philip Barry, 1975.

Krutch, Joseph Wood. *The American Drama Since 1918: An Informal History*, 1939, 1957.

Lavery, Emmet. "The World of Philip Barry," in *Drama Critique*. III (November, 1960), pp. 98-107.

Lippman, Monroe. "Philip Barry and His Socio-Political Attitudes," in *Quarterly Journal of Speech*. XLII (1956), pp. 151-156.

Mantle, Robert Burns. "Philip Barry," in *Contemporary American Playwrights*, 1938.

Roppolo, Joseph Patrick. *Philip Barry*, 1965.

Sievers, W. David. *Freud on Broadway: A History of Psychoanalysis and the American Drama*, 1955.

Charles L. P. Silet

FRANCIS BEAUMONT

Born: Grace-Dieu, England; c. 1584
Died: London, England; March 6, 1616

Principal drama

The Woman Hater, pr. c. 1606, pb. 1607 (with John Fletcher); *The Knight of the Burning Pestle*, pr. 1607, pb. 1613; *The Coxcomb*, pr. c. 1608-1610, pb. 1647 (with Fletcher); *Philaster: Or, Love Lies A-Bleeding*, pr. c. 1609, pb. 1620 (with Fletcher); *The Captain*, pr. c. 1609-1612, pb. 1647 (with Fletcher); *The Maid's Tragedy*, pr. c. 1611, pb. 1619 (with Fletcher); *A King and No King*, pr. 1611, pb. 1619 (with Fletcher); *Cupid's Revenge*, pr. 1612, pb. 1615 (with Fletcher); *Four Plays, or Moral Representations, in One*, pr. c. 1612, pb. 1617 (with Fletcher; commonly known as *Four Plays in One*); *The Masque of the Inner Temple and Grayes Inn*, pr., pb. 1613 (with Fletcher); *The Scornful Lady*, pr. c. 1615-1616, pb. 1616 (with Fletcher); *The Tragedy of Thierry, King of France, and His Brother Theodoret*, pr. 1617(?), pb. 1621 (with Fletcher; commonly known as *Thierry and Theodoret*).

Other literary forms

Known almost exclusively as a dramatist, Francis Beaumont did publish one verse satire, *Salmacis and Hermaphroditus* (1602), and several lyrics. A collection of his verse, entitled *Poems*, was published in 1640.

Achievements

Francis Beaumont's imprint on seventeenth century drama cannot be distinguished from that of John Fletcher, since their jointly written plays secured the reputations of both men. Indeed, the success of their collaboration from about 1606 until 1613 was such that later editors assumed their few solo plays to have been joint productions; moreover, Fletcher's many collaborations with other writers, most notably Philip Massinger, were widely regarded throughout the seventeenth century as the works of Fletcher and Beaumont.

Though rarely produced after the Restoration and without critical stature since that time, the Beaumont-Fletcher collaborations, including, among others, *Philaster*, *The Maid's Tragedy*, and *A King and No King*, captured large, fashionable audiences with their blend of satire, sophisticated dialogue, and sexual titillation. These plays perfectly suited the tastes of the more affluent theatergoers who patronized the indoor Blackfriars playhouse, while the outdoor theaters catered to the middle-class taste for farce, romance, and patriotic heroism. Beaumont and Fletcher's comedies and tragicomedies expose middle-class optimism as mere naïveté or ignorant ambition. Though never creating worlds as darkly depraved as those of John Webster or George Chapman, Beaumont and Fletcher nevertheless pictured society as corrupt, its rulers as venal, its populace as stupid and conniving. Their main characters, neither heroes nor villains, typically represent the educated gentry; worldly, well-spoken, vain, they assume aristocratic privilege almost as a virtue and thus are frequently boors, though never unwitty ones. Good and evil have little relevance in the Beaumont-Fletcher world; favor is granted those who can seduce or acquire wealth with the greatest aplomb, the most studied indifference. Overt ambition, lack of humor, bad manners, and slow wits mark the losers.

Though the Beaumont-Fletcher partnership ended in 1613 and both playwrights were dead by 1625, their collaborations stayed popular for the rest of the century, Restoration critics regarding them as contemporary masterpieces while reducing the works of William Shakespeare and Ben Jonson to the status of mere classics. William Wycherley, Sir George Etheredge, William Congreve, and, to some extent, John Dryden all wrote as followers of the Beaumont-Fletcher tradition. Those tastes in drama to which the pair had appealed at the Blackfriars were confirmed and intensified in the self-consciously fashionable audiences after 1660.

When fashions changed early in the eighteenth century, the Beaumont-Fletcher collaborations disappeared from the stage and have rarely been revived. Ironically, the least popular play in the canon, Beaumont's *The Knight of the Burning Pestle*, has been increasingly performed, particularly in this century, and is now critically regarded as one of the greatest Renaissance comedies. Structurally a daringly original play, *The Knight of the Burning Pestle* deliberately blurs the distinctions between players and audience, play and reality. In an era when taste in drama has been molded by Eugène Ionesco, Samuel Beckett, and Thornton Wilder, *The Knight of the Burning Pestle* is perhaps more at home than at any previous time.

Biography

Francis Beaumont's life varied significantly from that of the stereotypical Elizabethan playwright, who emerged from the trade class, worked his way through Oxford or Cambridge, and struggled for an insecure living by writing for the stage, the press, and occasional patrons. As the son of a wealthy Leicestershire judge descended from the Norman nobility, Beaumont seems not to have pursued either his education or his writing out of burning ambition or necessity. Entering Broadgates Hall (later Pembroke College), Oxford, at age twelve, Beaumont left a year later, upon the death of his father, and never returned to the university. He turned instead to the family profession, law, being admitted to the Inner Temple in 1600, but, again, he did not complete his studies.

During this time, Beaumont became one of the habitués of the London literary scene, befriending such luminaries as Michael Drayton and Ben Jonson. Drayton called Beaumont and his brother John, a poet, "My deare companions whom I freely chose/ My bosome friends," while the first quarto of Jonson's *Volpone* (pr. 1606) includes commendatory verses by one "F. B.," probably Beaumont. The playwright's famous association with fellow dramatist John Fletcher began in these years also, with the first of their collaborations occurring about 1606. A bishop's son, Fletcher shared with Beaumont an aristocratic heritage; in addition, he shared Beaumont's Bohemian tastes. According to contemporary chronicler John Aubrey, the friends enjoyed "a wonderful consimility of phansey": "They lived together on the Banke side, not far from the Playhouse, both batchelors; lay together; had one Wench in the house between them, which they did so admire; the same cloathes and cloake, etc. between them."

Though immersed in the life of the city, Beaumont remained a member of the gentry, having inherited the family holdings upon the death of his elder brother Henry in 1605. A verse letter to Jonson indicates his occasional sojourns at Grace-Dieu throughout his London years. Finally, in 1613, the same year that Shakespeare left London for Stratford, Beaumont ended his collaboration with Fletcher in order to marry Ursula Isley, heiress of Sundridge Hall in Kent, and return to country life. The marriage, which produced two daughters, abruptly ended three years later with Beaumont's death, on March 6, 1616.

Analysis

To describe the style of a writer whose greatest body of work was done in collaboration is, to say the least, difficult. Three centuries of commentators have arrived at widely differing judgments of the contributions of John Fletcher and Francis Beaumont to the plays they are known to have written together. Since nothing is known of their characteristic collaborative process, it is presumptuous to look at linguistic cues or at staging patterns as indicators of the dominant hand in certain plays or even in particular scenes. Moreover, since their collaboration produced works remarkably distinct in style from the few solo works by either man, one cannot say which characters or ideas seem typical of Beaumont and which of Fletcher.

What one can do is compare a typical work of the Beaumont-Fletcher collaboration with the single play, *The Knight of the Burning Pestle*, which is believed to be wholly Beaumont's, in order to understand his work; in these different contexts, remarkably different pictures of Beaumont the playwright emerge.

Though the first version of *The Woman Hater* is considered to have been Beaumont's alone, the only extant version of the play is that revised by Fletcher in 1607, the first year of their collaboration; it well represents the typical features of the Beaumont-Fletcher plays. Acted early in 1606 by the

Children of St. Paul's, *The Woman Hater* was among those plays taken over by the King's Men when the children's company disbanded later that year. The play was acted periodically, to some acclaim, throughout the decades before the closing of the theaters in 1642. Its longevity is attested by the publication of two quartos, the first in 1607, the second in 1648-1649.

The 1607 prologue proclaims the play neither comedy nor tragedy: "A Play it is, which was meant to make you laugh, how it will please you, is not written in my part." This vagueness about form is understandable: Though the play holds together, at least somewhat, as a satire of classes and mores, the trivial plot and superficial characters make it incoherent and formless as a complete play. The pleasure it gave its audiences derives primarily from the satire—and, perhaps, from its mildly titillating dialogue between Gondarino, the misogynist, and the coquettish, though technically virginal, Oriana. The satire bites broadly rather than deeply, cutting across the ranks and occupations of society rather than exploring the corruption of a few significant individuals. One reason for the thinness of the play is that both playwrights are satisfied to have all characters function as mere caricatures of familiar court and city types: the officious minister, Lucio, a would-be Machiavel; the feckless nobleman, Count Valore, who whiles away his hours with petty practical jokes; a nameless mercer, representative of the London middle class, a man easily gulled by a pimp into marrying a prostitute. Skulking through the play are also two anonymous intelligencers, courtiers of the most base and vicious sort, who feed the appetite of a decadent court for scandals and plots.

Perhaps the most extreme caricatures are the principals, Gondarino and Oriana, who embody in almost grotesque form the essential pointlessness, in the playwrights' view, of court life. In a Shakespearean comedy, the pair, a professed enemy of womankind and a clever, rich maiden, would gradually fall in love and, in the finale, marry. Beaumont and Fletcher continually tease the audience with this expectation, but the play ends with the two still mutual enemies and love nowhere to be found. At different points in the play, each professes eternal devotion to the other, but these exclamations are nothing more than tricks. There is, however, no real malice in their actions; the overwhelming impression one receives is that these deceptions are motivated merely by boredom.

The only genuine passion in *The Woman Hater* is that of the gluttonous courtier Lazarello, who gives his all in word and deed to win dinner invitations. His particular quest throughout the play is for the head of an umbrana fish, a rare delicacy, which is passed from courtier to courtier in return for favors. Though Lazarello's interest is the basest, he sparks more interest than any other character, because he seems to be the only figure who clearly attaches value to anything.

Although many commentators consider *The Woman Hater* primarily the work of Beaumont, with relatively few scenes exhibiting characteristic Fletcherian diction, the play must be considered essentially a collaboration. Its tone of cynical ennui, besides its structural emphasis on the individual scene rather than on the architectonics of the whole play, makes it very similar to *Philaster*, *A King and No King*, and other Beaumont-Fletcher tragicomedies. It is also so different in every way from *The Knight of the Burning Pestle* that one has no reason to consider *The Woman Hater* substantially the work of Beaumont alone.

The differences in tone and structure between *The Woman Hater* and *The Knight of the Burning Pestle* are so great that they can hardly be overstated. Where the earlier play exemplifies the typical jadedness of court life in the Beaumont-Fletcher world, the play of one year later offers an optimistic, highly original vision of human harmony. *The Knight of the Burning Pestle* is a boldly imaginative play, unconventional in some startling ways, yet fruitfully adapting conventions of the Elizabethan comic stage to Beaumont's fresh purpose. For example, the play features even more music and song than a typical Shakespearean comedy, with popular tunes and love lyrics helping to create and sustain an atmosphere of romance that would be for Beaumont's audience both idyllic and familiar. From Jonson's early comedies, such as *Every Man in His Humour* (pr. 1598, pb. 1601), Beaumont borrows a satiric perspective within which human foibles and pretensions are seen not as evil but as humbling and ironic. To Robert Greene, Thomas Dekker, and Thomas Heywood, he owes the ebullience of his middle-class characters, who carry his message of joy and harmony, even though his satire frequently makes sport of the outspoken citizen.

The Knight of the Burning Pestle is clearly Beaumont's work alone. The Beaumont-Fletcher plays have been frequently characterized as dominated by the sensational scene rather than moved forward by the plot. In plays such as *Philaster* and *A King and No King*, the plots often seem absurdly manipulated to bring certain volatile characters into confrontation; little thought seems to have been paid to the dramatic working out of a key idea or to the meaning of a conflict beyond the voltage which it can generate. In *A King and No King*, for example, the audience knows that the hero and heroine are brother and sister; the characters do not. The plot is constructed so that the two fall in love, are brought together in a passionate love scene, and then are shocked to discover the truth. There is no exploration of the moral alternatives, no facing up to the conflict between taboo and instinct; there is only the voyeuristic titillation of the audience. Conversely, *The Knight of the Burning Pestle* de-emphasizes the individual scene; all scenes are brief, with dialogues frequently interrupted by the surprising arrival of new characters. Emphasis is on movement toward resolution of the central conflict, which is nothing less than the open clash of two bourgeois ideas: romantic optimism and the virtues of industry.

Through a plot that juggles two or three subplots simultaneously, so that even as one story progresses, the audience is aware of events occurring elsewhere, momentum builds to a romantic resolution that leaves all characters reconciled and the spirit of comedy triumphant.

A description of the play's movement suggests some of the complexity of its structure. The players enter, purporting to present a play entitled *The London Merchant*, presumably a typically anti-middle-class vehicle suited to Blackfriars taste. From the audience, however, comes a "Citizen," George the grocer, and his wife, Nell, who upbraid the players for their prejudice and demand that their apprentice, Rafe, be allowed to perform heroic scenes to honor the grocers of London. To humor the obstreperous pair, the players let Rafe give his speeches, similar to those that bourgeois audiences would have heard in the chivalric fantasies played at the outdoor theaters. At various points throughout the play, the intended performance is again interrupted by outbursts from the Citizens, so that Rafe can orate, sometimes alone but also in impromptu scenes hastily concocted between Rafe and one or two of the players. Surprisingly, Rafe turns out to be no ignorant blowhard, but a marvelously bright and multifaceted performer. Though the players never admit Rafe's talents, the audience observes as the play proceeds how readily they adapt themselves to meet the histrionic whims of George and Nell.

Meanwhile, the intended play also proceeds. As George had suspected, it does make "girds at Citizens," but, ironically, its hero and heroine are also middle-class; thus, the overall tone is not antibourgeois. Moreover, the satire always remains gentle. The play's most amazing character, old Merrythought, displays an utterly joyful faith in Providence that allows romantic optimism always to dominate the urge to find fault.

Simply told, *The London Merchant* begins by presenting the plan of Venturewell—the London merchant of the title—to marry his daughter, Luce, to a loyal but dull apprentice, Humphrey. Luce, however, loves Jasper Merrythought, another apprentice, who has been discharged by the merchant for his outspokenness—and for his attentions to Luce. Jasper has also been exiled from his home by his mother, who has decided to take the family belongings and leave her husband, whose carefree ways she can no longer tolerate. With no money and in fear of the merchant, Jasper and Luce run off to be married; they, like old Merrythought, believe that things will always turn out for the best, if one does not worry.

Lo and behold, they are right. Through a surprising set of coincidences and a clever stratagem engineered by Jasper, the couple eventually wins the father's blessings, and the Merrythoughts, husband and wife, mother and son, are reconciled. Indeed, the sense of harmony is so pervasive that even the interludes by Rafe contribute to the overall effect. The players' growing acceptance of Rafe as a performer parallels the merchant's acceptance of Jasper and Luce and Mistress Merrythought's return to her husband.

It is easy to see why *The Knight of the Burning Pestle* failed in its time. For one reason, Beaumont seems to have tried the play on the wrong audience. Romantic comedies about grocers (the pestle was the symbol of the grocers' guild) and other members of the middle class were doomed at the Blackfriars, even if they satirized tradesmen and their wives for their bluntness, ignorance, greed, and gullibility. Beaumont and the players perhaps thought, wrongly, that the sparkling good fun of this play would make the audience forget its animosities.

An equally important reason for its contemporary failure was its unconventional structure, and this might have ruined it for an audience at the outdoor theaters as quickly as it did for the viewers at the Blackfriars. Other plays, such as John Marston's *The Malcontent* (pr. 1604), include feigned confrontations between audiences and actors, but there are not any so fully instrumental to the play as those in *The Knight of the Burning Pestle*. No doubt the Blackfriars audience expected George and Nell to be harshly put down by the players when the couple first interrupted the action. When, however, their behavior was condoned and when, even worse, Rafe became a key performer, the audience was certainly confused, its dramatic expectations thoroughly thwarted. Though Elizabethan and Jacobean theatergoers tolerated many structural innovations, one does not find in this period any other play that so deeply questions the relationship between actor and spectator. One wonders indeed if Beaumont realized the originality of his venture before it was produced. Whatever the answer, one can speculate that the failure of this wonderful play led him to distrust his singular talents and to cultivate the partnership with Fletcher that won him popularity, but not lasting fame.

Other major works

POETRY: *Salmacis and Hermaphroditus*, 1602; *Poems*, 1640.

Bibliography

Gayley, Charles Mills. *Beaumont, the Dramatist*, 1914.

Sprague, Arthur Colby. *Beaumont and Fletcher on the Restoration Stage*, 1926.

Waith, Eugene. *The Pattern of Tragicomedy in the Works of Beaumont and Fletcher*, 1952.

Wallis, Lawrence B. *Fletcher, Beaumont, and Company: Entertainers to the Jacobean Gentry*, 1947.

Wilson, John Harold. *The Influence of Beaumont and Fletcher on Restoration Drama*, 1928.

Christopher J. Thaiss

SAMUEL BECKETT

Born: Foxrock, Ireland; April 13, 1906

Principal drama

En attendant Godot, pb. 1952, pr. 1953 (*Waiting for Godot*, pb. 1954, pr. 1955); *Fin de partie: Suivi de Acte sans paroles*, pr., pb. 1957 (*Endgame: A Play in One Act; Followed by Act Without Words: A Mime for One Player*, pr., pb. 1958; music by John Beckett); *All That Fall*, pr., pb. 1957, pr. 1968 (revised) (radio play); *Krapp's Last Tape*, pr., pb. 1958 (one act); *Embers*, pr., pb. 1959 (radio play); *Act Without Words II*, pr., pb. 1960 (one-act mime); *Happy Days*, pr., pb. 1961 (two acts); *Play*, pr. 1963, pb. 1963-1964 (German), pr., pb. 1964 (English) (one act); *Come and Go: Dramaticule*, pr., pb. 1965 (German), pr., pb. 1966 (French), pb. 1967, pr. 1968 (English) (one scene); *Film*, pr. 1965, pb. 1967 (screenplay); *That Time*, pr., pb. 1976; *Footfalls*, pr., pb. 1976; *A Piece of Monologue*, pr. 1979; *Rockaby*, pr., pb. 1981; *Ohio Impromptu*, pr. 1981, *Catastrophe*, pr. 1982; *Company*, pr. 1983.

Other literary forms

Samuel Beckett opened his literary career with a scattering of highly personal and almost completely hermetic poems in English, stylistically much in the manner of Arthur Rimbaud, Jules Laforgue, and their French successors. Of these, the most notable are *Whoroscope* (1930) and *Echo's Bones and Other Precipitates* (1935). From 1938 on, he also published a small number of poems in French. Finally, in 1958, he produced *An Anthology of Mexican Poetry*, a translation of an anthology of Octavio Paz.

As a writer of fiction, Beckett has exercised an enormous influence, comparable to that of his drama. An early collection of short stories, *More Pricks than Kicks* (1934), and his first two novels, *Murphy* (1938) and *Watt* (written between 1942 and 1944 but not published until 1953), were written in English. He began writing fiction in French with *Mercier et Camier* (written in 1946, published in French in 1970, and published in 1974 in English translation as *Mercier and Camier*), and since that time virtually all of his fiction has been written in French. His masterpiece is the trilogy of novels consisting of *Molloy* (1951; English translation, 1955), *Malone meurt* (1951; *Malone Dies*, 1956), and *L'Innommable* (1953; *The Unnamable*, 1958). Beckett has also turned to shorter forms, publishing a number of extremely brief texts, of which *Le Dépeupleur* (1971; *The Lost Ones*, 1972) is representative. Finally, he has produced one extended work of criticism, a monograph written early in his career, *Proust* (1931), a number of radio plays and teleplays, and a screenplay, *Film*.

Achievements

One of Beckett's principal achievements as a playwright is to have pointed the way toward a totally new concept of drama, in which the balance between verbal and visual elements can be varied in either direction, to the total exclusion of one or the other. Beckett turned to the theater comparatively late in his career; unlike most major dramatists, he did not possess from the outset a three-dimensional imagination. Wholly at variance, for example, with Antonin Artaud, he did not begin with a concept of space, subsequently to be filled with objects and people, but rather with a sound of voices which could be either infinite or, like the mind of his character Murphy, "bounded in a nutshell," so that for Beckett the dimensions of the stage itself are never more than arbitrary, or at best symbolic, restraints on the thoughts and movements of those who evolve within them. Of movement, moreover, there is virtually none—at best, formal and prearranged gestures, as in *Act Without Words II*, or mathematically conceived permutations and combinations of stage business, as in the exchange-of-hats scene in *Waiting for Godot*, or in the linking-of-hands scene in *Come and Go*.

This "theatre of immobility" had its predecessors in the French tradition, notably with Paul Claudel and with Henry de Montherlant, but no previous dramatist had conceived of an entire drama (*Play*, or *Not I*, 1972, or *Ohio Impromptu*) in terms of a *total* motionlessness. In the earlier plays, it might have seemed that this lack of a three-dimensional conception must prove to be a dead end. Instead, it has proved to be one of Beckett's major assets, for it has enabled him to transcend completely the traditional limitations of stage space and stage dimensions, and to move effortlessly from the space-free medium of radio drama, by way of the miniature two-dimensionality of the television screen, toward a concept of stage space as a series of geometrical blueprints on a drawing board.

The power and the fascination that emanate from this type of theater— barren of those devices normally required to hold an audience's attention— originate in Beckett's ability to penetrate the intellectual and metaphysical dilemmas that obsess the twentieth century mind.

Two final points need to be taken into account in any general assessment of Beckett's drama, and of these, the first is negative: his total lack of concern with social or political issues. The Brechtian invasion which so profoundly affected the French theater from 1955 onward left him completely untouched, in ideology no less than in technique. For Beckett, man is not, or never willingly, a social animal. All of Beckett's characters are in essence solitaries; even when, in the earlier plays such as *Waiting for Godot* and *Endgame*, a comparatively traditional dialogue is used, the protagonists, Vladimir and Estragon, Hamm and Clov, seem to represent the two voices of a single being rather than two genuinely autonomous characters.

Beckett's most characteristic form of expression is the monologue interrupted by silence; it is one of his most significant achievements to have
developed a form of drama based essentially, if paradoxically, on the
monologue.

The novels of Beckett's trilogy, *Molloy, Malone Dies,* and *The Unnamable,* consist of monologues almost entirely, but these have little to contribute to the drama as such. By contrast, in Beckett's first published novel,
Murphy, there occurs in the closing pages a passage which, by its interweaving of monologue and silence, clearly foreshadows the later plays. Celia is lamenting the death of Murphy:

> I was a piece out of him that he could not go on without, no matter what I did.
> (*A rest.*)
> He had to leave me to be what he was before he met me, only worse, or better, no
> matter what I did.
> (*A long rest.*)
> I was the last exile.
> (*A rest.*)

And so the passage continues. Technically, the pattern of Winnie's monologue in *Happy Days,* or the monologue of the Voice in *Footfalls,* is virtually identical to that of this passage in *Murphy,* and it is evident, therefore,
that the structure of the later dramas existed in embryo in Beckett's mind
almost from the outset of his career.

The last element which characterizes Beckett's dramatic progress is his
steady trend toward condensation. Only two of his plays are conventionally
full-length, *Waiting for Godot* and *Happy Days,* both in two acts, and even
during this first period, he was showing a preference for the compression
and the density imposed by the one-act form (*Endgame, Embers,* and so
on). Indeed, his last full-length work in any form was the novel *Comment
c'est* (1961; *How It Is,* 1964). From 1960 on—perhaps encouraged in this
direction by the discovery of the film or television scenario in which several
pages of dialogue can provide material for a program of forty minutes
duration or more—he began to experiment with "miniature" dramas, of
which the first of major significance was the "dramaticule" *Come and Go;*
all of his later dramatic work has adopted this form. These dramaticules
are, without exception, tragic meditations on the metaphysical condition of
man, composed of halting monologue, immobility, and silence, devoid of
color (significantly, in his teleplays, Beckett invariably uses black and
white), in which the words drop like stones into an empty well, bringing
Blaise Pascal to mind. Jean Anouilh, reviewing the world premiere of *Waiting for Godot,* observed most perceptively that it reminded him of Pascal's
Pensées (1670) performed by the Brothers Fratellini (a famous team of
clowns). Progressively the clownish element has evaporated (perhaps the
last trace of it can be discovered in *Film*), and one is left, in works such as

Footfalls, Ghost Trio (1977), or *Ohio Impromptu*, with the somber meditations of a twentieth century ascetic upon that most obsessive of all Pascalian themes: "The Wretchedness of Man without God."

Biography

Samuel Barclay Beckett was born in Foxrock, a prosperous suburb in the southern part of Dublin, on April 13, 1906 (there is some evidence that he was born a month earlier), the second son of a successful quantity surveyor of remote Huguenot extraction. His childhood was happy. He attended Earlsfort House, a preparatory school, in Dublin, and, from 1920 to 1923, he attended Portora Royal School, in Enniskillen, County Fermanagh, Northern Ireland. He showed a remarkable talent for sport, excelling at cricket and swimming. In October, 1923, he entered Trinity College, Dublin, whence he was graduated in 1927 with honors in French and Italian, together with a sound knowledge of German and Spanish. During these university years, he acquired his passionate interest in Dante; he also frequented both the Abbey and the Gate theaters. His intellectual curiosity for French life and culture was stimulated by a French *lecteur*, Alfred Péron, a Surrealist poet who later became his friend and companion.

In October, 1928, after a few months as a schoolteacher, Beckett received one of the most coveted of all appointments open to young graduates in French: that of *lecteur d'anglais* at the École Normale Supérieure in Paris. He was received on terms of intimacy into both French and Anglo-Irish circles; in particular, he was welcomed by James Joyce (then working on *Finnegans Wake*, 1939), Joyce's family and his collaborators, and Eugene Jolas and the group who ran the international avant-garde review *Transition*. It was during this period that he began writing seriously: poems (*Whoroscope*), short stories, and above all, criticism ("Dante . . . Bruno. Vico . . . Joyce," 1929; *Proust*). On the expiration of his appointment at the École Normale Supérieure, he was named assistant lecturer in modern languages at Trinity College, Dublin. In October, 1930, he took up the post, only to resign some fifteen months later.

There followed some five years of rather desultory wanderings, from London to Dublin, from Paris to Kassel and Munich. In 1934, Beckett's first volume of stories, *More Pricks than Kicks*, was published, and was immediately banned by the Irish censor, an occurrence which may have contributed to his vow never to live more than one month out of any year in his native country. In 1937, he definitively took up residence in Paris. There, on January 7, 1939, an incident occurred that had a considerable effect on his life: Walking out after dark, he was attacked and stabbed by a pimp. First aid was administered by a passing *conservatoire* student, Suzanne Deschevaux-Dumesnil, who thus entered Beckett's life and thereafter refused to leave it (they were married eventually in 1961). Moreover, when the pimp, having been arrested, was questioned by Beckett as to why he had attacked him, he replied simply that he had not the faintest idea. Beckett noted the point.

In June, 1940, when the German Army occupied Paris, Beckett and Suzanne retreated for four months to Arcachon, but as soon as the immediate danger was past, they returned to Paris. There, Beckett, though apolitical, was so disgusted by the Nazi treatment of the Jews that he joined a Resistance group; in March 1945, he would be awarded the Croix de Guerre by General Charles de Gaulle. In August, 1942, Beckett's group was betrayed to the Germans; with less than an hour or two to spare, he and Suzanne escaped from Paris and made their way, mainly on foot, toward the extreme south of France. There, in the isolated village of Roussillon, they spent the next two and a half years, Beckett's most dangerous enemy being not the Nazis but boredom. It was in Roussillon that he wrote *Watt*. With the liberation, he returned briefly to Ireland to see his mother (May Beckett died in August, 1950, thus severing his last ties with his native land), and for the last few months of 1945, he worked as storekeeper and interpreter with the Irish Red Cross at Saint-Lô, in the French province of Normandy.

By the end of 1945, Beckett was back in his flat in the rue des Favorites. He then began the now famous "siege in the room," which lasted for twelve or more years, in the course of which he wrote the majority of the works for which he is known throughout the world. Because of the efforts of Suzanne, who acted as his agent, he discovered an enthusiastic publisher in Jérôme Lindon, of the Éditions de Minuit, and in 1953, his name became internationally known with the success of *Waiting for Godot*. When he was awarded the Nobel Prize for Literature in 1969, the honor merely confirmed his unquestioned eminence; aside from the intrinsic merit of his works, he is among the two or three most influential writers of his time.

Analysis

Waiting for Godot, Samuel Beckett's first and best-known play, is a meditation upon the condition of man imprisoned within the obdurate and inexplicable dimension of time. In the bare scene—"A country road. A tree. Evening"—two down-and-outs, Vladimir and Estragon, are awaiting the arrival of Godot, that enigmatic figure who will decide their destiny, relieve them of the responsibility of living. Who Godot may be remains a mystery. "If I had known," replied Beckett in response to a query from his first American director, Alan Schneider, "I should have said so in the play." Godot is the "end," the impossible end which logically must exist yet which can never be reached or ascertained—the end which alone can vouchsafe to the human consciousness the privilege of ascertaining its own existence. About Vladimir and Estragon there is something clownish—their bouts of music-hall repartee, their battered bowlers—but there is something no less clownish about Godot. If God(*ot?*) created man in His own image, and if the existence of man is absurd, then, logically, God is absurd also. In French, the language in which the play was originally written, Charlie Chaplin, the supreme clown of all time, is known as Charl*ot* . . . (God)*ot*. In the absent image of Godot, however, there is something menacing as well. Vladimir and Estragon are all too human; God(*ot*), Who, before He created man, created "that double-headed monster of salvation and damnation, Time," is more sinister: a clown without a sense of humor. He is the ultimate tantalizer, promising that which can never be realized: the definitive knowledge of the Self.

Time was; time is; the problem is, whether time will continue to be, forever, or whether time *might* end (and Godot *might* come). Upon the endless verbal exchanges of Vladimir and Estragon, all designed as "games" to "kill" time, intrude two further characters: Pozzo and his slave Lucky. Pozzo exudes the company executive's confidence in the here and now; Lucky, who can talk only when he has his hat on, is gifted, Cassandra-like, with a terrifying vision of the future, when all life will have been extinguished for all eternity: "the stones so blue so calm alas alas. . . . " For Vladimir and Estragon, the vision is too overwhelming. They forcibly remove Lucky's hat, reducing him to silence, and the dialogue designed to kill time is resumed.

There is, however, a possibility even more disquieting than that of a time never-ending: a time that is cyclical. All that was, when it reaches its end, will begin all over again—perhaps an infinitesimal degree nearer the impossible ending, the impossible knowledge-of-self, but so little advanced that the progress (unless Godot should come, which he does not) is even more frustrating than if time had been annihilated altogether. Thus, act 2 of *Waiting for Godot*, which opens with a traditional bit of doggerel embodying a totally cyclical form of narrative, ends, as act 1 had opened, in total immobility: waiting for Godot.

Within this cyclical construction, however, Beckett, for purposes that are both illustrative and dramatic, has emphasized the contrast between time and timelessness. Pozzo, intruding a second time, has gone blind, and Lucky is now dumb. For Pozzo, time is moving ever faster, his watch recording not the hours but the years; for Estragon, time has slowed down so that it seems, momentarily at least, to have stopped altogether. Meanwhile, the tree, the standard of normal time, has put out leaves:

ESTRAGON: Leaves?
VLADIMIR: In a single night.
ESTRAGON: It must be spring.
VLADIMIR: But in a single night.
ESTRAGON: I tell you, we weren't here yesterday.

The audience knows, moreover, that the play will, on the next night, begin all over again; nothing ends, nothing *can* end. In this vision of the anguish of man at odds with time, all beginnings are illusions. The beginning holds a delusive promise of significance; time *is*, and through time come destruction, decay, and disillusionment, but the end, the one factor that can redeem the promise of the beginning, is as remote as is the resolution of the recurring decimal. Godot *is*, but Godot will not come—not today. "Christ have mercy on us!" exclaims Vladimir, as the play draws to its close. Christ, however, whose figure pervades the imagery of the play—Christ, too, was caught up in the web of time.

In *Endgame*, the setting is a single room, a closed system, the inside of a skull, with two windows like eyes, looking out on all that remains of an irrelevant world. In the center of the room sits Hamm, the Self, blind and motionless, not even a reality, but an actor acting the Self—scarcely that, perhaps, but rather a stage prop, from which, as from the seats in the stalls, the dust-sheets are removed before the performance and replaced as soon as it is over. About him revolves his servant, Clov, who is perhaps also his son. Clov is the "I" detached from the Self, having no reality save as a "vice-exister" of the Self, in the same way as the Self is a Nothing, a Void, without the I. Both are eternally incompatible with each other yet eternally inseparable.

Behind the present lies the past. Behind Hamm, each ensconced in a dustbin, live Nagg and Nell, Hamm's parents, unforgivable and arbitrary authors of that beginning which has no end. In his lifelong obsession with Dante's *The Divine Comedy*, Beckett's main interest has always resided in *Purgatory*. Both Hell and Paradise are outside time, but Purgatory is the place of waiting, waiting for time to run out. "Finished," says Clov, "It's finished, nearly finished, it must be nearly finished." Then, taking up one of the "dialectical demonstrations," or parables, of "that old Greek," the ancient philosopher Zeno, he continues, "Grain upon grain, one by one, and one day, suddenly, there's a heap, a little heap. . . ." Zeno had predicated a man with a sack of millet, a man who, first, tipped half of his load onto the ground in a heap, then half again, and so on. Pure mathematics can circumscribe the infinite; if ordinary man could do likewise, then the heap might one day be completed. Man, however, being circumscribed by temporality, can never do so, for the nearer the ideal sum approaches to the totality, the slower it increases. The heap becomes "the *impossible* heap." Without its completion, however, there is no release. The Purgatory of *Endgame* is a compass point or two nearer to Hell than had been the "Country Road with Tree" of *Waiting for Godot*. The note of despair, consequently, is intensified. The world beyond the windows, likewise, is a degree nearer to its ultimate annihilation: a desert of burned-out emptiness. Hamm and Clov are the last, the *very* last, of the living. The familiar objects which have given meaning to their existence are running out, even faster than time itself: "No more bicycles ... no more pain-killer. ..." Yet the idea of meaninglessness is the most difficult one of all for the human mind to accept, for what is mind, if not the apprehension of meaning?

> HAMM: We're not beginning to ... to ... mean something?
> CLOV: Mean something! You and I, mean something! Ah, that's a good one!

"End*game*": the "play" (in both senses of the word) is structured like a game of chess—Hamm as King, Clov as Knight—and the outcome, inevitably, is stalemate rather than checkmate. The end of the game implies both that theater is a game and that existence itself is a game—that is, an occupation contrived to pass the time—while time itself proceeds toward its end, or its beginning, indifferent and impervious. It is a game having its own rules, conventions, and inviolable commandments, yet in the end, it is gratuitous. The game that ends in stalemate, that concludes without concluding, is the most futile of all. Such is the conclusion of *Endgame*.

The same line of reasoning is pursued further in the radio play *All That Fall*. Man is futile, but man is created in God's image. Logically, therefore, God also is futile, but God, in addition to being futile, is dangerous—a criminal lunatic empowered with the management of the world that He has made. Man, for all the absurdity of his existence, is at least more sane than God, capable at least of recognizing the criminality of God and launching an accusation. For God, not man, invented death, and God, not man, endowed humanity with the knowledge of death. This is the theme of *All That Fall*, one of the more bitterly ironic commentaries on the notion of a benevolent God in the whole of the God-obsessed modern French theater.

The play takes its title from Psalms 145:14: "The Lord upholdeth all that fall and raiseth up all those that be bowed down." Old Maddy Rooney, scarcely able to walk, sets off down the road to meet her husband, blind Dan Rooney, arriving by train at the "pretty little wayside station"—with its view over the Leopardstown Racecourse—and is helped on her way by various clownlike local characters of the authentic Irish musical-comedy variety. The train is late, delayed, so it would appear, by a child's having fallen out of a carriage door and having been killed on the line. Infinitely slowly, the two decrepits walk home together. From their fragmentary conversation as they walk, the suggestion emerges (though it is never more than a suggestion) that it was old blind Dan who pushed the child out of the train. "The Lord upholdeth all that fall ... "?

Among Beckett's dramas, *All That Fall* is the most realistic and at the same time the most "Irish," but neither the realism nor the Irishness is, in the last analysis, more than outward show; they have little intrinsic value. Realism, in fact—as so often in Beckett—has as its primary functions those of disguising, and at the same time of rendering palatable, an underlying metaphysical reality. This reality is the factor of death—no longer the *angoisse* of the Self-that-cannot-die, but the arbitrary and intolerable fact of death itself: the ultimate Absurd. From the opening strains of Franz Shubert's *Death and the Maiden* quartet to the final revelation of Dan's participation in the death of the child, the drama is a litany of death. When the Preacher's text, proclaiming a merciful God, is announced, Dan and Maddy join in wild laughter. The function of *All That Fall* would seem to have been to get God out of Beckett's system once and for all. That accomplished, he could go ahead.

Embers, Beckett's next play for radio, while not one of his most outstanding achievements, marks a milestone in the development of his dramatic technique. It is constructed in three-part sonata form, a movement of dramatic dialogue encompassed by two lengthy sections of monologue; for the first time, in terms of pure drama, it is the monologue which predominates. This monologue itself, moreover, incorporates sections of dramatic dialogue, related second hand by Henry, the narrator:

> (. . . *following conversation, then back in the room.*)
>   HOLLOWAY: My dear Bolton, it is now past midnight, if you would be good enough—
> (*Gets no further.*)
>   BOLTON: please! PLEASE! . . .

The telegraphic style, the nagging repetitions, the stories within stories, all pointless and inconclusive, the old men of the narrative—"old men, great trouble, white world, not a sound"—all of these elements announce the dramatic meditations of the later Beckett. "White world, great trouble, not a sound, only the embers"—the embers of the fire of life, of love, of marriage, the past, dying but never dead, never ended, continue to smolder into the present.

In *Krapp's Last Tape*, Beckett's first uninterrupted dramatic monologue for the live theater, the Essential Self and the Apparent Self confront each other in the context of a tape recorder. Self-Past and Self-Present attempt, and fail, to resolve their discordances into a harmony of potential coexistence. As Krapp, a "wearish" and derelict old man addicted to whiskey and bananas, has lived, so he has recorded his life, at intervals, on tape, an innovation of the 1950's, not to be found in Dante's Purgatory. In this play, in a more literal sense than ever before in Beckett's work, the past consists of words—not the misleading words of memory, confused, or partially confused, with images, but words that are pure sound and nothing else. These words telescope all time into a continuous present, for Krapp *is* the voice of Krapp, yet the Krapp on the stage is the indecipherable future to the voice of Krapp on the tape. The voice of Krapp embodies a series of degrees of pastness yet exists only in the present: Switch off the apparatus, and there is no sound—Nothing. The machine itself is Krapp's identity—an identity that he contemplates with horror and disgust: "Hard to believe I was ever that young whelp. The voice! Jesus! And the aspirations!"

The machine, too, is caught up in time, in the cycles of eternity. Even when silent, Krapp's life in time is still there, on the spools: Press the button, and it all begins again, identically. "Here I end," speaks the voice of Krapp; promptly, Krapp switches off, winds the tape back, and switches on again. Once more, there is no end. Only if the tape contained nothing but silence could there be an end of speaking. To say "Here I end" is not to end, for now the words exist, repeatable *ad infinitum*. Each word is a Sartrean act: engendered out of Nothing, but once engendered, possessed of an indestructible existence. *Krapp's Last Tape* makes tangible the impasse of Existentialism.

Happy Days represents, with *Waiting for Godot*, Beckett's most important dramatic achievement. It is essentially a dramatic monologue, although Winnie's husband, Willie, contrives to contribute some forty-seven words (all mindless, irrelevant, and repetitive) to the human dialogue of marriage.

Winnie, from her opening prayer to her closing love-ditty, occupies the center of the stage, "stuck up to her diddies in the bleeding ground"—or rather, in the Zeno-heap of days. For Winnie, as for Estragon, time has staggered almost to a standstill, only to leave her entangled in eternal cycles of recurrence. The units of time have grown meaningless, yet she cannot resist them. They have a sort of "old-world flavor" about them which contributes to her "happiness," and she treasures them nostalgically, much as other women would treasure the decorations from a wedding cake. Vladimir and Estragon still hoped for night to come—not so Winnie. For her, the daylight is endless; she needs a bell to tell her when it is time to wake and when it is time to sleep. She is dead already, perhaps: This may be Hell ("this hellish sun," "this blaze of hellish light"); if so, then Hell is what lies between death and the end of time.

Winnie's strangest characteristic is her happiness, a happiness almost more frightening than the despair of *Endgame*. Winnie is resigned, eager to devour any old untruth, even poetry, to make use of any "pillow of old words" for her head, provided that it keep her "happy." She will believe that black is white if such a belief is comforting. She will even believe that God is good, as the Preacher in *All That Fall* promised, that Hell is Heaven. "Another heavenly day," her monologue begins, and her speech is studded with fragments of hymns and scraps of prayers. There is irony in this, and a great deal of bitterness, but there is also pity. Winnie is a victim, a victim of the human condition; if her only defense against the intolerable is to behave as though it were all natural and very understandable, who is there to blame her? She has the usual consolations of existence—

she tells herself stories, she has her "bag," her hoard of miscellaneous possessions, and she has the futile consolations of her sexuality. At times, she can even exercise her intellect. Nevertheless, her most formidable weapon of defense against the Absurd is her indifference.

Film, Beckett's screenplay, is silent and contains no indication of color. It is an impressive mime, set, according to Beckett himself, in a climate which is "comic and unreal," but in fact, judging by both versions which have reached the screen, realized against a background of stylized naturalism. Beckett's sad clown, "O," moves, like the later Chaplin, amid the shabby surroundings of urban semipoverty.

Perhaps as a consequence of the experiments carried out in the radio plays *Words and Music* (1962) and *Cascando* (1963), Beckett would seem to have singled out the mime as the form best suited to his profounder explorations of the purely abstract problems of Being and Perception. Hidden beneath the Buster Keaton-like antics of *Film* lies the illustrated working out of a Berkeleyan proposition: "To be is to be perceived; therefore he who ceases to be perceived ceases to be." The script is probably unique among those employed by the motion-picture industry, in that it opens with a philosophical disquisition:

> *Esse est percipi.*
> All extraneous perception suppressed, animal, human, divine, self-perception maintains in being.
> Search for non-being in flight from extraneous perception breaking down in the inescapability of self-perception. . . .

Add to this a variant of the Sartrean theme of the anguish induced by the perception of the Other, and the metastructure of the action is complete. The camera is not merely an instrument but also a perceiving eye ("E"): not merely "Others," but also *The* Other, the ultimate enemy, the Self-as-Other eternally perceiving the Self-as-Self, and thus everlastingly compelling it to exist, excluding it from the quietus of finality.

Film consists of three sections: O in the street, perceived by Others, hurrying frantically to escape; O on the staircase of his tenement, fleeing upward toward his room, his sole refuge now that the Others are left behind; and finally, O in his room, embattled against perception, door locked, window and mirror curtained, eye of dog and cat, of parrot and goldfish variously thwarted, Eye-of-God (print of the Face of God-the-Father) destroyed, photographs torn up. O sleeps in his rocking chair, quietus achieved at last, *percipi* defeated, all Others banished, balked, annihilated. Only E remains, now inside O (slight variation of focus). *Esse est percipi*—or rather, to reverse the proposition, to be perceived is to continue to be, even when the perceiver is the Self. O, his face now seen for the first time, slumps forward in anguish and despair.

As with all the best philosophical tales, and this is one of Beckett's masterpieces, *Film* works on two levels: It is a superb canvas for seriocomic clowning of the highest order, and it is a profound statement about the mystery of Being.

The bulk of Beckett's later dramatic works, whether written for the stage or for radio, may be termed meditations, condensed mini-dramas wholly symbolist in conception. In these works, as in Beckett's later, minimalist fictions, elements of an impoverished, erratically illuminated reality dissolve into the mystery of a menacing darkness.

In the opening sequence of *Waiting for Godot*, Vladimir hails Estragon: "Ah, there you are!" "*Am* I?" replies Estragon. This exchange epitomizes the whole of Beckett's technique. Beckett is certainly one of the most profound metaphysical dramatists of all time, yet the abstract conundrums of Being and Not-Being that he is exploring are consistently disguised by being given an over exact and literal interpretation in terms of the most banal of everyday phrases and actions. Thus, in terms of drama, they emerge, not as portentous, but as grotesque—sometimes pathetic, sometimes wildly comic, but, like the similarly grotesque imaginings of Hieronymus Bosch, always disturbing. Hugh Kenner, in an early essay, once described Beckett as an "academic clown." The phrase is apt. Beckett-the-Clown—like all true clowns—relies on effects that are, at bottom, of supreme simplicity, yet handled with a professional mastery of touch, timing, and poetry which gives them universal significance, while Beckett-the-Academic—most eminent Professor of Nihilistic Philosophy that he is—remains discreetly in the prompter's corner.

Other major works

NOVELS: *Murphy*, 1938; *Molloy*, 1951 (English translation, 1955); *Malone meurt*, 1951 (*Malone Dies*, 1956); *L'Innommable*, 1953 (*The Unnamable*, 1958); *Watt*, 1953; *Comment c'est*, 1961 (*How It Is*, 1964); *Mercier et Camier*, 1970 (*Mercier and Camier*, 1974); *Le Dépeupleur*, 1971 (*The Lost Ones*, 1972); *Company*, 1980; *Mal vu mal dit*, 1981 (*Ill Seen Ill Said*, 1981); *Worstward Ho*, 1983.

SHORT FICTION: *More Pricks than Kicks*, 1934; *Nouvelles et textes pour rien*, 1955 (*Stories and Texts for Nothing*, 1967); *No's Knife: Collected Shorter Prose 1947-1966*, 1967 (includes *Stories and Texts for Nothing* with other short prose); *First Love and Other Shorts*, 1974; *Pour finir encore et autres foirades*, 1976 (*Fizzles*, 1976; also as *For to End Yet Again*, 1976).

POETRY: *Whoroscope*, 1930; *Echo's Bones and Other Precipitates*, 1935; *Poems in English*, 1961; *Collected Poems in English and French*, 1977.

NONFICTION: *Proust*, 1931.

TELEPLAYS: *Eh Joe*, 1966 (*Dis Joe*, 1967); *Not I*, 1972; *Tryst*, 1976; *Shades*, 1977 (includes *Ghost Trio*, *Not I*, ... *but the clouds* ...); *Quad*,

1981.

RADIO PLAYS: *Words and Music*, 1962 (music by John Beckett); *Cascando*, 1963 (music by Marcel Mihalovici).

TRANSLATIONS: "Zone," 1972 (of Guillaume Apollinaire's poem); *An Anthology of Mexican Poetry*, 1958 (of Octavio Paz's anthology).

Bibliography

Bair, Deirdre. *Samuel Beckett: A Biography*, 1978.

Coe, Richard N. *Beckett*, 1964.

Cohn, Ruby. *Just Play: Beckett's Theater*, 1980.

Duckworth, Colin. *Angels of Darkness: Dramatic Effect in Samuel Beckett with Special References to Eugène Ionesco*, 1972.

Eliopulos, James. *Samuel Beckett's Dramatic Language*, 1975.

Fletcher, John, and John Spurling. *Beckett: A Study of His Plays*, 1978.

Foucré, Michèle. *Le Geste et la parole dans le théâtre de Samuel Beckett*, 1970.

Kenner, Hugh. *Samuel Beckett: A Critical Study*, 1962, 1968.

Knowlson, James. *Light and Darkness in the Theatre of Samuel Beckett*, 1972.

Knowlson, James, and John Pilling. *Frescoes of the Skull: The Later Prose and Drama of Samuel Beckett*, 1980.

Lyons, Charles R. *Samuel Beckett*, 1984.

Reid, Alec. *All I Can Manage, More than I Could: An Approach to the Plays of Samuel Beckett*, 1972.

Rojtman, Betty. *Forme et signification dans le théâtre de Beckett*, 1976.

Webb, Eugene. *The Plays of Samuel Beckett*, 1972.

Richard N. Coe

BRENDAN BEHAN

Born: Dublin, Ireland; February 9, 1923
Died: Dublin, Ireland; March 20, 1964

Principal drama

Gretna Green, pr. 1947; *The Quare Fellow*, pr. 1954, pb. 1956 (translation and revision of his Gaelic play "Casadh Súgáin Eile," wr. 1946); *The Big House*, pr. 1957 (radio play), pr. 1958 (staged), pb. 1961; *An Giall*, pr. 1958 (in Gaelic); *The Hostage*, pr., pb. 1958 (translation and revision of *An Giall*); *Richard's Cork Leg*, pr. 1972, pb. 1973 (begun 1960, completed posthumously by Alan Simpson, 1964).

Other literary forms

Brendan Behan's literary reputation rests on the merits of three works: *The Quare Fellow* and *The Hostage*, his dramatic masterpieces; and *The Borstal Boy* (1958), published in England by Hutchinson and in the United States by Alfred A. Knopf. The two plays were performed several times prior to their publication, and the performance rights are still retained by the Theatre Workshop in East London. *The Borstal Boy*, although often considered a novel, is actually a compilation of stories, an autobiographical narrative of Behan's adolescent years in prison. Several of the stories included in *The Borstal Boy* appeared initially in literary magazines and journals. *Brendan Behan's Island* (1962) was intended by Behan to be similar in tone and structure to John Millington Synge's *The Aran Islands* (1907), but it does not stand up to this literary comparison. Unable to write for extended periods of time in his later years, Behan began taping his stories and subsequently had them edited by his publishing guardian angel and friend, Rae Jeffs. *Brendan Behan's Island, Hold Your Hour and Have Another* (1963), *Brendan Behan's New York* (1964), and *Confessions of an Irish Rebel* (1965) are all edited results of taping sessions. *The Scarperer* (1964) was published in book form the year Behan died but had been published first as a series in *The Irish Times*, in 1953, under the pseudonym "Emmet Street." Several of Behan's works were published posthumously. Among these are *Confessions of an Irish Rebel, Moving Out*, and *A Garden Party*, and *Richard's Cork Leg*, the latter of which was begun by Behan in 1960 and ultimately completed by Alan Simpson. In addition to his plays and books, Behan contributed scores of short stories and poems on a variety of subjects to journals and newspapers throughout his life. He was as renowned for his balladeering as he was for his writings, and he composed the songs for his plays. A recording entitled *Brendan Behan Sings Irish Folksongs and Ballads*, produced by Spoken Arts Inc., provides insight into Behan's passionate personality.

Achievements

Behan has been called the most important postwar Irish writer by contemporary Irish, English, and American critics. His works represent an extraordinary mixture of Irish romance, history, patriotism, and racism. All of his works reflect, in some measure, the Irish Republican Army's efforts to rid Northern Ireland of the English. Paradoxically, his major literary successes came first in England, and though productions of *The Quare Fellow* and *The Hostage* met with moderate success in America, his most receptive audience was always in London.

Stylistically, Behan has been compared to Jonathan Swift, James Joyce, Synge, and Sean O'Casey. His treatment of the Irish in his plays and stories is simultaneously warm and biting. Clearly a social critic, Behan's writings indict law, religion, Ireland, England, and the absurdity of politics. His literary career spans barely twenty years, though the most productive of these amount to less than a decade. His first story, "I Become a Borstal Boy," was published in June, 1942, after which he regularly contributed nationalistic essays, stories, and poems to various Irish periodicals, including organs of the Irish Republican Army (IRA) such as *Fianna: The Voice of Young Ireland* and the *Wolfe Tone Weekly*.

Behan's most productive years (1953-1959) were marked by the production of both *The Quare Fellow* and *The Hostage* and the publication of *The Borstal Boy*. During these years, Behan's fame began to wane, and his creative talent floundered in a sea of alcohol. Behan wrote principally of a world of men, yet ironically it was his association with two women that accounted for much of his artistic success. Joan Littlewood, director and manager of the Theatre Workshop at the Theatre Royal, Stratford East, London, directed *The Quare Fellow* in 1956 and catapulted Behan into the international limelight. Her production of *The Hostage* in 1958 earned for Behan equally high praise. His friend Jeffs can be credited with virtually all of Behan's productivity during his final years. The publicity manager for Hutchinson's Publishing Company, she was "assigned" the obstreperous Behan in 1957. From 1957 to 1964, Jeffs's formidable task included following Behan from pub to pub, trailing and assisting him on his trips from England to America to Ireland, all the while making sure he was writing or taping his work, to be edited later. Ultimately, she performed her task as a labor of love, serving as friend and confidante to both Behan and his wife, Beatrice. Without Jeffs's tenacity, Behan's literary career would have ended in 1957 in an alcoholic stupor. In his final years, Behan became a drunken caricature of himself. The early works evidence the true spark of genius that carried him through the years of honor to the dark years plagued by alcoholism and self-doubt. It is to these early works that one must turn to capture the real genius embodied in the literature of this twentieth century Irish phenomenon.

Biography

Brendan Behan was born February 9, 1923, in Dublin, Ireland, the first child of Stephen and Kathleen (Kearney) Behan, though his mother had two sons by a previous marriage. Born into a family with radical political leanings, Behan was reared on a double dose of IRA propaganda and Catholicism. The radical Left was part of his genetic makeup. His grandmother and a grandfather were jailed for their roles in the revolution, the former for illegal possession of explosives when she was seventy years old and the latter for his part in the murder of Lord Cavendish. Both of Behan's parents fought in the Irish Revolution and in the Troubles. Ultimately jailed for his participation in the violence, Behan's father saw his son for the first time through prison bars.

Behan was a precocious child whose reverence for writers was spawned by his father's readings of Samuel Pepys, Charles Dickens, Émile Zola, George Bernard Shaw, and various polemical treatises to his children. By Behan's own account, his home was filled with reading, song, and revolution. Juxtaposed to this violent heritage was Behan's conservative religious training. He attended schools run by the Sisters of Charity of St. Vincent de Paul, where he was a favorite, and another operated by the Irish Christian Brothers, where he found himself in constant disfavor. His militant disposition surfaced early, when at the age of nine he joined the Fianna Éireann, the junior wing of the IRA. Most of his early adult years were spent in prison. Arrested in Liverpool at the age of sixteen for participating in IRA bombings in England, Behan spent three years in the Borstal, the English correctional institution for juvenile delinquents. Released in 1941 and deported to Ireland, Behan was again incarcerated the following year for shooting at a policeman. He had served four years of a fourteen-year sentence when he was released in 1946. Additional stays in jail followed throughout his life.

The worldview projected in Behan's works recalls the environment in which he matured, one dominated by a radical family and by his prison experience. Cradled in the romance of revolution, Behan was cultured in a more traditional sense. Kathleen and Stephen Behan reared their children with a love for music and literature. Nurtured with a reverential attitude toward Kathleen's brother Peadar Kearney, a noted composer who wrote the Irish national anthem, the Behan children learned his marches and ballads in a home continuously filled with music. According to Colbert Kearney, Behan's precociousness as a child was largely attributable to the education he received at home. His father instilled in him a deep-seated respect for Irish writers and rhetoricians. He learned to read at an early age and was fond of memorizing speeches by Irish patriots such as Robert Emmet. Not as readily discernible in Behan's work is the influence of his strict upbringing in Catholicism. Behan had a love-hate relationship with the Church, and often his works condemn religion. Yet one of his most bitter disappointments came when he was excommunicated while serving time in prison. Some critics believe that this was a crisis in Behan's life from which he never recovered.

Behan began writing while in prison, and his first story, "I Become a Borstal Boy," was published in *The Bell* in 1942. The plays, poems, and short stories written during his prison terms are all autobiographical. The years from 1946 to 1956 were the most ambitious of his career. For a time he lived in Paris, but he was eventually drawn back to Ireland, where he worked as a housepainter and free-lance journalist. During this hiatus from serious encounters with the law, he married Beatrice ffrench-Salkeld, daughter of the noted Irish artist Cecil Salkeld. Behan's major break came when Alan Simpson agreed to produce *The Quare Fellow* at the Pike Theatre in Dublin in 1954. The play met with critical acclaim, but, to Behan's disappointment, the more prestigious Irish theaters such as the Abbey refused to stage it. This rejection spurred in Behan an overwhelming desire to be accepted as an artist in his own country. *The Quare Fellow* was noticed by Joan Littlewood, whose 1956 London production made Behan an international sensation. He followed this success with another play, *An Giall*, which he wrote in Gaelic and later translated as *The Hostage*. Littlewood's subsequent production of *The Hostage* proved an even greater success than *The Quare Fellow*.

Critics proclaimed Behan a literary genius, but he was destroyed by his success. His notorious interruptions of his plays with drunken speeches shouted from his seat in the audience and his intoxication during interviews for the British Broadcasting Corporation, enhanced the "bad boy" image he so carefully cultivated, but ultimately it killed him. The most tragic repercussion of his alcoholism proved to be his inability to sit and write for an extended period of time. *The Hostage* was Behan's last good work. When his writing sojourns to Ibiza, his favorite retreat, and America and Canada produced little, he resorted to taping sessions to meet his publication contracts. By 1960, after two major breakdowns as well as intermittent stays in hospitals to dry out, Behan was a shell of his former robust personality. Riding on his reputation of acknowledged artistry, he found himself incapable of writing, which led him to drink even more. Behan died March 20, 1964, at the age of forty-one. Several of his edited works published after his death created a brief, cultish interest in the man and his writing, but this adulation soon passed. What remains is the recognition that Behan was one of the finest twentieth century Irish writers. His talent will be recognized long after his colorful reputation has faded.

Analysis

To understand Brendan Behan's work, one must first recognize the underlying Behan legend, which is built on paradox. Frank O'Connor, writing in the *Sunday Independent* (Dublin), said of Behan that "under his turbulent exterior there was quite clearly the soul of an altar boy." Behan was a kind, gentle man who acted violently. He was insecure and feared publicity yet perpetrated outrageous stunts to capture attention; he wrote of reasonableness and absurdity in the world yet persisted in his personal irrationality. Behan was saint and sinner, moralist and profligate, and this dichotomy is carried over into his works. Even his overriding thematic consideration, a politically divided Ireland, is complex. Gordon Wickstrom believes Behan writes of three Irelands: the Ireland of contemporary, illegal Republican fanaticism, dedicated to the destruction of everything English; the Ireland of glorious memory of the Troubles and Easter Week, needing no justification beyond the private experience of valor and sacrifice; and Ireland as it actually exists, complete with police attacks, sirens, bloodbaths, and terror.

The principal themes in Behan's works are culled from his close association with the Irish Republican Army: death, freedom, and the absurdity of man's impermanence in a hostile world. Behan's major plays, *The Quare Fellow* and *The Hostage*, examine these themes through the eyes of a prisoner, a character-type that figures prominently in Behan's works. As his life stands as a series of paradoxes, so, too, does his style. Behan fills his works with unsavory gallows humor and swings erratically between comedy and tragedy in a decidedly Brechtian manner. Yet the early works are tightly structured and astonishingly poetic. Songs incorporated into his plays serve as lyric Gaelic laments but can quickly turn into obscene ditties. Behan's use of vernacular and the overwhelming sense of freedom in the lines contribute to the impressive strength of his writing. An unlikely coupling of naturalism and absurdism is characteristic of his best work. His characters are drawn from the lower classes, with Irish nationalism, bordering on racism, binding them together. Ironically, Behan's genteel audiences find it easy to empathize with his murderers, prostitutes, homosexuals, and radicals, perhaps because the sordid individuals in Behan's plays and stories are presented with a depth of compassion and understanding usually reserved for more noble literary characters.

Behan's prison years had a profound influence on him. During these stultifying periods, he became preoccupied with the two themes that dominate his works: death and freedom. In the cells and work yards of the Borstal and Mountjoy prisons, Behan mentally cataloged information about individuals, human nature, and the absurdity of the world and its systems. The examination of conflicts between gentleness and violence, a trademark of Behan's work, stems directly from his own divided nature as much as his early background. Major characters such as Dunlavin and the Warder in *The Quare Fellow*, Monsewer and Williams in *The Hostage*, or the prisoner in *The Borstal Boy* reflect various facets of his personality.

In November, 1954, *The Quare Fellow* was labeled "a powerful piece of propaganda" by A. J. Leventhal, writing in *Dublin Magazine*. This assessment of Behan's first literary and theatrical success holds true for all of his works. Though his plays do not strictly adhere to agitation-propaganda techniques used by earlier European playwrights, Behan's works are obviously propagandistic. *The Quare Fellow*, the most structured of his plays, examines the issue of capital punishment. Set in a prison, *The Quare Fellow* is a series of episodes in which the prison community prepares for the execution of the unseen titular character.

Tension is deftly established on two levels: the friction maintained in the relationship between prisoners and warders and the more insidious anxiety, hidden beneath the prattle and routine of the prison, that eats at the souls of both warders and prisoners as the moment of execution draws near. Every character waits in dread for the final moment when a man will die. Their empathetic response to ritualized, state-supported death reinforces the horror felt by the audience. The prison serves as Behan's microcosm of the world in which primal struggles of life and death as well as social struggles of promotion, acceptance, pretense, and charity are all in evidence.

The Quare Fellow opens with the singing of a man in solitary confinement, trying to keep his sanity. His haunting lament, floating over the prison grounds, becomes almost a dirge as the play progresses. The plot is moved by the institution's preparations for the day of execution. Each character fears the approach of the hour of death and manifests his uneasiness in a different way. The prisoners attempt a forced jauntiness and irreverence but are unable to call the condemned man by his Christian name, preferring instead to force on him anonymity, calling him only "the quare fellow." As the climax approaches and the moment of death is imminent, a prisoner cynically announces the offstage procession to the gallows as though it were the start of a horse race: "We're off, in this order: The Governor, The Chief, two screws Regan and Crimmin, the quare fellow between them. . . ." Yet this comic diversion is incapable of diluting the dramatic effect of the climax when the clock strikes the hour and the prisoners wail, howl, and roar in primal lamentation, as the trap drops and the quare fellow hangs. The hero of the play, the quare fellow, never appears onstage. Dunlavin, a crusty, experienced prisoner, and Regan, a compassionate warder, are the principal characters. This den of thieves and murderers has its own order, a social hierarchy based on criminal offenses and experience. Sex offenders are ostracized by the prison community, and Dunlavin bemoans his misfortune at having one placed in the cell next to his. The sex offender, for his part, is appalled that he must live among murderers and takes to quoting Thomas Carlyle.

Religion is brutally satirized in *The Quare Fellow*. The hypocritical representative from the Department of Justice is dubbed "Holy Healey" by the inmates, who paste religious pictures on their walls to curry favor during his visits. Dunlavin's friend and neighbor in the cellblock comments on the importance of the Bible to prisoners, stating, "Many's the time the Bible was a consolation to a fellow all alone in the old cell," not for its spiritual comfort, but because prisoners rolled mattress bits within its pages and smoked them. Dunlavin, in turn, recounts how in his first twelve months he smoked his way halfway through Genesis. The executioner, referred to imperially as "Himself," cannot face his job in a sober state and must be accompanied by a teetotaling, Bible-quoting, hymn-singing assistant to see him to his appointed rounds. The incongruity of this misallied pair is obvious as Jenkinson, the assistant, sings a hymn while the hangman audibly calculates the weight of the condemned man and the height of the drop needed to kill him.

Behan's vision of the value of life and the awesome power of death is painted in masterful strokes throughout *The Quare Follow*. The dignity of man, the worth of an individual life, and the inhumanity of a system devised for correctional purposes are powerfully juxtaposed in this play. The 1954 Pike Theatre production of *The Quare Fellow* was well received, but it was Joan Littlewood's direction in 1956 that made it a modern classic. Although the play has been criticized as being melodramatic, Behan mixes well-developed characters with stereotypes and caricatures to provide diverse opportunities for commentary on various levels. *The Quare Fellow* is not wholly a tragedy, nor is it merely black comedy. It is an unnatural two-backed beast that violently gives birth to Behan's pessimistic worldview.

The music-hall atmosphere of *The Hostage* differs radically from the sterile environment of *The Quare Fellow*. From the opening jig, danced by two prostitutes and two homosexuals, to the rousing chorus, sung by the corpse, Behan jars his audience with the unexpected. Like Bertolt Brecht's *The Threepenny Opera* (pr. 1928), *The Hostage* is populated by a cast of societal misfits. Brechtian influences can be noticed in the play's structure as well. *The Hostage*, according to Richard A. Duprey in *The Critic*, is an indictment of law, religion, home, country, human decency, art, and even death. What is espoused within its tenuous structure is IRA radicalism, but even this cannot escape Behan's satiric barbs. The IRA officer in the play is outraged by the shoddy accommodations—a brothel—afforded him and his political prisoner, while Pat, manager of the "brockel" and a veteran of the Easter Rebellion and the Troubles, denounces the new IRA soldiers as "white-faced loons with their trench coats, berets and teetotal badges."

Thematically, *The Hostage* compares with Behan's other major works in that the protagonist is a prisoner. Leslie Williams has committed no crime except that he is an English soldier in Ireland. Taken as a hostage by IRA reactionaries, Williams is offered in trade for a jailed Irish youth sentenced to hang. The IRA cause is felt most strongly in this play, and Behan's nationalistic biases are given ample voice in the songs about the Easter Rebellion, Monsewer's senile ravings about the days of glorious conflict, and Pat's diatribes against modern Ireland. Hidden beneath the brash, gaudy, and colorful language of the play, such weighty underpinnings emerge in flashes of seriousness.

A mélange of dramatic styles pushes the plot through a series of vignettes, comedy routines, and song-and-dance numbers. Songs, jokes, and malapropisms abound in this very political play. Individually, the characters lack depth and are only one step removed from the stereotyped clowns of burlesque houses. Collectively, they champion traditional Irish Republicanism while at the same time denouncing the absurdity of its violent contemporary manifestations. This is a play about the Republican cause; it is also a play about the value of life. Leslie Williams is an apolitical character who dies needlessly, an injustice which Behan adroitly condemns. Life and death in Behan's work are never equal forces; life always triumphs. He breaks the serious mood of his final scene, in which Williams' death is disclosed, by having the corpse jump up and sing, "The bells of hell go ting a ling a ling for you but not for me. . . ."

The original Gaelic-language version of the play, *An Giall*, was a much more serious play than the version presented in the internationally acclaimed 1958 London production. The seminal version had but ten characters, whereas *The Hostage* has fifteen. Colbert Kearney notes that *An Giall* is essentially a naturalistic tragedy, while *The Hostage* is a musical extravaganza. Certainly, the latter tolerates a greater degree of bawdiness than the original. Critics charged that Joan Littlewood's company substantially altered *An Giall* while in production for *The Hostage*, yet this was partially Behan's fault. During 1957 and 1958, he was committed to two projects: translating *An Giall* into *The Hostage* for Littlewood and finishing *The Borstal Boy*. He became preoccupied with the publicity and lavish promotion given the latter and neglected his commitments to Littlewood. Consequently, parts of *The Hostage* grew out of the improvisations of the Theatre Workshop and, though sanctioned by Behan, changed the play significantly from the original work. Ulick O'Connor believes several of the non sequitur scenes in *The Hostage* were invented by Littlewood and do not reflect Behan's hand in the revision. Nevertheless, the production was a hit. *The Hostage* was selected to represent Great Britain at the prestigious Théâtre des Nations festival in 1959, and it moved to the fashionable Wyndham Theatre on London's West End. Productions of Behan's plays opened in Dublin, New York, Paris, and Berlin.

The Hostage proved to be Behan's last theatrical success. His reputation sustained him as an artist for the next six years, but his talent abandoned

him. He began another play, *Richard's Cork Leg*, but it remained unfinished at his death. *The Hostage* is not as neatly structured as *The Quare
Fellow*, though Behan's genius for dialogue and *mise en scène* pervade the
work. Behan—patriot, nationalist, and racist—is plainly seen in *The Hostage*, yet his persona, so dominant in his plays, turns to reveal Behan the
humanitarian in equally sharp focus. Brendan Behan's works, like the man,
are paradoxical. His legend lives on, supported by contemporary interest in
Behan the revolutionary and artist.

Other major works

NOVELS: *The Borstal Boy*, 1958; *The Scarperer*, 1964 (serialized 1953, as
by Emmet Street).

SHORT FICTION: *Brendan Behan's Island*, 1962; *Hold Your Hour and Have
Another*, 1963.

NONFICTION: *Brendan Behan's New York*, 1964; *Confessions of an Irish
Rebel*, 1965.

RADIO PLAYS: *A Garden Party*, pr. 1952, pb. 1967; *Moving Out*, pr. 1952,
pb. 1967.

Bibliography
Behan, Dominic. *My Brother Brendan*, 1965.
Boyle, Ted E., ed. *Brendan Behan*, 1969.
Jeffs, Rae. *Brendan Behan*, 1965.
Kearney, Colbert. *The Writings of Brendan Behan*, 1977.
McCann, Sean. *The World of Brendan Behan*, 1966.
Mikhail, E. H., ed. *The Art of Brendan Behan*, 1979.
O'Connor, Ulick. *Brendan Behan*, 1970.
Porter, Raymond J. *Brendan Behan*, 1973.
Wickstrom, Gordon M. "The Heroic Dimension in Brendan Behan's *The
Hostage*," in *Educational Theatre Journal*. XXII (1970), pp. 406-411.

Susan Duffy

APHRA BEHN

Born: England; July(?), 1640
Died: London, England; April 16, 1689

Principal drama

The Forced Marriage: Or, The Jealous Bridegroom, pr. 1670, pb. 1671; *The Amorous Prince: Or, The Curious Husband*, pr., pb. 1671; *The Dutch Lover*, pr., pb. 1673; *Abdelazer: Or, The Moor's Revenge*, pr. 1676, pb. 1677; *The Town Fop: Or, Sir Timothy Tawdry*, pr. 1676, pb. 1677; *The Rover: Or, The Banished Cavaliers, Part I*, pr., pb. 1677, *Part II*, pr., pb. 1681; *Sir Patient Fancy*, pr., pb. 1678; *The Feigned Courtesans: Or, A Night's Intrigue*, pr., pb. 1679; *The Roundheads: Or, The Good Old Cause*, pr. 1681, pb. 1682; *The City Heiress: Or, Sir Timothy Treat-All*, pr., pb. 1682; *The Lucky Chance: Or, An Alderman's Bargain*, pr. 1686, pb. 1687; *The Emperor of the Moon*, pr., pb. 1687.

Other literary forms

In addition to her plays, Aphra Behn's literary legacy includes many noteworthy works of fiction and poetry. The three-part novel entitled *Love Letters Between a Nobleman and His Sister* (1683-1687) is both her earliest and her longest narrative effort. A fictionalized version of a notorious contemporary scandal, this novel was extremely popular at the time, but it is little read today. Of much more interest to present-day readers are the shorter novels such as *The Fair Jilt: Or, The History of Prince Tarquin and Miranda* (1688) and *Oroonoko: Or, The Royal Slave* (1688). The latter is undoubtedly Mrs. Behn's most enduring literary creation in any genre. Allegedly based on her own experiences in Surinam during the 1660's, the narrative relates the tragic history of a slave of African origin named Oroonoko and his wife, Imoinda, from the viewpoint of the author herself. As the story unfolds, Mrs. Behn repeatedly exposes the deceitful and greedy nature of the European settlers and underscores the innate virtue of the novel's eponymous hero. He is, therefore, one of the earliest fictional manifestations of the archetypical "noble savage." Because of its implicit condemnation of slavery and colonialism, the novel is highly regarded as a harbinger of the crisis in political and social morality that was to trouble the conscience of Europeans in their dealings with the nonwhite population of the globe over the succeeding centuries.

Mrs. Behn's poetry is widely diverse in character. In keeping with the convention of the time, she made it a practice to provide her plays with prologues and epilogues in verse form. She also interspersed many songs within the prose dialogue of her plays. In both instances, the quality of her poetry is usually of a high order. Two of her most successful poems, in fact, appear in *Abdelazer*. The song which begins with the line "LOVE in fantastick Triumph sat" comes at the opening of act 1, and the one commencing "MAKE haste, Amintas, come away" is to be found near the end of act 2. Both of these songs are frequently anthologized. Likewise commendable are two short narrative poems entitled "The Disappointment" and "The Golden Age." While most of her occasional poetry consists of overly rhetorical panegyrics to illustrious personages, a few of the elegies are moving expressions of private grief. Perhaps the best of these are "To the Memory of George, Duke of Buckingham" and "On the Death of Edmund Waller, Esq."

Being fluent in French, Mrs. Behn began making translations from that language as a source of income late in her career. Among the French works that she translated are the maxims of the Duke François de La Rochefoucauld and two works of fiction by Bernard le Bovier de Fontenelle. More in the nature of an adaptation is her translation of Abbé Paul Tallemant's *Le Voyage de l'isle d'amour* (1663), which she published under the title *A Voyage to the Island of Love* in 1684. Tallemant's piece of fantasy is, for the most part, a prose narrative interspersed with songs, but Mrs. Behn chose to render all the prose passages as rhymed couplets. In *Lycidus: Or, The Lover in Fashion* (1688), including an adaptation of Tallemant's second voyage to the Island of Love, however, she adheres to the prose and poetry distinctions of the original text. One of the songs in *Lycidus*, starting with the line "A thousand Martyrs I have made," has proved itself to be a perennial favorite with the reading public. The fact that Mrs. Behn knew little Latin and less Greek did not prevent her from "translating" works written in those tongues. With the aid of French and English translations, she managed to turn out excellent versions of Aesop's fables for an illustrated edition published in 1687. Working chiefly from a prose paraphrase, she also produced a rhymed translation of book 6 (*Of Trees*) from Abraham Cowley's poetic treatise entitled *Sex libri plantarum* (1668). The preceding five books were translated by others, and the complete text of the *Six Books of Plants* was published shortly before Mrs. Behn's death in 1689.

Achievements

Mrs. Behn came of age during the period in English history known as the Restoration. The epoch began in 1660 with the Stuart monarchy being restored in the person of Charles II. His Royal Highness was passionately fond of the theater, and one of his first acts was to rescind the laws prohibiting the performance of plays that had been enacted in 1642 by the Long Parliament under the domination of Oliver Cromwell. While all forms of drama were thenceforth permitted to flourish, the best plays written in the succeeding era turned out to be comedies. The masterpieces of this genre were created by Sir George Etherege, William Wycherley, and William Congreve, among others. While it would be injudicious to claim that any of Mrs. Behn's comedies should be ranked with the best of Etherege, Wycherley, or Congreve, many of her plays have withstood the test of time and are fully deserving of a contemporary readership. The same is true with respect to her novel *Oroonoko*. The dramatic vitality of *Oroonoko* and many of her other works of narrative fiction is attested by the fact that several of them have been successfully adapted for the theater by other hands. Using the novel *The History of the Nun: Or, The Fair Vow-Breaker* (1689) as the source for his plot, Thomas Southerne scored one of his greatest successes as a playwright with the tragedy entitled *The Fatal Marriage: Or, The Innocent Adultery* (pr. 1694). Two years later, in 1696, he repeated this success with a dramatization of *Oroonoko*. In the same year, moreover, Mrs. Catherine Cockburn offered the theatergoing public the opportunity of seeing a play based on Mrs. Behn's novel *Agnes de Castro* (1688). The popularity of these adaptations, it should be noted, continued well into the eighteenth century.

Literary historians will always accord an honorable place to Mrs. Behn for being the first Englishwoman to become a professional author and to support herself solely by means of income derived from her writings. While it must have been a bold decision on her part to defy conventional wisdom regarding the proper mode of existence for a woman of her class, she seems not to have been seriously disadvantaged on account of her gender in pursuing a literary career and may have actually been helped by it. The only apparent adverse effect which she suffered by being a woman stemmed from the generally held belief that women are innately more virtuous than men. As a consequence of this social attitude, there was a propensity on the part of some critics, as well as the public at large, to regard her comedies as being more immoral than those of her male colleagues. This charge has been immortalized in Alexander Pope's satire *The First Epistle to the Second Book of Horace* (1737). Here, in a couplet in which he refers to Mrs. Behn by a pseudonym under which she frequently published her poetry, Pope writes: "The stage how loosely does Astraea tread,/ Who fairly puts all Characters to bed." Pope's imputation is unfair, for Mrs. Behn's plays are no more licentious, and frequently less so, than others written in that era. These charges, moreover, never proved detrimental to public attendance at performances of her plays. That she was one of the most popular playwrights of her age is a matter of historical record.

Biography

Reliable information pertaining to the first half of Aphra Behn's life is virtually nonexistent. The sparse biographical information for this period is, moreover, frequently contradictory. The earliest account of her career is to be found in the introduction to an edition of her fictional works that was published posthumously in 1696, which purports to be memoirs on her life written by a "gentlewoman" of her acquaintance. It is now believed that the "gentlewoman" in question was, in fact, Mrs. Behn's personal friend and editor Charles Gildon (1665-1724). According to his account, she was born into a good family by the name of Johnson, whose ancestral roots lay in the city of Canterbury in Kent. Her father, furthermore, was reported as being related to Lord Francis Willoughby of Parham, a man who used his good offices to secure Johnson an appointment to the administrative post of lieutenant-governor over many islands in the West Indies and the territory of Surinam. When Gildon's memoirs were reprinted a year later in an anthology devoted to the lives of dramatic poets, the text was revised in such a way as to state explicitly that Mrs. Behn was herself born in the city of Canterbury.

Information that runs counter to Gildon's memoirs on two important issues, however, comes from the hand of another contemporary writer, Anne Finch (1661-1720). Finch, who is better known as the Countess of Winchelsea, left a marginal note in a manuscript copy of some unpublished poems of her own in which she mentions that the place of Mrs. Behn's birth was the small market town of Wye, near Canterbury, and that her father had been a barber by trade. Finch's account was first discovered by an English literary scholar in 1884, but it was not until the opening decade of the twentieth century that the pertinent entry in the baptismal registry at Wye received a thorough scrutiny. It was thereupon learned that a child listed as Ayfara, along with a brother named John, was duly baptized there on July 10, 1640, but that her family name was not Johnson at all. The parents of Ayfara and her brother are, in fact, identified as a couple named John and Amy Amis. Then, in the 1950's, another English scholar perused the burial registry at Wye and found that both of these children had died a few days after their baptism: Ayfara on July 12 and John on July 16. In neither the baptismal nor the burial registries, moreover, is there any reference to Mr. Amis' being a barber by trade. In the light of these discrepancies, it is difficult to avoid drawing the conclusion that Finch's marginal note is nothing more than a false lead.

The only other contemporary evidence pertaining to Mrs. Behn's birth comes from some manuscripts now held in the British Library that were composed before 1708 by a member of the gentry named Thomas Culpepper. Culpepper reports that Mrs. Behn was born at Canterbury or Sturry and that her maiden name was Johnson. He further claims that she was also his foster-sister by virtue of the fact that her mother was his nurse at one time. A subsequent check of the marriage registry at St. Paul's in Canterbury corroborated Culpepper's account insofar as a couple named

Bartholomew and Elizabeth Johnson was married there on August 25, 1638. It has also been ascertained that Bartholomew Johnson was a yeoman (that is, a member of the class of small freeholding farmers) and that he originally came from Bishopsbourne, a village situated three and a half miles from Canterbury. The first of the couple's four children was, moreover, named Eaffry (Aphra), but she appears to have been born in neither Canterbury nor Sturry. The baptismal records of St. Michael's in the village of Harbledown, located just outside the walls of Canterbury, list her as being baptized there on December 14, 1640. Since Culpepper himself was born on Christmas Day in 1637, there would appear to be some question whether Mrs. Johnson could have served him in the capacity of a wetnurse.

The question of Mrs. Behn's parentage is further complicated by a passage appearing in James Rodway's *Chronological History of the Discovery and Settlement of Guiana, 1493-1796*, a work first published in 1888. Here it is reported that a relative of Lord Willoughby named Johnson left his homeland toward the end of 1658 bound for Surinam in the company of his wife and children, along with an adopted daughter named Afra or Aphra Johnson. In the absence of any further corroborative evidence, however, the claim regarding Aphra's status as Johnson's foster child is still viewed with a large measure of skepticism by most literary scholars at the current time. Rodway goes on to assert that Johnson never assumed his administrative duties in Surinam, since he fell ill during the voyage and died at sea. The rest of the family, according to this history, duly disembarked at Surinam and spent the next two or three years residing on one of Lord Willoughby's estates in that land.

Rodway's assertion that Johnson died before reaching Surinam is corroborated by some autobiographical remarks that Mrs. Behn makes in her novel *Oroonoko*. Other statements in *Oroonoko*, however, are at variance with several items in Rodway's account of the surviving family's subsequent sojourn in the New World. For one thing, Mrs. Behn herself maintains that their stay in Surinam was a matter of months rather than the two or three years mentioned by Rodway. On the basis of references made to actual events and historical personages in the course of her narrative, it is also most likely that the period of young Aphra's residence in Surinam lasted from November, 1663, to February, 1664.

Shortly after her return to England, she married a London merchant of Dutch ancestry whose surname was Behn. This marriage ended quite abruptly in 1665 or 1666, owing to the death of Mr. Behn, an apparent victim of the plague which raged throughout London during these years. At this point in her life as at several others, Mrs. Behn appears to have been in need of money. Whether for financial or for idealistic reasons, she chose to become a spy for the recently restored British monarchy, which was at that point engaged in a war with the States of Holland—hostilities that were soon extended to France. She was to take up residence in Antwerp (then part of Holland) for the purpose of collecting information pertaining to the activities of dissident English exiles (supporters of Cromwell) as well as the military plans of the Dutch government. Her Dutch surname must surely have been advantageous to her in this mission.

Mrs. Behn is believed to have gone to Antwerp in July, 1666, and for the ensuing six months or so she continued to send cryptographic reports back to her superiors in England, using the code name Astrea to identify herself. It is widely held that she had already adopted this pseudonym while still in Surinam. Although Astrea (or Astraea) is the Greek goddess of justice, the name was quite likely suggested by Honoré d'Urfé's popular three-part novel *Astrea* (1607-1628). The eponymous heroine of this novel had a lover called Celadon, a name which came to be employed as a code name for Aphra's good friend William Scot. This individual was the son of Thomas Scot, a man who was one of the judges at the trial which ended with the execution of Charles I in 1649 and who was himself put to death as a regicide in 1660. Since William Scot was in both Surinam and Antwerp at the same time that "Astrea" was in these places, it is tempting to surmise that a close amorous relationship existed between them. It is, moreover, indisputable that Mrs. Behn diverted much of her energies while in Antwerp to the task of obtaining a royal pardon on behalf of William Scot for political offenses which he had committed against the crown in past years.

Whether Mrs. Behn received adequate financial compensation from the crown for her espionage mission on the Continent is still a debatable issue. There is no doubt, however, that she was in desperate need of money after her return from Antwerp, for she was jailed for a brief period in 1668, as a result of her inability to repay outstanding debts that she had lately contracted. Upon her release from debtors' prison, Mrs. Behn made a bold decision to try her hand at writing for the theater as a means of achieving financial independence. It is likely that her release from confinement was achieved through the intercession of Thomas Killigrew (1612-1683). Killigrew, himself the author of several noteworthy dramas, devoted most of his energies to managing the affairs of the Theatre Royal at Drury Lane. This organization, commonly referred to as the King's Company, was the first of two acting ensembles to be granted a monopoly over theatrical performances within the city of London. The other group, known as the Duke's Company, was managed by Sir William Davenant until his death in 1668. Both of these companies, incidentally, were the first in England to engage actresses to play the roles of women, rather than following the traditional practice of using boys and young men to perform these parts. Despite her close friendship with Killigrew, Mrs. Behn's own plays were staged by the Duke's Company, under the supervision of Davenant's successors, from the time that her first play was produced in 1670 to the year 1682. The plays that she composed during this period, except for an occasional failure, proved to be popular successes, and she soon established herself as one of the public's favorite playwrights.

Mrs. Behn's career as a playwright was nevertheless placed in severe jeopardy when she decided to promote the fortunes of the Stuart monarchy by using the stage to attack powerful Whig opponents of Charles II. Her chief contribution as a propagandist for the Tory cause is to be found in the pair of plays entitled *The Roundheads* and *The City Heiress*. What precipitated a crisis in Mrs. Behn's partisan political activity, however, was her composition of a sardonic prologue and epilogue for the production, in 1682, of *Romulus and Hersilia*, a play by an anonymous author. These supplementary contributions were deemed to be unwarranted aspersions upon the character of the Duke of Monmouth as well as other persons of quality, and a warrant for Mrs. Behn's arrest was issued by the Lord Chamberlain. Subsequent events remain unclear, but she appears to have gotten off lightly in terms of actual confinement. The effect on her literary creativity was far more profound, for she ceased writing plays for a period of nearly four years. During this hiatus from the theater, she found an outlet for her literary talents in composing poetry and narrative fiction. Even though she resumed writing for the theater in the spring of 1686, most of Mrs. Behn's succeeding plays never matched the success of her earlier ones, and she increasingly devoted her time to writing fictional works and to translating plays and novels of foreign authors, perhaps deeming this a superior means of earning a livelihood by the pen.

Since Mrs. Behn was both beautiful and witty, she was highly successful in forming close associations with a great number of prominent persons from literary and social circles in London. The literary figures among her acquaintance included John Dryden, Edmund Waller, and Thomas Otway. The full extent of her friendship with the rakish Earl of Rochester, John Wilmot, is still a matter of conjecture; whether he was among their number, it was common knowledge that Mrs. Behn had a variety of lovers during the 1670's and 1680's. Her most abiding romantic favor appears to have been bestowed upon John Hoyle, a lawyer noted for his witty repartee and ready swordsmanship. Mrs. Behn's relationship with Hoyle was greatly complicated by his unrepressed bisexual proclivities, and they parted ways several years before her death. She died after a long physical illness the exact nature of which is still not fully established. Mrs. Behn was buried in the cloisters of Westminster Abbey. On her tombstone is a wry couplet alleged to have been written by Hoyle himself that runs as follows:

> Here lies a proof that wit can never be
> Defence enough against mortality.

These lines proved to be even more apposite in regard to Hoyle's personal fate, for his own life came to an abrupt end as the result of a tavern brawl in 1692.

Analysis

Aphra Behn began her literary career with two plays whose technique and style are based on the romantic tragicomedies written in collaboration by Francis Beaumont and John Fletcher. Plays of this type permit a serious subject to be explored while avoiding a tragic resolution of the conflict. The first of her dramas in this vein was entitled *The Forced Marriage*, a work whose theme is the conflict between love and honor. This play was followed by *The Amorous Prince*; Mrs. Behn uses a double plot in which the worldly protagonist first seduces an innocent country lass and then proceeds to fall in love with his best friend's fiancée. The play thus contrasts rural innocence with urban corruption and probes the competing claims of love and friendship. The plot is resolved happily when the repentant prince agrees to marry the country lass and renounces his designs on the friend's fiancée. Neither of these plays has much to interest present-day readers, but they were received enthusiastically by London audiences at the time, and Mrs. Behn's future in the theater appeared to be assured.

The performance of her third play, however, ended in failure. Despite the fact that *The Dutch Lover* is much better than either of its predecessors, the public proved unreceptive. Much of the blame for its failure, however, may justly be attributed to a poor production. Based on a contemporary novel with a Spanish setting, the intricate plot of *The Dutch Lover* involves seven sets of lovers—four of them being of earnest intent and the other three being comic in nature. One of the males who is featured in a comic pair of lovers is a Dutchman, and the play derives its name from his prominence in many of the comedic scenes. The various strands of plot mesh nicely—with the aid of multiple disguises and mistaken identities reminiscent of plays constructed in the manner of Spanish intrigue. Such comedies emphasized action and intricate plotting at the expense of character development and usually incorporated the element of spectacle. Mrs. Behn's fondness for this kind of drama was an abiding one, and she persisted in writing works of this style long after its popularity with English audiences had waned.

Discouraged by the failure of *The Dutch Lover*, Mrs. Behn offered the public no new plays from February, 1673, to the time when *Abdelazer* was produced in July, 1676. This work is a romantic tragedy in the grand manner, with much turgid rhetoric. The plot was derived from an anonymous sixteenth century play, and its action takes place in a Spanish-Moorish milieu. Although it met with public approbation, it is decidedly inferior to plays of this genre written by Dryden and Otway. Sensing that she lacked the temperament needed to create heroic drama, Mrs. Behn did not again attempt to write tragedy. For her next play, she turned to more congenial subject matter and for the first time composed a play whose setting lay within the city of London. Entitled *The Town Fop*, it is a marked improvement over any of her previous works for the theater. Indebted in the main features of its plot to George Wilkins' *The Miseries of Enforced Marriage* (pr. 1605), it deals with a young man whose guardian forces him to marry against his will, despite the fact that he has already promised to wed a girl with whom he is deeply in love. The girl disguises herself as a young man and feigns an attempt to make love to the wife of her former fiancé before he has had a chance to consummate their marriage. Believing that his wife has been morally compromised by this encounter, the young man divorces her and then marries his former sweetheart. The problem of enforced marriage is a major theme in the works of Mrs. Behn and recurs in many of her other plays.

The problem of enforced marriage is, in fact, the chief dramatic conflict in Mrs. Behn's most famous play, *The Rover*. Like many of her plays, it is an adaptation of an earlier work by a different hand. In this case, the source was Thomas Killigrew's closet drama *Thomaso: Or, The Wanderer*. Killigrew's play has seventy-three scenes that are organized into ten acts. He wrote this work in 1654 while in exile, but it was not actually published until ten years later. While there is no direct evidence that Killigrew granted permission to Mrs. Behn to make the adaptation, it is quite unlikely that she would have done so without his express consent. Killigrew's *Thomaso* contains so much material that Mrs. Behn needed two full-length plays to encompass the entire story despite her drastic condensation of certain features of the original plot. The first part of *The Rover* was produced in March, 1677, and the second part almost four years later, in January, 1681. Whereas Killigrew's entire play is set in Madrid, Mrs. Behn shifted the setting for the first part of *The Rover* to Naples during the climax of its carnival season. Since mistakes in identity are rendered more credible when the populace at large is in masquerade, the change of scene has obvious advantages for a comedy of intrigue in which duels are fought based on mistaken identities.

The banished cavaliers referred to in the subtitle of *The Rover* are a group of Englishmen who are compelled to live in exile as a result of Oliver Cromwell's abolition of the Stuart monarchy in 1642. Although not as complex as *The Dutch Lover*, the plot of the first part focuses on the romantic maneuvers of three Englishmen and three Spanish ladies that eventually culminate in the matrimonial union of each pair. The central couple consists of a spirited young Spanish lady named Hellena and a witty Englishman known as Wilmore the Rover. Wilmore is believed to be a composite character based on two of Mrs. Behn's close friends: John Hoyle and John Wilmot, the Earl of Rochester. Wilmore is such an attractive rake that he is said to have made vice alluring to a good part of the audience. Hellena, on the other hand, was originally destined for life in a cloister. It is her sister, Florinda, who is being coerced into an arranged marriage for the sake of prestige and economic advantage. All ends well, and both sisters manage to avoid the respective forms of bondage that threaten their future happiness. There are, it must be acknowledged, many implausibilities in the plot, and some actions appear to be insufficiently motivated. These deficiencies, however, are transcended by the sparkling dialogue that flows from Mrs. Behn's pen, and it is this witty repartee that constitutes the play's chief virtue. Its sequel, generally regarded as inferior to the first part, is most noteworthy for the fact that Mrs. Behn introduced two *commedia dell'arte* figures into its plot: Harlequin and Scaramouche.

Of the plays produced after the first part of *The Rover*, *Sir Patient Fancy* and *The Emperor of the Moon* are probably the most outstanding examples of Mrs. Behn's dramatic craftmanship. Much of the inspiration for *Sir Patient Fancy* is derived from three of Molière's comedies—especially *The Imaginary Invalid* (1673). Her play, however, should be judged on its own merits, for she borrows incidents rather than themes from the French master. While Molière asserted that the purpose of comedy is to correct men by entertaining them, Mrs. Behn herself did not ascribe any pedagogical function to the theater. She wrote her plays solely for the sake of entertaining the public. In *Sir Patient Fancy*, Mrs. Behn succeeds perhaps too well, for the play is undoubtedly her bawdiest. Many women in the audience were offended by the play's overt sexual escapades, and Mrs. Behn had to go to great lengths to defend herself against charges of obscenity. Had the play been written by a man, she argued, the issue of licentiousness would never have arisen.

The Emperor of the Moon, on the other hand, is a model of decorum. This love intrigue successfully integrates a number of distinct styles, including those of grand opera and *commedia dell'arte*. Although the figures of Harlequin and Scaramouche were previously used in the second part of *The Rover*, they are incorporated much more effectively in *The Emperor of the Moon*. The plot centers on a pair of men who masquerade as the King of the Moon and Prince Thunderland as a stratagem of courtship in wooing the daughter and niece of a gullible astrologer. Before their ruse is uncovered, the two masqueraders succeed in marrying the objects of their affection. The astrologer, for his part, duly recognizes the folly of living in a world of fantasy. An immediate success when first performed in 1687, the play continued to be popular with London audiences for most of the eighteenth century.

Although Mrs. Behn lived in an age of great intellectual ferment, her ideas on politics and society are usually commonplace and traditional. In reading her plays, one is tempted to look for connections with current feminist concerns, but except for her deep concern that marriage be entered into on the basis of mutual affection and not contracted for social or monetary reasons, there is little that Mrs. Behn wished to change in the relationship between the sexes. She knew herself too well, furthermore, to attribute greater virtue to women than to men. If she did not appear to be interested in demonstrating the virtue of her sex, she at least used her plays to celebrate its power.

Other major works

NOVELS: *Love Letters Between a Nobleman and His Sister*, 1683-1687 (3 volumes); *The Fair Jilt: Or, The History of Prince Tarquin and Miranda*, 1688; *Oroonoko: Or, The Royal Slave*, 1688; *Agnes de Castro*, 1688; *The History of the Nun: Or, The Fair Vow-Breaker*, 1689; *The Lucky Mistake*, 1689; *The Nun: Or, The Perjured Beauty*, 1697; *The Adventure of the Black Lady*, 1698; *The Wandering Beauty*, 1698.

POETRY: *Poems upon Several Occasions, with A Voyage to the Island of Love*, 1684 (including adaptation of Abbé Paul Tallemant's *Le Voyage de l'isle d'amour*); *Miscellany: Being a Collection of Poems by Several Hands*, 1685 (includes works by others).

TRANSLATIONS: *Aesop's Fables*, 1687 (with Francis Barlow); *Of Trees*, 1689 (of book 6 of Abraham Cowley's *Sex libri plantarum*).

MISCELLANEOUS: *La Montre: Or, The Lover's Watch*, 1686 (prose and poetry); *The Case for the Watch*, 1686 (prose and poetry); *Lycidus: Or, The Lover in Fashion*, 1688 (prose and poetry; includes works by others); *The Lady's Looking-Glass, to Dress Herself By: Or, The Art of Charming*, 1697 (prose and poetry); *The Works of Aphra Behn*, 1915, 1967 (6 volumes; Montague Summers, editor).

Bibliography

Cameron, William J. *New Light on Aphra Behn*, 1961.
Duffy, Maureen. *The Passionate Shepherdess: Aphra Behn*, 1977.
Hargreaves, Henry A. "The Life and Plays of Mrs. Aphra Behn," 1961 (dissertation).
Link, Frederick M. *Aphra Behn*, 1968.
Phelps, Robert. "Introduction," in *Selected Writings of the Ingenious Mrs. Aphra Behn*, 1950.
Sackville-West, Victoria. *Aphra Behn: The Incomparable Astrea*, 1927.
Sutherland, James. *English Literature of the Late Seventeenth Century*, 1969.
Woodcock, George. *The Incomparable Aphra*, 1948.

                                                          Victor Anthony Rudowski

S. N. BEHRMAN

Born: Worcester, Massachusetts; June 9, 1893(?)
Died: New York, New York; September 9, 1973

Principal drama
Bedside Manners, pr. 1923, pb. 1924 (with J. Kenyon Nicholson); *A Night's Work*, pr. 1924, pb. 1926 (with Nicholson); *The Man Who Forgot*, pr. 1926 (with Owen Davis); *The Second Man*, pr., pb. 1927; *Serena Blandish: Or, The Difficulty of Getting Married*, pr. 1929, pb. 1934; *Meteor*, pr. 1929, pb. 1934; *Brief Moment*, pr., pb. 1931; *Biography*, pr. 1932, pb. 1933; *Rain from Heaven*, pr., pb. 1934; *End of Summer*, pr., pb. 1936; *Amphitryon 38*, pr. 1937, pb. 1938; *Wine of Choice*, pr., pb. 1938; *No Time for Comedy*, pr., pb. 1939; *The Talley Method*, pr., pb. 1941; *The Pirate*, pr. 1942, pb. 1943 (adaptation of Ludwig Fulda's play *Die Seerauber*); *Jacobowsky and the Colonel*, pr., pb. 1944 (based on Franz Werfel's play *Jacobowsky und der Oberst*); *Dunnigan's Daughter*, pr., pb. 1945; *I Know My Love*, pr., pb. 1949 (adaptation of Marcel Achard's play *Auprès de ma blonde*); *Jane*, pr., pb. 1952 (based on a story by W. Somerset Maugham); *Fanny*, pr. 1954, pb. 1955 (with Joshua Logan; music and lyrics by Harold Rome; based on Marcel Pagnol's plays *Marius* and *Fanny* and his screenplay *César*); *The Cold Wind and the Warm*, pr. 1958, pb. 1959; *Lord Pengo*, pr. 1962, pb. 1963; *But for Whom Charlie*, pr., pb. 1964.

Other literary forms
S. N. Behrman wrote two "profile"-type biographies: *Duveen* (1952) and *Portrait of Max: An Intimate Memoir of Sir Max Beerbohm* (1960). *The Suspended Drawing Room* (1965) is a collection of (mostly) familiar essays focusing on such notables as Robert E. Sherwood, Ferenc Molnár, and A. E. Kazan; *The Worcester Account* (1954), the best of Behrman's prose works, is a collection of pieces originally published in *The New Yorker*; *The Burning Glass* (1968) is a semiautobiographical novel; and *People in a Diary* (1972; reissued as *Tribulations and Laughter*, 1972) is a memoir containing brief, often poignant essays and sketches.

Behrman was also the author of numerous screenplays, including several adaptations of his own and others' works.

Achievements
Although Behrman's career as a dramatist spanned several decades, his major impact upon the American theater covered roughly two and a half decades, from 1927, with the great success of *The Second Man* (178 performances in New York City), to 1944, with *Jacobowsky and the Colonel*, which had a run of 415 performances, also in New York City. Excluding his

earlier apprenticeship plays, written during and after studies at Harvard University, Behrman's career as a dramatist ranged from 1923, with *Bedside Manners* (in collaboration with J. Kenyon Nicholson), to 1964, with *But for Whom Charlie*. During this period, the playwright offered to the New York stage—without counting other locales—a total of twenty-two plays in full production, most of them enjoying considerable or at least moderate success. Only three plays were (relatively speaking) unsuccessful—*Wine of Choice*, *Dunnigan's Daughter*, and *But for Whom Charlie*—and even these works attracted some favorable critical notice. Along with *Jacobowsky and the Colonel*, which later became a motion picture, *Fanny* (written as a musical comedy in collaboration with Joshua Logan) and *I Know My Love* enjoyed the longest runs. These works were essentially entertainments, written with a shrewd sense of the audience response yet without the writer's special touches of mannered comedy. Earlier, during the "vintage" years, as Kenneth T. Reed (*S. N. Behrman*, 1975) describes the period between 1927 and 1936, when the writer had seven plays in production on Broadway, a new comedy by Behrman was a special event, one eagerly awaited.

For this audience, a particular quality that marked the author's comedies was "sophistication." This term, still generally applied to Behrman, has only limited usefulness. For one matter, not all of his plays belong to this mode—the most significant exception is *The Cold Wind and the Warm*, a semiautobiographical work, impressionistic and poetic. Moreover, the word "sophistication" has negative connotations, perhaps carrying over from social criticism of the 1930's and 1940's. From this point of view, the word denotes, among other negative attitudes, frivolity, urbane elegance, and elitism. To be sure, most of Behrman's early comedies are set in the drawing rooms of the privileged class, with a clash between intellectuals (either true or sham), together with grasping middle-class parvenues whose special concerns are money, status, and advantageous marriage. Nevertheless, Behrman's judgment of privilege in these comedies is critical and gently satiric, not approving.

By more narrowly construing "sophisticated," the word may be applied with greater confidence to the wide range of Behrman's drama. In the general class of comic ironists such as Oscar Wilde, George Bernard Shaw, W. Somerset Maugham, and Noël Coward (also, arguably, Neil Simon), Behrman writes plays that resemble comedies of manners or polite comedies, but unlike Wilde (although he admired the Irishman's *The Importance of Being Earnest*, pr. 1895), Behrman never treats frivolity or triviality as a prime theme, and unlike Coward (although he also admired Coward's *Blithe Spirit*, pr. 1941), Behrman avoids sentimental fantasy. Curiously, Behrman's work more closely resembles the lighter drama of Shaw and the less farcical comedies of Maugham. Behrman's comedy does not propagandize in favor of socialistic causes, but beneath the surface banter of the American writer is a tough realistic edge, a sharp awareness of the vulgar display of wealth and the brutality of social intolerance. Also, in its satiric wit stopping short of misanthropy, Behrman's work reminds one of certain Maugham plays, such as *Our Betters* (pr. 1917) and *The Circle* (pr. 1921).

Judging the impact of his own work, Behrman was modest. In *People in a Diary*, he wrote: "For a time, Philip Barry, Paul Osborn, and I were the only American writers of high comedy." Of these playwrights, only the first is still remembered. By the late 1930's, Behrman had already established his reputation: In *The American Drama Since 1918: An Informal History* (1939), Joseph Wood Krutch wrote that Behrman had secured for himself "as sure a position in the contemporary American theater as any writer can claim."

Biography

Samuel Nathaniel Behrman was the third child of Joseph and Zelda (Feingold) Behrman and was born in Worcester, Massachusetts. The first two children in the Behrman family, Hiram and Morris, were born in Eastern Europe (in or near Vilna, Lithuania). Because no official record of the writer's birthdate was ever recorded in Worcester, he arbitrarily selected his own "birthday" as June 9, 1893. In *The Worcester Account*, Behrman humorously described the circumstances of his search for his true date of birth and concluded that "common sense tells me that 1893 must be reasonably close."

Readers interested in the details of Behrman's youth and schooling should turn to *The Worcester Account*, a colorful but by no means sentimentalized review of his adventures, the chapters originally written as short narratives for *The New Yorker*. From these pieces one learns that, although poor, Behrman's family enjoyed some distinction among the other Jewish residents of the neighborhood because the father was a Talmudic scholar. From him, Samuel learned "the Old Testament stories as if they had taken place recently—as if they constituted his personal past."

In 1899, Behrman entered Providence Street School, and in 1902, he heard a political speech delivered by Eugene V. Debs, then the Socialist Labor Party candidate for president. That chance occasion, as he later remarked, began in his life "an orientation it would otherwise not have had—a bias in favor of those who had suffered from cruelty or callousness." Another direction in his life was pointed by his friend Daniel Asher (who appears as the character Willie Lavin in *The Cold Wind and the Warm*); with Asher, he witnessed at Lothrops's Opera House in 1904 a melodrama entitled *Devil's Island*, and years later he still recalled the enchantment of that performance.

By 1907, when he entered Classical High School in Worcester, Behrman had begun his lifelong habit of omnivorous reading. Among his early favorites were William Shakespeare and Horatio Alger. He could, for his high school classes, recite from memory passages from *Hamlet* and *Macbeth*, and he acquired an elementary knowledge of Latin and Greek, useful tools in his cultivation of language skills. During these years, also, he deepened his friendship with Asher, who urged Behrman to write and who analyzed all the youth's fledgling manuscripts.

In 1911, Behrman toured on the Poli vaudeville circuit for some months with a skit that he had written himself, entitled "Only a Part." The circuit covered a number of theatrical points, including a New York vaudeville house on Fourteenth Street. Behrman's health, in those years precarious, obliged him to cut short the tour with two others, and he returned to Worcester. In 1912, at the family's urging, he entered Clark College. As a special student at this local school, he continued to write and act, also turning his attention to oratory. His academic work as an English major was successful, but he failed to report to physical education classes and was suspended from Clark. In the summer of 1913, he enrolled at Harvard, then reentered Clark in 1914, but was again suspended for neglecting physical education classes. The next year, he sold his first story, "La Vie Parisienne," which he wrote as a student in Charles Townsend Copeland's class at Harvard. By 1916, he had enrolled in Professor George Pierce Baker's Workshop 47, the only undergraduate admitted to Baker's famous playwriting course. Also in that year, Behrman was graduated from Harvard with a bachelor's degree. After failing to find a job in newspaper offices in several cities, he decided to continue his education at Columbia University, where he studied under Brander Matthews and other notable teachers. In 1918, Behrman earned his master's degree at Columbia. Offered a teaching appointment at the University of Minnesota, Behrman decided instead to hazard his fortune in writing. For the next two years, he worked for *The New York Times*, at first as a typist of classified ads and later as a book reviewer. Before and during this time, he sold stories and essays to several magazines. One of the most influential of them, *The Smart Set*, carried in its November, 1919, issue "The Second Man," a story that he later rewrote into the play of the same title.

For the young journalist with dreams of becoming a playwright, the early years of the 1920's were arduous, mostly frustrating, with only occasional periods of publishing success. This period came to an end in 1926, when Behrman developed a working friendship with a more established dramatist, Owen Davis, with whom he collaborated on a play entitled *The Man Who Forgot*. Later that year, *A Night's Work*, written in collaboration with J. Kenyon Nicholson, was produced on Broadway. Through these efforts and the contacts that he established with producers Ned Harris and Crosbie Gaige, Behrman was able to supplement his income with publicity work for other New York-based plays.

Finally, on April 11, 1927, Behrman's years of apprenticeship came to an end when the Theatre Guild presented *The Second Man*. After that popular and critical success, Behrman's labors were often divided between playwriting and scriptwriting for Hollywood. Also dating from this period was his long-lasting association and friendship with Harold Ross of *The New Yorker*. Over the years, Ross commissioned Behrman to write many essays, including "profiles," for his magazine—the first of which was on George Gershwin and appeared in 1929.

During the late 1920's and the decade of the 1930's, Behrman attained to considerable prominence in his craft, as a playwright and as a producer-writer. In 1928, he sailed to England to oversee a production of *The Second Man* in London, with Noël Coward in the leading role. Indeed, over the years, the production of a Behrman play usually called for the talents of America's and England's most distinguished players: Alfred Lunt and Lynn Fontanne, Ina Claire, Catherine Cornell, and Laurence Olivier, among others. From 1929 to 1939, Behrman's work was produced on Broadway stages with general approval: *Serena Blandish*, *Meteor*, *Brief Moment*, *Biography*, *Rain from Heaven*, *End of Summer*, and *No Time for Comedy*. For Behrman, these years brought both regret (with the death by suicide of Daniel Asher in 1929) and personal fulfillment (including his marriage in 1936 to Elza Heifetz and the birth of their only child, David Arthur, in 1937).

In 1938, Behrman joined the Playwrights' Company, an independent guild of writer-producers that included Robert E. Sherwood, Maxwell Anderson, Elmer Rice, and Sidney Howard. Until 1945, when Behrman withdrew from the company, he produced *The Talley Method*, *The Pirate*, *Jacobowsky and the Colonel*, and *Dunnigan's Daughter*. During this time, he received a significant award, as well as academic recognition: In 1943, he was admitted to the Department of Arts and Literature of the National Institute of Arts and Letters, and in 1944, his *Jacobowsky and the Colonel*, based originally upon a sketch by Franz Werfel but almost completely reinterpreted by the playwright, won the New York Drama Critics Circle Award as the best foreign play of the season.

After 1945, Behrman divided his literary work—that is to say, writing not commissioned by Hollywood studios—between the stage and various kinds of prose. His later plays include *I Know My Love*, *Jane*, *Fanny*, *The Cold Wind and the Warm*, *Lord Pengo*, and his final production, *But for Whom Charlie*. Toward the end of his career, he turned with greater avidity to the expanded essay, which prose he called his "one hobby." In 1952, he published *Duveen*, a biography of Joseph Duveen, a notorious art dealer about whom Behrman had earlier written a profile entitled "The Days of Duveen" for *The New Yorker*. The autobiographical volume *The Worcester*

Account, as noted above, also had its genesis in *The New Yorker*. In 1960, he published *Portrait of Max*, in 1965, a sheaf of essays entitled *The Suspended Drawing Room*; in 1968, his only novel, *The Burning Glass*; and in 1972, a book of memoirs and appreciations, *People in a Diary*. Among the awards he received during the final decades of his life were an honorary degree from Clark University (1949) and the Brandeis University Creative Arts Award (1962); in the latter year, he was also appointed Trustee of Clark University. On September 9, 1973, Behrman died in New York of apparent heart failure.

Analysis

Although S. N. Behrman was not, except in *The Cold Wind and the Warm*, basically an autobiographical playwright, many of his themes can be traced to circumstances in his life. His economically deprived youth and his years of struggle as a journalist lay behind his frequent depiction of the clash between characters emerging from deprivation with those already privileged by birth or class. At the same time, his culturally enriched childhood, one that particularly emphasized traditional Jewish values of social justice and strict moral probity, sensitized him to the contrast between superficially upright but morally corrupt people and those of genuine integrity. Finally, in his early comedies—particularly those prior to 1936— Behrman transformed Horatio Alger stories that he had enjoyed as a youth into moral tales concerning the Midas touch that turns gold into dross.

Typically in Behrman's variations on these ambition myths, the major (sensible) character abandons his childish illusions, discovers his limitations, and accepts in a mature way his responsibilities or potentialities. Rarely, as in *Serena Blandish*, the character is a woman; on the whole, Behrman's female leads are more astute than their romantic counterparts. For men and women alike, the tests for Behrman's pattern of discovery/initiation are through friendship or through marriage. As a youth, Behrman was not physically robust or socially assertive; perhaps by way of compensation, he cherished throughout his lifetime generous friendships (an assumption supported by *People in a Diary*), and in his plays he established the values of supportive relationships. The greater test of maturity, however, was in the courtship clash that precedes marriage. Married late in life, at the age of forty-three, Behrman tended to view on the stage the "war of the sexes" from the vantage point of rationality, not idealistic romance. If couples in his plays achieve the promise of a satisfactory (rational) union, the credit always goes to the woman, whom Behrman—like Shaw—championed as the more sensible of the sexes. In all relationships—those of competition, of friendship, and of courtship—Behrman holds up the exemplary pattern of tolerance. Without tolerance, his characters could never come to self-knowledge, and their world of high comedy would fall apart.

In *The Second Man*, Mrs. Kendall Frayne, a wealthy widow whose chief asset is her common sense, and Monica Grey, a younger woman, are romantically interested in Clark Storey. Storey is a would-be poet and novelist, handsome but passionless. His counterpart is Austin Lowe, a chemist with meager social graces to match his rival's. Nevertheless, he wins the love of Monica; for her part, Mrs. Frayne is too worldly-wise to fall for the superficial Storey. By the end of the play, Storey escapes both romantic entanglements but discovers the unsettling truth that he possesses a "second man" in his nature, one that is "calm, critical, observant, unmoved, blasé, odious." Thus, Storey attains, at the very least, the reward of painful illumination.

For Behrman's original audience, the play offered both entertainment and a moral lesson that they were prepared to accept. By challenging the playgoers' intelligence, the writer allowed them to discern, without the heavy hand of editorial intrusion, that Mrs. Frayne's "sophistication" would prevent her from choosing a poor mate. In addition to flattering the audience's urbanity, Behrman taught them a sound moral lesson. For all of his protestations that he speaks honest truth, Clark Storey must—to protect his vanity—conceal his emotional shallowness and his greed to achieve status. Thus, the audience learns to reject an ambition that lacks the solid basis of integrity.

This lesson, presented with different variations upon the theme, appears in *Serena Blandish* and *End of Summer*. In both plays, fortune hunters attempt, without hiding their motives, to secure a marriage that will advance their ambitions. Subtitled *The Difficulty of Getting Married*, *Serena Blandish* showcases a charming, witty young woman who has emerged from an impoverished background. Serena catches the eye of Sigmund Traub, a wealthy, middle-aged, Jewish businessman. He takes her under his wing, provides her with social advantages and money (he even lends her a diamond ring), and generally acts like a Pygmalion to her Galatea. Her ambitions, however, are never realized. The money she displays to her rich suitors she does not really possess, and by the end of the play she remains unmarried. Similarly, in *End of Summer*, Dr. Kenneth Rice pursues but fails to snare two wealthy women. A "self-made man," as he likes to call himself, he courts Leonie Frothingham and her daughter Paula for the sake of their money, but Leonie, a sensible woman in the mold of Mrs. Frayne, rejects his advances, as does her idealistic daughter. At the "end of summer," he has neither wife nor money.

Dr. Rice, a Freudian psychoanalyst, resembles other power-obsessive character-types in Behrman's plays: Hobart Eldridge (*Rain from Heaven*), Allan Frobisher (*Jane*), Orrin Kinnicott (*Biography*), Raphael Lord (*Meteor*), Lord Pengo (*Lord Pengo*), and Dr. Axton Talley (*The Talley Method*). Although different in certain respects, all of these personalities are rigid, authoritarian, self-centered, and intolerant; most are politically conservative. They contrast with other male characters who, although less assertive, have more attractive personal qualities. Among these sensitive (but often unfocused and self-indulgent) types are a number of second-rate artists or aesthetes in the pattern of Clark Storey of *The Second Man*. They include Aaron (*The Cold Wind and the Warm*), Sasha Barashaev (*Rain from Heaven*), Daniel Chanler (*I Know My Love*), Roderick Dean (*Brief Moment*), Peter Crewe (*Jane*), Melchoir Feydak (*Biography*), Edgar Mallison (*Serena Blandish*), Derek Pengo (*Lord Pengo*), Willard Prosper (*But for Whom Charlie*), Miguel Riachi (*Dunnigan's Daughter*), and Warwick Wilson (*Biography*). Although these would-be artists range in appeal from the fragile Aaron to the radical Marxist painter Riachi, they share the qualities of self-indulgence, independence, and (to varying degrees) fecklessness.

In general, Behrman's male figures—whether petulantly dictatorial or dreamy—lack the balanced common sense of their female counterparts. Among his "strong" women in the pattern of Mrs. Frayne are Emily Chanler (*I Know My Love*), Fern Dunnigan (*Dunnigan's Daughter*), Linda Esterbrook (*No Time for Comedy*), Abbey Fane (*Brief Moment*), Marion Froude (*Biography*), Enid Fuller (*The Talley Method*), and Lael Wyngate (*Rain from Heaven*). To these may be added Leonie Frothingham (despite her naïveté) and Serena Blandish, whose good sense compensates, in large measure, for her deficiency in exaggerating the values of money and status.

Along with their common sense and emotional maturity, these women share a quality of tolerance. For Behrman, tolerance greatly humanizes his protagonists. To be sure, several leading males are wisely tolerant—chief among them Jacobowsky, but the "strong" women (as contrasted to frivolous types) best exemplify the virtue. In *The Second Man*, Clark Storey tells Mrs. Frayne that she possesses the two "great requirements" for marriage: money and tolerance. Running through many of Behrman's comedies is a conflict between the tolerant, blessed with habits of kindness and serenity, and the intolerant. In *Biography*, three characters hold narrowly rigid opinions: Orrin Kinnicott, Richard Kurt, and Bunny Nolan. Responding to Marion Froude's open nature, Kurt upbraids her, for "what you call tolerance I call sloppy laziness." The audience, comparing the two personalities—the woman cheerful and emancipated, the man egotistic, wrapped up in radical politics—can be expected to draw a different conclusion.

In *Rain from Heaven*, Behrman stigmatizes, in the words of Lael Wyngate, an "epidemic of hatred and intolerance that may engulf us all." Perhaps the playwright best expresses this theme in *Jacobowsky and the Colonel*. In the second act, the Nazi Colonel warns Marianne that he cannot tolerate being treated in any fashion that he believes is disrespectful.

The Nazi's counterpart in this moral tale of "strange bedfellows" is Jacobowsky, the "wandering Jew" who has learned to accept life's evils with a redeeming sense of good humor. Through his example, the Colonel undergoes an initiation in the rites of true manhood. By the end of the play, the Colonel is not entirely "mature," not wholly tolerant, but he has at least learned to make compromises.

Behrman's insights into the corrosive effects of intolerance derive, at least in part, from his life's education as a Jew. Curiously, most of his apprenticeship work and the plays of the late 1920's and early 1930's avoid all mention of Jews. To be sure, Sigmund Traub in *Serena Blandish* is a Jew, a Bond Street merchant, but Behrman reveals little about the man's psychological reasons for pampering a beautiful woman not linked to him by passion. Not until 1934 in *Rain from Heaven* did Behrman create a Jewish character who functions as spokesman for his own ideas: Hugo Willens, who, despite his Nordic appearance, had to flee Europe because his grandmother was a Jew.

Among the later plays, *The Cold Wind and the Warm* explores autobiographical themes already presented in Behrman's essays for *The New Yorker*; in this, his most touching play, Behrman comes to terms with his Jewishness, without evasion or apology. A drama of recollection, *The Cold Wind and the Warm* surprised some critics, who were accustomed to Behrman's usual "high comedy"; although reviews were mixed, the play lasted for 120 performances at the Morosco. The playwright's final stage offering, *But for Whom Charlie*—one of his least successful plays—included the minor character Seymour Rosenthal, a Jew who had once been excluded from a college fraternity because of his religion. Also in the play, however, was Brock Dunaway, a Jewish novelist seventy years old—a survivor, just as Behrman was to survive the hardships of his own past.

Fortunately for the decent characters in the author's drama, they do not stand alone in their struggle against prejudice. For Behrman, the links of friendship, perhaps more enduring than those of romantic passion, unite men and women of goodwill. By the final act of *Amphitryon 38*, Jupiter and Alkmena move toward a deeper appreciation of each other. Jupiter asks the rhetorical question: What is the object of friendship? Alkmena's answer is probably also Behrman's: "To bring together the most totally dissimilar people and make them equal." This judgment is crucial in accepting the friendship of men as dissimilar as the Colonel and Jacobowsky. The audience must grasp the idea that they not only tolerate each other but also become friends. If social antagonists can appreciate each other's values, then people of goodwill have an even greater obligation to join forces. In *Biography*, Marion Froude's friendship with Melchoir Feydak is based upon mutual respect and admiration. As decent, emphathetic persons, they stand out as the only fully tolerant characters in the play. Conversely, when

Behrman's characters lack a capacity for friendship, they become self-centered and obnoxious. Like Dr. Kenneth Rice (*End of Summer*), who cannot trust another person deeply enough to make him (or her) a friend, Raphael Lord (*Meteor*) and Dr. Axton Talley (*The Talley Method*) ultimately become monsters. Without meaningful attachments, Behrman believes, human beings lose their spiritual bearings and destroy themselves.

It is noteworthy that Behrman's defective characters invariably lack humor. For the dramatist, a sense of the comic, no less than a capacity for friendship, marks the true human being. In an interview with *The New York Times* in 1952, Behrman remarked: "The essence of the comic sense is awareness: awareness of the tragedy as well as the fun of life, of the pity, the futility, the lost hopes, the striving for immortality, for permanence, for security, for love."

Although Behrman's plays were crafted for theatrical performance, they are also admirably suitable for reading. Modeled after the scintillating comedies of Wilde and Shaw, Behrman's plays similarly are, by turn, clever, ironic, provocative. That is not to say, however, that Behrman was an original thinker on social issues, as Shaw was, or that his plays match Wilde's sense of whimsy. Indeed, Behrman's drama is uneven in quality. Plays such as *The Pirate* (adapted from Ludwig Fulda's play *Die Seerauber*) and *I Know My Love* (adapted from Marcel Achard) or the musical *Fanny* must be judged as entertainments, not against the highest standards of the dramatic art. Other plays are quite dated, products of their time. In particular, the comedies of the 1930's, for all of their surface brilliance, resemble certain clever mating comedies of the motion pictures of that decade. During the hard years of the Great Depression, many theatergoers appreciated escapist fantasies that would carry them in imagination away from their troubles. The drawing-room settings of Behrman's plays, with furnishings opulent and refined, provided an alternative world, one inhabited by mostly clever, attractive characters whose major problem in life was to find an appropriate mate. Behrman's characters—mostly upper-class, worldly, and well-educated—fit comfortably into this world, but for modern theatergoers, the Depression-era frame of reference has vanished.

Nevertheless, Behrman's plays still appeal to audiences interested in comedy of manners. He isolates universal human traits and observes them faithfully, without exaggeration. At his best, his comedies offer the viewer (or reader) moral choices that exercise the heart. Never vulgar, rarely sexually provocative, his comedies sparkle with ample appreciation for human potentialities: for the happiness of a true marriage; for friendship based upon trust; for common sense that cannot be swayed by political or social bias; for discovery of the authentic self; above all, for tolerance of others' foibles, together with the resolve never to injure innocent people through malice or ignorance.

Other major works

NOVEL: *The Burning Glass*, 1968.

NONFICTION: *Duveen*, 1952; *The Worcester Account*, 1954; *Portrait of Max: An Intimate Memoir of Sir Max Beerbohm*, 1960; *The Suspended Drawing Room*, 1965; *People in a Diary*, 1972 (reissued as *Tribulations and Laughter*, 1972).

SCREENPLAYS: *He Knew Women*, 1930 (adaptation of his *The Second Man*); *The Sea Wolf*, 1930 (adaptation of Jack London's novel); *Surrender*, 1931 (with Sonya Levien); *Rebecca of Sunnybrook Farm*, 1932 (with Levien; adaptation of Kau Douglas Wiggin's children's novel); *Brief Moment*, 1933 (adaptation of his play); *Anna Karenina*, 1935 (with Salka Viertel and Clemence Dane; adaptation of Leo Tolstoy's novel); *The Scarlet Pimpernel*, 1935 (with Lajos Biro, Robert E. Sherwood, and Arthur Wimperes); *Quo Vadis*, 1951 (with John Lee Makin and Levien; adaptation of Henryk Sienkiewicz's novel).

Bibliography

Asher, Donald. *The Eminent Yachtsman and the Whorehouse Piano Player*, 1973.

Dodd, Loring Holmes. *Celebrities at Our Hearthside*, 1955.

Heniford, Lewis Williams. *S. N. Behrman as a Social Dramatist*, 1964 (dissertation).

Krutch, Joseph Wood. *The American Drama Since 1918: An Informal History*, 1939.

Reed, Kenneth T. *S. N. Behrman*, 1975.

Seivers, David W. *Freud on Broadway*, 1953.

Leslie B. Mittleman

DAVID BELASCO

Born: San Francisco, California; July 25, 1853
Died: New York, New York; May 14, 1931

Principal drama

L'Assommoir, pr. 1879 (adaptation of Émile Zola's novel); *Within an Inch of His Life*, pr. 1879 (with James A. Herne); *Hearts of Oak*, pr. 1879 (with Herne; originally as *Chums*; adaptation of Henry Leslie's play *The Mariner's Compass*); *La Belle Russe*, pr. 1881, pb. 1882; *The Stranglers of Paris*, pr. 1881, pb. 1941 (adaptation of Adolphe Belot's novel *L'Estrangleur*); *May Blossom*, pb. 1883, pr. 1884; *Valerie*, pr. 1886 (adaptation of Victorien Sardou's *Fernande*); *Baron Rudolph*, pr. 1887, pb. 1941 (with Bronson Howard); *The Highest Bidder*, pr. 1887; *The Wife*, pr. 1887, pb. 1941 (with Henry C. De Mille); *Lord Chumley*, pr., pb. 1888 (with De Mille); *The Charity Ball*, pr. 1889, pb. 1941 (with De Mille); *Men and Women*, pr. 1890, pb. 1941 (with De Mille); *Miss Helvett*, pr. 1891; *The Girl I Left Behind Me*, pr. 1893, pb. 1941 (with Franklyn Fyles); *The Younger Son*, pr. 1893 (adaptation of O. Vischer's play *Schlimme Saat*); *The Heart of Maryland*, pr., pb. 1895; *Zaza*, pr. 1898 (adaptation of Pierre Berton and Charles Simon's French play); *Madame Butterfly*, pr. 1900, pb. 1935 (with Long; adaptation of John Luther Long's story); *Naughty Anthony*, pr. 1900, pb. 1941; *DuBarry*, pr. 1901, pb. 1928; *The Darling of the Gods*, pr. 1902, pb. 1928 (with Long); *Sweet Kitty Bellairs*, pr., pb. 1903 (adaptation of Agnes and Egeron Castle's *The Bath Comedy*); *Adrea*, pr. 1905, pb. 1928 (with Long); *The Girl of the Golden West*, pr. 1905, pb. 1928; *The Rose of the Rancho*, pr. 1906, pb. 1936 (with Richard W. Tully adaptation of Tully's *Juanita*); *A Grand Army Man*, pr. 1907, pb. 1908 (with Pauline Phelps and Marion Short); *The Lily*, pr. 1909; *The Return of Peter Grimm*, pr. 1911, pb. 1928; *The Governor's Lady*, pr., pb. 1912 (with Alice Bradley); *The Secret*, pr. 1913; *The Son Daughter*, pr., pb. 1919 (with George Scarborough); *The Comedian*, pr. 1923; *Laugh, Clown, Laugh*, pr. 1923 (adaptation of Fausto Maria Martini's play *Ridi, pagliaccio*); *Fanny*, pr., pb. 1926 (with Willard Mack); *Mima*, pr. 1928 (adaptation of Ferenc Molnár's play *The Red Mill*); *Six Plays*, pb. 1928 (Montrose J. Moses, editor); *The Plays of Henry C. De Mille, Written in Collaboration with David Belasco*, pb. 1941 (Robert Hamilton Ball, editor).

Other literary forms

David Belasco published a number of human-interest essays and articles about stagecraft, including "How I Stage My Plays" and "Stage Realism of the Future." A serialized autobiography, "My Life's Story," was published in *Hearst's Magazine* from March, 1914, to December, 1915, followed four years later by a full-length memoir, *The Theatre Through Its Stage Door* (1919). With two of his most popular plays later turned into novels, Belasco was one of the first in the United States to capitalize on the success of dramatic works by revising them for a new reading audience.

Achievements

While contemporary critics frequently criticized Belasco's penchant for melodrama, his immense popular success was a product of his reliance upon heart-interest as well as a strict interpretation of the fourth-wall convention. Belasco paid meticulous attention to details, often rewriting extensively in rehearsal. Indeed, he is best remembered for his directing methods, his realism, and his technical effects.

Belasco was the directing genius behind many actors and actresses. David Warfield, for example, who began his career with the burlesque company Weber and Fields, under Belasco's tutelage moved from the farcical *The Auctioneer* to Belasco's own seriocomic *The Return of Peter Grimm* and later appeared in William Shakespeare's *The Merchant of Venice*. Perhaps "Mr. Dave's" greatest success was Leslie Carter, a society divorcée who undertook two years of acting lessons from Belasco. Best remembered for her electrifying performance in *The Heart of Maryland*, the fiery-haired actress exemplified the sensationalism that Belasco's audiences enjoyed. Such individual triumphs by no means detracted from Belasco's attention to his entire company. On the one hand, he encouraged every expression of individual talent, no matter how slender; on the other, he held long, painstaking rehearsals commencing at least six weeks before opening night.

Belasco believed that the purpose of the theater was to mimic nature, and he attempted to immerse his actors not merely in a realistic scene but in a mood as well. As Lise-Lone Marker points out, his goal seems similar to that of the proponents of the New Stagecraft, yet Belasco saw both light and color to be as essential to dialogue as music is to a song. He is noted for his ultrarealistic stage sets—sets that seem to answer August Strindberg's objection, in the preface to *Miss Julie*, to unstable canvas scenery. Belasco imported antique furniture and draperies for his sets; he offered his company his collection of authentic jewelry; he even introduced a flock of sheep on stage for his production of Salmi Morse's *The Passion Play*, and *The Governor's Lady* featured an exact replica of fashionable Child's restaurant. He followed the fourth-wall convention to its logical conclusion, forcing the famous tenor Enrico Caruso to sing his arias with his back to the audience in Giacomo Puccini's operatic version of *The Girl of the Golden West*.

Belasco's stage sets were complemented by his innovations in the use of movable spots, diffused lighting, and, above all, the baby spotlight (invented by Belasco's light man, Louis Hartmann), which eliminated the harshness of the ever-present footlight. His experiments with colored silks as filters and his discovery of the scrim, which was used in staging *The Darling of the Gods*, produced the spectacular effects that earned him the nickname "The Wizard."

Biography

David Belasco was born in San Francisco, California, on July 25, 1853. His father, Humphrey Abraham Belasco, was a London actor who, with his bride, Reina Martin Belasco, had succumbed to Gold Rush fever. Once in San Francisco, however, the couple settled into shopkeeping after David's birth. Five years later, news of a gold strike in British Columbia lured them north, where David's three brothers were born and where Humphrey Belasco maintained a tobacco shop while investing in real estate and digging for gold.

Belasco's published memories of British Columbia are highly imaginative accounts, containing references to a monastic education as well as to his appearance as "Davido, the Boy Wonder," with the Rio de Janeiro Circus. More sober accounts place him first at the Colonial School and then at the Anglican Collegiate School in 1862. Two years later, he made his first professional stage appearance, as the Duke of York in Charles Kean's *King Richard III*. Belasco's other theatrical efforts took place in San Francisco, to which his family returned when he was eleven. *The Roll of the Drum*, a childhood play strongly influenced by the penny dreadfuls, and a gold medal at Lincoln Grammar School for his impassioned rendition of Matthew Gregory Lewis' poem "The Maniac" were among Belasco's early achievements.

After graduation from Lincoln, Belasco entered a self-imposed, five-year apprenticeship during which he took a touring company up and down the West Coast, deriving much of the material by copying prompt books and pirating uncopyrighted Continental works. At twenty, he began a fifty-two-year marriage with Cecelia Loverich. His subsequent career in California was furthered by Tom Maguire, an unschooled Tammany barkeeper who opened a series of successful California theaters. As Maguire's prompter at the Baldwin, a magnificent hotel/theater, Belasco oversaw Salmi Morse's *The Passion Play*, which scandalized the citizens of San Francisco. During this period, he staged his Naturalistic version of Émile Zola's *L'Assommoir* and collaborated with James Herne in such works as *Chums*, which became known as *Hearts of Oak* after its New York success under that title. Before Maguire retired in 1882, Belasco had written and directed a number of works, among them *La Belle Russe* and *The Stranglers of Paris*, an adaptation of Adolphe Belot's earlier work.

Belasco's first New York assignment was as stage manager at the Madison Square Theatre, backed by Marshall and George Mallory, who sought wholesome productions by American playwrights. The interference and parsimony of the Mallory brothers caused Belasco to leave after only a few years, in 1885. After brief stints with Steele MacKaye and Lester Wallack, Belasco was hired by Daniel Frohman to direct the Lyceum Theatre. There, he collaborated with Henry C. DeMille to produce *The Wife, Lord Chumley, The Charity Ball,* and *Men and Women.* In 1889, Belasco undertook the training of a red-haired society divorcée, Leslie Carter, for the stage; finally, at forty, he had his first unqualified success with *The Heart of Maryland,* a Civil War drama written expressly for Carter, whose role called for her to swing on a bell clapper to keep the bell from ringing and to save her escaping Northern lover. After winning a lawsuit against N. K. Fairbank, Carter's financial backer, for withdrawing funding for another play, Belasco produced *Zaza*—inspired, in part, by Carter's determination to go upon the stage—and began training another star, Blanche Bates, who initially appeared in Belasco's *Naughty Anthony.* Ironically, the afterpiece with which Belasco bolstered his slender farce—an adaptation of John Luther Long's story "Madame Butterfly"—proved the more memorable production; in later years, it became one of Puccini's best-known operas.

In 1901, Belasco produced a dramatization of the life of Madame DuBarry, the mistress of King Louis XV. In staging *DuBarry,* another Carter vehicle, Belasco imported French antique draperies and furniture. The next year, he leased Oscar Hammerstein's theater, the Republic, which was remodeled and renamed the Belasco; his first new play, a collaboration with Long called *The Darling of the Gods,* featured the back-lit scrim. Although leasing the Republic gave him relative freedom from the Theatrical Syndicate which for sixteen years controlled bookings in New York and throughout the United States, Belasco entered a 1903-1904 lawsuit charging hidden partnerships and bribery against Marc Klaw and Abe Erlanger, a lawsuit often credited with breaking the syndicate's power. Immediately after the altercation, Belasco produced his very successful melodrama *The Girl of the Golden West,* which Puccini produced as *La fanciulla del West.*

In the same year, Carter deserted Belasco by remarrying; consequently, in 1907, it was Blanche Bates who helped inaugurate Belasco's new theater, the Stuyvesant, whose ornamental façade hid not only the finest lighting equipment then available but also Belasco's own private studio. Shortly thereafter, Belasco shocked his public by producing *The Easiest Way* (pb. 1908, pr. 1909), Eugene Walter's play about an unreformed prostitute. Belasco recouped with a production of his own *The Return of Peter Grimm,* a play known as much for its masterly lighting as for its afterlife theme—validated, according to the program notes, by psychologist William James himself.

From 1910 to 1920, Belasco produced thirty-two plays, mostly melodramas by other authors; his masterly 1920 production of *Deburau* (Harley Granville-Barker's adaptation of Sacha Guitry's play about pantomime) and his 1922 production of Shakespeare's *The Merchant of Venice*, with David Warfield, demonstrated that he was still a powerful figure in the theater. In November, 1930, Belasco fell ill with pneumonia during rehearsals of Frederic and Fanny Hatton's *Tonight or Never* and died the following year, on May 14, in New York.

Analysis

While David Belasco experimented with Naturalism, an overriding number of his plays are either melodramas or farces, whose strong emotion, light wit, and happy endings appealed to his audiences. Indeed, when Belasco was not writing adaptations of foreign novels and plays, he relied on a number of well-worn themes and used his magic realism to disguise the similarities. Many of his well-made plays feature the trials and tribulations of young lovers; his fascination with the lives of outcast women is equally evident.

A number of Belasco's melodramas have historical or ethnic backgrounds. *DuBarry*, set in the time of Louis XV, and *The Darling of the Gods*, set in Japan during the Samurai period, exhibit the same melodramatic characteristics as *The Girl of the Golden West*—slender character motivation, a romantic plot, strong appeal to the emotions, and a denouement characterized by poetic justice. Of the three heroines, DuBarry is the only one who fails to win a happy ending; the French milliner turned king's mistress, executed by the revolutionaries as an aristocrat, does nevertheless achieve a final reunion with Cossé, her former sweetheart. Yo-San, who dies for betraying the hide-out of her Samurai lover's band, meets Kara in the afterlife. Of the three, the Girl—Minnie—achieves the most enduring happiness, for although she leaves her beloved Sierra Nevada mountains, she does so in the company of Johnson, a reformed thief who has become her sweetheart. Perhaps the most sensational of Belasco's historical plays, *The Heart of Maryland* feature a pair of Civil War lovers divided by opposing North/South sympathies and reunited after an act of heroism on the part of Maryland Calvert herself.

Belasco's farces were much less sumptuous in staging and considerably lighter in plot; like *Lord Chumley*, *Naughty Anthony* relies on complicated, improbable situations for its humor. Professor Anthony Depew, a teacher of moral behavior, when caught kissing one of his patients in a darkened park gazebo, gives his landlord's name instead of his own. An incompetent lawyer, another love triangle, and a vengeful wife are coupled with what was then a mildly shocking episode in which Cora, a hosiery saleswoman, strips off her stockings onstage. Handled differently, *Naughty Anthony* might have succeeded as a satire of moral hypocrisy; as it stands, however, the tangled skeins of the well-made play are too much in evidence.

Belasco attempted to deal with the outcast woman in historical plays like *DuBarry* and in sheer melodrama like *La Belle Russe*, in which a notorious prostitute tries to profit from the good fortune of her innocent twin. La Belle Russe herself is saved by the love for her illegitimate child; similarly, in *Zaza*, the heroine redeems herself by becoming a great actress. Other characters, not nearly as well received, face a more realistic end.

A lavish and sensational Civil War melodrama, *The Heart of Maryland* made Belasco independent. The play, backed by Max Blieman, a dealer in art, opened on October 9, 1895, in Washington, D.C., and moved to the Herald Square Theatre in New York two weeks later for a run of 229 performances.

The property and light cues for the play show that Belasco paid extraordinary attention to detail, even visiting Maryland so he could duplicate the atmosphere. The first scene opens on The Lilacs, a nostalgically reproduced mansion replete with fragrant lilac bushes and water lilies. In the near distance is a stream crossed by a rustic bridge; in the far appear the hills of Maryland. The plot interprets the conflict between North and South romantically: Maryland Calvert's Northern lover is Colonel Alan Kendrick, whose father commands the Southern forces; Nanny, a sharp-witted Yankee of sixteen, is wooed by Robert Telfair, a lieutenant in the Southern artillery unit encamped at The Lilacs. Further complications arise when Colonel Thorpe, a Southern officer in the employ of the Northern Secret Service, uses the information given to him by Lloyd Calvert—Maryland's brother, a Northern sympathizer—to further his own career rather than to warn General Hooker of General Kendrick's advance. When Alan is brought as a prisoner to The Lilacs, Maryland, despite her strong Dixie bias, passes the information to him.

In act 2, Lloyd is killed while he is carrying information, but not before he asks his sister to detain an anonymous "friend" of his—Alan. Captured while awaiting Maryland, Alan confronts his father, who keeps his military bearing with difficulty. Maryland becomes hysterical upon learning of her brother's death and impulsively accuses his "friend" of spying. As the scene closes, she understands that she has accused her lover in order to save her brother's name.

At the beginning of act 3, Alan is incarcerated in an old church that serves as a prison. Maryland, crossing the lines, brings a stay of execution, but Thorpe realizes that had the letter reached the now-dead Colonel Kendrick, he himself would have been indicted for spying. He brings Alan from the prison to torment him with the sight of Maryland; Alan, bound and helpless, watches as Maryland—like the operatic heroine Tosca—stabs her attacker and urges Alan to run. The climax of the scene occurs when she races up the stairs and leaps to grasp the clapper on the bell that is rung to alert the Southern artillery. As the act closes, Maryland swings back and forth on the bell, a tour de force supposedly reminiscent of Belasco's childhood fascination with Rosa Hartwicke Thorpe's poem "The Curfew Must Not Ring Tonight."

The resolution in the fourth act finds Nanny nursing the wounded Telfair while the Northern troops, led by Alan, cannonade The Lilacs, where Thorpe has imprisoned Maryland. Thorpe negotiates a retreat to Richmond but insists that Maryland accompany him to stand trial. Alan accepts but then, given safe conduct, delivers a letter from General Lee court-martialing Thorpe for double treachery and appointing Telfair commander. The curtain closes as Maryland and Alan are reunited.

Although Belasco, in a first-night curtain speech, had said, "Now I am encouraged to hope I have proved myself a dramatist," critical praise was not forthcoming; nevertheless, the play ran for nearly nine months and had a successful season in London. Although some British critics praised Leslie Carter's histrionics as Maryland and likened Belasco to the wildly popular French playwright Victorien Sardou, George Bernard Shaw (who also disliked Sardou) made sharp-tongued fun of American melodrama while conceding that the actors themselves were better trained than their British cousins and that Carter's intensity showed her to be an actress "of no mean powers."

One of the works that held the most personal meaning for Belasco, *The Return of Peter Grimm* is permeated not only by a sense of loss for departed family members but also by a belief in an afterlife. During the play's first performance at the Boston Hollis Street Theatre on January 2, 1911, Belasco's younger daughter Augusta, terminally ill with tuberculosis, impressed her father with her belief that dying is another form of living— or, in Peter Grimm's words, "knowing better." Other personal facts contributed to the production of the play about the old horticulturist who returns from the dead to right his mistakes, most notably Belasco's insistence in 1898 that his mother had appeared to him in a waking dream; the next morning, news was brought during the rehearsals for *Zaza* that she had died in San Francisco during the night.

Despite rumors to the contrary, Belasco reiterated publicly that Cecil B. DeMille was responsible only for the idea of the play and not for the actual script—a script which, Belasco noted presented the serious problem of how to make Grimm's return believable. Three factors contributed to his success in solving this problem: naturalistic stage setting, acting, and lighting. First, the props were carefully selected to suggest not only a real room but also a wealth of memories that might be evoked by a cosy, homey house; likewise, the view shown from the onstage window conveys the close tie between Grimm's sense of well-being and his thriving business. Second, Belasco instructed his other actors to look *through* the Grimm "apparition" so as to highlight the reaction of the eight-year-old child medium. Third, the complex lighting system made use of the baby lens developed by Louis Hartmann. This lens concentrated spots of flesh-toned light on all of the characters but Grimm, who was bathed in a colder, bluer light; consequently, he seemed in contrast always to be shadowed. In addition, Belasco abolished the footlights and substituted bridge lights on beams above the set. The lighting schematic took almost a year to develop but was called "perhaps the most perfect example of stage lighting ever exhibited."

The melodramatic plot includes a love triangle, a villainous family member, and a child who dies young. In the long first act, the love that James Hartman, Grimm's secretary, has not only for Catherine Staats—Grimm's adopted daughter—but also for the plants themselves is juxtaposed to the money-hungry courtship of Grimm's nephew Frederick, whose dearest wish is to sell the house and nursery. Warned by his doctor that the condition of his heart may cause his death at any moment, Grimm forces an engagement between Catherine and Frederick so that he may be, he thinks, assured of the continuance of his business and of Catherine's happiness. William, the eight-year-old illegitimate son of a runaway servant, is also put under the protection of Frederick, who clearly dislikes him. At the end of the act, Peter dies.

An approaching storm, James's and Catherine's manifest unhappiness, an altercation among Grimm's old friends over their legacies—all produce a mood of suspense that builds toward the arrival of the ghost in act 2. When the ghostly Grimm does appear, however, it is very quietly; moreover, since he can make himself felt only indirectly, his efforts to save the business, to make Catherine break her engagement, and to reveal Frederick as William's father are all subtle (or else, indeed, the play would end abruptly). It is only to William, who is ill, that Grimm can speak directly; through Grimm's influence, William points out the incriminating letter from his mother, Annemarie. Frederick's perfidy revealed and the marriage broken off, the third act centers on William's death, a scene that escapes the bathetic partly by the circus motif that carries over from the first act and partly by Peter's insistence that he is taking William away "to know better." As the curtain falls, the two dance away to the clown's tune, "Uncle Rat Has Gone to Town." The play, which moved to the New York Stuyvesant Theatre on October 18, 1911, ran for 231 performances. Critical reception was warm, citing Belasco's triumph in making the impossible appear actual by his magic of lighting and directing.

A compound of memories of California (as well as of Bret Harte, as some contemporary critics charged), *The Girl of the Golden West* opened on October 3, 1905, at the Belasco Theatre in Pittsburgh and moved to New York on November 14. Puccini adapted the play, which Belasco believed his best, under the title *La fanciulla del West* (Puccini had brought about a similar musical transformation with Belasco's *Madame Butterfly* in 1904). As Belasco notes, teaching acting techniques to opera singers—Enrico Caruso among them—familiar only with vocal flourishes was a difficult task, considering that both he and Arturo Toscanini, the conductor, were autocratic in their methods. The December 10, 1910, premiere at the Metropolitan Opera House was, nevertheless, a success.

The melodramatic plot, which Belasco insisted was based on his father's stories, features the trusting, unlettered Minnie, owner of The Polka, a Western saloon. Most of her customers, including the gambler/sheriff Jack Rance, are in love with her. While the bartender, Nick, slyly keeps up business by encouraging her suitors, Minnie, who has fallen in love with a nameless stranger she has met on the road, cheerfully and faithfully serves as a "bank" for the prospectors' nuggets. In act 1, the stranger, Dick Johnson—in reality, Ramerrez, a bandit who has plotted to rob The Polka—appears. While Johnson is at The Polka, the Pony Express brings news that Ramerrez is in the area, and the Girl, who innocently admires Johnson, stoutly declares that she will protect the prospectors' hard-earned gold.

In act 2, Minnie welcomes Johnson to her cabin for dinner, where he becomes convinced that she is the one woman for whom he would reform. Trapped by a snowstorm, he hides when Rance and his men appear at the cabin to ascertain Minnie's safety. While there, they arouse Minnie's jealousy by mentioning Ramerrez's supposed lover, Nina Micheltorena. Minnie angrily sends Johnson out into the storm, but he is wounded by Rance and returns to take refuge in her loft. Rance is almost convinced that Ramerrez has escaped until a drop of blood from the loft falls on his handkerchief. As the act ends, Rance and the Girl play poker to win Ramerrez; during a diversion, Minnie uses the three aces she had hidden in her stocking to make a better hand, wins the right to let Ramerrez escape, and frees herself from Rance's power.

In act 3, Minnie opens the "Academy," a grammar school for prospectors, but is distracted by happiness at the thought of meeting Johnson and sadness at leaving The Polka. A crisis occurs when the Wells Fargo agent recaptures Johnson, much to the glee of Rance, who has kept his promise not to interfere but who can now take revenge. Rance proposes lynching Johnson, and the boys in The Polka are willing to follow his lead until they witness the reunion between Johnson and the Girl. Hearing her prayer, they become convinced that Providence protects Johnson. As the play concludes, Johnson and the Girl are leaving California for a new start in the "promised land" in the East.

Belasco introduced a number of special effects that enhanced the play's atmosphere. Before the first act, audiences saw a detailed panorama of the

Sierra Nevada, complete with the Girl's cabin on Cloudy Mountain. The panorama, a transparency painted in evocative colors and lit from behind, slowly unrolled to the bottom of the mountain, where The Polka appeared blazing with light. The sound effects were introduced at this point; Belasco discarded the usual orchestral accompaniment, using instead a small band of concertina and banjo playing such favorites as "Camptown Races" and "Pop Goes the Weasel," partly, Belasco claimed, in memory of the famous mining camp banjo player Jake Wallace. After the houselights were dimmed and the panorama removed, the act opened on the interior of The Polka, where all props were handled with meticulous detail, from the real pineboards in the walls to the riding paraphernalia piled carelessly on the floor. In addition, even the minor characters were costumed in distinctly in-dividualistic ways to suggest a realistic and motley selection of prospectors. Perhaps the greatest tour de force of the play was the snowstorm that trapped Johnson in Minnie's cabin. Making use of the pathetic fallacy—the idea that natural events parallel emotional and moral situations—Belasco built the suspense of the scene. Blowers, fans, rock salt, snow bags, and air tanks to reproduce the sound of the storm were operated by a cadre of thirty-two stagehands, who formed, as William Winter notes, "a sort of mechanical orchestra."

On the whole, Belasco's plays are not classics and do not even lend themselves to serious criticism. In his own day, his appeal to the emotions did as much as his wizardry in the areas of lighting and directing to guar-antee his plays full houses and long runs. Today's more sophisticated audi-ences would judge them overly sentimental, melodramatic, and simplistic. Yet Belasco did have an enduring impact on the theater, setting an example with his imaginative approach to extending what had become the usual boundaries of staging and his meticulous attention to the details of production.

Other major works

NOVELS: *The Girl of the Golden West*, 1911; *The Return of Peter Grimm*, 1912.

NONFICTION: *My Life's Story*, 1916 (2 volumes); *The Theatre Through Its Stage Door*, 1919.

Bibliography

Marker, Lise-Lone. *David Belasco: Naturalism in the American Theatre*, 1975.

Timberlake, Craig. *The Bishop of Broadway: The Life and Work of David Belasco*, 1954.

Winter, William. *The Life of David Belasco*, 1918.

Patricia Marks

RUDOLPH BESIER

Born: Java; July 2, 1878
Died: Elmhurst, England; June 13, 1942

Principal drama

The Virgin Goddess, pr. 1906, pb. 1907; *Olive Latimer's Husband*, pr. 1909; *Don*, pr., pb. 1909; *Apropos*, pr. 1910; *The Crisis*, pr. 1910 (adaptation of P. F. Berton's play *Le Rencontre*); *Lady Patricia*, pr., pb. 1911; *Kipps*, pr. 1912 (with H. G. Wells; adaptation of Wells's novel); *Kings and Queens*, pr. 1915; *Kultur at Home*, pr. 1916 (with Sybil Spotiswoode); *A Run for His Money*, pr. 1916 (also as *Buxell*, pr. 1916); *Robin's Father*, pr. 1918 (with Hugh Walpole); *The Prude's Fall*, pr. 1920 (with May Edginton; originally as *The Awakening of Beatrice*); *The Ninth Earl*, pr. 1921 (with Edginton); *Secrets*, pr. 1922 (with Edginton); *The Barretts of Wimpole Street*, pr., pb. 1930.

Other literary forms

Rudolph Besier is noted only for his dramatic works, although he was also engaged in journalism and translated from the French.

Achievements

Though he wrote a large number of plays, Besier's international reputation depends upon a single work, the historical drama *The Barretts of Wimpole Street*. This perennial favorite was produced for the first time at the Malvern Festival in England in 1930 by Sir Barry Jackson, following its rejection by two London producers. After twenty-seven American producers turned it down, Katharine Cornell accepted it and the play opened in Cleveland and, shortly thereafter, at the Empire Theatre in New York.

At the turn of the century, dramatic language on the English-speaking stage had increasingly tended to become dry and uninteresting, and, as a result, dialogue seemed stilted. Besier's first play, *The Virgin Goddess*, a classical tragedy written during a visit to the United States, clearly showed his eagerness to return colorful and lively dialogue to the stage. The play was greeted with mixed reviews. Three years later, Besier received considerable praise for his comedy *Don*, which centers on an eccentric and magnanimous poet. The play's formal language and heavy sentimentality have dated badly. *Lady Patricia*, a satire on English affectations, and *Kultur at Home*, which delighted audiences for the manner in which it depicted German domestic life at its worst, kept Besier before the critics and the public.

Besier first achieved genuine popular success with the dream play, *Secrets*, in which he used the device of allowing the first act to take shape as a prologue, commencing the main action with the second act. In the opening episode, Lady Carlton, old and exhausted from constantly tending her dying husband, falls asleep in an armchair beside his bed. The drama itself consists of a series of flashbacks presented in the form of a dream. In these, the lives of the couple are presented as they marry, endure initial poverty, and gradually attain affluence. During this time, the husband has an affair with another woman; his wife forgives him, despite her bitter jealousy, because of her realization that he needs her. Like several of Besier's earlier plays, *Secrets* is highly sentimental, but it is distinguished by its acute perceptions into the psychology of the two main characters.

The success of *Secrets* did not prepare the public for Besier's masterpiece, which appeared some eight years later. Though many playgoers were surprised by the general popularity of *The Barretts of Wimpole Street*, one can see in retrospect the groundwork for this achievement. At the beginning of his career, Besier had demonstrated his ability to draw a portrait of a peculiar poet, and in *Secrets* he demonstrated his sharp and sensitive knowledge of human feelings. Further, several of his earlier plays revealed a flair for melodrama. Though *The Barretts of Wimpole Street* exhibits characteristics of the comedy (it was labeled by Besier as such), the psychological drama, and the historical drama, the play contains many of the traits of the melodrama. Above all, it is the intrinsic appeal of the story of Elizabeth Barrett and Robert Browning which has given the play its enduring appeal, yet Besier must be given full credit for realizing the dramatic potential in this well-known romance—particularly the role of Elizabeth Barrett's father, the quintessential Victorian tyrant.

Biography

Born in Java of Dutch extraction on July 2, 1878, Rudolph Besier was the son of Margaret (née Collinson) and Rudolph Besier. He was educated in England and Germany: at St. Elizabeth College, Guernsey, and at Heidelberg, respectively. For several years he was engaged in journalism, being for a time on the staff of C. Arthur Pearson, Ltd. In 1908, however, Besier left journalism, having decided to devote his efforts entirely to the theater. He married Charlotte Woodward, the daughter of the Reverend J. P. S. Woodward, of Plumpton, Sussex. He wrote a large number of plays; the most famous of these plays and the one that confirmed his dramatic reputation is *The Barretts of Wimpole Street*. Critics praised the play, but it was severely criticized by members of the Barrett family, who objected to the Freudian implications in the portrayal of Edward Moulton Barrett. Later, a film version of the play was made. An extremely tall, handsome man who shunned public exposure, Rudolph Besier spent the last part of his life at his home in Elmhurst, Surrey, where he died suddenly of heart failure on June 13, 1942.

Analysis

Like any work that deals with actual personages, a play demands some understanding of the lives of its characters and the times in which they lived if it is to be thoroughly appreciated. Understanding the fullness of *The Barretts of Wimpole Street* necessarily entails historical knowledge not only of Elizabeth Barrett and Robert Browning but also of the general nature of Victorian customs, manners, and class distinctions. The oldest child in a wealthy, upper-middle-class family, Elizabeth Barrett was educated at home. As a result of a back injury at the age of fifteen, she became a chronic invalid. From her early teens until the end of her life, she read widely and concentrated on writing poetry. At the time of the play, Elizabeth for a number of years had been confined to her room in her father's London house on Wimpole Street. From there, she pursued her education, including the study of Greek, took frequent medication, and, with the exception of visits by her family and a few friends, remained by herself to write articles and the poetry which brought her recognition. Robert Browning, a poet then ignored by the public, one day came to pay his respects, and the celebrated literary romance began. The pair seemed ill-matched; she was six years older than he and her health was frail. Her father, moreover, had decided that none of his children should marry.

Despite such unpromising conditions, the two lovers secretly married and moved to Italy, where they lived for most of the fifteen years that remained of Elizabeth Barrett Browning's life. There, they wrote most of their now famous poems and had a son. Elizabeth Browning strongly devoted herself to the Italian struggle for independence against Austria. She wrote not only *The Cry of the Children* (1854), in which she passionately argued against child labor in England, but also *Sonnets from the Portuguese* (1850), her famous sonnet sequence celebrating her love for her husband. In 1861, she died and was buried in her beloved Italy.

The hero of Besier's play, Robert Browning, was strong, spirited, and optimistic; like Elizabeth, he began writing when he was young. The criticism that attended his poetry early in his career failed to discourage him, for he continued to write prolifically. His whirlwind courtship overwhelmed Elizabeth's initial resistance, and their romance ended only with her death, after which he returned to England. His reputation today rests primarily on his dramatic monologues, in which the speakers' own words provide psychological insights into their characters. He died in Venice in 1889, but his body was returned to England and buried in Westminster Abbey, where many of England's great poets are buried.

Set against Browning in the play is the antagonist, Elizabeth's father, Edward Moulton Barrett, who at the age of nineteen left Cambridge University to marry a woman more than five years older than he. The union produced twelve children; one child, a girl, died in childhood, and two boys died as adults. After his wife died, Barrett ruled his nine remaining children like a despot, refusing to explain any of his commands and forbidding any of the children to marry. Three eventually disobeyed him, and as a result, he disinherited them and refused to see them again.

The Barretts of Wimpole Street takes place during the early years of Queen Victoria's reign. Though the living and working conditions of the lower classes were slowly improving, the poor found it difficult to make gains through their employment. The exploitation of women and child laborers was common. Putting in long hours for pitifully low wages under oppressive and unhealthy conditions, workers were barely able to survive. Then, too, the class distinctions were rigidly structured and observed, with opportunities to rise to a higher class practically nonexistent. Though not of the aristocracy, Edward Moulton Barrett had inherited large sums of money and had land holdings on the British island of Jamaica. Consequently, he was able to attend Cambridge University. Supported by his own means and the wealth that came to him through his wife, Barrett lived comfortably in a fashionable London district and reared his large family, though he was temporarily inconvenienced financially when all slaves were freed in the British Empire.

Both sons and daughters of the upper classes were dependent on their fathers for financial support. Robert Browning was himself supported by his parents until his poetry began to earn money for him. The various Barrett sons assisted their father in his office, taking orders while he attended to business in the financial quarter of London or while he was abroad supervising his land holdings. Daughters were never permitted to engage in business affairs, and, as a result, some, like Bella, became social butterflies, while others, like Arabel, worked in support of various social or religious causes. Certain others became little more than house decorations, awaiting the opportunity to marry. Elizabeth Barrett, therefore, stands out in contrast, for she had both a career of her own and a limited inheritance. Elizabeth was fortunate also in being able to secure a respectable education. Girls of the upper classes were generally encouraged to pursue only the refined graces of music, manners, and needlework. Elizabeth gained additional education through her own intense and varied reading and from her brothers' tutors.

Characterized by prudery, repression, and formality, the Victorian period was highlighted by a fear of outspokenness and by the evasion of facts. In *The Barretts of Wimpole Street*, for example, Arabel upbraids Bella for speaking of the birth of children and scolds Henrietta for describing their father with language she considers ugly. Houses of the wealthy were heavily and formally furnished. Women, moreover, dressed in voluminous layers of clothing, and men indulged in formal attire. When first calling on Elizabeth, Robert Browning faultlessly dressed in the manner of the times—a cape fastened around his neck, a high hat, lemon-colored gloves, and a cane. Mr. Barrett, together with his sons, wore evening clothes for dinner with the family each night. The wealthy also were transported in fine carriages that were attended by coachmen and footmen wearing powdered wigs.

Besier's purpose necessitated many of the dramatic techniques he used in the play. His intention was not so much to present the love affair between Elizabeth Barrett and Robert Browning as to portray a family dominated by a tyrannical, repressed father. The revolt of the most unlikely family member of the Barretts of Wimpole Street constitutes the romantic and dramatic climax, and, appropriately enough, the play is set entirely in Elizabeth's room. The use of only one setting focuses audience attention on the one room which every family member visited. By this means, Besier could portray the attitudes of the various sons and daughters toward their father and, in turn, his effect on them. The play's conclusion maintains and reinforces this dramatic focus: The audience does not view Elizabeth's marriage, nor is there any scene in Italy. The play closes with Mr. Barrett's frustrated endeavor to destroy Elizabeth's dog, Flush, a final indication of his unreasoning cruelty.

Terror affects each member of the Barrett family. Elizabeth continues to drink the porter that she so detests in order not to displease her father, while Henrietta, ever rebellious, accedes to Barrett's demands and swears upon the Bible that she will neither see nor communicate with her suitor, Captain Surtees Cook. Representing all the boys who through fear of their father are leading "a life which isn't a life at all," Octavius calls Barrett "His Majesty." The whole family is elated when informed that the father is undertaking a two-week business trip. Arabel, more placid than most of the other children, hopes that he will be detained. Elizabeth herself later declares that "our family life was one of unrelieved gloom." Besier relieves the tense, strained, family atmosphere with scenes of a lighter, even humorous, quality. The Browning story primarily supplies these brief interludes, but to a degree, the story of Henrietta and Captain Cook does so as well. Entertainment also is provided by the refreshingly frivolous Bella, whose ostentatiousness reveals an aspect of Mr. Barrett not brought out by any of the other characters.

Because his primary intention was not simply to dramatize the romance between two gifted poets, Besier was confronted by the problem of subordinating the literary activities and interests of his principal characters to the analysis of a family's spirit in the household of a tyrannical father. Besier's dramatic maturity is evident in the masterful manner in which he resolves the problem. He employs the play's various references to poetry either to delineate character or to move the plot forward. When Elizabeth, for example, is reflecting on what she perceives to be the obscure nature of

Browning's poetry ("No—it's quite beyond me! I give it up!"), the audience is prepared for the tender, more intimate scene in which the shared poetic sensibilities of the lovers establish their rapport and suggest their determination to overcome the obstacles that life sets before them.

The play is divided into the classical five acts, as opposed to the more modern three, and each act is given a title: "Porter in a Tankard," "Mr. Robert Browning," "Robert," "Henrietta," and "Papa." All five acts revolve around the commanding presence (or absence) of the father: act 1, his insistence that Elizabeth drink porter as medicine; act 2, the appearance of his as yet unknown opponent; act 3, Browning's deepening hold on Elizabeth's affections; act 4, the father's cruelty to Henrietta and Elizabeth's realization that she must agree with Browning's wedding plans; and act 5, Elizabeth's final interview with her father, in which she is so revolted by his words that she becomes distraught. Indeed, Barrett's influence, even when he is not actually onstage, is so extensive, so tangible, that in many ways he, and not Elizabeth or Browning, is the main character of the play.

Much of Besier's portrayal of Barrett accords with the known facts of his life and personality. Not only did the father terrorize his children, but also he prohibited them to marry and actually disowned three who disobeyed his injunction. In other details, however, Besier used dramatic license. He collapsed the actual time of Elizabeth's romance with Browning from one year to approximately four months, and he inserted into the dialogue a remark that was not to achieve acclaim until some years later. When Browning finally achieved recognition, Browning societies were established all over England for the express purpose of discussing and analyzing his poetry. Browning, after receiving a letter from a member of one of these societies asking for an explanation of one particularly obscure poetic passage, replied: "When that passage was written, only God and Robert Browning understood it. Now only God understands it." Besier felt at liberty to include the remark in a conversation between Elizabeth and Browning, thereby reinforcing the warmth and the humanness of their relationship.

The reader can trace in *The Barretts of Wimpole Street* the change in Elizabeth's feelings for her father and, at the same time, her increasing health and desire for life as she comes increasingly under the influence of Robert Browning. When the first act begins, she is "so tired—tired—tired of it all," and later she admits that she "was often impatient for the end." To Browning, she declares that love can have no place in the life of a dying woman. Three months later, however, she is miraculously revitalized, full of energy and desirous of experiencing nature's passionate embrace, all of which she attributes not to the doctors or the porter but to Browning himself: "I wanted to live—eagerly, desperately, passionately—and only because life meant you—you—and the sight of your face, and the sound of your voice, and the touch of your hand." Carried along by Browning's inspiring vitality, she nevertheless continues to resist the idea of marriage simply because of the difference in their ages. When she views her father's brutal treatment of Henrietta, however, she becomes more sure about marriage, and following her final interview with her father, when she realizes that he is "not like other men," all of her doubts disappear. With a self-assurance and determination not earlier evident, she whispers to herself: "I must go at once—I must go—I must go. . . ."

Besier raised *The Barretts of Wimpole Street* from what could have been mere sentimentalism to the genuinely dramatic. The result was a play that has continued to please audiences on stage, television, and film.

Bibliography
Brown, John Mason. *Seeing Things*, 1946.
Craik, T. W. *The Revels History of Drama in English*, 1976-1983 (8 volumes).
Mikhail, E. H. *English Drama, 1900-1950*, 1977.
Nathan, George Jean. *The Theatre Book of the Year, 1944-1945*, 1946.
Nicoll, Allardyce. *English Drama, 1900-1930: The Beginnings of the Modern Period*, 1973.
Palmer, Helen H. *European Drama Criticism, 1900-1975*, 1977.
Shipley, Joseph T. *Guide to Great Plays*, 1956.

A. Gordon Van Ness III

ROBERT MONTGOMERY BIRD

Born: New Castle, Delaware; February 5, 1806
Died: Philadelphia, Pennsylvania; January 23, 1854

Principal drama

The Cowled Lover, wr. 1827, pb. 1941; *Caridorf: Or, The Avenger*, wr. 1827, pb. 1941; *'Twas All for the Best*, wr. 1827, pb. 1941; *The City Looking Glass: A Philadelphia Comedy*, wr. 1829, pr., pb. 1933; *Pelopidas: Or, The Fall of Polemarchs*, wr. 1830, pb. 1919; *The Gladiator*, pr. 1831, pb. 1919; *Oralloossa: Son of the Incas*, pr. 1832, pb. 1919; *The Broker of Bogotá*, pr. 1834, pb. 1917; *The Life and Dramatic Works*, pb. 1919 (includes *Pelopidas, The Gladiator, Oralloossa*); *News of the Night: Or, A Trip to Niagara*, pr. 1929, pb. 1941; *The Cowled Lover and Other Plays*, pb. 1941 (includes *Caridorf, 'Twas All for the Best, News of the Night*).

Other literary forms

Robert Montgomery Bird is better known as a novelist than as a dramatist. In his dramas, Bird was clearly moving toward the subject matter that would form the basis for his two earliest novels, *Calavar: Or, The Knight of the Conquest* (1834) and *The Infidel: Or, The Fall of Mexico* (1835)—romances dealing with Mexican Indians. Yet Bird is better remembered for his novels that are set in indigenous North American settings—*The Hawks of Hawk-Hollow: A Tradition of Pennsylvania* (1835) and *Nick of the Woods: Or, The Jibbenainosay, a Tale of Kentucky* (1837)—than he is for his Mexican romances. In addition, Bird published a volume of short fiction, *Peter Pilgrim: Or, A Rambler's Recollections* (1838), and several works of nonfiction, including *Sketch of the Life, Public Services, and Character of Major Thomas Stockton of New-Castle, the Candidate for the Whig Party for the Office of Governor of Delaware* (1844) and *A Brief Review of the Career, Character, and Campaigns of Zachary Taylor* (1848).

Achievements

How one ranks the achievement of Bird depends on the backdrop against which one is viewing him. Compared with American dramatists since Eugene O'Neill, Bird must be viewed as a less than successful artist whose plays were somewhat contrived and stereotyped. Viewed against a different backdrop, that of the dramatists of the first half of the nineteenth century, Bird figures as one of the two or three most promising figures in the American drama of his time. It must be remembered that American theater audiences were unsophisticated and, at times, uncouth during this period. Bird himself called them "foolish and vulgar," and he was probably not much off the mark. Refined and cultivated Americans did not go to the theater. British audiences were not much better than those in the United States, and audiences in both countries preferred to attend performances of Shakespearean plays rather than performances of contemporary drama. Bird knew his audiences, and if he ever forgot their salient characteristics, Edwin Forrest, the great actor of the day, was always nearby to remind him, as Forrest's notations in surviving manuscripts of Bird's dramas attest.

Certainly, Bird's earliest plays are dramatically substandard. Some of them have never been performed and a few had their first performances only after Arthur Hobson Quinn drew scholarly attention to Bird, in his 1916 article in *The Nation*, "Dramatic Works of Robert Montgomery Bird," and in his compendious *A History of American Drama from the Beginning to the Civil War* (1923). It must be borne in mind, however, that Bird was only twenty-one or twenty-two years old when he wrote his earliest plays and that he was at the time a student in medical school, which surely distracted him substantially from his literary pursuits.

Bird began to come into his own as an American dramatist in 1830 with Forrest's acceptance as a prize play in the dramatic contest that the actor sponsored annually of *Pelopidas*, a work surging with the Romantic spirit that Bird brought to American drama. Although *Pelopidas* was never produced during Bird's lifetime, Forrest continued to hold ownership of the play. The next year, Forrest awarded the dramatic prize to Bird's *The Gladiator*, which turned out to be Bird's most popular play with audiences and which certainly vies with *The Broker of Bogotá* as his best drama. Forrest took *The Gladiator* to London in 1836, where it was received less enthusiastically than was Forrest himself as Spartacus. Nevertheless, it is significant that this was the first American drama to be transported to England. The play was performed at the Theatre Royal in Drury Lane in a run that began on October 17, and despite the less than warm reception it received, its author was elected to honorary membership in the English Dramatic Authors' Society within a fortnight of its opening.

Two more of Bird's plays were to win Forrest's drama prizes in the years immediately following the award given to *The Gladiator*. *Oralloossa*, one of Bird's Latin American plays, won the prize in 1832, and the following year *The Broker of Bogotá*, also set in Latin America, received the coveted award.

Bird had great literary ambitions. By the time he was twenty-two, he had a clearly laid plan for his career as a writer. He intended initially to establish himself as a dramatist and had already sketched the plans for fifty-five plays he hoped to write. Once established as a dramatist, he planned to write a series of romances, and finally he anticipated devoting the talents of his later years to the writing of history.

It is impossible to say whether Bird might have followed his plan had he not had a severe falling out with Edwin Forrest in 1837, confirming for him his earlier contention that one cannot fill one's purse with the proceeds that the writer receives from drama. Forrest was growing rich on Bird's plays, and Bird received little more than the prize money (one thousand dollars in each instance) awarded to the winning play. No copyright laws, as we know them today, existed in Bird's time to protect playwrights from the sort of exploitation that Bird was experiencing.

Bird turned his efforts to writing romances, the first two of which, *Calavar* and *The Infidel*, were set in Mexico and were well received. In 1835, Benjamin H. Brewster turned *The Infidel* into a play. *The Hawks of Hawk-Hollow* and *Nick of the Woods*, however, had the kind of indigenous North American setting for which Americans longed and for which many American intellectuals were calling in their writings—Washington Irving in his "English Writers on America" (1820), William Cullen Bryant in his *Lectures on Poetry* (1884), William Ellery Channing in his "On National Literature" (1830), Henry Wadsworth Longfellow in his "The Defence of Poetry" (1832), and, most notably, Ralph Waldo Emerson in his Phi Beta Kappa address, "The American Scholar" (1837). Bird's first two American romances established him as an outstanding writer capable of dealing seriously and successfully with indigenous American themes. *Calavar* told about the life of a Tory family in Pennsylvania a year after the Battle of Yorktown; *The Infidel* told the tale of Nathan Slaughter, an Indian-hating Quaker living in Kentucky, who, because of his Quaker pacifism, refused to join his Kentucky neighbors in 1782 in taking up arms against the Indians. Given the temper of Bird's times, one would have to consider his ability to produce such writing as his outstanding literary achievement.

In the fifteen years between the publication of his last novel, *The Adventures of Robin Day* (1839), and his death, Bird, afflicted by recurrent ill health, wrote only two more significant works of any length: his sketch of Major Thomas Stockton in 1844 and *A Brief Review of the Career, Character, and Campaigns of Zachary Taylor* in 1848. He also revised his dramas, hoping that he might publish them; Edwin Forrest, however, would not relinquish his ownership of the works, so that Bird was unable to follow through on this idea.

Toward the end of his life, Bird joined forces with George H. Boker, renowned for his drama *Francesca da Rimini* (pr. 1855), to agitate for a copyright law that would protect writers. It was not until two years after Bird's death, however, that the Copyright Act of 1856 was finally passed. Certainly its passage must be numbered among Bird's notable achievements, because the passage of this act made careers in writing more attractive to Americans than they had previously been.

Biography

Robert Montgomery Bird's father died in 1810, when Robert was only four years old. Because the elder Bird was bankrupt at the time of his death, his young son went to live in the home of his kindly uncle, Nicholas Van Dyke, who had been a member of the Council for Safety in 1776, a framer of the constitution of the state of Delaware, and president of the state of Delaware from 1783 until 1786. Bird remained in his uncle's house for ten years. The young boy led a relatively happy life with his uncle and with his uncle's family, although he was not overly happy in school and was subjected to frequent beatings. When his uncle discovered this, he withdrew Robert from the New Castle Academy, which the boy had been attending. Bird had a passion for books and for reading, and he drew heavily upon the resources of the New Castle Library Company during these early years of his life. He became interested in music and in writing during this period, and by the time he moved to Philadelphia in 1820 to live with his mother and to attend a school run by Mr. Pardon Davis, he had written considerable verse. In Philadelphia, he became interested in drawing, an avocation that he continued to pursue in his later years.

Bird returned to New Castle in 1821 and enrolled in the same New Castle Academy from which his uncle had earlier withdrawn him. While there, he wrote some of his earliest descriptive pieces. He remained at New Castle Academy until 1823, when he entered Germantown Academy to pursue courses preparatory to his entering the University of Pennsylvania as a medical student. In the summer between leaving Germantown Academy and entering the university, Bird studied medicine, as was the custom in his day, with a practicing physician, Dr. Joseph Parrish.

Bird attended the University from 1824 until 1827, receiving the M.D. degree upon the completion of his studies. By that time, he had published a great deal of poetry in *Philadelphia Monthly Magazine* and had begun to write plays, although they all remained fragmentary at that point. He had also laid specific plans for his literary career and had begun reading widely in classical literature, in Shakespearean and Jacobean drama, and in Latin American history, archaeology, and literature as a means of implementing his literary plans.

Life as a physician did not appeal to Bird, although in 1827 he established himself as a doctor in Philadelphia and had a substantial number of patients. After a year in medical practice, during which time he completed a comedy, *'Twas All for the Best*, and two tragedies, *The Cowled Lover* and *Caridorf*, he left the medical profession to support himself by writing.

In 1828, Bird began work on three more plays, "King Philip," "The Three Dukes," and "Giannone." He also began work on his long poem, "The Cave," and on a novel, "The Volunteers." Although none of these works was ever produced or published, within a short time Bird had also finished *The City Looking Glass*, a comedy that would finally be staged in 1933, some hundred years after it was written.

Bird was working so unrelentingly that his health began to be adversely affected, and in 1829, he sought diversion in painting as a means of regaining his health. At the end of that summer, he began a long journey to what was then considered frontier territory, Pittsburgh and Cincinnati. He spent the winter in Cincinnati with John Grimes, an artist, and his circle. During that trip, Bird visited Kentucky and imbibed some of the local color that later was to appear in his most successful novel, *Nick of the Woods.*

Upon returning to Philadelphia in 1830, Bird learned that Edwin Forrest was again offering an annual prize, which he had instituted in 1828, for the best play written by an American author. The prize was one thousand dollars, and Forrest, who was to act in the prize play, was to own the property in return for awarding the prize. Bird entered the contest with *Pelopidas*, a classical tragedy set in Thebes, and this play won the prize quite handily. Forrest ultimately decided against producing the play, because it did not have the sort of clearly defined central character that he required in any play that was to be a vehicle for his talent. This being the case, Bird wrote for him another play, *The Gladiator*, which was declared a prize play but for which Forrest did not give the author another one thousand dollars in prize money, reasoning that this play was a substitute for *Pelopidas.*

The Gladiator provided Forrest with the perfect role, that of Spartacus, and the play opened to enormous acclaim in New York on September 26, 1831. It soon had played in both Boston and Philadelphia, and it always played to full houses and enthusiastic audiences. By the time Bird died in 1854, *The Gladiator* had been presented more than one thousand times, and its success was to continue until the turn of the century. Forrest grew rich from the proceeds, none of which he shared with the author.

Forrest and Bird were born in the same year, and they became not only close professional associates but also close friends. Bird was to win two more of Forrest's prizes, one for *Oralloossa* in 1832 and one for *The Broker of Bogotá* in 1834. In all, Forrest awarded nine prizes for American plays, and Bird took four of them, although he was paid for only three.

In 1833, Bird and Forrest traveled together for some months. They had planned to go to Mexico; they turned back at New Orleans, however, because of a cholera epidemic. Bird went on to Nashville, where he had a reunion with John Grimes, with whom he went to Mammoth Cave, which the two explored fully. As a result of this exploration, Bird returned to his work on the long poem "The Cave," which had occupied him earlier. He began work on *The Broker of Bogotá*, his last drama, which he completed the next year.

By that time, Bird had concluded that he could not support himself as a playwright, and he decided to devote his time to writing romances. His explanation was that "novels are much easier sorts of things and immortalize one's pocket much sooner. A tragedy takes, or should take, as much labor as two romances; and one comedy as much as six tragedies."

Drawing on the extensive reading he had done about Latin America, Bird wrote *Calavar* in 1834, following it the next year with *The Infidel: Or, The Fall of Mexico*. These novels were meticulously researched and found a ready audience, but Bird was to find his real métier in *The Hawks of Hawk-Hollow*, published in the same year as *The Infidel*, and in *Nick of the Woods*, published in 1837.

Bird set *The Hawks of Hawk-Hollow* in the area around the Delaware Water Gap on the Pennsylvania-New Jersey border, a region with which he had a particular affinity. A second edition of the novel was released in the first year of the book's publication, and that was followed by three English editions of the work by 1842. Because international copyright laws did not exist at that time, Bird did not profit financially from the English editions.

Nick of the Woods was published in 1837, the year of Bird's marriage to Mary Mayer, and was a resounding success. By 1839, the novel had been dramatized by J. T. Haines, and two other dramatizations of it were to follow, one in 1856 and another in 1940. *Nick of the Woods* was also translated into several foreign languages.

In 1837, largely at his wife's urging, Bird tried to convince Forrest to pay him some six thousand dollars that Bird believed was rightfully his. Forrest argued bitterly with Bird over this debt and stormed out of Bird's house, claiming to have complete ownership of Bird's major dramas—a claim that Forrest exercised through Bird's remaining years. Bird was never to write another play, although he revised his dramas in 1843, planning to publish them. That hope, however, was thwarted by Forrest's claim to exclusive rights to the plays.

Afflicted by a complete nervous collapse in 1840, Bird turned to farming on acreage he had bought two years earlier near Elkton, Maryland. He underwent substantial losses of his crops because of violent weather, but his health improved greatly during this interlude of intense physical activity as a farmer. In 1841, Bird was well enough to return to Philadelphia, where he had been appointed a professor at Pennsylvania Medical College, a post in which he served with high distinction until 1843, when the medical college disbanded.

Meanwhile, Bird had become active in politics. He attended the Whig Convention in Delaware as a delegate in 1842 and felt reasonably sure that he would be nominated as a representative to the United States Congress. This plan went awry when George Brydges Rodney, the incumbent, who had intended not to run for reelection, changed his mind, leaving no place for Bird on the Whig ticket. Nevertheless, Bird received a minor political appointment in 1846 when he was named to be a director of the New Castle Branch of the Farmers' National Bank. The following year, Bird was nominated for the positions of assistant director and librarian of the

Smithsonian Institution but was not appointed. Using thirty thousand dollars borrowed from his close friend Senator John M. Clayton, Bird bought a one-third interest in Philadelphia's *North American*, a newspaper that thrived under Bird's editorship, although the paper's success was marred by the mismanagement of his partners. Bird gave his full energies to his newspaper work and was considered an excellent literary editor.

During the presidential campaign of 1848, Bird was a vigorous supporter of Zachary Taylor, whose biography he wrote specifically to aid the candidate in his campaign. Bird hoped for some sort of government appointment, but, despite a meeting with President Taylor in 1849, Bird was not appointed to office. He spent his final years working hard on the *North American* to the detriment of his own health, as well as working with George H. Boker to help bring about copyright laws that would protect authors from the sort of exploitation that he, Bird, had suffered at the hands of Forrest and of English publishers who had pirated his work.

Bird was in ill health during the latter months of 1853. His condition worsened in the first days of 1854, and on January 23, he died of a cerebral hemorrhage at his country residence, Kittatiny House, in Delaware Water Gap. His wife and fifteen-year-old son, Frederick Mayer Bird, survived him.

Analysis

Robert Montgomery Bird's earliest plays were essentially derivative, at times suggestive of the closet dramas of the Elizabethan Revival, at times recalling Ben Jonson's plays or the Restoration drama of William Congreve, with whose work Bird was well acquainted. Most of the plays of this early period are set in such romantic locations as Spain ("The Three Dukes"), Italy ("Giannone"), or other foreign places. They depend heavily upon highly intricate plots in which the key characters are amply disguised; mistaken identity is central to the resolution of the plot, and coincidence is a *sine qua non* of the plays' rising action and denouement. Like many of the Restoration dramatists, Bird selected names that were either ironic— for example, "Nathan Slaughter" for a Quaker who refused to fight in *Nick of the Woods*—or descriptive—Sluggardly, the innkeeper; Ha'penny, the debtor; and Agony, the miserly uncle. These plays are no worse than much of the Restoration drama that sometimes served as Bird's model, but they can hardly be called good.

'Twas All for the Best is a complicated comedy of manners set in England. The language is stilted to the point of being painful to the modern reader. The plot revolves around Sir Noel Nozlebody, who steals his brother's daughter, rears her as his own child, and declares his own daughter to be a foundling. This play contains some scenes that are essentially tragic and that seem to have no place in a play that purports to be a comedy. In

'Twas All for the Best, Bird was not yet in control of his medium.

Similarly complicated in plot is another Bird farce of the same general period, *News of the Night*, which is set in Philadelphia but which follows a classical Roman story line with strong overtones of the comic spirit of Jonson. This play, with its stereotypical props of old chests, rope ladders, and women dressed as men, was first produced by the Columbia University Laboratory Players in New York on November 2, 1929.

The City Looking Glass, first published in an edition by Arthur Hobson Quinn in 1933, was subtitled *A Philadelphia Comedy*. It is ostensibly about the seamy side of life in Philadelphia, but there seems to be little that is American about it. Again, the plot is reminiscent of Jonson and involves two low-life creatures, Ravin and Ringfinger, who pursue two commonplace young ladies, only to discover that one of these girls, Emma, is really the daughter of a highly respected and wealthy Virginia gentleman. Act 4 provides small glimpses into Southern life and into the views of the times, but except for that act, the play has little relationship to anything authentically American. This drama was first performed by the Zelosophic Society of the University of Pennsylvania on January 20, 1933.

"The Fanatick," based on Charles Brockden Brown's Gothic novel *Wieland* (1798), was planned but was never completed. "The Three Dukes" and "Giannone" also exist only in fragments which are a part of the Robert Montgomery Bird Collection at the University of Pennsylvania; "Giannone" is the most promising of these fragmentary plays. It is interesting to note that in these works, members of the nobility speak in blank verse while the other characters speak in prose.

Bird all but completed two tragedies, *The Cowled Lover* and *Caridorf*. *The Cowled Lover* is modeled after William Shakespeare's *Romeo and Juliet*. The ardent Raymond disguises himself as a monk in order to be near his beloved, Rosalia. Ultimately, he and Rosalia are killed by the young woman's father. The play is highly Romantic and shows the strong Gothic influence of some of the authors Bird was reading at the time—Percy Bysshe Shelley and Lord Byron, for example.

Caridorf suffers from having a quite unconvincing hero, a man who refuses to come to the bedside of his dying father and who first seduces Genevra, then upbraids her for having lost her chastity. The audience is asked to overlook these inhumane acts and see through to Caridorf's essential goodness, a demand which strains credulity.

With *Pelopidas*, Bird showed signs of maturing into a significant playwright. Gone are the stereotypical plots of his earlier plays; gone are the heavy-handed props of a play such as *News of the Night*. *Pelopidas* has a typical Romantic setting, that of Thebes after the Spartans had conquered and grasped political power in the city. The tale of Pelopidas is told in Plutarch's *Parallel Lives*, which is the basic source for Bird's play. Bird, however, showing excellent critical judgment, distorted the Plutarchan version to suit his own artistic needs.

Pelopidas was a great hero of Thebes, and, with the conquest of the city by Sparta, he was forced into exile. His wife remained behind in the city, which was now controlled by four polemarchs. In Plutarch's account, these polemarchs were native Thebans who were appointed to their dictatorial positions by the conquerors. Bird, however, made two of the polemarchs, Philip and Archias, Spartan, thereby setting up an interesting contrast between them and the two Theban polemarchs, Leontidas and Philidas. Bird also established contrasts within the two pairs. Philip is the typical Spartan, businesslike, aggressive, suspicious; Archias is trusting, fun-loving, somewhat lazy. Of the two Thebans, Leontidas is a libertine whose actions really trigger the action of the plot; Philidas is a more complex character, a seeming traitor to his city who is in truth working with his fellow Thebans to unseat the Spartans.

Pelopidas leaves his exile and sneaks back into Thebes, drawn irresistibly to the city because word has reached him that Leontidas is trying to seduce his wife, Sibylla. Upon his return, it becomes known that Philidas, the seeming turncoat, is planning a feast with the Spartans and that he is plotting their destruction. During the very tense banquet scene, the Spartans come close to learning what is about to happen; Bird manages to keep the suspense high until Pelopidas arrives and sees that the Spartans are dispatched. Pelopidas returns to the prison-room of his house just in time to save his wife and son from being murdered by the evil Leontidas, whom he kills.

Pelopidas is well drawn. He is a brave, rash idealist. When he first returns to Thebes, he brashly tries to rescue his wife and is captured by the enemy, only to escape and, chastened, make his more calculated and successful attempt at the rescue.

Edwin Forrest appreciated the dramaticality of *Pelopidas*, but he never allowed the play to be performed, because the role of Philidas tended to overshadow the leading role, in which Forrest would have been cast. When William E. Burton, manager of Philadelphia's National Theater, wanted to produce *Pelopidas* in 1840, Bird demurred, despite the generosity of Burton's terms, because he did not wish to enter into a disagreeable fray with Forrest, who claimed ownership of the property.

Had the Copyright Act of 1856 been passed twenty-five years earlier, *The Gladiator* would have made Bird an exceptionally wealthy man. As it turned out, Forrest reaped the full benefit of this play's success, while Bird received nothing for it. The story of Spartacus was well-known in the early nineteenth century, and Bird adapted this popular tale to serve his purposes in *The Gladiator*. Spartacus is a Thracian, recently captured by the Romans. His fame as a fighter has preceded him to Rome, where

Phasarius, one of Rome's most renowned gladiators, is plotting with the other gladiators to overthrow the city while its generals and soldiers are away. Phasarius, however, delays the planned overthrow because he wants the challenge of fighting Spartacus. Spartacus agrees to the combat because by doing so he can win the freedom of his wife and child, who have been enslaved.

The combat is arranged, and the gladiators enter the ring, but upon seeing each other, they realize that they are brothers. They lay down their arms, reunite, and organize the gladiators into an army that is soon on the brink of conquering Rome. At this point, Phasarius wants to destroy Rome utterly, whereas Spartacus wishes only to take his family and return to Thrace. Phasarius, like Leontidas in *Pelopidas*, wants to seduce Julia, the daughter of a high Roman official and a captive of the gladiatorial forces. Spartacus intervenes and saves Julia. The gladiators are divided between loyalty to Phasarius and loyalty to Spartacus, and thus the Romans are able to defeat them. When Spartacus' wife and child are killed, largely through Phasarius' duplicity, Spartacus loses his will to live. Although offered a pardon from the Romans, who are grateful for his protection of Julia, Spartacus chooses to die with his sword in his hand.

Like *Pelopidas*, *The Gladiator* is concerned centrally with the human quest for liberty. Led by Spartacus as the strong, central hero, the gladiators are glorified for rebelling against their oppressors. Like many Americans of his day, Bird could appreciate the impulse toward freedom in the classical characters he idealized in this play, while at the same time supporting slavery in his own country and refusing to buy property in Philadelphia, opting instead for the eastern shore of Maryland, because he feared that Pennsylvania would soon enfranchise black people.

Plays about Indians were popular in America during the 1830's and 1840's. The idea of the noble savage was in the air, and Forrest had already been playing John Augustus Stone's *Metamora* (pr. 1829), which focused on these topics, for two years when he first met Bird. Indeed, in 1836, Forrest gave Bird *Metamora* to revise; although no copy of Bird's revision is extant, it is generally thought that he in essence wrote an entirely new play, the only copy of which he delivered to Forrest. *Oralloossa* was awarded another of Forrest's drama prizes and was a resounding success when it was first performed. Forrest did not perform the play often after its initial run, partly because it was an expensive play to stage and partly because he was more at home in the role of Spartacus in *The Gladiator*.

Oralloossa bears certain surface resemblances to *Pelopidas*. In it, the Peruvian Incas are pitted against Pizarro's invading forces. Pizarro and his young compatriot Almagro are roughly comparable to Philip and Archias in *Pelopidas*, while the two Incas, Oralloossa and Manco, are roughly comparable to Philidas and Leontidas. Oralloossa serves both Pizarro and

Almagro simultaneously, but he is planning the downfall of each. As in *Pelopidas*, the crucial scene is a banquet at which Pizarro's forces are to dispatch Almagro. Oralloossa, however, who has put Pizarro up to this, has also arranged that Almagro will first kill Pizarro. Only the latter event comes to pass, and Almagro, who loves Oralloossa's sister, Ooallie, survives.

Oralloossa and Ooallie are both imprisoned by the Spanish because Manco has betrayed them, but Oralloossa escapes. So infuriated is Oralloossa at his fellow Inca, Manco, that he forsakes his kinsmen and tells the new Spanish viceroy, De Castro, where Manco and Almagro are hiding. Meanwhile, Oralloossa's sister Ooallie is buried alive and dies, because the priest who is supposed to save her from this fate never arrives. Oralloossa kills Almagro and then dies himself, leaving the Christian Spanish firmly in charge of the pagan Incas.

The play presents some extremely intense moments, but the climax comes so early in the action that the last act seems unbearably anticlimactic. *Oralloossa* might better have been a three-act play, ending shortly after Pizarro's murder, but three-act plays were not in vogue at the time.

The Broker of Bogotá, Bird's last play, is better crafted than *Oralloossa*; many regard it as his finest play. It is set in Bogotá, in the Spanish territory of New Grenada, which comprised present-day Colombia, Ecuador, Panama, and Venezuela. The play's protagonist is Febro, a bourgeois moneylender who has two sons of opposite temperaments. Ramon is unbridled and unruly, although he shows regret at times when his demeanor causes his father pain. He is counterbalanced by a much more dutiful brother, Francisco, who is a comfort to his father. A daughter, Leonor, is in love with the viceroy's son, Fernando. In a plot that runs rather like that of an Italian opera, Ramon falls in love with Juana, but Juana's father will not permit Ramon, who has been disowned by his own father, to pay court to his daughter.

At this point, the villain enters in the person of the nobleman Cabarero; he convinces Ramon to steal from his father's safe, the key to which he has just found, a substantial sum of money that the viceroy has left with Febro for safekeeping. Coincidentally, right at this point, Febro is considering a reconciliation with his errant son, but Ramon is unaware of this. To complicate matters further, Febro is accused of the theft and is brought before the viceroy. Febro has no defense unless Ramon is willing to admit to his own guilt, and he does not have the strength of character to do this. Just at this point, the distraught Febro is told that his daughter has eloped with a suitor.

All might have ended happily because, through Juana, it is revealed that Ramon, not Febro, is the thief, and at the same time it is revealed that the lover with whom Leonor has eloped is the viceroy's son. In the tradition of

Elizabethan tragedy, however, Bird cannot allow this to happen: Ramon commits suicide, and Febro dies.

The Broker of Bogotá is contrived, as were most of the plays of its period. Nevertheless, the play has a great deal to recommend it. The trial scene has much of the dramatic tension of a modern television mystery; Febro's fatherly efforts to defend Ramon when his guilt becomes known are well presented. Here, Bird's characters are multidimensional, in contrast to the relatively stereotyped figures of his earlier works. Finally, the basic conflict between the father and son, out of which the central action of the play develops, is convincing and tenable.

Although he cannot be classified among the greatest authors the United States has produced, Bird was a highly gifted, ambitious literary figure who had a clear sense of what he hoped to accomplish artistically. His writings brought him considerable celebrity in his own time and have won for him an enduring place in America's literary history.

Other major works

NOVELS: *Calavar: Or, The Knight of the Conquest*, 1834; *The Infidel: Or, The Fall of Mexico*, 1835; *The Hawks of Hawk-Hollow: A Tradition of Pennsylvania*, 1835; *Sheppard Lee*, 1836; *Nick of the Woods: Or, The Jibbenainosay, a Tale of Kentucky*, 1837; *The Adventures of Robin Day*, 1839.

SHORT FICTION: *Peter Pilgrim: Or, A Rambler's Recollections*, 1838.

NONFICTION: *Sketch of the Life, Public Services, and Character of Major Thomas Stockton of New-Castle, the Candidate for the Whig Party for the Office of Governor of Delaware*, 1844; *A Brief Review of the Career, Character, and Campaigns of Zachary Taylor*, 1848.

Bibliography

Bird, Mary Mayer. *The Life of Robert Montgomery Bird*, 1945 (C. Seymour, editor).

Blanck, Jacob. "Robert Montgomery Bird," in *Bibliography of American Literature, Volume I*, 1955.

Dahl, Curtis. *Robert Montgomery Bird*, 1963.

Foust, Clement E. *The Life and Dramatic Works of Robert Montgomery Bird*, 1919.

Quinn, Arthur Hobson. "Dramatic Works of Robert Montgomery Bird," in *The Nation*. CIII (August 3, 1916), pp. 108-109.

_____. *A History of American Drama from the Beginning to the Civil War*, 1923, 1943.

R. Baird Shuman

GEORGE H. BOKER

Born: Philadelphia, Pennsylvania; October 6, 1823
Died: Philadelphia, Pennsylvania; January 2, 1890

Principal drama

Calaynos, pb. 1848, pr. 1849; *Anne Boleyn*, pb. 1850; *The Betrothal*, pr. 1850, pb. 1856; *The World a Mask*, pr. 1851, pb. 1940; *Leonor de Guzman*, pr. 1853, pb. 1856; *Francesca da Rimini*, pr. 1855, pb. 1856 (revised); *The Bankrupt*, pr. 1855, pb. 1940; *The Widow's Marriage*, pb. 1856; *Königsmark*, pb. 1869; *Nydia*, wr. 1885, pb. 1929 (early version of *Glaucus*); *Glaucus*, wr. 1885-1886, pb. 1940.

Other literary forms

Although George H. Boker is remembered primarily as a dramatist, he wanted to be remembered as a poet. To this end, he wrote hundreds of poems.

The Book of the Dead, written in 1859 and 1860 and published in 1882, is his vindication of his father's name. After his father, a banker, died, the Girard Bank tried unsuccessfully to sue his estate for more than a half million dollars. The emotion in these 107 poems is sincere and the events prompting the collection are interesting, but the poems are less well crafted than those in Boker's other volumes of poetry.

After Boker ceased to write about the problems of his father's estate, he wrote many poems about the Civil War. Nearly every poem of this type is precisely dated, offering a narrative of a particular battle. Published soon after they were written in periodicals and leaflets, these poems, sentimental yet sincere and richly detailed, inspired patriotism in Northern readers. In 1864, Boker collected his Civil War verse in *Poems of the War*.

Boker's third important collection of poetry, *Sonnets: A Sequence on Profane Love*, comprises poems written between 1857 and 1887, but the work was only published posthumously in 1929. Of the 313 sonnets in the sequence, the first 282 seem to be about one woman, the next thirteen about another, and the last eighteen about a third woman. Written in the Italian form, these sonnets are generally well constructed and evoke intense images. The classical allusions are forced, but the descriptions of nature are powerful. Writing in 1927, Edward Sculley Bradley, the eminent critic who served as Boker's biographer and as editor of the sequence, argued that Henry Wadsworth Longfellow was the only American to equal Boker as a sonneteer.

Achievements

Important American literary figures of the nineteenth century respected

Boker as both a dramatist and a poet. He received praise from William Cullen Bryant, Oliver Wendell Holmes, James Russell Lowell, and Henry Wadsworth Longfellow. He was also elected to the Authors' Club of New York and the American Philosophical Society. Boker failed, however, to achieve comparable recognition from the American public: *Francesca da Rimini* and *The Betrothal* were his only popular plays.

Although fame eluded him, Boker was a master of the romantic tragedy. Romantic tragedy, like classical tragedy, depicts a hero or heroine, usually an admirable aristocrat, who suffers defeat or death because of fate or a fatal character flaw. For example, Leonor, the noble mistress of a king in *Leonor de Guzman*, dies a victim of circumstance and her own determination to see her son crowned king. In *Francesca da Rimini*, Paolo and Francesca, both of royal birth, die because of their predestined love for each other and their inability to assert reason over emotion.

The conventions of romantic tragedy are less rigid than those governing classical tragedy; also, in contrast to classical tragedy, romantic tragedy emphasizes the emotions and personalities of the characters rather than the plot. In *Francesca da Rimini*, the personality of Lanciotto, Francesca's deformed and savage husband, is more interesting than the play's inevitable end. Similarly, Leonor's passionate and forceful personality is more interesting than the palace intrigue.

Other characteristics of romantic tragedy include blank verse and remote, exotic settings. Boker's two best tragedies, *Francesca da Rimini* and *Leonor de Guzman*, are both written in blank verse and take place during the fourteenth century, the former in Italy and the latter in Spain.

William Shakespeare was the finest playwright in the tradition of romantic tragedy. If Boker's works clearly do not belong in such company, he nevertheless wrote romantic tragedies superior to those of any of his contemporaries. The only other American to approach Boker's success with romantic drama was Robert Montgomery Bird, an earlier nineteenth century novelist and playwright. *Francesca da Rimini* marks the end of romantic tragedy as a viable form in America and stands as the best play written by an American before the twentieth century.

Biography

George Henry Boker, a lifelong citizen of Philadelphia, was born in 1823. He attended the College of New Jersey (now Princeton University), where he developed a keen admiration for Shakespeare and other Elizabethan dramatists. He was still at college when he published his first poems. When Boker was graduated in 1842, his father wanted him to be a businessman or diplomat. He tried to study law, but he could not commit himself to a business career and did not pursue law. In 1844, he married Julia Riggs, a woman he had courted for some years. They had three children, but only the first, George, survived into adulthood. This son married but did not have children.

Boker had a literary group of friends, all poets, including Charles Godfrey Leland, Bayard Taylor, Thomas Bailey Aldrich (also editor of the *Atlantic Monthly*), Edmund Clarence Stedman, and Richard H. Stoddard. Boker generously used his wealth and literary influence to help his friends become published writers.

From 1847 to 1853, Boker wrote the bulk of his work. *The Lesson of Life and Other Poems* (1848), containing several sonnets, anticipates his later sequence of sonnets. *Calaynos*, his first play, is a romantic tragedy about a man whose Moorish ancestry is not apparent. It was produced in London in 1849, apparently without the author's permission; and then produced with his permission in the United States in 1851. Angered by a playwright's lack of rights, Boker supported the Dramatic Authors' Bill which Congress passed in 1856.

Anne Boleyn, Boker's second play, was never produced. His next two plays, which were produced, were *The Betrothal*, a comedy in blank verse, and *The World a Mask*, a social satire written largely in prose. In 1852, he published *The Podesta's Daughter*, a dramatic dialogue. That year he also wrote two more plays, *The Widow's Marriage*, a comedy which was never produced, and *Leonor de Guzman*, a romantic tragedy about two women trying to secure the Castilian throne for their sons. Boker began a sequel to this latter play but never finished it.

In nineteen intense days in March of 1853, Boker wrote his masterpiece, *Francesca da Rimini*, a reworking of Dante's account of Paolo and Francesca. It was first produced with moderate success in 1855. After writing his best play, he wrote one of his worst, *The Bankrupt*. Like *The World a Mask*, it is poorly written and shows Boker's inability to handle a contemporary setting well. Boker had it produced anonymously.

After *The Bankrupt*, Boker's dramatic production slowed down. He published *Plays and Poems* in 1856, a popular collection in two volumes which contained no new works. He labored longer than usual on *Königsmark*, a dramatic sketch never produced. Boker's dramatic career was impeded by a series of events—what appears to have been a long affair with a woman from Philadelphia, a lawsuit against his father's estate, his involvement in the Civil War, and, finally, his work as a diplomat.

From 1857 until 1871, Boker apparently carried on a love affair, and during this time he wrote almost three hundred sonnets in celebration of his love. These sonnets, along with two other short sequences probably inspired by subsequent affairs, were discovered in his daughter-in-law's house after his death and were published in 1929 with the help of his biographer, Edward Sculley Bradley. Boker was also preoccupied by a suit against his father's estate that lasted fifteen years. Soon after Boker's father died, representatives of the bank he had managed initiated a suit against his estate. Although Boker did not share his father's interest in business, he admired his father's business acumen and respected his integrity. Depressed and fearful of bankruptcy, Boker spent 1859 and 1860 writing vindictive poems against his father's enemies.

From 1861 to the end of the Civil War, Boker vigorously supported the Northern position. He wrote many poems in support of the war effort; they were published individually and were instantly successful. Boker had them published as a collection, *Poems of the War*, and they became his most widely read publication. He also helped to organize The Union League, a Philadelphia club in support of the Northern stance. Boker was its first secretary and served in that capacity until he began his diplomatic career. In 1871, Boker began an appointment in Turkey, and in 1875, he became a diplomat in Russia. He and his wife returned to the United States permanently in 1878.

Upon returning home, Boker finally achieved some of the recognition he had sought. He became president of the Union League and was elected to both the Authors' Club of New York and the American Philosophical Society. He also published previously written works—*The Book of the Dead*, comprising his poems in support of his father, and a reprint of *Plays and Poems*, in 1883. Most important, however, in 1883, Lawrence Barrett, a famous nineteenth century actor, successfully revived *Francesca da Rimini*.

Boker wrote only two more plays after his return to the United States, *Nydia*, a tragedy, and *Glaucus*, apparently a revision of *Nydia*. Neither version was produced. Ill for the last three years of his life, Boker died of a heart attack in 1890.

Analysis

Francesca da Rimini, in spite of its imitative blank verse, is the best dramatic rendering of the love story recorded both by Giovanni Boccaccio and by Dante. The first version of George H. Boker's masterpiece, written in 1853, was never published; the final version was published in 1856. There are important differences between these two versions. In the published version, the participants in the love triangle—Lanciotto, Francesca, and Paolo—are emphasized more or less equally. In the 1853 version, in contrast, Lanciotto was the central figure. Further, the love scenes involving Francesca and Paolo, including the one immediately preceding the consummation of their love, were largely absent in the 1853 version. These changes served not only to decrease Lanciotto's importance but also to increase the audience's sympathy for the two young lovers.

Because it is shorter, the 1853 version moves more briskly to the conclusion. For example, in the 1853 version, Boker immediately prepares the audience for the climax by having Francesca, the inadvertent cause of

Lanciotto and Paolo's strife, appear in the first scene. In the 1856 version, however, Francesca does not appear until act 2, and Boker uses the first act to reveal the personalities of the two brothers and their relationship to each other. On the other hand, the published play is generally superior to the earlier version because it allows for richer characterizations. Both versions, though, to Boker's credit, emphasize character rather than plot.

Paolo loves his brother, but, an idler, he has not the discipline necessary to ignore his feelings for his brother's wife. Francesca, while she has the audience's sympathy, is too much a victim to have their unreserved admiration. Forced to become engaged to a man she has never met, she is deceived about Lanciotto's hideous appearance by the three most important people in her life—her father, Guido; her servant and confidante, Ritta; and the man with whom she has just fallen in love, Paolo. She recognizes that Lanciotto has a more noble character than Paolo, but she is nevertheless repelled by his deformities. She displays free will in a single scene only, one not present in the 1853 version, where she, more than Paolo, seeks consummation of their love. Francesca becomes a victim again in the last scene when Lanciotto, in an effort to force Paolo to kill him, kills her.

Lanciotto, a more complex figure than the young lovers, both repels and attracts the audience. He first appears as a hideously deformed and vicious, almost barbaric, warrior. While his father pities the defeated citizens of Ravenna, Lanciotto wants to see the city burn and its women crying. An uncivilized man, he is also deeply superstitious. He believes a warning by his nurse that his blood will be mixed with Guido's, and later he fears doom when he thinks he sees blood on his sword. Paolo and Maletesta, the brothers' father, are more civilized than he and chide him for his superstitions, but he remains convinced that evil awaits him.

Juxtaposed to Lanciotto's savagery and superstition are his deeply felt emotions, which gain the audience's sympathy. The audience understands his desire to destroy Ravenna when he reveals the reason for such rage: His first memory is of the death of his nurse's husband at the hands of a citizen of Ravenna. Lanciotto ironically evokes the most sympathy from the audience when he discloses how much he hates his deformed body for creating fear and pity in others. He also wins the audience over when he says he will not force Francesca, who so obviously loathes his sight, to touch him.

The last act shows Lanciotto at war with himself, fighting both his savagery and his love for his brother. When Lanciotto learns that his brother and wife have betrayed him, he, the savage soldier, feels that he cannot live with such dishonor unavenged. He races to the lovers, only to find he cannot attack his beloved brother. He asks the lovers to lie about their adultery. When they refuse, he tries to goad Paolo into killing him, but Paolo, never a fighter, remains passive. Even when Lanciotto stabs Francesca, Paolo refuses to act. Finally, Lanciotto kills his brother, too. Momentarily, he is relieved to have avenged his honor, but as the play concludes, he falls upon Paolo, declaring that he "loved him more than honor—more than life." Paolo, paralyzed by his love for Lanciotto, cannot save himself or Francesca. Lanciotto, wrongly believing that his honor is more important than his love for Paolo, forces himself into violence. Thus, the play ends with two brothers—one passively, one actively—led into destruction.

Pepe, Maletesta's jester, is one reason that critics admire *Francesca da Rimini*. As Boker's own addition to the story of Francesca and Paolo, Pepe hastens the inevitable tragedy. Pepe frequently suggests to Lanciotto that Paolo and Francesca love each other, and he tells Lanciotto when their love is consummated. To assure that Lanciotto seeks vengeance, he also lies, telling Lanciotto that Paolo has hired him to kill his brother. As Pepe expects, in anger, Lanciotto kills him, but he dies glad that the two brothers will also be destroyed.

Pepe would be a completely malevolent figure except for the motivation behind his hatred for Paolo and Lanciotto. A proponent of democracy, he hates the brothers because they represent royalty. He tells Lanciotto that he would like to see marriage abolished so that everyone would be born equal. Later, in a scene not present in the 1853 version, Paolo reports that he overheard Pepe ranting about being treated as a toy. Both brothers indeed treat him like that; generally unconcerned about his desires, they expect him to do their bidding, and they fatally underestimate his anger. Pepe is a modern antihero, supporting the cause of democracy.

Critics agree that two other plays by Boker approach the excellence of *Francesca da Rimini*: *Leonor de Guzman*, another romantic tragedy, and *The Betrothal*, a romantic comedy.

In *Leonor de Guzman*, the King of Castile and Leon dies, leaving three rivals competing for power: his wife Maria, who wants the throne to remain with her son; his mistress Leonor, who wants her son to become king; and Alburquerque, the prime minister, who wants the power for himself. The play is effective particularly because of the struggle between Leonor, the spiritually pure mistress who unwaveringly manipulates events to ensure that her son will be king, and Maria, the betrayed wife whose bitterness leads her to murder Leonor. The play ends with Leonor dead and Maria's son ill and successfully manipulated by Alburquerque. It seems that the Prime Minister will be victorious, but Leonor, before her death, has prophesied her son's triumph and Alburquerque's downfall so convincingly that, even as he watches her die, the Prime Minister already feels the sting of defeat.

Centering as it does on three strong characters, each with his or her distinctive personality, the play sustains the audience's interest. Nevertheless, it is inferior to *Francesca da Rimini*. In *Leonor de Guzman*, too many humorous scenes inappropriately distract the audience from the ensuing tragedy, and too many characters participating in palace intrigue blur the development of the three principal characters.

The Betrothal is a comedy about Costanza, who unhappily agrees to marry the evil Marsio to save her aristocratic father from poverty and possibly from prison. When she falls in love with Count Juranio, the Count's kinsman Salvatore manipulates events so that Costanza may marry the man she loves without ruining her father. Like *Francesca da Rimini* and *Leonor de Guzman*, *The Betrothal* is written in blank verse and centers on characters of aristocratic birth, but in addition to the expected difference in tone, the differences in plot, character, and theme distinctly set this comedy apart from Boker's tragedies. Murder is plotted in *The Betrothal*, but, as is consistent with its comic tone, no death occurs. Furthermore, the romance between Costanza's cousin and Juranio's kinsman is developed into a subplot, something Boker avoids in the two tragedies.

The characters of *The Betrothal* are interesting figures, but, unlike the prominent characters in the two tragedies, they are merely types— Costanza and Juranio as the virtuous lovers, Filippia and Salvatore as the loyal confidants, and Marsio as the evil suitor. Little exists in their portrayal to make them other than hero, heroine, or villain.

All three plays have a major character who is not a proper aristocrat. Pepe is a mere jester in *Francesca da Rimini*; Leonor, by becoming a mistress, has relinquished the status with which she was born; Marsio represents the nouveau riche. An important theme of the two tragedies is that those set apart from elite society may defeat the aristocracy. Pepe dies victorious, knowing that he has made royalty suffer. Leonor also dies victorious, knowing that her son, a bastard, will be king. In *The Betrothal*, however, Marsio, who is despicable partly because he lacks aristocratic graces, suffers ignominious defeat so that two aristocrats may appropriately marry each other. Boker's admiration for democracy is not apparent in this comedy.

One reason Boker is little remembered today is that he excelled at romantic drama, a form which modern readers, with their love of realism, seldom appreciate. *Leonor de Guzman*, with its emphasis on palace intrigue, and *The Betrothal*, with its assumption that aristocrats are better than others, understandably have little appeal for the twentieth century American reader. *Francesca da Rimini*, however, deserves the attention of modern readers: The play's complex characterization and democratic theme can sustain interest even today.

Other major works

POETRY: *The Lesson of Life and Other Poems*, 1848; *The Podesta's*

Daughter and Other Poems, 1852; *Poems of the War*, 1864; *The Book of the Dead*, 1882; *Sonnets: A Sequence on Profane Love*, 1929 (Edward Sculley Bradley, editor).

MISCELLANEOUS: *Plays and Poems*, 1856, 1883 (2 volumes).

Bibliography

Bradley, Edward Sculley. *George Henry Boker: Poet and Patriot*, 1927.

Mayorga, Margaret G. *A Short History of the American Drama: Commentaries on Plays Prior to 1920*, 1932.

Moses, Montrose J. *The American Dramatist*, 1939.

Quinn, Arthur Hobson. *A History of the American Drama from the Beginning to the Civil War*, 1943 (2nd edition).

_____. *Representative American Plays from 1767 to the Present Day*, 1966 (7th edition).

Vaughn, Jack A. *Early American Dramatists from the Beginnings to 1900*, 1981.

Margaret Ann Baker

ROBERT BOLT

Born: Sale, England; August 15, 1924

Principal drama

A Man for All Seasons, pr. 1954 (radio play), pr. 1957 (televised), pr. 1960 (staged), pb. 1960; *The Last of the Wine*, pr. 1955 (radio play), pr. 1956 (staged); *The Critic and the Heart*, pr. 1957; *Flowering Cherry*, pr. 1957, pb. 1958; *The Tiger and the Horse*, pr. 1960, pb. 1961; *Gentle Jack*, pr. 1963, pb. 1965; *The Thwarting of Baron Bolligrew*, pr. 1965, pb. 1966 (children's play); *Brother and Sister*, pr. 1967, 1968 (revision of *The Critic and the Heart*); *Vivat! Vivat Regina!*, pr. 1970, pb. 1971; *State of Revolution*, pr., pb. 1977.

Other literary forms

Robert Bolt began his career in drama as a writer of radio plays for the British Broadcasting Company, starting in 1953 with *The Master*, a play about the wandering scholars of the Middle Ages. He wrote sixteen scripts for the British Broadcasting Corporation, including eight for children. The first version of *A Man for All Seasons* was broadcast as a radio drama in 1954, and his very first production on the legitimate stage, *The Last of the Wine*, originated as a radio script a year earlier.

Bolt's most noteworthy achievements outside the legitimate theater, however, have been as a screenwriter. He worked with the renowned British director David Lean on *Lawrence of Arabia*, creating a screenplay based on T. E. Lawrence's own writings. The film received the Academy Award for Best Picture of 1962, and Bolt's scenario received a special award from the British Film Academy. His adaptation of Boris Pasternak's novel *Doctor Zhivago*, another script written for David Lean, won an Oscar for the Best Screenplay of 1965, an honor repeated in 1966 when Bolt adapted his own play, *A Man for All Seasons* (directed by Fred Zinnemann). The movie version also earned for Bolt the British Film Academy Award and the New York Film Critics Circle Award in 1966. His next project was an original treatment of *Ryan's Daughter* for David Lean in 1970. In 1972, he wrote and directed *Lady Caroline Lamb*, based on the life of the mistress of Lord Byron, the famous English poet.

Achievements

Bolt has earned the reputation of being a serious dramatist whose sense of stagecraft has made him popular with theater audiences. Critics have also recognized his talent for structure and his concern with language from the time of his appearance in the West End theaters of London with

Flowering Cherry in 1957. This play, a popular and critical success during its 435 performances at the Haymarket Theatre, won for him the *Evening Standard* Drama Award for Most Promising Playwright of that year. Although Bolt launched his career in the heyday of the Angry Young Men, when playwrights as diverse as John Osborne, Harold Pinter, John Arden, and Arnold Wesker challenged the then reigning conventions of English theater, he has never been associated with the avant-garde. In fact, as John Fuegi has emphasized, Bolt has deliberately rejected many features of the new drama while responding to those influences that he could accommodate to his traditional aesthetic.

Bolt's own statements about his approach to his art reflect his conviction that conventional dramatic structure, with a clearly articulated plot and an organic unity, not only satisfies the legitimate expectations of the audience but also provides an effective vehicle "for conveying delicate but immediate insights." He compares highly conventional theater, "where both sides of the footlights understand thoroughly what's going on," to a taut drumskin that resounds at the lightest tap. "Take away these conventions and you find yourself with a slack drumskin; you've got to jump up and down on it before you get even the slightest tinkle." Bolt also maintains that the slice-of-life dramatists who let the audience supply the ending use the theater "as a therapeutic rather than dramatic medium."

Bolt's earliest dramas were traditional well-crafted plays, largely naturalistic in approach, with a fourth-wall style of dramaturgy. Even as early as *Flowering Cherry*, however, Bolt was striving to break out of the purely naturalistic mode while maintaining a clear, unified structure. *A Man for All Seasons* realizes these ambitions; the play that established Bolt as one of the most popular playwrights in the London theater, it ran more than nine months in London and enjoyed an even longer New York run of more than a year and a half, starting in November, 1961. Despite some demurrers such as the influential critic Kenneth Tynan, the drama won widespread critical acclaim. Robert Corrigan was among those who considered *A Man for All Seasons* "one of the finest achievements of the modern theatre." Jerry Tallman of *The Village Voice* could think of no play that surpassed it in almost forty years for dramatic tension, structure, meaning, and language. The stage version received two American drama awards in 1962: the Tony Award of the American Theatre Wing for the best play of that year and the New York Drama Critics Circle Award for the best foreign play.

Biography

Robert Oxton Bolt was born in 1924, the younger son of Ralph Bolt and Leah Binnion Bolt. His family lived in the small town of Sale in Lancashire, where his father owned a shop carrying mostly furniture, glass, and china. His mother was a schoolteacher. The playwright has spoken of his parents as loving, concerned, and not unduly strict, despite their high standards. Though Bolt has described his religious position as between agnosticism and atheism, he was reared a Methodist. He has stated, "I ought to be religious in the sense that I'm comfortable thinking in religious terms and altogether I seem naturally constituted to be religious."

Despite his good home background, Bolt distinguished himself as a youngster by constantly getting into trouble and remaining at the bottom of his class in the Manchester Grammar School until his graduation in 1940. Not really prepared to enter any career or qualified to go on to a university, he became an office boy for the Sun Life Assurance Company in Manchester in 1942—a position he thoroughly loathed. Determined to escape from this whole way of life, he leaped at the opportunity to study for a degree in commerce under special wartime arrangements for admission to a university program. Through intensive preparation for his Advanced Level examinations, he gained a place in an honors school at Manchester University rather than the school of commerce. There, he began work for a degree in history in 1943. During this period, he also became a Marxist; from 1942 to 1947, he was a member of the Communist Party, inspired by youthfully idealistic visions of the Party's ability to change the world. He has since described himself as a Marxist with so many reservations that he would be scorned by a true Marxist.

After a year at Manchester University, Bolt joined the Royal Air Force and later transferred to the army, serving as an officer with the Royal West African Frontier Force in Ghana. At the end of the war, he returned to the university, where he was awarded an honors degree in history in 1949. That same year, he married Celia Ann Roberts, a painter; the couple had three children—Sally, Benedict, and Joanna—prior to their divorce in 1967. Bolt has been remarried twice since then; his second wife was the actress Sara Miles, by whom he had one son and from whom he was divorced in 1976. In 1980, he married Ann Zane.

Following his graduation from Manchester, Bolt prepared for a career in education by studying for his teaching diploma, which he received from the University of Exeter in 1950. For the next eight years, he worked as an English teacher, first at a village in Bishopsteignton in Devon and then at Millfield School in Street, Devon. His desire to become a dramatist first developed in 1954 while he was searching for a nativity play to perform with the children at the village school. Finding none of the plays he had read satisfactory, he decided to compose his own. Bolt recalls vividly "the electric tension" that built up inside him after he had composed some of the dialogue, and he remembers telling his wife, "Listen, I think I've found what I want to do." At this point, he decided to combine teaching with writing and began composing his radio scripts.

An adaptation of his 1955 radio script, *The Last of the Wine*, was staged in London at Theatre in the Round in 1956. The success of Osborne's play *Look Back in Anger* that same year made Bolt feel that young playwrights might have a chance of breaking into the West End theaters, and Bolt sent his play *The Critic and the Heart* to the Royal Court Theatre, where the reader—Osborne himself—rejected it, claiming that it was a promising play but not the particular kind of drama that the theater was seeking. Although Bolt did not succeed in getting a West End showing, *The Critic and the Heart* was produced at the Oxford Playhouse in 1957 and was well received. This play represents Bolt at his most traditional. Bolt himself criticized the play for being too orthodox and completely naturalistic in form. He tells how, being inexperienced in the theater, he modeled the play on W. Somerset Maugham's *The Circle* (pr. 1921), doing a detailed structural analysis and following it closely in his own play, even down to the placement of climaxes and the lengths of acts. As Ronald Hayman emphasizes, however, the content and dialogue are distinctly Bolt's own; the playwright also demonstrates his capacity for closely interweaving characters and plot. Bolt later rewrote the play as *Brother and Sister*, which was produced at Brighton in 1967; another revised version appeared at Bristol in 1968.

With his next play, *Flowering Cherry*, Bolt caught the attention of director Frith Banbury, known for his promotion of promising young playwrights. Banbury arranged Bolt's first West End production in 1957 with a stellar cast, including Ralph Richardson and Celia Johnson in the leads. The highly successful London run was followed by a New York production in 1959, when critics received it far less enthusiastically. Bolt's next work, *The Tiger and the Horse*, about the effects a petition to ban the hydrogen bomb have on a middle-class university family, is another basically naturalistic domestic drama of the same type as *Flowering Cherry*. Like its predecessor, it was directed by Banbury, beginning a successful London run in August, 1960.

A Man for All Seasons began its run at the Globe Theater in July, 1960, with Paul Scofield as Sir Thomas More; *The Tiger and the Horse*, though written first, opened a month later. Thus, Bolt had the distinction of having two very different types of plays enjoying success at the West End theaters simultaneously. The 1960's also found Bolt branching out into screenwriting and winning distinction in that field as well. In 1961, he also went to jail briefly, along with other members of Bertrand Russell's Committee of One Hundred, for antinuclear protests that involved token breaches of the law. Bolt had been working on the screenplay for *Lawrence of Arabia* at the time, and progress on the film stopped while he was away from the scene. Finally, producer Sam Spiegel angrily pressured him into binding himself over and coming out of prison because people's jobs and thousands of dollars were at stake. Bolt speaks of this as a surrender, an action he has regretted, despite the good reasons for doing it.

Bolt's next drama for the legitimate stage was *Gentle Jack*, a highly experimental drama in which he sought to move even further away from naturalism. John R. Kaiser aptly described the play as "an adult fairy tale or an allegorical fantasy" dealing with the appearance of the god Pan in the modern world. Produced in 1963, with Dame Edith Evans and Kenneth Williams in the leading roles, *Gentle Jack* is perhaps the least successful of Bolt's major theatrical works, running for only seventy-five performances. Neither the critics nor the public received it favorably; many found it puzzling and obscure, a marked departure from Bolt's usual clarity and even from the types of drama that had made him one of the leading popular playwrights of his time.

For his next stage venture, Bolt turned to another fairy tale, but this time a highly successful one for children, *The Thwarting of Baron Bolligrew*, first performed in December, 1965, by the Royal Shakespeare Company at the Aldwich Theatre in London. It has been noted that Bolt's penchant for larger-than-life figures served him well in creating his fairy-tale characters, including the stout, elderly hero, Sir Oblong Fitz-Oblong, a knight with a strong sense of duty, and the villainous Baron Bolligrew. The knight is a humorous version of the uncommon man of principle who must fight against the evil and deception in the society around him. Ronald Hayman notes that, "like some children, he tries too hard to be good." Bolt also makes use of a Storyteller who, like the Common Man, provides a narrative link between episodes and occasionally takes part in the action, such as by making the moon rise when Sir Oblong asks for it.

Bolt has returned to historical subjects for the adult dramas that he has written since *Gentle Jack*. *Vivat! Vivat Regina!*—his treatment of the rival queens Mary Stuart and Elizabeth Tudor—had its premiere at the Chichester Festival in 1970; it then moved to the Piccadilly Theatre in London, where it proved a major hit of the season. The play also had a successful New York engagement in 1972. A play dealing with the Russian Revolution and Vladimir Ilich Lenin's central role in it, *State of Revolution*, was first produced in 1977 at the Birmingham Repertory Theatre and later at the National Theatre.

Analysis

The full range of Robert Bolt's achievements can be illustrated most effectively through a more detailed consideration of four major plays. *The Tiger and the Horse* demonstrates the "uneasy straddling between naturalism and non-naturalism" that he found in his earlier plays; it also represents one of his attempts to give his contemporaries the larger-than-life significance he finds appropriate in theatrical characters. Marking a signifi-

cant development in Bolt's dramaturgical skills, *A Man for All Seasons*
shows how he turned to historical settings to escape the pitfalls of naturalism and to present individuals of significant dramatic dimension; the play
remains his most penetrating examination of the individual in conflict with
society. In *Vivat! Vivat Regina!*, he draws upon the artificiality of the theater in presenting the conflict between two striking historical figures.
Finally, *State of Revolution* represents a serious attempt to explore some
decisive events in contemporary history and the towering figure who gave
them shape.

The Tiger and the Horse is a well-plotted domestic drama in which a
petition to ban the bomb serves as a major catalyst in the action; its effects
are skillfully interwoven with the crises of a seduction and growing insanity
to provide some intensely pitched action.

The title alludes to an aphorism by the poet William Blake, from *The
Marriage of Heaven and Hell*: "The tygers of wrath are wiser than the
horses of instruction"; it suggests that the logic of the heart can express a
higher wisdom than can the reasoning of the mind. In his review of the
play, Richard Findlater aptly summarized the theme embedded in the
drama "as the relative values of commitment in private and public life, and
the balance of power between heart and head among members of the English thinking class." Through Bolt's craftsmanship, public issues and private
concerns are skillfully intertwined in the development of the plot.

Jack Dean, the Master of a university college who is in line for the vice
chancellorship, is the horse of the play. Though a kindly, tolerant, and
highly principled man, he has developed as his personal philosophy a
detachment that is essentially a refusal to become involved, an emotional
neutrality that he unwittingly carries over into personal relationships as well
as into his approach to larger issues. Even his having abandoned astronomy
to take up philosophy becomes significant in Bolt's careful delineation of
his character. When his daughter Stella is looking through his telescope and
taking comfort in the order she finds in nature, Dean launches into one of
the "big speeches" found here and in *Flowering Cherry*; he speaks of the
darkness, "ignorant of human necessities," that fills the spaces between the
stars, and he adds that what appears to be a meaningful pattern in the universe is actually merely "Scribble." Thus, staid, imperturbable Dean reveals
the terrifying vision of the existential void that led him to turn away from
investigating the world around him and to take refuge in abstract philosophical speculation.

When Louis Flax, a research fellow from a working-class background,
circulates a petition urging nuclear disarmament, Dean refuses to sign; one
vote, he says, does not really matter, and he claims that he does not understand all the political and diplomatic considerations involved. The same
lack of engagement is apparent in his personal life. When Stella tries to

warn Dean that her mother is acting strangely and seems mentally unbalanced, he refuses to take her concern seriously. At first, too, he fends off Stella's confidences about Louis; only when she tells her father that she is pregnant and has no intention of marrying Louis because he does not really love her does she crack that mask of imperturbability. Dean responds with natural fatherly concern for Stella and indignation against Louis, yet while he offers his daughter his firm support and expresses distress on her behalf, he still insists, "I am not involved."

Dean's wife, Gwendoline, is the tiger of the play, a woman capable of passionate intensity, though she has obviously submerged her own feelings in her role as the Master's wife. A biologist before her marriage, she is profoundly moved by the issue of the bomb, aware of the mutation that radiation can cause in unborn children. She is ready to sign Louis' petition until Sir Hugo Slade, the present Vice Chancellor of the university, reminds her that such an action on her part could cost her husband the Vice Chancellor's post. She tries to find out what Dean wants her to do, but he refuses to coerce her in any way, even offering her the pen and urging her to sign the petition. She holds back out of concern for his position, even though she continues to brood over the petition—to the point of arousing Stella's concern.

Louis Flax, like Dean, is an intellectual who is out of touch with his emotions. The general concern for humanity that underlies his petition against the hydrogen bomb does not extend itself to a genuine love for the woman bearing his child. Even though he dutifully proposes marriage to Stella, he, too, must discover the place love should occupy in his life.

The climax comes when Dean discovers that Gwendoline has gone mad and has slashed the Holbein painting belonging to the college (one that depicts a deformed child); she has attached the petition to the damaged portrait. In the confrontation that follows, Dean realizes that he bears the responsibility for his wife's troubled state. His philosophy of dissociation, his unwitting failure to share anything with her, has led her to believe that he does not really love her and that he tolerated her only out of his "goodness." Her concern over the issues raised by Louis' petition finally pushed her over the edge. Though Sir Hugo Slade urges Dean publicly to dissociate himself from his wife's action, Dean accepts responsibility for what he has done to her. He expresses his love for her and refuses to dismiss her gesture as merely the aberration of an insane woman, even going so far as to add his own signature to the petition.

In many respects, *The Tiger and the Horse* is a conventional, well-made play, integrating a serious contemporary theme with the stuff of traditional domestic drama. The reservations that Hayman and others have expressed about the play are valid; in particular, the plot is so tightly developed that there is no room to develop the characters as effectively as Bolt might have done. For example, the progression of Gwendoline's madness is never really dramatized; her eccentricity and troubled behavior are only mentioned in the dialogue. Thus, her breakdown has a certain melodramatic edge. Similarly, Louis' changed attitude after his son is born—his discovery that he really does love Stella—is not dramatized; rather, it is tacked on to provide a conventional happy ending.

With *A Man for All Seasons*, Bolt shifted to a historical subject, but one that embodies themes relevant to contemporary life. He felt that the distancing effect of a play set in past centuries would provide a way of escaping from some of the constraints of naturalism, such as an overriding concern for the skillful use of realistic plot detail.

The play's protagonist, Sir Thomas More, exemplifies the man who has realized his full potential. The historical Thomas More was a charming, urbane man, extraordinarily successful in his public and private life—happy in his family and in his friendships, accomplished as a statesman, renowned for his intelligence and wit. Unlike Jack Dean, he was intensely involved in the life of his times, yet he retained enough detachment to keep his sense of values intact. As Bolt stresses in his preface to the play, he found More's most distinctive quality to be "an adamantine sense of his own self. He knew where he began and left off, what area of himself he could yield to the encroachments of his enemies, and what to the encroachments of these he loved." Though More loved life and did not court martyrdom, he was willing to die rather than betray his deepest principles. More could not falsely express approval of King Henry VIII's divorce and subsequent marriage to Anne Boleyn, particularly when this meant swearing an oath, pledging his integrity as a guarantor of the truth. Thus, Bolt describes More as "a hero of selfhood."

Tynan objected that Bolt does not show the audience what More's underlying convictions were or why he embraced them so uncompromisingly. He notes that the playwright is not concerned with whether these convictions are right or wrong but only that More clung to them and would not disclose them under questioning. More's speech before the death sentence is passed succinctly states his position that the Act of Parliament making King Henry Supreme Head of the Church is contrary to divine law, but Bolt's concern is not with exploring the soundness of More's view; rather, he dramatizes More's twofold struggle—to preserve his life, if possible, but above all to preserve his soul, or essential self.

Corrigan has described the main action of the play as a series of confrontations between More and those who seek to make him retreat from that last stronghold of the self and accede to the king's behest. Bolt effectively uses the Brechtian device of a series of semi-independent scenes to develop these confrontations. The scenes show More adroitly facing powerful opponents, as well as interacting with his family, which is deeply involved with his fate. Because of Bolt's emphasis on More's domestic life, Hayman has found *A Man for All Seasons* thin on social texture, a drama focusing on personal relationships rather than showing the individual pitted against society. Yet Bolt has correctly noted that More himself attached great importance to his family life. Moreover, the conflicts Bolt presents are skillfully orchestrated to show More facing questions, opposition, and misunderstandings in the small world of his home at the same time that he is battling them in the world at large.

Perhaps the two most important foils for More are Richard Rich and the Common Man. When Rich first appears, he is arguing with More, maintaining that "every man has his price," an opinion that his own subsequent career aptly illustrates. Not adequately defined by any strong sense of personal values, as More is, he is readily tempted to sell himself in order to procure advancement. Rich undergoes something of an interior struggle when he finds himself drifting toward betrayal of his king, but he soon sheds any semblance of self-respect to become a useful tool to Thomas Cromwell. Unlike More, who will not compromise himself by a false oath that is a mere formality, Rich boldly perjures himself in a capital case to help Cromwell secure More's conviction.

The Common Man, who assumes various roles within the play, starting as More's steward Matthew and ending as his executioner, provides another foil to the man of uncommon moral courage. Bolt indicates that he used "common" in the sense of "that which is common to us all"; he intended to have the audience identify to a degree with the character. In each role, the Common Man demonstrates his overriding concern with two basic human instincts, self-interest and self-preservation. Anselm Atkins has argued that, despite essential differences, the Common Man is made to resemble More sufficiently to have the audience recognize themselves in both characters. More represents what we could be, at our best; the Common Man indicates what we all too often are—concerned finally with slipping by comfortably in life, getting what we can without too many moral scruples. Both characters are extremely rational and both seek with great care to keep themselves out of trouble. Like More, the Common Man draws a firm boundary between what he will and will not do, only in his case he draws a line where risks outweigh gains, as when Cromwell offers the jailer a dangerously large sum for information about his prisoner More. The Common Man, unlike More, is concerned with preserving his bodily life at all costs, not with the essential self, his soul.

Bolt's masterful handling of language, blending a Tudor flavor into modern dialogue and skillfully interpolating More's own words where appropriate, is a notable feature of the play. The dramatist has indicated that he sought to make thematic use of images, with dry land representing society and the sea and water representing "that larger context which we all inhabit, the terrifying cosmos." These references are so naturally interwoven into the rest of the play that they generally escape notice, yet the pattern is there; such remarks as King Henry's passing allusion to *his* river, where he is playing the role of pilot, and Matthew's reference to More's fear of drowning have additional resonance when seen in this context.

Bolt's preface to *Vivat! Vivat Regina!* makes evident his conviction that setting plays in the past is one method of giving characters the particularity they need to emerge as people rather than as archetypes while still enabling them to be "theatrical." By this the playwright means that the characters have "a continuously high pitch of speech and action" obviously different from the pace of real life but appropriate to the heightened intensity of drama and made convincing within the dramatic framework. Bolt feels that the audience accepts theatrical speech and action more readily in characters from the past "not because we seriously think they really did continuously speak and act like that but because we don't know how they spoke and only know the more dramatic of their actions."

Certainly Bolt selected a highly dramatic subject in the parallel careers of Elizabeth I of England and Mary, Queen of Scots, and the tragic rivalry between the two monarchs. Here the tension between the individual and society emerges as a study of the conflict between fulfillment in personal relationships and the exigencies of political power. Both women are strong-willed queens; as they steer their courses through troubled political waters, each recognizing a potential threat in the other, they must make crucial choices between love and political expediency. Elizabeth, who from her youth has had to be extremely self-controlled and politically calculating, can subordinate her needs as a woman to the requirements of her office, though at great psychological cost; she suppresses part of her personality, becoming hardened and neurotic even as she achieves greatness as a monarch. By contrast, Mary refuses to suppress the emotional side of her nature; she willfully chooses love, even though she risks political disaster.

Bolt's mastery of structure is evident in his handling of complex historical events unfolding over a number of years. He employs a series of parallel scenes, with the action shifting back and forth between Mary and Elizabeth in the same type of fluid staging that characterized *A Man for All Seasons*. He also uses patently theatrical devices to advance the action and to underscore the interconnections between the two monarchs' careers; in one such scene, Elizabeth is seated aloft on the throne as the baptism of Mary's son James, heir of the Tudor line, takes place in the foreground. The most stylized piece of action occurs at the Kirk o' Field incident, where Mary is shown acting in collusion with Bothwell, the murderer of her second husband, Darnley. She is seen dancing "puppet-like under Bothwell's compelling stare," then dancing alone and frightened. After an explosion rocks the stage and scatters the dancers, John Knox steps into the spotlight vacated by Mary and denounces her. When the lights come up, the other dancers are revealed to include Elizabeth and Lord Cecil, Philip of Spain, and the pope, who remonstrate with Mary over her involvement with Bothwell.

In discussing how he gave dramatic shape to the involved story of the two monarchs, Bolt notes that he sought "to present the confused eventfulness of Mary's life as a series of single theatrical happenings, and to present the torturous complexities of Elizabeth's policy as an immediate response." Bolt draws a sharply dramatic contrast between the two monarchs in terms of sexual politics. At the beginning of the play, Elizabeth, though deeply in love with Robert Dudley, reluctantly takes Lord Cecil's advice not to marry him because of his suspected involvement with his wife's death. The queen believes him innocent but realizes that such a marriage might cost her the throne. Her decision is partially affected by the knowledge that Mary, Queen of Scots, would welcome such a move. So much has she learned to subordinate her personal feelings to concerns of state that she later agrees to let Cecil propose Robert Dudley, now Earl of Leicester, as a "safe" suitor for Mary, Queen of Scots.

Instead, Mary makes a politically advantageous second marriage to Henry Stuart, Lord Darnley, which strengthens her claim to the English throne, yet even this marriage reflects Mary's determination to have a husband she can love. When Darnley proves weak and faithless, participating in the plot to kill the queen's favorite, David Rizzio, Mary falls deeply in love with Lord Bothwell. Unlike Elizabeth, she is portrayed as all too ready to risk her throne for love. Not only does she bring Darnley to Kirk o' Field under threat of otherwise losing Bothwell's love; she also refuses to repudiate Bothwell later, acting against Elizabeth's own admonition. Mary stubbornly maintains that he was tried and found innocent, despite the questionable nature of the verdict; she further reveals that she has married him. Even after she has surrendered herself to the Scottish nobility on condition that they let Bothwell go, she refuses to conciliate the lords by repudiating the marriage as a forced one and thus reclaiming her throne. Passionately, she declares, "I would follow him to the edge of the earth—in my shift!" When Bothwell is driven into exile and Mary is living as a royal prisoner in England, she still clings to the hope that he will keep his promise and return. Mary's pained acknowledgment that Bothwell will not return—she learns that he has taken service with the King of Denmark and has another woman in his house—leads her to renounce love to "study policy." This "policy," however, involves her in a conspiracy against Elizabeth and leads to her execution.

Because the two queens never met historically, Bolt does not invent any scene involving a direct confrontation between them as other dramatists, including Friedrich Schiller, have done. A key scene in the latter's *Mary Stuart* (pr. 1800) is a meeting between Elizabeth and Mary at Fotheringhay

Castle, where Mary wins a moral victory over Elizabeth that ensures her death. In *Vivat! Vivat Regina!* the monarchs exchange words onstage twice in scenes that are obviously representational of exchanges that took place in letters. In addition, Bolt gains considerable dramatic impact by emphasizing the psychological effects of the rivalry. Elizabeth's reaction to the news of Mary's escape (following the murder of Rizzio) reveals her envy of Mary's more intense involvement in life; she particularly envies the passionate response the Queen of Scots can evoke in men such as Lord Bothwell, who "raises men, half-naked men . . . and drives her enemies from Edinburgh—and for what? Why, for herself." The English queen's envy is heightened by the awareness that the child Mary is carrying will be heir to the English throne, since Elizabeth is "barren stock." When Elizabeth is thought merciful for giving Mary refuge in England, even after hearing an impassioned letter from Mary to Bothwell that furnishes proof of Mary's involvement in the plot to kill Darnley, Lord Cecil astutely observes, "I do not think that this is altogether mercy. I think our Queen sees Mary in the mirror." On the other hand, Mary signs the letter giving her approval of the conspiracy against Elizabeth after she has learned that her son, James, has never received any of the letters and gifts she has sent and that Elizabeth "has played the mother's part." Her fury against the English queen impels Mary to an action that she knows might entrap her and lead to her death.

Bolt's psychobiographical approach presents both Mary and Elizabeth in human terms while fashioning an extremely effective structure for dramatizing the intertwined careers of the two monarchs. Hayman finds that the emphasis on personal relationships, which he sees as characteristic of Bolt's dramas, prevents Bolt from mining the complexity of his subject sufficiently. Similarly, Irving Wardle has called the play "an immensely skillful piece of cosmetic surgery: adding the common touch and the free-flowing action of epic theatre, while leaving the assumptions of heroic costume drama untouched." Other critics, however, such as Samuel Hirsch, have found *Vivat! Vivat Regina!* "exciting theater" that "illuminates history by putting it in the perspective of human personality."

When Bolt turned to twentieth century history and the Russian Revolution for the subject of his next play, *State of Revolution*, he focused on another uncommon man—this time a leader at odds not only with the capitalist society he sought to replace but also with his fellow revolutionaries. What fascinated the playwright was Vladimir Lenin's uncompromising dedication to the Marxist view of history and the Socialist Revolution as he saw it developing. Adopting the Marxist ethic that anything which promoted the establishment of the Socialist State was justified, Lenin often sanctioned extreme and brutal measures as necessary means to this great end. In an interview with Sally Emerson, Bolt stressed the paradox this man presented: "Viewed in one light, he was an indefensible monster, in another he was a great and good man. He did and said quite impermissible things but he was also selfless with no love of cruelty for its own sake."

Once again employing an episodic structure, Bolt moves from the pre-Revolutionary period in 1910, when the Bolshevik leaders were running a school to train Party activists at Maxim Gorky's villa in Capri, through the Revolution and its aftermath, ending with Vladimir Ilich Lenin's death and Joseph Stalin's rise to power in 1924. In order to provide a frame for the chronicle, the playwright uses as his narrator a historical figure, Anatole Lunacharsky, an associate of Lenin who became Commissioner for Education and Enlightenment in the Soviet State. Lunacharsky is portrayed as addressing a meeting of Young Communists around 1930, on the anniversary of Lenin's death. As critic David Zane Mairowitz has emphasized, Lunacharsky, a humane intellectual, reflects the original idealism within the revolutionary movement as well as the questioning and moral scruples that surfaced as its promise was betrayed. Mairowitz and others have also shown the basic problem with this particular framing device; the staged events purport to dramatize Lunacharsky's speech to his 1930 audience, yet such an account of the origins of Stalinism is inconceivable in that context: By 1930, the Stalinist rewriting of history was already well under way.

Nevertheless, Lunacharsky's account does present a compelling portrait of Lenin as a complex, driven man who acted with a terrible consistency in pursuing the goal of establishing a Socialist State. The play provides glimpses of the human warmth that Lenin too often suppressed in the name of revolutionary ideal, yet it also shows the cold detachment and ruthless determination he could exercise when personal feelings or human considerations seemed contrary to these greater goals. Despite his feeling of friendship for Lunacharsky, Lenin can brutally question why he is still in the Party with his baggage of humanistic notions. Lenin argues that "unconditional human love is nothing but a dirty dream" at a moment in history that requires "unconditional class hatred." He further indicates that he is willing to sacrifice cultural values, even the "moral amenities," to achieve the new society that will beget its own virtue—"its own new form of love and unimaginable music." Yet Lenin's words also suggest his own brand of revolutionary idealism and his intensity of purpose.

One of the deepest ironies underscored in the drama is the contradiction that Lenin's career offers to the Marxist view of history he embraced, which postulates that history finds the men it needs, contrary to the doctrine that great men shape events. At many crucial points, it is Lenin's "overwhelming, ruthless will" that determines the course of events, prevailing over the opposition of other Bolshevik leaders. Convinced that a Russian Revolution would lead to a worldwide Socialist revolution, he argues for an end to Russian participation in World War I and the immediate pursuit of a civil war. He is also determined to use the discontent of the peasants in promoting a Socialist revolution, even though the realistic Gorky emphasizes the disparity between the goals of the peasants and the aims of the Bolsheviks; the peasants desire individual ownership of the land, not the establishment of a collectivist society. Lenin also argues for the adoption of the Brest-Litovsk Treaty with Germany despite its harsh conditions, since his first priority is continuing the Revolution on any possible terms. After the Bolsheviks assume power, he continues to play the prime role in charting the development of the Socialist State. Following the Kronstadt uprising, he is the prime force shaping the New Economic Policy that permits a measure of capitalistic enterprise, because he deems this a necessary expedient. He also favors using the Cheka as a counterrevolutionary police force to root out the bourgeois elements in the Party.

The greatest irony, however, is the failure of Lenin's last supreme effort to exert his will and to influence the Party's choice of leader after his death. The Central Committee suppresses Lenin's "Testament" as the work of a sick man, even though its warning proves fatefully accurate. In this important document, Lenin expresses his preference for Leon Davidovich Trotsky as the next Party leader and warns that Stalin is too brutal. The irony is compounded by the fact that Stalin has been considered the ideal Party functionary for years, doing what needs to be done (like Thomas Cromwell in *A Man for All Seasons*). When he hears Lenin's warning that he will not use his power as Party Secretary with sufficient caution, Stalin can remind the Committee that he carried out all the jobs that Lenin asked him to do. He can also remind them that revolution is brutal—a statement Lenin himself often made. Lenin's collapse takes place onstage in the background during Stalin's delivery of his triumphant speech before the Thirteenth Congress—dramatically emphasizing Lenin's unsuccessful struggle to combat the menace he sees in Stalin. Bolt's drama portrays the development of Stalinism as a perverted outgrowth of Marxism-Leninism and makes clear the dangers of a philosophy that can dispense with the "moral amenities" in seeking to establish the dictatorship of the proletariat.

State of Revolution evoked mixed responses from the critics. Although the play confirms Bolt's talent for providing a clearly developed structure in treating the complex events of the Russian Revolution and its disastrous aftermath, Mairowitz has pointed out a number of oversimplifications in Bolt's treatment of the material, such as his failure to make clear that a civil war was in progress and his focusing upon the Bolshevik leaders with relatively little attention to the lower classes and their part in these historic events. Mairowitz and other critics have observed that the Bolshevik leaders tend to represent attitudes rather than fully articulated characters; Mairowitz adds that they sound like Englishmen in debate rather than impassioned Socialists. Despite such limitations, Bolt has managed to construct a compelling portrait of Lenin tragically caught up in the Marxist view of history, a drama culminating in a terrifying vision of the logical consequences of the Marxist ethic as Lenin himself formulated it.

Though Bolt has not matched the success of *A Man for All Seasons* in his subsequent dramas, he has effectively employed the open or epic style of that work to explore other historical subjects in *Vivat! Vivat Regina!* and *State of Revolution*. He has also continued to use the technical devices associated with a consciously theatrical style of dramaturgy for carefully planned effects. Bolt has never lost his concern for a realistic examination of human behavior or his ability to interweave close connections between plot and character. He continues to be one of the most skillful craftsmen in contemporary British theater, a popular playwright who has taken drama seriously and merits serious regard.

Other major works

NONFICTION: "English Theatre Today: The Importance of Shape," 1958 (in *International Theatre Annual*).

SCREENPLAYS: *Lawrence of Arabia*, 1962 (based on T. E. Lawrence's writings); *Doctor Zhivago*, 1965 (adaptation of Boris Pasternak's novel); *A Man for All Seasons*, 1966; *Ryan's Daughter*, 1970; *Lady Caroline Lamb*, 1972.

RADIO PLAYS: *The Master*, 1953; *Fifty Pigs*, 1953; *Ladies and Gentlemen*, 1954; *Mr. Sampson's Sundays*, 1955; *The Window*, 1958; *The Drunken Sailor*, 1958; *The Banana Tree*, 1961.

Bibliography

Atkins, Anselm. "Robert Bolt: Self, Shadow, and the Theater of Recognition," in *Modern Drama*. X (September, 1967), pp. 182-188.

Corrigan, Robert W. "Anger and After: A Decade of British Theatre," in *The Theatre in Search of a Fix*, 1973.

Emerson, Sally. "Playing the Game: Robert Bolt and William Douglas Home," in *Plays and Players*. XXIV (June, 1977), pp. 10-15.

Free, William J. "Robert Bolt and the Marxist View of History," in *Mosaic*. XIV (1981), pp. 51-59.

Fuegi, John. "Like a Woman They Keep Going Back To," in *Drama*. XCVIII (Autumn, 1970), pp. 57-64.

_____ . "Robert (Oxton) Bolt," in *Contemporary Dramatists*, 1977. Edited by James Vinson and D. L. Kirkpatrick.

Hayman, Ronald. *Robert Bolt*, 1969.

Kaiser, John R. "Robert Bolt" in *Dictionary of Literary Biography, Volume VIII: British Dramatists Since World War I*, Part 1, 1982. Edited by Stanley Weintraub.

Mairowitz, David Zane. "State of Revolution" in *Plays and Players*. XXIV

(August, 1977), pp. 16-17.

O'Connor, Garry. "Bolt, Robert Oxton," in *Contemporary Dramatists*, 1982. Edited by James Vinson and D. L. Kirkpatrick.

Taylor, John Russell. *The Angry Theater: New British Drama*, 1969.

"Teaching Is for Schools: An Interview with Robert Bolt," in *Encore*. VIII (March/April, 1961), pp. 17-33.

Tynan, Kenneth. *A View of the English Stage, 1944-63*, 1975.

Gertrude K. Hamilton

EDWARD BOND

Born: Hollaway, North London; July 18, 1934

Principal drama

The Pope's Wedding, pr. 1962, pb. 1971; *Saved*, pr. 1965, pb. 1966; *Early Morning*, pr., pb. 1968; *Narrow Road to the Deep North*, pr., pb. 1968; *Black Mass*, pr. 1970, pb. 1971; *Lear*, pr. 1971, pb. 1972; *Passion*, pr., pb. 1971; *Bingo: Scenes of Money and Death*, pr. 1973, pb. 1974; *The Sea*, pr., pb. 1973; *The Fool*, pr. 1975, pb. 1976; *A-A-America!*, pr., pb. 1976; *Stone*, pr., pb. 1976; *We Come to the River*, pr., pb. 1976 (music by Hanz Werner Henze); *The Bundle: Or, New Narrow Road to the Deep North*, pr., pb. 1978; *The Woman*, pr. 1978, pb. 1979; *The Cat*, pr. 1980, pb. 1982; *Restoration*, pr., pb. 1981 (music by Nick Bicat); *Summer*, pr., pb. 1982.

Other literary forms

Edward Bond has adapted or translated classic plays, published several volumes of poetry and essays, and written a number of screenplays; he cowrote with Michelangelo Antonioni the screenplay for *Blow Up* (1967), also directed by Antonioni. Generally, Bond's essays deal with politics and the political responsibility of the artist.

Achievements

Bond's first major achievements occurred in the law court and in Parliament. His play *Saved* was the last British play prosecuted for obscenity; his *Early Morning*, the last banned entirely by the Lord Chancellor's office. The controversy stirred by these two plays focused attention on Britain's censorship laws and helped rally support to repeal them. Because of this notoriety and his association with London's Royal Court Theatre, long the home of experimental drama, Bond's detractors now dismiss him as an *enfant terrible* intent on shocking a complacent middle class. This view not only underestimates the excellence of Bond's early work but also denies the scope and richness of what has followed. A serious leftist, Bond has been concerned to show how social conditions generate moral ideas and how the past weighs on the present. Not surprisingly, then, Bond's later work has concentrated on mythic or historical subjects; he has written a play based on the Lear legend (*Lear*) and another about William Shakespeare in retirement (*Bingo*). *Early Morning* is set in Victoria's reign and *The Sea* in Edward's; *The Fool* is about the Romantic poet John Clare. In short, no other contemporary British playwright has explored the British past as thoroughly as has Bond in his search to find the sources of British ideas.

Bond disparages his film scripts because he believes that work in this medium cannot escape commercialism. Nevertheless, two of his screenplays, *Blow Up* (based on a story by Julio Cortázar) and *Walkabout* (1971) deserve mention. In *Blow Up*, a photographer discovers that he has accidentally taken a picture of what appears to be a murder. The film then explores the reactions of the photographer and his friends to this act of violence. This theme seems very close to those of Bond's major works. Similarly, *Walkabout*, the story of two children lost in the Australian Outback who are befriended by an aborigine, is informed by Bond's notion that innocence is available to primitives and children in a way that it is not available to civilized adults.

Biography

Born into a working-class family, Edward Bond, one of four children, was evacuated to Cornwall at the beginning of World War II, after which he returned to his grandparents' home near Ely. These country experiences were important to Bond and may be the source of his exceptional ability to capture a wide variety of speech mannerisms. After the war, he returned to London for grammar school; like many of his classmates, he left school at fifteen. He later attributed his interest in playwriting to two childhood experiences: first, his early exposure to the music hall, where one of his sisters was a magician's assistant, and second, his seeing, at age fourteen, the actor Daniel Wolfit in Shakespeare's *Macbeth*. Bond says of this experience, "It was the first thing that made sense of my life for me."

After leaving school, Bond worked in a factory until he was eighteen and then fulfilled his national service obligation. After basic training, he found himself stationed in Vienna, where he began seriously to try to write fiction. He returned to London in 1955 and again worked in factories. After submitting some plays to the Royal Court, he was asked in 1958 to join the writers' group there and to become a regular play reader for the theater. His first produced play, *The Pope's Wedding*, was directed by George Devine, who became Bond's favorite director and a champion of his work. Since 1966, Bond has lived by his writing, although his income has come more from the cinema than the theater. He has developed a coterie following in England and America and has been a very popular playwright in Germany. His plays have won a number of awards, and in 1977 Yale University awarded him an honorary doctorate.

Analysis

Edward Bond's early plays, *The Pope's Wedding* and *Saved*, realistically depict the English working class. His later plays move toward mythological and historical drama whose form seems to have been influenced by the works of both Bertolt Brecht and Shakespeare. In all of his work, Bond considers the connections of political power and violence in a society that reduces human beings to commodities.

Bond's second play, *Saved*, created a *succès de scandale*, and much of his subsequent fame depended on the notoriety of this first production at the Royal Court Theatre. The play tells the story of a young man, Len, who is picked up by a young woman, Pam, and taken home by her. The first scene depicts Pam's seduction of Len and his embarrassment at being interrupted by her father, Harry. Len rents a room in Pam's parents' flat, but the affair ends when Pam falls in love with another young man, Fred. All of these characters are clearly South London working class, but none is unemployed or desperate for money. The play instead examines emotional poverty and destructive relationships. Although Pam bears Fred's child, Len continues to live with her parents, who have arranged their lives so that they hardly see or speak to each other.

Fred abandons Pam, who continues to pursue him and enlists Len's aid in doing so. In scene 4, Len, Pam, Harry, and Mary, Pam's mother, studiously ignore the crying baby as the audience witnesses the emotional poverty of their lives. After a short domestic scene between Len and Pam, scene 6 provides the play's central action. It begins with Fred and Len talking to each other about Pam. Some of Fred's friends arrive and describe their rowdy activities. Pam enters, pushing the baby's carriage. She tells Fred that the baby will be quiet because she has doped it with aspirin, but eventually she argues with the men and exits. Len exits shortly afterward. More of Fred's friends arrive, and rough male joking begins. Soon, the youths notice the baby and begin pushing the carriage violently across the stage. As Fred watches passively, their actions escalate until they remove the baby's diaper and rub its own excrement on its face.

One of the men, Pete, then throws a stone to Fred, who lets it drop. There is a moment of silence, then some taunting. At last, Fred picks up the stone and throws it into the carriage. The other men then stone the child. The men run off and Pam enters and wheels the carriage away, cooing all the time to the baby, at whom she has not yet looked closely. In scene 7, the last in the first act, Pam and Len visit Fred in jail. Fred will be convicted of manslaughter, but, more important, the audience learns that Len witnessed the entire scene but did not come forward to the police. It is also apparent that Pam still loves Fred.

As Sir Laurence Olivier pointed out in his defense of the play, *Saved* is like Shakespeare's *Macbeth* and *Julius Caesar* in that a horrifying act of violence happens in the first part of the play, with the rest of the play devoted to examining the consequences of that action. The remaining six scenes of *Saved* portray Len's continuing efforts to establish human contact and to work out his feelings about the killing. Act 2 opens with Harry and Len talking about Harry's work. The audience is unclear about how much time has lapsed since Fred's trial. Pam enters and an argument erupts.

Bond uses this scene to show how Pam has not been changed by the baby's death and how Len is still searching for a viable human relationship. In the next scene, Mary and Len are alone together; she tears her stocking, which Len repairs. As he kneels beside her to work on the stocking, the audience sees that despite their age difference there is a powerful sexual attraction between them. In a clear parallel to scene 1, Harry also interrupts this scene.

Scene 10 shows Fred's return to his friends after his prison sentence. Pam and Len both go to the pub in which this reunion occurs. Several times, Len tries to find out what Fred felt during the stoning of the baby. Fred has objectified the experience and refuses to talk to Len. Indeed, his comments are all about the awfulness of prison. At the end of this scene, he rejects Pam brutally and takes up with another girl. Pam blames Len for this rejection.

Scene 11 shows a violent fight between Mary and Harry, who has accused his wife of "goin' after [her] own daughter's leftovers." Pam and Len interrupt this scene but are unable to prevent Mary from breaking a teapot (significantly, a wedding present) over Harry's head. Pam, still distraught because of her rejection by Fred, blames Len for all of her troubles.

Scene 12 is a scene of reconciliation between Harry and Len, in which Harry, among other things, tells Len that he has missed his chance because there is no war. Harry remembers killing with fondness. This scene, in which Harry and Len acknowledge their similarities, is the closest to real human contact that any of the characters come. The final scene of the play presents the entire family onstage while Len attempts to fix a chair; they sit self-absorbed and silent as he works.

This plot summary, which suggests how Bond mixes the tedious and ordinary to reveal the deeper evils in human nature, cannot convey the real power of *Saved*. His control of speech rhythms enhances the believability of the characters, revealing the depth of feeling that lies beneath the mere content of their speeches. Their very inarticulateness motivates their violence; they can only lash out.

Most of the early critics of the play were so appalled by its violence that they overlooked its devastating and insightful comments on society as well as its literary merit. Bond himself chides these critics in his introduction to the play when he writes, "Clearly the stoning to death of a baby in a London park is a typical British understatement. Compared to the strategic bombing of German towns it is a negligible atrocity, compared to the cultural and emotional deprivation of most of our children its consequences are insignificant."

The play, in fact, has two intertwined stories—the death of the child and Len's growing attraction for Mary. This second plot Bond calls an "Oedipal comedy" which is resolved by Harry's and Len's reconciliation. The death of the baby, however, must be seen in context. Scene 4, in which the baby is ignored, the personal relations within Pam's family, and the personality of Fred and his friends all suggest the bleakness of the life that would await this child if it grew up; at best, it would become like its murderers. The stoning, then, is a metaphor for the life of such children and shows in one brief, horrid moment the damage that accumulates over a lifetime.

Len constantly seeks a way out of these destructive relationships. Instinctively, he knows the importance of human contact, and instinctively he seeks it. His world offers virtually no language and no social structure to facilitate these contacts. Actions, often small and discontinuous, are thus the characters' only real means of expression. The last scene, in which Len repairs the chair, is a fitting end to the play. Len's commitment to Harry, Mary, and Pam is affirmed by this action; the others' indifference to him is affirmed by the trivial tasks they perform. The only speech in the last scene is Len's request for a hammer—a request the others ignore. Bond calls *Saved* "almost irresponsibly optimistic" because Len retains his "natural goodness." To the extent that Len survives the horrors of the play, Bond may be right in his judgment.

In an early *Theatre Quarterly* interview, Bond suggested that *Saved* suffered from "too much realism." His next play, *Early Morning*, a political satire set vaguely in Victoria's court, suffers from no such disadvantage. The Prince of Wales is portrayed as Siamese twins; Victoria is having a lesbian relationship with Florence Nightingale; and Disraeli plans a coup. Many critics, notably Malcolm Hay, see *Early Morning* as the play which holds the clue to Bond's later work. Bond's next play, *Narrow Road to the Deep North*, however—also performed in 1968—uses similar themes and techniques, won wider critical acclaim, and is more accessible to the non-British audience.

Bond says that *Narrow Road to the Deep North* began from his reading of *The Narrow Road to the Deep North* (1933), by the seventeenth century Japanese poet Matsuo Bashō, who is a character in the play. In one section of this celebrated travel journal, "The Records of a Weather Beaten Skeleton," Bashō reports that he came across a child abandoned by a river and decided that it was fate or "the irresistible will of heaven" which had caused its abandonment. Bashō then concludes, "If it is so child, you must raise your voice to heaven, and I must pass on leaving you behind."

Bond was so shocked by this incident that he put the book down and refused to go on reading it. The memory of it festered, however, and Bond's play resulted. This genesis would suggest that Bond's play is about the social responsibility of the artist—a theme clear in two of Bond's later plays, *Bingo* and *The Fool*. Bond's Bashō, however, is a religious poet; he seeks enlightenment in his travels and therefore seeks the "Deep North." The play is thus about religion and society, and as Tony Coult observes, "Edward Bond is an atheist and a humanist. These facts are basic to what goes on in his plays. His work invariably embodies a tough critique of the unholy alliance between religion and politics."

There are numerous formal and stylistic differences between *Narrow Road to the Deep North* and *Saved*. First, *Narrow Road to the Deep North* makes no pretense at historical accuracy: The seventeenth century poet invites nineteenth century English missionaries into Japan. The audience is firmly in the world of fable. Second, Bond is willing to address the audience directly. In the introduction, as Bond calls his prologue, Bashō says, "I'm the seventeenth century poet Bashō." Scene 1 begins, "Thirty years since I was here!," and the next scene Bashō begins, "I've been back two years now." In short, Bond ignores the conventions of exposition and simply tells the audience directly what it needs to know and moves on. Third, Bond develops two techniques beyond their use in *Saved*. His ability to create the symbolic stage picture has increased, and he is more at home in an extended episodic structure which allows him to trace the development of a story through time. History is important to Bond, and he seeks forms that allow him to trace its consequence.

Narrow Road to the Deep North opens with a prologue in which Bashō leaves the abandoned child by the river. He returns thirty years later, having been "enlightened," to find the city ruled by the tyrant Shogo, who is discovered at the end of the play to be the child that Bashō left to die. Kiro, a young seeker after truth, wants to become Bashō's disciple, but Bashō rejects him. During this scene, prisoners are marched to the river to be drowned. Bashō is confronted face-to-face with Shogo's cruelty.

Two years later, Shogo summons Bashō to the palace to become the tutor of the Emperor's son, the legitimate ruler of the city. On the same day, Kiro, clowning about with two other monks, gets his head stuck in a sacred pot. Bashō brings him before Shogo and challenges him to resolve this dilemma. Shogo, having no respect for the sacredness of the pot, simply smashes it. Kiro is so entranced by the power of direct action that he becomes Shogo's follower despite reservations about his cruelty. Bashō, appalled by this sacrilege, persuades the British to invade and take over the city.

The British are represented by Georgina, a missionary, and the Commodore, her military brother. Bashō mistakenly assumes he can control the Commodore, only to discover that Georgina is the real power and that her morality is as destructive as Shogo's barbarity. Posing as priests, Kiro and Shogo escape to the deep north, where Shogo raises an army. He retakes the city and determines that the boy emperor shall not be used against him again. When Georgina, who has been left in charge of the children, cannot tell him who is the boy emperor, he kills them all. This act drives Georgina mad. The Commodore returns with reinforcements and retakes the city, capturing Shogo in the process.

The play's last scene shows Bond's growing strength and sophistication as a playwright. Shogo has been executed offstage. A procession of cheering townspeople enters carrying parts of Shogo's mutilated body on placards. After the crowd passes, Georgina and Kiro are left onstage. Kiro opens his robe, and Georgina comically and anxiously awaits rape. Instead, Kiro performs hari-kari. Two British soldiers enter and lead the still expectant Georgina away. A shout is heard offstage, and a man, dripping wet, emerges from the river. Naked, except for a loincloth, he asks, "Didn't you hear me shout? I shouted 'help.' You must have heard and didn't come. . . . I could have drowned." He wrings out his loincloth and dries himself with a banner from the procession as Kiro's body pitches forward in its death spasm. Thus, Bond ends the play with a complex of rhythms and images that bring his humanist view center. The audience is left with the nude body of the bather drying himself, unaware of the corpse beside him. Men must help men. Magic pots, prayers, and ritual suicide are all useless. The play echoes Brecht's heroine Joan Dark, who learns "that only men help where men are."

Unquestionably Bond's greatest achievement so far is his play *Lear*, which is not an adaptation or rewrite of Shakespeare's *King Lear* but a new play based on the Lear story. In fact, because Cordelia survives and rules in Bond's play, he claims that his play more closely follows the sources. Many of his statements about his own work must be taken with a grain of salt; like George Bernard Shaw, Bond makes extreme statements to annoy his critics. Nevertheless, part of the power of Bond's play derives from the comparison with *King Lear*, and in many ways it forms an anti-*Lear*—that is, it acknowledges the very different social worlds that produced the two plays.

In their book on Bond's plays, Malcolm Hay and Philip Roberts describe how Bond worked and the changes he made in the manuscript during the year and a half it took him to write the play. In his notes, Bond says of *King Lear*, "As a society we use the play in the wrong way. And it's for that reason that I would like to rewrite it so that we now have to use the play for ourselves, for our society, for our time, for our problems."

Lear's plot is too complex to summarize in detail, but there are some essential similarities and differences between it and *King Lear*. Like Shakespeare's Lear, Bond's king moves from arbitrariness through insanity to understanding. Daughters rebel against their father, the kingdom is divided, and blindness and the imprisonment of father and daughter occur. Like *King Lear*, Bond's play presents its themes and characters through animal imagery.

The differences between the plays seem more important. Bond renames Regan and Goneril as Bodice and Fontanelle. Cordelia is not Lear's daughter but a guerrilla leader who overthrows Bodice and Fontanelle and finds herself condemned to repeat Lear's mistakes. The action does not start from Lear's laying down of his authority but from his arbitrary exercise of it. As Bond's play opens, Lear and his daughters are inspecting a wall that Lear is building around the entire kingdom to protect it from his enemies. Because the wall drains the local people of both land and money, they attempt to sabotage the wall. Lear executes a malingering worker without a trial; his daughters, appalled at this abuse of power, marry his enemies and lead a revolt.

All the positive characters (Edgar, Kent, Albany, Gloucester) disappear from Bond's play. Lear himself is blinded onstage. The Fool is transformed into the Ghost of the Gravedigger's Boy and functions opposite Shakespeare's fool. Instead of leading Lear to wisdom, the ghost offers Lear refuge in noninvolvement and self-pity; he is less responsible than the king.

The eighteenth century found *King Lear* too violent, and it was rewritten into a decorous tragedy. Bond seems not to have found it violent enough. Warick, Lear's counselor, is beaten onstage, and his eardrums are pierced by Bodice's knitting needle. The death of the Gravedigger's Boy is accompanied by the squeals of slaughtered pigs. A medical orderly blinds Lear with a suction device after trapping his head in a specially designed chair. Like a good doctor, he sprays an aerosol on the wound to "encourage scabbing." The play ends when Lear is shot trying to destroy the wall that Cordelia is in the process of rebuilding. Bond might not argue that human beings today are more cruel than they were in the seventeenth century, but he will not allow his audience to forget that the modern technology of cruelty far exceeds the devices of the past.

In his preface written after the first production, Bond defends himself against those critics who find his work too violent:

> I write about violence as naturally as Jane Austen wrote about manners. Violence shapes and obsesses our society and if we do not stop being violent, we have no future. People who do not want writers to write about violence want us to stop writing about us and our time. It would be immoral not to write about violence.

To see and to accept mankind's role in violence leads one to see clearly, to understand. In act 2, Fontanelle, imprisoned with Lear, is executed onstage, and the medical orderly performs an autopsy on her. Lear watches with intense interest, saying: "She sleeps inside like a lion and a lamb and a child. The things are so beautiful. I am astonished. I have never seen anything so beautiful. . . ." The human body is not as it is for King Lear, "a poor bare forked thing." Bodice, the other daughter, is brought in as a prisoner during the autopsy. In their ensuing argument, Lear "puts his hands into Fontanelle and brings them out with organs and viscera." He says to Bodice:

> Look! I killed her! Her blood is on my hands! Destroyer! Murderer! And now I must begin again. I must walk through my life, step after step, I must walk in weariness and bitterness. I must become a child, hungry and stripped and shivering in blood, I must open my eyes and see.

Lear's inability to shirk the violence that his world has created leads him to pity and sanity, but Bond will not stop here. At the end of this scene, Lear is blinded after witnessing the death of both of his daughters. In his blindness, he is led to insight. Bond's Lear finds no redemption; revolt, not order, is established at the end of the play. Cordelia's revolution leads to more violence because her "morality is a form of violence."

Between them, *Lear* and *Narrow Road to the Deep North* suggest most of the concerns and techniques of Bond's theater. He stands to Shakespeare as the Greek tragedians stood to Homer. Like them, he rewrites old stories for a new time. Like Shakespeare, he makes myths out of English history—or rather, he deconstructs the myths of the past. In Bond's play *Bingo*, for example, Shakespeare is a character. Bond is not, however, concerned with the great playwright, but with the middle-class investor who allows himself to be bought off so that the big landlords can enclose the common fields. Bond's play, *The Fool*, centers on the Romantic poet John Clare. Instead of a private madness or the divine madness of the great poet, Bond shows a working-class writer driven mad by upper-class expectations and attitudes. In both of these plays, Bond attacks the romantic myth of the artist who is separated from and superior to society. By negative examples, he insists that the artist is shaped by his time and his responsibilities to it.

Major British playwrights have to move Shakespeare; he sits on their horizons like a threatening cloud. Shaw railed at him all the time; Bond has sought to demythologize him in *Lear* and in *Bingo*. Bond is a writer now at the height of his powers; it is, perhaps, early to make definitive judgments. Like Shaw and Shakespeare, Bond can tell a story about interesting people in compelling language. Above all, he creates a stage picture that burns into the memory.

Other major works

POETRY: *Theatre Poems and Songs*, 1978.

SCREENPLAYS: *Blow Up*, 1967 (with Michelangelo Antonioni; adaptation of Julio Cortázar's short story "Las babas del diablo"); *Laughter in the Dark*, 1969 (adaptation of Vladimir Nabokov's novel); *Walkabout*, 1971.

Bibliography

Coult, Tony. *The Plays of Edward Bond*, 1977.

Hay, Malcolm, and Philip Roberts. *Edward Bond: A Companion to His Plays*, 1978.

_____ . *Edward Bond: A Study of His Plays*, 1980.
Loney, Glenn. "Interview: Edward Bond," in *Performing Arts Journal*. I (Fall, 1976), pp. 37-45.
Scharine, Richard. *The Plays of Edward Bond*, 1976.
Trussler, Simon. *Edward Bond*, 1976.
_____ . "Edward Bond: The Long Road to Lear," in *Theatre Quarterly*. II (January, 1972), pp. 4-14.

Sidney F. Parham

GORDON BOTTOMLEY

Born: Keighley, England; February 20, 1874
Died: Oare, near Marlborough, England; August 25, 1948

Principal drama

The Crier by Night, pb. 1902, pr. 1916 (one act); *Midsummer Eve*, pb. 1905, pr. 1930 (one act); *Laodice and Danaë*, pb. 1909, pr. 1930 (one act); *The Riding to Lithend*, pb. 1909, pr. 1928 (one act); *King Lear's Wife*, pr. 1915, pb. 1916; *Britain's Daughter*, pb. 1921, pr. 1922; *Gruach*, pb. 1921, pr. 1923; *Scenes and Plays*, pb. 1929 (includes *Ardvorlich's Wife*); *The Acts of Saint Peter*, pr., pb. 1933; *Lyric Plays*, pb. 1932; *Choric Plays and a Comedy*, pb. 1939.

Other literary forms

Gordon Bottomley has also written nondramatic poetry, much of it published privately, in anthologies and in the small literary magazines of his time. Bottomley also favored a form of minor dramatic poetry which appears in the form of monologues, "duologues" (his term), and preludes. He also wrote many one-act plays, a form fashionable in small theaters and theater festivals, religious and secular, in the early part of the twentieth century. Examples of such miniatures of dramatic experimentation include *Ardvorlich's Wife*, in *Scenes and Plays*, and the short plays with Celtic themes in *Lyric Plays* and *Choric Plays and a Comedy*.

In addition to his lyric poetry and poetic drama, Bottomley took an active interest in visual arts and the careers of colleagues in a wide range of the arts. Thus, he introduced works by Sir James Guthrie, the graphic artist, and poetry by William Morris and Isaac Rosenberg, prominent poets of his time. He left also a lengthy correspondence with the painter and illustrator Paul Nash. It was Bottomley's conviction that serious drama must embrace music and the visual arts.

Bottomley also practiced the art of the dedicatory poem or prologue. Nearly every one of his theatrical works is dedicated in verse to a prominent artistic friend or colleague, including those mentioned above. In this practice the playwright followed and enlivened a long-standing tradition. Often Bottomley's prologue poems contain not only the standard praise for their recipient but also a brief apologia for his work.

Achievements

Bottomley was the recipient of the Femina Vie Heureuse prize, given in Paris in 1923, and three honorary degrees, from the universities of Aberdeen, in Scotland, and Durham and Leeds, in England. Perhaps, however, the playwright's achievement should be measured less by official acknowledgment than by his influence on contemporaries and disciples. The intense artistic friendships which Bottomley maintained helped to give momentum and focus to the efforts of the Georgian poets and to aid the movement of poetic and dramatic theme, structure, and language toward a distinctly modern mode. Bottomley was a recognized leader of his contemporaries, reading other playwrights' work in progress, writing frequent letters in response, and providing opportunities for stimulating work to designers, producers, and actors.

One of Bottomley's principal contributions to the arts was his insistence upon proper vocal training and delivery of lines of verse on the stage. Seeking to reestablish verse as a proper medium for drama, Bottomley was active in the formulation of a verse-speaking society whose efforts were copied elsewhere in Britain, Ireland, and the United States. By working with this society—with John Masefield, the poet laureate, who maintained a small theater in Oxford, and with experimental groups at the theater at Dartington Hall in Devon—and by aiding in the production of his and others' works by smaller groups and amateur groups, such as the Festival Theatre in Cambridge and the Yale University Drama School, Bottomley revived emphasis on the words used by playwrights to convey their dramatic ideas. *A Stage for Poetry: My Purposes with My Plays*, published in the year of his death, encapsulates Bottomley's views on the necessity for an artistic theater, definitely not aimed at mass audiences and their tastes; appendices in this text delineate his views on the need for the spoken word, in formal verse lines, to predominate on the stage.

Biography

Gordon Bottomley was the son of Alfred and Ann Maria Bottomley (née Gordon). The senior Bottomley worked as a cashier in a Yorkshire worsted mill, and sent his son to Keighley Grammar School. After he left school, Bottomley worked as a bank clerk until illness caused him to go into near-seclusion. He married Emily Burton of Arnside in 1905, and lived quietly, settling permanently in 1914 in The Shieling, Silverdale, near Carnforth in Lancashire. The Bottomleys took lengthy holidays in North Wales and often stayed with literary friends. Although Gordon Bottomley shunned the literary life of London, he was always current with literary and artistic trends, enjoying frequent communication and correspondence with such men of letters as Lascelles Abercrombie, a fellow Georgian poet-dramatist; John Drinkwater, who wrote poetic plays and produced one of Bottomley's; Paul Nash, the painter, who produced sketches and studies of scenes from those plays; and Sir Edmund William Gosse, who would eventually respond negatively to the work of Bottomley and the Georgians. Perhaps Bottomley's greatest literary friend and supporter, however, was Sir Edward Marsh, the editor of several volumes bearing the title *Georgian Po-*

etry (1912-1922), in which Bottomley's work figured prominently.

For all of his Georgian traits, it should be noted that Bottomley was deeply influenced by the Celtic Twilight movement of the late nineteenth century, as well as by the closely related Pre-Raphaelite Brotherhood. These movements were both interdisciplinary; both celebrated an idyllic, nearly prelapsarian, era of innocence and a setting in the more remote Celtic regions of Britain. Much of Bottomley's work is set in Scotland and draws from its folklore and mythology. In this, he is seen often as imitating or paralleling the dramatic experiments of William Butler Yeats, who found his inspiration in specifically Irish material.

There is little of event to record of Bottomley's personal life, but the publication and performance of one of his plays brought him a certain notoriety. When *King Lear's Wife* was first published, it appeared as the first offering in one of Marsh's anthologies, *Georgian Poetry II, 1913-1915* (1916). The preceding volume had been published to nearly unanimous acclaim, and literary critics hailed the harder, cleaner images of the modern Georgian poets, who were self-proclaimed anti-Victorians. The young poets of the new century were successfully freeing themselves from the limitations of the past. When *Georgian Poetry II, 1913-1915* was issued, however, the general critical response was negative—in some cases outraged—by what was judged to be excessive realism. The works of Bottomley and Abercrombie in particular were singled out as being representative of a new form of ugliness which offered violent and negative images of nature and mankind. Following productions of *King Lear's Wife* in Birmingham in 1915 and in London the next year, this negative response continued, with its focus on a corpse-washing sequence and a song, based on a child's nursery rhyme, which was considered shocking. It should be noted, however, that later critics, such as Frank Lawrence Lucas and Priscilla Thouless, have not been offended by Bottomley's harshness, generally viewing his work as transitional: He was aware of and influenced by the past, but he looked to the modern age.

Although Bottomley was in poor health for most of his life, he lived to see literary fashion change a number of times and to witness a small rekindling of interest in his drama in the 1940's, shortly before his death.

Analysis

In his *A Stage for Poetry*, Gordon Bottomley, near the end of his life, gave a tidy history of his dramatic career, complete with photographs and sketches of sets and costumes. More important, he left his own record of his dramatic intentions and accomplishments. He divided his works into two parts: "A Theatre Outworn" and "A Theatre Unborn." The former includes all the major works of his early career, which are written in traditional blank verse and hold generally to the nineteenth century model of heroic drama in aristocratic settings. From this group came Bottomley's commercial, if limited, successes. The plays that constitute his "Theatre Unborn" are considerably starker, using black or white cloths as backdrops, avoiding the proscenium stage, reverting to classical choric groups in robes, and featuring not aristocrats but characters who are often only partially human—either supernatural or animalistic or both. These theatrical experiments never found a proper audience, but they were not totally alien from Bottomley's earlier works. The playwright maintained an interest in Celtic mythology which runs through his work until the very end of his career. Although he came too late to be considered a playwright of the Celtic Twilight, Bottomley's themes and their execution stay true to that late nineteenth century movement's ideals. Bottomley's plays, many of them set in Scotland, contain frequent references to humans' dealings with supernatural creatures who hold power over them. His heroes and heroines are also frequently dreamers, incapable of dealing with the rigors of the real world; such refined sensibility was the Romantic legacy to the Celtic Twilight.

The Riding to Lithend is, in many ways, a characteristic one-act play by Bottomley. It features a long dedicatory poem to a prominent contemporary, and it is based, however loosely, on saga and myth. It includes a small cast of characters, not all of which are entirely or identifiably human, and its female characters are atypically strong, if not ferocious.

The play, written in 1908 but not performed until 1928, opens with a poem to the poet Edward Thomas, who died in World War I. In the poem, Bottomley refers to a visit from Thomas in 1907 during which he encouraged Bottomley to breathe new life into the adventures of the Icelandic hero Gunnar. Bottomley also compares Thomas himself to this early type by emphasizing his Welsh heritage, likening him to one of the heroes of *The Mabinogion* (c. 1100-1200), the Welsh saga cycle.

The *dramatis personae* include Gunnar Hamundsson, the hero-warrior; his wife, Hallgerd Longcoat; his mother, Rannveig; three female servants, Oddny, Astrid, and Steinvor; and a female thrall (a slave, taken in war), Ormild. There are also three beggar-women—Biartey, Jofrid, and Gudfinn—and many Riders, or warrior-vigilantes. The play is set in an "eating hall" in Gunnar's manor in the year 990. The female servants are combing and spinning wool and stitching a royal garment. In many of Bottomley's plays, an elaborate garment, representing its owner and symbolic of wealth and power, is prominently displayed in the opening scene.

The servant women have a sense of foreboding because all the men of the manor have been sent by Gunnar, rather unwisely it is feared, to a late harvest on the islands nearby. The abnormality of the harvest season is emphasized, and the audience learns that the seemingly capricious decision is in keeping with Gunnar's irregular hours and habits. He is an outcast from local law, and it is believed that his house is haunted by ghostly victims of his past misdeeds. Despite the foreboding occasioned by the unseasonal harvest, it is noted that Gunnar's "singing bill" (or sword) is silent, so that imminent danger seems unlikely. (The convention of the enchanted singing sword is prominent in early Northern European sagas and tales, most notably in Excalibur of Arthurian legend.) Once the concept of magic or unnatural power is introduced, there is a reference to a minor clairvoyant character who has foretold Gunnar's death. So strong is the power of this prophecy that Gunnar's brother, previously his stalwart lieutenant, has left Iceland as a result, and also to fulfill an injunction imposed upon Gunnar to exile himself for three years to atone for political and other misdeeds. All of this is related by the four serving women, who conclude that Gunnar, to defy such a prophecy, must be "fey"—that is, in the power of supernatural forces.

Rannveig enters and, as mother to two sons, one in exile, wishes Gunnar would fulfill the "atonement" and thus avoid being murdered by enraged noblemen. Hallgerd, the source of the trouble, enters preoccupied and angry about her fading beauty. Gunnar and Hallgerd argue over their predicament, and as a defiant gesture she looses her hair from its covering—signifying widowhood. It is then revealed that she was a widow when Gunnar first met, wooed, and won her. Theirs has been a turbulent marriage, and in the past, when Hallgerd stole food so as not to shame her husband in time of famine and in the presence of guests, he publicly humiliated her by slapping her face. By law, he could have killed or maimed her for such an offense. In this and others of Bottomley's plays, thievery, in keeping with the era and the culture he is representing, is a crime of great import and beneath the dignity of gentlefolk. This instance of thievery was the beginning of the blood feud which has resulted in Gunnar's being under injunction of exile.

Three witchlike figures from Icelandic myth enter, posing as beggar-women. They admit to traveling by flying through the night sky in a westerly direction (which signifies death), but Gunnar nevertheless agrees to house them for the night. These crones tell of Gunnar's heroic reputation, which remains solid throughout the country, and explain that there is still one ship by which he can escape. Here it is related that he did try once to leave the country, but his horse threw him and he experienced a vision of his homeland which made him vow to stay.

The crones also engage in traditional witch behavior, taking over the spinning (which they destroy), speaking of curses, and reciting the aristocratic lineage of Hallgerd, who in many respects is a worthy wife for the heroic Gunnar. The witches incense Hallgerd, who eventually drives them out. Their true nature becomes apparent when entering characters cannot see them; they become invisible after they leave the manor.

The noblemen who have awaited Gunnar's compliance with the law arrive at his home, and a battle ensues. Gunnar fights single-handedly, while Rannveig urges prudence and Hallgerd thirsts for blood. Gunnar's bowstring is broken, and he asks Hallgerd for some of her hair to repair it. She refuses—choosing this moment to avenge the public humiliation of her that he inflicted years earlier. Gunnar dies in battle with Hallgerd laughing. Rannveig, the grieving mother, keeps Hallgerd from her son's corpse, pulling her by the hair she denied to her husband. Rannveig then tries to murder Hallgerd to avenge her son's death, and hers is the play's final soliloquy—including a lullaby which uses images of sleep and death to good effect. In a final tableau, she raises the singing bill aloft over the corpse of her son. It is still singing, signifying Gunnar's victory even in death.

The Riding to Lithend makes significant use of Irish references, indicating the playwright's knowledge of the early links of custom and commerce between Iceland and Ireland and thus allowing for the Celtic Twilight influence seen elsewhere in his work. Also prominent is bird imagery, especially sinister imagery of birds of prey. The witch figures resemble in appearance and powers the Morrigan, a bird-woman of Celtic mythology who is usually a figure of death or misfortune, and Gunnar is identified with a bird-god which appears on his family crest.

The play delivers a primitive message in a primitive setting, and its characters retain the necessary two-dimensional qualities of figures in saga literature, who are more important as types than as individuals. The law is irrevocable, and although Gunnar is viewed as the best of the warrior mold of his homeland, he is not above the law. Appropriately, he dies in battle.

The blank verse, in this and in nearly all of Bottomley's plays, is at times merely neo-Elizabethan, deriving from the Shakespearean model used so much in the nineteenth century theater, but it can rise to eloquence when the playwright molds an honored verse form to modern language and expression. Bottomley's servant characters often have lines of a cleaner, more precise language; unlike Shakespearean servants, they too speak in blank verse, like their masters and mistresses.

King Lear's Wife begins with a lengthy dedicatory poem to Thomas Sturge Moore, another multifaceted artist who wrote verse plays of Bottomley's type and who also achieved distinction as an illustrator and designer of books, costumes and stage sets. The poem, written in iambic quadrameter, is composed in three stanzas of irregular length, each of which opens and closes with a triplet, while the remainder is formed in couplets. Bottomley praises *The Dial*, a literary magazine of the day, in which he had first encountered Moore's poetry from his seclusion in Lancashire. He hails Moore as "prince of poets in our time" and reminisces about conversations they enjoyed at a meeting in Surrey. Bottomley closes by offering *King Lear's Wife* as a "token . . . of admiration and loyalty."

The *dramatis personae* include Lear, King of Britain; Hygd, his queen;

Goneril and Cordeil, his daughters; Gormflaith and Merryn, servants to the queen; a Physician and two Elderly Women. The setting is a primitive English castle, fitted with harsh fabrics which deny a hospitable atmosphere. Highlighted is an elaborate robe and crown which belong to the "emaciated" Queen Hygd, whose large four-poster bed dominates the stage. She is being attended by Merryn, a Cornish servant of many years' service, and it is very early in the morning—a bleak time for a bleak setting.

The immediate subject is death. Hygd wants to die, feeling unneeded in middle age, but lingers mournfully in her illness. Merryn, quite old, is characterized as superstitious and alien because of her Cornish heritage; she dreads the idea of her own death. Enter a very vital middle-aged Lear, not the old and crazed figure of Bottomley's Shakespearean model. He is accompanied by the court Physician, and he has arranged for Gormflaith, a young Scotswoman, to tend the queen.

The Physician, seeking a psychological explanation for the queen's failing health, asks what long-term bitterness nursed in secret is the cause. The king responds vituperatively, and then the Physician suggests a cure, of juniper berries, marrow of adder, and emerald dust. Only Lear has a valuable emerald, a gift from an Irish king whose daughter mothered many British kings. He refuses to destroy it to save his wife's life.

Hygd awakens alone and is joined by Goneril, who is on the edge of womanhood. Dressed in hunting garb, Goneril is described in terms associated with Diana, the Greek virgin goddess and hunter. Both Goneril and Gormflaith are representative of "life." It is Lear's belief that his wife will benefit from their presence, but Hygd is repelled by their vitality. Goneril describes a visionary encounter at a Druidic site (a holy place of the priest class which had earlier controlled Britain). In contrast, Hygd describes and dismisses the new Christian religion of Merryn. Hygd then asks about Regan (the third daughter of Lear, who appears as an important character in Shakespeare's play but not at all in Bottomley's).

Hygd warns Goneril to enjoy her freedom now because soon she will be obliged to marry. The aging queen offers a philosophy frequent in Bottomley's work—that the domestication of fine, brave young women in marriage yields bitter results. At best, claims Hygd, women can only be venerated in age, whereas men fare better and have wider choices later in life.

They are interrupted by the child Cordeil (Cordelia in Shakespeare), who is at the door seeking her father. She is called "my little curse" and "an evil child" by her mother, who denies her access to the sickroom. Hygd claims that she conceived Cordeil to keep Lear faithful, adding that Cordeil's birth has left her an invalid. After Goneril lulls her mother to sleep, Gormflaith enters, an attractive woman, too eager to please. She reads a letter arranging an assignation with Lear, who arrives and destroys the letter for the sake of security. He then softens the blow by allowing Gormflaith to wear his emerald.

The king intends to make Gormflaith his queen after Hygd's death, despite Gormflaith's cunning observations concerning the negative effect this will have in his court and within his family. In his desire for a male heir, Lear will not hear reason. Gormflaith, in a climactic moment, asks to wear Hygd's crown, and Lear chastises her: "You cannot have the nature of a queen/ If you believe that there are things above you." Lear softens again, however, and while Gormflaith is sitting on his knee, wearing Hygd's crown, the queen awakens and sees all. Hygd tries to follow the lovers to the garden, falls, has a dying vision of Lear's mother, and dies shouting to Goneril "Pay Gormflaith."

The play rapidly becomes less poetic as Merryn discusses the need to tend the dead queen before rigor mortis sets in. The irony and bitterness increase as Goneril mockingly pays homage when Gormflaith reenters, still wearing Hygd's crown. Since Gormflaith was meant to be tending the queen, the enraged Goneril demands of her father the penalty given for servants leaving their posts, knowing fully that Lear is the cause of Gormflaith's absence. Goneril snatches the crown and replaces it on the queen.

The momentum of the play, its imagery and tone, alter greatly with the entrance of two women to minister to the queen's body. Like the gravediggers in William Shakespeare's *Hamlet*, they are irreverent in the presence of death, haggling over Hygd's personal effects—traditional payment for such work. They sing a grisly work song to the tune of "Froggie's Gone a Courtin'," preparing the reader for the equally grisly entrance of Goneril with a bloody knife. In a somewhat surprising about-face, Lear, when confronted by his murderess-daughter, disowns the dead Gormflaith and calls Goneril his "true daughter." The play ends with Lear hoping to marry off and "break" Goneril, thus bearing out Hygd's earlier fear, and the corpse washers finish by enjoying the irony of Lear's having traded one predicament—a sick wife—for another—a fearless and cruel daughter.

King Lear's Wife observes the traditional dramatic unities scrupulously. It showcases Lear against a predominantly female cast to great effect, and it develops ideas seen often in Bottomley's corpus. Beauty is power, but it is transient; death and physical violence are always near. The play rings a gender change on the classic revenge drama, because here a daughter avenges the disgrace and death of her mother. Ultimately, it affirms the sense of hierarchy and order codified in the law: Evildoers receive their just deserts.

The language of *King Lear's Wife* is not as garrulous as it is in many of Bottomley's works, and the speeches of supporting characters, such as

Merryn and the two corpse washers, are effective in reinforcing the thematic message of the play. Animal imagery prevails and is well integrated. The corpse washers wear black, batlike or birdlike costumes, appropriate to their task, and the reader is prepared for Goneril's murderous role because as a huntress she has killed in cold blood and become exhilarated by the act.

Hygd, the title character, was first performed by Katherine Drinkwater, the producer's wife, and later by Lady Viola Tree, of the famous acting family. *King Lear's Wife* was the only play Bottomley wrote that provoked a significant critical response. Although that response was largely negative, it drew attention to Bottomley's work, and as a result, his plays were produced more readily in subsequent years.

Although Gordon Bottomley's work has evoked little interest among critics of his own or subsequent generations, it is an excellent example of the transitional nature of the Georgian movement. Like the work of his contemporary, Yeats, Bottomley's plays bridged the Victorian and modern eras. He employed ancient Celtic folklore and mythology as subject matter, the verse form of Elizabethan drama, and combined them with the realism and clarity of language characteristic of modern drama. The more realistic content and style already being employed by Henrik Ibsen and George Bernard Shaw, however, had moved Western drama into the twentieth century, while Bottomley's work remained part of an earlier era.

Other major works

POETRY: *Poems at White Nights*, 1899; *Chambers of Imagery*, 1907, 1912; *A Vision of Giorgione*, 1910; *Poems of Thirty Years*, 1925.

NONFICTION: *A Stage for Poetry: My Purpose with My Plays*, 1948.

Bibliography

Lucas, Frank L. *Authors Dead and Living*, 1926.

Nicoll, Allardyce. *English Drama, 1900-1930: The Beginnings of the Modern Period*, 1973.

Ross, Robert H. *The Georgian Revolt, 1910-1922: Rise and Fall of a Poetic Ideal*, 1965.

Sitwell, Edith. "Great Writers Rediscovered 5, Poets of Delight: Gordon Bottomley and Ralph Hodgson," in *Sunday Times* (London). May 5, 1957.

Spanos, W. V. *The Christian Tradition in Modern British Verse Drama*, 1967.

Thouless, Priscilla. *Modern Poetic Drama*, 1934.

Tindall, William York. *Forces in British Literature 1885-1946*, 1949.

Christina Hunt Mahony

DION BOUCICAULT
Dionysius Lardner Boursiquot

Born: Dublin, Ireland; December 7, 1820(?)
Died: New York, New York; September 18, 1890

Principal drama

London Assurance, pr., pb. 1841 (as Lee Moreton); *Old Heads and Young Hearts*, pr. 1844, pb. 1845; *The Knight of Arva*, pr. 1848, pb. 1868; *The Corsican Brothers*, pr., pb. 1852 (adaptation of Eugène Grangé and Xavier de Montépin's *Les Frères Corses*); *Louis XI*, pr., pb. 1855 (adaptation from the French); *The Poor of New York*, pr. 1857 (also known as *The Poor of Liverpool*, pr. 1864, and as *The Streets of London*; adaptation of Édouard-Louis-Alexandre Brisbarre and Eugène Nus's *Les Pauvres de Paris*); *Jessie Brown: Or, The Relief of Lucknow*, pr., pb. 1858; *Dot*, pr. 1859, pb. 1940 (adaptation of Charles Dickens' *The Cricket on the Hearth*); *The Octoroon: Or, Life in Louisiana*, pr. 1859, pr. 1861 (revised), pb. 1953 (adaptation of Mayne Reid's novel *The Quadroon*); *The Colleen Bawn*, pr. 1860, pb. 1953 (adaptation of Gerald Griffin's novel *The Collegians*); *Arrah-na-Pogue: Or, The Wicklow Wedding*, pr. 1864, pb. 1865 (in Gaelic); *Rip Van Winkle*, pr. 1865, pb. 1944 (with Joseph Jefferson; adaptation of the story by Washington Irving); *The Flying Scud: Or, Four-Legged Fortune*, pr. 1866, pb. 1940; *After Dark: A Tale of London Life*, pr., pb. 1868; *Formosa: Or, The Railroad to Ruin*, pr., pb. 1869; *Babil and Bijou*, pr. 1872 (with James Robinson Planché); *The Shaughraun*, pr. 1874, pb. 1880; *Forbidden Fruit*, pr., pb. 1876; *The Jilt*, pr. 1885, pb. 1904 (adaptation of a story by Hawley Smart); *Forbidden Fruit and Other Plays*, pb. 1940, 1963.

Dion Boucicault was responsible for well over one hundred plays during his lengthy career. Some have been anthologized, and the three Irish plays were published together as *The Dolmen Boucicault* (1964). The others are most accessible in the microprint series *English and American Drama of the Nineteenth Century*, edited by Allardyce Nicoll and George Freedley (1965-1971), which also includes promptbook reproductions for many of the plays.

Other literary forms

Dion Boucicault's only fictional work was a collaboration with Charles Reade, *Foul Play* (1868). A short, dramatized history, *The Story of Ireland* (1881), was also published in his lifetime; *The Art of Acting* (1926) and *The Art of Acting: A Discussion by Constant Coquelin, Henry Irving, and Dion Boucicault* (1926) were posthumous collections. Boucicault was a regular contributor to *North American Review* from 1887 to 1889 and had written two essays for that periodical: "The Decline of the Drama" (1877) and

"The Art of Dramatic Composition" (1878). Several of his articles appeared elsewhere.

Achievements

Boucicault was the mid-nineteenth century's complete man of the theater. For almost fifty years, on both sides of the Atlantic, he labored as playwright, dramaturge, actor, director, and manager. Many of his enduring contributions were in the realm of practical theater. He was, with playwright Thomas William Robertson, one of the early proponents of directed rehearsals and ensemble playing. This interest led later to his formation of touring casts to replace the traditional system in which traveling stars played virtually unrehearsed stock dramas with local companies. He improved theatrical conditions by shortening the lengthy triple bills frequently offered and by abolishing half-price admission for latecomers. As an author, he fought for changes in American copyright law and for the principle of the playwright receiving a percentage of the receipts from his play's performance. Late in his life, he invented a method of fireproofing scenery.

As a dramatist, Boucicault was both prolific and popular. Here it was his sense of what would work onstage that raised him above his contemporaries. While many of his productions were translations or adaptations of others' works, any piece was more stageworthy once he had left his mark on it. Notable examples of his talents in this area are *The Corsican Brothers*, which he adapted from a French adaptation of a story by Alexandre Dumas, *père*, and *Rip Van Winkle*, which Boucicault adapted for the actor Joseph Jefferson. The former Boucicault merely made more spectacular, but for the latter, he completely remodeled the title character. The early Rip became a young and thoughtless scamp, lovable but destructive of himself and his family. The contrast between the young and old Rip adds dramatic interest, as does the very real dilemma his early behavior creates for his wife.

Boucicault's earliest successes were original comedies of manners. With this form, he provides virtually the only link between the great comic dramatists of previous centuries and Oscar Wilde. Indeed, several of Boucicault's early plays have scenes and characters that are suggestive of *The Importance of Being Earnest* (pr. 1895). *London Assurance*, his first major comedy, has been revived successfully in this century.

Moving next to sentimental melodrama, the dominant form of his day, Boucicault quickly mastered the formulas that would please audiences. The plays themselves have been largely forgotten, but the spectacular scenes with which he enlivened all of them have had a more lasting effect. It was his *After Dark*, for example, that popularized the image of the hero rescued from railway tracks as a train thundered toward him. Here again,

Boucicault had taken his hint from another playwright, Augustin Daly, but had doubled the atmosphere of suspense and integrated the scene into a well-made plot. His presentation of sensational scenes has been seen to have parallels with later cinematographic techniques.

Boucicault's American career had a strong effect on the development of American theater, and playwright-producer David Belasco can certainly be considered his follower. In England, George Bernard Shaw included him on a brief list of dramatists worth reading. It is on the Irish dramas, however, that Boucicault has had his most lasting influence. The transformation of the stage Irishman that he effected in his three best Irish plays was a clear forerunner to John Millington Synge's and Sean O'Casey's greatest characters, and both acknowledged their debt to him. Aside from grand theatricality and memorable characters, these plays were full of a gentle patriotism that only once went too far for his English audience. It was Boucicault's new version of the old ballad "The Wearing of the Green," which is sung in *Arrah-na-Pogue*, that caused that song to be banned in Britain and hence popularized it in Dublin and New York.

Biography

Dion Boucicault was born Dionysius Lardner Boursiquot in Dublin, Ireland, apparently in 1820, although he claimed a date in 1822. His mother, née Anne Darley, was sister to George Darley the poet and editor, and to the Reverend Charles Darley, a minor playwright. She was married to Samuel Smith Boursiquot, a Dublin wine merchant from whom she separated in 1819. Nevertheless, his will acknowledged Boucicault as his legitimate son, and the latter always referred to Boursiquot as his father—although Dr. Dionysius Lardner, who lived with Boucicault's mother from the summer of 1820 and was the boy's guardian, was probably Boucicault's actual father. Lardner was the compiler of *Cabinet Cyclopedia* and the first professor of natural philosophy and astronomy at the University of London (from 1827). Although Lardner financed young Dion Boucicault's education in Dublin and in the London area, the affair with Boucicault's mother did not survive Lardner's relocation to England.

After a brief apprenticeship to Lardner as a civil engineer, Boucicault had embarked, by 1838, on a stage career under the name Lee Moreton. *London Assurance*, accepted for the 1841 season at Covent Garden, was a resounding success on whose proceeds Boucicault brought his mother to London. Living beyond his means, he soon exhausted the money his first few comedies and farces brought him. In 1845, he married a French widow, Anne Guiot, his elder by some twenty years. She died soon after their marriage, in the Swiss Alps, leaving Boucicault a large sum that kept him in Paris for several more years. There, he familiarized himself with the French plays that were becoming so popular in England and that were to bring him many later successes in his translated and adapted versions. Always the actor, he traveled as the Viscount de Bourcicault.

When Charles Kean took over the Princess Theatre in 1850, Boucicault, impecunious again, was hired as his literary adviser. The two learned from each other, for Kean always sought the spectacular in his productions, and Boucicault was soon presenting scenes such as the miraculous appearance of the ghost in *The Corsican Brothers*. After joining Kean, he met the young actress Agnes Robertson, the manager's ward, who was to be his companion and partner for thirty years. By September, 1853, the two were performing in New York. Boucicault was later to claim that they had never married, but all of their acquaintances believed that they were man and wife. They had six children.

Having written *The Colleen Bawn* in a white heat and opened it success-fully in New York, Boucicault returned with it to London in 1860, where the play ran an unprecedented 360 consecutive nights at the Adelphi. The next year, the piece opened in Dublin to enthusiastic Irish audiences. Until 1872, Boucicault was prospering in England. Then, an expensive collaboration with James Robinson Planché, *Babil and Bijou*, sent him once again to the United States in temporary disgrace. For the next few years, he toured on both sides of the Atlantic, and *The Shaughraun*, another Irish play, scored heavily wherever it played.

By then, Boucicault was often on the road without Agnes, and in 1885, while the company was performing in Sydney, Australia, he married Louise Thorndyke, a young actress in his last great success, *The Jilt*. Agnes sued for a formal divorce, which was eventually granted in England. Time was running out for Boucicault, whom William Archer had already branded "a playwright of yesterday." In 1888, his last company disbanded for lack of funds. For the next two years, he worked for an acting school in New York, where he died after a heart attack, complicated by pneumonia, on September 18, 1890.

Analysis

Dion Boucicault never had literary pretensions, but he was, and knew himself to be, a superb theatrical craftsman. He prefaced his first publication, *London Assurance*, with an apology that answers for much of his later work as well: "It will not bear analysis as a literary production. In fact, my sole object was to throw together a few scenes of a dramatic nature, and therefore I studied the stage rather than the moral effect." He later rationalized this concentration on the individual dramatic scene by arguing the decline of an audience whose chief literary form had become the newspaper. It is also true that he had to make his living from his work, and, as he once said, "More money has been made out of guano than out of poetry."

Certainly, Boucicault did not concentrate on fine language. Indeed, when he wrote his Aristotelian essay "The Art of Dramatic Composition," he listed only action, character, and decoration as the components of a drama. Diction and thought were never an issue for him, except as they were directly applicable to the presentation of plot and character. Nevertheless, a very serviceable acting drama can be written by concentrating on plot, characters, and spectacle.

Boucicault's drama was always based on his impression, invariably correct, of what would work in the theater. At the outset of his career, this impression was founded on his reading of the masters of English comedy. Oliver Goldsmith, Richard Brinsley Sheridan, George Farquhar, Sir John Vanbrugh, and William Congreve were his sources, and he wrote well in the comic style that they had established. His best work was always in the comic vein, but as his theatrical experience grew, he perfected his skills in melodrama. His great Irish plays represent the successful synthesis of these two strains.

What Boucicault learned above all from the earlier comic dramatists was the presentation of character-types. "By character," Boucicault wrote, "we mean that individuality in a person made by the consistency of feelings, speech, and physiognomy." The intricacies of character development were not for him, but in the creation of consistent comic caricatures, he excelled. From the gentleman freeloader Dazzle and the befuddled pastor Rural, through the thoughtlessly alcoholic Rip Van Winkle, to the rogue heroes of the Irish plays, Boucicault forged a gallery of memorable acting parts. The essential ingredient in each is individuality. Every major role has a certain dimension of stereotype, but the successful ones are not mere stereotypes.

As in his creation of spectacle, Boucicault exploits local color to the full. Thus, the clever servant is given a distinctively Irish flavor; the soldiers defending the empire are also clannish Scots; and the inventory of national types in *The Octoroon* includes an American Indian, good and bad Yankees, Southern gentry, a heroine of mixed blood, and a cosmopolitan hero who cannot understand why he should not marry her. A character such as Lady Gay Spanker, a typical domineering wife, is given an extra dose of realism by being the complete English horsewoman.

Character is subordinated to plot in Boucicault's theoretical article, and plot shows the characters "suffering their fate." As in all melodrama, calamity dogs the sympathetic characters until poetic justice raises them to some form of final triumph. Financial ruin is the omnipresent threat, but there are also physical dangers to be faced by the innocent. A typical Boucicault play involves a number of threats and rescues, with a continuing major danger increasing in intensity until the final resolution. Some of his melodramas are historical, but most are set in the present. While none of them could be called serious social drama, many do deal with real social problems: the plight of the poor, the evils of gambling and drink, even race relations. Boucicault's position is never controversial, and he is careful to balance good and evil characters in every social or national class.

The final element in the construction of a drama is decoration, which Boucicault recognized as at once the least essential and the most impressive. The realistic portrayal of locality, whether it was London, Lucknow, Louisiana, or Wicklow, was the first aim in his set design. This interest in decoration began early, and *London Assurance*, Boucicault's first success, was also the first play in London to be staged with a box set simulating a real room. For this, he had Madame Vestris, manager of Covent Garden, to thank, but scenery was to remain of vital importance to him. He often sought out the exotic, but the representation had to be believable. His realism, however, was designed to impress rather than to probe social issues. Each play offers at least one truly sensational scene: a steamboat explosion, a near-drowning, a boat race, or a burning building. These thrilling moments of spectacle join with the dangers presented by the plot to involve the audience in a world of vicarious peril.

Boucicault's best drama discards none of the sensationalism of his more commercial melodrama. Rather, it adds a true sense of comedy and a skill in the creation of characters, particularly of Irish characters. He kept a rich brogue all of his life and frequently acted parts calling for a stage Irishman. By setting plays in Ireland, he was able to exploit some traditional attributes of this stereotype without condescension. The audience laughs more *with* Myles-na-Coppaleen, for example, than *at* him. The witty dialogue of Boucicault's early comedies returns in full force in these Irish plays in such a way as to make the sentimentality of their main actions palatable even to an age unused to melodrama.

London Assurance and *Old Heads and Young Hearts* are theatrical curiosities. Boucicault took London by storm with comedies of manners, a dramatic form at least fifty years out of date. The plays are set in a time that might be the Regency (1811-1820) but draw heavily on the comic situations and characters of eighteenth century drama. While the plots of both plays are intricate, it is their characters that make them memorable.

London Assurance offers two fine female roles: Grace Harkaway is a witty heroine in the tradition of Congreve's Millamant, while Lady Gay Spanker, "glee made a living thing," carries the last three acts with her enthusiasm. Dazzle, the man nobody knows, is essentially the clever comic servant in his manipulation of the action. He brazenly attaches himself to the company, and his discovery provides the comic conclusion to the play when he acknowledges that he himself has "not the remotest idea" who he is. The moral tag which succeeds this quip, with its tedious definition of a gentleman, is the only Victorian thing about the play.

The main action, the father-and-son opposition in a love triangle, is the stuff of traditional comedy. An interesting variation is the "disguise" adopted by the son—simply denying his identity to his own father. This barefaced lie is so improbable that it works both in the play and on the stage. In this matter, Boucicault shows a spark of the assurance that characterizes Dazzle and Charles Courtly.

Old Heads and Young Hearts was Boucicault's second well-deserved success. In this play, there are now two pairs of lovers and two fathers to be placated. The background of hunting has been replaced by that of politics, and the country retreat is run as a military post by Colonel Rocket. The family relationships of the Colonel and his daughter and of Lord and Lady Pompion are sensitively drawn. The plot is deliberately confusing, and the old heads cannot follow what is going on. Jesse Rural, a well-meaning old minister, compounds the confusion with his efforts to help the young hearts and remains baffled at the final curtain. The wit is defter than that of *London Assurance*, but *Old Heads and Young Hearts* was to be Boucicault's last effort at true comedy of manners. He would argue later that the public only thought it wanted comedy, while what it really demanded was a mixture of genres.

The majority of Boucicault's original plays may be classed under the general heading melodrama, of which *The Poor of New York* and *After Dark* may be considered representative. The former was suggested by the commercial panic of 1857 in New York, but with its local allusions changed, it reappeared as *The Poor of Liverpool* and as *The Streets of London*. The plot, shamelessly based on coincidence, sentiment, and sensation, was loosely borrowed from a French play. The villainous banker Bloodgood, who has cheated or ruined virtually all the other characters, is finally exposed when two men break into a burning tenement to secure evidence against him that is about to be destroyed.

The plot of *After Dark* is incredible to an extreme that approaches self-parody. Father and daughter, husband and wife, jailer and convict, and former fellow officers are reunited by a series of coincidences, schemes, and discoveries that is utterly fantastic. The action, which is set in the lurid atmosphere of a gambling den, exploits the possibilities of the newly opened underground railway as well as providing an attempted suicide under Blackfriars Bridge.

The Octoroon is an altogether better play, although it depends on the same sort of sentimentality and coincidence. Boucicault walked a fine line between pro- and antislavery elements, and somehow managed to offend no one. Salem Scudder, a crusty Yankee who has a soft heart, is one of Boucicault's finest sentimental characters. The discovery of the murderer's identity by a self-developing photograph exploited a topical scientific discovery in a sensational manner. The ending, however, is tragic, as it must be. Zoe, the octoroon forbidden by her own society from marrying the man who loves her, had to die if the play was not to support miscegenation and offend many in the audience of Boucicault's day. The comic dialogue that was to lighten the sentiment of the Irish plays is also absent.

It is probably no coincidence that Boucicault's best plays were those with the largest roles for himself. He was a comic actor of some versatility, limited mainly by his accent, yet it was not until 1860 that he wrote a really meaty part that took advantage of this handicap. *The Colleen Bawn*, *Arrah-na-Pogue*, and *The Shaughraun* were his greatest successes, and Boucicault saved his best writing for them. Several other Irish plays were baldly commercial and had poor receptions.

The Colleen Bawn drew its plot loosely from Gerald Griffin's novel *The Collegians*, but Boucicault created the characters. Drawing on his reading of Irish playwrights Samuel Lover and Charles Lever, as well as on his own skill at comic dialogue, he quickly sketched a romantic comedy with the framework of melodrama. For spectacle, he added a dramatic dive to save the drowning heroine and an elaborate series of sliding Irish backdrops. For himself, he penned the character of Myles-na-Coppaleen, the heroic vagabond, a type he would re-create as Shaun the Post and Conn the Shaughraun in succeeding plays. Yet much of the wittiest dialogue is given to Anne Chute, a strong heroine in the mold of Grace Harkaway. Danny Mann, the villain, is given unusual depth in that he sincerely believes himself to be the faithful servant of the hero, Hardress Cregan.

As in Boucicault's two other major Irish plays, the villains are homegrown and the only Englishman is a noble romantic. *Arrah-na-Pogue* and *The Shaughraun*, however, both present heroes pursued by the English simply for being patriots. The political overtones are softened in that pardons are granted in both cases, but the atmosphere of oppression has been created. In the Irish plays, the dispossessed nobility are shown as the victims of an English system administered by greedy Irish speculators. The union between Cregan and Eily O'Connor, who belongs to a lower social station, is romantically satisfying but ultimately unrealistic. In the real-life episode fictionalized by Griffin, the young gentleman did find it necessary to have his peasant mistress murdered.

Arrah-na-Pogue brings back many of the character-types and sentiments of the earlier play. The trial of Shaun the Post, who has confessed in order to shield others, is a masterful comic scene that may well have influenced Shaw in *The Devil's Disciple* (pr. 1897). O'Grady seems symbolic of the Irish way of doing things in these plays when he asks for acquittal on the grounds of the prisoner's eloquence. Shaun's spectacular escape up an ivy-covered wall, just in time to rescue his Arrah, provides an appropriately melodramatic climax.

The Shaughraun is certainly Boucicault's finest play. The dramatist coined the title word from the Irish *seachran*, a participle that means "wandering." Conn is at his irrepressible best when he sneaks drinks at his own wake, after a popular Irish motif. The banter between Molineux, whose English birth was not his fault, and the spirited Claire is unforgettable. These two, however, are united in their reaction to Conn's pretended death. On that occasion, Molineux asks permission to exclaim "You Irish!" and Claire readily grants it. The playwright's confident introduction of the farcical hogshead barrel sequence into the midst of his melodramatic climax shows his complete control of the medium.

The cast of Irish characters includes the spirited heroine; the romantic heroine and her Fenian lover; the genial priest Father Dolan (once acted by Sean O'Casey); his housekeeper Moya, in love with Conn; the villainous squireen and his informer accomplice; and Conn's old mother, as well as his dog Tatthers, whose presence seems inseparable from Conn's yet who never appears onstage. This collection comprises the major types from the earlier two plays, and all are handled with a surer touch. As in many comic masterpieces, only the romantic lovers seem faceless.

Boucicault did not write any great drama after *The Shaughraun*. Some would argue that he had not done so before. Nevertheless, in this fantastic blend of melodrama, genuine comic wit, and facetious Irish blarney, Boucicault concocted truly memorable theater.

Other major works

NOVEL: *Foul Play*, 1868 (with Charles Reade).

NONFICTION: *The Story of Ireland*, 1881; *The Art of Acting*, 1926.

MISCELLANEOUS: *The Art of Acting: A Discussion by Constant Coquelin, Henry Irving, and Dion Boucicault*, 1926.

Bibliography

Fawkes, Richard. *Dion Boucicault*, 1979.

Hogan, Robert. *Dion Boucicault*, 1969.

Krause, David. "The Theatre of Dion Boucicault," in *The Dolmen Boucicault*, 1964.

Molin, Sven Eric, and Robin Goodfellowe, eds. *Dion Boucicault, The Shaughraun, I: The Early Years*, 1979.

Vardac, A. Nicholas. *Stage to Screen: Theatrical Method from Garrick to Griffith*, 1968.

Walsh, Townsend. *The Career of Dion Boucicault*, 1915.

Philip Oxley

JAMES BRIDIE
Osborne Henry Mavor

Born: Glasgow, Scotland; January 3, 1888
Died: Edinburgh, Scotland; January 29, 1951

Principal drama

The Sunlight Sonata: Or, To Meet the Seven Deadly Sins, pr. 1928, pb. 1930; *The Switchback,* pr. 1929, pb. 1930; *What It Is to Be Young,* pr. 1929, pb. 1934; *The Anatomist,* pr. 1930, pb. 1931; *The Girl Who Did Not Want to Go to Kuala Lampur,* pr. 1930, pb. 1934; *Tobias and the Angel,* pr. 1930, pb. 1931; *The Amazed Evangelist,* pb. 1931, pr. 1932; *The Dancing Bear,* pr. 1931, pb. 1934; *Jonah and the Whale,* pr., pb. 1932; *The Proposal,* pr. 1932 (adaptation of Anton Chekhov's play *A Marriage Proposal*); *A Sleeping Clergyman,* pr., pb. 1933; *Colonel Wotherspoon,* pr., pb. 1934; *Colonel Wotherspoon and Other Plays,* pb. 1934; *Marriage Is No Joke,* pr., pb. 1934; *Mary Read,* pr. 1934, pb. 1935 (with Claud Gurney); *The Black Eye,* pr., pb. 1935; *Moral Plays,* pb. 1936; *Storm in a Teacup,* pr. 1936, pb. 1937 (adaptation of Bruno Frank's play); *Susannah and the Elders,* pr. 1937, pb. 1940; *Babes in the Wood,* pr., pb. 1938; *The King of Nowhere,* pr., pb. 1938; *The Last Trump,* pr., pb. 1938; *The Golden Legend of Shults,* pr. 1939, pb. 1940; *What Say They?,* pr., pb. 1939; *The Dragon and the Dove,* pr. 1942, pb. 1944; *Holy Isle,* pr. 1942, pb. 1944; *Jonah 3,* pr. 1942, pb. 1944 (based on his play *Jonah and the Whale*); *A Change for the Worse,* pr. 1943, pb. 1944; *Mr. Bolfry,* pr. 1943, pb. 1944; *It Depends What You Mean,* pr. 1944, pb. 1948; *Lancelot,* pb. 1944, pr. 1945; *Plays for Plain People,* pb. 1944; *The Forrigan Reel,* pr. 1945, pb. 1949; *Hedda Gabler,* pr. 1945 (adaptation of Henrik Ibsen's play); *The Wild Duck,* pr. 1946 (adaptation of Ibsen's play); *De Angelus,* pr. 1947, pb. 1949; *John Knox,* pr. 1947, pb. 1949; *Gog and Magog,* pr. 1948; *Daphne Laureola,* pr., pb. 1949 (with George Munro); *John Knox and Other Plays,* pb. 1949; *The Tintock Cup,* pr. 1949; *Mr. Gillie,* pr., pb. 1950; *The Queen's Comedy,* pr., pb. 1950; *Red Riding Hood,* pr. 1950 (with Duncan Macrae); *The Baikie Charivari: Or, The Seven Prophets,* pr. 1952, pb. 1953; *Meeting at Night,* pr. 1954, pb. 1956 (with Archibald Batty).

Other literary forms

Two autobiographical volumes constitute the major nondramatic writings of James Bridie. *Some Talk of Alexander,* derived from his experiences in the field ambulance unit of the British army during World War I in India, Mesopotamia, Persia, Transcaucasia, and Constantinople, was published in 1926. A second autobiography, *One Way of Living,* published in 1939, is a creative memoir written when Bridie had turned fifty. It is divided into ten chapters, each covering a five-year period of his life. There is an overlay of italicized portions in each chapter, in which an interior monologue of the author ranges freely over some imaginative, associative reflection, evoking the style of James Joyce in *A Portrait of the Artist as a Young Man* (1916). In addition to his two autobiographical works, Bridie wrote a collection of essays entitled *Mr. Bridie's Alphabet for Little Glasgow Highbrows* (1934); a collection of short plays, fragments, essays, poetry, and film and radio scripts entitled *Tedious and Brief* (1944); criticism in *The British Drama* (1945); and still another collection of essays entitled *A Small Stir: Letters on the English* (1949; with Moray McLaren). Finally, Bridie was a prolific writer of articles, described by Winifred Bannister, his biographer, as "witty, teasing admonitions usually aimed at drawing people into the theatre, and even that part of the Scottish public not interested in the theatre could hardly avoid being aware of Bridie as a personality, for almost everything he said and did in public was news."

Achievements

Bridie, like John Keats and Anton Chekhov, belongs to a long tradition of writers who were educated for a medical career but who eventually became major literary figures. The author of more than forty plays, he complemented that impressive achievement with a lifelong, active participation in the development of the Glasgow Citizens' Theatre, Glasgow's equivalent of London's National Theatre. His civic work on the Scottish Arts Council, the Edinburgh International Festival of music and drama, the film section of UNESCO, and the Scottish Community Drama Association was unflagging. He also developed into a more than proficient artist, for a time illustrating the *Scots Pictorial* as "O.H." His drawings and paintings have been exhibited at Glasgow art galleries.

Bridie's position in modern British drama is firmly established, and certainly in Scottish theater history he is a major dramatist. Gerald Weales in *Religion in Modern English Drama* (1961) links Bridie and George Bernard Shaw as modern religious dramatists who, at their deaths in 1951 (Bridie) and 1950 (Shaw), left religious drama "almost completely in the hands of the more orthodox practitioners," few of whom "approach Shaw and Bridie as playwrights." J. B. Priestley, a consummate crafter of the well-made play, while calling attention to some of Bridie's weaknesses, calls his best scenes "blazing triumphs." He also asserted that Bridie's "characters appear to exist more in their own right than Shaw's."

Indeed, for Priestley, Bridie is Scotland's major dramatist. In the preface to the posthumous publication of *Meeting at Night*, Priestley offers a measured evaluation of Bridie's work. He concludes his personal tribute to Bridie with the comment that since his death, "the Theatre has seemed only half the size, half the fun, it used to be."

Biography

James Bridie was born Osborne Henry Mavor on January 3, 1888, in Glasgow, Scotland, the son of Henry A. and Janet (Osborne) Mavor. Bridie said that in 1931, he started calling himself "James Bridie," after his grandfather James Mavor and his great-grandfather John Bridie, a sea captain. Gradually, the name Bridie—the dramatist half of Osborne Henry Mavor, the doctor—took over, so that by the time of his death, friends such as Priestley had thought of him strictly as Bridie, never as O. H. Mavor.

Near the beginning of his autobiography, *One Way of Living*, Bridie writes that on January 3, 1938, he takes pleasure, at the age of fifty, in having lived ten different lives in cycles of five years. He describes himself as a Lowland Scot who has no English or Highland blood, no Unconscious Mind, and who therefore is ill-qualified to write an autobiography. Yet he must write one, even though he makes of it a matter of mathematics rather than art, since a Lowland Scot is so ordered in his life, dividing it into three planes—intellectual, moral, and physical—that anyone out of step with it is considered disordered and abnormal. Indeed, Bridie's life was ordered, at first by a father whom he admired and who, unable to enter medicine because of financial difficulties, wished his son to become a doctor. Later, the order was of his own making.

At twenty-five, Bridie was still an undergraduate, having failed some of his medical courses, particularly anatomy. Eventually, however, he became a resident at the staff of the Royal Infirmary in Glasgow as house physician to W. R. Jack; he then moved to the eye, ear, and nose department. He served in the army field ambulance unit during World War I, returning from Soviet Russia in 1919. Joining the staff of the Victoria Infirmary in Glasgow, he led a pleasant life, and began writing, he contends, to subsidize his consulting practice. In 1923, he married Rona Locke Bremner, bought himself a car, and settled into what he describes as a happy bourgeois life; indeed, he remarks in his autobiography that a childhood admiration for a doctor who owned a car was his reason for wanting to become a doctor. His medical career was rewarded with a doctorate of law from Glasgow University in 1939, and a C.B.E. in 1946. Of the honors conferred on him, he enjoyed most the governorship of Victoria Infirmary in Glasgow, where he had earlier served as assistant physician and honorary consulting physician.

Amid the events of a physicians's life, however, Bridie's writing and theatrical interests persisted. Undergraduate productions of his plays with titles such as *The Son Who Was Considerate of His Father's Prejudices*, *No Wedding Cake for Her*, *The Duke Who Could Sometimes Hardly Keep from Smiling*, *Ethics Among Thieves*, and *The Baron Who Would Not Be Convinced That His Way of Living Was Anything out of the Ordinary* were received with loud applause at school functions. He also wrote for the Glasgow University magazine under "unfamiliar names."

Because of his concern that playwriting, considered by some disreputable, could hurt his consulting practice, Bridie at first wrote under the pseudonym "Mary Henderson," who appears as a character in his first professionally produced play, *The Sunlight Sonata*. In addition, he feared that the hobby might become too absorbing. Another name, "Archibald Kellock" (a character in *Colonel Wotherspoon*) became the pseudonym under which he wrote other plays. In 1938, at the age of fifty, Dr. Osborne Henry Mavor and playwright James Bridie parted, and the latter devoted full time to his chosen career, one that included the development of the Glasgow Citizens' Theatre in particular and the Scottish theater in general.

Bridie died in 1951 of a vascular condition at the Edinburgh Royal Infirmary, one year after the death of George Bernard Shaw, whom Bridie knew and who attended some of Bridie's plays.

Analysis

At the heart of much of James Bridie's drama lies the conflict between science and religion. He explored this conflict in a variety of dramatic genres, including comedies, mystery and morality plays that have interesting resemblances to those of the medieval period, and problem dramas that suggest the influence of Henrik Ibsen. In all three general groupings, one can detect a stylistic hallmark: the use of medical language, characters who are members of the medical profession or who have something to do with a member of that profession, or situations in which science is involved in either a major or minor way. In Bridie's plays, however, as in his life, science takes second place to the moral problems of his characters, even when its virtues or vices are the basis for those problems. In a general sense, then, all of his dramas, including the most entertaining Shavian comedies, are morality plays.

Although Bridie's religious views were "so liberal minded, so humanitarian as to be unfixed," according to Bannister, they were, nevertheless, the driving force in his own life and in the characters of his plays. A moral fervor and rational humanism characterize his earliest performed play, *The Sunlight Sonata*, a comedy about seven characters affected by the traditional Seven Deadly Sins. Similarly, *The Baikie Charivari* is a Faustian confrontation between man and the Devil, containing seven potential evils in the form of visitors who would teach Bridie's "Faust." Indeed, Bridie's thesis resembles Johann Wolfgang von Goethe's: the necessity of never saying to the moment, "Stay, thou art fair."

Bridie's mystery plays, dramatizations of Bible stories, constitute an important part of his oeuvre. In the tradition of the medieval mystery play, in which Bible stories were dramatized for "plain people," Bridie modernizes the dilemmas in which biblical characters find themselves. In fact, he wrote three versions of the Jonah story: *Jonah and the Whale, The Sign of the Prophet Jonah*, and *Jonah 3*. Bridie's stories were drawn not only from the Bible but also from the Apocrypha and from contemporary religious events and figures.

Some of Bridie's plays have evoked comparisons with Shaw and Ibsen. Clever turns of phrase, witty dialogue, puns, outrageous situations in which societal "outlaws" (such as the father and daughter in *Meeting at Night* who conduct a mail-order confidence racket) have earned for Bridie the label the "Scottish Shaw." Bannister records a comment that Shaw is supposed to have made to Bridie: "If there had been no me there would have been no you." The two dramatists are dissimilar, however, in a major way, for with the exception of *Daphne Laureola*, Bridie's characterizations of women lack the strength and conviction of Shaw's. Among influences on Bridie, perhaps that of Ibsen is the strongest. It can be seen in his adaptations of Ibsen's plays but more subtly in the satiric thrusts at status-quo science and religion in plays such as *A Sleeping Clergyman, The Switchback*, and *The Anatomist*.

In his autobiography, Bridie claimed that *A Sleeping Clergyman* "was the nearest thing to a masterpiece I shall probably ever write." Completed at the end of 1932, before he had decided to give up medicine in order to devote himself to the theater, the play was produced in London in 1933. He had worked on the play off and on for two years, with earlier productions in Birmingham and Malvern. He stated that the play was an attempt to combine two themes with which he had dealt earlier: the scientist as dictator in *The Anatomist* and as lost sheep in the wilderness in *The Switchback*, and the relation of man to God in *Tobias and the Angel* and *Jonah and the Whale*.

The play is in two acts, the first preceded by a prologue and the second by a "chorus." In these two introductory portions, the framework for the story is established. At a respectable men's club in Glasgow, Dr. Cooper, a specialist in diseases of women, and Dr. Coutts, a neurologist, are relaxing with a drink. Nearby, a "huge, whitebearded" clergyman sleeps. Coutts has just returned from the funeral service of ninety-seven-year-old Dr. William Marshall, a former visiting physician at the Royal Infirmary of Glasgow. Coutts, whose father had been a friend of Marshall, represented the faculty at the funeral. The conversation then turns to another funeral attendee, Sir Charles Cameron, a noted bacteriologist. Interest in Cameron, a relative of the deceased, is aroused as the matter of his illegitimate birth is mentioned by Coutts. With a brief reference to Cameron's grandfather, a dissipated medical student, the prologue ends, and the narration shifts to a dramatization of events in the lives of three generations of Camerons. In flashback style, the drama consists of two acts, with four scenes in each act. The action moves swiftly through more than sixty years, from 1867 to 1872, 1885, 1886, 1907, 1916, and finally to the 1930's, in a fascinating tale in which genius eventually conquers the predilection to dissipation which the latest Cameron had inherited from his grandfather.

In act 1, the first Cameron is a young medical researcher, dying of consumption but, above everything else, bent on finishing the medical research project in which he is currently engaged. The efforts of Dr. Will Marshall and his sister, Harriet, to convince Cameron to spend some time with them at their shore residence are futile. After visiting Cameron in his untidy room, Will leaves, having loaned Cameron three pounds. Later, Harriet arrives to inform Cameron that she is pregnant. He agrees to her proposal of marriage, but it is later revealed, in a conversation between two relatives on the day of a birthday party for little Wilhelmina (daughter of Harriet and Cameron), that the marriage had never taken place.

The story of the second generation of Camerons is dramatized in scene 3 of act 1. Wilhelmina, now a young woman, shows the effects of heredity as she asks her Uncle Will for a cigar she wishes to try. The incident evokes the scene in Ibsen's *Ghosts* in which Oswald, an artist returning from Paris to his hometown in Norway, smokes a pipe and then recalls being sick as a child after his father had given him a pipe to smoke. Ibsen's play is about an inherited syphilitic condition; Bridie's is about inherited genius and its accompanying Bohemian life-style.

Wilhelmina, reared by her Uncle Will, follows in the footsteps of her mother and father in her disregard of stifling, conventional conduct. During a lovers' quarrel over her decision to marry another man, a man of her own class—even though she is pregnant by her lover, a lower-class employee of her uncle—she poisons the latter. In covering up her act, her uncle asks Dr. Coutts (father of Coutts of the prologue) to carry out the investigation of the death. In the ensuing trial, Wilhelmina is found innocent, and then, in a reversal of her earlier intentions, refuses to marry Sutherland even though he proposed. Act 1 ends on this note. Without regard for the puritanical mores of Scottish respectability, the Camerons continue to exercise their individualism.

A "chorus" introducing the second act parallels the prologue to act 1. The clergyman still sleeps as Dr. Cooper listens to Dr. Coutts's tale of the Cameron generations. The audience learns of the trial of Wilhelmina and of the birth of her twins, Charles and Hope. The birth is followed by Wilhelmina's suicide one month later.

Act 2 continues with the third generation of Camerons, as Will Marshall once more assumes the duties of child-rearing. Charles Cameron follows in his grandfather's footsteps in the sowing of his wild oats and in his genius for medical research. Like the ghosts of the past in Ibsen's plays, the present repeats the past. When Cameron cites the pressure of exams as the reason for his disorderly conduct and consequent arrest, Uncle Will provides the three pounds for his release, an amount similar to that which he had loaned Cameron's grandfather long ago.

After service in World War I, this third-generation Cameron, through both hard work and genius, eventually becomes a noted bacteriologist. At the age of fifty, he heads a medical research organization, the Walker Institute, financed by a wealthy relative, Sir Douglas Todd Walker. In his consistently blunt manner, he proposes marriage to Lady Katharine, saying that, if he wants descendants, he will have to hurry. Katharine, a worker who supplies the Institute with flowers, accepts, returning his bluntness in her acceptance.

Cameron's sister, Hope, appears on the scene from Geneva with a message from the League of Nations asking Cameron to expedite research on his cure for influenza. Both sister and brother have experienced the triumph of virtue over evil, even though it required three generations to do so. Old Will Marshall, now in his nineties, lives to see the rewards of his efforts. Vindicated, he comments to Hope at the play's end that "Charlie Cameron the First had the spark in his poor diseased body. Now lettest thou thy servant depart in peace. I did my best to keep the spark alive, and now it's a great flame in Charlie and in you. Humanity will warm its hands at you."

Bridie's view of genius as the divine force working through man is reflected in Katharine's comment that perhaps Cameron is a law of biology himself. God, like the sleeping clergyman in the two prologues, is removed from the immediate goings-on. Old Dr. Will Marshall, having lived ninety-seven years and having encouraged the spark of genius through three generations of Camerons, is a variation of the God-principle. Like the sleeping clergyman, who is oblivious to his surroundings, Dr. Will has devoted nearly a lifetime to practicing status-quo medicine. Unlike the clergyman, however, he has nourished the genius in which he never loses faith.

In addition to the Ibsenite concern with heredity already mentioned, there is in Bridie's play the Shavian concern with a life force that works through genius, emerging in the medical breakthroughs by the Camerons in their contributions to civilization. Religious, not in the conventional, doctrinaire sense but in his contribution to mankind, Cameron is the very essence of God. Bridie's God is a deistic entity that has provided man with laws and that has retired, like the sleeping clergyman, to a preprandial nap, to allow man to work out those laws. This working out of virtue is the personal and social morality of Bridie's plays. Weales claims that Bridie is one of the last two modern playwrights (Shaw is the other) to write religious plays based on a personal and unorthodox view of man's relationship to God.

The style of the play is as direct, unsentimental, and naturalistic as are the Camerons, whose disregard for the civilities of language and behavior provokes the censure of their conventional friends and relatives. Bridie's epic sweep of three generations has invited the criticism that the characters, particularly the supporting ones, are not fully developed.

Two of Bridie's last plays are companion pieces that deal yet again with man's relationship to his God or gods. The first of the two, *The Queen's Comedy*, is a reworking of books 14 and 15 of Homer's *Iliad*. Produced in 1950, a year before Bridie's death, the play is dedicated to its director, Tyrone Guthrie, famous in both England and the United States. On the title page appears Gloucester's famous line from William Shakespeare's *King Lear*: "As flies to wanton boys are we to the gods: they kill us for their sport." The title of the play derives from the various goddesses' attitudes toward Jupiter, particularly toward his entanglement in the affairs of men. In a conversation with Minerva, Juno reflects on the absurdity of Jupiter changing himself into "swans and things," a reference to his love affair with Leda and, consequently, his peopling the whole world "with his little lapses—all demanding special consideration because of their remarkable parentage. . . ."

Reflecting the ravages of World War II, in which Bridie lost a son, the play modernizes Homer's view of the gods. Jupiter comments that it was "easier to make a Universe than to control it. It was full of mad, meaningless forces. I got most of them bound and fixed and working to rules and all of a sudden I felt lonely. I felt that I would rather my mother had given me a puppydog or a kitten. . . ." An extension of the sleeping clergyman as a symbol for God, Jupiter feels helpless and, more pointedly, is saddened by his inability to provide answers to the overriding questions of man's existence. It is this fact that humans discover when, slain on the battlefield of Troy, they reach Olympus. The gods in their personal habits and relationships are no better than humans. Bridie wrote this fiercely antiwar play at a time when his own deteriorating health intensified his awareness of the bleakness that pervaded postwar Great Britain.

If *The Queen's Comedy* is about the relationship between God and man, its companion piece, *The Baikie Charivari*, is an allegory about the relationship between man and the devils that besiege him during his life. The play can be seen as Bridie's final comment on his lifelong concern with good and evil forces at work in the life of man. Produced the year after his death, the drama bears an interesting resemblance to his first professionally produced play, *The Sunlight Sonata*. Like the Seven Deadly Sins of that earlier play, seven devils confront Sir James MacArthur Pounce-Pellott, the leading character, whose name is derived from that of Pontius Pilate and the comic character, Punch, of magazine fame. His wife's name is Judy, and they have a daughter whom they still call Baby, even though she is of marriageable age. Pounce-Pellott has returned to the town of Baikie on the

Clyde Estuary in Scotland to retire at the age of fifty. He has spent his life in the British Civil Service in Junglipore, India.

In the surrealistic prologue, the Devil appears as a mask in the moon and speaks to a beadle, the Reverend Marcus Beadle, and to a local policeman, Robert Copper. The names of the Baikie residents, like those of the characters in a medieval morality play, symbolize their professions or qualities. In the style of the Book of Job in the Old Testament, the Devil inquires of Beadle and Copper, "Have ye considered my servant Pounce-Pellott?" When the cock crows and the Devil vanishes, Pounce-Pellott appears, a good-looking man in his fifties, announcing himself as "Knight Commander of the Indian Empire, King of Ghosts and Shadows, sometimes District Commander of Junglipore and other places."

Like Faust in his quest for wisdom, Pounce-Pellott wishes to be educated in the knowledge of the West. To this end, various neighbors (and a woman from America) appear as his teachers: the Reverend James Beadle (religion), Robert Copper (law), Councillor John Ketch (sociology, labor and left-wing thinking), Joe Mascara (art), Dr. Jean Pothecary (psychiatry), Lady Maggie Revenant (the old aristocratic order, actually a ghost from the past), and Mrs. Jemima Lee Crowe (an American publisher who offers Pounce-Pellott money for his memoirs). These figures represent the current wisdom of the West.

In the end, Pounce-Pellott, like his predecessor Pilate, washes his hands of them all and, asking for his stick, kills them all, except Lady Maggie, whom he cannot kill because she is a ghost. The Devil reappears, announcing that only time will tell whether he has been defeated. He vanishes, and Pounce-Pellott reflects on his inability to answer the riddle of life. He does know, however, that he killed those who pretended to know. Like Cameron of *A Sleeping Clergyman*, he knows that he cannot know, but also that he cannot stop seeking to know.

The tone of the play shifts between the surrealism of scenes such as that in which the Devil appears to Pounce-Pellott, and the ironic comedy of a Punch-and-Judy world, in which the realistic antics of his wife, daughter, and the seven representatives of Western wisdom are observed by Pounce-Pellott. As the play progresses to its conclusion in the form of arguments presented by the seven teachers, the prosaic style subtly gives way to poetic and lyric passages.

As a final, highly poetic statement, *The Baikie Charivari* is a sophisticated extension of Bridie's lifelong moral earnestness and a paean to the necessary effort of the human spirit to extend virtue, not in any narrow dogmatic sense or through high-flown idealism, but in the dogged persistence with which a rational humanism can create some order out of chaos, even out of the remnants of civilization left in the wake of a Trojan War or a World War II.

Responding to the long-standing criticism that he had difficulty in concluding a play, Bridie, at the close of *One Way of Living*, writes: "Only God can write a third act, and He seldom does." Bridie expresses his anger at "doctrinaire duds" and insists that audiences should leave the theater with their heads "whirling with speculation" and "selecting infinite possibilities for the characters . . . seen on stage." These possibilities find focus from time to time in men of genius such as Charles Cameron of *A Sleeping Clergyman* and Pounce-Pellott of *The Baikie Charivari*, who can stand alone if necessary. The miracle, mystery, and morality plays of medieval times are given contemporary significance in Bridie's theater, in that it is the miracle of individuated man that gives meaning to the existence of a Maker. As reflected in the very structure of Bridie's plays, there is no concluding "third act" to man's Faustian effort to work miracles on earth.

Other major works

NONFICTION: *Some Talk of Alexander*, 1926; *Mr. Bridie's Alphabet for Little Glasgow Highbrows*, 1934; *One Way of Living*, 1939; *The British Drama*, 1945; *A Small Stir: Letters on the English*, 1949 (with Moray McLaren).

RADIO PLAY: *The Sign of the Prophet Jonah*, 1942 (based on his play *Jonah and the Whale*).

MISCELLANEOUS: *Tedious and Brief*, 1944.

Bibliography

Bannister, Winifred. *James Bridie and His Theatre*, 1955.
Luyben, Helen L. *James Bridie: Clown and Philosopher*, 1965.
Priestley, J. B. *Bridie and the Theatre*, 1956.
_____ . "Introduction," in Bridie's *Meeting at Night*, 1956.
Tobin, Terence. *James Bridie*, 1980.
Weales, Gerald. *Religion in Modern English Drama*, 1961.

Susan Rusinko

RICHARD BROME

Born: England; c. 1590
Died: England; c. 1652-1653

Principal drama

Christianetta, pr. 1623(?) (with George Chapman?; no longer extant); *A Fault in Friendship*, pr. 1623 (with "Young Johnson"; no longer extant); *The Love-sick Maid: Or, The Honor of Young Ladies*, pr. 1629 (no longer extant); *The Northern Lass*, pr. 1629, pb. 1632; *The City Wit: Or, The Woman Wears the Breeches*, pr. c. 1629, pb. 1653; *The Queen's Exchange*, pr. 1631-1632(?), pb. 1657; *The Novella*, pr. 1632, pb. 1653; *The Covent-Garden Weeded*, pr. 1632, pb. 1659; *The Love-sick Court: Or, The Ambitious Politique*, pr. 1633-1634(?), pb. 1659; *The Late Lancashire Witches*, pr., pb. 1634 (with Thomas Heywood); *The Life and Death of Sir Martin Skink*, pr. c. 1634 (with Heywood; no longer extant); *The Apprentice's Prize*, pr. c. 1634 (with Heywood?; no longer extant); *The Sparagus Garden*, pr. 1635, pb. 1640; *The New Academy: Or, The New Exchange*, pr. 1635(?), pb. 1659; *The Queen and the Concubine*, pr. 1635-1636(?), pb. 1659; *The Jewish Gentleman*, pr. 1636(?) (no longer extant); *The English Moor: Or, The Mock-Marriage*, pr. 1637, pb. 1659; *The Antipodes*, pr. 1638, pb. 1640; *The Damoiselle: Or, The New Ordinary*, pr. 1638(?), pb. 1653; *Wit in Madness*, pr. 1638-1639(?) (no longer extant); *A Mad Couple Well Matched*, pr. 1639, pb. 1653; *The Court Beggar*, pr. 1640, pb. 1653; *A Jovial Crew: Or, The Merry Beggars*, pr. 1641, pb. 1652.

Other literary forms

Besides plays, Richard Brome wrote only some brief commendatory poems attached to other writers' collections of poetry or plays. He also edited John Fletcher's play *Monsieur Thomas* (pb. 1639) and probably edited *Lachrymae Musarum: The Tears of the Muses* (1649), a collection of elegies, to which Brome contributed, on the death of Henry Hastings in 1645.

Achievements

The reputation of Caroline playwright Richard Brome has generally been haunted by some ambiguity or doubt. During his own time, Brome was extremely popular, but even then his success was marred by criticisms that he pandered to his audience's poor tastes. Such criticisms might have been motivated to some extent by irrelevant factors, such as envy of his success and scorn for his humble background as a servant. His popularity continued during the Restoration, when his work influenced the form of Restoration comedy, and lasted into the eighteenth century. During the Victorian period, Brome was roundly condemned as the most obscene of the Renaissance dramatists and frequently contrasted with Ben Jonson—Jonson and Brome respectively epitomizing a "good" versus a "bad" comic dramatist. Again, irrelevant factors appear to have clouded the critical estimates of Brome.

Brome's ambiguous reputation has continued into the modern period, when he has been known as the most outstanding minor Caroline dramatist, but his status has also been on the rise. Kathleen Lynch demonstrated that Brome is an important link between Renaissance and Restoration comedy in *The Social Mode of Restoration Comedy* (1926), and R. J. Kaufmann valued Brome's work as an accurate reflection of Brome's time, a pivotal period in English history, in *Richard Brome: Caroline Playwright* (1961). Brome, however, is not merely of historical interest: His plays, particularly his best works, are still entertaining, and the social conditions he depicts bear some close resemblances to conditions today. T. S. Eliot believed that Brome should be read more, and Catherine M. Shaw, Brome's latest chronicler, in her book *Richard Brome* (1980), states that his plays could be revived on stage.

A highly professional playwright, eclectic and practical, Brome had the ability to judge public taste and had the theatrical skills to satisfy it—through his use of both satiric and romantic elements, his plotting, his characters, and his language. Of these, his characters are perhaps most appealing today, offering an engaging cross section of Caroline England. Brome's diversity of characters resembles Jonson's, but, unlike Jonson, Brome seems to like his characters: His satire is tolerant rather than indignant or disgusted.

Also appealing is Brome's style. It is clear and direct, easy to follow, already anticipating the Restoration style, which T. S. Eliot called the first "modern" style. At the same time, it retains some of the old Renaissance figurative richness. Finally, Brome had an excellent ear for conversation, including cant, dialects, and speech mannerisms. The resulting blend is a particularly effective style for the theater. Brome's style is another indication that he was in tune with the theater and with his time.

Brome's success was consistent throughout his career, beginning with the early plays *The Love-sick Maid* (now lost) and *The Northern Lass*, but his art improved as he went along. To modern tastes, his best plays might include *The Covent-Garden Weeded* and *The Sparagus Garden*, written near the midpoint of his career, and *The Antipodes*, *A Mad Couple Well Matched*, and *A Jovial Crew*, written near the end. *A Jovial Crew* has generally been the favorite.

Biography

Little is known of Richard Brome's personal life, including date and place of birth and death. The conventionally accepted estimate of his birth date is 1590, but evidence for the date is scanty: In 1591, a Richard Brome was listed as the son of Henry Brome in the St. James Clerkenwell parish register, and depositions in 1639 and 1640 Chancery Court suits identified a Richard Brome "aged 50 years or thereabouts." Whether these records refer to Richard Brome the playwright is uncertain, since marriage and burial records of the period indicate several Richard Bromes in the London area alone. For the same reason, Brome's marriage and family relationships cannot be clearly identified, though he did apparently marry and rear a family: In 1640, he complained that the Salisbury Court Theatre's refusal to pay him caused him and his family to suffer hardship. His death can be pinned down only to the years 1652-1653.

Much more interesting information is available on Brome's career as a playwright. The most interesting fact is that, before becoming a playwright, Brome was the servant of Ben Jonson, a leading playwright and the main theorist of Renaissance English drama. The induction of Jonson's comedy *Bartholomew Fair* (pr. 1614) refers to "his man, Master Broome, behind the arras," and Jonson wrote a commendatory poem for Brome's *The Northern Lass* that includes the following lines:

> I had you for a servant, once, Dick Brome;
> And you performed a servant's faithful parts.
> Now, you are got into a nearer room,
> Of fellowship, professing my old arts.
> And you do do them well, with good applause,
> Which you have justly gained from the stage,
> By observation of those comic laws
> Which I, your master, first did teach the age.
> You learned it well, and for it served your time
> A prenticeship: which few do nowadays. . . .

Similarly, Brome gratefully acknowledged Jonson's influence and tutelage, proud to be one of the "Sons of Ben."

How well Brome learned from his mentor is indicated by an incident that occurred in 1629. That year, Jonson's *The New Inn* failed miserably at the Blackfriars Theatre; shortly afterward, the same company and theater presented Brome's *The Love-sick Maid*—to extraordinarily popular acclaim. Jonson was so upset that, in "Ben Jonson's Ode to Himself," he blasted popular taste in the theater, complaining that "Broom's sweepings do as well/ There as his master's meal." Other Sons of Ben seconded their master with puns on Brome's name and status and with allusions to the sweepings or dregs he was serving up. Apparently this incident ruffled Jonson and Brome's relationship only briefly, however, since Jonson left out the snide allusion to Brome when he published his ode in 1631, and in 1632, Jonson wrote his commendatory verses to Brome's *The Northern Lass*.

The coincidence of Jonson's failure and Brome's success in 1629 also indicates that Brome learned from other contemporary playwrights besides his mentor. Brome collaborated with Thomas Heywood and possibly with George Chapman, and a number of fellow dramatists, including James Shirley and John Ford, wrote commendatory verses for Brome's works. In addition, Brome's work shows the influence of still other playwrights, such as John Fletcher, Francis Beaumont, and Philip Massinger. These collaborations, commendations, and influences confirm that, if Jonson was Brome's mentor, Brome was also widely acquainted with other dramatists and their work.

Such a view of Brome is further supported by his associations with various companies and theaters. His early play with "Young Johnson," *A Fault in Friendship* (now lost), was produced by the Prince's Company, probably at the Red Bull Theatre. In 1628, Brome was listed with the Queen of Bohemia's Players, who apparently toured the provinces and sometimes acted at the Red Bull Theatre in London (whether Brome was an actor for the company is in dispute). From 1629 to 1634, Brome wrote for the King's Men, the leading troupe in London and also Jonson's company, who produced Brome's work at court and at the Globe and Blackfriars theaters. In 1635, Brome returned briefly to the Prince's Company at the Red Bull, then signed a three-year contract to write for the King's Revels (later Queen Henrietta's Men) at the Salisbury Court Theatre. Brome found this association unsatisfactory—there was a dispute about proper payment—and did not sign a new seven-year contract with Salisbury Court Theatre when it was offered to him in 1638. Instead, in 1639 he moved over to write for Beeston's Boys at the Cockpit Theatre—a happy association which continued until the end of Brome's career.

Brome's career ended abruptly, at its height, when the English Civil War started in 1642 and Parliament closed all the theaters. A creature of the theater, Brome lived on, sadly and in poverty, until 1652 or 1653. Appropriately, his last known literary effort involved a collection of elegies entitled *Lachrymae Musarum.*

Analysis

As R. J. Kaufmann observes, Richard Brome's work forms "an intelligible and complex commentary on a central phase of an historical evolutionary process." That historical process, though highly complex itself, with its many social, religious, and nationalistic side issues, can be briefly summarized as the growing challenge of the English middle class to the old aristocratic order. Although individuals did not line up neatly, the middle class as a group found its symbol of power in Parliament, while the king was the figurehead of the old order. The middle class also leaned toward the Puritan sects, while the aristocracy generally hewed to the established Anglican Church. These deep-rooted tensions and others came to a head during the ill-fated reign of Charles I, from 1625 to 1649, when Brome practiced his art, and culminated in the English Civil War and the beheading of King Charles in 1649.

As these bloody events show, Brome lived and wrote on the eve of destruction. While his tone is comic, Brome nevertheless sets forth the conditions which led to social paroxysm. As a playwright, he sets forth those conditions in human terms, in the terms of feeling individuals. Therefore, for students of seventeenth century English history, Brome has particular significance, but there are also some strong parallels between the social conditions in his plays and those of today. For people living in unstable times, possibly on the edge of cataclysm, Brome has a message.

Brome's message centers mostly on money, which dominates the life depicted in his plays, and money's erosion of all other values. Marriages and alliances are formed on the basis of money as much as on the basis of love or friendship. Degraded aristocrats, short on cash, join with the middle class or with crooks and coney-catchers in pursuit of lucre. Groups of beggars roam the countryside. Everywhere the middle class is rampant, feeling its oats and hoping to purchase the manners and pedigrees of the aristocracy it is replacing. The world itself seems turned upside down, former values inverted. For the general theme of Mammon-worship, Brome was probably indebted to his mentor, Jonson, but Brome elaborates the social details of his theme that were apparent in the society around him. Brome might also have been indebted to Jonson for his conservative, aristocratic sympathies; with the changing makeup of the Caroline audience, Brome had to tone down those sympathies and appeared to be a more evenhanded observer.

The Northern Lass is an example of Brome's early work. The play's immediate success, combined with that of *The Love-sick Maid*, which was produced the same year, firmly established Brome's popularity in his time. These two early hits proved Brome's ability to satisfy his audience's tastes, but *The Northern Lass* makes one question those tastes and wonder whether Jonson was not right, after all, to attack them. The play's overdone intrigue and disguising become tedious, and its main attraction is its sentimental portrait of Constance from England's North Country. Yet *The Northern Lass* does illustrate the typical Brome: It introduces the all-pervasive theme of money and Brome's use here, in one play, of both satiric and romantic elements.

Money's power is underlined by the play's opening scene: Sir Philip Luckless, a court gentleman, has contracted to marry Mistress Fitchow, a rich city widow. The marriage represents a common social expedient of the time, the uneasy alliance of aristocrats and members of the middle class as the aristocrats sought to replenish their funds while the middle class sought to obtain titles. Sir Philip learns how uneasy the alliance is when he meets his bride's relatives, "a race of fools," and discovers that the bride herself is a loud shrew. He regrets the marriage bargain even more when Constance, the sweet-voiced Northern lass who is in love with him, appears on the scene. Eventually, Sir Philip gets a divorce on a technicality (since he and Mistress Fitchow quarrel on their wedding day, their marriage is never consummated) and is able to marry Constance. Significantly, the conflicts between love and money, aristocracy and middle class, end in compromise: Half of Constance's rich uncle's estate comes with her hand, and Fitchow marries Sir Philip's cousin Tridewell, who rather unconvincingly falls in love with her. By Brome's time, dramatists had to give money and the middle class their due.

As the play's title suggests, it was the sentimental portrait of Constance—the romantic element—that charmed Brome's audience. Innocent and direct, Constance speaks in a fetching North Country dialect: "But for my life I could not but think, he war the likest man that I had seen with mine eyne, and could not devise the thing I had, might be unbeggen by him." Mistaking Sir Philip's courtly compliment for a marriage proposal, she pursues him all the way to London. Naïve and loving, Constance introduces another perspective into the scheming context of the play, particularly in contrast to Fitchow and the prostitute Constance Holdup. Yet even the prostitute, through confusion with Constance, takes on some of her halo, thus enabling the audience to sentimentalize both innocence and its loss. In short, Constance is a reminder that innocence exists out there somewhere—or so Brome's audience wanted to believe.

A much better play than *The Northern Lass* is *The Sparagus Garden*, written around the midpoint of Brome's career. A comedy in which the satiric element predominates, *The Sparagus Garden* might well win the appreciation of a modern audience. Brome warns in the prologue that the audience should not "expect high language or much cost," since "the subject is so low." In fact, the language is sharp, colorful, and varied (including courtly and Somersetshire accents and satire of gentlemen's cant), not to mention full of sexual innuendo. The "low subject" is the Sparagus Garden, a suburban garden-restaurant with beds upstairs—the best little rendezvous for lovers in London. Here they can also sate themselves with asparagus, which is described as full of wonderful properties in both its erect and limp states.

Aside from the sexual appetites of Londoners, much else is satirized in *The Sparagus Garden*. For example, neighborly feuding is satirized in the characters of Touchwood and Striker, two rich old justices whose enmity over the years has grown into a close and sustaining relationship: They love to hate each other, and the desire of each to strike the final blow keeps them alive. Marital strife is satirized through the relationship of Brittleware and Rebecca: Brittleware fears that Rebecca will make him a cuckold, and

Rebecca plays on her husband's anxiety by reciting her sexual yearnings and Brittleware's inability to satisfy them—"you John Bopeep." Anxiety about sexual promiscuity is also satirized through the figure of Sir Arnold Cautious, "a stale bachelor" and "a ridiculous lover of women" (a voyeur) who will marry no woman because he can find no virgin. Other objects of incidental satire in *The Sparagus Garden* are lawyers and poets.

The social change occurring in the Caroline period is strikingly drama-tized in *The Sparagus Garden*. Not only is the Sparagus Garden a resort for gentlemen accompanying city wives, such as Mrs. Holyhock, the "pre-cise" (that is, puritanical) draper's wife, but also its main agent (pimp/pro-curator/publicist) is Sir Hugh Moneylacks, a degraded knight who "lives by shifts." Having run through his own estate and that of his middle-class wife, whom he drove to an early grave, Sir Hugh is now Striker's disowned son-in-law.

A hardened hustler, Sir Hugh is not at all abashed by his father-in-law's rejection, nor is the Sparagus Garden his only money-making project. In addition, he and his confederates are instructing the Somersetshire bump-kin Tim Hoyden, who has four hundred pounds to invest in the project, on how to be a gentleman—a subject of further satire in *The Sparagus Garden*.

In contrast to *The Sparagus Garden*, *A Jovial Crew* is a Brome comedy in which the romantic element predominates. The last of Brome's plays, *A Jovial Crew* is generally considered his best. It was a favorite of the Res-toration and of the eighteenth century, when it was turned into a comic op-era at Covent Garden—a version no doubt suggested by the play's numer-ous songs and dances. Performed by a jolly crew of raffish beggars, the rousing songs and dances embody the beggars' carefree philosophy, which stands in stark contrast to the middle-class ethos. The bands of beggars roaming the countryside are both an indictment of and an alternative to the emerging middle-class order. Coming from all walks of life—soldiers, lawyers, courtiers, and poets as well as peasants—the beggars turn neces-sity into a virtue: They form a "beggars' Commonwealth" with its own lan-guage and values, values based on fellowship rather than money. In fact, they scorn money.

The middle-class characters view the beggars' commonwealth with fear and fascination. Oldrents, an old country esquire whose home epitomizes middle-class prosperity, stability, and dullness, is vexed by a fortune-teller's prediction that his two daughters will become beggars. His friend Hearty, "a decayed gentleman," urges him to laugh at the prediction (to look upon the carefree beggars and birds of the field and be as they) but to little avail. As it turns out, Oldrents has good reason to fear for his daughters—particularly since his rapacious grandfather wrested the family estate from a "thriftless heir," Wrought-on, whose own posterity became beggars. Oldrents fathered a son with one of Wrought-on's beggar-descendants; now the son, unknown to him, is his steward, Springlove, who has a yearning, each spring, to go wandering with the beggars.

Oldrents' daughters also feel the attraction of the wandering life, which promises an escape from Oldrents' dull household and worried disposition. The daughters, Rachel and Meriel, look on their begging venture as a lark, and they impose it upon Vincent and Hilliard, their boyfriends since childhood, as an ordeal, a test of loyalty more significant than such childish games as "tearing of books" or "piss and paddle in't." In fact, they are all failures at alternative life-styles, even though they have the services of Springlove, who equips and instructs them and gives them an introduction to the beggars. After experiencing the hardships of pricking their "bums" on a straw bed and waking without a mirror, they fly back to their middle-class nests.

Despite its fun and folly, its reminder of Shakespearean couples running through the forests of Arden and Athens, *A Jovial Crew* is a strong record of a deteriorating society on the verge of civil war. It was Brome's final statement. The record had been building, however, throughout his works— a record of growing middle-class dominance, of money's power, of declin- ing loyalties and eroding values, of a vacuum at the heart of life. It is a record that today's world might do well to examine carefully.

Bibliography
Kaufmann, R. J. *Richard Brome: Caroline Playwright*, 1961.
Lynch, Kathleen. *The Social Mode of Restoration Comedy*, 1926.
Shaw, Catherine M. *Richard Brome*, 1980.

Harold Branam

ROBERT BROWNING

Born: Camberwell, England; May 7, 1812
Died: Venice, Italy; December 12, 1889

Principal drama

Strafford, pr., pb. 1837; *Pippa Passes*, pb. 1841; *King Victor and King Charles*, pb. 1842; *The Return of the Druses*, pb. 1843; *A Blot in the 'Scutcheon*, pr., pb. 1843; *Colombe's Birthday*, pb. 1844, pr. 1853; *Luria*, pb. 1846; *A Soul's Tragedy*, pb. 1846.

Other literary forms

Robert Browning is better known as a major Victorian poet and, in particular, as one who perfected the influential verse form called dramatic monologue. His achievement in poetry, for which he forsook the theater altogether in 1846, was unquestionably much greater than what he accomplished as a writer of stage plays, yet it is difficult and unwise to distinguish the subject matter and techniques of Browning's "failed" dramas from those of his successful poems. Although he was by nature and inclination a dramatic writer, it became apparent that his peculiar interests and talent in that line were more suited to the finer medium of poetry than to the practical exigencies of stagecraft. The verse confirms his acknowledged preoccupation with interior drama ("Action in character, not character in action"). Browning's verse masterpieces in this mode include "Porphyria's Lover," "My Last Duchess," "The Bishop Orders His Tomb at St. Praxed's Church," "Andrea del Sarto," "Love Among the Ruins," "The Last Ride Together," and *The Ring and the Book* (1868-1869). A dramatic monologue by Browning typically features an incandescent moment of crisis or of self-realization in the mental life of some unusual, often morally or psychologically flawed, character. Rather like a soliloquy except in being addressed to a present but silent listener, this type of poem enabled Browning to let his speakers' personalities, motives, obsessions, and delusions be revealed—inadvertently or otherwise—in speech and implied gesture. This preoccupation with inward, psychological drama—with the springs of action rather than with action itself—is the origin of Browning's greatness as a poet and of his limitations as a stageworthy playwright.

Achievements

In nineteenth and early twentieth century criticism, Browning was widely considered to be the best English writer of dramatic literature (though not of stageable plays) since the Renaissance. That judgment was probably accurate enough, if only because of the remarkable dearth of fine drama during the two hundred years in question. Even today, especially if Browning's splendid dramatic monologues are included in the estimate, there can be little doubt that his achievement was, under the circumstances, extraordinary. Nevertheless, any evaluation of his plays must begin by conceding that, despite his hopes, practical theatrical craft in the ordinary sense was never in Browning's vein of genius. He was a first-rate dramatic poet, not a good technical playwright. Indeed, the very themes and methods that mark the plays' literary value are the source of their unsuitability for successful performance. One historical explanation of this "failure" is the Romantic concept of acted and unacted drama, documented in Michael Mason's contribution to *Robert Browning* (1975). Mason associates Browning with a widespread and consciously antitheatrical attitude among authors that resulted in plays composed with indifference to performative—as opposed to literary or expressive—criteria. If Browning did believe on principle that actual staging is not necessary to serious drama, it is less surprising that his own plays are satisfactory chiefly as reading texts. On the other hand, we should remember that Browning did press persistently to see some of his work upon the boards. In any case, Browning's plays have never been popular and, with the exception of *Pippa Passes*, are not usually numbered among his most important contributions to the history of English dramatic writing. Their lasting excellence, then, is in their objective poetry and prose. As in the verse collections to which he gave titles such as *Dramatic Lyrics* (1842; in *Bells and Pomegranates*, 1841-1846), *Dramatis Personae* (1864), *Dramatic Idyls* (1879, 1880), and *Men and Women* (1855), Browning's mastery of inward action is demonstrated in the plays' delineation of moral and psychological crises and in their vivid intellectual and emotional energy. Understood as searching critiques of modern life, the psychological and moral bearings of some of these dramas—and their subversive frankness (about eroticism, for example, or respectability)— were original and significantly ahead of their time. Formal innovations in the reading plays (*Pippa Passes* and *A Soul's Tragedy*) and Browning's special gift for creating memorable female characters have also been praised.

Biography

As a young man, Robert Browning was tutored at his prosperous family's home near London. He spent much of a sheltered adolescence reading eagerly and eclectically in the fine library there, absorbing philosophical, artistic, and historical lore that would later emerge—sometimes rather obscurely—in his plays and poems. Devoted always to a literary career, Browning lived for many years dependent upon his indulgent parents. They exerted a deep personal influence: the father intellectually, the mother religiously. In literature, the works and example of Percy Bysshe Shelley were Browning's first and most enduring inspiration, though in drama itself the constant model would be, wisely and otherwise, William Shakespeare. The privately published verse and plays of Browning's early maturity were eccentric and poorly received. Most of the drama in particular was ill-suited to theatrical production, and in disappointment, he turned increasingly to a new type of poetry, the dramatic monologue, in order to fuse the variousness and objectivity of plays with the subtle effects of poems. Yet even after 1846, when elopement and marriage crowned his long, ardent courtship of Elizabeth Barrett, she was still the better-known writer of the two. The blithe years of his wedded life were spent mostly in Italy, where Browning's fascination with the rich and enigmatic sociocultural heritage of the Mediterranean bloomed and reflected itself in the great new poems collected in *Men and Women*. Mrs. Browning's sudden death in 1861 ended this golden era and was personally devastating for her husband. Thereafter, Browning resided in both England and Italy, continuing to write poetry— notably *The Ring and the Book*—and gradually winning a wide and appreciative audience for all of his work. This late adulation, including the international Browning Society's admiration of his religious and philosophical outlook, was in striking contrast with the humiliation he had felt during the early years. In 1889, he saw the publication of a seventeen-volume collection of his dramatic and poetic canon.

Analysis

Robert Browning's best plays, whether for reading or performance, are the ones in which we are most aware of his genius for evoking "action in character": the drama of human personality in conscious or unconscious conflict with itself. Outward action and scenic spectacle are perhaps more incidental in Browning than in any other significant English playwright, though the extended implications for social morality are usually apparent. Instead, Browning concentrates on the self-articulation of minds that are devious or deviant or otherwise exceptional. One effect is to cast doubt upon the normative values and impulses contending in (or generated by) such mentalities, notably in politics or love. Indeed, love of one sort or another among socially prominent characters is usually the symbolic field in which Browning's flawed or obsessive personalities perform most ineffectually or tragically. Rationalizers of selfishness, greed, hypocrisy, or cruelty are frequently presented, as are characters who let themselves and others be destroyed by the paradoxes inherent in artificial codes or standards of conduct. In particular, egomania and other faults of willful pride (including excessive shame or guilt) would appear to be Browning's diagnosis of the moral neuroses and complacencies he detected in Victorian society at large. The characters are not so much evil as inveterately and anxiously deluded.

It is easy to misconstrue the sometimes grotesque, sentimental, or over-wrought behavior of Browning's characters as a lapse or compromise with popular taste on the playwright's part. In Browning, the trite or melodramatic overreaction is symptomatic—it is his subject, not his technique. The presence and perspective of intelligent, realistic, and sensible characters such as Guendolen in *A Blot in the 'Scutcheon* confirms Browning's deliberate exhibition of abnormality in others, such as the histrionic Mildred and Thorold Tresham. That contemporary readers and audiences (including Charles Dickens) could apparently value Browning's pathos for its own sake is a separate consideration. A more significant problem for Browning, and for modern readers, is the atheatricality of such refined psychological and metaphoric aims. The artistic intention may in fact be too subtle, the rendering too opaque, the intended medium too visual to elicit onstage anything like the appropriate effect. Nevertheless, as a reading text the typical Browning play yields the same kind of dramatic significance that is to be found in his poetry.

The verse tragedy *A Blot in the 'Scutcheon*, considered Browning's best play, indicates his special effort to create something both subtle and stageworthy. In fact, he described it to the celebrated actor-manager William Charles Macready as "a sort of compromise between my notion and yours. . . . There is *action* in it, drabbing, stabbing, et autres gentillesses." Nevertheless, the observable action and strong dialogue in this drama of eighteenth century aristocratic honor remain subordinated to Browning's real interest in portraying inward conflicts and destructive ideals. Moreover, the tragic situation derives entirely from the flawed psyches of proud, rash Lord Tresham and his guilt-tormented sister Mildred. The distraught girl and her illicit lover Lord Mertoun attempt through an elaborate charade of formal betrothal to bring their relationship within the bounds of social and class respectability. Here, then, is a combination of Browning's favorite dramatic themes: unusually heightened emotion, symbolic moments of intense individual crisis, thwarted or misdirected love and sexuality, and the inhibiting force of pride or conventionality upon free feeling and action. In all of these respects, *A Blot in the 'Scutcheon* shows divided loyalties and misguidedly good intentions causing tensions that explode in impulsive and fatal choices. Mildred Tresham is visibly going to pieces throughout much of the play, her virtual derangement the price she pays for being torn between her passionate love for Mertoun and her terror of offending her imperious brother. It is her panic that has necessitated the young lovers' gamble for respectability, and she thus initiates the sequence of disastrous dissimulations, exposures, and misunderstandings. Both men are doomed when, cracking under the strain, she blurts out half the truth; Tresham and Mertoun feel bound by honor to suppress the simple word that could avert the needless catastrophe. It is the kind of situation in which Browning excelled: dilemmas in which men and women are too hampered by mixed motives to act with candor, charity, courage, or imagination.

The proud folly of Thorold Tresham is likewise responsible for the tragic denouement in *A Blot in the 'Scutcheon*. He whips himself into a rage about Mildred's "dishonorableness" and the reputation of his ancestral house, despite having seen earlier the wisdom of embarrassed concealment. In his fury, he so aggravates her already excessive shame that she is unable to reveal that her secret paramour and her formal suitor are the same person. Again in the duel scene, Tresham's selfish, intemperate anger and taunting compel the unwilling Mertoun to fight and die. Thereafter, sorrowful but still obsessed with observing the niceties of maintaining the family name, Tresham kills himself in a gesture that would seem ludicrously melodramatic were it not so poignantly in keeping with the pernicious notions of heroism and dynastic obligation he has displayed all along. Guendolen's wry epitaph confirms that one is expected to pity Tresham but by no means to admire his "perfect spirit of honor" or to condone his pointless, self-righteous suicide. Here and elsewhere, Guendolen seems to reflect the author's bemusement by what she calls "the world's seemings and realities." If the Treshams are unstable and haunted, young Mertoun seems overly casual until it is too late, at which point he overreacts in dignified fatalism. His contribution to the tragedy, apart from maintaining, all too incautiously, the liaison with Mildred and misjudging her brother, is to defy Tresham unnecessarily before the duel and to perish more or less suicidally on the latter's sword. Murders, suicides, and (as in Mildred's case) expirings under stress are almost always associated in Browning's plays with willful or simplistic escapism, albeit in the name of some illusory notion of justice. The three deaths in *A Blot in the 'Scutcheon* are good examples of this tendency.

The thematic focus of this play is on the inhumanity of what is perversely done for the sake of personal, social, and dynastic honor. In scene after scene, Tresham, Mildred, and Mertoun are either driven or betrayed by such considerations, their relationships becoming increasingly complicated, frustrated, and dangerous. At the same time, Guendolen's frank and genial perspective reminds us (and ought to have convinced the other characters) that with a little more candor and a lot less preoccupation with "name" and "blots," the whole problem could have been resolved comedically rather than tragically. She notices almost prophetically, for example, how overready the others are to announce principles for which they are prepared to die. It is also Guendolen who gaily sees through Mertoun's pretence, Tresham's gullible complacency, and Mildred's guilty secret. Her insights are ignored or come too late, but her bright and ironic personality commands the stage at the end. It is significant that Tresham, Mildred, and Mertoun apparently die uncontrite: They regret the ghastly effects, but not the causes, of their actions. Tresham's dying utterances, which he imagines to embody heroic penance and self-sacrifice, are as banal, code-bound, and monomaniac as anything he has said before. Mildred likewise persists in considering her own death as a just retribution and relief from anguish. Mertoun, like the others, is none the wiser for bringing on his own end. Each demise is a wholly destructive martyrdom to some abstract, over-scrupulous notion of "duty" or "wrong." Moreover, these unexpected deaths are shocking; as in some of Browning's other plays (and in such dramatic monologues as "Porphyria's Lover" and "My Last Duchess"), the customary tragic effects of fear and pity are mingled with surprise and even revulsion. The conventions of drama do not easily embrace Browning's emphasis on extravagance and perversity in characters' motives and reactions. If pathology and tragedy do not mix, Browning is no tragedian. His work may nevertheless be a finer, more modern, and more disturbing criticism of life for having deviated from literary tradition.

Pippa Passes is Browning's most famous (though possibly least stageable) play and ranks among his best works. An early and experimental composition, the drama comprises four symbolic vignettes from Renaissance life in an Italian town. These independent scenes are structurally and thematically connected by the momentary overhearing, in each, of young Pippa's voice. The girl's innocent singing crucially affects the outcome of interviews that she unknowingly bypasses in her holiday journey. In every case, her song induces a hearer to make, at a point of personal crisis, a guilty choice in favor of just or noble action. *Pippa Passes* reveals Browning at his dramatically strongest and weakest. The situations, subtle effects, psychological focus, and tenuous framing story are quite unsuitable for theatrical performance. In reading, however, the play is successful and undoubtedly dramatic. The issues raised by the various personalities, conflicts, and resolutions of the four scenes are likewise typical of Browning at his best.

Perhaps the most memorable and evocative vignette in *Pippa Passes* is the scene that presents two adulterous lovers, Ottima and Sebald, who have just murdered Ottima's wealthy old husband. Even as the couple begin to talk, it becomes evident that their former "wild wicked" passion has become wearied and cloying. The crime designed to set them free has already started to gnaw the heart out of their love. Sebald in particular seems irritable, distracted, and resentful from the outset. He is also grimly obsessed with the man whose killing he now half regrets. Like Macbeth, he is weaker and more morbidly sensitive than his accomplice. Sebald surprises, and then alarms, Ottima by dwelling on his troubled conscience, self-disgust, and frank doubts about her value as his reward. The pace and drama intensify as Ottima grasps the seriousness of this threat to their relationship and fearfully sets out to argue and finally to seduce him back into her control. In lines of lush and powerfully sensual poetry, accompanied by indications of alluring gesture, she soon succeeds in diverting and arousing the febrile Sebald. As he excitedly begs forgiveness and names her his "queen ... magnificent in sin," they embrace and ardently undress. At this instant, the passing song of Pippa is heard from outside the window—the famous little lyric ending, "God's in his heaven—/ All's right with the world." Grateful for being rescued by the intervention of this "miracle," a remorseful Sebald recoils at once from Ottima, bitterly repudiates her fascinations, and abruptly kills himself. It is typical of Browning that the impulsiveness and startling effect of the suicide, rather than its moral implications, are highlighted: The act's dramatic interest is in its psychology, its convincing exhibition of how that haunted mind might react, edifyingly or not, under such stress. Ottima's immediate responses—shock, envy, tender generosity, and self-recovery—are likewise rendered by Browning with skillful realism and irony. She is another of his brilliant portraits of women, and for all of her sins (a murder among them), the sanity of her final outlook underlines the strange extremism of Sebald's.

Each of the other sections of *Pippa Passes* similarly portrays two characters whose dilemma is interrupted and in some sense resolved by the passing voice of unworldly little Pippa, and, like the Ottima-Sebald scene, the others are Browningesque in their psychological verisimilitude, dramatic patterning, unusual feeling, and apparent moral opaqueness. Two parts employ a robust and naturalistic prose that confirms Browning's versatility and also indicates how emphatically his preference for "outmoded" verse drama was based on positive and theoretical considerations, not on any inability as a prose stylist. He never composed another play with the ingenuity and variety of *Pippa Passes*, but in the separate vignettes can be seen the germ of the great dramatic monologues to come, as well as the peculiarly psychological (or psychosocial) bearings of speeches and soliloquies in the later plays.

Briefer analyses of Browning's other dramas will suffice. Of these, *Strafford*, *King Victor and King Charles*, *The Return of the Druses*, and *Luria* are undistinguished. The first two are historical studies. *Luria* is a tragedy strongly reminiscent of (but much inferior to) Shakespeare's *Othello*. A convoluted romance, *The Return of the Druses* fails to integrate the politics with the love story. Features of two other plays do deserve attention. These are *Colombe's Birthday* (important as the happiest and most stageworthy Browning drama) and *A Soul's Tragedy* (very significantly the last).

Colombe's Birthday is a fairly conventional romantic comedy about the personal feelings and minor diplomatic stir associated with a young duchess' marriage. Graceful and gently satiric, the story interestingly follows good Duchess Colombe's birthday tribulations (both a threatened insurrection and the advent of a rival claimant to the throne, followed by two attractive marriage proposals) and the sound judgment (and luck) by which she satisfies both love and public duty. There are pleasing and eloquent characters, much fine verse, a genially searching critique of "courtier-ways," and a satisfying conclusion in which all receive as much or as little as their behavior warrants. Moreover, as a stage play *Colombe's Birthday* is workmanlike, accessible, and sedately agreeable. There is, however, a notable scarcity of Browning's customary dramatic concerns, tensions, and techniques. Indeed, to some extent this play indicates the literary limitations of work in which he most compromises with practicality and with popular taste. It may not be coincidental, then, that *Colombe's Birthday* was the last drama Browning designed expressly for theatrical presentation and that he soon abandoned playwriting altogether.

A Soul's Tragedy, Browning's most politically and philosophically serious play, has often been praised even though it is his last and his least stageable. Written in evident indifference to theatrical expectations, it dexterously traces the development and decline of a sixteenth century revolutionary's mind. The title itself seems to express the lifelong orientation of Browning's writing and the inevitability of his forsaking the theater. An entirely interior, possibly allegorical, process is being enacted in *A Soul's Tragedy*, called by its author a "wise metaphysical play." Only the inward action—defeat in the soul—is tragic, moreover; to all outward appearances the pattern and outcome are comedic. Well-articulated theories of statecraft, and much rhetoric about public responsibility, are simply vehicles for the playwright's exploration of moral psychology. The "tragedy" lies in the latter—in the conscious and unconscious mental life underlying an individual's outward behavior and rationalized principles. As critic Trevor Lloyd has shrewdly pointed out in connection with the political dramas, Browning handles well "the frame of mind of a man undertaking an imposture for the sake of something that he can convincingly regard as a good purpose." The mind that undergoes change in *A Soul's Tragedy* is that of Chiappino. During the first half of the play, he utters, in excellent verse, all the idealism (sincere and otherwise) of unselfish aspiration. Then, in the second part, he speaks—this time in lively prose—all the disillusionment (justifiable and otherwise) of realpolitik. That switch from "poetical" to "prosaic" thought and expression is not simply a political metaphor or an elegant gimmick on Browning's part. Both "voices" are rhetorical projections of what the self-preoccupied "soul" imagines or requires itself to believe at the moment. The touchstones against which Chiappino's development can be charted are two alter-ego characters: Luitolfo is the simple and genuine radical, while Onigben is the cynical legate whose droll Machiavellianism here is unsurpassed in English drama. As we might expect in Browning, Onigben gets the last word.

Browning published *A Soul's Tragedy* with *Luria* in 1846 as the eighth and last issue of the *Bells and Pomegranates* series. In more ways then one, this pamphlet marked the end of an era in his artistic life. The dedication to Walter Savage Landor announced the work as Browning's "last attempt for the present at dramatic poetry." He never wrote another play.

Other major works

POETRY: *Pauline*, 1833; *Paracelsus*, 1835; *Sordello*, 1840; *Dramatic Lyrics*, 1842 (in *Bells and Pomegranates*, 1841-1846); *Dramatic Romances and Lyrics*, 1845 (in *Bells and Pomegranates*); *Christmas Eve and Easter Day*, 1850; *Men and Women*, 1855 (2 volumes); *Dramatis Personae*, 1864; *The Ring and the Book*, 1868-1869 (4 volumes); *Balaustion's Adventure*, 1871; *Prince Hohenstiel-Schwangau: Savior of Society*, 1871; *Fifine at the Fair*, 1872; *Red Cotton Nightcap Country: Or, Turf and Towers*, 1873; *Aristophane's Apology*, 1875 (sequel to *Balaustion's Adventure*); *The Inn Album*, 1875; *Pacchiarotto and How He Worked in Distemper*, 1876; *La Saisiaz, and The Two Poets of Croisac*, 1878; *Dramatic Idyls (First Series)*, 1879; *Dramatic Idyls (Second Series)*, 1880; *Jocoseria*, 1883; *Ferishtah's Fancies*, 1884; *Parleyings with Certain People of Importance*, 1887; *Poetical Works*, 1888-1894 (17 volumes); *Asolando*, 1889; *Robert Browning: The Poems*, 1981 (2 volumes).

NONFICTION: *The Letters of Robert Browning and Elizabeth Barrett 1845-1846*, 1969 (Elvan Kintner, editor); *Browning's Essay on Chatterton*, 1948 (Donald A. Smalley, editor); *New Letter of Robert Browning*, 1950 (W. C. DeVane and Kenneth Knickerbocker, editors).

TRANSLATION: *The Agamemnon of Aeschylus*, 1877.

MISCELLANEOUS: *Bells and Pomegranates*, 1841-1846 (poetry and plays).

Bibliography

Armstrong, Isobel, ed. *Robert Browning*, 1975.

DeVane, William Clyde. *A Browning Handbook*, 1955.

Honan, Park. *Browning's Characters: A Study in Technique*, 1961.

Langbaum, Robert. *The Poetry of Experience*, 1957.

Nicoll, Allardyce. *History of Early Nineteenth Century Drama, 1800-1850*, 1930.

Pearsall, Robert B. *Robert Browning*, 1974.

Rolfe, William J., and Heloise E. Hershey. *A Blot in the 'Scutcheon and Other Dramas by Robert Browning*, 1887.

Thomas, Donald. *Robert Browning: A Life Within Life*, 1983.

Michael D. Moore

ED BULLINS

Born: Philadelphia, Pennsylvania; July 2, 1935

Principal drama

Dialect Determinism: Or, The Rally, pr. 1954, pb. 1973; *Clara's Ole Man*, pr. 1965, pb. 1969; *How Do You Do?*, pr. 1965, pb. 1968; *The Theme Is Blackness*, pr. 1966, pb. 1973; *A Son, Come Home*, pr. 1968, pb. 1969; *The Electronic Nigger*, pr. 1968, pb. 1969; *Goin' a Buffalo*, pr. 1968, pb. 1969; *In the Wine Time*, pr. 1968, pb. 1969; *The Gentleman Caller*, pb. 1968, pr. 1969; *Five Plays*, pb. 1969 (includes *Clara's Ole Man, A Son, Come Home, The Electronic Nigger, Goin' a Buffalo, In the Wine Time*); *We Righteous Bombers*, pr. 1969 (as Kingsley B. Bass, Jr.; adaption of Albert Camus' play *Les Justes*); *In New England Winter*, pb. 1969, pr. 1971; *A Ritual to Raise the Dead and Foretell the Future*, pr. 1970; *The Pig Pen*, pr. 1970, pb. 1971; *The Duplex*, pr. 1970, pb. 1971; *Street Sounds*, pr. 1970, pb. 1973; *The Devil Catchers*, pr. 1971; *The Fabulous Miss Marie*, pr. 1971, pb. 1974; *House Party*, pr. 1973 (lyrics; music by Pat Patrick); *The Theme Is Blackness*, pb. 1973 (collection); *The Taking of Miss Janie*, pr. 1975, pb. 1981; *Home Boy*, pr. 1976 (lyrics; music by Aaron Bell); *Jo Anne!*, pr. 1976; *Daddy*, pr. 1977; *Storyville*, pr. 1977, 1979 (revised, music by Mildred Kayden); *Sepia Star: Or, Chocolate Comes to the Cotton Club*, pr. 1977 (lyrics; music by Kayden).

Other literary forms

Although known primarily as a playwright, Ed Bullins has also worked in forms ranging from fiction and the essay to the "revolutionary television commercial." His novel *The Reluctant Rapist* (1973) focuses on the early experience of Steve Benson, a semiautobiographical character who appears in several plays, including *In New England Winter, The Duplex*, and *The Fabulous Miss Marie*. *The Hungered Ones: Early Writings* (1971), a collection of Bullins' early stories and essays, some of which are loosely autobiographical, provides an overview of his early perspective. Active as an editor and a theorist throughout his career, Bullins has written introductions to anthologies such as *The New Lafayette Theater Presents* (1974) and *New Plays from the Black Theatre* (1969). Along with the introduction to his own collection *The Theme Is Blackness* (1973), these introductions provide a powerful and influential theoretical statement on the aesthetics and politics of Afro-American theater during the late 1960's and early 1970's. *The Theme Is Blackness* also contains scripts for "rituals" and mixed-media productions, including "Black Revolutionary Commercials," which reflect the concern with electronic media visible in many of his later plays.

Achievements

As much as any contemporary American playwright, Bullins has forged a powerful synthesis of avant-garde technique and revolutionary commitment challenging easy preconceptions concerning the relationship between politics and aesthetics. Like Latin American writers Carlos Fuentes and Gabriel García Márquez and African writers Ngugi wa Thiong'o and Wole Soyinka, Bullins sees no inherent contradiction between the use of experimental techniques and the drive to reach a mass audience alienated from the dominant social/economic/racial hierarchy. Separating himself from the cultural elite which has claimed possession of the modernist/postmodernist tradition, Bullins adapts the tradition to the frames of reference and to the immediate concerns of his audience, primarily but not exclusively within the Afro-American community. While he frequently comments on and revises the philosophical and aesthetic concerns of Euro-American modernism, he does so in order to clarify his audience's vision of an American culture riddled by psychological and political contradictions which intimate the need for a basic change.

Paralleling the political modernism advocated by Bertolt Brecht in his aesthetic/political debate with Georg Lukács, Bullins' synthesis takes on particular significance in the context of the Black Arts Movement of the late 1960's. As a leading figure in the movement for specifically black cultural institutions and modes of expression, Bullins refuted through example the casual stereotypes of black revolutionary artists as ideologically inflexible and aesthetically naïve. Although he supports the confrontational strategies of radical playwrights committed to what he calls the "dialectic of change," he works primarily within what he calls the "dialectic of experience," which entails a sophisticated confrontation with a "reality" he understands to be in large part shaped by individual perceptions. Drawing on Brecht, Jean Genet, Albert Camus, Amiri Baraka, Eugene O'Neill, John Cage, Anton Chekhov, and Langston Hughes with equal facility, Bullins is not primarily a literary dramatist or a political agitator. Rather, he is a playwright in the classic sense, concerned above all with bringing the experience of black Americans alive onstage in a manner which forces the audience to confront its metaphorically ambiguous but politically explosive implications. His most successful plays, such as *In New England Winter* and *The Taking of Miss Janie*, demonstrate conclusively that a revolutionary artist does not need to circumscribe his vision in order to defend a preestablished ideological position. Demonstrating his affinities with Brechtian theory, as opposed to Brechtian practice, Bullins creates tensions between presentation style and content to alienate his audience, white or black, from its assumptions concerning race, class, sex, and ultimately the nature of perception.

Not surprisingly, this challenge frequently disturbs mainstream audiences and critics; typical is the response of Walter Kerr, who complained in a review of *The Taking of Miss Janie* that "no one likes having to finish—or trying to finish—an author's play for him; but that's the effort asked here." Ironically, Kerr's criticism accurately identifies the reason for Bullins' success in contexts ranging from the black community theaters of San Francisco and New York to the La Mama theater in New York's Soho district. Challenging the audience to confront the experience presented rather than to accept a mediated statement about that experience, Bullins rarely presents didactic statements without substantial ironic qualification. By refusing to advance simple solutions or to repress his awareness of oppression, Bullins attempts to force the audience to internalize and act on its responses. Effective as literature as well as theater, Bullins' plays have won numerous awards and grants from both Afro- and Euro-American organizations. The best of them, especially the early sections of the Twentieth-Century Cycle, a projected twenty-play series, have led some critics to compare Bullins with O'Neill. While his ultimate stature depends in large part on the development of the cycle and his continuing ability to generate new forms in response to changing audiences and political contexts, Bullins' place in the history of American and Afro-American theater seems assured.

Biography

Intensely protective concerning the details of his private life, Ed Bullins has nevertheless been a highly visible force in the development of Afro-American theater since the mid-1960's. Reared primarily by his civil-servant mother in North Philadelphia, Bullins attended a predominantly white grade school before transferring to an inner-city junior high, where he became involved with the street gang called the Jet Cobras. Like his semiautobiographical character Steve Benson (*The Reluctant Rapist*, *In New England Winter*, *The Duplex*), Bullins suffered a near-fatal knife wound, in the area of his heart, in a street fight. After dropping out of high school, he served in the United States Navy from 1952 to 1955. In 1958, he moved to California, where he passed his high school graduation equivalency examination and attended Los Angeles City College from 1961 to 1963.

Bullins' 1963 move to San Francisco signaled the start of his emergence as an influential figure in Afro-American culture. The first national publication of his essays in 1963 initiated a period of tremendous creativity extending into the mid-1970's. Actively committed to black nationalist politics by 1965, he began working with community theater organizations such as Black Arts/West, the Black Student Union at San Francisco State College, and Black House of San Francisco, which he founded along with playwright Marvin X. The first major production of Bullins' drama, a program including *How Do You Do?*, *Dialect Determinism*, and *Clara's Ole Man*, premiered at the Firehouse Repertory Theater in San Francisco on August 5, 1965. At about the same time, Bullins assumed the position of Minister of Culture with the Black Panther Party, then emerging as a major force in national politics. Breaking with the Panthers in 1967, reportedly in disagreement with Eldridge Cleaver's decision to accept alliances with white radical groups, Bullins moved to Harlem at the urging of Robert MacBeth, director of the New Lafayette Theater.

Bullins' first New York production, *The Electronic Nigger*, ran for ninety-six performances following its February 21, 1968, debut at the American Place Theatre, where it was moved after the original New Lafayette burned down. Combined with his editorship of the controversial Summer, 1968, "Black Theatre" issue of *The Drama Review*, the success of *The Electronic Nigger* consolidated Bullins' position alongside Baraka as a major presence within and outside the Afro-American theatrical community. Between 1968 and 1976, Bullins' plays received an average of three major New York productions per year at theaters including the New Lafayette (where Bullins was playwright-in-residence up to its 1973 closing), the American Place Theatre, the Brooklyn Academy of Music, Woodie King's New Federal Theatre at the Henry Street Settlement House, Lincoln Center, and the La Mama Experimental Theater. Bullins won the 1968 Vernon Rice Award for *The Electronic Nigger*, the 1971 Obie Award for *In New England Winter* and *The Fabulous Miss Marie*, and in 1975 both the Obie and the New York Drama Critics Circle Award for *The Taking of Miss Janie*. In addition to teaching at Fordham, Columbia, the University of Massachusetts (Boston), Bronx Community College, Manhattan Community College, and Amherst College, Bullins has received grants from the Guggenheim Foundation (1971, 1976), the Rockefeller Foundation (1968, 1970, 1973), the Creative Artists Program Service (1973), the Black Arts Alliance (1971), and the National Endowment for the Arts (1974). As public interest in Afro-American theater diminished in the 1980's, Bullins continued supporting community theater in California, working on the Twentieth-Century Cycle and occasionally acting in New York productions, including the revival of *Clara's Ole Man* and Wallace Shawn's *The Hotel Play* (pr. 1981). Despite his critical success, however, no Bullins play has been produced on Broadway and no collection of his work remained in print as of the mid-1980's.

Analysis

A radical playwright in both the simple and the complex senses of the term, Ed Bullins consistently challenges the members of his audience to test their political and aesthetic beliefs against the multifaceted reality of daily life in the United States. Committed to a revolutionary black nationalist consciousness, he attacks both liberal and conservative politics as aspects of an oppressive context dominated by a white elite. Equally committed to the development of a radical alternative to Euro-American modernist aesthetics, he incorporates a wide range of cultural materials into specifically black performances. The clearest evidence of Bullins' radical sensibility, however, is his unwavering refusal to accept any dogma, white or black, traditional or revolutionary, without testing it against a multitude of perspectives and experiences. Throughout a career that has earned for him serious consideration alongside Eugene O'Neill and Tennessee Williams as the United States' greatest dramatist, Bullins has subjected the hypocrisies and corruptions of Euro- and Afro-American culture to rigorous examination and reevaluation. Refusing to accept any distinctions between aesthetics and politics or between the concerns of the artist and those of the mass community, Bullins demands that his audience synthesize abstract perception and concrete experience. Providing a set of terms useful to understanding the development of these concerns in his own work, Bullins defines a constituting dialectic in the black theatrical movement which emerged in the mid-1960's:

> This new thrust has two main branches—the *dialectic of change* and the *dialectic of experience*. The writers are attempting to answer questions concerning Black survival and future, one group through confronting the Black/white reality of America, the other, by heightening the dreadful white reality of being a modern Black captive and victim.

Essentially, the dialectic of change focuses attention on political problems demanding a specific form of action. The dialectic of experience focuses on a more "realistic" (though Bullins redefines the term to encompass aspects of reality frequently dismissed by programmatic realists) picture of black life in the context in which the problems continue to condition all experience. Reflecting his awareness that by definition each dialectic is in constant tension with the other, Bullins directs his work in the dialectic of change to altering the audience's actual experience. Similarly, his work in the dialectic of experience, while rarely explicitly didactic, leads inexorably to recognition of the need for change.

Bullins' work in both dialectics repudiates the tradition of the Western theater, which, he says, "shies away from social, political, psychological or any disturbing (revolutionary) reforms." Asserting the central importance of non-Western references, Bullins catalogs the "elements that make up the alphabet of the secret language used in Black theater," among them the blues, dance, African religion and mysticism, "familial nationalism," myth-science, vodun ritual-ceremony, and "nigger street styles." Despite the commitment to an Afro-American continuum evident in the construction and content of his plays, Bullins by no means repudiates all elements of the Euro-American tradition. Even as he criticizes Brechtian epic theater, Bullins employs aspects of Brecht's dramatic rhetoric, designed to alienate the audience from received modes of perceiving theatrical, and by extension political, events. It is less important to catalog Bullins' allusions to William Shakespeare, O'Neill, Camus, or Genet than to recognize his use of their devices alongside those of Baraka, Soyinka, and Derek A. Walcott in the service of "Black artistic, political, and cultural consciousness."

Most of Bullins' work in the dialectic of change, which he calls "protest writing" when addressed to a Euro-American audience and "Black revolutionary writing" when addressed to an Afro-American audience, takes the form of short satiric or agitprop plays. Frequently intended for street performance, these plays aim to attract a crowd and communicate an incisive message as rapidly as possibly. Influential in the ritual theater of Baraka and in Bullins' own "Black Revolutionary Commercials," this strategy developed out of association with the black nationalist movement in cities such as New York, Detroit, Chicago, San Francisco, and Newark. Reflecting the need to avoid unplanned confrontations with police, the performances described in Bullins' influential "Short Statement on Street Theater" concentrate on establishing contact with groups unlikely to enter a theater, especially black working people and individuals living on the margins of society—gang members, junkies, prostitutes, street people. Recognizing the impact of the media on American consciousness, Bullins frequently parodies media techniques, satirizing political advertising in "The American Flag Ritual" and "selling" positive black revolutionary images in "A Street Play." Somewhat longer though equally direct, "Death List," which can be performed by a troupe moving through the neighborhood streets, alerts the community to "enemies of the Black People," from Vernon Jordan to Whitney Young. Considered out of their performance context, many of these pieces seem simplistic or didactic, but their real intent is to realize Bullins' desire that "each individual in the crowd should have his sense of reality confronted, his consciousness assaulted." Because the "accidental" street audience comes into contact with the play while in its "normal" frame of mind, Bullins creates deliberately hyperbolic images to dislocate that mind-set in a very short period of time.

When writing revolutionary plays for performance in traditional theaters, Bullins tempers his rhetoric considerably. To be sure, *Dialect Determinism*, a warning against trivializing the revolutionary impulse of Malcolm X, and *The Gentleman Caller*, a satiric attack on master-slave mentality of black-white economic interaction, both resemble the street plays in their insistence on revolutionary change. *Dialect Determinism* climaxes with the killing of a black "enemy," while *The Gentleman Caller* ends with a formulaic call for the rise of the foretold "Black nation that will survive, conquer and rule." The difference between these plays and the street theater lies not in message but in Bullins' way of involving the audience. Recognizing the different needs of an audience willing to seek out his work in the theater but frequently educated by the dominant culture, Bullins involves it in the analytic process leading to what seem, from a black nationalist perspective, relatively unambiguous political perceptions. Rather than asserting the messages at the start of the plays, therefore, he developed a satiric setting before stripping away the masks and distortions imposed by the audience's normal frame of reference on its recognition of his revolutionary message.

Along with Baraka, Marvin X, Adrienne Kennedy, and others, Bullins helped make the dialectic of change an important cultural force at the height of the black nationalist movement, but his most substantial achievements involve the dialectic of experience. Ranging from his impressionistic gallery plays and politically resonant problem plays to the intricately interconnected Twentieth-Century Cycle, Bullins' work in this dialectic reveals a profound skepticism regarding revolutionary ideals which have not been tested against the actual contradictions of Afro-American experience. *Street Sounds*, parts of which were later incorporated into *House Party*, represents Bullins' adaptation of the gallery approach pioneered by poets such as Robert Browning, Edgar Lee Masters (*Spoon River Anthology*, 1915), Melvin B. Tolson (*Harlem Gallery*, 1969), Gwendolyn Brooks (*A Street in Bronzeville*, 1945) and Langston Hughes (*Montage of a Dream Deferred*, 1951). Montaging a series of thirty- to ninety-second monologues, Bullins suggests the tensions common to the experience of seemingly disparate elements of the Afro-American community. Superficially, the characters can be divided into categories such as politicians (Harlem Politician, Black Student), hustlers (Dope Seller, The Thief), artists (Black Revolutionary Artist, Black Writer), street people (Fried Brains, Corner Brother), working people (Errand Boy, Workin' Man), and women (The Loved One, The Virgin, Harlem Mother). None of the categories, however, survives careful examination; individual women could be placed in every other category; the Black Revolutionary Artist combines politics and art; the Harlem Politician, politics and crime. To a large extent, all types ultimately amount to variations on several social and psychological themes which render the surface distinctions far less important than they initially appear.

Although their particular responses vary considerably, each character in *Street Sounds* confronts the decaying community described by The Old-timer: "They changin' things, you know? Freeways comin' through tearin' up the old neighborhood. Buildings goin' down, and not bein' put up again. Abandoned houses that are boarded up, the homes of winos, junkies and rats, catchin' fire and never bein' fixed up." As a result, many share the Workin' Man's feeling of being "trapped inside of ourselves, inside our experience." Throughout the play, Bullins portrays a deep-seated feeling of racial inferiority which results in male obsession with white women (Slightly Confused Negro, The Explainer) and a casual willingness to exploit or attack other blacks (The Thief, The Doubter, Young West Indian Revolutionary Poet). Attempting to salvage some sense of freedom or self-worth, or simply to find momentary release from the struggle, individuals turn to art, sex, politics, or drugs, but the weight of their context pressures each toward the psychological collapse of Fried Brains, the hypocritical delusions of the Non-Ideological Nigger, or the unfounded self-glorification of The Genius. Even when individuals embrace political causes, Bullins remains skeptical. The Theorist, The Rapper, and The Liar, who ironically echoes Bullins' aesthetic when he declares, "Even when I lie, I lie truthfully. . . . I'm no stranger to experience," express ideological positions similar to those Bullins advocates in the dialectic of change. None, however, seems even marginally aware that his grand pronouncements have no impact on the experience of the black community. The Rapper's revolutionary call—"We are slaves now, this moment in time, brothers, but let this moment end with this breath and let us unite as fearless revolutionaries in the pursuit of world liberation!"—comes between the entirely apolitical monologues of Waiting and Bewildered. Similarly, the Black Revolutionary Artist's endorsement of "a cosmic revolution that will liberate the highest potential of nationhood in the universe" is followed by the Black Dee Jay's claim that "BLACK MEANS BUY!" The sales pitch seems to have a great deal more power than the nationalist vision in the lives of the Soul Sister and the Corner Brother, whose monologues frame the Black Revolutionary Artist-Black Dee Jay sequence.

One of Bullins' characteristic "signatures" is the attribution of his own ideas to characters unwilling or unable to act or inspire others to act on them. Reflecting his belief that without action ideals have little value, Bullins structures *Street Sounds* to insist on the need for connection. The opening monologue, delivered by a white "Pig," establishes a political context similar to the one that Bullins uses in the dialectic of change, within which the dialectic of experience proceeds. Reducing all blacks to a single type, the nigger, Pig wishes only to "beat his nigger ass good." Although Bullins clearly perceives the police as a basic oppressive force in the ghetto, he does not concentrate on highlighting the audience's awareness of that point. Rather, by the end of the play he has made it clear that the Afro-American community in actuality beats its own ass. The absence of any other white character in the play reflects Bullins' focus on the nature of victimization as experienced within and perpetuated by the black community. The Harlem Mother monologue which closes the play concentrates almost entirely on details of experience. Although she presents no hyperbolic portraits of white oppressors, her memories of the impact on her family of economic exploitation, hunger, and government indifference carry more politically dramatic power than does any abstraction. This by no means indicates Bullins' distaste for political analysis or a repudiation of the opening monologues; rather, it reflects his awareness that abstract principles signify little unless they are embedded in the experience first of the audience and, ultimately, of the community as a whole.

While Bullins consistently directs his work toward the Afro-American community, his work in the dialectic of experience inevitably involves the interaction of blacks and whites. *The Taking of Miss Janie*, perhaps his single most powerful play, focuses on a group of California college students, several of whom first appeared in *The Pig Pen*. In part a meditation on the heritage of the 1960's civil rights movement, *The Taking of Miss Janie* revolves around the sexual and political tensions between and within racial groups. Although most of the characters are readily identifiable types—the stage directions identify Rick as a cultural nationalist, Janie as a California beach girl, Flossy as a "soul sister"—Bullins explores individual characters in depth, concentrating on their tendency to revert to behavior patterns, especially when they assume rigid ideological or social roles. The central incident of the play—the "rape" of the white Janie by Monty, a black friend of long standing—provides a severely alienating image of this tendency to both black and white audiences. After committing a murder, which may or may not be real, when the half-mythic Jewish beatnik Mort Silberstein taunts him for his inability to separate his consciousness from Euro-American influences, Monty undresses Janie, who does not resist or cooperate, in a rape scene devoid of violence, love, anger, or physical desire. Unable to resist the pressures which make their traditional Western claim to individuality seem naïve, both Janie and Monty seem resigned to living out a "fate" which in fact depends on their acquiescence. Monty accepts the role of the "black beast" who rapes and murders white people, while Janie plays the role of plantation mistress. While these intellectually articulate characters do not genuinely believe in the reality of their roles, their ironic attitude ultimately makes no difference, for the roles govern their actions.

While the rape incident provides the frame for *The Taking of Miss Janie*, Monty and Janie exist in a gallery of characters whose collective inability to maintain individual integrity testifies to the larger dimensions of the problem. Rick and Len enact the classic argument between nationalism and eclecticism in the black political/intellectual world; Peggy tires of confronting the neuroses of black men and turns to lesbianism; "hip" white boy Lonnie moves from fad to fad, turning his contact with black culture to financial advantage in the music business; several couples drift aimlessly into interracial marriages. Alternating scenes in which characters interact with monologues in which an individual reflects on his future development, Bullins reveals his characters' inability to create an alternative to the "fate" within which they feel themselves trapped. While none demonstrates a fully developed ability to integrate ideals and experiences, several seem substantially less alienated than others. In many ways the least deluded, Peggy accepts both her lesbianism and her responsibility for her past actions. Her comment on the 1960's articulates a basic aspect of Bullins' vision: "We all failed. Failed ourselves in that serious time known as the sixties. And by failing ourselves we also failed in the test of the times." Her honesty and insight also have a positive impact on the black nationalist Rick, who during a conversation with Peggy abandons his grandiose rhetoric on the "devil's tricknology" (a phrase adopted from the Nation of Islam)—rhetoric which masks a deep hostility toward other blacks. Although he has previously attacked her as a lesbian "freak," Rick's final lines to Peggy suggest another aspect of Bullins' perspective: "Ya know, it be about what you make it anyway." Any adequate response to *The Taking of Miss Janie* must take into account not only Peggy's survival strategy and Rick's nationalistic idealism but also Janie's willed naïveté and the accuracy of Mort's claim that, despite his invocation of Mao, Malcolm X, and Franz Fanon, Monty is still on some levels "FREAKY FOR JESUS!" Bullins presents no simple answers nor does he simply contemplate the wasteland. Rather, as in almost all of his work in both the dialectic of change and the dialectic of experience, he challenges his audience to make something out of the fragments and failures he portrays.

The Twentieth-Century Cycle, Bullins' most far-reaching confrontation with the American experience, brings together most of his theatrical and thematic concerns and seems destined to stand as his major work. Several of the projected twenty plays of the cycle have been performed, including *In the Wine Time, In New England Winter, The Duplex, The Fabulous Miss Marie, Home Boy*, and *Daddy*. Although the underlying structure of the cycle remains a matter of speculation, it clearly focuses on the experience of a group of black people traversing various areas of America's cultural and physical geography during the 1950's, 1960's, and 1970's. Recurring characters, including Cliff Dawson, his nephew Ray Crawford, Michael Brown (who first appeared in a play not part of the cycle, *A Son, Come Home*), and Steve Benson, a black intellectual whose life story resembles Bullins' own, serve to unify the cycle's imaginative landscape. In addition, a core of thematic concerns, viewed from various perspectives, unites the plays.

In the Wine Time, the initial play of the cycle, establishes a basic set of thematic concerns, including the incompatibility of Ray's romantic idealism with the brutality and potential violence of his northern urban environment. Stylistically, the play typifies the cycle in its juxtaposition of introverted lyricism, naturalistic dialogue, technological staging, and Afro-American music and dance. Individual plays combine these elements in different ways. *In New England Winter*, set in California, draws much of its power from a poetic image of the snow which takes on racial, geographical, and metaphysical meanings in Steve Benson's consciousness. Each act of *The Duplex* opens with a jazz, blues, or rhythm-and-blues song which sets a framework for the ensuing action. *The Fabulous Miss Marie* uses televised images of the civil rights movement both to highlight its characters' personal desperation and to emphasize the role of technology in creating and aggravating their problems of perception. Drawing directly on the reflexive rhetoric of Euro-American modernism, *In New England Winter* revolves around Steve Benson's construction of a "play," involving a planned robbery, which he plans to enact in reality but which he also uses as a means of working out his psychological desires. Ultimately, Bullins suggests that each of these approaches reflects a perspective on experience actually present in contemporary American society and that any vision failing to take all of them into account will inevitably fall victim to the dissociation of ideals and experience which plunges many of Bullins' characters into despair or violence. While some of his characters, most notably Steve Benson, seem intermittently aware of the source of their alienation and are potentially capable of imaginative responses with political impact, Bullins leaves the resolution of the cycle plays to the members of the audience. Portraying the futility of socially prescribed roles and of any consciousness not directly engaged with its total context, Bullins continues to challenge his audience to attain a perspective from which the dialectic of experience and the dialectic of change can be realized as one and the same.

Other major works

NOVEL: *The Reluctant Rapist*, 1973.
POETRY: *To Raise the Dead and Foretell the Future*, 1971.
SCREENPLAYS: *Night of the Beast*, 1971; *The Ritual Masters*, 1972.
ANTHOLOGIES: *New Plays from the Black Theatre*, 1969 (with introduction); *The New Lafayette Theater Presents: Plays with Aesthetic Comments by Six Black Playwrights*, 1974 (with introduction).
MISCELLANEOUS: *The Hungered Ones: Early Writings*, 1971 (stories and essays).

Bibliography

Fabre, Geneviève. *Drumbeats, Masks, and Metaphors: Contemporary Afro-American Theater*, 1983.
Gayle, Addison, Jr., ed. *Black Expression*, 1969.
Harrison, Paul Carter. *The Drama of Nommo*, 1972.
King, Woodie, Jr. *Black Theatre: Present Conditions*, 1981.

Craig Werner

EDWARD BULWER-LYTTON

Born: London, England; May 25, 1803
Died: Torquay, England; January 18, 1873

Principal drama

The Duchess de la Vallière, pb. 1836, pr. 1837; *The Lady of Lyons: Or, Love and Pride*, pr., pb. 1838; *Richelieu: Or, The Conspiracy*, pr., pb. 1839; *The Sea-Captain: Or, The Birthright*, pb. 1839; *Money*, pr., pb. 1840; *Dramatic Works*, pb. 1841; *Not So Bad as We Seem: Or, Many Sides to a Character*, pb. 1851.

Other literary forms

Edward Bulwer-Lytton was one of the most versatile and prolific writers of a far-from-laconic age. Though he held the stage during the late 1830's as the foremost contemporary English playwright, Bulwer-Lytton was more generally known in his own day for his novels, which gained an international readership. Today, what reputation remains to this once celebrated Victorian writer rests on a handful of his twenty-odd novels. Bulwer-Lytton the fiction writer was deft in many veins. Among his works are witty and elegant society novels, the best being *Pelham: Or, The Adventures of a Gentleman* (1828); the so-called Newgate novels, dealing with the dark impulses of the criminal mind, such as *Eugene Aram* (1832); historical romances, such as the famous *The Last Days of Pompeii* (1834); metaphysical works in the *Bildungsroman* tradition of Johann Wolfgang von Goethe, including *Ernest Maltravers* (1837) and its sequel *Alice: Or, The Mysteries* (1838); and even, at the end of his life, a precursor of utopian science fiction, *The Coming Race* (1871). Bulwer-Lytton, who despite his aristocratic background was obliged to support himself through his literary labors, also wrote short stories, his best pieces being "The Haunted and the Haunters" (1857) and *A Strange Story* (1862), and poetry, including *The New Timon* (1846), now chiefly remembered for having provoked Alfred, Lord Tennyson, and *King Arthur* (1848-1849, 1870). His *England and the English* (1833), a multifaceted study of pre-Reform Bill England, remains one of the most insightful social histories of early nineteenth century British culture, politics, education, and manners.

Achievements

Bulwer-Lytton is an author whose breadth leads the public, rightly or wrongly, to undervalue the depth of his achievements. When he aimed for high seriousness in the philosophical novels devoted to such abstractions as the Ideal and the Beautiful, he proved himself superficial, but when he set his sights lower, he excelled. He produced in *Pelham* one of the earliest and finest examples of the "silver fork" novel, a genre that proved its intrinsic worth in its culminating work, William Makepeace Thackeray's *Vanity Fair* (1847-1848), and demonstrated its endurance by continuing to flourish, if only in a debased form, down to the present day. He wrote historical novels exemplary in their learning and accuracy, books that remain models for that genre, whatever one chooses to make of its worth. Finally, Bulwer-Lytton's utopian novel *The Coming Race*, though less than a finished literary achievement, prefigures in its title, theme, and format the sort of "scientific romances" produced by H. G. Wells at the turn of the century.

Bulwer-Lytton's achievements as a dramatist are less substantial. Solidly researched, structurally sound, but inexcusably melodramatic by modern standards, his historical dramas served at best to keep playwriting alive in an age when few good British writers were making the effort to do so. In *Money*, Bulwer-Lytton offered for the Victorian world what *Pelham* had given the Regency: an incisive and detailed study of the forms folly, pretension, hypocrisy, and honor take in a particular milieu at a particular time.

Biography

Edward George Earle Lytton Bulwer (later, on inheriting his mother's estate, to be called E.G.E.L. Bulwer-Lytton, and later still, E.G.E.L. B.L., first Baron Lytton) was the third and last son of General William Bulwer and his wife Elizabeth Barbara Lytton, the heiress of Knebworth. Both of his parents were descendants of ancient families. Bulwer's early education was erratic but intensive. He read widely and deeply in the notable library of his maternal grandfather, Richard Warburton Lytton, and instead of attending a public school, he was placed with a tutor at Ealing. In 1822, Bulwer went up to Cambridge. He earned a bachelor of arts degree in 1826 and a master of arts in 1835. His university awarded him an honorary doctor of laws in 1864.

Having finished his education, Bulwer led the life of traveler and man of fashion. He toured the Lake District and Scotland and frequented the most exclusive circles of society in London and Paris. Handsome, elegantly dressed, proficient at all the fashionable sports and pursuits, he was one of the great dandies of England's "age of cards and candlelight." Like many another literary gentleman of his day, Bulwer had been dazzled by the glamour and notoriety of the late Lord Byron, and he made the mistake of embarking upon a curious romance with one of Byron's former mistresses, the mentally unbalanced Lady Caroline Lamb. This liaison led him to a yet worse error: In 1827, he married Lady Caroline's protégée Rosina Doyle Wheeler, a lovely but volatile Irishwoman, against the wishes of his mother, upon whose inclinations all of his financial prospects rested.

As short of income as they were lavish in their tastes, the young couple had to rely upon Bulwer-Lytton's pen to pay their bills. It proved dependable. Throughout the 1820's and 1830's, Bulwer-Lytton worked rapidly and industriously to churn out a succession of novels that gained for him a wide public and a sufficient income. This taxing labor impaired his temper and ultimately contributed to the breakdown of his marriage, however, for Rosina was suited by neither temperament nor training to suffer neglect and ill-use with composure. After traveling abroad to Naples in 1833, the Bulwer-Lyttons reached the point at which they could no longer live together. They agreed to a legal separation in 1836, but Rosina's financial dependence and monomaniacal hatred made her a recurring torment to her husband throughout the rest of his life.

Besides working hard as an author and as editor of the *New Monthly Magazine*, Bulwer-Lytton had in 1831 been elected to Parliament as member for St. Ives. A Radical Reformer, he was acquainted with the younger members of the utilitarian school. He supported liberal causes throughout his first parliamentary period, which ended when he lost his seat in 1841. The late 1830's and 1840's found him continuing his career as novelist, launching himself as a successful dramatist, and traveling, often for his health. On returning from one such trip abroad in 1849, he joined his friend Charles Dickens in forming a Guild of Literature and Art for the relief of impoverished authors. To benefit this guild, he wrote *Not So Bad as We Seem*, which an amateur troupe managed by Dickens staged in 1851. The philanthropic venture did not prosper, but the friendship of the two men of letters did. Dickens was to name one of his own sons after Bulwer-Lytton; at his fellow author's urging, he rewrote the ending of *Great Expectations* (1860-1861), so that the Victorian reading public could have the affirmative sort of conclusion it tended to prefer.

In 1852, after having published his political *Letters to John Bull, Esquire* in 1851, Bulwer-Lytton was returned to Parliament as member for Hertfordshire, a position he was to hold until his elevation to the peerage in 1866. On rejoining the ranks of the Commons, he stationed himself among the conservatives, though his positions were more philosophical than were those of the usual Tory gentleman. In 1858, Lord Derby made him secretary for the Colonies. He was to raise Bulwer-Lytton to the peerage as first Baron Lytton of Knebworth in 1866.

On receiving his barony, Bulwer-Lytton retired from political life but continued his literary efforts until his death at Torquay early in 1873. His son Edward Robert Bulwer-Lytton (later the first Earl of Lytton and himself a man of letters) was with him in his last days.

Analysis

A combination of versatile talent and personal glamour made Edward Bulwer-Lytton a literary star of the first magnitude in his own day. His apparent brilliance has waned considerably in the century since his death, and readers no longer see him as the literary peer of such novelists as Dickens or Thackeray—or Anthony Trollope, for that matter. Instead, he is remembered for writing a handful of works quite different from one another: an urbanely witty "silver fork" novel, an abstruse metaphysical romance, an impressively learned historical novel or two. Even though Bulwer-Lytton was more widely read and diversely educated than were many better-remembered literary figures of his day and despite the fact that his literary craftsmanship is sound, there are several reasons for his descent, if not into obscurity at least into a sort of twilight.

First, the passage of time has made the personal notoriety that surrounded Bulwer-Lytton's literary image—his violently unhappy marriage, his friendship with the "most gorgeous" Lady Blessington and the still more decorative Alfred, Count d'Orsay, his political adventures and editorial skirmishes—matters of historical curiosity rather than compelling contemporary interest. Second, the "high moral tone" so agreeable and edifying to Victorian readers sounds bombastic or bathetic to twentieth century ears; thus, the grandiose rhetoric to which Bulwer-Lytton, no less than most of his fellow writers, regularly resorted often blights what might otherwise be engaging books. Finally, and most important, Bulwer-Lytton's very ambition works against him for a modern audience. He was a writer who, as Sir Leslie Stephen acutely remarked, had talent enough to believe himself a genius; perpetually straining to be more of a philosopher or poet than he had power to be, Bulwer-Lytton conveyed the impression of being more superficial and insincere than he actually was. Thus, even Bulwer-Lytton's soundest literary achievements today have a smaller audience than they deserve. His plays, which are very far from being masterpieces, would no doubt have been completely forgotten had they not been written in what may be the Dark Age of British drama, that mediocre century between Richard Brinsley Sheridan and Oscar Wilde.

Bulwer-Lytton's literary detractors have accused him, both in his own day and subsequently, of being an opportunist who shrewdly gauged the reading public's desires and accommodated them. This charge is not entirely accurate—one of Bulwer-Lytton's ruling characteristics was that temperamental mobility that makes its possessor innately responsive to shifts in the climate of his milieu—but a clear sense of the marketplace does dominate his career as a dramatist. His interest in the public theater of the day predated his writing for it. He worked in Parliament to correct or simplify certain legal abuses or complexities that handicapped the contemporary theater, and his sociocultural study *England and the English* (1833) contains a chapter assessing the state of the British stage. By the early 1830's, he had even written two dramatic pieces: a stage version of his novel *Eugene Aram* (the play, in fact, preceded the novel) and a historical drama centering on Cromwell. Bulwer-Lytton's serious theatrical career, however, dates from February, 1836, when he invited the popular actor-manager William Charles Macready, renowned for his championing of "true" Shakespearean texts and his partisanship of contemporary British ventures in legitimate theater, to meet him at the Albany. With this visit began a fruitful professional relationship that is chronicled in the two men's letters to each other. Macready's advice on dramatic affairs enabled Bulwer-Lytton to discard one embryonic play ("Cromwell") and to strengthen another (*The Duchess de la Vallière*) until it became stageable—though despite Macready's presence in a leading role, this maiden venture failed when presented in January, 1837. Bulwer-Lytton was to write a number of other mediocre and unsuccessful plays in his career, but between 1837 and 1840, he created for Macready, at this time managing a theatrical company, three plays that attained a measure of distinction and considerable popular success: *The Lady of Lyons*, *Richelieu*, and *Money*.

Three of Bulwer-Lytton's plays—*The Duchess de la Vallière*, *The Lady of Lyons*, and *Richelieu*—take French incidents for their subject matter and contemporary French drama for their inspiration: Bulwer-Lytton, a political liberal and a writer who believed in giving his politics literary embodiment, admired the early promise of France's republican revolution of 1830 and her political playwrights, particularly Victor Hugo and Alexandre Dumas, *père*. Bulwer-Lytton's own French plays, as he observes in the introductory remarks to his *Dramatic Works*, offer a trilogy that follows the passage of France's reins of power from the one (in *Richelieu*) to the many (in *The Lady of Lyons*).

As theater, the first of these plays fails. Dealing with the career of Louise de la Vallière, one of Louis XIV's mistresses, *The Duchess de la Vallière* offers an always melodramatic and sometimes downright hysterical moral battle waged within and on behalf of the heroine. A virtuous provincial maiden, Louise goes to court, where she both falls (morally) and rises (socially) when the Sun King makes her his mistress and a duchess. Too good a woman to be continually interesting, too sincere a lover of Louis the man to be a stimulating and appreciative companion for Louis the King or the sort of intermediary courtiers find useful, Louise is soon supplanted by a more worldly mistress. After many a scene of debate, escape, pursuit, and lament, the duchess takes her leave of the king and the world and enters a nunnery.

The Lady of Lyons: Or, Love and Pride, based on a slight tale called "The Bellows Mender," proved more successful than had its predecessor, for a number of reasons. As the critic Charles Shattuck observes, Bulwer-Lytton the Radical selected just the sort of story—"that of the noble commoner winning out against the entrenched social prejudices of decadent aristocracy"—to please the public in an age of reform. In addition, the play is not high drama but romantic comedy: The temptations to grandiose posturing, moralizing, and philosophizing are less frequent. The lady of the play's title is Pauline Deschappelles, the beautiful daughter of a rich merchant. She inspires the love and possesses the pride that combine in the subtitle.

As the play opens, Pauline, with the encouragement of her mother, a woman as stupid and matrimonially obsessed as is Mrs. Bennet in Jane Austen's novel *Pride and Prejudice* (1813), has refused the proposal of Beauseant, *ci-devant* marquis, who bitterly states the absurdity of the lovely girl's goals in life: "Now as we have no noblemen left in France,—as we are all citizens and equals, she can only hope that, in spite of the war, some English Milord or German Count will risk his life, by coming to Lyons, that this *fille du Roturier* may condescend to accept him."

To revenge himself on the proud beauty and her family, Beauseant enlists the aid of one of "Nature's noblemen"—Claude Melnotte, the handsome and self-educated son of a gardener. Melnotte, known ironically, because of his efforts at self-improvement, as "Prince Claude," is himself a man who loves and has been brutally scorned by Pauline. Disguised as the Prince of Como and financed by Beauseant, Claude is to woo, win, and thereby disgrace the ambitious girl. Because he has been insulted by her, the gardener's son agrees, but because he truly loves her, he repents of his deception as soon as Pauline agrees to marry him, for in so doing, she reveals herself partly charmed by his title but also partly alive to his real excellence. No sooner has he wed the girl than Claude nobly offers her an annulment, which Pauline, by now seriously attached to him, is not disposed to accept. Having thus won her love, Claude goes off as a soldier to acquire a name and fortune worthy of the lady he has gained.

Two and a half years pass, and Claude, now known as the mysterious and heroic Colonel Morier, returns to Lyons to claim Pauline's hand. He is crushed to learn that the woman who vowed to wait for him is on the verge of marrying Beauseant—but relieved to discover that her apparent fickleness is only filial concern to save her now-bankrupt father's good name by giving him a rich son-in-law. Having arrived at the eleventh hour, the gardener's son, now risen to eminence in the Grande Armée, can stoop to save the little bourgeoise who once scorned him. Thus, the play's outcome is shrewdly calculated to please both republicans and romantics.

Whereas *The Lady of Lyons* offered a timely political message in a palatable comic form, Bulwer-Lytton's next play for Macready, *Richelieu*, proved more ambitious. Initially conceived as a romance set in the days of Louis XIII, and only incidentally dealing with the cardinal, the play gradually changed, as Bulwer-Lytton's fascination with the complex man who was one of the great architects of the prerevolutionary French state drew Richelieu to center stage.

Accordingly, the romantic comedy was elevated to a blank-verse drama. The love conflict—a triangular relationship whose three parties are the cardinal's ward Julie de Mortemar; her honorable admirer the Chevalier de Mauprat, at first the cardinal's foe, then his stout ally; and Louis XIII, who wants Julie for his mistress—was subordinated to a political problem: a conspiracy against the cardinal's strategies and life by a cabal allied with the Spanish powers. Bulwer-Lytton, well-read in French history, condensed a number of events occurring between 1630 and 1642 for his *Richelieu*. In one grand chain of events, the shrewd, brave, ruthless, but jovial cardinal successfully deals with the Duc de Bouillon's conspiracy, the "Day of Dupes," the apostasy of Baradas, and the treason of Cinq Mars. Not surprisingly, then, the play is full of melodramatic action. It contains an abundance of the intrigues and counterintrigues, betrayals, escapes, and pursuits admired by nineteenth century audiences. Bulwer-Lytton's chief interest, though, is in doing justice to the cardinal's character: His preface and occasional footnotes guarantee that the reader's attention remains on the cardinal's character as revealed through events, rather than on the events themselves. As statesman and private person, the Richelieu that Bulwer-Lytton presents is a plausible mixture of vices and virtues. For a reading audience, the playwright comes close to his professed goal of "not disguising his foibles or his vices, but not [being] unjust to the grander qualities (especially the love of country), by which they were often dignified, and, at times, redeemed."

Bulwer-Lytton's third play for Macready, the piece first called "Norman," then "The Inquisition," next "The Birthright," and finally *The Sea-Captain*, failed disastrously in 1839; and Bulwer-Lytton was not immediately eager to resume his playwriting. In May, 1840, however, Macready's company was having a slow season at the Haymarket, so Bulwer-Lytton, willing to oblige a friend in need, embarked upon the composition of a social comedy. He began and then abandoned "Appearances," a play conceived as "a satire on the way appearances of all kinds impose on the public." The play he then proceeded to write, *Money*, is a refinement on this theme.

In *Money*, which is the most enduring of his plays, Bulwer-Lytton deals rather as Molière might have done with the manner in which the hypocritical world's regard for a man changes as his financial position improves or deteriorates. The play's hero is Alfred Evelyn, a high-minded but impoverished gentleman serving as private secretary to his worldly cousin Sir John Vesey, a man who lives luxuriously on the reputation of wealth, as do more than a few suave deceivers in Bulwer-Lytton's society novels. Evelyn loves and proposes to his equally poor and equally admirable cousin Clara, who, like him, is an exploited retainer of the Vesey family. Clara returns his love but knows from her parents' experience that affection without money is not enough to make a man happy. With Evelyn's best interests at heart, she refuses him. Directly thereafter, Evelyn inherits a great fortune, and Clara proves too scrupulous to confess the love she had not permitted herself to avow when he was poor. He therefore engages himself to the mercenary Sir John's charming, calculating daughter Georgina, but, suspicious of her avowed attachment, pretends to ruin himself through extravagant spending, particularly gambling. As a result of this test, Georgina's insincerity and Clara's generous love become evident. The play ends with the virtuous man whom money alone cannot please gaining true wealth: As Evelyn tells his fiancée, Clara, "You have reconciled me to the world and to mankind."

As a comedy of manners, *Money* falls short of such masterpieces as William Congreve's *The Way of the World* (pr. 1700) or Wilde's *The Importance of Being Earnest* (pr. 1895), but it is of all Bulwer-Lytton's plays the one that proves most rewarding to twentieth century readers. *Money* demonstrates how a chronic moral disease, the avarice of the fashionable world, afflicts the denizens of a particular place and time. The Victorian symptoms of this malaise, the coldhearted courtships, the mutual deceptions of extravagant worldlings and greedy tradesmen, the compelling drama of the gaming table, are interesting historical curiosities for a modern audience. Thus, ironically, the one play that Bulwer-Lytton chose to set in the present is the one in which posterity finds the most telling observations of a vanished age.

Other major works

NOVELS: *Falkland*, 1827; *The Disowned*, 1828; *Pelham: Or, The Adventures of a Gentleman*, 1828; *Devereux: A Tale*, 1829; *Paul Clifford*, 1830; *Eugene Aram*, 1832; *Godolphin*, 1833; *The Last Days of Pompeii*, 1834; *Rienzi, the Last of the Roman Tribunes*, 1835; *Ernest Maltravers*, 1837; *Alice: Or, The Mysteries*, 1838; *Zanoni*, 1842; *The Last of the Barons*, 1843; *Harold, the Last of the Saxons*, 1848; *The Caxtons: A Family Picture*, 1849; *My Novel*, 1852; *What Will He Do with It?*, 1859; *The Coming Race*, 1871; *Kenelm Chillingly: His Adventures and Opinions*, 1873; *The Parisians*, 1873.

SHORT FICTION: "The Haunted and the Haunters," 1857; *A Strange Story*, 1862.

POETRY: *The New Timon*, 1846; *King Arthur: An Epic Poem*, 1848-1849, 1870.

NONFICTION: *England and the English*, 1833; *Letters to John Bull, Esquire*, 1851.

Bibliography

Christensen, A. C. *Edward Bulwer-Lytton: The Fiction of New Regions*, 1976.
Lytton, Victor A. *The Life of Edward Bulwer, First Lord Lytton*, 1913.

Sadleir, Michael. *Bulwer: A Panorama*, 1931.
Shattuck, Charles H. *Bulwer and Macready: A Chronicle of the Early Victorian Theatre*, 1958.
Stewart, C. N. *Bulwer Lytton as Occultist*, 1927.

Peter W. Graham

ALEXANDER BUZO

Born: Sydney, Australia; July 23, 1944

Principal drama
Norm and Ahmed, pr. 1968, pb. 1969; *The Front Room Boys*, pr. 1969, pb. 1970; *Rooted*, pr. 1969, pb. 1973; *The Roy Murphy Show*, pr. 1970, pb. 1973; *Macquarie*, pb. 1971, pr. 1972; *Tom*, pr. 1972, pb. 1975; *Batman's Beachhead*, pr. 1973; *Coralie Lansdowne Says No*, pr., pb. 1974; *Martello Towers*, pr. 1975, pb. 1976; *Makassar Reef*, pr., pb. 1978; *Big River*, pr. 1980, pb. 1981; *The Marginal Farm*, pr. 1984.

Other literary forms
Alexander Buzo has written for both film and television, coauthoring the script for the television production of *Ned Kelly* (1970) and writing the screenplay for the short film *Rod* (1972). He has also contributed articles to journals such as *The Australian Financial Review*, *National Times*, and *POL Magazine*.

Achievements
Buzo was playwright-in-residence for the Melbourne Theatre Company in 1972-1973. During that period, his historical play *Macquarie* and a satire on big business, *Tom*, were produced. He was awarded the Australian Literature Society Gold Medal for those two plays in 1972. Buzo also received a fellowship from the Commonwealth Literary Fund in 1970 and a grant from the Literature Board of the Australia Council in 1973 and 1979.

One of Buzo's greatest achievements has been to alter the image of the Australian theater. He belongs to the "New Wave" of Australian playwrights who began to come to prominence in the 1960's and whose spiritual mentor was Ray Lawler, whose *Summer of the Seventeenth Doll* (pr. 1955) was the first Australian play to win international attention.

Buzo's first important play, the one-act *Norm and Ahmed*, won for him as much notoriety as fame. It was the subject of a number of prosecutions for indecency, provided by the play's obscene closing line. *Norm and Ahmed* was introduced to the public in 1968, at the Old Tote Theatre in Sydney, as part of an experimental Australian play season; it was accompanied by another one-act play, *The Fire on the Snow* (pr. 1941), by Douglas Stewart, which had been first produced as a radio play. In the original production, the closing line was delivered onstage in a Bowdlerized form, but in the play's production in Brisbane, in April and May of 1969, the final speech was delivered as written in Buzo's script. The actor playing Norm, who speaks the offending line, was arrested after about two weeks of production, having ignored warnings by the police. He was tried, convicted, and fined, but he took the case to the State Supreme Court of Queensland, where the conviction was overturned. The state authorities appealed to the High Court of Australia, which upheld the State Supreme Court's decision.

The play was produced in Melbourne, the capital of the state of Victoria, in July of 1969, and the producer and the actor playing Norm were prosecuted for indecency in that state as well. After a number of adjournments, during one of which the magistrate, counsel, and witnesses saw a special performance, the producer and actor were each fined ten dollars. They appealed, but the appeal was dismissed, and the judge decided that the line in question violated contemporary standards of decency.

Norm and Ahmed was first published as a supplement to *Komos*, the journal of drama and theater arts of Monash University in Victoria, Australia. The publishers mentioned that they had had extreme difficulty obtaining a firm to set the type because of the obscenity charge which was then before the courts.

The controversy over *Norm and Ahmed* received a considerable amount of publicity. The net effect was to liberate Australian drama from censorship, and many playwrights have followed Buzo's lead, using strong language wherever they feel it to be appropriate.

Biography

Alexander Buzo was born in Sydney, the capital of the state of New South Wales, on July 23, 1944, the son of an Albanian-born, American-educated civil-engineer father and an Australian mother. Buzo spent his childhood in Armidale, an inland town in New South Wales, near the border between New South Wales and Queensland, an area devoted primarily to the raising of sheep.

Buzo attended primary school in Armidale and high school at the International School in Geneva, Switzerland. After completing high school, he returned to Australia. He was graduated from the University of New South Wales in Sydney.

Buzo has firmly committed himself to earning a living as a writer and has succeeded in doing so—no mean feat in Australia. Producing plays almost annually since the age of twenty-five, he has achieved world renown as a dramatist. His plays reflect many of his personal beliefs; he detests bullies and cowards and satirizes them mercilessly, as demonstrated by his portrayal of the central character of Norm in *Norm and Ahmed*; he is sympathetic to women's attempts to achieve equality and to make a mark in the traditionally male-chauvinist society of Australia; and, finally, he deplores the insularity of Australia and Australians, and his writings reflect his attempts to change his people's view of themselves.

Analysis

All Alexander Buzo's plays may be classified as socially pertinent and controversial. He writes to shock, or at least to make his audience uncomfortable, even when they are laughing uproariously. In his earlier plays, his tone is satiric, bordering sometimes on the morbid, while in his later work it tends to be ironic. If his plays seem to lack a definite structure much of the time, this failing is balanced by his superlative dialogue.

There is a universality of character and setting that more than makes up for the Australian idioms that Buzo employs, particularly in his early plays—idioms that will frequently baffle the non-Australian playgoer (or reader). Indeed, as Buzo has matured, his characterizations have become increasingly rich and complex. His early characters, although representing recognizable types, border on caricature. Norm, in *Norm and Ahmed*, for example, is drawn in bold strokes but with little detail. In contrast, Coralie Lansdowne, of *Coralie Lansdowne Says No*, is a fine character portrait of a troubled woman, uneasy with herself, and Weeks Brown, the protagonist of *Makassar Reef*, has a depth of character seldom met in modern drama, Australian or European, American or English.

As noted above, Buzo's recurring theme as a playwright is Australia's national identity. While he has many other concerns as well, it is this theme that links plays as diverse as *Norm and Ahmed*, *Macquarie*, and *Makassar Reef*. *Norm and Ahmed*, which has been called "probably the best Australian one-act play staged for many years," is primarily a study of an uncertain Australian, one who cannot come to terms with the "invasion" of his country by immigrants who have different values and different mores. Indeed, Norm is portrayed as the archetypal Australian; the attitudes he expresses are those ascribed to the conservative middle-class, median-educated "Aussie." Ahmed personifies everything that this class of Australian has come to dislike: the immigrant who is not only disturbingly "different" but also ambitious, hardworking, and self-possessed. Confronted by a "boong" such as Ahmed, the typical Aussie feels a need to reestablish his uneasy sense of superiority.

The historical background to the play, which needs no explanation for an Australian audience, will be less familiar to non-Australians. Traditionally, immigrants to Australia, of whom there were more than two million after World War II, were drawn from Great Britain and continental Europe, and for many years there was in effect a "White Australia" policy. This policy has changed, however, as the Australian government has come to realize that the country is situated in Southeast Asia, with many nonwhite neighbors. While nonwhites have been permitted to immigrate to Australia, attitudes toward them have changed slowly, and many white Australians have retained racist tendencies.

Both Norm and Ahmed are types rather than fully developed characters.

Norm, who mentions that his father was Irish, fits the stereotype of the Irish-Australian: antigovernment but politically conservative, boozing, rebellious, suspicious of foreigners. Ahmed is a leftist, unhappy with the government both in Australia and in Pakistan. He is formal, polite, and reserved.

Buzo's gift for dialogue is evident in this early play. Indeed, the play depends entirely on dialogue to hold the audience's attention. There is no plot and, with the exception of the kick to Ahmed's stomach that provides the conclusion, no action. Norm is a natural storyteller, and he keeps Ahmed engaged with tales of himself and his exploits during the war, at the same time freely expressing his attitudes toward various facets of Australian life. Norm is not only a fine raconteur but also a born actor, and he acts out many of his tales for Ahmed. His speech is glib, and he cleverly conceals his true self from Ahmed throughout the play, until the culmination. The play made a deep impression in Australia, and much has been written about why Norm kicks Ahmed. Why indeed?

Norm has received only politeness from Ahmed, but Ahmed's reserve implies a feeling of superiority, which Norm cannot tolerate. As Katherine Brisbane observes in her introduction to *Three Plays by Alexander Buzo* (1973): "His powers of reasoning may have betrayed him in the past but his prejudice he can rely on."

Buzo's first historical play, *Macquarie*, is about one of Australia's early colonial governors, Lachlan Macquarie. The play is important in that it marks Buzo's first foray into the roots of Australia's national identity. One must remember that the first settlement in Australia took place in 1788. Buzo uses the historical genre to draw parallels between the past and the present. He makes his audience realize that no matter how much things have changed, there are certain human characteristics that are constant. Greed, avarice, honesty, and high-mindedness are still as significant in maintaining societal values as they were in the nineteenth century.

The play retains a twentieth century flavor by a series of rapid changes on a permanent set—using lighting to focus on particular parts of the set, leaving other parts darkened, and employing a commentator to narrate the action. These devices, given currency by the epic theater of Bertolt Brecht, reminds the audience that they are in contemporary times. Stage presentations of *Macquarie* rely heavily on technical effects of this nature, and the sparse setting that Buzo calls for compels the playgoer or reader to use his imagination to fill in the blanks. The play is not naturalistic; it does not try to present the history of the era as much as it delves into the motivations of an honorable man who is opposed by a number of self-interested factions. It stresses moral struggles which are universal.

Governor Macquarie is opposed by the ultraconservative, anticonvict faction of "established" Australians, among whom are his lieutenant governor and a prominent Methodist minister, Samuel Marsden, one of the wealthiest landowners of the time. The latter group wishes to maintain the status quo and violently opposes Macquarie's reform efforts.

The action opens in Sydney, in the colony of New South Wales, which, at the time, constituted all of settled Australia, except for Tasmania, then known as Van Diemen's Land. The colony extended along the entire east coast of Australia, much of which had not yet been explored. There are rapid shifts in time and place (between Sydney and London) and a lot of action. So many changes in locale occur at such a rapid pace that the audience will wonder, now and then, exactly where the action is taking place.

Considerable social commentary is included in the play, amounting almost to allegory. The clergyman Marsden represents the evil forces in the colony, whereas Macquarie represents the forces of good, overcome by deceit, greed, and politicizing. The play dramatizes the visions of fairness and right as exemplified in a just, farsighted governor, who, although he makes errors in judgment, is basically a sincere and compassionate man. While he made mistakes because of his own character faults, nevertheless he was a heroic figure in early Australia.

Macquarie provides audiences with an insight into the beginnings of Australia and, implicitly, a standard by which to judge the present. That judgment is made more explicit in *Makassar Reef*, a play which differs in style from *Macquarie* as much as *Macquarie* differs from *Norm and Ahmed* yet which continues Buzo's investigation of the Australian experience.

The setting for *Makassar Reef* is the Celebes Islands of Indonesia. The plot concerns a no-longer-young Australian couple: Weeks Brown, a government economist in his thirties, and his fiancée, Beth Fleetwood. Other characters are Wendy Ostrow and her daughter, recently back from Geneva and now on their way to Australia, where Wendy was born but which her daughter has never seen; Perry Glasson, an Australian yachtsman-drifter, who will do almost anything to make a little money; Silver, a thief who passes as a Dutch hippie but who was really born in Australia; and two Indonesians: Karim, a corrupt government official, and Abidin, a disillusioned but still politically active journalist who earns his living as an English teacher and guide. There is also an offstage character, Madame Yu, who owns the hotel and restaurant in which much of the action takes place, and who also has a hand in prostitution, drugs, and, presumably, many other illegal affairs.

There are many parallels between this play and William J. Lederer's novel *The Ugly American* (1958). As travel has become cheaper and Australians more mobile, they have usurped the place of the American, especially in locations closer to Australia, displaying all the characteristics despised for so many years in American tourists: smug superiority, conspicuous display of wealth, and disregard for local customs.

Disillusionment pervades *Makassar Reef*. Weeks either is on vacation, has resigned, or has been fired from his post as a government economic adviser in Australia; it appears that one of the policies he advised his superiors to put into effect has had disastrous results. Almost penniless in Makassar, reduced to selling his personal possessions, Weeks is drunk through much of the play.

In this demoralized state, Weeks looks for solace in an affair with Wendy, and thus the plot is set in motion. Beth is aware of the affair but will not relinquish Weeks. Wendy's daughter, Camilla, thinks that Weeks and Beth are married; indeed, they have lived together for nine years and it would appear there is nothing left for them to do but marry. Camilla is shattered by the revelation of Weeks's affair with her mother.

Beth retaliates by having an affair with the yachtsman, Perry, who is subsequently falsely arrested in a conspiracy between the Indonesian official, Karim, and the thief, Silver. Silver, however, learns that Madame Yu, determined to rid her territory of all competition, intends to eliminate him. Needing passage from the island, he strikes a bargain with Weeks to liberate Perry, who, in return, is supposed to take Silver with him to Singapore, far from Madame Yu's influence. Upon liberation, however, Perry leaves the island by himself, abandoning Silver to his well-deserved fate.

At the close of the play, the audience learns that Weeks has obtained work with the World Bank in Washington, and Beth, who earlier claimed that she was pregnant by him but who casually mentions that she is now menstruating, is to go with him. Wendy and Camilla are booked on the next plane to Australia, much to Camilla's distress: She wants to return to her friends and school in Geneva, the only life she has ever known.

Makassar Reef is a dark play enlivened with occasional sparks of humor. The dialogue, as is typical of Buzo, is fast-paced, and the action shifts rapidly from point to point on the set. As noted above, there is a feeling of senselessness about life, an utter disillusionment pervading this play, a pressing-in of the world that is forcefully communicated to the audience. The mood of the play reminds one of post-World War I European theater and film; it is redolent with a feeling of defeat.

The play is noteworthy for its superb characterizations, its trenchant examination of the difficulties people experience in establishing and maintaining intimacy. The stereotyped characters and broad satire of Buzo's early plays have given way to fully rounded characters and subtle irony. At the same time, Buzo has developed the theme of Australia's isolation introduced in *Norm and Ahmed*. In *Makassar Reef*, he stresses Australia's position, geographically and economically, as a Southeast Asian nation. Thus, both stylistically and thematically, *Makassar Reef* gives evidence of Buzo's continuing growth as a dramatist.

Other major works

SCREENPLAY: *Rod*, 1972.

TELEPLAY: *Ned Kelly*, 1970.

Bibliography

Brisbane, Katherine. "Introduction," in *Three Plays by Alexander Buzo*, 1973.

Holloway, Peter, ed. *Contemporary Australian Drama: Perspectives Since 1955*, 1981.

Horler, Ken. "Preface," in *Coralie Lansdowne Says No: A Play by Alexander Buzo*, 1974.

Rees, Leslie. *A History of Australian Drama, Volume II: Australian Drama in the 1970's*, 1978.

Sumner, John, and Richard Wherrett. "Introduction," in Buzo's *Martello Towers*, 1976.

Peter Goslett

GEORGE GORDON, LORD BYRON

Born: London, England; January 22, 1788
Died: Missolonghi, Greece; April 19, 1824

Principal drama

Manfred, pb. 1817, pr. 1834; *Marino Faliero, Doge of Venice*, pr., pb. 1821; *Sardanapalus: A Tragedy*, pb. 1821, pr. 1834; *The Two Foscari: A Tragedy*, pb. 1821, pr. 1837; *Sardanapalus: A Tragedy, The Two Foscari: A Tragedy, Cain: A Mystery*, pb. 1821; *Heaven and Earth*, pb. 1822 (fragment); *Werner: Or, The Inheritance*, pb. 1823, pr. 1830; *The Deformed Transformed*, pb. 1824 (fragment).

Other literary forms

George Gordon, Lord Byron, is considerably better known as a poet than as a dramatist, and the relative importance of the poetry is quickly evident in any review of Byron's literary career. His first book, *Fugitive Pieces,* was printed at his own expense in November of 1806, and though it consisted primarily of sentimental and mildly erotic verse, it also contained hints of the satiric wit that would be so important to Byron's later reputation. The volume is also notable for having inspired the first accusations that Byron lacked poetic chastity; at the urging of some of his friends, he withdrew the book from private circulation and replaced it with the more morally upright *Poems on Various Occasions*, printed in Newark in January of 1807 by John Ridge, who had also printed *Fugitive Pieces.*

In his first attempt at public recognition as a man of letters, Byron published *Hours of Idleness* in June of 1807. The volume shows the obvious influence of a number of Augustan and Romantic poets, but despite its largely derivative nature, it received several favorable early reviews. Fortunately for Byron's development as a poet, however, the praise was not universal, and subsequent critical attacks, notably by Henry Brougham of *The Edinburgh Review*, helped inspire the writing of Byron's first poetic triumph, *English Bards and Scotch Reviewers* (1809). In the tradition of Alexander Pope's *The Dunciad* (1728-1743) but written under the more direct influence of *Baviad* (1794) and *Maeviad* (1795), by William Gifford, *English Bards and Scotch Reviewers* is the earliest significant example of Byron's satiric genius. Three more satiric poems soon followed, but none of these—*Hints from Horace* (1811), *The Curse of Minerva* (1812), and *Waltz: An Apostrophic Hymn* (1813)—attracted as much admiring attention as *English Bards and Scotch Reviewers*.

During this same period, Byron was composing the poem with which he would be most closely associated during his lifetime and which would make him the most lionized literary figure of his day, *Childe Harold's Pilgrimage,*

Cantos I-IV (1812-1818, 1819). The first two cantos of the poem, an imaginative meditation loosely based on two years of travel on the Continent, were published on March 10, 1812, and produced an immediate sensation. In his own words, Byron "awoke one morning and found myself famous." Cantos III and IV were greeted with equal excitement and confirmed the identification of Byron in the popular mind with his poem's gloomy protagonist.

In the meantime, Byron published a series of poetic tales that further exploited the knowledge derived from his Eastern travels and that continued the development of the Byronic hero, the brooding, titanic figure whose prototype within Byron's canon is Childe Harold. These tales include *The Giaour* (1813), *The Bride of Abydos* (1813), *The Corsair* (1814), *Lara* (1814), *Parisina* (1816), and *The Siege of Corinth* (1816). Illustrative of the diversity of Byron's poetic output is the publication, during this same period, of *Hebrew Melodies Ancient and Modern* (1815), short lyrics based largely on passages from the Bible and accompanied by the music of Isaac Nathan. Although Byron lacked the lyric mastery of a number of his extraordinary contemporaries, he produced well-crafted lyrics throughout his literary career, none of which is more admired or more often quoted than the first poem of *Hebrew Melodies Ancient and Modern*, "She Walks in Beauty."

Also published in 1816 was "The Prisoner of Chillon," a dramatic monologue on the theme of human freedom, which Byron was inspired to write after a visit to the castle where François de Bonivard had been imprisoned during the sixteenth century. *The Lament of Tasso* (1817), written during the following year, is a less successful variation on the same theme and, more important, an early manifestation of Byron's fascination with the literature and history of Italy. This fascination is also seen in *The Prophecy of Dante* (1821), "Francesca of Rimini" (inspired by Canto V of Dante's *Inferno*), and the translation of Canto I of Luigi Pulci's *Morgante Maggiore* (1483), which were produced in the years 1819 and 1820.

The importance of Pulci to Byron's poetic career is immeasurable. Through *Whistlecraft* (1817-1818), by John Hookham Frere, Byron became indirectly acquainted with the casual, facetious manner of the *Morgante Maggiore* and adapted the Pulci/Frere style to his own purposes in his immensely successful tale of Venetian dalliance, *Beppo: A Venetian Story*. Written in 1817 and published in 1818, *Beppo* is the direct stylistic precursor of *Don Juan*, Cantos I-XVI (1819-1824, 1826), the seriocomic masterpiece whose composition occupied Byron at irregular intervals throughout the last six years of his life.

Although the final years of Byron's literary career are important primarily for the writing of *Don Juan*, several other of Byron's works deserve passing or prominent mention. *Mazeppa* (1819) is a verse tale in Byron's earlier manner which treats heavy-handedly a theme which the first cantos of *Don Juan* address with an adroit lightness: the disastrous consequences of an illicit love. *The Island* (1823) is a romantic tale inspired by William Bligh's account of the *Bounty* mutiny, a tale that possesses some affinities with the Haidée episode of *Don Juan*. The years from 1821 to 1823 produced three topical satires, *The Blues: A Literary Ecologue* (written in 1821 but first published in *The Liberal* in 1823), *The Vision of Judgment* (1822), and *The Age of Bronze* (1823), the second of which, a devastating response to Robert Southey's obsequious *A Vision of Judgment*, is one of Byron's undoubted masterworks.

Finally, no account of Byron's nondramatic writings would be complete without making reference to his correspondence, among the finest in the English language, which has been given its definitive form in Leslie A. Marchand's multivolume edition, *Byron's Letters and Journals* (1973-1982).

Achievements

In his *The Dramas of Lord Byron: A Critical Study* (1915), Samuel C. Chew, Jr., makes it abundantly clear that Byron was simultaneously fascinated with the theater and contemptuous of the accomplishments of contemporary dramatists. He was frequently to be found in the playhouses, especially during his days as a student and during the period immediately following his Eastern travels, and on at least two occasions, he acted, with considerable success, in amateur theatrical productions. His comments on the stage suggest, however, that he was appalled by the reliance of early nineteenth century playwrights on melodramatic sensationalism and visual spectacle. His letters mention the scarcity of fine plays, and his poetry castigates modern dramatists for their tastelessness. *English Bards and Scotch Reviewers*, for example, calls contemporary drama a "motley sight" and deplores the "degradation of our vaunted stage." It cries out to George Colman and Richard Cumberland to "awake!" and implores Richard Brinsley Sheridan, who had achieved a recent success with *Pizarro: A Tragedy in Five Acts* (pr. 1799), an adaptation of a play by August von Kotzebue, to "Abjure the mummery of the German schools" and instead to "reform the stage." It asks, in indignant mockery, "Shall sapient managers new scenes produce/ From Cherry, Skeffington, and Mother Goose?" and makes sneering reference to the extravagances of Matthew Gregory "Monk" Lewis' *The Castle Spectre* (pr. 1797). It suggests, on the whole, that the once glorious English theater is in woeful decline.

Despite Byron's sense of the theater's decay, or perhaps because of it, evidence exists, in epistolary references to destroyed manuscripts and in a surviving fragment or two of attempted drama, that, as early as 1813-1814, he had ambitions of becoming a playwright, but he had completed nothing for the stage when, in 1815, he was appointed a member of the Drury

Lane Committee of Management. Although he found his committee work "really good fun," it did nothing to improve his opinion of the taste of contemporary dramatists and their audiences, and when he finally finished a dramatic work, it was not intended for popular presentation.

Like the rest of his completed drama, *Manfred* was written during Byron's final, self-imposed exile from England. Begun in Switzerland and finished in Venice, the play is psychosymbolic rather than realistic and may have been inspired, as any number of commentators have pointed out, by Byron's acquaintance with Johann Wolfgang von Goethe's *Faust* (pb. 1808, 1833). Byron appears to have known of Goethe's masterpiece through translated passages in Madame de Staël's *De l'Allemagne* (1810) and through an extensive oral translation by Monk Lewis during a visit to the poet in August of 1816. Considerable controversy has occurred, however, over the extent of *Faust*'s influence on *Manfred*, the consensus now being that *Faust* is simply one of many sources of the play's intricate materials, albeit an important one. Chew makes mention of Chateaubriand's *René* (1802), Goethe's *The Sorrows of Young Werther* (1774), Horace Walpole's *The Castle of Otranto* (1764) and *The Mysterious Mother* (1768), Samuel Taylor Coleridge's *Remorse* (1813), John Robert Maturin's *Bertram: Or, The Castle of St. Aldobrand* (1816), William Beckford's *Vathek* (1782), and Lewis' *The Monk* (1796) as other works with which *Manfred* has affinities and from which borrowings may have occurred. More important, however, *Manfred* is a cathartic projection of Byron's own troubled psyche, an attempt, which some critics have called Promethean rather than Faustian, to cope with the seemingly unconquerable presence of evil in the world, to deal with his frustrated aspirations toward an unattainable ideal, and, on a more mundane level, to come to terms with his confused feelings toward his half sister Augusta. With respect to *Manfred*'s place in theatrical history, Malcolm Kelsall, in *The Byron Journal* (1978), has made an excellent case for grouping Byron's play both with *Faust* and with Henrik Ibsen's *Peer Gynt* (pb. 1867). Kelsall states that "the new kind of stage envisaged" in these plays "is unfettered by any kind of limitation of place, and that assault, which is as much upon the conceived possibilities of stage allusion as upon unity of place, demands of the imagination that it supply constantly shifting visual correlatives for the inner turmoil of the hero's mind."

Byron's next play, *Marino Faliero, Doge of Venice*, is of an entirely different sort and ushers in a period in which Byron attempted to return to classical dramatic principles to produce plays whose themes are essentially political. He sought to counteract the undisciplined bombast and sprawling display of the drama with which he had become familiar in England by making use, without becoming anyone's slavish disciple, of theatrical techniques exploited by the ancient Greeks and Romans, the neoclassical French, and the contemporary Italians, notably Conte Vittorio Alfieri.

Because he did this during a time when his involvement in Italian political intrigue was beginning to develop, Byron's decision to center his play on Marino Faliero, the fourteenth century Doge of Venice who was executed for conspiring to overthrow the oppressive aristocratic class to which he himself belonged, is hardly surprising. He wrote the play as a closet drama—to be read rather than staged—considering its classical regularity an impossible barrier to its popular success, and he was furious when he learned of Drury Lane's intention of producing it. As he summarized the matter in a journal entry of January 12, 1821, how could anything please contemporary English theatergoers which contained "nothing melodramatic—no surprises, no starts, nor trap-doors, nor opportunities 'for tossing of their heads and kicking their heels'—and no *love*—the grand ingredient of a modern play"?

In *Sardanapalus*, Byron extended his experimentation with classical regularity and continued his exploration of political themes while at the same time appealing in two particular ways to popular taste. The play's setting, ancient Nineveh, accorded well with popular interest in Eastern exoticism, an interest that Byron's own Eastern tales had intensified, and the devotion of the slave Myrrha to Nineveh's troubled ruler satisfied the public's desire to witness pure, selfless love.

The Two Foscari, the third of the classically constructed political plays, again makes use of Venice for its setting. Although generally considered to be less successful than the earlier of the Venetian dramas, *The Two Foscari* contains autobiographical elements, embodied in Jacopo Foscari, that give a certain fascination to the play. Jacopo, after a youth of aristocratic gaiety, has been unjustly exiled from his native land. He had been the boon companion of the city's most promising young men, had been admired for his athletic vigor, particularly in swimming, and had drawn the attention of the city's most beautiful young women. Then the powerful had intrigued against him, and his banishment had begun. Byron's contemporaries could hardly have missed the personal significance of this situation or have overlooked the note of defiant anguish in such an exchange as the following:

> GUARD: And can you so much love the soil which hates you?
> JAC. FOS: The soil!—Oh no, it is the seed of the soil
>   Which persecutes me; but my native earth
>   Will take me as a mother to her arms.

Jacopo's persecution is carried out as an act of vengeance by an enemy of the Foscari family, an act which corrupts its perpetrator, but unlike Percy Bysshe Shelley's *The Cenci* (pb. 1819), whose theme is much the same, *The Two Foscari* is not effective theater.

Cain was published as part of a volume that also contained *Sardanapalus* and *The Two Foscari*, but it ought instead to be grouped with *Heaven and*

Earth, which was written at about the same time but whose publication was delayed because of the controversy inspired by *Cain*. In *Cain* and *Heaven and Earth*, Byron returned to the style of *Manfred*, but he derived his materials from biblical lore and from previous literary treatments of these same stories. He called the plays "mysteries," a reference both to the medieval mystery plays and to the mystified response Byron was expecting from the general public. *Cain* is a reinterpretation of the tale of the primal murder, a reinterpretation in which Cain is clearly the superior of his brother Abel and kills his brother, as Chew observes, in an "instinctive assertion of freedom against the limitations of fate." *Heaven and Earth* is based on the passage in Genesis which states that "the sons of God saw the daughters of men that they were fair; and they took them wives of all which they chose." Its plot culminates in the nearly total destruction of the flood, a destruction so general and arbitrary that the play becomes, in Chew's summary, "a subtle attack on the justice of the Most High." The heretical themes of the two works suggest why Murray, during a period of reactionary conservatism, was involved in litigation over the publication of *Cain* and was reluctant to associate himself with *Heaven and Earth*.

Werner was much more in keeping with the literary tastes of the time than Byron's other plays, a fact that can be at least partially explained by its having been begun in 1815, during the period of Byron's closest association with Drury Lane. A surprisingly faithful rendering of "The German's Tale" from Sophia and Harriet Lee's *The Canterbury Tales* (1797-1805), *Werner* centers on the title character and his perfidious son, Ulric, an ambitious villain of the deepest dye. Making no pretense of adhering to the classical unities, the play moves with Gothic ponderousness toward its dark conclusion, in which Ulric is revealed to be the cold-blooded murderer of his own fiancée's father, Stralenheim, the one man who stood between Ulric's family and their return to hereditary wealth and power.

The Deformed Transformed is one of Byron's two dramatic fragments (the other being *Heaven and Earth*). As its prefatory "Advertisement" states, Byron based it on Joshua Pickersgill's novel *The Three Brothers* (1803) and on Goethe's *Faust*. Chew points out the autobiographical significance of Byron's adding lameness to the other deformities from which his central character, Arnold, escapes by dealing with the Devil, but the play's incompleteness and incoherence make it difficult to comment further on Byron's dramatic intention. The fragment was composed in 1822 and published in February of 1824 by John Hunt.

The history of Byron's plays in theatrical production appears largely to be a tale of creative misinterpretation in the twentieth century and commercial adaptation and exploitation in the nineteenth. Margaret Howell's 1974 account in *The Byron Journal* of Charles Kean's June 13, 1853, production of *Sardanapalus* is particularly instructive. Reduced from its full length of 2,835 lines to 1,563, the play was presented almost solely as spectacle and required the approval of the local fire inspectors, because of one of its more impressive effects, before it could be performed. The production seems to have embodied everything that most disgusted Byron about London theater.

Biography

Born in London, England, on January 22, 1788, George Gordon, Lord Byron, who, since birth, suffered from a deformed foot, was the son of Captain John Byron, nicknamed "Mad Jack" because of his wild ways, and the former Catherine Gordon. On his mother's side, the poet claimed descent from James I of Scotland and on his father's, with less certainty, from Ernegis and Radulfus de Burun, estate owners in the days of William the Conqueror. Newstead Abbey, which the poet would inherit at age ten as the sixth Lord Byron, had been granted to Sir John Byron by King Henry VIII, though the title of lord was first held by General John Byron, follower of Charles I and Charles II, the latter of whom is said to have seduced the general's wife. The poet received the title upon the death, in 1798, of his great-uncle, William Byron, nicknamed "the Wicked Lord."

Because the poet's grandfather, Admiral John Byron, himself something of a rake, had disinherited Mad Jack for his even greater irresponsibility and because his father, before his death at age thirty-six, had squandered nearly all the wealth of both of the heiresses he had married, the poet's earliest years were spent in genteel poverty in his mother's native Aberdeen, Scotland, where he attended Aberdeen Grammar School. During these years, he developed his lifelong interests in both athletics and reading and was imbued, under the influence of his nurse, Agnes Gray, and his Presbyterian instructors, with the sense of predestined evil that marked so much of his later life.

After coming into his inheritance in 1798, Byron and his mother moved to Nottinghamshire, the location of Newstead Abbey, in which the young lord proudly took up residence despite the warning of John Hanson, the family attorney, that the abbey was in such disrepair that it ought not to be lived in. During 1799, Byron's clubfoot was incompetently treated by a local quack physician, Dr. Lavender, and Byron was physically and sexually abused by his new nurse, May Gray, events that left the poet with permanent emotional scars. Later in the same year, Byron was taken to London to be treated by a more reputable physician. He was also placed in the Dulwich boarding school of Dr. Glennie, who was to prepare young Byron for admission to Harrow.

Byron entered Harrow in April of 1801, and despite an occasional period of haughty aloofness, he soon became a favorite of his schoolmates. Some of his most intense friendships dated from his Harrow days, friendships the intensity of which was probably an expression, as his biographers have pointed out, of his fundamentally bisexual nature. Nevertheless, the instances of Byron's overt amatory passion, especially early in his life, more often involved women than men. He had become infatuated with a cousin, Mary Duff, perhaps as early as age seven; had written his first love poetry for another cousin, Margaret Parker, at age twelve; and had fallen so deeply in love with Mary Chaworth during a hiatus in Nottinghamshire in 1803 that he at first refused to return to Harrow. Nevertheless, he did return, and after completing his course of studies, he enrolled in Trinity College, Cambridge, during the fall of 1805.

During his Cambridge days, Byron formed romantic attachments with two male friends, won acceptance by the university's liberal intellectual elite, kept a bear in his living quarters, and became thoroughly acquainted with the distractions of London, including the theater. He also assembled his first books of poetry, most notably *Hours of Idleness*, and, almost incidentally, earned a Cambridge master's degree, which was granted in July of 1808. After a short retirement to Newstead Abbey, during which he worked on *English Bards and Scotch Reviewers*, Byron left for London, where he became a member of the House of Lords on March 13, 1809, and where *English Bards and Scotch Reviewers* was anonymously published several days thereafter. The authorship of the scathing satire was soon discovered, and Byron had the satisfaction of being lauded for his poem by Gifford and others before his departure on July 2, 1809, for his Continental tour.

Traveling with John Cam Hobhouse and several retainers, Byron disembarked in Lisbon and made the journey to Seville and later to Cadiz by horseback. The frigate *Hyperion* then took them to Gibraltar, after which they sailed for Malta, where he managed a romantic interlude with the fascinating Mrs. Constance Spencer Smith. The brig *Spider* next delivered them to Patras and Prevesa in Greece, then ruled by the Turks, whence they set out for Janina, capital of the kingdom of the barbarous Ali Pasha, sovereign of western Greece and Albania and prototype of *Don Juan's* piratical Lambro. Ali Pasha's court was located seventy-five miles away, in Tepelene, where Byron arrived on October 19, 1809, and where the colorful ruler flattered the young poet with an audience. The Tepelene adventure was one of the most memorable of Byron's memorable life, and when he returned to Janina, he began *Childe Harold's Pilgrimage* in an attempt to capture the poetic essence of his travels.

Following his perilous return to Patras by way of Missolonghi, where he was to die fifteen years later, Byron journeyed on to Athens, stopping first at Mount Parnassus and writing several stanzas to commemorate the event. In Athens itself, he and Hobhouse lived with the Macri family, whose twelve-year-old Theresa was immortalized by Byron as "the Maid of Athens." The two travelers explored the city and its historic surroundings from Christmas Day, 1809, through March 5, 1810. The sloop *Pylades* then carried them to Smyrna, where they took a side trip to Ephesus, after which they embarked for Constantinople aboard the frigate *Salsette*. On May 3, 1810, during a pause in the voyage, Byron swam the Hellespont from Sestos to Abydos, an accomplishment about which he would never tire of boasting.

Byron's stay in Constantinople brought him further invaluable knowledge of the decadent splendors of the East and also involved him in several petty disputes over matters of protocol, disputes in which Byron's aristocratic arrogance, one of his least attractive traits, came repulsively to the fore. Such matters appear to have been smoothed over, however, by the time Byron left Constantinople on July 14, 1810.

Hobhouse returned directly to England, but Byron spent the next several months in Greece, where he added to his sexual conquests, contracted a venereal disease, saved a young woman from threatened execution, and continued his exploration of a country for whose freedom he was eventually to offer up his life. On April 22, 1811, he sailed from Greece for Malta, where he temporarily renewed his affair with Mrs. Smith, and then returned home to England, stepping ashore on July 14, 1811.

Within a month of his landing, Byron's mother died, an event which caused him considerable distress despite the uneasy relationship that had long existed between them. The year also brought news of the deaths of three of Byron's closest friends. The poet dealt with his grief as best he could and continued preparations for the publication of *Childe Harold's Pilgrimage*, Cantos I and II. He also resumed his place in the House of Lords, delivering his maiden speech on February 27, 1812, an effective denunciation of a bill requiring the execution of frame breakers (workers who violently resisted the mechanization of the weaving trade). Byron delivered two more parliamentary speeches, on April 21, 1812, and June 1, 1813, but the sudden fame that *Childe Harold's Pilgrimage* brought him after its appearance on March 10, 1812, drew his attention away from politics and changed his life forever.

The immediate effect of Byron's renown was that he became the most sought-after guest in London society and the most avidly pursued of handsome bachelors. In particular, Lady Caroline Lamb, despite being already married, descended upon him with extraordinary enthusiasm. She found him "mad—bad—and dangerous to know," a description which might, with equal or greater justice, have been applied to Lady Caroline herself. Their tempestuous liaison occupied much of Byron's attention during the spring and summer of 1812 and involved indiscreet meetings, plans of elopement, threats of suicide, and a great deal of public scandal. Although they parted in September, to Byron's infinite relief, occasional further storms broke out in the months thereafter.

During the years 1812 and 1813, Byron began the series of Oriental tales that would solidify his literary fame and involved himself in affairs with various other women, most peculiarly and most deeply with his half sister, Mrs. Augusta Leigh. He spent much of the summer of 1813 with Augusta, and Elizabeth Medora Leigh, born on April 15, 1814, has always been assumed to be the poet's daughter. Though Byron never publicly acknowledged her, various passages in his letters, especially those to his close confidante, Lady Melbourne, suggest his paternity.

Lady Melbourne's brilliant niece, Annabella Milbanke, also figured prominently in Byron's life during this period. Although he despised "bluestockings" (intellectual women), Byron was unaccountably drawn to Annabella, whose intelligence and wide reading distinguished her so completely from the impulsively romantic Lady Caroline and the passively maternal Augusta. Perhaps as a means of escaping the chaos of his unstable love life, Byron proposed to Milbanke on two occasions, in September of 1812 and again in September of 1813. Unfortunately for both of them, Byron's second proposal was accepted. After various delays, apparently involving visits to Augusta, Byron and Annabella Milbanke were married on January 2, 1815.

The several months of Byron's marriage were marked by continuing literary activity (especially work on the later Oriental tales and on *Hebrew Melodies Ancient and Modern*), by visits to and from Augusta, by Byron's association with the Drury Lane Committee of Management, and by fits of temper, related to the poet's marital and financial problems, which terrified both his wife and his half sister. The birth of the poet's only legitimate child, Augusta Ada Byron, in December of 1815, did nothing to improve the situation, and when mother and daughter left on January 5, 1816, for what was purportedly a temporary visit to Annabella's parents, the marriage was effectively at an end. By March of 1816, a separation had been agreed upon, and Byron affixed his signature to the necessary legal documents on April 21, 1816. A week earlier, he had spoken for the last time to his beloved Augusta, and on April 25, still experiencing financial difficulties and being roundly denounced by the press for his marital problems, Byron left England forever.

Once more on the Continent, Byron visited the Waterloo battlefield, journeyed up the Rhine Valley, crossed into Switzerland, and began looking for accommodations near Lake Geneva. Along the lakeshore, he and his traveling companion, Dr. John Polidori, were approached by Claire Clairmont, who, as a result of an affair earlier in the spring, was pregnant with Byron's child. Clairmont was accompanied by her stepsister, Mary Godwin (later to become Mary Shelley), and Percy Bysshe Shelley. The poets were soon fast friends and by early June had established households very near each other and within two miles of Geneva. Their animated conversations deeply influenced the lives of both poets, with the inspiration of their contact communicating itself, on one particular evening, to two other members of the group. During a gathering at the Villa Diodati, where Byron had taken up residence, a challenge to compose ghost stories resulted in the eventual publication of Dr. Polidori's *The Vampyre* (1819), the first English vampire tale, and Mary Shelley's classic Gothic novel, *Frankenstein* (1818). During the several weeks of his almost daily talks with Shelley, Byron himself wrote "The Prisoner of Chillon" and worked diligently on *Childe Harold's Pilgrimage*, Canto III.

Although Claire had at first kept her relationship with Byron a secret from Mary and Percy, they inevitably became aware of Claire's pregnancy, after which Percy and Claire approached Byron in an attempt to resolve matters. Because Byron did not feel the same affection for Claire that she felt for him, it was decided that they should not live together. It was further decided that the child should be cared for by Byron, with Claire being addressed as its aunt. The child, Allegra Byron, was born in Bath, England, on January 12, 1817, and died in Ravenna, Italy, on April 20, 1822.

John Cam Hobhouse arrived at the Villa Diodati with another of Byron's friends, Scrope Davies, on August 26, 1816, and following the departure for England of the Shelley household on August 29, the two toured the Alps with Byron and Polidori. Another tour, with Hobhouse only, began on September 17. Byron's combined impressions of the Alps helped inspire *Manfred*, whose composition was well advanced when the poet gave up the Villa Diodati on October 5 and journeyed with Hobhouse to Milan.

After a sojourn of less than a month in Milan, during which he met the Italian poet Vincenzo Monti and the French novelist Stendhal, rescued Polidori from an encounter with the local authorities, and came under the surveillance of the Austrian secret police, Byron left with Hobhouse for Venice, where they arrived on or about November 10. Hobhouse soon departed to see other areas of Italy, but Byron, having fallen in love with Venice and with Marianna Segati, his landlord's wife, settled in for an extended stay. In the several months of this first Venetian interlude, he completed *Manfred* and overindulged during the Carnival period.

On April 17, 1817, Byron set out, by way of Arqua, Ferrara, and Florence, for Rome, where Hobhouse showed him the local antiquities. He returned on May 28 with the completed *The Lament of Tasso* and with vivid impressions that would be incorporated in *Childe Harold's Pilgrimage*, Canto IV. Soon thereafter, he and Marianna established themselves at the Villa Foscarini in La Mira, outside Venice. There, Byron formed another liaison, this time with the beautiful Margarita Cogni; worked at what was to become the final canto of *Childe Harold's Pilgrimage*; and began the precursor of *Don Juan*, the charming *Beppo*. Late in 1817, he returned to

Venice with the visiting Hobhouse and, on January 7, 1818, said goodbye to his friend after a last ride together. Byron entrusted Hobhouse with the manuscript of *Childe Harold's Pilgrimage*, Canto IV, whose publication in April brought the poet further literary fame during a time when his personal life had rendered him infamous.

In 1818, Byron's Venetian dissipations reached a level of obsessive frequency that threatened his health. Nevertheless, he continued to write, producing *Mazeppa* and Canto I of *Don Juan* and beginning Canto II. He was showing signs of physical exhaustion by April of 1819, when he became reacquainted with a woman whom he had casually encountered during the previous year. With this woman, the nineteen-year-old Countess Teresa Guiccioli, he was soon involved in one of the most long-lasting and passionate relationships of his life. In June, he followed her to Ravenna, in August to Bologna, and in September back to Venice, where they spent some of their time at Byron's quarters in the Palazzo Mocenigo and longer periods at the Villa Foscarini in La Mira. At the end of the year, when Teresa's husband cajoled her to return to Ravenna, Byron followed again.

The continuation of *Don Juan* had been one of Byron's primary literary projects in 1819, and further material was written in 1820. The year was significant for other reasons, too, including the writing of *Marino Faliero, Doge of Venice*, Byron's increasing entanglement in the revolutionary Carbonari movement, and Teresa's formal separation from Count Guiccioli. When the Carbonari movement collapsed in 1821 and Teresa's family was exiled from Ravenna, Byron accepted Shelley's invitation to move himself, his lover, and her banished relatives to Pisa, where Shelley had taken up residence. Despite this political and personal upheaval, Byron completed three plays during 1821 (*Sardanapalus*, *The Two Foscari*, and *Cain*) and wrote the magnificent *The Vision of Judgment*.

Byron became part of the Pisan Circle in November of 1821, and he remained a resident of the general Pisa area until September of 1822. These months witnessed the writing of much of *Don Juan*, which Byron had previously ceased composing upon the request of Teresa and which he now resumed with her permission. The period also saw the beginnings of Byron's acquaintance with the colorful Edward John Trelawny and the less satisfactory relationship between Byron and the improvident Hunt family. Most sadly, however, these were the months in which Byron's daughter, Allegra, died in a convent at Ravenna and in which Shelley, with Edward Williams, was drowned off the Italian coast. What ultimately drove Byron from Tuscany, however, was the latest banishment of Teresa's family, this time to Genoa, where Byron joined them in late September.

In Genoa, Byron wrote his last Augustan satire, *The Age of Bronze*, and a romantic verse narrative, *The Island*, while continuing *Don Juan*. He also began making serious plans to leave for Greece, where a war of independence had recently broken out. After a traumatic parting with Teresa, he set sail from Italy aboard the *Hercules* in July of 1823, accompanied by Trelawny and Teresa's brother, Pietro Gamba. In early August, they reached Cephalonia, and in late December, they left for Missolonghi, where Byron arrived on January 4, 1824, to be greeted the next day by Prince Alexandros Mavrocordatos, the Greek military leader.

During the previous August, Byron had been taken ill after an excursion to Ithaca. At Missolonghi, on February 15, he became ill once again. His recovery was slow and was hampered by terrible weather, the disunity of the Greek leadership, and their constant demands that he supply them with money. After riding through a rainstorm on April 9, he experienced a relapse. His condition worsened during the following days, and after being bled by his physicians until his strength was gone, he died on April 19, 1824. His remains were returned to England, where they were denied burial in Westminster Abbey. Instead, he was interred on July 16, 1824, in Hucknall Torkard Church, near his ancestral home of Newstead Abbey.

Analysis

Although a number of George Gordon, Lord Byron's, plays are more easily approached as dramatic poetry than as theatrical drama, the political tragedies are readily accessible to dramatic analysis. The following discussion will center on three such works, the classically constructed *Marino Faliero, Doge of Venice* and *Sardanapalus*, and the Gothic, melodramatic *Werner*.

Because it more closely resembles the popular theater of Byron's day, *Werner* will be considered first. Despite being the last play which Byron completed, *Werner* is the earliest of the plays in terms of initial composition, having been begun during the year preceding Byron's final exile from England. Byron's fascination with the story upon which the play is based dates from an even earlier period. As he explains in the play's preface, he had read "The German's Tale" from the Lees' *The Canterbury Tales* at about age fourteen, and it had "made a deep impression upon" him. It "may, indeed, be said to contain the germ of much that" he wrote thereafter, an admission that suggests the importance of the play within the Byron canon, despite the play's obvious literary deficiencies.

The play's title character embodies many of the traits of the Byronic hero and has much in common, too, with Byron's father, "Mad Jack" Byron. As the play begins, Werner is a poverty-stricken wanderer, who, like Mad Jack, has been driven out by his father because of various youthful excesses resulting from the indulgence of his overly passionate nature. Although a marriage that his father considered improvident was the immediate cause of this estrangement, Werner was guilty of other, unstated transgressions before this, transgressions that prepared the way for the final severing of the parental tie. Since then, Werner has been a proud exile, burdened by a sense of personal guilt and too familiar with the weaknesses of human nature to rely on his fellowman for consolation. His love for Josephine, herself an exile, partially sustains him, but his realization that her sufferings are a product of his own foolish actions exacerbates his gloom.

The one embodiment of hope for Werner and Josephine is their son, Ulric, who has been reared by Werner's father, Count Siegendorf, after Werner's banishment. Ulric, however, possesses his father's passions without possessing the sense of honor that would prevent those passions from expressing themselves in hideous crimes. As the play begins, Ulric is missing from his grandfather's court, disturbing rumors are circulating concerning his possible whereabouts, and the nobleman Stralenheim, a distant relation, is poised to usurp the family inheritance in the event of Werner's father's death.

The play's elements of Gothic melodrama are obvious from the opening of the first scene. The play begins at night during a violent thunderstorm, and act 1 is set in "The Hall of a decayed Palace" in a remote section of Silesia. The palace is honeycombed with secret passages, which receive considerable use during the course of the play's action. The Thirty Years' War has just ended, rendering the profession of soldier superfluous and lending glamour to professional thievery, that favorite occupation of many a *Sturm und Drang* hero-villain. Ulric, as we eventually discover, is himself the leader of a band of soldiers turned marauders.

Ulric, another avatar of Byronic heroism, is something of a superman, possessing traits that render him capable of great good and great evil. One of the play's characters, the poor but honorable Gabor, describes him as a man

> Of wonderful endowments:—birth and fortune,
> Youth, strength and beauty, almost superhuman,
> And courage as unrivall'd, were proclaim'd
> His by the public rumour; and his sway,
> Not only over his associates, but
> His judges, was attributed to witchcraft,
> Such was his influence. . . .

Ulric's dual nature expresses itself most clearly in his treatment of the potential usurper, Stralenheim. When Ulric is unaware of Stralenheim's identity, he courageously rescues him from the floodwaters of the River Oder, but later, when he learns that Stralenheim is a threat to his family's wealth and power, he cold-bloodedly murders him. He then conceals his responsibility for the crime and hypocritically questions his father about his possible role in Stralenheim's death. Werner has compromised his honor by stealing gold coins from Stralenheim's room, a crime that suggests the family's moral weakness, but he is incapable of murder. Freed of restraint by one additional generation of moral decay, Ulric, by contrast, is capable of almost anything.

Because of Stralenheim's murder and the nearly simultaneous death of Werner's aged father, Werner becomes Count Siegendorf and Ulric his heir apparent. All goes well for a year, although Werner, troubled by his possession of the tainted gold and by the mysterious circumstances of his rise to power, is plagued by a guilty conscience. There are manifestations of guilt in Ulric's behavior, too, but that strength of will which allowed him to rescue Stralenheim from the flood and later to cut his throat sustains him through subsequent unsavory deeds. He continues his clandestine command of the marauders who threaten the fragile peace and accepts betrothal to the loving and innocent Ida, daughter of the murdered Stralenheim. The ultimate proof of Ulric's reprobate nature occurs when Gabor, who had witnessed the hideous crime and had been unjustly branded as its likely perpetrator, comes forward to accuse Ulric. In an attempt to silence this threat to everything he has striven to accomplish, Ulric sends his minions in pursuit of the innocent man, at the same time uttering a defiant confession of his guilt before the startled Ida, who immediately falls dead in shocked disbelief.

Werner deviates from classical restraint in both content and form. In addition to relying on melodramatic plot devices, *Werner* violates the unities of place and time, a major shift in location and period occurring between acts 3 and 4. *Marino Faliero, Doge of Venice* and *Sardanapalus*, on the other hand, are much more regular, with only slight changes in setting and time taking place from one scene to the next. Like *Werner*, however, both plays center on the consequences of having men of powerful but uncertain character in positions of responsibility.

The tenuous thread on which the plot of *Marino Faliero, Doge of Venice* hangs is the apparent historical fact that the title character, while he was Doge of Venice, conspired against the tyrannous Venetian oligarchy partly because he found their rule unjust and, more important, because they failed to punish one of their number severely enough for a scrawled insult to the Doge's wife. When Faliero discovers that Michel Steno is to receive one month of imprisonment instead of death for an unsavory comment inscribed on the ducal throne, he becomes furious, although his wife, Angiolina, counsels restraint. His rage is motivated by his disgust that the oligarchy, with its facelessly diffused and inflexibly selfish power, refuses, on the one hand, to recognize the rights of the common people and neglects, on the other, to show the deference due superior spirits. His rebelliousness (like Byron's own) is simultaneously an assertion of individual, proud will and a genuine concern for democratic principles. He detests the oppressive rule of the privileged few and joins a conspiracy against them, but he maintains an aristocratic haughtiness among the "common ruffians leagued to ruin states" with whom he throws in his lot.

Ultimately, his joining the conspirators is an expression of that irrepressible, restless pride which he shares with Byron's other heroes. He exhibits not simply the temporal pride of a Coriolanus but also the everlasting, self-assertive pride of a Lucifer. Indeed, his is

> . . . the same sin that overthrew the angels,
> And of all sins most easily besets
> Mortals the nearest to the angelic nature:
> The vile are only vain: the great are proud.

In addition to treating, with considerable complexity, the frequently self-contradictory motivations of the rebel, *Marino Faliero, Doge of Venice* explores the moral ambiguities of instigating violent actions to achieve just ends. Like the French revolutionaries, the Venetian conspirators are about to sweep away the old order in a bath of blood, but one of their number, Bertram, refuses to abandon his humanity and warns an aristocratic friend that his life is in danger. The ironic result of this humane gesture is that the rebellion is discovered and the conspirators themselves, including the proud Doge, are put to death. Victory belongs to those whose ruthlessness wins out over their compassion, and he who would be kind becomes a Judas.

In *Sardanapalus*, this conflict between humanity and harsh political reality is again examined. Sardanapalus is a lover of life whose mercy and whose desire for peace, love, and pleasure bring down a dynasty. As a descendant of Nimrod and the fierce Semiramis, he is expected to conduct the affairs of state by means of bloodshed and unrelenting conquest. Instead, he allies himself with the forces of vitality against those of death and thereby earns a reputation for weakness. He knows the harem and the banquet hall better than the battlefield and is judged effeminate because he prefers the paradisiacal celebration of life to the ruthless bloodletting of war and political persecution. Even when he knows that two of his most powerful subjects, the Chaldean Beleses and the Mede Arbaces, have plotted against him, he refuses to have them killed and thereby opens the way to successful rebellion. After merely banishing the two from Nineveh, he finds himself, during a symbolically appropriate banquet, beset by a usurping army.

Despite his seeming weakness, Sardanapalus, like Byron's other heroes, possesses unquenchable pride and courage. Assuming the weapons of the warrior but refusing to wear full armor, so that his soldiers will recognize and rally to him, he enters battle and temporarily staves off defeat. His lover, Myrrha, a character added to the play, significantly enough, at the suggestion of Teresa Guiccioli, shows an equally fierce courage, as do Sardanapalus' loyal troops, and for a time, victory seems possible. Still, the kingly worshiper of life is troubled in his dreams by the image of the worshiper of death, Semiramis, and there are dark forebodings of approaching catastrophe.

When it finally becomes clear that defeat is inevitable, Sardanapalus expresses regret that the fallen world in which he found himself was unwilling to accept the temporary renewal which he attempted to offer:

> I thought to have made mine inoffensive rule
> An era of sweet peace 'midst bloody annals,
> A green spot amidst desert centuries,
> On which the future would turn back and smile,
> And cultivate, or sigh, when it could not
> Recall Sardanapalus' golden reign.
> I thought to have made my realm a paradise,
> And every moon an epoch of new pleasures.

When the world refuses his great gift, he turns to the only paradisiacal sanctuary available in a universe of spiritual disorder. He unites himself with the one individual who most loves him. He has his last loyal subjects build a funeral pyre, symbolic of his and Myrrha's passion, and the lovers die amid its flames.

Byron's political tragedies are literary explorations of the relationship, in an unregenerate world, of the extraordinary individual to the state. They examine the place of the almost superhumanly proud and passionate man within corporate humanity. They express the fascination with the link between earthly power and individual freedom and fulfillment that manifested itself in Byron's first speech before Parliament and that would lead him, finally, to his death at Missolonghi.

Other major works

POETRY: *Fugitive Pieces*, 1806; *Poems on Various Occasions*, 1807; *Hours of Idleness*, 1807; *Poems Original and Translated*, 1808; *English Bards and Scotch Reviewers*, 1809; *Hints from Horace*, 1811; *Childe Harold's Pilgrimage*, Cantos I-IV, 1812-1818, 1819 (4 cantos published together); *The Curse of Minerva*, 1812; *Waltz: An Apostrophic Hymn*, 1813; *The Giaour*, 1813; *The Bride of Abydos*, 1813; *The Corsair*, 1814; *Ode to Napoleon Buonaparte*, 1814; *Lara*, 1814; *Hebrew Melodies Ancient and Modern*, 1815; *Monody on the Death of the Right Honourable R. B. Sheridan*, 1816; *Parisina*, 1816; *Poems*, 1816; *The Prisoner of Chillon, and Other Poems*, 1816; *The Siege of Corinth*, 1816; *The Lament of Tasso*, 1817; *Beppo: A Venetian Story*, 1818; *Mazeppa*, 1819; *Don Juan*, Cantos I-XVI, 1819-1824, 1826 (16 cantos published together); *The Prophecy of Dante*, 1821; *The Vision of Judgment*, 1822; *The Age of Bronze*, 1823; *The Blues: A Literary Eclogue*, 1823; *The Island*, 1823.

NONFICTION: *Letter to [John Murray] on the Rev. W. L. Bowles' Strictures on the Life and Writings of Pope*, 1821; "A Letter to the Editor of *My Grandmother's Review*," 1822; *The Parliamentary Speeches of Lord Byron*, 1824; *Byron's Letters and Journals*, 1973-1982 (12 volumes; Leslie A. Marchand, editor).

Bibliography

Chew, Samuel C., Jr. *The Dramas of Lord Byron: A Critical Study*, 1915.

Howell, Margaret J. "*Sardanapalus*," in *The Byron Journal*, 1974.

Kelsall, Malcolm. "Goethe, Byron, Ibsen: The Faustian Idea on Stage," in *The Byron Journal*, 1978.

Marchand, Leslie A. *Byron: A Portrait*, 1970.

Taborski, Boleslaw. *Byron and the Theatre*, 1972.

Trueblood, Paul G. *Lord Byron*, 1969, 1977.

Robert H. O'Connor

MRS. SUSANNAH CENTLIVRE

Born: Whaplode(?), England; c. 1667
Died: London, England; December 1, 1723

Principal drama

The Perjur'd Husband: Or, The Adventures of Venice, pr., pb. 1700; *The Beau's Duel: Or, A Soldier for the Ladies*, pr., pb. 1702; *The Stolen Heiress: Or, The Salamanca Doctor Outplotted*, pr. 1702, pb. 1703; *Love's Contrivance: Or, Le Medecin Malgré Lui*, pr., pb. 1703; *The Gamester*, pr., pb. 1705; *The Basset-Table*, pb. 1706, pr. 1905; *Love at a Venture*, pr. 1706(?), pb. 1706; *The Platonick Lady*, pr. 1706, pb. 1707; *The Busie Body*, pr., pb. 1709; *The Man's Bewitch'd: Or, The Devil to Do About Her*, pr., pb. 1709; *A Bickerstaff's Burying: Or, Work for the Upholders*, pr., pb. 1710; *Mar-Plot: Or, The Second Part of the Busie Body*, pr. 1710, pb. 1711; *The Perplex'd Lovers*, pr., pb. 1712; *The Wonder: A Woman Keeps a Secret*, pr., pb. 1714; *The Gotham Election*, pb. 1715; *A Wife Well Manag'd*, pb. 1715, pr. 1724; *The Cruel Gift: Or, The Royal Resentment*, pr. 1716, pb. 1717; *A Bold Stroke for a Wife*, pr., pb. 1718; *The Artifice*, pr., pb. 1722; *The Dynamic Works of the Celebrated Mrs. Centlivre*, 1872 (3 volumes); *The Plays of Susanna Centlivre*, 1982 (3 volumes).

Other literary forms

In addition to her plays, Mrs. Susannah Centlivre published literary letters and some verse celebrating state occasions. None of it, however, has much literary value.

Achievements

From 1700 until her death in 1723, Mrs. Centlivre was probably the most prolific and popular playwright in England. In her first ten years as a professional, she turned out a dozen plays for the stage; in the second half of her career, another seven.

Some of her plays closed after one or two nights, but others became exceptionally popular. *The Busie Body*, *The Wonder*, and *A Bold Stroke for a Wife* were major successes for Mrs. Centlivre, although these pieces had their longest runs after 1750. *The Busie Body*, her most popular play, was mounted at least 475 times between its premiere and 1800. David Garrick, the greatest actor of the century, gained at least part of his fame by his frequent portrayal of Marplot, the good-natured bungler in *The Busie Body*. For the last role of his career, Garrick chose Don Felix, a jealous lover in *The Wonder*. *The Busie Body* and *The Wonder* even survived the doldrums of Victorian theater, becoming repertory pieces on the modern British stage and the American stage.

Mrs. Centlivre never became rich writing plays, but she did achieve some celebrity in literary circles. As a woman playwright, she was something of a novelty; other women published plays, but very few. In her lifetime, Mrs. Centlivre had only two serious female rivals, Mary Manley and Mary Pix. Neither woman wrote so much or so well. Mrs. Centlivre competed with male writers also, becoming a friendly rival to such accomplished dramatists as George Farquhar, Nicholas Rowe, and Sir Richard Steele.

Modern critics generally view Mrs. Centlivre as a competent professional whose plays make great theater, if not great literature.

Biography

The life of "celebrated Mrs. Centlivre," as she is commonly known to stage history, is poorly documented. A Susannah Freeman, born in Lincolnshire, probably to William and Ann Freeman of Whaplode, who had her baptized on November 20, 1669, is thought to have become Mrs. Susannah Centlivre. She was educated at home, but she left in her teens, evidently to escape a stern stepmother. Legend has it that she had some "gay adventures" during her early wanderings. One contemporary of Mrs. Centlivre related that when she left home, she stopped by the side of the road one day to rest, where she was spotted by a passing student from Cambridge University, Anthony Hammond, who—as the story goes—took pity on the fatigued and tearful girl and brought her to his quarters at the university. Disguised as Hammond's cousin Jack, Mrs. Centlivre is said to have studied at the university for two months, after which she left with Hammond's letter of recommendation. The story is probably apocryphal, but it exemplifies the kind of mythology that contemporaries used to explain Mrs. Centlivre's mysterious early years.

Mrs. Centlivre joined a company of strolling players around 1684. By most accounts she was always attractive to men, including, some sources say, a Mr. Fox, who either married her or simply shared the same quarters with her for a while. Fox apparently died, and she seems to have married a Mr. Carroll, an army officer, in 1685. Carroll died within a year and a half from wounds sustained in a duel.

By 1700, Mrs. Centlivre had settled in London, where she began life as a professional playwright. Her early plays were not well received; not until *The Gamester* was produced in 1705 did she have a genuine success.

After three more failures, Mrs. Centlivre enjoyed another success with *The Busie Body*, which, premiering in 1709, became her most popular play ever. Still, the kind of success that she enjoyed with *The Gamester* and *The Busie Body* did not provide an adequate living. For her income, Mrs. Centlivre, like most playwrights, depended on three sources: gifts from patrons of the arts, sales of play copies, and author benefit nights at the theater, in which she would receive all the ticket receipts, less the house's operating expenses. None of these sources was reliable, and there is evidence that between 1700 and 1707 Mrs. Centlivre spent some time as a strolling actor in the provinces, presumably supplementing the income she made from playwriting.

The burden of supporting herself was relieved considerably when, in 1707, she married the man with whom she would live for the rest of her life, Joseph Centlivre. As a cook for the Crown, Joseph could expect to make at least fifty-five pounds per annum, not a negligible income at the time.

After *The Busie Body*, Mrs. Centlivre was never to see another true success. She tried to take advantage of the play's popularity by writing the sequel, *Mar-Plot*; but, like most sequels, it had a short run, lasting only six days during the 1710-1711 season. *The Wonder* in 1714 and *A Bold Stroke for a Wife* in 1718 had respectable runs, but they did not achieve real popularity until after 1750.

Mrs. Centlivre died on December 1, 1723, in her house in London's Buckingham Court, where she had lived the last ten years of her life. She was buried in St. Paul's, Covent Garden.

Analysis

If Mrs. Susannah Centlivre became the most popular playwright of her time, there was good reason for it. As a professional playwright, she wrote to eat, and thus to please. She gave the audience what they wanted, and she gave them plenty of it.

Writing to please the audiences of the early eighteenth century was no easy task. In the preface to *Love's Contrivance*, Mrs. Centlivre complains that "Writing is a kind of Lottery in this fickle Age, and Dependence on the Stage as precarious as the Cast of a Die; the Chance may turn up, and a Man may write to please the Town, but 'tis uncertain, since we see our best Authors sometimes fail." If audiences were notoriously fickle, playwrights were careful also not to anger the moral reformers, who needed only the scantest traces of profanity or bawdy language to brand a play licentious.

Mrs. Centlivre's solution was to write entertaining plays that would offend very few theatergoers and, with any luck, please most of them. Thus, she avoided tough satiric material. Her plays may poke fun, but they rarely abuse; they mock, but rarely malign. In English drama written between 1660 and 1685, so-called Restoration drama, comedy was often savagely satiric—and there was a good stock of comic butts: merchants, Puritans, fops, pedants, coquettes, and old lechers. Mrs. Centlivre adopted many of the comic types of the Restoration stage but treated them with a tolerance uncharacteristic of her models.

Indeed, the stock character is a major component of Mrs. Centlivre's drama and is usually found in formulaic plots, often variations on the boy-gets-girl theme. Mrs. Centlivre created characters not for the ages but for the Friday-afternoon show. She expected that her audience would recognize the character types and take delight in the predictable action, as the greedy merchant loses his money or the resourceful maid wins her beau. Indeed, in a play by Mrs. Centlivre, plot is often preeminent, featuring disguises, chance meetings, lovers' assignations, schemes and counterschemes—all the elements that we would expect from a busy play of intrigue. No Centlivre character ever stops to ponder aloud the ethics of his actions; rather, he pursues his aims until they are either fulfilled or frustrated. Much of Mrs. Centlivre's art, then, depended on giving new life to old characters and old plots, and in this she was very successful.

In *The Gamester*, she wrote a didactic play showing the reformation of a compulsive gambler. The main action concerns Valere, who is in love with Angelica. Angelica returns his love but will not marry him unless he gives up gambling. Valere has another reason to forsake the dice when his father, Sir Thomas Valere, announces that he is tired of paying his son's debts and that he must marry Angelica or lose his inheritance. Thus, Valere asks Angelica's forgiveness one more time, which she bestows, giving him a diamond-studded portrait of herself to seal the bargain.

Predictably, Valere cannot resist the gaming tables even now, and he loses all of his money to a pert young gentleman who turns out to be Angelica disguised in breeches; she has come to verify a rumor that Valere has broken his promise. Having won all of his cash, Angelica convinces him to stake the precious portrait, which she also wins, and she dashes out before he has a chance to win it back.

When Valere goes to Angelica to claim her hand, she demands the portrait as proof of his faith. When he cannot produce it, she reveals it herself, making Valere believe that their relationship is over. Indeed, the situation looks desperate: When Sir Thomas enters the scene and learns what has happened, he disinherits his son. Sir Thomas' severity seems to shock Angelica, though, and she takes Valere back, recognizing, perhaps, her own hand in his downfall. Convinced that the couple will marry, Sir Thomas restores his son's fortune.

In writing *The Gamester*, Mrs. Centlivre was trying to capitalize on the vogue for didactic comedy that developed in the first decade of the eighteenth century. Didactic comedy, in which a character is reformed from vicious ways, never dominated the stage, but professionals such as Colley Cibber, Sir Richard Steele, and Sir John Vanbrugh all wrote plays of this type, with various degrees of success. Steele's *The Lying Lover* (pr. 1703) was a failure, but, as noted above, *The Gamester* enjoyed a successful run. Steele had written a ponderous, preachy play; Mrs. Centlivre wrote something quite different.

Unlike *The Lying Lover*, *The Gamester* does not take itself too seriously. In his play, Steele works in a sermon on the evils of dueling, but Mrs. Centlivre never rails against gambling. Her prime interest is in the gamester, not in gaming itself. By reclaiming a gambler, she gives her play a moral pretext and a handy plot formula. Shocking people into giving up gambling was not her purpose; in fact, as a compulsive gambler, Valere does not have a bad life. He must occasionally avoid his creditors, and his dealings with Angelica and Sir Thomas are sometimes a bit awkward, but, ultimately, his vice causes him relatively little hardship or distress. At the end of the play, he is a bit richer, and he has the girl.

In one sense, Valere's gaming works as Angelica's rival for his attentions. Since Mrs. Centlivre does not portray the life of a gamester as a difficult one, Valere's prime motive in giving up the dice is to win Angelica (and his inheritance). Mrs. Centlivre is, in effect, giving us another version of the boy-gets-girl plot. As in many dramatic versions of this old story, the couple must overcome some difficult elders, represented by Sir Thomas, who threatens disinheritance, and his brother Dorante, a minor character with amorous designs on Angelica.

In keeping with the spirit of the play, Mrs. Centlivre makes neither her characters nor any of their fates very nasty. Perhaps she was worried that her play could be considered immoral if she portrayed vice too graphically. Valere is not Vice incarnate, nor is he even vicious—he simply has a vice, gaming. His habit is like a disease, and the audience is free to hate the disease while sympathizing with Valere himself. The audience forgives him and celebrates his happy end.

In *The Busie Body*, a different kind of play, Mrs. Centlivre produced what some critics have called a romantic intrigue. Sir George Airy, a rich young gentleman, is in love with Miranda, who lives with her amorous old guardian, Sir Francis Gripe. Miranda wants no part of her guardian's romancing, but she is also rather coy with Sir George, whom she does fancy. The situation has a parallel in the plight of Isabinda, who is sequestered by her father, Sir Jealous Traffic. Traffic wants to save his daughter for a Spanish merchant, but Charles, the poor son of Sir Francis, provides some competition. The young lovers do eventually marry, but not before having many of their best-laid plans dashed by ill luck and by the good-natured but witless bungling of Marplot, the "busie body" of the title.

After viewing *The Gamester*, Mrs. Centlivre's audience could conceivably debate whether Valere deserved such good fortune at the end of the play. He does very little to earn it. *The Busie Body* does not pose the same kind of question. The play exhibits plot with a vengeance, and the characters are all familiar types, preventing the audience from taking any of them seriously. Sir Francis and Sir Jealous, for example, are typically stubborn, overbearing fathers who hinder true love by proposing and championing unsuitable matches for their children. In the rebellious lovers of *The Busie Body*, the audience recognizes more stock characters. Miranda is the familiar resourceful woman who seems to control much of the play's action and wins her man as much as he wins her. Miranda does not immediately express her love for Sir George: She keeps him dangling for a while. (The type is coy as well as cunning.) For all of her schemes, though, the resourceful woman is generally a sympathetic character. So, too, is the sequestered maiden, the damsel in distress, of which Isabinda is a prime example. Locking up fair maidens for inevitable rescue was a staple of Spanish romance, but playwrights such as William Wycherley and Mrs. Centlivre put the device to good use on the English stage.

Mrs. Centlivre's rescuers, Sir George and Charles, would also have been familiar to the audience of 1709. As in many comedies with two pairs of lovers, the gentlemen are good friends. Both characters resemble the male half of Restoration comedy's "gay couple." Typically, the gay couple, while trying to outmaneuver scheming elders, engage in battles of wit, man and woman guardedly measuring the depth of each other's affection. Contests of wit were not Mrs. Centlivre's strong point, but there is a sparring match of sorts in the first meeting between Miranda and Sir George.

In Marplot, Mrs. Centlivre presented to her audience a character-type less familiar than the others but still not entirely original. As the well-meaning bungler, Marplot has forebears in John Dryden's Sir Martin in *Sir Martin Mar-All: Or, The Feign'd Innocence* (pr. 1667), for example. Of all the characters in *The Busie Body*, Marplot may be the most attractive. Although his mere presence is ruinous to the plans of the couples, his good heart and feeble wit keep one from really blaming him. In trying to delay Sir Jealous, Marplot succeeds only in confirming the father's suspicions that Charles is in his daughter's bedroom. At one point in the play, Sir George, to escape the eyes of Sir Francis, hides behind the chimney board. The fastidious Sir Francis wants to throw an orange peel in the chimney, so Miranda tells him that she is keeping a monkey there, a monkey that should be released only when the trainer is present. Sir Francis accepts this story and walks off, but Marplot cannot contain his curiosity and reveals George behind the board. Marplot yells out, and Sir George must bolt out of the room to remain undetected by the returning Sir Francis. Perhaps the audience never really becomes emotionally attached to Marplot—after all, he remains a type—but he is fresher than the other characters, charming and amusing.

No character, however, overshadows the action of *The Busie Body*. The play offers virtually a smorgasbord of comic plot devices. Secret meetings between lovers are interrupted by the unseasonable return of parents. Charles dispatches a letter to Isabinda, but the woman servant, Patch, accidentally drops it for Sir Jealous to find. Miranda gets rid of Sir Francis by telling him that he must attend the funeral of Squeezum the Usurer, but her guardian meets Squeezum on the street, hastening his return. There is little suspense—the audience knows that young love will conquer parental tyranny—but great pleasure in seeing the complex plot brought to a satisfactory conclusion.

Mrs. Centlivre's last great success, *A Bold Stroke for a Wife*, is a comedy with some scenes that border on pure farce. The business of the play is to get Colonel Fainwell, a soldier, married to his lover, Ann Lovely, whose dead father has left her the ward of four eccentric guardians: Sir Philip Modelove, an aging fop; Periwinkle, an antiquarian; Tradelove, a stockbroker; and Obadiah Prim, a Quaker. Ann cannot claim her fortune unless she marries a man agreed upon by all four of her guardians—a requirement which, given their radically different dispositions, appears to be impossible to satisfy. The couple could not live on a soldier's wages; thus, Fainwell must find a way to trick all four into accepting him as Ann's match. This he accomplishes through disguise and deception.

Unlike *The Busie Body*, *A Bold Stroke for a Wife* does not give the audience an endless series of comic devices. Fainwell uses one basic tactic throughout the play: impersonation. He appears as a fop to Sir Philip, as a collector of odd facts and curios to Periwinkle, as a Dutch trader to Tradelove, and as a Quaker to Prim. After winning the confidence of each guardian, he uses transparent tricks to gain their consent. For the most part, his ploys run smoothly, although there are some predictable complications. In general, the plot of *A Bold Stroke for a Wife* is not very compelling. We enjoy seeing the guardians duped, but our pleasure comes from the justice, not the methods.

The play works, in part, because some comic butts get their richly deserved rewards. Fops, stockbrokers, antiquarians, and puritans had long been targets of satire when Mrs. Centlivre wrote her play. Rarely, however, had so many types of butts appeared in one play. If tricking one kind of butt was funny, tricking four kinds would be even funnier—the more, the merrier.

The audience laughs because each of the butts, in his own way, is prideful and narrow-minded. Sir Philip affects French dress and the French language and disdains anything associated with his native England. Periwinkle is obsessed with the unauthentic artifacts of ancient history. The prime mover of Tradelove's existence is money, while Prim cares only for parading his piety and condemning the wicked ways of others.

In Restoration comedy, such figures would be abused and ridiculed. In contrast, Mrs. Centlivre does not treat her butts ruthlessly. Refusing to heap scorn upon them, she laughs good-naturedly at their follies and invites us to do the same. She may have realized that there is a bit of Prim and Periwinkle in everyone.

Other major works

POETRY: *The Masquerade*, 1713; *A Poem Humbly Presented to His Most Sacred Majesty George* . . . , 1714; *An Epistle to the King of Sweden from a Lady of Great Britain*, 1715.

Bibliography

Bowyer, John Wilson. *The Celebrated Mrs. Centlivre*, 1952.

Hume, Robert D. *The Development of English Drama in the Late Seventeenth Century*, 1976.

Lock, F. P. *Susannah Centlivre*, 1979.

Mackenzie, John H. "Susan Centlivre," in *Notes and Queries*. CXCVIII (1953), pp. 386-390.

Sutherland, James R. "The Progress of Error: Mrs. Centlivre and the Biographers," in *Review of English Studies*. XVII (1942), pp. 167-182.

Douglas R. Butler

GEORGE CHAPMAN

Born: Hitchin, England; c. 1559
Died: London, England; May 12, 1634

Principal drama

The Blind Beggar of Alexandria, pr. 1596, pb. 1598 (fragment); *An Humourous Day's Mirth*, pr. 1597, pb. 1599; *All Fools*, wr. 1599, pr. 1604, pb. 1605 (also known as *The World Runs on Wheels*); *Sir Giles Goosecap*, pr. c. 1601 or 1603, pb. 1606; *The Gentleman Usher*, pr. c. 1602, pb. 1606; *Bussy d'Ambois*, pr. 1604, pb. 1607; *Monsieur d'Olive*, pr. 1604, pb. 1606; *Eastward Ho!*, pr., pb. 1605 (with John Marston and Ben Jonson); *The Widow's Tears*, pr. c. 1605, pb. 1612; *The Conspiracy and Tragedy of Charles, Duke of Byron*, pr., pb. 1608; *May Day*, pr. c. 1609, pb. 1611; *The Revenge of Bussy d'Ambois*, pr. c. 1610, pb. 1613; *The Masque of the Middle Temple and Lincoln's Inn*, pr. 1613 (masque); *The Wars of Caesar and Pompey*, pr. c. 1613, pb. 1631; *The Ball*, pr. 1632, pb. 1639 (with James Shirley); *Chabot, Admiral of France*, pr. 1635, pb. 1639 (with Shirley).

Other literary forms

George Chapman was a poet and scholar as well as a playwright. His literary career began with the publication of the poem *The Shadow of Night* in 1594 and included the completion of a poem begun by Christopher Marlowe, *Hero and Leander* (1598). Chapman seemed to have been proudest of his achievements as a self-taught scholar. He translated Homer's *Iliad* (part of book 18 appeared in 1598, and the entire work was published in 1611) and *Odyssey* (1614). He also translated the lesser works of Homer (*The Crown of All Homer's Works*, 1624) and Hesiod's *Georgics* (1618). Although a few of Chapman's plays enjoyed popularity into the eighteenth century, he was best known for his translations. His versions of Homer's works were read well into the nineteenth century and influenced John Keats, among others. Chapman regarded his work on Homer as his life's mission and believed that Homer's spirit had visited him and urged him on in his labors; his translation ends with the assertion, "The work that I was born to do, is done."

Achievements

With the exception of *Chabot, Admiral of France*, Chapman's plays were written and first produced over a seventeen-year span, from 1596 to 1613. Chapman regarded himself as a scholar; he wrote plays simply to earn a living. In his own day, his plays enjoyed varying degrees of success, with his comedies and *Bussy d'Ambois* meeting with the greatest public favor. Today, Chapman's plays are seldom performed. They are generally well-written, usually reflect his scholarly interests, and have dialogue that is sometimes difficult to speak. In his own day and in subsequent eras, Chapman's dialogue has been cited as the principal weakness of his plays. The syntax is sometimes so convoluted that actors would have difficulty speaking their lines. On the other hand, the good-natured wit of his best comedies, such as *All Fools*, makes them appealing even to modern audiences. Chapman lived when both William Shakespeare and Ben Jonson were writing some of the best plays written in any language. His plays suffer in comparison with theirs and thus are not performed as often as they might be. Nevertheless, his comedies have their own special qualities that make them interesting apart from the writings of his great contemporaries.

Chapman's dark and brutal tragedies lack the universal appeal of the comedies. They are interesting studies of character and moral issues and make for good reading. They are so seldom performed that one has difficulty ascertaining how they might be received by a modern audience.

Scholars place Chapman among the historically important English playwrights. He is credited with several innovations—such as the comedy of humors—that were later used by Ben Jonson and the Restoration dramatists. In overall achievement, he must rank behind Shakespeare and Jonson, but he might be fairly rated as ahead of his other contemporaries, although many of them, such as John Marston, Francis Beaumont, and John Fletcher, might be his superior in some aspects of drama. Having written in an era of great playwrights and great dramas, Chapman has the distinction of having been an innovator and of having created a style uniquely his own.

Biography

Little is known of George Chapman's life before the publication of *The Shadow of Night*. He was born near Hitchin, a town in rural Herfordshire, England, in about 1559. His parents were Thomas and Joan Chapman; Thomas was wealthy, and Joan was the daughter of George Nodes, who had served Henry VIII. Chapman's older brother, Thomas, inherited nearly all the family estate, and Chapman was in financial straits for most of his adult life.

In about 1574, George Chapman may have attended a university, possibly Oxford. If he did so, he did not attend for long. He eventually joined Sir Ralph Sabler's household and was there until 1583 or 1585. From 1591 to 1592, he served in the battles against Spain in the Low Countries. After returning to England, Chapman fell under the influence of a group of prominent young men that included Christopher Marlowe and was nominally led by Sir Walter Raleigh. Their theories about philosophy and the occult provide much of the substance of Chapman's first poem, *The Shadow of Night*. With the publication of this poem and *Ovid's Banquet of*

Sense (1595), Chapman became a prominent poet, but he remained poor.

Much of Chapman's adult life was marred by periodic imprisonment and battles with creditors. He had bad luck with his patrons, and his plays, even when successful, did not pay him enough to achieve permanent security. In 1600, he was jailed on fraudulent charges of failing to pay his debts. After certain passages of *Eastward Ho!* were perceived as insulting to the king, he was jailed in 1605 along with one of his coauthors, Ben Jonson. Chapman adamantly protested his innocence of intent to mock the king; he and Jonson were eventually released. He was almost imprisoned again in 1608 for some offending scenes in *The Conspiracy and Tragedy of Charles, Duke of Byron*. This play angered the ambassador of France, whose protests resulted in heavy cutting of scenes by censors. In 1612, one of Chapman's few patrons, Prince Henry, died; King James did not fulfill Henry's pledge to support Chapman, and the playwright was again imprisoned for debt. Good fortune seemed his at last when the Earl of Somerset became his patron and he gained favor in the royal court, but the earl was arrested for murder in 1615. Chapman remained loyal to Somerset, who was eventually pardoned (although he was not guilty) and released in 1622. During the intervening years, Chapman had to fight the old legal charges of debt until he was acquitted in 1621.

Chapman's public life was filled with difficulties, but what his private life was like is unclear. Certainly, his financial and legal problems must have clouded his personal relationships, but whether he was married or had a family is unknown. What little is known of his friendships indicates that he was loyal and formed long-lasting bonds. He seems to have been faithful to the memory of Christopher Marlowe; he was loyal to the Earl of Somerset during the nobleman's most difficult moments; and he had a close friendship with Inigo Jones, the Jacobean court's chief architect and designer of sets for masques. His long friendship with Ben Jonson was stormy, particularly because of Jonson's bitter enmity with Jones.

Throughout debts, his imprisonment, and other setbacks, Chapman remained dedicated to an ideal. His life and achievements are colored by his determination to render in English the works of Homer. The classical structures of some of his plays reflect his researches; his studies of the nature of power are informed by his classical readings; his style is influenced by the classics of antiquity. He endured hardship, in part, because of his belief that he had a special purpose in life and because of his belief in the importance of literature.

Analysis

George Chapman's plays are diverse in structure, topic, and style, yet they are united by his interests in learning and learned people, his dismay at the unfairness of human society, and his moral beliefs. Beginning with boisterous and exuberant comedy, moving through satire and tragicomedy, then through violently dynamic tragedies, and ending with philosophical tragedies, Chapman's plays reveal a remarkably coherent ethos and a mastery of poetry and prose that allows for wonderful diversity in the dramas.

The first extant play by Chapman, *The Blind Beggar of Alexandria*, exists only in a truncated version. It was very popular and was often performed, but only its subplot was printed in 1598. Its main plot can be interpolated only from fragments found in the subplot's story of Iris, the blind beggar. It shares with the play that followed it, *An Humourous Day's Mirth*, the distinction of being a comedy of humours—a play in which each of the characters represents an aspect of human nature, such as greed or sloth. Although Ben Jonson's *Every Man in His Humour* (pr. 1598) is sometimes credited with being the first comedy of humours, both of Chapman's plays predate it. Thus, Chapman's first two plays have historical importance as the earliest extant examples of an important late Renaissance form of comedy, although the question of who actually invented the form is problematic. It is a form that remained important for Jonson throughout his career, but one that was abandoned by Chapman after 1602.

Neither *The Blind Beggar of Alexandria* nor *An Humourous Day's Mirth* is important for its artistry. Both are funny, and both have intricate plots typical of much of Chapman's comedy. The first shows his use of classical sources for inspiration, also typical of much of his dramatic writing. *The Blind Beggar of Alexandria* is peopled by Greek characters—King Ptolemy, Aegiale, Cleanthes, Prince Doricles, and others. The elements of Greek comedy, such as magic, are combined with Renaissance themes, such as comedy inspired by social manners. In his later plays, Chapman combines classical and contemporary forms to refresh stock ideas. *An Humourous Day's Mirth* is a weak play overcrowded with superfluous characters and is awkwardly constructed. Its significance for Chapman's later achievements is found in its scholarly heroine Florilla, whose true learning is contrasted with the pretenses of those around her. The assuming by characters of false humors, such as melancholy, in order to appear learned or sensitive, and the gulling of fools are reminiscent of the comedies of Jonson, but the concern for genuine learning, as personified by Florilla, distinguishes Chapman's work. Other playwrights of Chapman's day, including Jonson, mocked false learning and admired true scholarship, but none examines them as consistently as Chapman.

An Humourous Day's Mirth was followed by a minor masterpiece of comedy, *All Fools*. The play is about Rinaldo, a schemer roughly related to the Vice of medieval morality plays and to the intriguing servant of classical drama; Valerio, Rinaldo's friend and favored son of Gostanzo; and Fortunio, Rinaldo's virtuous brother. Around these three young men revolve their fathers, a jealous husband, and the women—Gratiana and

Bellanora—whom Valerio and Fortunio love. The intricate plot of the play is representative of comedies of its day. Rinaldo schemes to dupe various characters, and according to the weaknesses in their personalities, various characters are duped; some, such as Gostanzo, think that they are gulling others even as they are gulled.

The plot of Chapman's *All Fools* comes mainly from Terence's comedy *Heautontimorumenos* (163 B.C.; *The Self-Tormentor)*, although Chapman reworks it into a play that is more Elizabethan than classical in character and colors it with a strong moral point of view not found in Terence's play. Gostanzo is deluded about himself and his son Valerio; he believes himself to be wise and his son to be virtuous when, in fact, he is foolish and his son is a profligate gambler who is heavily in debt. Valerio marries Gratiana but keeps the marriage secret from Gostanzo because she is not wealthy enough for Gostanzo's approval and because he is supposed to be innocent of worldly matters such as male-female relationships. Gostanzo also has a daughter, Bellanora, who loves Fortunio, a modest and virtuous young man who is also not wealthy enough to satisfy Gostanzo. Once, when Valerio, Gratiana, Fortunio, and Rinaldo are together, they see Gostanzo approaching them, and all save Rinaldo flee. Rinaldo tells Gostanzo that Gratiana and Fortunio are secretly married and wish to keep the marriage secret from Fortunio's father, Marc Antonio. Gostanzo believes Rinaldo's story and tells it to Marc Antonio at the first opportunity, even though he had promised to keep the story secret. Under Rinaldo's influence, Gostanzo convinces Marc Antonio that Fortunio is in danger of becoming a dissolute young man and that Valerio might prove to be a good influence on him if Fortunio and Gratiana lived in Gostanzo's home. Thus, without his knowing it, Gostanzo arranges for Valerio and Gratiana to live together and leaves Fortunio free to court Bellanora.

All Fools might remain a funny but unexceptional comedy, but Chapman is enough of an artist to allow his characters to learn, grow, and change. The plot becomes increasingly complex as Gostanzo suspects that Valerio is having a love affair with Fortunio's wife (who is really Valerio's wife), and under Rinaldo's influence, he pretends to Marc Antonio that Gratiana is really Valerio's wife (which she is, but Gostanzo does not know it) and persuades Marc Antonio to take Gratiana into his house and to allow Valerio to visit her. Gostanzo, proud of his wisdom, believes he has gulled Marc Antonio. The plot expands to include Cornelio, a jealous husband, and Gazetta, his wife. Rinaldo tricks Cornelio into believing that Gazetta has a lover, and Cornelio attacks the supposed lover and arranges to divorce his wife. In the meantime, Gostanzo is tricked into giving his blessing to the marriage of Valerio and Gratiana, believing that he is tricking Marc Antonio because he thinks Fortunio is married to Gratiana. Cornelio learns of Rinaldo's deceit and decides to trick Rinaldo and Valerio. He tells Rinaldo that Valerio has finally been arrested for his debts and is held at the Half Moon Tavern. Rinaldo and Gostanzo rush to the tavern and find Valerio gaming and drinking. Gostanzo, learning of his son's profligacy and recognizing the trick that has been played on him, is at first enraged. He discovers that Fortunio and Bellanora have also married and that he is not as clever and wise as he thought. He has acquired enough wisdom to recognize his own limitations, however, and he accepts what has happened. With Cornelio's reconciliation with Gazetta, all parties are reconciled, and *All Fools* ends with its characters happy.

Although the play's ending seems a bit contrived, Gostanzo's growth is believable. His pride was immoral; it helped to drive Valerio and Rinaldo to their deceitful behavior. Rinaldo is also proud; he takes pride in his ability to manipulate Gostanzo, Marc Antonio, and Cornelio. The comeuppance delivered by Cornelio is a necessary lesson for Rinaldo; he, too, can be tricked. Happiness is possible at the end of the play because the characters learn to accept themselves and others as they are; pride and trickery had prevented such acceptance.

All Fools has much charm and much good comedy; its mad plot can still entertain a modern audience. *May Day* also retains the ability to entertain, although it is not as strong a play as *All Fools*. In *May Day*, the schemer is Lodovico; other figures based on classical conventions appear in the play, including Quintiliano, a representative of the *miles gloriosus* (braggart soldier) commonly found in classical comedies. As in *All Fools*, conventions, classical or otherwise, serve as foundations for Chapman's development of complex characterizations and his sophisticated comedy. Like *All Fools*, *May Day* is a comedy of humors; Chapman wrote one more such play, *Sir Giles Goosecap*. Although still amusing, it lacks the spirited activity of its predecessors. By 1602, Chapman was working on a new kind of comedy.

A tragicomedy is a play that has a plot like that of a tragedy but ends like a comedy. It is a genre that allows for much variety in plot and character, and one that can incorporate elements of other genres, such as romantic comedy. Shakespeare's *Measure for Measure* (pr. 1604), for example, could be classified as a tragicomedy because its plot focuses on the possible execution of an innocent man and the potential debauchment of a chaste woman. The potential tragic ending is averted only when the Duke of Vienna reappears as himself. Of Chapman's tragicomedies, *The Gentleman Usher* is notable for its excellent characterizations and variety of action; it does not match Shakespeare's plays for depth of feeling or suspenseful plotting, but it compares well with any Elizabethan comedy in its richness of ideas and events. On the other hand, *Monsieur d'Olive* is a good play but not as well designed as its predecessor. It is notable more for its subplot than for its romantic central plot.

As in *All Fools*, notions of what constitutes virtuous conduct are called into question by *The Gentleman Usher* in the conflict between a father and his son. This time, the father and son both love the same woman. The son, Prince Vincentio, must, like Valerio, hide his intentions and behavior from his father, Duke Alphonso. Like Gostanzo, Alphonso is deluded about his own nature and that of his son. The rivalry of father and son is played out in a plot of treachery and danger. In *All Fools*, the scheming Rinaldo was mostly playful; he did some harm but was not inherently malicious. His counterpart in *The Gentleman Usher* is Medice, who is vengeful, ambitious, and willing to murder to get what he wants.

The malice of Medice is balanced by the pompous foolishness of Bassiolo, usher to Count Lasso, the father of Margaret, who is loved by Alphonso and Vincentio. Bassiolo fancies himself to be a schemer and agrees to be the go-between for Margaret and Vincentio after Vincentio flatters him. The bumbling Bassiolo provides much of the play's laughter, but even in his character, there is an element of menace. While Vincentio has been privately making fun of Bassiolo, he and his friend, Count Strozza, have also mocked Medice. Favorite of Alphonso, and ambitious, the proud Medice is angered by the two men. He graphically shows how the seemingly innocent conniving of Vincentio can be turned into tragedy. Alphonso has arranged for a boar hunt near the home of Count Lasso and Margaret; Strozza joins him in the hunt. Medice arranges for Strozza to be shot by an arrow and Strozza barely lives. This near-tragedy is a prelude to a seemingly complete tragedy. The foolish Bassiolo comes to know that he has been tricked; forced by Vincentio to continue as go-between, he overplays his role, and Alphonso and Medice discover that Vincentio has secretly courted Margaret. Vincentio flees, and Margaret, who has promised herself to Vincentio, covers her face with an ointment that disfigures it horribly; she hopes to repel Alphonso with her hideous looks. Only a doctor, acting as a *deus ex machina*, saves a comic ending by curing her disfigurement after Vincentio has shown that he loves her regardless of her looks. Medice is exiled and the other characters are reconciled.

The characters of *The Gentleman Usher* are well drawn, with the villain Medice comparing well even with the villains of Shakespeare's comedies. The play is full of activity, merriment, and suspense. Its main plot and subplot are well interwoven, and no event is without importance to the play as a whole. *The Gentleman Usher* ranks with *All Fools* as the best of Chapman's comedies and is representative of the best in English comedic traditions.

On the other hand, *Monsieur d'Olive* is more satiric, with its subplot portraying the silliness of courtly ambassadorships. Its comic variety has been admired by such critics as Algernon Charles Swinburne. It, too, might be well received by a modern audience. Chapman would write only one more comedy, *The Widow's Tears*.

Chapman's first tragedies, *Bussy d'Ambois* and *The Conspiracy and Tragedy of Charles, Duke of Byron* (consisting of two mated plays, *The Conspiracy* and *The Tragedy*), feature angry and robust protagonists whose courage is offset by ignorance of human nature and misguided ambition. Both Bussy d'Ambois and the Duke of Byron are betrayed and murdered. Although both plays are good and make for interesting reading, *Bussy d'Ambois* is superior in thematic construction and dramatic structure.

Bussy gains access to the court of Henry III, King of France, through Monsieur, the king's brother. A proud man, Bussy rapidly alienates the venal courtiers surrounding the king. He excites the jealousy of the Duke of Guise by making pleasant conversation with Guise's wife, Eleanor, and he persists even after Guise asks him to stop. Bussy also angers the courtiers Barrisor, l'Anou, and Pyrhot; they duel Bussy and two of Bussy's friends. All are killed save Bussy. Even though his blunt manner of speaking and proud demeanor have resulted in the deaths of five men and jeopardized his own life, Bussy learns little from his experiences. He receives a pardon for the killings from King Henry, who grants the pardon at Monsieur's behest, and he then begins a love affair with Tamyra, the wife of the Count of Montsurry; she is also coveted by Monsieur. The play gains momentum and moves toward a seemingly inevitable conclusion. Bussy becomes the favorite of the king, and Monsieur grows jealous of his status in the court.

A friar acts as go-between for Bussy and Tamyra and in a secret chamber invokes spirits to show them the future. They warn Bussy of the conspiracy of Monsieur, Guise, and Montsurry to murder him. Later, Montsurry stabs and then tortures Tamyra on the rack in order to force her to confess to her affair with Bussy. The friar is exposed as the go-between and is killed. His ghost warns Bussy of danger. Proud, headstrong, and not given to thoughtfulness, Bussy ignores all warnings and is tricked by Montsurry into walking into an ambush. He struggles mightily but is mortally wounded; in a gesture of defiance, he dies while leaning on his sword and speaking forgiveness of those who had betrayed him.

Bussy d'Ambois is one of the most popular of Chapman's plays. Its bloody scenes rival the most awful scenes of the revenge tragedies of the period, and its atmosphere is rank with the corruption and perversity characteristic of the Jacobean theater, but it is superior to most plays of its time in its intellectual themes and fully drawn characters. All of Chapman's tragedies are concerned at least in part with knowledge and the lack of it, especially self-knowledge. None of the characters in *Bussy d'Ambois* truly understands his or her nature, even after that nature is exposed; thus, these characters are unable to control events fully. King Henry cannot save his favorite; Monsieur cannot use Bussy to advantage; the friar cannot save himself; Tamyra cannot save her lover; Montsurry is driven to murder; and Bussy walks into his own death trap. Bussy, like Byron in *The Conspiracy and Tragedy of Charles, Duke of Byron*, is a man of action and forthright in speech and behavior, but he lacks tact and thoughtfulness. Without intellectual substance, he is all bluster and blunder—a killing machine who cannot adequately battle lies, conspiracies, and corruption.

Bussy d'Ambois can be interpreted as an elaborate satire on the Renaissance individualist. Bussy's blunderings are unheroic and even silly. His loud manner of speaking is more offensive and egotistical than it is honest. The notion that he can reshape society is shown to be foolish by his susceptibility to the trickeries of those who are his moral inferiors. The horrible sufferings of his lover and the deaths of his friends are made to seem pointless by his empty gesture of standing and mouthing clichéd forgiveness as he succumbs to treachery he could easily have avoided if he had taken only a moment to think about what he was doing.

Chapman's *The Revenge of Bussy d'Ambois*, *The Wars of Caesar and Pompey*, and *Chabot, Admiral of France* complete his study of character and knowledge and give his dramatic canon a well-rounded wholeness. These tragedies lack the dynamism of Chapman's other plays; they are static and devoted more to contemplation than to action. They make good reading and are moving in their portraits of good, thoughtful men trapped in insane events and corrupt societies.

The Wars of Caesar and Pompey suffers from a corrupt text. It depicts Cato's efforts to save Rome from war and Pompey's downfall: The man of action, Pompey, and the thoughtful man, Cato, both die nobly, with Pompey having learned some wisdom and Cato having learned to act. Their deaths seem futile in terms of Rome's survival, but they both grow into better, more complete men than they were at the play's start.

Clermont d'Ambois of *The Revenge of Bussy d'Ambois* is a thoughtful man like Cato, and he is typical of Chapman's introspective heroes. Scholarly, contemplative, and courageous, Clermont displays the potential weakness of the thoughtful person—he tends to hesitate and to accept evils he might change through well-considered action. A capable fighter, he nevertheless lacks the boldness of his recently murdered brother, Bussy. He does not believe that revenge is a worthy act, but the ghost of his brother exacts from him a promise to avenge his murder. Charlotte, the sister of Clermont and Bussy, shares Bussy's active and thoughtless nature. She exacts from her husband, Baligny, his promise to avenge Bussy's murder, and her foolish and poorly considered actions contrast with Clermont's caution.

Through Baligny, Clermont tries to challenge Montsurry to a duel, but Montsurry is frightened of him and avoids the challenge. Baligny is a malicious man who contrives to make trouble for those around him. He talks his way into King Henry III's confidence by arguing that crimes committed on behalf of a king are justified. The Duke of Guise, who has atoned for his role in Bussy's death, has become Clermont's friend and a powerful

member of the king's court. While behaving in a friendly manner toward
Guise, Baligny encourages King Henry to fear and distrust the duke and
the duke's friend Clermont. The flatteries and lies of Baligny do not sway
Clermont one way or another because of his secure self-knowledge, but
Clermont's insistence on not thinking ill of his brother-in-law makes him
susceptible to trickery. When warned that Baligny has arranged his ambush, Clermont repeats his brother's error and ignores the warning. When
ambushed, Clermont fights with great strength, drives away his attackers,
and flees on foot until exhaustion forces him to stop. Once captured, he is
surprisingly calm and accepting of his fate.

The Duke of Guise persuades King Henry, who often vacillates under
the influence of others, to release Clermont from prison, and Clermont
goes to Guise's house. There, the ghost of Bussy again urges revenge. King
Henry, angered by Guise's defense of Clermont, orders the duke's death.
The king's men murder him as he comes to visit Henry.

Tamyra, wife of Montsurry and once Bussy's lover, helps Clermont enter
Montsurry's house. Inside, his sister Charlotte has been stopped by Bussy's
ghost in her own scheme to kill Montsurry. In a duel, Montsurry fights well
but is slain by Clermont. A short time later, Clermont learns of the death
of his close friend Guise, and in grief, he kills himself.

Clermont is a fine figure. The play is an exploration of his character
and the nature of worldly knowledge and self-knowledge. The focus on
Clermont's character, however, detracts from the action of the play. Some
scenes are set pieces for expositions, and the action scenes come as bursts
in the middle of a contemplative play. Clermont is like Shakespeare's Hamlet in his tendency to think rather than act, and like Hamlet, he is urged
into revenge by a ghost. Unlike Hamlet, he exacts revenge not in an out-
burst forced by events but in a planned duel. In addition, Clermont is a
man who does not worry about fate; although introspective, he does not
waffle in indecision. He does not act because he does not want to act.

Chapman devoted much of his life to the scholarly ideal. His characters
Clermont and Cato reflect the learning and self-understanding that enable
people to know themselves well enough to endure most of life's vicissitudes
with calm and to be impervious to flattery and the dangerous lure of personal ambition. His plays are united by characters such as Florilla, the
knowledgeable heroine of *An Humourous Day's Mirth*, by his themes of
knowledge and ignorance and wisdom and foolishness, by his mastery of
dramatic forms and techniques, and by his humane point of view. The
range of human emotions is covered by his plays, from joy to sorrow and
from laughter to pathos. The plays reflect Chapman's high-minded seriousness about his art and his compassion for humanity. That Chapman is a
good playwright, not a great one, speaks well for the great ones. His plays
will reward those who read them, stage them, or attend them.

Other major works

POETRY: *The Shadow of Night*, 1594; *Ovid's Banquet of Sense*, 1595; *Hero and Leander*, 1598 (a completion of the poem begun by Christopher Marlowe); *The Tears of Peace*, 1609; *Andromeda Liberata*, 1614.

TRANSLATIONS: *Iliad*, 1598, 1609, 1611 (of Homer's *Iliad*); *Odyssey*, 1614 (of Homer's *Odyssey*); *Georgics*, 1618 (of Hesiod's *Georgics*); *The Crown of All Homer's Works*, 1624 (of Homer's lesser-known works).

Bibliography

Grant, Thomas M. *The Comedies of George Chapman: A Study in Development*, 1972.

MacLure, Miller. *George Chapman: A Critical Study*, 1966.

Rees, Ennis. *The Tragedies of George Chapman: Renaissance Ethics in Action*, 1955.

Spivak, Charlotte. *George Chapman*, 1967.

Swinburne, Algernon Charles. "George Chapman," in *The Complete Works, Volume XII*, 1875.

Kirk H. Beetz

COLLEY CIBBER

Born: London, England; November 6, 1671
Died: London, England; December 11, 1757

Principal drama

Love's Last Shift: Or, The Fool in Fashion, pr., pb. 1696; *Woman's Wit: Or, The Lady in Fashion*, pb. 1697, pr. 1699; *The Tragical History of King Richard III*, pr. 1699, pb. 1700 (adaptation of William Shakespeare's play *Richard III*); *Xerxes*, pr., pb. 1699; *Love Makes a Man: Or, The Fop's Fortune*, pr. 1700, pb. 1701; *The School Boy: Or, The Comical Rivals*, pr. 1702, pb. 1707; *She Wou'd and She Wou'd Not: Or, The Kind Imposter*, pr. 1702, pb. 1703; *The Careless Husband*, pr. 1704, pb. 1705; *Perolla and Izadora*, pr. 1705, pb. 1706; *The Comical Lovers*, pr., pb. 1707; *The Double Gallant: Or, The Sick Lady's Cure*, pr., pb. 1707; *The Lady's Last Stake: Or, The Wife's Resentment*, pr. 1707, pb. 1708; *The Rival Fools*, pr., pb. 1709; *The Rival Queens*, pr. 1710, pb. 1729 (burlesque); *Ximena: Or, The Heroic Daughter*, pr. 1712, pb. 1719; *Myrtillo*, pr., pb. 1715 (masque); *Venus and Adonis*, pr., pb. 1715 (masque); *The Non-Juror*, pr. 1717, pb. 1718; *The Refusal: Or, The Ladies' Philosophy*, pr., pb. 1721; *Caesar in Aegypt*, pr. 1724, pb. 1725; *The Provok'd Husband: Or, A Journey to London*, pr., pb. 1728 (completion of Sir John Vanbrugh's play); *Damon and Phillida*, pr., pb. 1729 (ballad opera); *Love in a Riddle*, pr., pb. 1729 (ballad opera); *Papal Tyranny in the Reign of King John*, pr., pb. 1745; *The Lady's Lecture*, 1748.

Other literary forms

Colley Cibber wrote a number of nonfiction works in his later years: *An Apology for the Life of Colley Cibber* (1740), *A Letter from Mr. Cibber to Mr. Pope* (1742), *The Egoist: Or, Colley upon Cibber* (1743), *A Second Letter from Mr. Cibber to Mr. Pope* (1743), *Another Occasional Letter from Mr. Cibber to Mr. Pope* (1744), *The Character and Conduct of Cicero* (1747), and *A Rhapsody upon the Marvellous* (1751). In addition, having been made poet laureate in 1730, he wrote a series of annual New Year's and birthday odes celebrating the virtues of George II.

Achievements

Cibber's reputation rests on his career as an actor, manager, and playwright. As an actor, he was one of the principal comedians of his time, winning fame for his portrayals of a particular character-type, the foppish fool. As one of several actor-managers, he was the reader for Drury Lane and determined which new plays were performed and which were rejected. As a playwright, he wrote a series of successful dramas, including the first

sentimental comedy, *Love's Last Shift*. Today, his plays have chiefly historical interest, but a good half dozen became staples of the theatrical repertory during the eighteenth century. In his autobiography, *An Apology for
the Life of Colley Cibber*, Cibber likened his plays to his children: "I think
we had about a dozen of each sort [that is, children and plays] between us;
of both which Kinds, some dy'd in their Infancy, and near an equal number
of each were alive, when I quitted the Theatre." Cibber's autobiography
provides not only a record of his life but also a theatrical history of London
during the Restoration and early eighteenth century. Today, it is Cibber's
most widely read work.

Biography

Colley Cibber was the son of Jane Colley and Caius Gabriel Cibber, a
master sculptor from Flensburg, Schleswig. Cibber's father had intended
his son for the Church, but Cibber became stagestruck at an early age and
in 1689 joined the Theatre Royal as an unsalaried apprentice. Even though
his early years were not marked by financial success, in 1693, Cibber married Katherine Shore, the daughter of Matthias Shore, who held the post
of Sergeant Trumpet at court.

Discouraged by the poor roles he was assigned, Cibber wrote a play
(*Love's Last Shift*) with a role for himself. Sir Novelty Fashion was not the
main character in the play, but the part gave Cibber a chance to demonstrate his comic abilities. Shortly after the play's premiere in 1696, Sir John
Vanbrugh wrote *The Relapse: Or, Virtue in Danger* as a sequel to *Love's
Last Shift*. Cibber's performance as Lord Foppington (the new title for Sir
Novelty) in Vanbrugh's play confirmed his success in *Love's Last Shift* and
established him as one of the leading comedians of his day. As a playwright
and an actor, Cibber did not limit himself to comedy, but it was in this
genre that he enjoyed his greatest successes. In addition to writing and acting, Cibber became increasingly involved in the administration of Drury
Lane, eventually becoming one of the triumvirate of actor-managers who
ran the company.

The 1720's were marked for Cibber by well-publicized quarrels with
Alexander Pope, Henry Fielding, John Dennis, and Nathaniel Mist.
Cibber's popularity also declined during this decade; there appeared to be
a permanent claque in the audience that disapproved of everything Cibber
did. As reader for Drury Lane, Cibber was the most influential of the
three actor-managers. Many of his problems stemmed from his cavalier
treatment of new works that were submitted to the company for possible
performance.

In 1730, Cibber was named poet laureate. This new post proved a source
of both pleasure and aggravation for Cibber. It gave him an entry into the
highest levels of society but also made him the target of new volleys of ridi-

cule, since he was not a skilled poet.

In 1733, Cibber retired from the stage, but he continued to make guest appearances until 1745, when his play *Papal Tyranny in the Reign of King John* was presented, with the author playing Cardinal Pandulph. Neither the play nor Cibber's performance was well received; it marked his last appearance on the stage.

In 1740, his autobiography appeared and became an immediate success, quickly going through several editions. In 1743, Pope immortalized Cibber as the King of the Dunces in *The Dunciad* (1728-1743), thus bringing to a head their long-standing feud. Despite the attacks by Pope and other men of letters, Cibber enjoyed his final years, for he had achieved the status of a celebrity and was accorded preferential treatment by the finest families of England.

Analysis

As the reader for Drury Lane, Colley Cibber was widely hated for his many rejections of plays on the basis of their lack of theatricality. According to Richard Hindry Barker in *Mr. Cibber of Drury Lane* (1939), for Cibber, theatricality meant "effective situations, plenty of opportunities for stage business, good acting parts suitable for [Robert] Wilks, [Barton] Booth, Mrs. [Anne] Oldfield, and himself." These criteria are surely the outstanding characteristics of his own dramas. He knew what worked on the stage, and he fashioned his plays accordingly.

Today, Cibber is remembered as the creator of the first eighteenth century sentimental comedy; this accomplishment can best be understood in terms of the theatricality of his plays. Cibber did not set out to write a new kind of comedy. Rather, he set out to write a play that would show off the skills of his actors and that would leave his audience pleased and satisfied at the end of the evening. In his first play, he discovered a number of formulas that worked well on the stage. In a Cibber comedy, there are two plots involving a series of deceptions that lead up to discovery scenes in acts 4 and 5, in which the complications of the evening are resolved in a moral, decorous way. Usually, a leading character in the main plot comes to recognize that he has been living according to a false set of values. When he sees the errors of his ways, the problems of the evening are resolved. What makes Cibber a less than compelling dramatist is that this reversal usually does not grow out of characterization. Cibber's heroes and heroines perform what F. W. Bateson in *English Comic Drama, 1700-1750* (1929) calls a "psychological *volte-face*" in act 5, brought about by manipulations in the plot rather than by a process of self-discovery. The action in the secondary plot usually resembles the action in the main plot, but it does not depend on a character's sudden transformation for its resolution.

Cibber's plays are well crafted. No matter how complicated the plots become, they are always easy to follow, all conflicts being neatly resolved by the end of the performance. Cibber gave his audiences the satisfaction of seeing virtue rewarded and lovers correctly matched. His characters are, by and large, stock figures taken from the world of the Restoration comedy of manners. Many of the situations and plot complications also are part of the stock-in-trade of the Restoration stage. Nevertheless, his plays do represent a quite significant departure from the dramatic world of William Wycherley, Sir George Etherege, and William Congreve, in whose plays the endings are rarely so neat and uncomplicated.

Love's Last Shift was Cibber's first play and immediately established him as an important playwright. The main plot involves the reconciliation of a debauchee with the wife he had abandoned eight years before: Loveless "grew weary of his Wife in six Months; left her, and the Town, for Debts he did not care to pay; and having spent the last part of his Estate beyond Sea, returns to *England* in a very mean Condition." He thinks his wife Amanda is dead, but she in fact is alive, having remained faithful to him and come into an estate of her own with the death of a rich uncle. Amanda is not the witty heroine of Restoration comedy but a precursor of the noble heroine of eighteenth century drama, a model of fidelity and moral strength as she sets herself an all but impossible task:

> Oh! to reclaim the Man I'm bound by Heaven to Love, to expose the Folly of a roving Mind, in pleasing him with what he seem'd to loath, were such a sweet Revenge for slighted Love, so vast a Triumph of rewarded Constancy, as might persuade the looser part of Womankind ev'n to forsake themselves, and fall in Love with Virtue.

Loveless is a more familiar figure from the world of Restoration comedy, a rake who has lived according to a delusion of his sex and class about marriage: "an affectation of being fashionably Vicious, than any reasonable Dislike he cou'd either find in" his wife's "Mind or Person." Amanda, who has been altered (but not for the worse) by smallpox since Loveless last saw her, is persuaded by Young Worthy to trick her husband into her bed. This plot involves two transformation scenes. In act 4, the audience has the titillating experience of seeing the apparently virtuous Amanda abandon herself to the pleasures of "a lawless Love: I own my self a Libertine, a mortal Foe to that dull Thing call'd Virtue, that mere Disease of sickly Nature." In act 5, when Loveless discovers the mistake he has made, he admits the errors of his ways and returns to his faithful wife, a scene which reportedly brought tears to the eyes of the first-night audience.

These characters are one-dimensional figures committed to particular moral points of view, but the clash between these opposing views gives their scenes dramatic tension. Cibber also managed to leaven their scenes with laughter by introducing a subplot involving Loveless' servant Snap and Amanda's maid. Snap is placed under a table throughout Loveless' assignation with Amanda. After Loveless and Amanda retire, Snap sneaks up on Amanda's maid, who is listening at her mistress' door, and begins to take advantage of her. When she gets a chance, the maid tricks him into falling into the cellar, but Snap pulls her down with him and they spend the night together. Their brief scenes form an appropriate low-comedy contrast to the more serious affairs of their master and mistress.

The secondary plot ostensibly involves the correct mating of the Worthy brothers. Young Worthy loves Narcissa, who is betrothed to Elder Worthy, who loves Hillaria, Narcissa's cousin. At the end of the play, the couples are correctly matched, but Cibber's working out of this plot was perfunctory, since his real interest in this part of the play was Sir Novelty Fashion, the role which helped to establish him as an actor. One might expect Sir Novelty, a stock figure from Restoration drama modeled after Sir Fopling Flutter in Etherege's *The Man of Mode* (pr. 1676), to function as a possible rival for the hands of Narcissa and Hillaria, but he is so obviously a fool that no one, save himself, takes him seriously. Rather than using Sir Novelty to add complications to the secondary plot, Cibber used the plot as an occasion to display Sir Novelty. As a prank, the four young lovers lure Sir Novelty to St. James' Park with the promise of a rendezvous with Narcissa, whom he assumes must be enamored of his charms. Instead, he meets Mrs. Flareit, a used mistress he wants to get rid of. The scene, like so many of Cibber's big comic scenes, is filled with physical action. At its climax, the emotional Mrs. Flareit attempts to run Sir Novelty through with a sword. Occurring at the beginning of act 4, this scene with its broad humor balances the almost melodramatic meeting between Loveless and Amanda at the end of the act. In addition, the scenes thematically resemble each other, since both involve tricks played on male characters who are overly concerned with following the false dictates of fashion. Unlike Loveless, Sir Novelty experiences no moral reformation. He is simply exposed as the fool he is, to the general amusement of all.

In *The Careless Husband*, written eight years later, Cibber used more artfully many of the elements that had worked so well in *Love's Last Shift*. Sir Novelty reappears as Sir Foppington, but now he furthers the plot. He is still a fantastic fool, but not so ludicrous that he cannot make a devoted lover jealous when he ogles the lover's mistress. The double plot once again involves a similar situation played out with two couples, but here the characters in both plots are from the same genteel level of society and interact with one another. In the main plot, Sir Charles Easy is married to a faithful woman who sincerely loves him. Only at the end of the play does he learn to value her devotion and cast off the conventional role of jaded husband who must look outside his home for pleasure. In the secondary plot, Lady Betty Modish is pursued by a faithful suitor, Lord Morelove, who sincerely loves her. Only at the end of the play is she able to come to grips with her true feelings for him and to cast off her conventional role of the desirable beauty who delights in exercising her power over men and in keeping them on a string.

These characters neatly complement one another. Lady Easy is a model of virtue. Even when she discovers her husband sleeping with her maid, she suppresses her anger and thinks instead of his needs by placing a scarf "gently over his head" so he will not catch cold. Her only concern is that he should not wake and be irritated: "And if he should wake offended at my too-busy care, let my heart-breaking patience, duty, and my fond affection plead my pardon." Lady Betty Modish is a flirt. She cannot resist engaging in battle with the opposite sex and is satisfied with nothing less than victory: "Let me but live to see him once more within my power, and I'll forgive the rest of fortune." Sir Charles Easy is a man of the world, careless in his affairs, weary of the complicated games lovers play: "I am of late grown so very lazy in my pleasures that I had rather lose a woman than go through the plague and trouble of having or keeping her." Lord Morelove is so timid that he would never even attempt such an affair: "The shame or scandal of a repulse always made me afraid of attempting a woman of condition."

The reconciliations in act 5 are better prepared for here than in *Love's Last Shift*. Sir Charles Easy and Lady Betty Modish may not be in touch with their true feelings, but the audience is well aware of them. In this context Lady Easy is extremely useful. To a modern reader, she may appear impossibly prim and virtuous, but she is aware of the true feelings of Sir Charles and Lady Betty, and she helps expose what the characters themselves do not know. Here, for example, Lady Easy probes the feelings of Lady Betty:

> LADY BETTY MODISH: But still, to marry before one's heartily in love—
> LADY EASY: Is not half so formidable a calamity. But if I have any eyes, my dear, you'll run no great hazard of that in venturing upon my Lord Morelove. You don't know, perhaps, that within this half hour the tone of your voice is strangely softened to him, ha! ha! ha! ha!

At the end, the reader does not feel that the reconciliations have been imposed by the law of happy endings; they are rather the natural consequence of character in action.

Cibber's last successful play, *The Provok'd Husband*, was presented twenty-four years after *The Careless Husband*. Like so many of Cibber's works, it is not a completely original play. In this instance, Cibber revised an unfinished play which came into his hands after the death of its author, Sir John Vanbrugh. The changes Cibber made give a good indication of his theatrical interests. Vanbrugh's play consisted of two plots and was entitled *A Journey to London*. The main plot involved a well-to-do family from the country, the Headpieces, who come to London only to fall easy victims to the lures of the big city. The secondary plot involved the battling Loverules, who fight over Lady Loverule's extravagances. Peter Dixon suggests in his edition of the play that if Vanbrugh had finished the work, the Loverule plot would have issued "in an angry separation, without hope of reconciliation, but also without the possibility of divorce." Cibber, who had a reputation as the dramatist of genteel society, reversed the importance of the two plots. The disputes between the Townlys (the new name for the Loverules) became the primary plot, while the misadventures of the Wrongheads (the new name for the Headpieces) became the secondary plot. In act 5, Cibber provided a moral conclusion with the reconciliation of the Townlys.

The theme of a wife's financial excesses dominates the Townly plot. Lady Townly is addicted to gambling. Her fault is not simply a matter of extravagant expenditures, for she virtually abandons her husband for the pleasures of the hazard table, associating with the least reputable people in polite society and sleeping until five in the afternoon. In act 5, however, Lady Townly reforms when she is threatened with the possibility of being cut off from her husband's wealth and her position as his wife. Her reformation is as unprepared for as Loveless' in *Love's Last Shift*. Both characters renounce their wicked ways after having spent a whole play demonstrating how committed they are to their profligate habits. In her recantation, Lady Townly sounds suspiciously like another Cibber character, Lady Betty Modish in *The Careless Husband*. Both ladies are great beauties who use their allure to gain power over men. Not surprisingly, both of these parts were written for Cibber's favorite actress, Anne Oldfield.

The secondary plot is also dominated by a conflict between spouses. Lady Wronghead quickly learns the main vice of the married lady in town—to spend money. She starts with knickknacks and fripperies, since "the greatest distinction of a fine lady in this town is in the variety of pretty things that she has no occasion for," but soon moves on to the pleasures of the hazard table, to which she is introduced by Lady Townly. At the end of the play, there is no recantation scene for Lady Wronghead. Rather, she is whisked back to the country, where she belongs and where she will do herself and others no harm. The Wrongheads, like Sir Novelty Fashion, exist to amuse the audience; moral reform is not possible for them.

In this late comedy, Cibber once more manipulated the character-types and situations with which he had worked for thirty years. Cibber's career as a dramatist does not reveal growth; rather, it reveals an early mastery of the requirements of the stage which sustained him for the rest of his career and made him the most important writer of comedies in the early eighteenth century.

Other major works

NONFICTION: *An Apology for the Life of Colley Cibber*, 1740; *A Letter from Mr. Cibber to Mr. Pope*, 1742; *The Egoist: Or, Colley upon Cibber*, 1743; *A Second Letter from Mr. Cibber to Mr. Pope*, 1743; *Another Occasional Letter from Mr. Cibber to Mr. Pope*, 1744; *The Character and Conduct of Cicero*, 1747; *A Rhapsody upon the Marvellous*, 1751.

Bibliography

Barker, Richard Hindry. *Mr. Cibber of Drury Lane*, 1939.
Bateson, F. W. *English Comic Drama, 1700-1750*, 1929.
Krutch, Joseph Wood. *Comedy and Conscience After the Restoration*, 1924.

Edward V. Geist

AUSTIN CLARKE

Born: Dublin, Ireland; May 9, 1896
Died: Dublin, Ireland; March 19, 1974

Principal drama

The Son of Learning, pr., pb. 1927 (as *The Hunger Demon*, pr. 1930); *The Flame*, pb. 1930, pr. 1932; *Sister Eucharia*, pr., pb. 1939; *Black Fast*, pb. 1941, pr. 1942; *As the Crow Flies*, pr. 1942 (radio play), pb. 1943, pr. 1948 (staged); *The Kiss*, pr. 1942, pb. 1944; *The Plot Is Ready*, pr. 1943, pb. 1944; *The Viscount of Blarney*, pr., pb. 1944; *The Second Kiss*, pr., pb. 1946; *The Plot Succeeds*, pr., pb. 1950; *The Moment Next to Nothing*, pr., pb. 1953; *Collected Plays*, pb. 1963; *The Student from Salamanca*, pr. 1966, pb. 1968; *Two Interludes Adapted from Cervantes: "The Student from Salamanca" and "The Silent Lover,"* pb. 1968; *The Impuritans: A Play in One Act Freely Adapted from the Short Story "Young Goodman Brown" by Nathaniel Hawthorne*, pb. 1972; *The Visitation*, pb. 1974; *The Third Kiss*, pb. 1976; *Liberty Lane*, pb. 1978.

Other literary forms

Austin Clarke was most prolific as a poet; all of his dramatic writings are also in verse form. Between 1917, when his first major poem, the narrative epic *The Vengeance of Fionn*, was issued by Maunsel in Dublin and London, and 1974, when his *Collected Poems* appeared just before his death, Clarke published numerous books of nondramatic verse as well as many individual poems. *Selected Poems*, edited and introduced by Thomas Kinsella, was published posthumously in 1976.

In addition to his dramatic verse, Clarke wrote in a variety of poetic genres—narrative epic poems, satires and epigrams, religious poems, confessional and meditative works, and erotic and love poetry. He also translated poems from the Gaelic. The subjects of his poetry—though diverse in some ways—are all related to aspects of Irish life and Irish culture, past and present.

Clarke wrote three novels, *The Bright Temptation* (1932), *The Singing Men at Cashel* (1936), and *The Sun Dances at Easter* (1952). Although these works are in the form of prose romance, full of adventure and fantasy, they also express Clarke's preoccupation with the problems of the development of the individual within the limits imposed by society, specifically Irish society. All three novels were banned at publication by the Irish Free State government. *The Bright Temptation* was reissued in 1973, but copies of Clarke's other two novels have virtually disappeared.

Besides poetry and novels, Clarke produced three book-length memoirs: *First Visit to England and Other Memories* (1945), *Twice Round the Black*

Church: Early Memories of Ireland and England (1962), and *A Penny in the Clouds: More Memories of Ireland and England* (1968). These books offer important insight into Clarke's development as a major writer in twentieth century Ireland.

Finally, Clarke was a prolific journalist, a frequent contributor of essays, reviews, and criticism to several major publications: *The Daily News and Leader* (London), which later became *The News Chronicle*; *The Spectator*; and *The Irish Times*. Between 1940 and 1973, he contributed more than a thousand articles on both narrowly literary as well as wide-ranging non-literary topics to *The Irish Times*. Clarke also wrote longer prose pieces for *The Dublin Magazine* and *The Bell*.

Achievements

In the judgment of many critics of Irish literature, Austin Clarke was the most important of the poets of the generation of Irish writers after William Butler Yeats. As a poet, Clarke's achievements are impressive. He wrote almost exclusively of Irish themes, myth, tradition, and history, and his own experience of Irish life and culture. Indeed, he has been called the "arch poet of Dublin," and his commitment to Gaelic poetic forms and pros-ody—assonantal patterns, vowel rhymes, tonic words—helped revise and preserve that poetic tradition.

Clarke was also a significant force in the revival of verse drama in Ire-land. In 1941, partly as a vehicle for performance of his own dramatic writings, Clarke, with Robert Farren, founded the Dublin Verse-Speaking Society, which performed on Radio Éireann and at the Abbey Theatre. In 1944, he and Farren founded the Lyric Theatre Company, which presented plays in verse form at the Abbey until the disastrous fire there in 1951.

Austin Clarke was a prolific man of letters, publishing a large amount of nonfiction and criticism for more than four decades in such respected out-lets as *The Bell*, *The Dublin Magazine*, and *The Irish Times*. Clarke's founding of a private small press, the Bridge Press, inspired other Irish writers to found small presses of their own that were later influential in the resurgence of Irish writing in the 1960's and 1970's. For thirteen years, Clarke presented a weekly broadcast on Radio Éireann on Irish poetry. He was president of the Irish branch of the International Association of Poets, Playwrights, Editors, Essayists and Novelists (PEN) for six years, and in 1952, he became president of the Irish Academy of Letters.

Clarke received many awards and prizes in recognition of his achieve-ments as a writer. For his early lyric poetry, he was honored with the National Award for Poetry at the Tailteann Games in 1928. Later in life, Clarke was recognized and honored by the Arts Council of Ireland, Irish PEN, the Irish Academy of Letters, and the American Irish Federation. He was nominated by the Irish PEN for the Nobel Prize.

In 1966, on the occasion of his seventieth birthday, Clarke was presented with a festschrift containing poems and tributes by major Irish literary figures. A special issue of the *Irish University Review* was devoted to Clarke shortly before his death in 1974.

Austin Clarke's commitment to a literature that spoke most directly to the Irish themselves, within Irish literary and social traditions, about Irish themes, issues, and conflicts, has exerted unfortunate limitations on his general appeal, despite the fact that much of his work ultimately transcends its Irish context to deal with universals in human experience. The increasing critical focus on Clarke's works may help extend his reputation beyond the confines of Ireland.

Biography

Augustine Joseph Clarke was born in Dublin, Ireland, on May 9, 1896. His parents, Augustine Clarke and Ellen Patten Browne Clarke, produced twelve children; three daughters and one son, Austin, survived. The young Clarke was educated at Belvedere College (1903-1912) and then at University College of the National University of Ireland on a three-year scholarship of forty pounds a year.

At University College, Clarke studied with such prominent figures in Irish literary life as Douglas Hyde and Thomas MacDonagh, and he read Yeats, George Russell (Æ), George Moore, and other English and Anglo-Irish writers. Clarke began to immerse himself in Irish culture and the Celtic Twilight and to explore the literary movements of the time.

Clarke received his bachelor of arts degree with first class honors in English language and literature in 1916, the year of the Easter Rising, and the next year, his master of arts degree, again with first class honors in English. He was then appointed assistant lecturer in English at University College, to replace his teacher, MacDonagh, who had been executed by the British after the Easter Rising.

Clarke published his first significant poem, *The Vengeance of Fionn*, an epic in the Irish mythic tradition, in 1917. The poem was much praised and Clarke was hailed as a "new Yeats." For the next several years, Clarke devoted himself to the study of Gaelic prosody and Irish myth and folklore. In 1920, Clarke married for the first time, but the marriage was to last only ten days. He married again in 1930. In 1921, he was appointed assistant examiner in matriculation, National University of Ireland, a post he held until 1970.

By the mid-1920's, Clarke had shifted his attention away from early Irish themes and had turned instead to the Celtic-Romanesque medieval period as a source of poetic inspiration. The poems in Clarke's *Pilgrimage and Other Poems* (1929) deal with themes from this period and illustrate his commitment to Gaelic prosody.

In 1927, Clarke completed his first verse drama, *The Son of Learning*, and saw it produced at the Cambridge Festival Theatre in October of that year. Between 1922 and 1937, Clarke lived in England. During this period of "exile," he wrote several more verse plays. In 1932, Clarke's first novel, *The Bright Temptation*, was banned by the Irish Free State government; that same year, Clarke was made a member of the Irish Academy of Letters at the invitation of Yeats and George Bernard Shaw.

Between 1933 and 1937, Clarke served as a judge for the annual Oxford Festival of Spoken Poetry. In 1936, when he turned forty, his *The Collected Poems of Austin Clarke* was published with an introduction by Padraic Colum, and his second novel, *The Singing Men at Cashel*, was banned in Ireland.

In 1937, Clarke returned to take up permanent residence in Ireland and to become engaged in all aspects of Irish literary life. Clarke's next book of verse, *Night and Morning* (1938), marked another turn in his poetic career, from medieval Irish traditions to more complex themes dealing with the struggle between the individual conscience and constituted authority, between personal faith and belief and the Catholic Church in Ireland.

Though he would produce no more poetry for many years, Clarke engaged in a variety of literary activities during the time of his poetic silence. He began to offer literary broadcasts on Radio Éireann; he made regular contributions to newspapers and literary magazines; he set up his own private press, the Bridge Press; he held regular literary evenings at home on Sundays; he established the Dublin Verse-Speaking Society and the Lyric Theatre Company in cooperation with Robert Farren; and he worked with dramatic productions by these groups. During this period, Clarke also continued to write verse plays, and he completed his third novel, *The Sun Dances at Easter*, in 1952.

In 1955, Clarke published *Ancient Lights: Poems and Satires*, his first book of verse in nearly two decades. After a period of ill health, Clarke published his *Later Poems* (1961), a volume that helped establish his reputation as a modern Irish poet. This was followed in 1963 by the publication of his *Collected Plays*, which contained all the plays he had written up to that time.

In 1964, for *Flight to Africa and Other Poems* (1963), Clarke won the Denis Devlin Memorial Award for Poetry from the Arts Council of Ireland. Like the best of his later poetry, the poems in *Flight to Africa and Other Poems* depart from the themes in his earlier works, dealing with issues of universal significance and exhibiting a more mature style.

The next year, Clarke was awarded a prize by the Arts Council of Britain. In 1966, an honorary degree was conferred on him by Trinity College. During the 1960's, Clarke published two memoirs, *Twice Round the Black Church* and *A Penny in the Clouds*.

In the closing years of his impressive career, Clarke was awarded the Irish Academy of Letters' highest award for literature, the Gregory Medal. He also received the American Irish Foundation's Literary Award. In 1972, Irish PEN nominated him for the Nobel Prize.

Clarke died in 1974, only a few months after the publication of his *Collected Poems*. Several of his plays were published posthumously, and a volume of his verse, *Selected Poems*, edited by Thomas Kinsella, appeared in 1976.

Analysis

Austin Clarke began his literary career as a poet. His first published works were several simple poems that appeared in 1916 and 1917 in a Dublin weekly, *New Ireland*. His first significant published poem was *The Vengeance of Fionn*. This epic poem and the other poems Clarke wrote early in his career drew heavily on Irish myth and the legends of pre-Christian Ireland. During the 1920's, Clarke turned from these themes to medieval Ireland and the monastic tradition as a source of poetic inspiration. In the 1930's, he abandoned these influences to write what could be called confessional poetry, particularly on subjects concerning the conflict between man's intellect and the limits imposed by religious dogma. His own Catholic upbringing and subsequent difficulties with the Irish Catholic Church served as an important source of inspiration during this period in his poetic career.

After a self-imposed exile in England that began in 1922, Clarke returned to Ireland in 1937. Between 1937 and 1955, there was a long silence in Clarke's poetic output. Instead, he turned to the writing of verse drama and worked actively for the support of the production of his own verse plays and those of other Irish verse playwrights, including Yeats. Clarke's first two verse plays had been written in England: *The Son of Learning* and *The Flame*. All of his subsequent dramas were written in Ireland between 1939 and 1974. Two plays, *The Third Kiss* and *Liberty Lane*, were published posthumously.

None of the major writers of drama in post-Revival Ireland—Sean O'Casey, Lennox Robinson, George Shiels, Paul Vincent Carroll, the collaborators Frank O'Connor and Hugh Hunt—wrote verse plays. Clarke was essentially alone in his continued commitment to this dramatic form. At the Abbey Theatre, the only verse plays to have been presented in the first third of the twentieth century were those of Yeats.

Clarke's first play, *The Son of Learning*, was written in 1927 while he was in England. Although Yeats rejected it on behalf of the Abbey, it was performed at the Cambridge Festival Theatre in October, 1927. The performance was repeated by the Lyric Theater Company at the Abbey in 1945.

Clarke's poetic drama drew, like the poetry of his early and middle career, on Irish myth, the folklore and legends of pre-Christian Ireland,

and medieval Ireland and its monastic traditions. Although Clarke followed Yeats as a writer of verse drama, and although his own verse drama company performed Yeats's plays, the tenor of Clarke's own verse plays differs significantly from the austerity, formality, and symbolic structures Yeats favored. Like his own later poetry, Clarke's verse dramas focus on human conflicts and dilemmas, on the problems of individual freedom in the face of religious dogmatism. They blend, in an essentially satisfying way, comedy and tragedy. A comic view of life and a well-developed sense of the absurdity of the human condition motivate many of the major and minor characters in Clarke's dramas.

The plays in Clarke's dramatic canon are clearly uneven in quality. Although critics have varied in the rigor with which they have addressed and judged Clarke's drama, there is general agreement that a good part of the dramatic writing will today sustain the interest of only the most serious student of modern Irish literature.

Some of the less successful plays, such as *Black Fast*, *Sister Eucharia*, and *The Plot Is Ready*, are of interest mainly because of the intellectual questions and conflicts of conscience they present and the ambiguity in which the "resolution" in each play leaves the reader/viewer. *The Moment Next to Nothing* was simply an unsuccessful attempt to translate into dramatic form Clarke's last novel, *The Sun Dances at Easter*, which had been banned in Ireland.

Seven short, minor plays on various themes are of little dramatic consequence, except that they often display Clarke's fine sense of language and his ability to work within such earlier dramatic traditions as masque and farce. *The Kiss* and *The Second Kiss*, both written in couplets, are light, short pieces that deal amusingly with the amorous adventures of Pierrot and his love, Columbine. Two short plays drawn from Miguel de Cervantes, *The Student from Salamanca* and *The Silent Lover*, are bawdy little farces written in the form of the interlude, the brief diversions typically presented between medieval morality plays. Clarke's other minor plays are *The Impuritans*, *The Third Kiss*, and *Liberty Lane*. *The Visitation* appeared in a special issue of *Irish University Review* (1974) devoted to Clarke.

At least one critic has observed that several of the later minor plays, especially *The Impuritans* and the interludes from Cervantes, might most properly be considered along with the poems of Clarke's old age, which focus happily on erotic themes and celebrate human sexuality.

Clarke's remaining five plays, which will be considered briefly here, offer a sense of the kind of dramatic achievement in verse of which Clarke was clearly capable and also indicate the wide range of types and styles of verse drama he undertook.

The Son of Learning, as Clarke himself recalled, found its inspiration in a translation by Kuno Meyer of an Irish legend about King Cathal of Munster, who falls in love with Ligach, a noblewoman whose brother disapproves of the match. The brother causes Cathal to be cursed with a hunger demon. The unfortunate king is taken to the monastery in Cork to be rid of the demon. The play's central character, a wandering scholar, also arrives at the monastery, enrages the monks because of his audacious lack of piety, and is condemned to death. By virtue of his skill with words, however, it is the scholar, not the monks, who lures the demon out of Cathal and packs him off to Hell.

Within this simple framework, particularly in the conversations between the scholar and the monks, the scholar and the demon, Clarke explores the effects of religious dogmatism, the traditional discord between scholar and monk, intellect and faith. The overall tone is comic, based on exaggerated character, action, and speech.

In the end, which is characteristically ambiguous, the king is cured—but by what agency, exactly, Clarke is cunningly silent. Audience members are left to decide for themselves.

This first play shows how Clarke's verse dramas differ from the verse dramas of Yeats. They are less solemn, more comic; the speeches of the characters, while expressed in verse, are more human and idiomatic. In all, Clarke's plays are peopled not only by distant, legendary heroes but also by real people who have real foibles and who are faced with truly human dilemmas and choices.

Clarke's next play, *The Flame*, takes place in a convent and explores the conflict between the individual and the religious community. In *The Flame*, a young medieval nun secretly violates her order's rules by permitting her once luxuriant hair to grow again. Her preoccupation with herself causes her to neglect her duty—to tend the flame of Saint Brigid, which has burned at the convent for centuries. She is brought before the abbess for punishment. At the end of the play, the young nun is vindicated by an event one might call "miraculous." About its actual dimensions, the author is once again ambiguous.

As the Crow Flies is Clarke's most fully mature dramatic work in verse, written especially for presentation on radio. In it, he confronts all the challenges posed by an art form that must rely for effect almost entirely on voices, and he is particularly successful.

The play has a seemingly simple plot. Three monks, waiting out a terrible storm, take refuge in a cliffside cave that may have once been the dwelling of an ancient holy hermit. Over the din of the storm, they hear the voices of animals from Irish myth.

In an eagle's nest on the top of the cliff, the Crow of Achill, who has wrought evil for centuries, tells tales to the eaglet nestlings. When the eaglets wonder whether the storm that crashes about them is the worst storm there ever was, the Crow prompts the mother eagle to ask first the Stag of Leiterlone and then the Blackbird of Derrycairn. When they cannot answer her, the Crow urges the mother eagle to fly off to question Fintan, the Salmon of Assaroe, the wisest of all creatures. Fintan tells the eagle that he can recall the Deluge, surely the worst storm in history. He also tells her that through his endless existence, he has found no explanation for the violence, war, greed, and slaughter that seem to be the "unchanging misery of mankind." The eagle's joy in her newly found knowledge is dreadfully quenched: She returns to her nest to find that the evil Crow of Achill has devoured her babies.

All through the night, the three monks have listened to the conversations of the animals and, except for Aengus, seem to have comprehended their meaning only partially.

After the storm subsides, the monks, who have returned to their boat, watch the eagle hurl herself against the cliff where her babies perished. As he watches, Aengus shivers. He tells the others, "I know/ The ancient thought that men endure at night/ What wall or cave can hide us from that knowledge?"

As the Crow Flies is very probably Clarke's most fully realized verse drama. The dialogue is rich, vital, and evocative. The verse forms are intricate and challenging. The sound effects implied in the text suggest that a well-mounted production would be particularly haunting and memorable. Clarke effectively uses the voices of the blackbird and the other animals—creatures he has taken from Irish myth—to present and explore the theme of the duality of nature that is at the heart of this play. The responses of the three monks to the conversations they overhear convincingly represent three different ways of dealing with reality.

Overall, *As the Crow Flies* is a satisfying, if unsettling, presentation of Clarke's own inner conflicts, themes he had explored in earlier works and continued to probe until his death: the problems of good and evil in the world, of the clash between faith and reason, of the continuing tension between the rational and the irrational in human existence.

The Viscount of Blarney was written for performance on either stage or radio; it illustrates particularly well Clarke's depth and versatility in the creation of meaning-laden dialogue in verse. This play, the only one of Clarke's major works to be set more or less in the present, concerns the personal development of Cauth Morrissey, who has been reared in an orphanage and who is naïve in her interpretation of the world she encounters as a young adult. Some critics have suggested that the play is about the situation of youth in modern Ireland, caught between the oppressive teachings of the Catholic Church and their own natural desires, interests, and inclinations. Cauth is confronted by a variety of phantoms and demons, a pooka, and various primordial fears. She is finally rescued from her terrors and ignorance by a schoolmaster who coolly and methodically helps her get at the irrational roots of her fear.

Finally, there is *The Plot Succeeds*, not to be confused with the earlier, lesser work, *The Plot Is Ready*, mentioned above. The former is a poetic pantomime, a frankly easygoing work in which the comedic elements eclipse the weightier themes typical of most of Clarke's other verse plays. The play is a pleasant mélange of mistaken identities, magic spells, and clowning; the basic action turns on the attempt of the main character, Mongan, to "win back" his wife, Dulaca, whom he has lost in a card game. *The Plot Succeeds* demonstrates that Clarke had a genuine gift for comedy, had he chosen to develop it.

The best writing in Clarke's verse plays emphasizes his range and versatility as both poet and dramatist. Even in the least successful of his plays, Clarke's effects are neither entirely unsatisfactory nor entirely frivolous. Nearly every one of his plays is, at heart, a study of the conflict between the individual and the community—more specifically, between the Irish Church and Irish society, and the natural instincts of the common Irishman and Irishwoman. Clarke recast this basic conflict in settings as wide-ranging as those of his nondramatic poetry.

Other major works

NOVELS: *The Bright Temptation*, 1932, 1973; *The Singing Men at Cashel*, 1936; *The Sun Dances at Easter*, 1952.

POETRY: *The Vengeance of Fionn*, 1917; *Pilgrimage and Other Poems*, 1929; *The Collected Poems of Austin Clarke*, 1936; *Night and Morning*, 1938; *Ancient Lights: Poems and Satires*, 1955; *Too Great a Vine: Poems and Satires*, 1957; *The Horse-Eaters: Poems and Satires*, 1960; *Later Poems*, 1961; *Flight to Africa and Other Poems*, 1963; *The Echo at Coole and Other Poems*, 1967; *Collected Poems*, 1974; *Selected Poems*, 1976 (Thomas Kinsella, editor).

NONFICTION: *First Visit to England and Other Memories*, 1945; *Twice Round the Black Church: Early Memories of Ireland and England*, 1962; *A Penny in the Clouds: More Memories of Ireland and England*, 1968.

Bibliography

Brown, Ray B., et al. *The Celtic Cross: Studies in Irish Culture and Folklore*, 1964.

Flower, Robin. *The Irish Tradition*, 1947.

Halpern, Susan. *Austin Clarke: His Life and Work*, 1974.

Hogan, Robert. *After the Irish Renaissance: A Critical History of Irish Drama Since "The Plough and the Stars,"* 1967.

Hyde, Douglas. *A Literary History of Ireland*, 1967.

Irish University Review, IV (Spring, 1974). Special Clarke issue.

McHugh, Roger, and Maurice Harmon. *A Short History of Anglo-Irish Literature*, 1982.

Schirmer, Gregory. *The Poetry of Austin Clarke*, 1983.

Tapping, G. Craig. *Austin Clarke: A Study of His Writing*, 1981.

Patricia A. Farrant

PADRAIC COLUM

Born: Longford, Ireland; December 8, 1881
Died: Enfield, Connecticut; January 11, 1972

Principal drama

The Children of Lir, pb. 1901 (one act); *Broken Soil*, pr. 1903; *The Land*, pr., pb. 1905; *The Fiddler's House*, pr., pb. 1907 (revision of *Broken Soil*); *The Miracle of the Corn*, pr. 1908; *The Destruction of the Hostel*, pr. 1910; *Thomas Muskerry*, pr., pb. 1910; *The Desert*, pb. 1912; *The Betrayal*, pr. 1914; *Three Plays*, pb. 1916, 1925 (revised), 1963 (revised; includes *The Land*, *The Fiddler's House*, *Thomas Muskerry*); *Mogu the Wanderer: Or, The Desert*, pb. 1917, pr. 1932 (revision of *The Desert*); *The Grasshopper*, pr. 1917 (adaptation of Eduard Keyserling's play *Ein Frühlingsofer*); *Balloon*, pb. 1929, pr. 1946; *Moytura: A Play for Dancers*, pr., pb. 1963; *The Challengers*, pr. 1966 (3 one acts; includes *Monasterboice*, *Glendalough*, *Cloughoughter*); *Carricknabauna*, pr. 1967 (also as *The Road Round Ireland*).

Other literary forms

Padraic Colum's career as a writer spanned nearly three-quarters of a century. His first one-act play was published in 1901, and he continued to write poetry until his death in 1972. For most of his life, his living was made largely from his children's books, many of which have become classics. Like all truly good books of their kind, they are readable and engaging for adults as well as for children. Such works as *A Boy in Eirinn* (1913), *The King of Ireland's Son* (1916), *The Adventures of Odysseus* (1918), *The Children of Odin* (1920), *The Golden Fleece and the Heroes Who Lived Before Achilles* (1921), and *Legends of Hawaii* (1937) won for him respect both as a children's writer and as an expert on folklore and mythology. Their popularity owes much to the wisdom with which he approached them. "The storyteller," he wrote, "must have respect for the child's mind and the child's conception of the world, knowing it for a complete mind and a complete conception. If a storyteller has that respect, he need not be childish in his language. . . . If children are to will out of the imagination and create out of the will, we must see to it that their imaginations are not clipped or made trivial."

Colum's literary output also included two novels, *Castle Conquer* (1923) and *The Flying Swans* (1957), several travel books, a literary recollection of James Joyce (written with Mary Colum), and a biography of Arthur Griffith, one of his earliest friends and the first president of the Irish Free State. A bibliography of Colum's separately published books would run to more than seventy titles. If miscellaneous works were added to this—books he edited, prefaces, introductions, and periodical publications of poems, stories, and essays—the number would be in the thousands.

In all Colum's prose works, his style is direct, lucid, and graceful, but his literary reputation rests most securely on his poetry, which has been widely anthologized and warmly praised by writers and critics since his poems first began to appear in the opening years of the twentieth century. The poet George Russell (Æ), one of Colum's earliest and most enthusiastic admirers, wrote in 1902 that he had "discovered a new Irish genius: . . . only just twenty, born an agricultural labourer's son, laboured himself, came to Dublin two years ago and educated himself, writes astonishingly well, poems and dramas with a real originality. . . . I prophesy about him." By 1904, Colum's poems had begun to appear in anthologies in Ireland and the United States, and since then every major collection of Irish poetry has included his work. Critics have consistently placed his name high on lists of the best Irish poets, but his poems have inspired few detailed scholarly studies. His poetry, in fact, resists such treatment: It is not easily identified with any particular school or movement, and it contains no esoteric philosophy to be glossed or obscure passages and patterns of symbolism to be unraveled. Indeed, its most distinguishing characteristics are simplicity and clarity. Often the poems are dramatic lyrics spoken by Irish peasants. Many are acutely accurate observations of commonplaces, as are those in his *Creatures* (1927) and *The Vegetable Kingdom* (1954).

Achievements

Although few scholars have written about Colum's poetry, scholars and poets have been generous in honoring him. He was elected president of the Poetry Society of America in 1938 and won its medal in 1940. He also received honorary doctorates from the University of Ireland and Columbia University and awards from the Academy of Irish Letters and the American Academy of Poets. Critic Edmund Wilson, after reading a collection of Colum's poems, wrote to him that "I wept while reading . . . some of them—not for sentiment, which doesn't often make me weep, but for the beauty of the lines. If everybody in Ireland hadn't been so overshadowed by Yeats, you would certainly have stood out as one of the best poets in English of your time."

Colum's reputation as a poet was well deserved, but it was one that did not altogether please him. He did not disown the title of poet, but he frequently objected to the exclusiveness of the label when it overshadowed his accomplishments in the theater. On one occasion, while discussing with a friend how future generations would remember him, he insisted that the popular notion that he was primarily a poet was a misconception. "I am primarily a man of the theatre," he argued, "and always have been." Colum repeated this judgment several times toward the end of his life. A few weeks before his death at the age of ninety, he told a reporter from *The*

New York Times that he was often prouder of his plays than of anything else he had written. Whenever he was in a position to influence the shaping of his public identity, he was careful to point out the close connection between his poetry and his plays. One such opportunity came when he was being interviewed by a writer who was preparing an introductory study of his works. "In the early part," Colum directed, "put my poems and plays together. The sort of plays I was writing for the theatre and the sort of poems I was writing are about the same sort of people and treat them in the same sort of way." Referring to such early poems as "The Plougher" and "An Old Woman of the Roads," he suggested that "you would put it best by saying that they were dramatizations. They're really characters in a play that hadn't been written." He was given another opportunity when Irish Radio invited him to sketch a prose portrait of himself. "Anything I have written, whether verse or narrative," he said during the broadcast, "goes back to my first literary discipline, the discipline of the theatre."

Biography

Padraic Colum wrote his first play when he was nineteen and his last when he was eighty-five. In all, he wrote about two dozen plays of varying lengths, many in several different versions. His plays have been produced at the Abbey and Gate theaters in Dublin, on Broadway by David Belasco and Iden Payne, Off-Broadway, at the Dublin Theatre Festival, on Irish television, in the little theaters that flourished in Dublin in the 1960's, and by amateur groups in Ireland, England, the United States, the Middle East, and Australia.

There was little in Colum's family background to suggest a career as a playwright. Unlike William Butler Yeats, John Millington Synge, Lady Augusta Gregory, and most of the other playwrights of the Irish Literary Renaissance with whom he became associated, his background was rural, Catholic, and working-class. His mother was the daughter of a gardener, and his father the son of a tenant farmer. Colum's father seems to have been temperamentally unsuited to handle the responsibilities of a growing family and, according to Colum, "was always unlucky looking for jobs." He worked first as a teacher in a national school and later taught the children of paupers at Longford Workhouse in the Irish midlands; he eventually became master of the workhouse but had to resign the position because of his drinking and mishandling of funds. He left Ireland for a few years to work at various jobs in the United States but returned when Colum was nine and moved the family to Sandycove outside Dublin, where he had found a job as a clerk in the railway station. Padraic entered the local national school, though his attendance became irregular when he was old enough to take a part-time job. He and his brother Fred worked as delivery boys for the railroad and took turns attending school, one going one day, the other the next. When he was seventeen, Colum left school after passing his examinations and began work as a clerk at the Railway Clearing House on Kildare Street in Dublin.

Colum soon became interested in drama, though all he knew about plays and playwriting was what he had learned from the national school curriculum, from books he found in the local library, and from rare visits to the theater in Dublin, where the fare tended to be a mixture of music-hall variety shows and popular English comedies. He recalled later that when he began writing his first play, he "knew nothing whatever about the theatre. I had seen [Dion Boucicault's] *The Colleen Bawn*, *The Shaughraun*, and some shows put on by amateurs, and I had gone to the Gaiety Theatre, and spent a whole shilling for a seat in the pit... to see Mr. and Mrs. Kendall in a play called *The Elder Miss Blossom*." This was in 1899, and there was as yet no such thing as a native Irish drama, apart from the melodramas of Boucicault. The Abbey Theatre, which would provide models for the next generation of playwrights, was still six years from being founded, and the Irish Literary Theatre, which Yeats, Lady Gregory, and Edward Martyn had established with the aim of creating a native drama, was only in its first year of production. Colum saw none of the Irish Literary Theatre's plays that year and, in fact, saw none of its subsequent productions except the final one on October 21, 1901. This was a double bill featuring *Diarmuid and Grania* by Yeats and George Moore and *Casad-an-Sugan (The Twisting of the Rope)*, Douglas Hyde's play in Irish.

Colum's first effort at playwriting was, instead, a result of his attendance at the *tableaux vivants* that the patriotic Daughters of Ireland were staging to promote nationalistic sentiment. "They were statuesque groups introduced by some familiar piece of music, and holding their pose for some minutes—an elementary show in which costume, music and striking appearance were ingredients," Colum later wrote. "I was in an audience that witnessed 'Silent, O Moyle, Be the Roar of Thy Waters.' I felt there should be words to give life to the pathos of children transformed by an enchantress stepmother; my mind was already on plays. I began a one act play in verse, *The Children of Lir*, and sent it to [the Daughters of Ireland]." Although they did not produce the play, Colum succeeded in getting it published in *The Irish Independent* on September 14, 1901. It was his first published work. During the next three years—what Colum called his apprentice period—he published several more one-act plays, including plays based on Irish history and mythology, Ibsen-like problem plays, a dramatic monologue, and a melodramatic propaganda play, written to discourage enlistments in the British Army. As might be expected, these early plays are, for the most part, awkward and immature, and Colum made no later effort to revise or republish them. They do, however, show a precocious grasp of dramatic techniques and a rapidly developing skill.

Colum's full-length play *Broken Soil* was produced by the Irish National Theatre Society in 1903, the same year it produced the first plays of Synge and Lady Gregory. Almost immediately he was recognized as a playwright of great promise and sound dramatic judgment. When he was only twenty-three, he was selected by the National Theatre Society to be a member of its first reading committee, a role he shared with Yeats and Æ. Yeats was particularly impressed by Colum's work, describing him in 1904 as "a man of genius in the first dark gropings of his thought" and noting that "some here think he will become our strongest dramatic talent." Colum's plays and poems also won for him the patronage of Thomas Hughes Kelly, an American millionaire living near Dublin, who awarded him a five-year grant—beginning at seventy pounds and increasing by ten pounds per year—to support his literary work. With this subsidy, Colum was able to quit his job as a railway clerk in 1904 and devote his full time to writing. He quickly developed into an accomplished playwright, and the popularity of his next play, *The Land*, helped to confirm Yeats's prediction. Produced in 1905 after the Irish National Theatre Society was reorganized as the Abbey Theatre, it gave the Abbey what it much needed when many were criticizing it for being something less than the national theater it purported to be—a play that was both a critical and a popular success. Irish and English critics hailed it as "the best play yet given us by the dramatic movement" and "one of the most important plays which have appeared in English for a long time." Although this praise was perhaps extravagant, the play did add a new dimension to the dramatic movement. As one reviewer explained: "What we have been waiting for is a play that should be at once good and popular. Mr. Yeats has proved a little too abstruse, and Mr. Synge a little too bizarre to get fully down to the hearts of the people."

The Land was the first of a series of three plays dealing with life in the Irish midlands that firmly established Colum's reputation as a major playwright and a pioneering figure in the realistic movement. The second in the series was a thorough reworking of *Broken Soil*, which he retitled *The Fiddler's House*. It was performed in 1907 by the Theatre of Ireland, a splinter group formed after Colum and others had left the Abbey in a dispute over theater policy a year earlier. By all accounts, the Theatre of Ireland production was inept. As a result, the play did not receive the public exposure it deserved, even though most critics thought it a much better play than *The Land*. Andrew E. Malone, for example, described it as "in every respect Colum's best play" and considered it "equal to the greatest in the Irish theatre." After Colum left the Abbey Theatre, he never fully reestablished his association with it. He did, however, give it *Thomas Muskerry*, the third of his realistic Irish plays, for production in 1910. The public reception of this play was mixed, with opinions turning on the harshness of its characterization of small-town merchants: While some reviewers found the play brilliant, others damned it as libeling the Irish national character. The issues raised by *Thomas Muskerry* were debated for several weeks in the columns of Dublin's newspapers. Like Synge's *The Playboy of the Western World* (pr. 1907) and Sean O'Casey's *The Plough and the Stars* (pr. 1926), however, the play survived the controversy it aroused and is now generally considered to be Colum's masterpiece.

In 1912, Colum married Mary Catherine Gunning Maguire, whom he had met while she was a student at University College, Dublin. By then, his five-year grant had expired, and his income was now dependent on his free-lance writing. He and Mary supplemented this by teaching in a private school but soon decided that if Colum was to earn a living as a writer, he would have to find a wider market than Dublin offered. When his aunt in Pittsburgh offered to pay their fare to the United States, they accepted, hoping to make careers for themselves there as writers. They left for the United States in 1914, and both subsequently succeeded in their goals, Colum by his voluminous output of books, essays, and literary journalism, and Mary by becoming a highly respected literary critic, writing reviews for *The New York Times* and several other major newspapers and literary journals and serving as literary editor of *Forum*.

In the ten years between the end of his apprenticeship in 1904 and his emigration to the United States, Colum wrote a number of other plays. None was in the manner of his three major realistic plays, and none was given a successful production until several years after he left Ireland. *The Miracle of the Corn*, written for the Irish National Theatre Society, was accepted and put into rehearsal in 1904 but for some reason was not performed. The Theatre of Ireland staged it in 1908 in a production that seems to have been less competent than that of *The Fiddler's House*. One critic in the opening-night audience commented that the actors spoke their lines so softly that they could not be heard in the first row. Colum wrote an adaptation of the medieval miracle play *The Second Shepherds' Play* at Yeats's suggestion in 1911, but the Abbey did not produce it. Of the other plays, only *The Destruction of the Hostel* was staged while Colum still lived in Ireland, and this was in an amateur production by the boys' acting class of St. Enda's School. After leaving the Abbey, Colum hoped to make a name for himself in the London theater and wrote three plays for production there. He was unable, however, to find a producer for *The Desert* or "Theodora of Byzantium," and a London production of *The Betrayal* was canceled after Lady Gregory refused to grant permission for a group of actors under contract with the Abbey to act in it.

Colum's interest in the theater continued after his arrival in the United States. His first job there was at the Carnegie Institute in Pittsburgh, where he was hired to assist in the production of a series of Irish plays. His *The Betrayal* was given its first production as part of the series. In 1915,

Colum moved to New York, where he lectured on Irish drama and announced his intention of joining John P. Campbell, a former artistic director of the Ulster Literary Theatre, in establishing the Irish Theatre of America, to be modeled after the Abbey Theatre. Colum and Campbell held an organizational meeting, issued a statement of plans to the press, and produced their first play in February, 1915, but the group failed to gather momentum and disbanded soon afterward. Over the next forty-five years, Colum's contacts with the theater became less frequent. *The Grasshopper*, his adaptation of Eduard Keyserling's *Ein Frühlingsofer*, was produced on Broadway in 1917 and at the Abbey in 1922. *The Fiddler's House* received its first Abbey Theatre production in 1919 and was revived in New York in 1941. *Mogu the Wanderer*, a revised version of *The Desert*, was produced at Dublin's Gate Theatre in 1932 with a young Orson Welles in a leading role. Michael Myerberg, who had successfully produced Thornton Wilder's *The Skin of Our Teeth* (pr. 1942), bought the option on *Balloon*, an experimental play modeled partly on the Italian *commedia dell'arte* and partly on American comic strips, published by Colum in 1929, and tried it out for two weeks in 1946 in Ogunquit, Maine, but did not take it into New York. Myerberg also commissioned Colum to write the screenplay for a 1954 adaptation of Engelbert Humperdinck's opera *Hansel and Gretel* (pr. 1893), in which the actors were animated dolls. Also in 1954, Colum assisted Marjorie Borkenstein in adapting James Joyce to the stage in *Ulysses in Nighttown*.

Such activities kept Colum sporadically in touch with the theater but were not enough to keep alive the reputation as a playwright he had established decades earlier in Dublin. Although his notebooks for these years show that the theater was rarely far from his mind, most of his writing efforts for the stage went into adaptations of other people's work and seemingly endless revisions of plays he had written years before. He produced only one wholly new play between 1912 and 1961. This was *Balloon*, and an anecdote about it reveals how difficult it was for Colum to keep alive his reputation as a man of the theater. His friend Charles Burgess tells of an encounter with him in New York during the 1950's. "You are talking to a dead man," Colum said, and Burgess recalls:

> That afternoon he had called on a producer to whom he had recently sent a play. . . . As they had discussed the possibility of a production, the producer had said to him, off-handedly, that of course they'd have to use a different name.
>
> Colum, rising to his work's defense, had replied, "Well, I don't know. . . . Most of the people who know the play tell me that *Balloon* is a very good name for it."
>
> "Oh, I don't mean the title of the play," the producer had countered, "it's the name Padraic Colum I'm referring to. There was another playwright by that name at the turn of the century and I think we'd be criticized if we used his name."

In the last ten years of his life, Colum stepped up his efforts in the drama and succeeded to some degree in bringing his name again before the playgoing public. In 1960, he began work on a cycle of Yeatsian Nō plays, the first of which, *Moytura*, was published in 1963. Also in 1963, he published a significantly revised edition of his realistic *Three Plays*. The revisions demonstrated a good sense of dramatic structure and revealed that Colum's mastery of dialogue was better than it had ever been. *Moytura* was performed at the Pike Theatre in Dublin in 1963, and productions of it and of other Nō plays followed on Irish radio and television. Three of the plays, *Monasterboice*, *Glendalough*, and *Cloughoughter*, were gathered together under the title *The Challengers* and staged in 1966 at Dublin's Lantern Theatre. The following year, *Carricknabauna*, a dramatic adaptation of some of Colum's poems, was performed Off-Broadway and, as *The Road Round Ireland*, at the Lantern.

Despite Colum's final flurry of activity, his dramatic efforts, spaced over a period of more than sixty years, do not add up to a distinguished career in the theater and hardly seem to justify his insistence that "if I am not a playwright, I am nothing." There is clearly an element of exaggeration in such a statement, but if there is, Colum's need to exaggerate is at least partially understandable as a protest against premature burial by literary historians who persisted in reporting that he had abandoned the stage for good in 1910 and Broadway producers who thought him long dead. There is also a temptation to dismiss Colum's repeated assertions that he was primarily a playwright as the wishful thinking of an old man who had never quite got over his first flush of success on the stage. Such an attitude does not do Colum justice, for his plays have never been fully evaluated, and the importance of their position in his identity as an artist has never been acknowledged.

Analysis

Padraic Colum was a major figure in Ireland's Literary Renaissance both because he was the first to deal realistically with the Irish peasant farmer and because of the influence his plays had on the playwrights who followed him. Something of the pervasiveness and power of his influence comes through in the open letter that Yeats wrote to Lady Gregory in 1919, in which he announced that he was giving up public theater for a more private theater of the drawing room. Yeats wrote that while he had sought to create a poetic drama, the Abbey playwrights, following Colum's lead, had instead succeeded in "the making articulate of all the dumb classes each with its own knowledge of the world, its own dignity, but all objective with the objectivity of the office and the workshop, of the newspaper and the street, of mechanism and of politics." It was, nevertheless, the realistic drama of peasant life that won for the Abbey Theatre its international recognition.

Colum himself did not claim to have been the inventor of the peasant play; he said that he shared the distinction with Synge. "My *Broken Soil* and Synge's *In the Shadow of the Glen* were produced within a month of each other," he wrote. "These two plays inaugurated the drama of peasant life. W. B. Yeats' *Cathleen ni Houlihan*, in which the characters are peasants, was produced first, but *Cathleen ni Houlihan* is symbolic and not a play of actual peasant life." "A play of actual peasant life" aptly describes what Colum sought to write, and it was with this type of play, in his view, that Ireland began to have a truly native drama—plays he described as being "authentic in idiom and character" and expressing "the sum of instincts, traditions, sympathies that made the Irish mind distinctive." Probably the most important concept in Colum's view of drama was that plays should *express* Irish life. Synge and others poeticized the life of the peasant; Colum saw a poetry within that life and expressed it realistically. In doing so, he saw his work as being distinctly "democratic, not only because it deals with the folk of the country and the town, but because it is written out of recognition of the fact that in every life there are moments of intensity and beauty." Other Irish playwrights wrote about peasants, but none accepted them on their own terms. They saw them as outsiders would see them: Yeats's peasants are romantic idealizations, Lady Gregory's are caricatures—only slightly less broad than the nineteenth century "stage Irishmen"—and Synge's, for all the richness and beauty of their language, are exaggerations of the Irish peasant. Of all the early Abbey Theatre playwrights, only Colum, who grew up among peasant farmers and small-town merchants, accurately reflected their character, their language, and their concerns.

Because of their realistic portrayal of Irish life, Colum considered *The Land*, *The Fiddler's House*, and *Thomas Muskerry* to be his most important and most influential plays. Most literary historians agree with this judgment. What gives each of the plays its dramatic vigor and depth of characterization is the tension inherent in Colum's view of Ireland. Each presents a pair of characters whose energy or imagination is too strong to be held back by the dreary inertia of Irish country life. Matt Cosgar and Ellen Douras in *The Land*, Maire Hourican and her father, Conn, in *The Fiddler's House*, and Muskerry and Myles Gorman in *Thomas Muskerry* all experience a conflict between their feelings of responsibility to something in this spiritually cramped existence and a deeper need to rise above it. The attention which Colum gives to realistic detail in the plays is a means of emphasizing the part in the conflict played by everyday life in Ireland. Permeating the three plays as a motivating force and linking them thematically is the struggle for freedom that is resolved in *Thomas Muskerry*'s final triumphant symbol, Myles Gorman, whom Colum described as "a man of energy set free on the roads."

Because he considered these plays so central to his reputation as a playwright, Colum revised them frequently throughout his life. He first gathered them together as *Three Plays* in 1916 and later published revised editions of the collection in 1925 and 1963. With the exception of *The Land*, which received only light revision, the plays in the 1963 edition differ significantly from the versions that were staged nearly a half a century earlier. *The Land* was inspired, Colum said, by the Land Act of 1903, which enabled Irish tenant farmers to purchase their land. The play's central conflict is between two generations: the farmers, who have fought to win their land, and their children, who are tempted by the call of the larger world outside. The younger generation prevails in the end, with Matt Cosgar and Ellen Douras departing for the United States and leaving their claims to their fathers' farms to Ellen's less imaginative brother Cornelius and Matt's slow-witted sister Sally.

Although Colum referred to it in 1910 as only "a sketch for a play" and wrote in 1963 that "if staged these days *The Land* would have to be played as an historical piece and for character parts," the play is notable for its strong characterization of Sally and the two fathers, Murtagh Cosgar and Martin Douras. It also has a strongly unified plot and a clean story line. By unfolding his plot against the larger historical backdrop of the farmers' progress from tenants to landowners, Colum managed to reinforce the irony of the exodus of Ireland's most gifted young people at the very time when the country had something to offer them.

The Land plays well on the stage—when the Dublin International Theatre Festival was inaugurated in 1957, it was the only early full-length Abbey Theatre play selected—but it is inferior to Colum's other two realistic dramas. The plot is perhaps too neatly constructed and the characters too conveniently paired off; the son and daughter of Murtagh Cosgar wed the son and daughter of Martin Douras, and six young emigrants to America in act 2 are balanced against six farmers who commit themselves to the land in act 1. Matt and Ellen, moreover, are too thinly characterized for the parts they play, and Cornelius' curtain speech is too obviously propagandistic. Nevertheless, because of both the popular support it won for the Abbey and its value as a commentary on social and political changes, the play has undeniable historical importance. *The Land*, in fact, is the only one of the three plays about which it can be said with any justice that historical value outweighs literary worth.

The Fiddler's House is similar to *The Land* in both theme and plot: An aging fiddler, Conn Hourican, leaves the farm that his daughter Maire has inherited to follow the roads, playing at festivals and in public houses. Maire, whose increasing sense of affinity with her father is matched by a growing aversion to Brian McConnell, the man whom she had intended to marry, decides to follow her father on the roads and deeds the farm to her younger sister, Anne. *The Fiddler's House* was probably Colum's most frequently revised play, and through several revisions the focus switched back and forth between the two main characters. In a letter to his patron, Kelly, in 1910, Colum revealed his fascination with the characters of Conn and Maire and suggested that Maire dominated the unpublished *Broken Soil.* "Now that I read the plays," he wrote, "Conn Hourican and [Maire] Hourican in *The Fiddler's House* are more vivid to me than any of the people in *The Land.* I know that you prefer *Broken Soil* to *The Fiddler's House*, the play that has taken its place. . . . But I thought Conn Hourican worth a play, and I tried to make a new one for him." Conn dominated both the 1907 and 1925 versions of the play. Later, however, Maire began to grow in Colum's imagination. In the preface of the 1963 edition of *Three Plays*, he says:

> The motive in its early version was simply "the call of the road." It became *The Fiddler's House* when a real conflict was seen as developing in it, the conflict between father and daughter in which reconciliation came when Maire Hourican becomes aware that she, too, has the vagrant in her. Later, when produced in New York by Augustin Duncan, something else in her character was made explicit. Her recoil from her lover is due to her fear of masculine possessiveness—a recoil not extraordinary in a girl brought up in the Irish countryside.

In the 1963 revision of the play, Maire regained the ground that she had lost in the versions of 1907 and 1925, and the characters settled into a state of equilibrium, each interesting for different reasons. While the divided focus of the play kept it from greatness, it also gave the Irish stage two memorable characters. The complexly motivated Maire is particularly well drawn. When Brian tries to dominate her and threatens to carry her off by force to marry him, she begins to realize that, more than marriage, she wants freedom. When she leaves to follow her father at the play's close, the possibility of reconciliation with Brian is more remote than it had been in the earlier plays. Through the various revisions, Colum gradually transformed her from a girl who wants only a home and a husband to a woman who wants to shape her own life.

Thomas Muskerry went through a similar evolutionary process of revision, and by the time he completed the process, Colum had transformed his weakest play into his strongest. Andrew E. Malone, writing about the early Abbey Theatre version of the play, termed it "in every respect inferior to *The Land* and *The Fiddler's House*; Robert Hogan, writing in 1967 about the final revision, called it Colum's "masterpiece." Most critics concur with Hogan's judgment. In writing the play, Colum drew on his earliest childhood experiences at the Longford Workhouse. As the play begins, Muskerry, master of a workhouse in the Irish midlands, is at the end of a successful career and looking forward to a pleasant retirement in the cottage he plans to buy with his life savings. By the play's end, he lies dead in a pauper's bed at the workhouse. In the intervening scenes, it is discovered that he had accidentally mismanaged the workhouse's funds, and the Crilly family, into which his daughter had married, persuades him to resign as master to save the family's reputation in the village. They also persuade him to give up his plan of buying a cottage and to live with them behind their shop. Once he abdicates his power to the Crillys, however, they become increasingly neglectful of him, even as he uses his savings to keep their shop from foundering. At the end of the play, he is penniless and spiritually broken by the ingratitude of his daughter and her in-laws and by the humiliating taunts of Felix Tournour, the workhouse porter. The only person who shows him any sympathy is Christy Clarke, an orphan whom he had befriended.

The 1910 version of *Thomas Muskerry* was little more than the bare bones of a play and had succeeded only on the merits of an unusually moving final act; it had little else to recommend it. The first act did scarcely more than lay an Ibsen-like foundation of complex exposition and introduce a large cast of sparsely drawn characters—each arriving and departing at too obviously opportune moments. The succession of events necessary for the play's later developments was more mechanical than dramatic and too rapid to be credible. The second act moved along at the same quick pace, carrying Muskerry mechanically through the events that led finally to his death. Muskerry in the closing scenes achieved—in his mixture of pathos and tragedy, failure and triumph—a grandeur reminiscent of Lear. The play, in fact, resembled William Shakespeare's tragedy in many ways and gained strength from the underlying but unspoken allusion to *King Lear* that reverberated through the unfolding pattern of filial ingratitude.

The later version of *Thomas Muskerry* more than compensates for the artistic deficiencies of the early version. Structurally, Colum's innovations slow the pace and allow the play to build more powerfully to its climax. What was merely a mechanical succession of events in the first version takes on an aura of inevitability in the revision. In rewriting the play, Colum divided the first act into two scenes by reshuffling the exposition and spreading the action over two evenings instead of one. He also suggests early in the first scene that Felix Tournour has information that may later damage Muskerry's reputation and jeopardize his pension. In the earlier version, Tournour's knowledge had come as a surprise late in the play and had no real effect on the action. With this small change, Colum was able to foreshadow the most important turning point in Muskerry's fortunes and to orchestrate Tournour into a nemesis who lurks through four acts before he finally strikes.

Between the original first and second acts, Colum inserted a new act that accomplishes several things. It begins with the senile bantering of two elderly inmates who reflect on the change in masters and, in the process, reveal to the audience the old master's record of humane kindliness. Their reverential comments continue in choric counterpoint behind the main action, in which Muskerry is quietly shunted aside to make room for his successor. Like the early slights of Goneril and Regan in *King Lear*, the early shifts in the way his daughter and her in-laws treat the retired Muskerry provide the first glancing blows at his dignity and prefigure the larger insults that follow. Into the new second act Colum also introduced a traveling photographer whose uncertainty about whether Muskerry is still master of the workhouse helps to bring into focus the other characters' attitudes toward the protagonist.

The third act of the 1963 play is the original second act; in the revision, Colum polished and augmented the dialogue to improve characterization and made the act a third again as long by the introduction of another character, Peter Macnabo, who, like Muskerry, is a former workhouse master fallen into disgrace. The addition of Macnabo alone would have been enough to improve the overall quality of the play. His indomitability, industrious self-sufficiency, and rising fortunes as he begins a new life for himself provide a strong contrast to Muskerry's decline. The positioning of his visit between the petty quarrels of the Crilly family and examples of Tournour's growing arrogance gives the new version's third act a dramatic intensity almost equal to that of act 4, and the combination of naïveté and shrewdness that prompts Macnabo at the age of sixty to attempt a new career manufacturing traditional Irish clay pipes makes him one of the play's most finely drawn characters.

The fourth act differs little from the strong concluding act of the original. Colum's major change was to expand the part of Muskerry's young ward, Christy Clarke, so that in the closing scenes he functions as something of an adopted Cordelia in ironic contrast to the Goneril and Regan of Muskerry's daughter and the Crilly family. Colum's changes in the play involved more than simply improving its structure and adding new characterization and dialogue. While the 1910 version presented an array of broadly sketched characters, the revision contains a gallery of fully delineated personalities. Muskerry, already a powerfully conceived protagonist in the original, is a truly memorable one in the final version. The revised play also features three unusually strong supporting characters in Christy Clarke, Peter Macnabo, and Felix Tournour. The remaining characters in the revised version all have the fullness and clearly defined identities that they lacked in the original. The dialogue, moreover, shows the sure hand of an artist with more than fifty years of experience as both a poet and a playwright.

Despite the high quality of his art and the glowing predictions of fellow writers such as Yeats and Æ, Colum never became truly famous. His emigration to the United States probably had much to do with this. His best plays were the early Abbey Theatre works about rural Irish life; when he left Ireland, he lost the stimulus of a convenient stage and an appreciative audience. Though he had been famous as a poet and playwright in Dublin, he was virtually unknown in New York and had to begin again to make a name for himself while expending much of his creative energy on the children's books and literary journalism that provided his income. Perhaps he was partially a victim of his own personality and of his ability to do many things well. If he had been flamboyant, irascible, or conspicuously tormented, he might have become a literary personality, as have many writers of less talent. Instead, he was a quiet, good-natured, and apparently happy man. If anything, he was conspicuously unflappable. "Every serious Irish writer has a pain in his belly," Æ once chided Frank O'Connor, who was complaining of indigestion. "Yeats has a pain in his belly; Joyce has a terrible pain in his belly; now you have a pain in your belly. Padraic Colum is the only Irish writer who never had a pain at all."

Other major works

NOVELS: *Castle Conquer*, 1923; *The Flying Swans*, 1957.

SHORT FICTION: *Selected Short Stories of Padraic Colum*, 1985 (Sanford Sternlicht, editor).

POETRY: *Wild Earth and Other Poems*, 1907; *Dramatic Legends, and Other Poems*, 1922; *Creatures*, 1927; *Way of the Cross*, 1927; *Old Pastures*, 1930; *Poems*, 1932; *Flower Pieces: New Poems*, 1938; *The Collected Poems of Padraic Colum*, 1953; *The Vegetable Kingdom*, 1954; *Ten Poems*, 1957; *The Poet's Circuits: Collected Poems of Ireland*, 1960; *Images of Departure*, 1969; *Irish Elegies*, 1976.

NONFICTION: *My Irish Year*, 1912; *The Road Round Ireland*, 1926; *Cross Roads in Ireland*, 1930; *A Half-Day's Ride: Or, Estates in Corsica*, 1932; *Our Friend James Joyce*, 1958 (with Mary Colum); *Ourselves Alone: The Story of Arthur Griffith and the Origin of the Irish Free State*, 1959.

SCREENPLAY: *Hansel and Gretel*, 1954 (adaptation of Engelbert Humperdinck's opera).

CHILDREN'S LITERATURE: *A Boy in Eirinn*, 1913; *The King of Ireland's Son*, 1916; *The Adventures of Odysseus*, 1918; *The Boy Who Knew What the Birds Said*, 1918; *The Girl Who Sat by the Ashes*, 1919; *The Boy Apprenticed to an Enchanter*, 1920; *The Children of Odin*, 1920; *The Golden Fleece and the Heroes Who Lived Before Achilles*, 1921; *The Children Who Followed the Piper*, 1922; *At the Gateways of the Day*, 1924; *The Island of the Mighty: Being the Hero Stories of Celtic Britain Retold from the Mabinogion*, 1924; *Six Who Were Left in a Shoe*, 1924; *The Bright Islands*, 1925; *The Forge in the Forest*, 1925; *The Voyagers: Being Legends and Romances of Atlantic Discovery*, 1925; *The Fountain of Youth: Stories to Be Told*, 1927; *Orpheus: Myths of the World*, 1930; *The Big Tree of Bunlahy: Stories of My Own Countryside*, 1933; *The White Sparrow*, 1933; *The Legend of Saint Columba*, 1935; *Legends of Hawaii*, 1937; *Where the Winds Never Blew and the Cocks Never Crew*, 1940; *The Frenzied Prince: Being Heroic Stories of Ancient Ireland*, 1943; *A Treasury of Irish Folklore*, 1954; *Story Telling, New and Old*, 1961; *The Stone of Victory, and Other Tales of Padraic Colum*, 1966.

Bibliography
Bowen, Zack. "Ninety Years in Retrospect," in *The Journal of Irish Literature*. II (January, 1973), pp. 14-34.
_____ . *Padraic Colum: A Biographical-Critical Introduction*, 1970.
Burgess, Charles. "A Playwright and His Work," in *The Journal of Irish Literature*. II (January, 1973), pp. 40-58.
Clarke, Brenna Katz. *The Emergence of the Irish Peasant Play at the Abbey Theatre*, 1982.
Denson, Alan. "Padraic Colum: An Appreciation with a Checklist of His Publications," in *The Dublin Magazine*. VI (Spring, 1967), pp. 50-67.
Ellis-Fermor, Una. *The Irish Dramatic Movement*, 1939.
Fay, W. G., and Catherine Carswell. *The Fays of the Abbey Theatre*, 1935.
Hickey, Des, and Gus Smith. "Colum: Life in a World of Writers," in *A Paler Shade of Green*, 1972.
Hogan, Robert, and Richard Burnham. *The Art of the Amateur, 1916-1920*, 1984.
Hogan, Robert, Richard Burnham, and Daniel P. Poteet. *The Rise of the Realists, 1910-1915*, 1979.
Hogan, Robert, and James Kilroy. *The Abbey Theatre: The Years of Synge, 1905-1909*, 1978.
_____ . *Laying the Foundations, 1902-1904*, 1976.
Malone, Andrew E. *The Irish Drama*, 1929.
Robinson, Lennox. *Ireland's Abbey Theatre*, 1951.
Weygandt, Cornelius. *Irish Plays and Playwrights*, 1913.

Gordon Henderson

WILLIAM CONGREVE

Born: Bardsey, England; January 24, 1670
Died: London, England; January 19, 1729

Principal drama

The Old Bachelor, pr., pb. 1693; *The Double Dealer*, pr. 1693, pb. 1694; *Love for Love*, pr., pb. 1695; *The Mourning Bride*, pr., pb. 1697; *The Way of the World*, pr., pb. 1700; *The Judgement of Paris*, pr., pb. 1701 (masque); *Squire Trelooby*, pr. 1704 (with Sir John Vanbrugh and William Walsh; adaptation of Molière's *Monsieur de Pourceaugnac*); *Semele*, pb. 1710 (libretto), pr. 1744 (modified version); *The Complete Plays of William Congreve*, pb. 1967 (Herbert Davis, editor).

Other literary forms

Although William Congreve is remembered today as a dramatist, his first publication was a novella, *Incognita: Or, Love and Duty Reconcil'd*, which appeared in 1692. He also published a translation of Juvenal's eleventh satire and commendatory verses "To Mr. Dryden on His Translation of Persius" in John Dryden's edition of *The Satires of Juvenal and Persius* (1693), as well as two songs and three odes in Charles Gildon's *Miscellany of Original Poems* (1692). Later, Congreve reprinted these odes, together with translations from Homer's *Iliad*, in *Examen Poeticum* (1693). His other translations from the classics include Ovid's *Art of Love, Book III* (1709) and two stories from Ovid in the 1717 edition of *Metamorphoses*. His original poetry was first collected with his other writings in *The Works of William Congreve* (1710) and frequently reprinted throughout the eighteenth century. After 1700, Congreve abandoned serious drama in favor of social and political interests, although he did write a masque and an opera after that date and collaborated with Sir John Vanbrugh and William Walsh on a farce. In response to Jeremy Collier's attacks on Restoration playwrights, Congreve wrote a short volume of dramatic criticism, *Amendments of Mr. Collier's False and Imperfect Citations* (1698). Congreve's letters have been edited by John C. Hodges and are available in *William Congreve: Letters and Documents* (1964).

Achievements

Congreve's first play, *The Old Bachelor*, was an instant success; its initial run of fourteen days made it the most popular play since Thomas Otway's *Venice Preserved* (pr., pb. 1682). *The Double Dealer* was not as instantly successful, but *Love for Love* was so popular that Congreve was made a manager of the theater. *The Mourning Bride* was still more successful; in 1699, Gildon said of the work that "this play had the greatest Success, not only of all Mr. Congreve's, but indeed of all the Plays that ever I can remember on the English Stage." Congreve's last comedy, *The Way of the World*, though now universally regarded as his best and arguably the best Restoration comedy as well, met with little support at the time, and its cool reception drove Congreve from serious drama.

Throughout the eighteenth century, Congreve's reputation remained high, both for his poetry and his plays. Edward Howard, in his *Essay upon Pastoral* (1695), said that Congreve possessed the talent of ten Vergils. Dryden, who equated Congreve to William Shakespeare on the stage, declared that in his translations from the *Iliad* Congreve surpassed Homer in pathos. Alexander Pope's translation of the *Iliad* (1715-1720) was dedicated to Congreve, as were Sir Richard Steele's *Poetical Miscellanies* (1714) and his 1722 edition of Joseph Addison's *The Drummer: Or, The Haunted House*. In the nineteenth century, Congreve's reputation declined, along with the public's regard for Restoration comedy in general, because of the sexual licentiousness depicted in the plays. With the twentieth century, however, came a reevaluation; when *The Way of the World* was revived at Cherry Lane Theatre in New York in 1924, it ran for 120 performances. That work and *Love for Love* remain among the most frequently acted of Restoration plays, and Congreve's other two comedies are also occasionally staged. Although Congreve's one tragedy has not worn as well, he may be today the most popular and most highly regarded English dramatist between Shakespeare and George Bernard Shaw.

Biography

William Congreve was born on January 24, 1670, at Bardsey, Yorkshire, England. In 1674, his father, also named William, received a lieutenant's commission to serve in Ireland, and the family moved to the garrison of Youghal. In 1678, the elder William was transferred to Carrickfergus, another Irish port, and again, the family accompanied him. Congreve's knowledge of port life may have contributed to his depiction of the sailor, Ben, in *Love for Love*; Ben's use of nautical terms demonstrates the playwright's familiarity with this jargon. When the elder Congreve joined the regiment of the Duke of Ormond at Kilkenny in 1681, his son was able to enroll in Kilkenny College, which was free to all families who served the duke. Here, Congreve received his first formal education and his first exposure to the high society that gathered around the wealthy Duke of Ormond. After spending four and a half years at Kilkenny, Congreve entered Trinity College, Dublin (April 5, 1686), where he had the same tutor as Jonathan Swift, St. George Ashe. The theater in Smock Alley, Dublin, was at this period being run by Joseph Ashbury, who, like Congreve's father, served under the Duke of Ormond. Congreve may already have known Ashbury before coming to Trinity College, and Congreve's frequent absences from college on Saturday afternoons suggest that he was spending his time at the theater. Here, he would have seen a fine sampling of contemporary drama and could have begun to learn those dramatic conventions that he perfected in his own works.

In 1688, James II fled to Ireland. Perhaps fearing a massacre of Protestants in retaliation for their support of William of Orange against the Catholic Stuart king, the Congreves left Ireland for their family home in England. Congreve went first to Staffordshire to visit his grandfather at Stretton Manor; there, he wrote a draft of *The Old Bachelor* before coming to London to enroll in the Middle Temple to study law. Congreve was not, however, an ideal law student. Like Steele's literary Templar in *The Spectator*, he frequented the Theatre Royal in nearby Drury Lane and Will's Coffee House rather than the Inns of Court.

At Will's, Dryden held literary court; by 1692, Congreve had become sufficiently friendly with the former laureate that he was asked to contribute a translation of Juvenal's eleventh satire to Dryden's forthcoming edition of the satires of Juvenal and Persius. Together with Arthur Manwayring and Thomas Southerne, Dryden was helpful to Congreve in revising *The Old Bachelor*. (In 1717, Congreve partially returned the favor, editing and writing an introduction to a posthumous edition of Dryden's *Dramatick Works*.) The play opened at the Theatre Royal in Drury Lane on March 9, 1693, with a brilliant cast, including Anne Bracegirdle as Araminta. Congreve was soon in love with Bracegirdle, who would play the heroine in each of his succeeding works and who may have been his mistress. In December, 1693, Congreve's second comedy, *The Double Dealer*, was performed. Though Dryden praised it profusely, the play was not initially well received. After Queen Mary requested a special performance, however, its popularity increased.

Love for Love needed no royal sponsorship for its success. The first play to be performed in the restored Lincoln's Inn Fields Theatre (April 30, 1695), it ran for thirteen nights. Congreve was made one of the managers of the theater in return for a promise of a play a year, if his health permitted. Congreve needed two years to complete *The Mourning Bride*, which opened on February 27, 1697. The tragedy was worth the wait, for it was eminently successful. Three more years elapsed before Congreve's next play. Meanwhile, in 1698, Jeremy Collier attacked the Restoration stage in general, and Congreve in particular, for immorality. Congreve replied with his *Amendments of Mr. Collier's False and Imperfect Citations*. Between ill-health and the controversy with Collier, Congreve was unable to stage *The Way of the World* until March, 1700. Dryden recognized its genius, writing to Mrs. Steward on March 12, "Congreve's new play has had but moderate success, though it deserves much better." Coupled with Collier's attacks, the poor reception of *The Way of the World* convinced Congreve to abandon serious drama, but he continued to write and remain interested in the theater.

On March 21, 1701, *The Judgement of Paris*, an elaborate masque, opened at Dorset Garden with Anne Bracegirdle as Venus. With Vanbrugh and Walsh, Congreve adapted Molière's *Monsieur de Pourceaugnac* as *Squire Trelooby*, which was performed in March, 1704. He also wrote the libretto to an opera, *Semele*, which was not performed in his lifetime. For a brief time, too, Congreve, Vanbrugh, and Walsh managed a theater in the Haymarket.

Although Congreve held a variety of government posts throughout his life—the type of minor posts with which men of letters were often rewarded in that era—he did not have a lucrative position until 1705, when he was made a commissioner of wines, with an annual salary of two hundred pounds. Congreve was an ardent Whig, but he had so agreeable a personality that when the Tories came to power, Jonathan Swift and Lord Halifax (to whom Congreve had dedicated *The Double Dealer*) intervened to help him retain this income. Dryden was not merely flattering when he wrote, "So much the sweetness of your manners move,/ We cannot envy you, because we love." Not until almost a decade later, when the Hanoverians came to power, did Congreve enjoy a substantial income, receiving the post of Secretary of the Island of Jamaica. He discharged his duties by a deputy, continuing to lead a placid, retired life in London during the winter and in various country houses during the summer. As he wrote to Joseph Keally, "Ease and quiet is what I hunt after. If I have not ambition, I have other passions more easily gratified."

One passion was for Henrietta, Duchess of Marlborough, whom he met in 1703. In 1722, Congreve went to Bath for his health, and Henrietta accompanied him, even though she was married to the son of Lord Treasurer Godolphin. The following year, when she gave birth to her second daughter, Mary, it was assumed that Congreve was the child's father. Henrietta was by his side when he died on January 19, 1729, and when she died four years later, she was buried near him in Westminster Abbey.

Analysis

William Congreve began writing some thirty years after the Restoration, yet his plays retain many of the concerns of those written in the 1660's and 1670's. Foremost among these concerns is what constitutes a gentleman; that is, how one should act in society. The seventeenth century, particularly after 1660, was very interested in this matter; some five hundred conduct books were published during the century, the majority of them after the Restoration.

The response that Congreve gives, which is identical to that of Sir George Etherege, William Wycherley, and other Restoration dramatists, may be summed up in a single word: wit. This wit encompasses far more than mere verbal facility. By the time Sir Richard Blackmore attacked wit as suitable "only to please with Jests at Dinner" ("A Satyr Against Wit," 1700), the term had lost much of its significance. For Congreve, Dryden's definition is more relevant than Blackmore's: "a propriety of thoughts and words"—and, he might have added, of conduct. As Rose Snider wrote in *Satire in the Comedies of Congreve, Sheridan, Wilde, and Coward* (1937), "Decorum (true wit) might be defined simply as a natural elegance of thought and conduct, based on respect for sound judgment, fidelity to nature, and a due regard for beauty."

What constitutes propriety and fidelity to nature is subject to varying interpretation. To the nineteenth century, Restoration comedy was at best "the Utopia of gallantry, where pleasure is duty, and the manners perfect freedom" (Charles Lamb, "On the Artificial Comedy of the Last Century"), at worst the height of immorality. Chastity was not a requirement for the late seventeenth century gentleman, though it was for the lady. Charles de Saint-Denis de Saint-Évremond expressed well the age's sexual ethics: "As for the Hatred of villainous Actions, it ought to continue so long as the World does, but give leave to Gentlemen of refin'd Palates to call that Pleasure, which gross and ill-bred People call Vice, and don't place your Virtue in old musty Notions which the primitive Mortals derived from their natural Savageness."

In keeping with this genial libertinism is a rejection of prudence, financial as well as sexual. Money is not to be saved but spent, and spent on pleasure. Business is rejected as an improper pursuit. In the first scene of *The Old Bachelor*, Congreve presents in the dialogue between Bellmour and Vainlove a catalog of unworthy occupations for the genteel and indicates that the proper pursuits are witty conversation and love.

To a certain extent, this hedonism was a reaction to the restraints imposed by the Puritan Protectorate. After the Restoration, playwrights, who had lost their occupation under Cromwell, continued to portray the final victory of Cavalier over Roundhead. The Puritan cleric is a standard butt of Restoration satire. So, too, is the "cit," the merchant—not only because he was likely to be a Dissenter rather than an Anglican but also because mercantile London supported Cromwell while in general the country squires remained loyal to the Crown. Those who suffered the most under the Protectorate, the Court party, took their revenge in their plays when they returned to power.

Restoration comedy does not, however, restrict itself to negatives, nor to rejecting conventional morality and ridiculing its followers. The Truewit is indeed a libertine and often a spendthrift and freethinker, but he espouses positive values that offset these signs of youthful exuberance. Bravery, for example, is highly prized. The wit will not tolerate an insult; a sign of wit is a willingness to defend one's honor. A character such as Captain Bluffe (in *The Old Bachelor*), who draws his sword only when all danger is past, or Fainall (in *The Way of the World*), who draws his sword on a woman, shows himself to be no true wit.

Urbanity is another attribute of the Truewit. He must be able to engage in brilliant repartee; his conversation must never be dull, vulgar, overly serious, or abstruse. A wit must never lose his temper, for reason should always control emotion. He must be aware of the latest fashions and observe them. Excesses in dress, manner, or speech are scorned, as are rusticity and bad taste. Because the wit must fit into polite society, the rustic is a butt of humor on the stage even though his political views probably harmonized with those of the playwrights who were mocking him.

Yet another virtue is intelligence, of which one outward sign is again brilliant conversation. A further indication is the ability to outsmart those who would thwart the wit's desires—generally comic villains who try to prevent his attaining a suitable wife and estate. Although these villains make a pretense of being clever and urbane, their speeches and action expose their flawed nature, which leads to their punishment at the end of the play.

Selflessness is also a Restoration ideal. Prodigality is not a vice but rather a manifestation of generosity. Fondlewife (*The Old Bachelor*) leaves his wife to secure five hundred pounds and is almost cuckolded during his absence. By contrast, Valentine (*Love for Love*) is willing to give money to a discarded mistress (though not to a creditor). When wits scheme, they are trying to secure what should rightfully be theirs; when fools and Witwouds plot, they are trying to secure what should belong to another. The latter are greedy and so are frustrated.

Restoration comedy is thus moral in its intent, punishing those who deviate from societal values and rewarding those who are faithful to those norms. These values are not Victorian, nor are they the values of religious fanatics, Puritans, or nonjurors such as Jeremy Collier—hence the repeated charges of immorality brought against Congreve and his contemporaries. In emphasizing intelligence, generosity, urbanity, and bravery, though, these dramatists were drawing on a tradition that went back to Aristotle's *Nicomachean Ethics* (fourth century B.C.), and their view of comedy is Aristotle's as well. Defending himself against Collier, Congreve conceded that he portrayed vice on the stage; but he did so because comedy, according to Aristotle, depicts "the worst sort of people." It portrayed such people, Congreve continued, because "men are to be laugh'd out of their Vices in Comedy; the Business of Comedy is to delight, as well as to instruct: And as vicious People are made asham'd of their Follies or Faults, by seeing them expos'd in a ridiculous manner, so are good People at once both warn'd and diverted at their Expense." Collier and his successors did not find this response persuasive; they saw little to choose between Bell-mour and Heartwell (*The Old Bachelor*) or between Mirabell and Fainall (*The Way of the World*). On the other hand, Congreve's appreciative audiences have always understood the important distinction.

At the same time that Congreve's plays are the artistic consummation of the traditions of Restoration comedy, they also reveal a breaking away from those traditions. Though these plays accept societal norms, and though the hero and heroine must be able to conform to societal expectations, they recognize the flaws of society also. Instead of trying simply to blend into society, the true wits seek to establish a private world beyond it. They recognize that beneath the glittering costumes and language lurk hypocrisy and brutality. Marriages are more often made in countinghouses than in heaven; a wedding is often the beginning of a domestic tragedy rather than the end of a social comedy. Life does not always proceed smoothly, and even when it does, it leads to a loss of youth, beauty, attractiveness. Congreve reaffirms the *carpe diem* spirit—eat, drink, and be merry—but he does not blink from the rest of the refrain—for tomorrow we die.

The sadness beneath the surface of Congreve's plays also derives from his refusal to dehumanize the targets of ridicule. Restoration comedy is social rather than psychological, and Congreve's plays are primarily concerned with how one should act in society. For the first time in the period, though, those who do not conform are not simply dismissed as fools. In fact, Pope wondered whether Congreve actually portrayed any fools, and in his dedication of *The Way of the World*, Congreve noted that audiences had difficulty distinguishing "betwixt the character of a Witwoud and a Truewit" in that work. Congreve probes beneath action to motivation to reveal what Heartwell, Fondlewife, Lord Plyant, and Lady Wishfort are thinking. These characters recognize their weaknesses; they are not merely two-dimensional types but three-dimensional people capable of suffering. By granting humanity to would-be wits and fools, Congreve was unconsciously moving away from the purely satiric toward sentimental comedy.

His one tragedy, which is actually a tragicomedy, similarly uses many of the conventions of the period while showing significant variations. The diction is inflated, as is typical of heroic tragedy. The action is remote in time and place, the characters of noble birth and larger than life, the conflict Hobbesian as rivals ruthlessly contend. Unlike earlier heroic tragedy, however, the resolution to the conflict comes not through a Leviathan, not through some divinely ordained ruler, but rather through a Glorious Revolution that overthrows unjust, though otherwise legitimate, authority in favor of a benign, popularly proclaimed monarch as exponents of power yield to advocates of love. The influence of John Locke and the deposition of James II echo in the play, especially when contrasted with Dryden's tragedies, which espouse the divine right of kings.

Congreve may have begun *The Old Bachelor* as early as 1689, at the age of nineteen. Although Dryden proclaimed it the best first comedy he had ever seen, it shows in many ways evidence of being an apprentice piece. It is the only one of Congreve's comedies that lacks dramatic tension. There is no reason why Bellmour and Belinda could not marry in the first scene, since there are no blocking characters to prevent the match. Another flaw is Congreve's ambiguous attitude toward Belinda. In the *dramatis personae*, he describes her as "an affected Lady," and in his *Amendments of Mr. Collier's False and Imperfect Citations*, he indicates that she is not intended to be admirable. Anne Bracegirdle, who always played the heroine in Congreve's works, took the role of Araminta; Belinda was played by Susanah Mountfort, who performed as the obviously foolish Lady Froth in *The Double Dealer*. Since role and performer blended with each other in Restoration drama, audiences would expect that Belinda/Mountfort was intended as a butt of ridicule for her affectation and that Araminta would be the ideal to be admired. Yet at the end of the piece, Belinda is rewarded with marriage, while Araminta remains single.

The Old Bachelor also suggests its author's youth in its close adherence to the conventions of Restoration drama. It is, for example, the only one of Congreve's comedies that has for its hero a practicing, rather than a reformed, rake. It introduces, somewhat gratuitously, standard butts of Restoration satire: a rustic boor (Sir Joseph Wittol), a pretender to valor who is in fact a coward (Captain Bluffe), a Puritan merchant (Fondlewife), and an old man who, according to the *dramatis personae*, while "pretending to slight Women, [is] secretly in love."

Aside from the treatment of Belinda, the play does show a sure hand in exposing these various pretenders and in providing suitable punishment for them. Sir Joseph Wittol is tricked out of one hundred pounds and married to Vainlove's discarded mistress. Captain Bluffe is shown to be aptly named; he is valorous only in the absence of danger. He is beaten and kicked by Sharper and married off to Silvia's maid, Lucy, who had been Setter's mistress. Heartwell, who pretends to misogyny and candor, is punished by being made to believe that he has married Silvia and then being informed that she is not as chaste as he had assumed. Though he is again unmarried, he is tormented and mocked for his folly. Fondlewife has married a woman too young and sprightly for his years; additionally, he devotes himself to business, which Bellmour calls "the rub of life [that] perverts our aim, casts off the bias, and leaves us wide and short of the intended mark." Fondlewife narrowly escapes cuckolding, and one senses that the escape is only temporary. As Vainlove notes, "If the spirit of cuckoldom be once raised up in a woman, the devil can't lay it, 'till she has done 't."

Congreve shows great skill in handling the dialogue. Bellmour and

Belinda exemplify the witty couple of Restoration comedy; as is typical of duels between the witty man and woman, Belinda has the better of their exchanges. Vainlove and Araminta, too, engage in witty debate, and again the woman proves the wittier; in one dialogue, Araminta reduces Vainlove to a defeated "O madam!," at which point she dismisses the conversation— and her suitor—with a call for music. The men and women also engage in repartee among themselves, deftly leaping from one topic to another, devising fresh and apt similes, coining paradoxes, brilliantly sketching a character in a line. The play abounds in the sheer joy of words, as when Barnaby tells Fondlewife, "Comfort will send Tribulation hither." Restoration audiences attended comedies less for their plots than for their wit, and the success of *The Old Bachelor* shows that Congreve did not disappoint them in this regard.

While Congreve was offering largely conventional fare in his first comedy, even here one finds hints of sadness beneath the comic surface. John King McComb argues (in his essay "Congreve's *The Old Bachelor*: A Satiric Anatomy") that Bellmour, Vainlove, Heartwell, Fondlewife, and Spintext are stages in the rise and fall of the lover—from rake, to fop, to gull, and, finally, to cuckold. The "cormorant in love," as Bellmour describes himself in the first scene, admits that "I must take up or I shall never hold out; flesh and blood cannot bear it always." Vainlove has been a cormorant in love, too, but now contents himself with arousing desire and leaving to others the task of satisfying it. Heartwell, too, was a rake in his youth, but his passion has ebbed; unlike Vainlove, he no longer can excite women at those rare instances when he wishes to and so must attempt to purchase love. At the last stage are Fondlewife and Spintext; the latter never appears in the play but is mentioned as being a cuckold, while the audience sees Fondlewife first almost suffering the same fate and then refusing to believe the ocular proof. Bellmour, too, will age, Congreve seems to suggest; he will lose his looks and gaiety and perhaps be reduced to the state of a Heartwell or Fondlewife. The last speech of the play, which Congreve gives to Heartwell, projects such a fate for the youth.

Restoration satire is also muted in the play through the humanization of Heartwell and Fondlewife, both of whom show more sense than the typical comic butt. Heartwell's pretended aversion to "the drudgery of loving" must be exposed, since love is the chief concern of the Truewit and thus not to be slighted. Neither can pretense go unpunished. Yet Heartwell himself understands his dilemma as he is caught between reason and desire. Standing before Silvia's house he declares, "I will recover my reason, and begone." He is, however, fixed to the spot; his feet will not move: "I'm caught! There stands my north, and thither my needle points.—Now could I curse myself, yet cannot repent." After Heartwell is caught and exposed, Congreve does not mask his real anguish. In a speech reminiscent of Shylock's "Hath not a Jew eyes," Heartwell turns upon his mockers: "How have I deserved this of you? any of ye?" Vainlove urges Bellmour to stop ridiculing Heartwell—"You vex him too much; 'tis all serious to him"— and Belinda agrees: "I begin to pity him myself."

Similarly, Fondlewife, Puritan, banker, old man that he is—and any one of these characteristics would suffice in itself to render him ridiculous in a Restoration comedy—has moments of self-knowledge that grant him a touch of humanity. When he discovers Bellmour with his wife, he, too, speaks with dignity. Though Bellmour kisses Laetitia's hand at the very moment she is being reconciled to her husband, Fondlewife's tears and professions of kindness take some of the edge off the satire. If one must choose between the world of Bellmour and that of Fondlewife, one will certainly prefer the former; even so, Congreve understands that with all its admirable qualities, its wit, grace, youth, and intelligence, that World, too, is not devoid of faults.

Congreve's second play, *The Double Dealer*, demonstrates much greater control over his material; it also contains a more fully developed negative portrayal of society. In *A Short View of the Profaneness and Immorality of the English Stage* (1698), Jeremy Collier noted, "There are but Four Ladys in this Play, and Three of the biggest of them are Whores. A Great Compliment to Quality to tell them there is not above a quarter of them Honest!" Despite Congreve's efforts to dismiss Collier's observation, Congreve does indeed indict the fashionable world, and his epigram from Horace.— "Sometimes even comedy raises her voice"—suggests that he intended to go beyond the conventional butts of Restoration satire. Small wonder that fashionable society returned the favor with a cool reception of the piece.

Artistically, *The Double Dealer* is much more coherent than *The Old Bachelor*. As Congreve wrote in the dedication, "I made the plot as strong as I could, because it was single; and I made it single, because I would avoid confusion." This single plot revolves around the love between Cynthia and Mellefont, who wish to marry, and the efforts of Maskwell and Lady Touchwood to prevent the match. The intrigues of these blocking figures, though conventional in comedies of the period, provide dramatic tension lacking in Congreve's earlier piece.

Congreve's handling of this central conflict, however, is less conventional. Typically, the Truewit defeats the Witwoud through his greater intelligence and so proves himself worthy of the witty heroine. When Mellefont proposes that he and Cynthia elope and thereby end the plotting and counterplotting, she rejects so simple a solution, demanding "a very evident demonstration of" her lover's wit. Until Maskwell overreaches and betrays himself, though, Mellefont is powerless to direct the action of the play; instead, he acts as Maskwell directs.

The conversation is not as sprightly as in Congreve's other plays or in

Restoration comedy generally. Mellefont and Cynthia are too good-natured to take verbal advantage of the follies of those around them. While their benevolence makes them likable, it also tends to make them dull. They seem to anticipate the comedies of Steele rather than looking back to those of Etherege and Wycherley. Like Maskwell, the Witwouds are left to expose themselves: Lady Froth attempts a heroic poem on "Syllabub," for which Brisk provides inane commentary; Lord Froth claims that the height of wit is refraining from laughing at a joke, yet he laughs incessantly; Lady Plyant thinks herself a mistress of language but contrives such convoluted sentences that her lover, Careless, is driven to exclaim, "O Heavens, madam, you confound me!"

These Witwouds are as vain as they are foolish. In a telling piece of by-play, Lord Froth takes out a mirror to look at himself; Brisk takes it from him to admire himself. This sign of vanity is repeated when Lady Froth hands her husband a mirror, asking him to pretend it is her picture. Lord Froth becomes so enamored of the image he sees that his wife declares, "Nay, my lord, you shan't kiss it so much, I shall grow jealous, I vow now." Like false wit, vanity is left to mock itself.

Even sex, treated so cavalierly in other comedies of the period, is here largely a disruptive rather than a regenerative force. Each of the married women in the play is false to her husband. Lord Froth and Sir Paul Plyant are old and foolish and so "deserve" to be cuckolded, but the same cannot be said of Lord Touchwood. Lady Touchwood's passion for her nephew Mellefont threatens to upset Cynthia's marriage as well as her own and to subvert, through incest, proper familial relationships. Her passion for Maskwell, meanwhile, threatens to allow a member of the servant class to become a lord, as she contrives to have Maskwell supplant Mellefont as her husband's heir. The seriousness of this sexual promiscuity is manifest at the end of the play; Lady Touchwood is to be divorced and so lose her position in society.

Surrounded by vanity, infidelity, folly, and knavery, Cynthia has good reason to wonder whether she and Mellefont should continue to participate in the social charade. "'Tis an odd game we are going to play at; what think you of drawing stakes, and giving over in time?" she asks Mellefont. She understands that marriage is not a great improver: "I'm thinking, though marriage makes man and wife one flesh, it leaves them still two fools." The song that concludes this conversation with Mellefont warns of yet another threat: "Prithee, Cynthia, look behind you,/ Age and wrinkles will o'ertake you;/ Then, too late, desire will find you,/ When the power must forsake you." To become like her stepmother, Lady Plyant, or Mellefont's aunt, Lady Touchwood, may be the fate reserved for Cynthia. The melancholy implicit in *The Old Bachelor* here rises to the surface. Mellefont remains cheerful, but his optimism seems misplaced. He has grossly misjudged

Maskwell; he may be misjudging all of reality. Though the true lovers marry, and though Maskwell and Lady Touchwood are banished at the end of the play, Congreve had not yet found, as he did in his last play, a way to reconcile the private world of virtue with the public world of folly, sham, and pretense. Cynthia and Mellefont remain apart from society; they do not control their actions, nor do they appear much in the play. The implication is that one can preserve one's innocence only by avoiding the fashionable world. The play thus foreshadows the gloom of the Tory satirists as well as the sentimental comedy of the next age.

Congreve was stung by the cool reception of his bitingly satiric *The Double Dealer*. Although he believed that satire is the aim of comedy, in his next play, *Love for Love*, he disguised his attacks on fashionable society offering a more traditional Restoration comedy. As he notes in the prologue: "We hope there's something that may please each taste. . . ." Much of the satire of *Love for Love* is confined to Valentine's mad scenes in the fourth act. By putting these comments into the mouth of a seeming madman, Congreve can be harsh without offending; it is as if he were stepping outside the world of the play to deliver these observations. Valentine in his madness is utterly Juvenalian, railing against all aspects of the fashionable world. There is more truth than wit in such observations as, "Dost thou know what will happen to-morrow?—answer me not—for I will tell thee. Tomorrow, knaves will thrive through craft, and fools through fortune, and honesty will go as it did, frost-nipped in a summer suit." Scandal, Valentine's friend, is also harsh in his analysis of society: "I can shew you pride, folly, affection, wantonness, inconstancy, covetousness, dissimulation, malice, and ignorance, all in one piece. Then I can shew you lying, foppery, vanity, cowardice, bragging, lechery, impotence and ugliness in another piece; and yet one of these is a celebrated beauty, and t'other a professed beau." Beneath the surface, the way of the world is vicious and foul.

By the end of the play, though, Valentine abandons his feigned madness, and Scandal is willing to take a kinder view of the world than that expressed in the song: "He alone won't betray in whom none will confide;/ And the nymph may be chaste that has never been tried." Although society in *Love for Love* has its faults, these spring more from folly than from vice; the world here is closer to that of *The Old Bachelor* than to that of *The Double Dealer*. There are no villains such as Maskwell or Lady Touchwood, no divorce, no banishment from society.

As in *The Old Bachelor*, there *is* considerable pretense that must be exposed and, to an extent, punished. Tattle pretends to be a great rake, a keeper of secrets, and a wit. Foresight pretends to be wise, to be able to foretell the future, and to be a suitable husband for a "young and sanguine" wife. Sir Sampson Legend pretends to be a good father and a fit husband for Angelica. Each of these pretenders is exposed and punished. Tattle is married off in secret to Mrs. Frail, a woman of the town. Fondle-wife is cuckolded. Sir Sampson's plan to cheat his son of his inheritance and his fiancée is frustrated. These characters are Witwouds because they fail to adhere to the ideals of Restoration society. Sir Sampson is greedy; Foresight has failed to acquire wisdom with age; Tattle seeks a fortune rather than pleasure. They all want to be Truewits, but they are unable or unwilling to conform to the demands of wit.

Below them are Ben and Miss Prue, respectively a "sea-beast" and a "land monster." Neither has had the opportunity to learn good manners, Ben because he has spent his life at sea and Prue because she has been reared in the country rather than the town. They are no match for even the pretended wits. Tattle quickly seduces Prue; Mrs. Frail seduces Ben. Society has no place for these characters, who return to their element at the end of the play.

Above the fools and would-be wits are Valentine and Angelica. She is the typical Restoration witty lady, able to manipulate Foresight and Sir Sampson and control Valentine to attain her goal, which is a suitable marriage. Valentine has many of the characteristics of the wit—he is generous, he prefers pleasure to prudence, he is a clever conversationalist—but Angelica will not marry him until she is certain that he really is a proper husband.

At the beginning of the play, there is some question as to his suitability, not because he has been a rake, not because he has spent money reck-lessly—these are actually commendable activities—but because he has been trying to buy Angelica's love. Valentine's lavish entertaining has been to impress her; he seems to regard her as mercenary and must learn her true character. Having failed to purchase her with his wealth, Valentine next tries to shame her with his poverty; here, again, he fails. Then he tries to trick her into expressing her love by feigning to be mad. As a Truewit, Angelica is able to penetrate this disguise also. Only when Valentine abandons all of his tricks and agrees that Angelica should have free choice of a husband does she accept him. Marriage for her is a serious business; she must be certain she is not submitting to tyranny or being pursued solely for her large fortune.

The blocking figure in *Love for Love* is, then, Valentine himself, and the plot of the play concerns his learning how to interact in society. Ben and Miss Prue do not learn how to do so, in part because of their previous experiences, in part because their teachers are would-be instead of true wits, in part because they lack intelligence and so are easily deceived. Foresight, Tattle, and Sir Sampson fail to learn because their characters are flawed. Foresight thinks he will learn from astrology, while Sir Sampson and Tattle think so highly of themselves that they are not even aware that they need to be taught anything.

Congreve indicates in *Love for Love* that one must live within a society that is less than perfect but that one can do so pleasantly enough if one adheres to the ideals of Restoration comedy. The despair in *The Double Dealer* yields here to a happier vision. Valentine and Angelica, unlike Mellefont and Cynthia, understand their society and have shown their ability to survive in it.

Because Congreve recognizes the limitations of the fashionable world, he is sympathetic to characters who do not quite fit in. Ben is not simply a butt of ridicule because he is an outsider. Whereas Tattle is punished with Mrs. Frail, Ben escapes that fate. Because he does not share society's viewpoint, Ben is also able to make some telling comments. He speaks his mind, shuns pretense, is generous, and understands that he will be happier at sea than in London. Prue, too, is honest; though she is Tattle's willing pupil, she does escape marrying him. The innocent fools suffer less than do the Witwouds.

With *Love for Love*, Congreve has found his true voice—a combination of satire, compassion, and wit. His hero and heroine understand both the attractions and faults of society and therefore are able to skate deftly on the surface of their world without succumbing to its folly, as Bellmour and Belinda may, or being overwhelmed by its viciousness, as Mellefont and Cynthia may be. It is a shorter step from *Love for Love* to *The Way of the World* than from *The Old Bachelor* to this comedy.

Before making that step, however, Congreve turned to tragedy, though *The Mourning Bride* resembles Congreve's other plays, for, like the comedies, it explores the questions of how the individual should act in society and what constitutes a proper marriage. On the one hand are Zara and Manuel, who rely on royal birth and power. They believe that power can command even love; Manuel wants to compel his daughter to marry Garcia, the son of the king's favorite, and Zara seeks to force Osmyn to marry her. Manuel is therefore another version of Sir Sampson Legend, who would have his child act as he himself wishes, regardless of the child's desires. Zara is a tragic rendition of Lady Touchwood, who would rather murder the man she loves than see a rival marry him. Significantly, Elizabeth Barry played both Lady Touchwood and Zara. Zara and Manuel serve as blocking figures, much like Maskwell and Lady Touchwood, but with more power to do evil.

Contrasted to these two are Osmyn and Almeria. They, too, are of royal birth, but instead of using power to create love, they use love to get power. They are generous, brave, intelligent, like their comic counterparts. Like them, too, they are young, confronting a harsh world controlled by their elders. As in the comedies, the values of the young triumph, but in the process the villains are not simply exposed but, as befits a tragedy, killed.

The true lovers wed; Zara and Manuel also "marry"—at the end of the play, Zara drinks to her love from a poisoned bowl, embraces him, and dies by his side exclaiming, "This to our mutual bliss when joined above." Like Tattle and Mrs. Frail, the unworthy characters are joined. The analogy is strengthened by the masked wedding each undergoes. Just as Tattle and Mrs. Frail do not recognize their partners until it is too late, so Zara believes she is dying beside Osmyn rather than Manuel.

The deposition of the old by the young marks a triumph of love over power. It also addresses the question of what constitutes legitimate power. The older generation believes that birth and rank alone are sufficient; Manuel and Zara sense no obligation to anyone but themselves. Theirs is the belief in the divine right of kings to govern wrongly. Osmyn and Almeria have a different view. Though of royal birth, Osmyn is elevated to the throne by the people, who rebel against Manuel's tyranny. Congreve, staunch Whig, is portraying the Glorious Revolution, in which the hereditary monarch, because he has abused his power, loses his crown to a more worthy, because more benevolent, successor.

In the first scene of the fourth act of *The Way of the World*, Congreve directly addresses the issue of how two people can live harmoniously with each other while retaining personal autonomy and dignity on the one hand and remaining part of the social world on the other. This famous "Proviso" scene has a long theatrical history. A scene that first gained prominence in Honoré d'Urfé's *Astrea* (1607-1628), versions appear in four of Dryden's comedies—*The Wild Gallant* (pr. 1663), *Secret Love: Or, The Maiden Queen* (pr. 1667), *Marriage à la Mode* (pr. 1672, pb. 1673) and *Amphitryon: Or, The Two Socia's* (pr., pb. 1690)—in James Howard's *All Mistaken: Or, The Mad Couple* (pr. 1667), and Edward Ravenscroft's *The Careless Lovers* (pr.1673) and *The Canterbury Guests* (pr. 1694). As he did so often, Congreve used a well-established convention but invested it with new significance and luster. The proviso in *The Way of the World* is not only the wittiest of such scenes but also the most brilliantly integrated into the theme of the play. Indeed, the scene illuminates the plight of every witty heroine who had appeared on the Restoration stage and summarized the hopes and fears of all fashionable couples to that time.

Millamant does not want to "dwindle into a wife"; Mirabell does not want to "be beyond measure enlarged into a husband." She wishes to be "made sure of my will and pleasure"; he wants to be certain that his wife's liberty will not degenerate into license. In the Hobbesian world of self-love, rivalry, and conflicting passions, these two therefore devise a Lockean compact, creating a peaceful and reasonable accommodation between their individual and mutual needs. They will not act like other fashionable couples, "proud of one another the first week, and ashamed of one another ever after." They will act more like strangers in public, that they may act more like lovers in private. Millamant will remain autonomous in her sphere of the tea table, but she will not "encroach upon the men's prerogative." She will not sacrifice her health or natural beauty to fashion or whim; otherwise, she may dress as she likes. Together the lovers create a private world divorced from the follies and vices of the society around them while retaining the freedom to interact with that society when they must.

In contrast to this witty couple are Fainall and Marwood. As the names suggest, Fainall is a pretender to wit, and his consort, Marwood, seeks to mar the match between Mirabell and Millamant because of her love—and then hate—for Mirabell. She, too, is a pretender, a seeming prude who in fact is having an affair with Fainall. Whereas the witty couple seek to preserve their private world inviolate, Fainall and Marwood attempt to exploit private relationships. Fainall has married for money, not love, and once he has secured his wife's fortune, he intends to divorce her, marry Marwood, and flee society. Later, he and Marwood conspire to secure half of Millamant's and all of Lady Wishfort's estate by threatening to expose Mrs. Fainall's earlier affair with Mirabell, hoping that Lady Wishfort will pay to keep secret her daughter's indiscretion and prevent a public divorce.

On yet another level are Lady Wishfort, Petulant, and Witwoud, who have no private life at all. Lady Wishfort cannot smile because she will ruin her carefully applied makeup; the face she presents to society must not be disturbed by any unexpected emotion. All of her efforts are directed to appearing fashionable—hence her fear of Mrs. Fainall's exposure. Hence, too, her inflated rhetoric when she tries to impress the supposed Sir Rowland. Petulant wishes to appear the true Restoration wit and so hires women to ask for him at public places. He will even disguise himself and then "call for himself, wait for himself; nay, and what's more, not finding himself, sometimes [leave] a letter for himself." Witwoud, as his name indicates, seeks to pass himself off as a wit but must rely on his memory rather than his invention to maintain a conversation. His cowardice or stupidity prevents his understanding an insult, and he mistakes "impudence and malice" for wit. He will not acknowledge his own brother because he believes it unfashionable to know one's own relations, thus surrendering private ties to public show. Sir Willful, Witwoud's half brother, is the typical rustic. Like Ben and Prue in *Love for Love*, he has no place in society. He withdraws from social interaction first by getting drunk and then by returning to his element, leaving the urban world entirely.

Congreve thus offers four ways of coping with the demands of society. One may flee completely, as Sir Willful does and as Marwood, Fainall, and Lady Wishfort talk of doing. Mirabell and Millamant could adopt this solution, too. If they elope, Millamant will retain half of her fortune, enough to allow the couple a comfortable life together, but they would lose the pleasures of the tea table, of the theater, of social intercourse—of all the benefits, in short, that society can offer. One can also submit one's personality completely to society and abandon any privacy (Petulant and Witwoud). One can use private life only to serve one's social ends (Fainall and Marwood), or one can find a suitable balance between them. Presented with these choices, Mirabell and Millamant wisely choose the last.

The question posed here is not only one of surfaces, of how best to enjoy life, although that element is important. Additionally, Congreve here explores differing ethical stances. The opening conversation between Mirabell and Fainall establishes the moral distinction between them. Fainall states, "I'd no more play with a man that slighted his ill fortune than I'd make love to a woman who undervalued the loss of her reputation." Mirabell replies, "You have a taste extremely delicate, and are for refining on your pleasures." Fainall's may be the wittier comment, but it is also the more malicious. True wit in *The Way of the World* embraces morality as well as intelligence. Mirabell does prove more intelligent than Fainall, outwitting him "by anticipation" just as he has cuckolded Fainall by anticipation. Even so, in their conversations the difference in cleverness is not as apparent as it is between Witwoud or Mirabell or Lady Wishfort and Millamant. Congreve once more is moving toward sentimental comedy by creating an intelligent hero who is also sententious. He is foreshadowing Addison's attempt in the *Spectator* "to enliven Morality with Wit, and to temper Wit with Morality."

The tone is bittersweet—another anticipation of the next age. Like Belinda in Pope's *The Rape of the Lock* (1712, 1714) Millamant must grow up. Just as she cannot be a coquette forever, so Mirabell must put aside his rakish past. One has a sense of time's passing. Even amid the witty repartee of the proviso scene, Mirabell looks ahead to Millamant's pregnancy, and to the time beyond that when she will be tempted, as Lady Wishfort is now, to hide her wrinkles. Her maid will one day say to her what Foible tells her lady: "I warrant you, madam, a little art once made your picture like you; and now a little of the same art must make you like your picture."

With this new sense of the future coexists a new sense of the past, a sense that one's earlier actions have consequences. Valentine is able to dismiss a former mistress with a gift of money and to redeem his earlier extravagances through an inheritance and a good marriage. Mirabell is not so fortunate. His previous affair with Mrs. Fainall is not immoral—no one condemns Mirabell for it—but neither is it a trifle to be quickly forgotten. Because of that affair, Mrs. Fainall has had to marry a man she dislikes and who hates her; she is not merely asking for information when she inquires of Mirabell, "Why did you make me marry this man?" Nor has Mirabell escaped all consequences, for this affair gives Fainall the opportunity to seize half of Millamant's—and thus half of Mirabell's—estate.

The artificial world and golden dreams of *The Old Bachelor* have essentially vanished in *The Way of the World*. The form remains—the witty couple contending successfully against the Witwouds and the fools; the young struggling against the old; the flawed but brilliant urbane society opposing vulgarity and rusticity. Congreve has elevated this form to its highest point; there is no more lovable coquette than Millamant, no Restoration wit more in control of his milieu than Mirabell. Yet the substance, the sense of passing time, of the sadness of real life, is undermining the comedy of wit. Alexander Pope called Congreve *ultimus Romanorum* (the ultimate Roman). He is truly the greatest of the Restoration dramatists, but he is *ultimus* in its other sense as well—the last.

Other major works

NOVELLA: *Incognita: Or, Love and Duty Reconcil'd*, 1692.

POETRY: "To Mr. Dryden on His Translation of Perius," 1693; *Poems upon Several Occasions*, 1710.

NONFICTION: *Amendments of Mr. Collier's False and Imperfect Citations*, 1698; *William Congreve: Letters and Documents*, 1964 (John C. Hodges, editor).

TRANSLATIONS: *Ovid's Art of Love, Book III*, 1709; *Ovid's Metamorphoses*, 1717 (with John Dryden and Joseph Addison).

MISCELLANEOUS: *Examen Poeticum*, 1693; *The Works of Mr. William Congreve*, 1710; *The Complete Works of William Congreve*, 1923 (4 volumes).

Bibliography

Hodges, John C. *William Congreve the Man: A Biography from New Sources*, 1941.

Love, Harold. *Congreve*, 1974.

McComb, John King. "Congreve's *The Old Bachelor*: A Satiric Anatomy," in *Studies in English Literature*. XVII (Summer, 1977), pp. 361-372.

Morris, Brian, ed. *William Congreve*, 1972.

Muir, Kenneth. "The Comedies of William Congreve," in *Restoration Theatre*, 1965. Edited by John Brown and Bernard Harris.

Novak, Maximillian E. *William Congreve*, 1971.

Rosowski, Susan J. "Thematic Development in the Comedies of William Congreve: The Individual in Society," in *Studies in English Literature*. XVI (Summer, 1976), pp. 387-406.

Snider, Rose. *Satire in the Comedies of Congreve, Sheridan, Wilder, and Coward*, 1937.

Joseph Rosenblum

MARC CONNELLY

Born: McKeesport, Pennsylvania; December 13, 1890
Died: New York, New York; December 21, 1980

Principal drama

Dulcy, pr., pb. 1921 (with George S. Kaufman); *To the Ladies!*, pr. 1922, pb. 1923 (with Kaufman); *Merton of the Movies*, pr. 1922, pb. 1925 (with Kaufman; adaptation of Harry Leon Wilson's story); *The Deep Tangled Wildwood*, pr. 1923 (with Kaufman; originally as *West of Pittsburg*, pr. 1922); *Helen of Troy*, pr. 1923 (with Kaufman; music and lyrics by Bert Kalmer and Harry Ruby); *Beggar on Horseback*, pr. 1924, pb. 1925 (with Kaufman; based on Paul Apel's play *Hans Sonnenstössers Höllenfahrt); Be Yourself*, pr. 1924 (with Kaufman; music by Kalmer, lyrics by Ruby); *The Wisdom Tooth*, pr., pb. 1926; *The Wild Man of Borneo*, pr. 1927 (with Herman J. Mankiewicz); *The Green Pastures: A Fable*, pb. 1929, pr. 1930 (adaptation of Roark Bradford's sketches in *Ol' Man Adam an' His Chillun*); *The Farmer Takes a Wife*, pr., pb. 1934 (with Frank B. Elser; adaptation of Walter D. Edmond's novel *Rome Haul*); *Everywhere I Roam*, pr. 1938 (with Arnold Sundgaard); *The Flowers of Virtue*, pr. 1942; *A Story for Strangers*, pr. 1948; *Hunter's Moon*, pr. 1958; *The Portable Yenberry*, pr. 1962.

Other literary forms

Marc Connelly is known primarily for his plays, but he also wrote many short humorous stories for *The New Yorker* and other magazines, a number of essays, a novel (*A Souvenir from Qam*, 1965), and an autobiography (*Voices Offstage*, 1968).

Achievements

Connelly is known mainly as a writer of polite farce of a conventional stamp. He enjoyed the partnership of a first-rate collaborator (George S. Kaufman) in his early years, the services of the stars of Broadway to speak his words, and one enduring artistic and commercial success, *The Green Pastures*, which won the 1930 Pulitzer Prize for Drama and made him a millionaire. He broke new ground in wedding his romantic views to Expressionistic techniques in a way that was suitable for the popular audience of the day. While his early successes were generally predictable comedies of manners, he was never content to restrict his plays to a single type, freely using features of the progressive theater of the time. His greatest work, *The Green Pastures*, which may seem condescending and simplistic to readers in the 1980's, represented a breakthrough for the theater of 1930: an all-black cast in a recasting of the Bible, set in the rural South. Connelly's dreams of an earthly paradise where the common man can find fulfillment despite his self-doubt and his burden of anxiety about the world are realized most completely in this play, set far from New York with characters different from the often fatuous urban types he had drawn so successfully. When audiences of the mid-1920's wanted someone to celebrate their heady exuberance and make them laugh, Connelly provided the gags and the situations to which they could respond; when the audiences of the Depression era wanted to find some hope in the future, Connelly responded again with a worldview pure in its simplicity, self-assured in its happy resolutions of misfortune, and delightful in its crackling wit.

Four of Connelly's collaborations with Kaufman in the years prior to *The Green Pastures* were successful: *Dulcy* and *To the Ladies!* arose from a character already popular in a New York newspaper column; *Merton of the Movies*, one of the earliest satires on Hollywood, adapted cinematic techniques to the stage; and *Beggar on Horseback* introduced Expressionism to Broadway. Later, *The Wisdom Tooth*, written by Connelly alone and chosen by Burns Mantle for *Best Plays of 1925-1926*, once more employed two realistic scenes flanking a fantasy.

Connelly's good taste, solidly American values, and ready wit made him a successful writer in other areas as well, from his radio play, *The Mole on Lincoln's Cheek* (1941), to his fiction, both long and short. In the same year that *The Green Pastures* won the Pulitzer Prize, Connelly also won the O. Henry Award for the 1930 short story "Coroner's Inquest." He was given honorary degrees by Bowdoin College (1952) and Baldwin-Wallace College (1962).

Connelly's plays have been rarely revived in recent years, and except for *The Green Pastures* his works are read only by historians of the stage. Nevertheless, his lasting achievement, *The Green Pastures*, is a monument of the American theater, distinguished by the purity of its sentiment, the richness of its language, and the charm of its imagination and humor.

Biography

Marcus Cook Connelly was born December 13, 1890. The year before, his parents, Patrick Joseph and Mabel Louise Fowler (Cook) Connelly, two touring actors, had settled in McKeesport, Pennsylvania, blaming the death of their first child on the hardships of the touring life. His father managed the White Hotel, a favorite stop for traveling circus troupes and theatrical companies, who imbued young Marc with what he later described as "the early feeling that going to the theatre is like going to an unusual church, where the spirit is nourished in mysterious ways, and pure magic may occur at any moment."

Connelly's father died of pneumonia when his son was twelve, and following the failure of the White Hotel in 1908, Connelly's hopes for college were dashed. When he and his mother moved to Pittsburgh, Connelly began a career with local newspapers, finally becoming second-string drama critic and author of a humorous weekly column, "Jots and Tittles," for the Pittsburgh *Gazette Times*. He also spent his evenings writing, directing, and stage-managing skits for the Pittsburgh Athletic Association. In 1913, Connelly wrote the lyrics for Alfred Ward Birdsall's *The Lady of Luzon*, which so impressed local steel magnate Joseph Riter that Connelly was commissioned to write the lyrics and libretto for a play that Riter was producing on Broadway, *The Amber Princess*. The play, which after two years of rewriting finally contained only Connelly's title and the lyrics to one song, failed, and the hopeful young playwright was forced to return to newspaper work, this time far from home.

While covering the theater district for the New York *Morning Telegraph* in 1917, Connelly met George S. Kaufman, who was then second-string drama critic for *The New York Times*. At the suggestion of the producer George C. Tyler, Connelly and Kaufman collaborated on a vehicle for Lynn Fontanne entitled *Dulcy*, which opened August 13, 1921, and was so popular (running for 246 performances) that they immediately created a sequel as a vehicle for another young star, Helen Hayes, entitled *To the Ladies!* (which ran for 128 performances). The team again collaborated on a misguided effort, *The Deep Tangled Wildwood*, which was shelved following a disastrous out-of-town tryout in May, 1922, and later reworked and produced on Broadway on November 5, 1923, running for only sixteen performances. Their greatest success as a team came with *Merton of the Movies*, the story of an innocent shop clerk who seeks stardom in Hollywood. It opened in November 13, 1922, and played for 398 performances.

At this same time, Connelly was firmly entrenched as a member of that group of literary and theatrical wits who lunched together at the Algonquin Hotel. In addition to the charter members, Franklin P. Adams, Jane Grant, Harold Ross, and Alexander Woollcott, the group included Robert Benchley, Dorothy Parker, Ring Lardner, Heywood Broun, Robert E. Sherwood, and others. In 1925, Grant, Ross, Woollcott, Kaufman, Connelly, and others founded *The New Yorker*, to which Connelly contributed numerous essays and pieces of short fiction between 1927 and 1930.

Kaufman and Connelly collaborated on three more plays, two of them musicals: *Helen of Troy*, with songs by Bert Kalmer and Harry Ruby, and *Be Yourself*, which starred Queenie Smith; the third was the fantasy *Beggar on Horseback*. When *Be Yourself* closed, the partnership was effectively over, although the two remained friends and were said to have been working on a musical about a union boss at the time of Kaufman's death.

Connelly went to Hollywood in 1925 to write the screenplay of a Beatrice Lillie vehicle, *Exit Smiling* (1926), returning to Broadway for his directorial debut in his play *The Wisdom Tooth*, a showcase for the actor Thomas

Mitchell, which ran for 160 performances. Connelly next collaborated with Herman J. Mankiewicz on a failed production, *The Wild Man of Borneo*, which closed after fifteen nights. For the next two years, Connelly avoided the theater and concentrated his efforts on *The New Yorker*.

In the fall of 1928, Connelly's cartoonist friend Rollin Kirby recommended that he read a book by a New Orleans newspaperman, Roark Bradford, entitled *Ol' Man Adam an' His Chillun*, a series of stories from the Old Testament told in the language of a black Southern preacher. Connelly immediately took to the book and visited Bradford in Louisiana, where he refined his knowledge of the dialect and found the spirituals a chorus would sing between the scenes. Once the play was written, Connelly spent the better part of a year seeking financial backing, as most producers feared offending both blacks and whites, the religious and the nonreligious. Finally, a broker, Rowland Stebbins, put up the necessary money, and on February 26, 1930, *The Green Pastures* had the first of its more than sixteen hundred performances. This play, for which he derived not only great financial rewards but also the deepest sense of fulfillment, formed the summary moment of his long career in the theater, a moment he never approached later in his life.

In 1930, Connelly married the actress Madeline Hurlock; they were divorced in 1935. It was during this period that Connelly wrote his last hit, *The Farmer Takes a Wife*, written with Frank B. Elser from his play *Rome Haul* (based on Walter D. Edmond's novel) and starring Henry Fonda. None of Connelly's remaining plays—*Everywhere I Roam* (written with Arnold Sundgaard), *The Flowers of Virtue*, *A Story for Strangers*, *Hunter's Moon*, and *The Portable Yenberry*—played more than fifteen performances. During this time, Connelly became involved in projects outside the theater. He directed his own adaptation of *The Green Pastures* for film (1936) and wrote several other screenplays as well, including *Captains Courageous* (1937). He also wrote a successful radio play, *The Mole on Lincoln's Cheek*, and, much later, a humorous novel, *A Souvenir from Qam*, as well as his autobiography, *Voices Offstage*, all the while contributing numerous pieces, mostly on his travels, to popular magazines. He occasionally acted, playing the Stage Manager in a 1944 production of Thornton Wilder's *Our Town*, and Professor Charles Osnan in Russel Crouse and Howard Lindsay's *The Tall Story*, both on Broadway (1959) and in the film (1960); also he served as the Narrator for the Off-Broadway revue *The Beast in Me* (1963), drawn from the writings of James Thurber. A founder of the Dramatists Guild, past president of the Authors' League of America, he was president of the National Institute of Arts and Letters from 1953 to 1956. From 1946 to 1950, he taught playwriting at Yale and frequently conducted seminars in the years following. Connelly's quiet humor remained keen to the end. On his ninetieth birthday, after receiving a certificate of appreciation from Mayor Ed Koch of New York, he said, "Some days I feel like an old man of 137, and other days like a mere boy of 136."

Analysis

Marc Connelly's early plays were highly successful largely because they adequately fulfilled audience expectations. He chose his collaborators well, as he did the books and plays that he adapted. While not a man of surpassing originality, he nevertheless brought a distinctive tone of gentility and sweet romanticism to his humor, tempering the brusque manner of Kaufman or the cynicism of Paul Apel. Throughout his work runs an implicit faith in man's ability to act for the good of himself and of mankind. For Connelly, humor brings forth all the elements of an earthly paradise: happiness, laughter, freedom from care, and harmony with others.

After a brief friendship, Connelly and Kaufman began their collaboration with *Dulcy*. A popular character in Franklin P. Adams' New York *World* column "The Conning Tower," Dulcinea was a chic suburban wife given to wearing fashionable clothes and uttering fashionable platitudes. A kind of satiric weather vane of the rising New York social set, she was ripe for appropriation for the stage, and she was taken by Connelly and Kaufman with Adams' full support. Characteristically, they did not make her an object of satiric attack; rather, they made her language and that of her friends a vehicle for laughter. The play centers on Dulcy Smith, who in her Westchester home hosts a weekend party for her husband Gordon's new business partner, C. Roger Forbes. Forbes wants to acquire Gordon's jewelry business for only a fraction of its real value. Dulcy sets out to get more money from Forbes, a fairer price, and upon her efforts the action of the play turns.

The other houseguests provide the heroine with a sufficient variety of difficulties to resolve before the final curtain. Dulcy's brother, William Parker, falls in love with Forbes's daughter Angela, who is already loved by another guest, screenwriter Vincent Leach. Schuyler Van Dyck is an otherwise attractive man who continually talks about the fortune he does not have, while Henry is a reformed forger whom Dulcy has converted into a butler.

Leach is supposed to encourage Mrs. Forbes's desire to write for the movies, but Forbes is antagonized by Dulcy's ploy, for he does not want his wife to become involved in the movie business. Dulcy further angers Forbes by helping his daughter Angela, who plans to elope with Leach; indeed, Forbes becomes so angry that he threatens to leave at once, canceling his offer to buy Gordon's business.

Dulcy is "a clever woman," however, and in the third act, all the complications are resolved. Forbes agrees to pay twenty-five percent for Gordon's business, rather than the sixteen and two-thirds percent initially offered. Instead of eloping with Leach, Angela is married off to Dulcy's stockbroker brother, William, pleasing her father no end. Schuyler Van Dyck is taken by Forbes for what he pretends to be, and Henry is exonerated of the charge of having stolen a pearl necklace.

If the action is uninspired, the *au courant* dialogue charmed contemporary audiences. Dulcy's trite expressions are played off against those of the clever characters, the most clever of whom is her brother, who is rewarded with the girl of his dreams. The jargon of various professions is exquisitely mocked: Leach speaks the language of Hollywood (particularly in his account of his movie *Sin*, the play's finest satiric set piece); Forbes speaks the language of Wall Street; and an incidental character, Tom Sterrett, an "advertising engineer," speaks the lingo of Madison Avenue. Broadway found itself laughing at this congenial burlesque of jargon, for the authors never make their satire sting but rather invite one to pardon these amiably foolish types.

Adams provided the impetus for another Connelly-Kaufman collaboration when he recommended in his column of February 3, 1922, *Merton of the Movies*, a novel by Harry Leon Wilson. The producer George C. Tyler then suggested it to the team, and the play opened November 13, 1922. Wilson's novel is a biting attack on the hypocrisy and meretriciousness of Hollywood and its reflection of the pervasive lack of culture in the United States; Connelly and Kaufman viewed Hollywood with an air of such superior amusement that they could not feel themselves threatened enough to knot the lash of their satire any more than they had with *Dulcy*. Instead, they made the play a story of one man realizing his dream to be a Hollywood star, ultimately becoming as vapid and cynical as those he had so long worshiped on the screen. The play was a critical and popular success, running for 398 performances.

Merton Gill is a clerk in a general store in Simsbury, Illinois, who gains stardom in Hollywood. His knowledge and interest in the "art" of the movies is limited to the fan magazines and public relations interviews he devours, and so at the beginning of the play he is as easy a butt for jokes as is the movie industry itself. The summation of all of his dreams is Beulah Baxter, the lead in the popular *Hazards of Hortense* serials to which Merton became addicted back in Simsbury. When he finally meets her, he finds not the sweet and simple ingenue she portrays but an oft-married, selfish starlet whose concerns about her art are as limited as her vocabulary. Tricked into appearing in a parody of his cinematic idol, Harold Parmalee, Merton becomes an overnight star. His gimmick is playing amusing roles seriously, which leads everyone (including the audience) to imagine that poor Merton is being used. In his final speech, however, which endeared him (and the play) to the Broadway audiences, Morton claims that he was not unwittingly used but that he had known what he was doing all along: He was creating satire so clever that most of his fans did not understand it.

Merton of the Movies was not the first parody of Hollywood, but it was one of the first stage productions to attempt the rapid scene shifts common to the medium it was satirizing. There are four acts and six scenes in this play, where *Dulcy* had three acts and one set only. Moreover, the action of the play unfolds before the audience as if they were watching a film in the process of being shot.

This play also presents the typical Connelly-Kaufman character: the innocent but honest man whose dreams are often compromised or negated by his own unwillingness or inability to act properly. Despite Connelly's dreamily romantic views of life, his leads tend to gain only ironic successes, as here, when Merton's very lack of talent makes him a star; the meaning of what he has learned about Hollywood (that is, that lack of talent does not make bad entertainment in the eyes of the moguls, but is perceived as "satire") is lost on him. Still, Connelly and Kaufman could not be accused of writing satire in *Merton of the Movies*, for the message of the play is too light and the attacks too gentle.

Beggar on Horseback declared itself more forcefully on the subject of the worthwhile in art and also represented a further advance in the team's stagecraft. Suggested by the German Expressionist Paul Apel's play *Hans Sonnenstössers Höllenfahrt* (pr. 1911), the play nevertheless is essentially Connelly and Kaufman's own, as Alexander Woollcott pointed out in his introduction to the printed version.

Beggar on Horseback develops the old chestnut, "Put a beggar on horseback and he'll outride the devil," by depicting, in Connelly's words, "a fantasy in which a young musician would go through a maze of kaleidoscopic experiences, the basic theme of which would be the ancient conflict of art and materialism." Neil McRae is a good composer but an improvident man who compromises his talent by writing cheap orchestrations of the sort that periodically drift in his window from the street. His wealthy neighbors are the Cady family: Mr. Cady is a businessman from Neil's hometown; Mrs. Cady is a society volunteer for worthy causes; their daughter, Gladys, is a ray of sunshine who brings Neil candy for his tea, while Homer, the son, is perpetually morose. Neil's friend, Dr. Albert Rice, suggests to Gladys that she marry Neil to give him the emotional and financial support he needs to get on with his writing. To calm his nerves, Neil takes a sleeping pill, and as he drifts off to sleep, Cynthia, to whom Neil has proposed, turns him down because she cannot support him as well as Gladys can.

The dream sequence that follows was remarkable for the Broadway stage of 1924: As Neil's future life is played out, he watches himself marry Gladys, whose bouquet is made of dollar bills, in a ceremony accompanied by the kind of sporty music he had heard in his apartment. The hectic pace of their social life prevents Neil from composing, and when he takes a job in Cady's widget business he begins to amass a fortune by day which he and Gladys will spend at jazz clubs by night. He finally sells his symphony, but Gladys destroys the manuscript, and Neil in a rage kills all four Cadys.

Neil comes to trial with Mr. Cady as the judge; the chief witness is Mrs. Cady, the prosecutor is Homer, and the members of the jury are all dance instructors. Neil loses his case after presenting as evidence on his behalf a ballet composed by himself and Cynthia, and he is sentenced by the jury to write popular songs for the rest of his life. Bent on suicide, he takes another pill, and Cynthia promises to stand by him forever.

The dream sequence ends with Cynthia knocking on the real door of Neil's apartment. Gladys breaks the engagement when she realizes that Neil's true love is Cynthia, and the lovers remain together.

Here, for the first time, Connelly and Kaufman do more than merely ridicule: They state clearly what is valuable for the artist both objectively (in the realistic sequences) and subjectively (in the dream sequence). The realistic sections are portrayals (in the manner of *Dulcy* and *Merton of the Movies*) of the lovable innocents and the mendicant fools of 1920's society. When in the dream one butler becomes two and those two become four, and so on, until the stage is literally filled with hustling butlers, the audience sees a dramatic representation of wealth overrunning the individual who possesses it. The play is also remarkable for the integral role that music plays in it. The authors were not afraid to follow their own artistic prescriptions, involving the music of Connelly's friend (and for a time, roommate), the composer and critic Deems Taylor, as an essential part of rather than accompaniment to the dramatic movement of the play, both in the realistic and in the dream sequences. While many more revolutionary developments were taking place in the 1920's in American experimental theaters—as well as in Europe—*Beggar on Horseback* introduced Expressionism to Broadway, and for this alone the play deserves a place in American theatrical history.

The Green Pastures marked a significant advance in Connelly's ambitions as a dramatist. In his previous plays, he had focused on a limited area of modern life: society life, Hollywood, business. In *The Green Pastures*, he attempted a unified retelling of the principal document of our culture within the context and language of rural Southern blacks. He was interested not in theological exactitude but rather in the humanistic message that even "De Lawd" comes to accept through His suffering: Man's essential imperfection must be accepted, for man's nature is to sin without regard to De Lawd's praise or damnation; this is the cross both man and God, as symbolized by Jesus on the Cross at the end of the play, must bear. Suffering ennobles the sufferer, be he man or God, and the anguish of the realization of man's nature is, in the closing words of the play, "a terrible burden for one man to carry."

The first part of the play covers events from Creation to the Flood. These ten episodes begin with a Sunday school lesson presided over by Mr. Deshee, who tells his children about Heaven, Creation, Adam and Eve, Cain and Abel, and Noah, showing how man fell from grace and how, with the Flood, he must begin again. Here is where *Dulcy*, *Merton of the Movies*, and *Beggar on Horseback* would have ended, full of promise, but Connelly was no longer satisfied to end on such a note. The end of part 1 finds De Lawd merely hopeful of the success of His new start and Gabriel downright uncertain.

Part 2 begins with two Heavenly Cleaners in De Lawd's office complaining that a little speck on De Lawd's horizon, Earth, is taking up too much of His time; Gabriel reports that the supply of thunderbolts is depleting without sufficient benefit for their use. De Lawd resolves to try once again with mankind, and He shows Moses how to trick Pharoah into letting His people out of Egypt. Joshua finally gets them to the Promised Land, but soon, in the words of Mr. Deshee, "dey went to de dogs again." The scene changes to a Harlem-style nightclub with golden idols and money-changing priests that bring De Lawd to renounce His creation and declare that He will not save man again.

In scene 6 of part 2, the fall of Jerusalem is played out. De Lawd is so moved by the statement of faith in the God of Hosea given by Hezdrel—a character created without biblical authority and in certain respects morally superior to even De Lawd—that He turns to a dialogue with Gabriel on the nature of man, who can be so evil, yet so noble and courageous in the face of suffering. De Lawd realizes that He, too, must suffer for each new thing He learns about mankind, and the joint suffering of God and man is made manifest in the Crucifixion, seen in shadow on De Lawd's wall. With this scene witnessed, the severe, noble black Lawd, now given hope in His creation for the first time, smiles broadly as the chorus sings "Hallelujah, King Jesus."

The play was received with overwhelming critical and popular praise, even from blacks, who, if they were offended by the stereotypical poverty and near-illiteracy of Mr. Deshee and his charges, were nevertheless elated at the acceptance Broadway audiences gave this all-black cast, behaving, with the exception of the Harlem-speakeasy Babylon scene, in a good and proper way. To what extent the simplistic figures of De Lawd and His minions and the hot-tempered, immoral, and occasionally violent characters such as Cain, Zeba, the Children of Noah, and the Children of Israel represented caricatures with which the New York audience could feel comfortable, and to what extent they represented behavioral archetypes that transcend race, is an open question. Connelly himself left no doubt about how he viewed them:

I never saw my play—and I certainly don't now—as part of any civil rights movement, as for or against *any* movement. It was no more simply about a race of people than [Gerhart Hauptmann's] *The Weavers* say, or [Maxim Gorky's] *The Lower Depths* was simply about one particular class of people. My play had little to do with Negroes—or, rather, it had as much to do with yellow and white and red as it did with black. *Green Pastures* was, at heart, about humanity, but maybe that's a little hard to explain today.

This play of simple faith in mankind came at the right time, as the United States was sinking into the Depression; with confusion and despair all around, Connelly brought hope and laughter to a darkening country.

Other major works

NOVEL: *A Souvenir from Qam*, 1965.

SHORT FICTION: "Luncheon at Sea," 1927; "Gentlemen Returning from a Party," 1927; "Barmecide's Feast," 1927; "The Committee: A Study of Contemporary New York Life," 1928; "The Guest," 1929; "Coroner's Inquest," 1930.

NONFICTION: *Voices Offstage: A Book of Memoirs*, 1968.

SCREENPLAYS: *Whispers*, 1920; *Exit Smiling*, 1926; *The Suitor*, 1928 (short); *The Bridegroom*, 1929 (short); *The Uncle*, 1929 (short); *The Green Pastures*, 1936; *I Married a Witch*, 1936; *Captains Courageous*, 1937 (with others); *Crowded Paradise*, 1956.

RADIO PLAY: *The Mole on Lincoln's Cheek*, 1941.

Bibliography

Brown, John Mason. "The Ever Green Pastures," in *Dramatis Personae*, 1963.

Nolan, Paul T. *Marc Connelly*, 1969.

Phillips, John L. "Before the Colors Fade: *The Green Pastures* Recalled," in *American Heritage*. XXI (February, 1970), p. 28.

Quinn, Arthur Hobson. *History of the American Drama from the Civil War to the Present Day*, 1927.

Ward W. Briggs